Employee Relations

We work with leading authors to develop the
strongest educational materials in business and finance,
bringing cutting-edge thinking and best learning
practice to a global market.

Under a range of well-known imprints, including
Financial Times Prentice Hall, we craft high quality print
and electronic publications which help readers to
understand and apply their content, whether studying
or at work.

To find out more about the complete range of our
publishing, please visit us on the World Wide Web at:
www.pearsoned.co.uk

Employee Relations

Second Edition

Edited by

Graham Hollinshead
Peter Nicholls
Stephanie Tailby

FT Prentice Hall
FINANCIAL TIMES

An imprint of **Pearson Education**
Harlow, England • London • New York • Boston • San Francisco • Toronto • Sydney • Singapore • Hong Kong
Tokyo • Seoul • Taipei • New Delhi • Cape Town • Madrid • Mexico City • Amsterdam • Munich • Paris • Milan

Pearson Education Limited
Edinburgh Gate
Harlow
Essex CM20 2JE
England

and Associated Companies throughout the world

Visit us on the World Wide Web at:
www.pearsoned.co.uk

First published in Great Britain 1999
Second edition 2003

© Financial Times Professional Limited 1999
© Pearson Eduction Limited 2003

ISBN-10: 0-273-65586-8
ISBN-13: 978-0-273-65586-2

British Library Cataloguing-in-Publication Data
A catalogue record for this book is available from the British Library

Library of Congress Cataloging-in-Publication Data
Employee relations / edited by Graham Hollinshead, Peter Nicholls, Stephanie Tailby.–2nd ed.
    p. cm.
  Originally published: London ; San Francisco : Financial Times/Pitman Pub., 1999.
  Includes bibliographical references and index.
  ISBN 0-273-65586-8
   1. Personnel management–Great Britain. 2. Industrial relations–Great Britain.
3. Personnel management–Europe. 4. Industrial relations–Europe. I. Hollinshead,
Graham. II. Nicholls, Peter, 1951- III. Tailby, Stephanie, 1954-

  HF5549.2.G7 E474 2002
  658.3'0094–dc21

2002190993

10 9 8 7 6 5 4
08 07 06 05

Typeset in 10/12.5pt Sabon by 35
Printed and bound in China
WC/04

Contents

Part Four
Patterns and practices

**Part Five
Conclusion**

Contributors

Editors

Graham Hollinshead, **Peter Nicholls** and **Stephanie Tailby** are all members of the School of Human Resource Management, Bristol Business School, University of the West of England.

Contributors

Philip Cox, **Jane Evans**, **Sally Howe**, **Mike Richardson** and **Martin Upchurch** are also members of the School of Human Resource Management, Bristol Business School, University of the West of England.

Andy Danford is Head of the School of Human Resource Management, Bristol Business School, University of the West of England.

Paul Stewart is Professor of Sociology of Work and Employment, School of Human Resource Management, Bristol Business School, University of the West of England.

Huw Morris is Associate Dean, Bristol Business School, University of the West of England.

Mike Leat is Head of School of Human Resource Management, University of Plymouth.

Ann Parkinson is a member of the part-time faculty at Henley Management College and lectures in human resources, career and management development. She is also Visiting Lecturer in the School of Human Resource Management, at Bristol Business School, University of the West of England, and an independent consultant.

Mike Salamon is Visiting Fellow at the School of Human Resource Management, Bristol Business School, University of the West of England.

Jackie Sinclair is College Lecturer in the Department of Industrial Relations at University College, Dublin.

Brian Willey is Director of the postgraduate programme in employment relations and law at Kingston University, Surrey and a member of the ACAS panel of arbitrators for unfair dismissal.

Preface

When the first edition of this book was published in 1999, following the election of a Labour government, there were signs that familiar contours on the UK 'map' of employee relations would be subject to redefinition. Associated with the vision of a 'stakeholder society', conciliatory statements abounded across industry and commerce concerning the need for the representatives of management and labour to modernise and harmonise their modes of interaction. Indeed the language of 'partnership' is now widely spoken, implying a listening ear on the part of employers to the expression of employee 'voice'. The agenda of employee consultation is also a lynchpin of European social policy, to which the UK is now a signatory. Nevertheless, as the optimism associated with the onset of a new era gives way to realistic appraisal of progress, it is clear that, for many, the workplace continues to be a source of stress and insecurity as well as satisfaction. Despite an increase in the volume of statutory regulation in the field of employment, impinging upon matters such as working time, minimum pay and equal opportunities, close scrutiny of contemporary organisational life reveals that many of the negative facets of previous employment traditions in the UK persist into the present. These include a legacy of low and variable pay, employment insecurity as well as excessive working hours and inadequate attention being given to the issue of employee well-being. In consequence, in charting a trajectory for the study of contemporary employee relations, it is important to recognise that, by its nature, the employment relationship is marked by conflict, tension and insecurity as well as the aspiration towards harmonious engagement. Related to this, in seeking to unravel the reality of work, there is not a single or correct version of events. Instead it is necessary to envisage the terrain of the discipline as remaining contested, in which the views of management, employees and their representatives, agencies of government and others need to be counterbalanced.

In this text our approach is underpinned by analysis and theoretical insight derived not only from the literature in this field but also from related disciplines such as sociology, politics, economics and psychology. The aim of the book is to convey, in an accessible and stimulating form, an understanding of the prominent features and dynamics of employee relations in Britain. It is aimed primarily at student readers, who are likely to be engaged on undergraduate courses in business studies or related areas, or on postgraduate programmes embracing this field of study. While up-to-date analyses and descriptions are provided, a discursive approach is taken, highlighting contemporary issues in the public and commercial domains, and relevant theoretical and conceptual frameworks underpin analysis. The book has a number of key distinguishing features:

- A 'user friendly' style has been adopted, which includes clear chapter objectives, illustrative case study material and newspaper articles, chapter summaries, questions, activities, a list of useful websites and further reading.

- It is written mainly by a team of staff who lecture and research in employee relations and human resource management at Bristol Business School and by their former colleagues. The approach therefore draws upon the specialist areas of the staff while retaining the coherence of a fully collaborative project. The relevance and accessibility of the material are also bolstered by the involvement of authors, over a period of years, in teaching constituencies of the book's target audience.

- The book, while adhering to many traditional conceptions of the disciplinary area, aims to take a fresh look at these, and also to emphasise some areas of growing significance. Consequently, particular attention is given to coverage of, for example, emerging areas of policy and law, international influences and the European employment agenda, non-union employee relations and the transformation of the public sector of industry.

- The book is accompanied by lecturer resources. PowerPoint slides and a seminar activity to support each chapter can be found at www.booksites.net/hollinshead.

March 2002

Graham Hollinshead
Peter Nicholls
Stephanie Tailby

Plan of the book

Part One · Perspectives on the employment relationship	
Chapter 1 Context and theory in employee relations	**Chapter 2** Values and their impact on the changing employment relationship

Part Two · The parties in employment		
Chapter 3 Management	**Chapter 4** Employee representation: trade unions	**Chapter 5** The state

Part Three · International influences and changing regulations		
Chapter 6 The European Union	**Chapter 7** Multinationals and employee relations	**Chapter 8** Regulating the employment relationship

Part Four · Patterns and practices		
Chapter 9 Collective bargaining	**Chapter 10** Employee participation and involvement	**Chapter 11** Pay
Chapter 12 Discrimination	**Chapter 13** Flexibility	**Chapter 14** Public sector employment

Part Five · Conclusion
Chapter 15 The rediscovery of conflict in the employment relationship

Introduction

The way that work is organised and understood in a society can reveal some of the features of underlying beliefs and values of that society or, perhaps more accurately, the views and values of key decision-makers. From slavery to the recent increasing use of short-term employment contracts, the manner in which work is translated into employment says much about the nature and structure of that society. Within modern capitalism, decisions are made which have significant consequences for levels and patterns of employment. In turn, 'tolerable' levels of unemployment are established whereby a consensus is sought as to what is considered reasonable objectives for 'full employment'. These standards of employment have clearly changed over time as politicians and pressure groups seek to alter the balance of opportunities and rewards within the labour market. Standards associated with the immediate post-war era saw the elimination of mass unemployment as a duty on the government of the day. In the 1980s, figures in excess of 2 million unemployed were defended as a necessary medicine for restructuring the labour market and Britain's level of industrial efficiency.

The national context for employee relations does not stand still and clearly must be addressed in this second edition. However, it would be surprising not to mention the international context as a source of change in the period since we were writing the first edition at the end of the 1990s.

This national context and the broad features of work and employment are clearly modified by international events, as 11 September 2001 has demonstrated. Such events also serve to remind us just how far these patterns of work and employment are increasingly embedded within an international set of relationships and connections. Creating and understanding a national picture of work and employment is just the starting point for an adequate analysis. Capturing the features of national politics and policies is essential, but increasingly we are coming to appreciate the influence and impact of supranational organisations like the OECD (Organisation for Economic Cooperation and Development), the IMF (International Monetary Fund) and GATT (General Agreement on Tariffs and Trade). Such international bodies appear to be playing an increasingly influential role in shaping the context of work and employment in the UK by providing constraints for national governments.

To make sense of employee relations is clearly dependent upon a wide range of factors. This book identifies a number of what we consider to be essential elements, which continue to have a profound effect on the character and direction of the subject.

Recent developments in the study of employee relations

This second edition seeks to capture some of the more salient developments that have shaped the subject of employee relations. These range from concrete issues such as changes in legislation, employment practices or facets of trade union structure and membership, to those issues of a more interpretative nature, where alterations in outlook have opened up the discipline to a wider set of intellectual and academic influences. A number of authors such as Kelly (1998), Wood (2000) and Wajcman (2000) have challenged the old boundaries of the discipline which concentrated on a set of institutions selected for their relevance for explaining the control and regulation of the employment relationship. In this mould, collective bargaining structures and practices became a central tenet of the discipline and trade unions and their membership.

To reflect a world of employment where trade union membership has reduced in numbers and collective bargaining no longer covers the majority of the workforce, Wood has called for a wider remit for the study of industrial relations, drawing upon research on a range of issues related to employment. Secondly, he has invited the subject to draw upon a wider range of disciplines and intellectual currents to more adequately reflect the contributions and insights from neighbouring social sciences.

As we indicated in the introduction to the first edition of this book, the 1980s were seen by some as a watershed in British political history and industrial relations, the divide between a post-war pluralist consensus and a more overt individualistic and business oriented regime. If that is the case, then perhaps academics in the area are adjusting their mode of analysis to reflect the new contours of the subject and admit fresh disciplinary insights to help make sense of new features within employment. For example, do the low levels of trade union membership really indicate some fundamental adoption of individualistic value systems within the British workforce, or, have the rhetorics of human resource management, 'competitiveness' and work intensification, among many other factors, led to a displacement of conflict into other forms and locations? Recent strikes reported in several chapters might also indicate the cyclical nature of some of the features traditionally associated with the full map of industrial relations. In other words, the work of employee relations continues to attempt to reveal the realities of work experience and the structures and processes which inform the systems of employment enacted across organisations. In so doing, it maps out the practices and procedures of management set within a legislative framework.

The form taken by these features of employment have clearly altered over time. For many commentators this has can provide important evidence of fundamental changes in employment and result in exaggerated claims for novelty within the area of study. Such claims might seek evidence for end of trade unionism, the benefits and success of non-standard employment or the end of careers. An important role for employee relations is therefore to provide solid evidence upon which to judge many such fanciful claims. Part of the intrigue of the subject is bound up in weighing the evidence of trends and developments within employment and setting these in context. Such analysis is central in discriminating between continuity and change and can provide important correctives to those who would benefit from establishing caricatures of employment conditions for political or personal gain.

■ A framework for employee relations

This edition is organised into five parts. Part One 'Perspectives on the employment relationship' seeks to re-establish the role of theory interpretation and theory construction as an integral part of the discipline. After the 1980s, when it appeared that legitimacy of this pursuit was being called into question, it is now considered important that effort is expended on developing or extending perspectives which can make sense of many of the new developments in the discipline.

Part Two adopts the traditional classification of parties to identify some of the key agencies in this area of study. These chapters reflect the fundamental differences of interests between the various parties and makes it clear that such institutional arrangements result in the existence of different sets of objectives leading to tension and periods of conflict. That this exists within an institutional arrangement, which itself is being redefined, is an important contribution of the chapters in this section.

Part Three 'International influences and changing regulations' groups together some of most significant external factors for determining the context of employee relations. With ever increasing volumes of international trade and the existence of substantial flows of foreign direct investment, employment is increasingly at risk from seemingly capricious decisions from distant boardrooms. The degree to which this encourages policy-makers to engage in regulating the economy and labour market is an area of considerable debate and a matter discussed in this section.

Part Four 'Patterns and practices' observes the structures and systems outlined above and represents the dynamic interplay of all these components of employee relations. How the key players make sense of their position within the field of employment, establish their objectives and conduct themselves provides a complex map of interactions. The consequent outcomes provide much of the content of this section. The section observes processes, practices and procedures in the field of employment and examines the impact of these on the experience of work.

Lastly, the Conclusion provides a review set within a discussion of the rediscovery of conflict associated with the workplace. Like several other features of the field of employee relations, the passage of time has allowed for the rhetoric and wishful thinking from some quarters to settle, revealing many of the persistent thorny problems of modern capitalism. Now within our gaze, it is time to try to make sense of their latest forms.

References

Kelly, J. (1998) *Rethinking Industrial Relations: Mobilisation, Collectivism and Long Waves*. London: Routledge.

Wacjman, J. (2000) 'Feminism facing industrial relations in Britain', *British Journal of Industrial Relations*, 38(1).

Wood, S. (2000) 'The BJIR and industrial relations in the new millennium', *British Journal of Industrial Relations*, 38(1).

Acknowledgements

We are grateful to the following for permission to reproduce copyright material:

Table 1.1 after 'Comparing modernism with post-modernism,' *Management of Human Resources*, Blackwell (Storey, J., 1992), Table 9.1 and Figure 9.1 from 'The employment contract: from contract to collective procedures to individual rights,' *British Journal of industrial Relations*, Vol. 38(4), 611–629, Blackwell (Brown, W. *et al.*, 2000); Figure 1.2 from *Industrial Relations System, 1st edition*, by © 1959. Reprinted with permission of South-Western College publishing a division of Thomson Learning. Fax 001 800 730 2215 (Dunlop, J.T., 1959); Figure 2.3 reprinted with the permission of The Free Press, an imprint of Simon & Schuster Adult Publishing Group, from MANAGING HUMAN ASSETS by M. Beer, B. Spector, P.R. Lawrence, D.Q. Mills, and R.E. Walton. Copyright © 1985 by The Free Press (Beer, M. *et al.*, 1985); Figure 2.4 from *New Deals: The Revolution in Managerial Careers*, © 1995 John Wiley & Sons Limited, reproduced by permission of John Wiley & Sons Limited (Herriot, P. and Pemberton, C., 1995); Figure 2.5 from *The changing nature of the employment relationship: mapping the subjective terrain of the psychological contract*, doctoral thesis, Henley Management College, © Ann Parkinson 2002 (Parkinson, A., 1998) and Figure 2.6 adapted from 'Sustaining constructive relationships across cultural boundaries,' in Joynt, P. and Morton, E. (eds) *The Global HR Manager*, IPD Books, © Ann Parkinson 2002 (Parkinson, A., 1999); Table 3.2 and Table 3.3 after *British Industrial Relations*, 2nd Edn, Routledge (Gospel, H.F. and Pimlott, G., 1993), Table 4.3, Table 1 (Conclusion) and Figure 3 (Conclusion) from *Britain at Work: As Depicted by the 1998 Workplace Employee Relations Survey*, Routledge (Cully, M.I. *et al.*, 1999); Table 3.4 after *Changing Patterns of Employee Relations*, © Harvester Wheatsheaf (Marchington, M. and Parker, P., 1990); Table 4.1 from *Social Trends 26*, p. 92 (HMSO, 1996); Table 4.2 from *Annual Report of the Certification Officer*, p. 62 (HMSO, 2001); Table 4.6, Table 4.7, Table 4.8, Table 4.9, Table 4.10 and Figure 4.2 from *Labour Market Trends*, September (ONS, 2001b), Figure 12.1, Figure 1 (Conclusion) and Figure 2 (Conclusion) from *Labour Market Trends*, June (ONS, 2001a), Table 13.4 from *Labour Market Trends*, November, p. 510 (ONS, 2001c); Figure 12.3 and Figure 12.4 from *Labour Force Survey* (HMSO, 1998), Table 13.1 and Table 13.3 *Labour Force Survey (ONS) Historical Supplement*, Table 13.5 from *Labour Force Survey*, Winter (ONS, 2000/1), Crown copyright material is reproduced with the permission of the Controller of HMSO and the Queen's Printer for Scotland; Table 4.2 from *TUC Directory 2002*, Table 4.5 data from *Struggling for Equality – A Survey of Women and their Unions* (SERTUC Women's Rights Committee, 1994), Table 14.1 from *TUC Annual Reports*, reproduced with permission of the TUC; Table 4.5 adapted from 'Still a long road to equality,' *Labour Research*, Vol. 83(3), pp. 5–7 (Labour Research Department, 1994); Table 4.11 adapted and reprinted by permission of Sage Publications Ltd, and the author William Brown, from 'The effect of British industrial relations legislation 1979–97,' *National Institute Economic Review*, Vol. 161, pp. 69–83, copyright © National Institute of Economic and Social Research (Brown, W. *et al.*, 1997); Table 13.2 from *Employment in Europe 2000*, only European Community legislation as printed in the *Official Journal of the European Communities* is deemed to be authentic (European Commission, 2000).

Guardian Newspapers Limited for extracts adapted from 'Wild cat postal strikes spread' by Seamus Milne published in *The Guardian* 24th May 2001 © The Guardian 2001, 'Now there's a four hour time difference when you cross the Channel' by John Crace published in *The Guardian* 11th August 2001 © The Guardian 2001, 'UK still a nation of workaholics' by Lucy Ward published in *The Guardian* 4th February 2002 © The Guardian 2002 and 'Dyson, champion of British industry, switches production to fareast' by Geoff Gibbs published in *The Guardian* 6th February 2002 © The Guardian 2002; HMSO for extracts from *Employment Trends* 1995, and 'New partnership channels at Thames Water' and 'Thames Water Utilities' published in *IRS Employment Trends* No. 715 November 2000; icBirmingham for an extract adapted from 'Choc workers in pioneer pay deal' by Chris Morley published in *The Evening Mail* 30th July 2001; Independent Newspapers (UK) Limited for an extract adapted from 'Keep the porshe, I'd rather have a life' by Emma Cook published in *The Independent on Sunday* 20th July 1997; National Funeral Directors Association, USA, for an extract adapted from 'A job with life . . . not a job for life' by F. Hecht published in *The Director*; TES Syndication for an extract adapted from 'Cash first, details of performance pay later, unions say' by Nic Barnard published in *Times Educational Supplement* 8th September 2000; and the Wainwright Trust for an extract adapted from 'Equal Value Training Manual' published in Ware, Hertfordshire: *The Wainwright Trust*.

In some instances we have been unable to trace the owners of copyright material and we would appreciate any information that would enable us to do so.

Part One

Perspectives on the employment relationship

Chapter 1

Context and theory in employee relations

Peter Nicholls

Learning objectives

By the end of this chapter, readers should be able to:

- appreciate the role of theory in providing a method for organising and making sense of knowledge and information within the discipline of employee relations;

- outline the differing theoretical frameworks to have emerged during the lifetime of the discipline, noting their major features, contributions and limitations;

- make connections between the impetus for particular theoretical frameworks, their intellectual origins and their social context;

- explore these theoretical frameworks, recognising the ability of all theories to sustain their utility for particular social groups over time;

- appreciate the 'architecture' of a theory for informing and influencing the definition of an employee relations problem and subsequently the design of appropriate policies to resolve such problems.

Introduction

When we wrote the first edition of this book, the Labour Party had just been elected to government. There was a mood of cautious optimism among many observers of the world of work and employment. It is now possible to assess how Labour's policies have impacted on this area of study.

Accepting that there has been change in the political and legal context does not alter the general intent of this chapter. Its aim is to argue that to understand the complexity and diversity of the world of work and employment requires theories and frameworks to organise and make links between a wide range of disparate data and ideas.

If there is a shift in emphasis, then it is the additional effort taken to make sense of the deepening divisions within the workforce and the continuity of regimes of control. These regimes appear to have created many areas of employment where individuals are obliged to respond to the tune of management, often at the risk of their own well-being and dignity. It would seem that, irrespective of the government in office, the advanced capitalist state cannot break its role of promoting the interests of certain sections of the economy at the expense of others. The growth of insecurity and instability in employment is redrawing the map of employee relations, and those who write about it need to provide insight into how to make sense of such trends and developments.

This chapter commences by looking at the history of theory within the subject of employee relations to better appreciate the relationship between its content and context. In turn it looks at the present to capture what might be some of the emerging theories and frameworks that hold the potential for providing new understandings and insights. Finally, it is important to note the significance of the Labour government's commitment to a 'third way' and to assess how far this has removed the polarities of capital/labour, private/public, individual/collective which traditionally have been such powerful dichotomies for informing the employee relations debate, theory and analysis.

The promise of a new form of social democracy has unleashed a series of reforms that, we are told, will lead to greater efficiencies in the labour market. Investigation might indicate that these efficiencies are obtained by creating further schisms within the labour market and setting one section of it against another. There is, therefore, an urgent need to make sense of such developments, and theories are the starting point for this task. Without theory construction and development, disciplines can remain trapped in a process of mapping evidence with little sense of the purpose and direction, and little assessment of the significance of broader changes. As Kelly (1998) observes, 'not only are we lacking answers to many fundamental questions, but we often lack the conceptual and theoretical tools that would enable us to think about these questions in a fruitful way'.

This chapter therefore reviews the variety of theories used within the discipline and observes the shifting emphasis reflected in each theory, set within its own historical context. Overall the chapter attempts to:

- better appreciate the nature of these theories;
- understand the reasons for adopting such theories at particular period of time;
- capture the interests of those adopting a particular theory or framework;
- appreciate the implications of adopting these theories for the consequent policy-making process.

These and many other issues related to the role of theory and the context within which employment is located form the main areas of concern for this chapter.

Perhaps to reflect this growing concern for establishing the significance and direction of change, many writing in this discipline talk of 'new industrial relations' (Marchington and Parker, 1990; Farnham and Pimlott, 1995; Beardwell, 1996) and substitute 'industrial relations' with 'employee relations' to indicate a significant shift in the context and content of the employment relationship. The very existence of this debate indicates the contentious nature of the discipline.

As if to underscore this change in the context of employee relations, moves in 2001 by the government to return Railtrack to public ownership after a troubled period of private sector control has triggered a series of industrial disputes. Both the original privatisation of the railways under the previous Conservative government and the continued problems of operating a fragmented system provide an important example of the failed attempt at introducing market competition into a major public service like the railways (Baldry and Ellison, 2000; Wolmar, 2001).

The outbreak of industrial conflict needs to seen in the context of some of lowest strike records in British history. Passengers and unions appear to have lost patience after years of poor management, inadequate investment and contradictory government policies (see Exhibit 1.1). How do we interpret this event? How do we evaluate the different arguments put forward for understanding the reasons that led up to this strike?

Exhibit 1.1

South West Trains strike

On 3 January 2002, the Rail, Maritime and Transport Union (RMT) called a four-day strike affecting nearly 1,700 daily services on commuter routes around London. Both the government and employers denounced the strike as unhelpful and inappropriate.

According to the *Financial Times* (FT) newspaper of 5 January 2002:

> The Rail Maritime and Transport Union yesterday refused to call off the remainder of the four days of strikes on South West Trains over pay and discipline for non-driver staff, raising the prospects that most of the company's 1,700 services will be cancelled on Monday and Tuesday...
> ...Barney Stringer, the Confederation of British Industry's head of infrastructure, said yesterday: 'To get [private sector investment] the industry needs stability and the unions need to consider whether their actions will contribute to that'. The department of trade said the strikes could 'degrade' the industry, which is already losing money.
> SWT [South West Trains] owned by Stagecoach Group, said that talks with the RMT failed because the union refused to postpone next week's strike during negotiations, and 'hardened' its stand.
> The RMT said that 'meaningful discussions were just not possible' because SWT refused to discuss the problems until the next strike was called off by the union. 'We remain available to talk and we are still urging South West Trains to restart negotiations', said Vernon Hince, RMT acting general-secretary.

On 9 January 2002 the FT's front page story was entitled 'Pressure on Blair as rail union calls for more strikes'. The article stated that the estimated losses to SWT caused by the strike were of the order of '£6m out of expected pre-tax profits this year of £64m, rising to nearly £10m if the union continues its action'. In the same edition, another story of the strike entitled 'Rail delays set to continue as unions flex their muscles', commented that: 'After years of relative peace, Britain's railways are once again the centre of industrial chaos.'

The article, by Christopher Adams, goes on to describe the prospect of strikes spreading from South West Trains to Arriva Northern and companies in Scotland. 'Since privatisation most of the rail companies have faced acute shortages. The main reason is that many former British Rail employees were encouraged to take voluntary retirement or voluntary severance. SWT said yesterday that the industry was taking steps to address staff shortages. The operators have about 9,100 drivers in employment, 300 short of what they need. Another 1,000 are being trained.'

On 10 January the FT ran another article, 'Train company criticised by industry for its record and handling of the dispute'. The article comments that 'several industry executives criticised SWT yesterday for not having acted sooner to avert two 48-hour strikes and attacked its industrial relations record'. Another executive said the company had adopted a 'very robust' negotiating style, which suggested it has had a long period of worsening industrial relations. 'They seemed to get into their trenches very quickly. It takes two to make a fight and we've usually managed to avoid getting to that state.' SWT rejected the criticism. 'We don't have any old scores to settle. We are not persecuting anyone with involvement in the RMT.' An official said that management had done everything it could to prevent a strike. 'We've bent over backwards.' The group defended its tactic of imposing a pay increase on its employees, a move that seemed to inflame union officials. 'We felt we had to take a positive step to break the stalemate that was costing the economy millions of pounds. We did not intend to be combative but to find a way forward that everyone could claim a win in.'

The brief extracts in Exhibit 1.1 display a variety of competing positions and associated explanations that exist not only in the British press but also in academic studies of employee relations. Clearly, the facts do not speak for themselves. That a set of events becomes classed as a problem is in itself a complex process which is not at all obvious. Once outside parties become involved, such as the press and academic commentators, we move on from establishing the situation as an 'issue' to trying to explain the events as they unfold and to account for this particular sequence of events.

Exhibit 1.1 demonstrates that a variety of explanations can exist for the same issue. Which interpretation is adopted will determine how an issue might be researched or what particular policy options might be chosen. If a single strike can evoke so much controversy, then it is not difficult to appreciate that in a subject such as employee relations, a considerable number of frameworks exist, some of which might claim the title of theories while others might remain frames of reference or perspectives.

What is implied here is a continuum, from a frame of reference that contains a series of related factors, to theories that rely upon the interrelationship of concepts, themselves reflecting well-established definitions, and the existence of indicators with which to measure these. In this chapter a distinction is made between those theories that might be classified as integral to the discipline – unitary and pluralist systems and Marxist theories – and those that have been significant for influencing and modifying these core theories and their variants, including feminist theory, comparative theory and postmodernist theory. Figure 1.1 summarises some of the distinguishing features of the chapter.

Theories and explanations in employee relations

Understanding and operationalising theories can sound a threatening prospect for those newly arrived at the discipline of employee relations. Yet in our day-to-day lives we engage in very similar activities without even stopping to consider the process. For instance, we all gather information, evaluate and analyse it and make decisions on the basis of that imperfect procedure.

Our individual social lives are composed of an appreciation that we just cannot know for certain that the answers to most of our questions are comprehensive. What makes our life possible and manageable is the continuous use of theories, which we are forced to create as a way of organising ourselves to cope with the pressures of our daily lives. In the workplace, for example, management would collapse if it were not able to utilise our own theories. For instance, we learn to adopt a whole repertoire of behaviour to deal with individuals at different levels of the organisational hierarchy. From one job to another, we carry patterns of behaviour that 'have worked for us'. In doing so, we have, in a simple sense, generated our own theory based upon observation, interpretation and experience. This is often called common sense (Berger and Luckman, 1966).

When it comes to employee relations, academics need to organise knowledge to enable them to generalise rather than remain in the detail of specific instances, in the detail of common sense. The contribution of the discipline is to make sense of the employment relationship and understand this relationship within the complexity of its context.

Theories are therefore helpful in thinking beyond particular cases and enabling us to summarise and generalise. As Adams and Meitz (1993: 12) put it: 'By choosing a theory one organises reality'. From this activity we can start to make sense of a wide range of instances and establish common themes and guidelines for interpreting the world

Perspectives	Genealogy	Status	Features in workplace	Manifestations
Unitary	Now post-industrial associated with ascendancy of management power	Stereotypical integration of unilateral management control of employment relationship	Omnipotent management exercising unilateral control	Unilateral PRP (performance related pay), emphasis on communication and performance evaluation
Pluralist	Reflects ideas of modern democracy legitimating trade union recognition	Stereotypical view of managerial acceptance of limited power-sharing in certain areas of decision making	Limited power sharing between major interested parties	Negotiated with interest groups, latterly stakeholder perspective
Marxist	Mid-nineteenth century analysis of gross inequalities creating capitalism	Theory of society emphasising opposing interests within workplace and beyond	Focus on exploitation and structured inequalities	Conflict absenteeism. Sabotage, false consciousness and consumerism
Systems	Interwar. Importance of pseudo-scientific conceptual analysis underpinning discipline	A conceptualisation in order to classify the discipline	Institutions in equilibrium governed by rules. Open systems, inputs and outputs affected by environment	Refinement of descriptive tools. Scope for international comparisons
Feminist	Two stages. Earlier recognition of the existence of patriarchy. Latterly, industrial relations recognising male domination	Theory of society emphasising structural inequalities between sexes in workplace and beyond	Male advantages embedded in institutions, culture and hence workplace	Agitation to improve policies and conditions of employment
Postmodern	Disputes nature of knowledge. Emphasis on subjective individual. Interpretation and verification of meaning	Reaction to scientific/empirical explanations of the world. Emphasis on individual experience and meaning	Belief in post-industrial world of work where meanings disputed by ambiguity and ambivalence	Adopts a rhetoric of human resource management plus associated ideologies

Figure 1.1 **Theories in employee relations**

of work and employment. Not surprisingly, the existence of competing explanations can result in continuous debate leading to particular groupings of academics around particular theoretical positions.

That such debates exist in employee relations explains the 'health' of the discipline. Theories therefore provide a more rigorous analysis than common sense and can be distinguished from it in two principal ways:

■ Breadth of coverage. How broad is the application of that theory? If it relates to a wide variety of situations, will it measure up to being an academic theory?

■ Coherence of its concepts. Do the different concepts, which are the building-blocks of the theory, logically relate to each other and remain consistent in a variety of different situations?

As we constantly transfer knowledge and experience from one setting to another and select from a wide diversity of facts and situations that which is relevant to our own tasks and activities, we generate our own theories.

In this chapter we are looking at theories created and refined by a wide variety of authors who have used them to interpret the information and data related to work and employment. As various commentators have noted, this information does not speak for itself. How it is collected, and subsequently analysed, means that there is considerable variety in interpretations within the discipline. This dynamic nature of the discipline is part of its intrigue but also part of its problem.

If no one theory is 'right' then what causes one theory to be replaced by another? This is what Kuhn (1970) calls a 'shift in the dominant paradigm', that is, an established set of explanations and research procedures which become established as the 'normal' way of creating knowledge in a given area. Furthermore, if several major theories emerge, how can they coexist within the same discipline at the same time?

Outlining the major features of the more significant theories, perspectives and frameworks of employee relations, and referring back to these related questions, it is argued, is important for understanding not just the content of employee relations but something of the character of the discipline and its changing concerns.

Employee relations and theoretical interpretation

In the Introduction we alluded to the specific meanings associated with the title 'employee relations' as compared with 'industrial relations'. Such distinctions were discussed there and so to avoid reworking those arguments, the two terms will be treated as synonymous in this chapter.

Clearly, employee relations can be seen as distinctive from industrial relations as a way of describing the employment relationship. Authors like Gospel (1992) and Beardwell (1996) make the claim for such a distinction; they argue that a difference of level of analysis exists between the two and that employee relations clearly suggests a value orientation and therefore leans towards a modern form of managerialism.

How far the discipline has changed as a result of changes in its context is a point of considerable debate (Undy, 1997). Agreement upon the existence of changes in the context of employee relations is extensive; what is harder to establish is the degree of consensus associated with the changes in interpretation adopted by researchers in the area (Keenoy, 1991).

Some of the contextual changes are associated, for example, with the growing role of the state, which influences and shapes employment through fiscal policy and changes in employment law and privatisation. Alongside state influences, discussed in Chapter 5, the private sector continues to change the shape and level of influence through size, scale and increasing global practices (Eldridge et al., 1991).

Management itself continues to refine its technologies whether through manufacturing, financial, marketing or human resource policies, as discussed in Chapter 3. Unions, too, have looked again at their *raison d'être* and entered into many new areas and activities to maintain their position within the employment relationship (see Chapter 4). To understand and interpret employee relations in the twenty-first century, therefore, requires by definition an analysis guided by theoretical insights.

Understanding and utilising a variety of theories should constitute some of the basic skills of any social science student and yet according to Hyman in the case of industrial relations, the development and cultivation of theory have been limited (Hyman, 1989).

In more detail, a concern to demonstrate the need for a greater awareness of the role of theory is linked to a point raised by Gospel and Palmer (1993: 11), when they discuss the bias towards description and prescription in many explanations within the discipline:

> Prescription lies at the centre of government and trade union debates on the subject. Over the last quarter-century there has been a succession of prescriptions for changes in industrial relations, for new ways of managing resources and for the introduction of industrial legislation of various kinds. In industrial relations, the existence of contentious and conflicting proposals from the different participants suggest that, whatever the assumptions are, they are certainly not 'common to all'.

As Gospel and Palmer go on to explain, there is considerable overlap within the discipline among academic theories, policy prescriptions and descriptive accounts. With so much attention focused upon the employment relationship in an advanced competitive industrial nation, the mixture of these forms of explanation is inevitable. Added to this, the media have an inbuilt interest in portraying the substance of the employment relationship in the most dramatic fashion for generating public interest (Philo *et al.*, 1977).

To start to make sense of theories in employee relations the next section outlines one of the earlier explanations, which like so many of these theories has continued to provide management with a useful analysis of work and employment since its inception. In this sense it is as important to acknowledge these theories for their contribution to explaining employment as it is in appreciating their ideological role.

Unitary theory

> In any executive work which involves the co-operation of two different men or parties, where both parties have anything like equal power or voice in its direction, there is almost sure to be a certain amount of bickering, quarrelling, and vacillation, and the success of the enterprise suffers accordingly. If, however, either one of the parties has the entire direction, the enterprise will progress consistently and probably harmoniously, even although the wrong one of the two parties may be in control. The essence of task (scientific) management lies in the fact that the control of the speed problem rests entirely with management. (Taylor, 1903, quoted by Clawson, 1980)

The story of scientific management has been told by many, but the essential point for us is Taylor's unquestioning assumption that management should maintain control of the organisation and control of work to ensure that business objectives are met. That belief in the 'right to manage' or the managerial prerogative provides an important assumption for those adopting a unitary perspective.

In essence, the unitary theory portrays the employment relationship as harmonious, with employer and employed working together to achieve success. It assumes a common set of values which binds the two parties together and ensures there is no potential source of conflict. Although this might be considered the earliest theory used to describe the employment relationship, it clearly connects with many of the contemporary ideas associated with corporate culture and the use of human resource management (HRM). For this harmonious relationship to exist requires a high level of consensus between the two parties in the employment relationship (see Chapter 3).

This begs the question as to how that consensus is achieved, which starts to explain how this theory – which was inspired by a set of conditions in the nineteenth century – can appear to sustain considerable currency today. Clearly, consensus about the objectives of an organisation can be produced by:

- ideas and values between employers and employees being absolutely identical as a result of a happy coincidence;
- ideas and values being a condition of entry to the organisation, their existence therefore being established at the recruitment and selection stage of employment;
- ideas and values originating with management being learnt by those entering the organisation on a voluntary basis and subsequently adopted by employees;
- ideas and values being part of a socialisation programme and, through corporate induction courses and other training activities, being involuntarily learnt and adopted;
- employees being confronted with these ideas and values and their adoption being a condition of continuing employment. The ideas and values are then adopted or not by employees, depending on their own circumstances.

Seen in this light, the consensus needs to be understood in a dynamic way and not as an unproblematic given. How it is reached, if it is reached at all, really depends on a whole series of factors existing within the employment relationship at that time.

In the nineteenth century, when workers were, for example, forced to move to the cities in search of jobs or join companies like the railways, they had no reference points to evaluate their employment conditions, and in many circumstances they were not sufficiently well informed to question the authority of the employer (Pollard, 1958). The unitary approach, as its name suggests, is therefore emphasising the existence of employers and employees working together, collaborating in the pursuit of these shared objectives. In these circumstances there appears to be little point in allowing a third party to intervene on behalf of either of the two parties.

Systems of ideas like Social Darwinism provided a strong moral justification for these arrangements at this time. It suggested that what took place in nature provided a compelling justification for many in positions of power and privilege in society. The process of natural selection and the survival of the fittest appeared to accord with life at this time and further legitimated the absolute control of employers backed up by the law. It provided a ready-made explanation for those who might wonder why such inequalities in the workplace persisted (Hofstader, 1955).

Trade unions were therefore of no value to either management or employees; it is as if some unnatural force had inserted itself into a natural arrangement. This natural quality to the theory is interesting and today some employers who adopt this theory appear to speak about it as good business sense or even common sense, in much the same way as earlier economists talked about the natural and inevitable need for the 'hidden hand' of the market to exist (Hayek, 1960). In other words, the labour market is depicted as a natural structure composed of an omnipotent management backed up by the state and of labour dependent on those two parties for its well-being (Gospel, 1992).

If trade unions are considered unnecessary by the theory then we have to explain how the consensus outlined above is maintained. Employees might accept a set of objectives when they start a new job, but the long-term cooperation of a workforce is unlikely. So what cements these employees into their jobs and sustains that consensus?

In the nineteenth century, paternalism played an important role in binding individual workers to their employers. Accounts of nineteenth-century work practices constantly refer to the personalised manner in which work and thereby employees were organised (see, for example, Laslett, 1971; Landes, 1972; Bendix, 1974). Employers treated their employees as if they belonged to them. Sometimes this was conducted in such a way that they were treated more like children and had to obey their 'parents'; in other circumstances they were made to feel that they 'belonged' to a family (Laslett, 1971). Clearly, a whole continuum of experiences existed but they all held the potential for overlaying the employment relationship with a sense of obligation to a person in authority.

Nineteenth-century business and employment

The railways in the mid-nineteenth century provide an interesting example of systematic management of employee relations. Their employment policies reflected many ideas originating in the navy at this time, which provided a suitable training for those confronting the coordination of an uneducated workforce with the demands of a modern technology itself set within a complex organisational structure, dependent upon a series of policies to provide both cooperation and control (Gourvish, 1972; McKenna, 1980). Added together, the experience of these practices clearly led many employees to believe that their needs and those of the company were not far apart. As McKenna (1980: 45) describes in an excellent account of employment conditions on the early railways:

> The railwaymen were from the beginning ruled by instructions as detailed as the Koran. They were the first 'organisation men', stitched firmly into the fabric of their company, noted for punctuality, cleanliness and the smart execution of orders. A railway worker was 'in the service'. He reported for duty, and left it only after being relieved. Failure to report for duty meant he was absent without leave. He took unpaid leave only after written permission had been granted; unauthorised leave could lead to suspension, fines, dismissal and even prosecution.

The railway workers very much 'belonged' to the company, which would usually demand testimonials; if accepted, individual employees would be assigned to particular directors, who then became responsible for the future behaviour and performance at work.

This type of employment relationship, which ensured that there was no strike on the railways for the first 50 years of their operation, established practices and assumptions about employee relations that were bound to inform those trying to develop general explanations and theories of employment. So where did the ideas for the unitary theory come from?

It is impossible to trace exactly the genealogy of such ideas but ultimately they may become the parts or concepts that form a theory. Here the historical context provided evidence of the structure and practices of employment, which could provide observers with inspiration for generalising the organisation of work about employment practices.

As Pollard (1958) suggests, the biggest worry for entrepreneurs and employers generally in the nineteenth century was the management of labour. Most firms were family firms or partnerships, with very few joint stock companies in existence. Firms were based upon small to medium-sized employment units for most of the nineteenth century guided by family members (Hobsbawm, 1974). In other words, most employees' experience of employment was contained within relatively intimate arrangements with close contact with their 'masters', whether they were family entrepreneurs or leading craftsmen – what Burawoy called the 'despotic regime' displaying a strong relationship of dependence and coercion between employers and employees (Burawoy, 1979, 1985).

In these circumstances, employees' experience of work was that of constantly being exposed to the organisation's objectives and where employment legislation was very much in favour of employers – for example, the requirements contained within the Master and Servants Act 1867. It was apparent that employees were under considerable pressure to submit themselves to the requirements of the law to ensure their survival.

Unitary theory is associated in the first instance with a version of employment as it existed in the nineteenth century and reflects a set of interests that clearly expresses employers' concerns and not those of employees – in other words, a managerialist perspective. It is based on an idealised employment relationship reflecting a set of desirable arrangements for management which, if operationalised, would ensure that management could maximise its objectives at the expense of its employees, as in the case of the early railway companies.

Some shortcomings of unitary theory

As an explanation of employment, unitary theory certainly does not take account of the real needs of the employees nor does it recognise the very real differences in objectives that exist between employers and employees.

To summarise its weaknesses:

- It fails to recognise the existence of differing interests between management and labour. The assumption is made that managers' decisions are rational and contain within them the interests of all employees.
- The explanation for the existence of a countervailing force, whether in the form of an individual, group or trade union, rests on the failure to understand the objectives of management. Better means of communication are often exhorted as the cure for such ills.
- Where this conflict persists, it is explained by what Palmer calls deviance (Palmer, 1983). The behaviour of those acting against management has to be dealt with by dismissal or the law (Palmer, 1983).
- With ever more sophisticated management techniques, many modern managers point to the existence of a conflict of interests resulting from a failure to establish a sufficiently clear corporate culture against which potential employees' qualities can be established.

Although few would admit to such a simple view of management today, the theory retains an attraction, as Palmer suggests, resulting from its prescriptive connotations and an ideological stance that has mirrored many of the management nostrums of the 1980s and 1990s (Palmer, 1983).

Farnham calls unitary theory's latest form 'neo-unitary' theory and suggests that since the 1980s it appears to correspond closely with many features associated with the 'new', more aggressive styles of management (Farnham and Pimlott, 1995). This 'new' management is associated with the decline of union power and the ascendancy of the managerial prerogative, by which we mean management's increasing ability to shape and control employment relations. That the unitary theory should once again appear to provide a way of understanding the employment relationship is not surprising. If the context of the 1990s had many features in common with that of the nineteenth century, then why should not the theory inspired by those arrangements re-emerge now to correspond to employment relations which, for many researchers, have more than a passing resemblance to those earlier conditions when management power was in the ascendant, resulting in polarities and divisions within the workforce? Not only do some of the same conditions relate to the earlier period, but clearly, for those adopting the theory, it defines the employment relationship in such a way as to ensure that management retains a privileged position and can continue to claim a defining role in the management of labour.

In summary, unitary theory was originally linked to a type of nineteenth-century employment that seems to reflect employers' managerial interests rather than the interests of employees. It is based on a kind of idealised relationship at work which suits management and which, if put into practice, would ensure that management could usually achieve all its objectives at the expense of employees.

More sophisticated versions of the theory have emerged to create images of consensus, teams and a shared vision of company objectives. The theory's managerialist bias is unmistakable and its account of employee relations one-sided.

If we took this approach and looked at the original case study of emerging rail strikes (Exhibit 1.1), then it would not be difficult to see such a theory concentrating on the business needs of the company articulated by management. In such circumstances, the claim by management that the company must be allowed to operate in a 'stable' environment would reflect a unitary analysis. Additionally when South West Trains stated that 'we felt we had to take a positive step' by *imposing* a pay award they clearly felt that such a decision could be made unilaterally without union involvement. To behave in this unilateral manner would normally indicate a unitary position.

Pluralist theory

With the growing complexity and scale of business units, a more appropriate explanation was required which might move beyond the simplicity of the unitary approach and more accurately reflect the experience of those working in larger and complex employment units. The exponents of pluralist theory acknowledged the existence of a limited level of conflicting interests in the workplace and the need for all parties to work towards achieving consensus.

In a 1997 policy document published by the Trades Union Congress (TUC, the umbrella organisation of the trade union movement), a description of the employment relationship is outlined which clearly acknowledges the differing interests of management and employees.

> The theme of this statement is partnership, a recognition that trade unions must not be seen as part of Britain's problems. At the workplace social partnership means employers and trade unions working together to achieve common goals such as fairness and competitiveness; it is recognition that, although they have different constituencies; it is a recognition that although they have different interests, they can serve these best by making common cause wherever possible. (TUC, 1997)

Although the potential for a conflict of interests exists, a very strong emphasis on a common purpose is evident.

If we could connect pluralist theories in employee relations to a particular historical juncture it would have to be the post-war period leading up to the high-point in the 1970s when such theories provided an explicit framework for government policy. Equally, they had a profound effect on the development of the discipline and its public role.

From this time onwards, no government, of whatever complexion, could allow employers and employees to settle things for themselves. As time went on, policies – whether explicit or not – such as incomes policies and the increasing use of the law and other institutional mechanisms, combined to demonstrate the growing level of intervention in employee relations (see Chapter 5).

Pluralist theory emerged in Britain at a time when post-war economic growth had led to a level of prosperity which, 20 years after the war, had started to spawn a number of cultural forms that were to challenge established ideas and assumptions and in a sense the 'establishment' of British society. Ideas of power vested in privileged positions and the right of old elites to dictate standards and values to the rest of society were under challenge as a new generation with greater disposable income and opportunities for employment set out with less reverence for the established ways of British society (Halsey, 1995). If the 'pop' and 'rock' culture in Britain signified some of these changes, the adoption of pluralist theory in industrial relations demonstrated to authors like Fox (1973) that the unitary theory had lost its credibility. As a consequence, the significance of pluralism grew and a change in emphasis within industrial relations theory ensued, as Fox (1973: 192) confirms:

> One alternative perspective which has developed, however, asserts the unitary view to be diminishingly useful. The increasing size and complexity of work organisations; shifts in the power relations within politics and industry; changes in social values; rising aspirations; weakening of traditional attitudes towards officially constituted governance: these are among the factors which are sometimes said to require managers to develop a new ideology and new sources of legitimisation if they are to maintain effective control.

Under the influence of Dahl (1957) and other political theorists, the idea that any form of governance should acknowledge the competing interests of the groups engaged in the process came to be recognised. As Fox points out, it was Cyert and March (1963) who talked about the existence of 'coalitions' where groups agreed to abide by a set of procedures to ensure the resolution of competing and often conflicting interests (Fox, 1973).

The implication of using this analysis was, unlike unitary theory, that it drew from accounts based upon a political heritage in democratic theory that portrayed decision-making as a process of reconciling the different claims made by a variety of competing groups.

In other words, it acknowledged the existence of a variety of competing interest groups, but in addition it accepted this variety as legitimate and normal. At the centre of this conception of the employment relationship was a fluid world where competing interests expended energy vying for the acknowledgement of their arguments and, ultimately, the successful adoption of their policies or proposals.

This fluidity stood in stark contrast to the unitary approach, which had always portrayed management policies as the only legitimate ideas for employment. In unitary theory, a consensus would result because of the common value system that was held to exist. Here, the existence of conflict was allowed for, and to an extent encouraged. Conflict led to creative tension, which encouraged effective arguments and debate. However, this could only be allowed as long as it remained within the 'creative' end of the continuum. As Fox (1973: 193) suggests: 'A certain amount of overt conflict and disputation is welcomed as evidence that not all aspirations are being either sapped by hopelessness or suppressed by power. On the other hand, conflict above a certain level is felt to be evidence that the ground rules need changing.' Therefore conflict exists in a way other theories find it hard to account for, yet there is still a restricted definition of conflict, one which sees the basis of that conflict resting in a clash over the means by which objectives are achieved. Further discussion of this feature of the theory will be explored in the section dealing with Marxist theory.

What the theory appears to offer is an account of the nature of industrial relations which achieves greater realism by reflecting the political realities of the situation at that time. This is hardly surprising when the details of that historical period are considered, along with the level of trade union activity and the incidence of industrial disputes in evidence at that time. Conflict was very much the norm (Bassett, 1987).

If the theory appeared to provide a more realistic account of this period of employment history by acknowledging the wider constituency of factors shaping the world of employment, it also had interesting consequences for the role of management.

- It reconfirmed management at the centre of this complex world of competing interests. The only group that possessed the capacity to ensure reconciliation between the different parties was management – not unlike the argument that Burnham had earlier espoused to place management at the middle of a 'new' technicist age (Burnham, 1957).
- If managers were the only group able to resolve the differences between the competing interests, then in the future they would have to develop logical and reasoned arguments to justify their final decisions, otherwise they would be unable to sustain the 'loose coalition'.

This was in stark contrast to the unitarist theory, which indicated that managements had a duty to impose their decisions on other groups.

Some shortcomings of pluralism

As with unitary theory, pluralism was ultimately premised upon the existence of a consensus, but differed from it in that it allowed for the existence of limited conflict to achieve that consensus. What is interesting to note in this theory, however, is the nature of that consensus and where it operates within the theory.

In the unitary approach the consensus is assumed and left as unproblematic; in the pluralist model it exists as a result of the acknowledged process of socialisation and the sustaining of roles, in other words, it is an active process which at times can fail the system. In the case of pluralist theory, it is given an active role although it becomes a more hidden process in the sense that it is assumed to exist at a fundamental level, as described by Fox (1973: 197):

> The assumption is being made that while, to be sure, conflicts arise over terms of economic collaboration, values and norms are not so divergent that workable compromises cannot be achieved. Underlying the cut and thrust of marketplace and organisational encounters, in other words, lies the rock-firm foundation of a stable and agreed social system.

Once again, the theory considered by some to provide a more realistic account of employment suffers from a series of assumptions for which there are serious misgivings:

- It believes in the existence of democracy which, through the franchise, ensures that individual rights are recognised.
- It assumes that the institutions of democracy operate to resolve what differences do occur between management and labour.
- It relies on the existence of a common set of rules and procedures which guide behaviour in the workplace.
- It depicts the differing parties to the employment relationship as possessing a rough equivalence of power and influence, competing for power on the basis of similar levels of influence.
- It relies on the power and success of negotiation and bargaining to overcome fundamental differences between management and labour.
- Its analytical focus is upon a continuous description of the 'given' institutions of modern capitalism and thereby fails to reveal the inbuilt biases and inequalities of such structures.

Such an emphasis on the institutions of modern capitalism for providing an understanding of the employment relationship plays down the political reality of employment and the very different worlds within which management and labour reside.

Salamon says of collective bargaining: 'the relationship is founded on mutual dependence. So too with pluralism – it relies upon the ability of both sides to appear to retain independent positions with room to maintain their independence of each other' (Salamon, 1998: 315).

From a more critical perspective, this misses the point that by entering into such collective agreements or negotiations, employees are unwittingly losing sight of the fact that the institutional arrangement in which they are operating is itself malformed or distorted in favour of those in powerful positions. As Crouch suggests: 'Management have usually succeeded in conceding pluralism over a limited range of issues (wage bargaining, low-level aspects of control of the work process), while maintaining intact a monist position on the more strategic issues of company or industry-level action' (Crouch, 1977: 47).

Post-war democracy and economic growth

This 'post-industrial' theory of employee relations is clearly associated with many features of the post-war period, when Harold Wilson could talk about the 'white heat of technology' coming to the aid of 'UK plc'.

Britain, although declining in terms of position in the world economy, had not yet been consigned to the remedial class. The discussion in social policy and the debates within various Labour governments had revealed a concern for the 'distribution of resources'. Inner city problems had been seen as necessitating the design of better delivery systems; the ideal of equality of access was still considered worthwhile.

In the world of employment, questions were being asked about the role and influence of trade unions as Britain's performance started to falter. The accepted architecture of pluralism – a modest role for the state, the continuation of voluntarism, trade unions as regulators of labour and an overall consensus over the existence of the pluralist coalition – was also under threat (Armstrong et al., 1991).

One particular event – the Donovan Commission – stands out as the epitome of the influence of the pluralist theory. This had been expressly set up to investigate what many saw as the uncontrolled growth of trade union disorder in 1968. The use of a pluralist frame of reference (sometimes known as the Oxford School or the institutional approach of industrial relations, involving Alan Flanders, Alan Fox and Hugh Clegg) had a major role in shaping this report, and in that capacity depicted the various elements of industrial relations in a way that was to have far-reaching consequences (Eldridge et al., 1991).

As a result of adopting this theoretical perspective, Eldridge et al. (1991: 97) suggest:

> The Donovan Commission in its attribution of cause and effect was itself taking part in this elaboration of trade union culpability but against a background where its recommendations could not directly address the roots of the 'disorder'.

Such developments tended to concentrate on achieving superficial adjustments to the distribution of work and rewards (Hyman and Brough, 1975). Like other areas of social policy, the coalition that comprised the area of employment had become ineffective and the balance of power needed to be recast. In this process it was the Donovan Commission that pointed to the imbalance between management and the unions as the cause of the breakdown in the coalition of interests. It was therefore the role of management within the relationship that needed redefining. The very theory that was intended to achieve a more realistic account of modern employee relations when operationalised by this commission had the effect of reinforcing the existence of unequal interests.

Pluralist theory confronted the question of competing interests in employment relations. It went beyond unitary theory and captured the political realities of the experience of employment in modern democracies. Ultimately it still portrayed the world of employment as resting upon a sufficient consensus to ensure that all parties would participate in resolving their restricted differences of interests.

If we consider the case study at the outset of the chapter (Exhibit 1.1), it is not difficult to see those accounts that acknowledge the potential for conflict between the two sides and consider the way forward to reside with the process of negotiation and conciliation, leading ultimately to a resolution of the conflict of interests, a position held by the government at the time. 'Tony Blair called yesterday for arbitration to resolve rail strikes and dismissed Conservative calls to stay at home and concentrate on domestic issues' (*Financial Times*, 10 January 2002).

To address some of the shortcomings identified above, we now turn to systems theory and its account of the organisation of employment, which, because of its ability to portray employment in a logical manner, did so much to enhance the role of the discipline.

Systems theory

Under a pluralist banner there appeared to be few attempts to question the underlying distribution of power and construction of hierarchies in work or employment. Alongside the growing influence of pluralist theory in employee relations in the post-war period, systems theory provided a version of pluralist thinking that sought to systematise knowledge of employee relations and establish the discipline as an equal to other areas of social science.

Systems theory, which is identified with the American writer John Dunlop and his landmark book *The Industrial Relations Systems* (1958), could be said to have provided one of the dominant paradigms in the field of employee relations. But why systems theory, why in 1958, and what has been the consequence of this virtual monopoly of the theoretical field for employee relations?

To answer the first question we need to establish what we mean by systems theory. General systems theory had been popularised by von Bertalanffy, who had established the theory within the field of biology (von Bertalanffy, 1950). The existence of systems has a seemingly natural base within biology. What we know about the operation of biological systems within an ecological context indicates that, for example, a cell requires inputs in the form of food, combines this with its own chemistry and converts this into energy, allowing it to survive in its environment. At the completion of this cycle the waste products of the process are expelled from the cell through its cell wall. Should the cell need more energy, then it absorbs more food from its environment and the whole cycle starts all over again. The logic of the entire system is guided by the need to survive. What was observed in nature appeared to correspond well with the world of work organisations. As Clegg (1990: 68) suggests, in relation to the impact of systems ideas on organisations:

> Not only did they produce a major reconceptualisation of organisations striving for orderliness in an otherwise chaotic world; they also successfully reinterpreted the past development of organisation theory. Reading backwards from the open systems perspective, much earlier conceptions could now be interpreted as an excessively internalist and closed system account of organisation structure and process.

What was true for organisations was certainly true of industrial relations at this time. Systems theory appeared to hold the prospect of making sense of a disparate set of phenomena composed of social movements, government organisations and a set of loosely structured procedures at a time of rapid industrial growth within the US economy in the immediate post-war era.

The attraction of systems theory has always been its ability to create an orderly description of its object of study, to provide an account of the variety of parts and connect them all together through the logic of the function each appears to play in sustaining the whole system. Dunlop, searching for a theory that could make sense of an apparently diverse set of factors, could see the opportunity of finding a device that could locate all of these factors within a single framework.

At that time in the US, one of the most powerful exponents of general systems theory was the sociologist Talcott Parsons. His work used the analogy of systems thinking as an entire framework for accounting for the nature and direction of American society (Parsons, 1952). Itself a system made up of subsystems with boundaries, his theory of society rested on the premise that maintained that society's structure was designed in such a way as to ensure its continued existence. The different subsystems had different jobs to fulfil and all complemented each other to help society to survive; they made it 'function'. That use of systems thinking could be applied to Dunlop's project; industrial relations could now be developed as a viable separate academic discipline and its disparate elements could be presented as logical components of a rational and ordered whole. For Dunlop, industrial relations could be established as a separate subsystem of the Parsons society, possessing identifiable inputs travelling across boundaries where they would engage in the process of transformation which ultimately would lead to outputs in the forms of rules that would subsequently guide the subsystem to its next stage (Figure 1.2).

One of the consequences of adopting this model was the creation of a set of terms that have become embedded in the language of employee relations. Inputs, as Figure 1.2 indicates, are composed of actors, environmental contexts and ideology. Actors refer to the employers and employees and representative organisations, while the contexts are composed of technological regimes, such as the type of production system itself, shaping the patterns of work and the composition of the workforce. Debates on whether the current production regime is Fordist (conforming to the dominant pattern of work organisation associated with the early production systems of Ford car plants), neo-Fordist (production similar to the Ford archetype but with the possibility of modifications and variations) or post-Fordist (production regimes that have passed on to different forms which display far greater flexibility in their arrangements as compared with the rigid control structures associated with the mass production of Ford) would

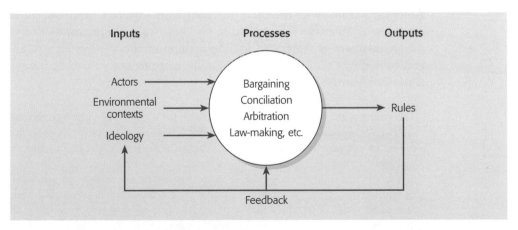

Figure 1.2 The industrial relations subsystem

Source: Dunlop (1958) From *Industrial Relations System, 1st edition*, by ©1959. Reprinted with permission of South-Western College publishing a division of Thomson Learning. Fax 001 800 730 2215.

determine the type of environmental input identified by the model, and, depending on which is identified, would have clear consequences for what effects this particular environmental factor might have on the transformation process (Allen, 1992).

The nature of markets and financial factors would also be regarded as contextual factors. With the emphasis since the late 1980s on the impact of markets on business performance and the capacity of firms to shape markets, markets and financial factors are bound to be significant for the model.

Finally, ideology plays a key role in explaining how the different parties in the industrial relations subsystem come to behave in a manner that sustains the desire to reconcile any differences in values and objectives. In Britain, with its strong tradition of voluntarism and an absence of strict legal constraints, an ideological system has emerged that is accessible to all of the different parties. Whether they are trade unions or employers' groups, they have been able to establish within the larger ideological system a set of ideas that sustains their own role and independence. At the heart of the model is the transformation process akin to the biological organism transforming food into energy for its continued existence.

In the same way, the different inputs mentioned above combine within a necessity to ensure that workplaces continue to operate and achieve agreements about the organisation and structure of work. Employers and employees negotiate and bargain to create workable practices enabling the organisation to continue to pursue its objectives. The output from this transformation is the creation of rules that, although temporary, guide the system to its next stage of development. This brief account of Dunlop's systems theory has to be viewed in the context of American society at that time.

The growth and integration of American industry

The late 1940s and 1950s in America were a period of enormous dynamism. During the 1930s, wave after wave of migrants had left war-torn Europe to establish new lives in the US. Many of the values and icons of American society were established during this period. Ideas of the openness of its social structure were born out of the stories of migrant success, climbing the economic ladder from the ghettos and achieving the American dream. With the energy deriving from this 'new' impetus, the institutions and practices of American society had to find new ways of integrating this population into the mainstream of American life. Something of this restless energy and opportunity is captured by Dos Passos (1952: 1) in his extraordinary novel spanning this period of American history:

> The young man walks fast by himself through the crowd that thins into the night streets; feet are tired from hours of walking; eyes greedy for warm curve faces, answering flicker of eyes, the set of a head, the lift of a shoulder, the ways the hands spread and clench; blood tingles with wants; mind is a beehive of hopes buzzing and stinging; muscles ache for the knowledge of jobs, the roadmender's pick and shovel work, the fisherman's knack with a hook when he hauls on the slithery net from the rail of the lurching trawler, the swing of the bridgeman's arm as he slings down the white hot rivet, the engineer's slow grip wise on the throttle, the dirtfarmer's use of his whole body when, whoaing the mules, he yanks the plow from the furrow. The young man walks by himself searching through the crowd with greedy ears taught to hear, by himself, alone.

In this immigrants' world, the American cities were a melting pot for those newly arrived as they searched for work and a place in the 'new' society. An earlier researcher had also seen this diversity and sought to establish a theory that might hold the potential to confront this restless and dynamic working population. Elton Mayo, and what was to become the human relations school, had seen the need to find a theory that could point to some process of integration. To be able to conceptualise the employment relationship in a way that could lead to integration through the creation of a 'system', held great value for those who might be considering the problem at a national political level.

The journey of systems theory from its biological starting point to the world of industrial relations did much the same. It suggested a framework for making sense of the rapidly changing world of employment, it labeled all manner of different phenomena and it provided an explanation that connected all these different parts (Roethlisberger and Dickinson, 1939; Carey, 1980).

Some shortcomings of systems theory

At this stage it is important to step back and assess this major theory in employee relations and perhaps start to understand its long life in the orthodoxy of the discipline. If employee relations is going to be accounted for in terms of a systems analogy, we need to get right to the heart of the theory to assess its capacity to explain that subsystem. Its main assumptions include the following:

- The term system implies something that is orderly and capable of description, as we mentioned above. It means more than this, however, it suggests that if the world of employment is a system, it displays a common set of values that binds it together and makes it a system. This is what Parsons (1952) called the 'central value system'. A belief in the existence of such a common value system appears at odds particularly with the experience of contemporary American society.
- An equilibrium – or, using the biological language, homeostasis – is achieved, that is, the employee relations subsystem reaches a point of balance within itself and its internal constituencies while at the same time reflecting the needs of the wider society of which it is a part. To use the modern idiom, it 'delivers' the world of employment in a way that is consonant with the requirements of that society at that time. As a result, the entire society continues to function and survive. With such a massive experience of social dislocation resulting in mass unemployment, skills shortages and industrial collapse in manufacturing sectors it is hard to see such equilibrium in operation.
- If all of these subsystems are to survive, the individuals within them must reflect as closely as possible the objectives of the organisation. How does this occur? According to systems theory it is produced by the socialisation of individuals into roles which, as individuals, we all learn to adopt. We learn to become a junior management trainee by observing others in that role, reading the relevant training literature and absorbing all manner of clues and information that will aid us in achieving a set of values and behaviours that are considered to correspond with the dominant definitions of that role at that time. For those who do not learn the right values and adopt the correct behaviour, their chance of achieving either access to work or success if they possess a job is limited.

In Dunlop's theory, the emphasis on rules starts to make sense. These outcomes from the industrial relations system are the product of those reconciliations between all the individual employees and their managers – or in systems language, all the values expressed by the workforce are reconciled with the organisation's objectives. The rules in whatever form, whether in what has been termed 'custom and practice' or some other form of collective agreement, express this process. In turn, these agreements come to be highly influential and shape employee relations from that moment into the future, until they are once again negotiated or allowed to be displaced by an entirely new set of agreements or rules.

This theory, although modified at times (Bain and Clegg, 1974; Clegg, 1979), has been dominant in the explanation of employee relations over the years.

Systems theory, which has a reputation for remaining extremely remote and abstract, has persisted in this area although it is claimed that many writers fail to acknowledge its nature and distinctiveness. In this sense it is important for us to ask about the limitations of this particular theory. Clegg and Dunkerley provide an excellent review of the major criticisms of general systems theory in their book *Organisation, Class and Control* (1980). They, with Silverman (1970) and Hyman (1989), provide a useful set of critiques that raise enough concerns about systems theory to make one wonder how it has survived so long (unless of course we start to appreciate its operational utility, which is a point we will come to later). Of the many criticisms, we need only outline those that explain the reservations certain authors have regarding the adoption of this particular theory. Its derivation from pluralist theory means that systems theory shares several of its features.

Some of the more significant limitations include:

- At the centre of the problem is the same question that was raised in relation to the unitary theory, that of consensus. The focus on values, socialisation and the resulting roles adopted by individuals all add up to a workplace where fairly passive individuals appear to sense the need to conform, collaborate and reconcile any differences that might exist between them. The theory appears to concentrate on the need to achieve equilibrium through the resolution of conflict.
- All of this further assumes that organisation members in the workplace read and interpret the rules in a similar manner and arrive at a rational and predictable answer.
- Conflict in employment is largely missing; in learning our roles we come to adopt the objectives of the firm according to this account, which implies conformity and cooperation.
- Related to this point is the question of unequal power. In the present context, with senior management in Britain accruing ever larger shares of the profits to their own reward schemes, it appears hard not to recognise the increasing gulf in pay and conditions, between those employing workers and those who are employed. Owners of enterprises clearly do not have the same level of influence on the system as ordinary employees.
- As far as the description of the inputs is concerned, it neither explains how they came into existence nor how they might change over time.
- At the most general level, the theory does not account for change, nor does it reflect the contradictions and failures of either the industrial relations system or the larger

society. The fact that we have youth unemployment, a segregated workforce divided on grounds of race and gender, and many other divisions, implies that we live in a society where conflict is normal and consensus is, at best, partial.

In systems theory, certainly at its inception in employee relations, we had a theory which once again appeared to reflect managerial concerns, but in this case they were very real problems facing American managers in the early post-war period. Like the unitary theory, systems theory in its earlier forms appeared to hold a method of analysis that contained within it a description of the problems of employee relations that were amenable to managerial initiatives and gave management a chance of sustaining its position in the employment relationship.

Finally, we should also note that, having contributed to the establishment of a whole new world of employee relations by providing a comprehensive theory to underpin what had been a fairly pragmatic discipline based upon 'fact-finding and description rather than theoretical generalisations' (Winchester, 1983: 101), it also opened the floodgates to empirical research. Its assumptions rooted in structural functionalism (a type of analysis that dwells on the role that the constituent elements of a system have in sustaining the function of that entity) meant that, once all of the different pieces of the system had been identified, empirical verification of the relationship between the parts would become a major task for those engaging in the discipline.

Looking back to Exhibit 1.1, we can see how a systems analysis could focus on the imbalance between the financial and human resource subsystems and label this a significant problem for management. South West Trains states that additional recruitment and training will help to solve the problem. Additionally, an adjustment would have to be reached through the process of collective bargaining, with each side establishing its own agenda. With the proper procedures followed, governed by the established rules and procedures, an outcome would be possible that would contain a new set of conditions and employment practices, reflecting a new point of balance within the organisation.

We would not claim that each of the theories discussed here follows some evolutionary path of advancement. Each has arisen at a particular time in a particular context, often with a particular purpose in the mind of its author. Over time they relate to particular policy practices and become modified to reflect the shifting patterns of interests prevailing at any one time. Of course, not all theories are as clear-cut as systems theory, where a single author can be connected initially to its development, as in the case of Dunlop.

Systems theory confronted the question of the changing shape of industry and employment and created a means of describing the specific arrangements and underlying processes identified as determining the employment relationship. With its emphasis upon the creation of rules and procedures it established the employment relationship as a central issue for research and policy development.

Marxist theory does not follow the foregoing theories in a neat and orderly progression. It too emerged in the nineteenth century but with an agenda to question the existing structure of society, with a concern to understand the nature and direction of the then new capitalist economy. In that sense, employment and the employment relationship, although of central concern to Marx's analysis of capitalism, are the focus of an explanation that seeks to understand the mechanism by which the 'whole' capitalist system operates. In that sense, they are not considered to be significant as separate elements within an 'academic' debate.

Marxist theory

For many, the fall of the Iron Curtain, the collapse of the Berlin Wall and attempts to introduce market-based policies into eastern bloc countries were all evidence of the end of socialism and the final proof of the lack of utility for Marxist-inspired theories. Here we need to make a distinction between the theories inspired by Marx's writing and the actual forms that took shape on the ground as a result of these theories.

The theories themselves emerged from Marx's observations at a time when capitalism was still in its infancy and employment was very much a matter of survival in a world where huge disparities of wealth and power existed. Faced with such a dramatic period of change, Marx set out to understand and identify the logic that drove the economic system to unfold in the way it did. Attached to this project was his ambition to explain how this understanding could in turn account for other features of capitalist society. If the dramatic features of the Industrial Revolution inspired Marx to seek a theory to explain the nature of capitalism, then, like all the other theories we have mentioned, it appears that Marxism continues to provide an important analytical device for understanding the employment relationship.

What is central in making sense of Marxist theory is therefore the connection between theory and practice. For Marx there was no distinction; theory existed to provide an account of society that, in the process of revealing the inner contradictions of the system, would lead to action to overcome these contradictions. In the process of elaborating a theory of capitalism he pointed to the constant exploitation of workers under capitalist employment conditions. Revealing the mechanisms by which these inequalities were generated through debate and policies of political movements, he believed, would lead to radical opposition to those in power and hence to the overthrow of the capitalist class. First and foremost, his theory was a product of the nineteenth century, a period of enormous social upheaval, as the 'new' capitalist society started to take shape (Mandel, 1978).

◼ Industrialisation and inequality

The Industrial Revolution provided Marx with the evidence for his theory of capitalism. What Marx saw was an industrial society in which divisions were being driven by the inevitable competition between classes. His particular insights and originality lay in his ability to connect so many of the different parts of that society within one overriding logic. At the heart of his analysis was the existence of the pursuit of profit by the entrepreneur; this was an 'inevitable' requirement of the capitalist system. This inevitable demand explained much about all the other features of that early society. This logic resulted in a system of work that invariably set one side of the employment relationship against the other. Entrepreneurs needed to maximise their return on investments and employees were bound to defend their standard of living by fighting for a 'decent' wage (Hobsbawm, 1974).

The conditions of work were often appalling, and employers had little regard for the well-being of their employees (Bendix, 1974). Hours were long, work was often dangerous and unhealthy, and pay, at least for the first half of the nineteenth century, was based on the principle of subsistence (Briggs and Saville, 1967).

In the contemporary labour market it is possible to see how these two sources of inequality become inescapable when experienced within a labour market that is becoming increasingly competitive, unstable and surrounded by unemployment. Whatever the inequality experienced, most workers in today's labour market would be far more likely to put up with it than risk the loss of their job. The ability to locate the employment relationship within this broader set of social relationships provides a persuasive account of how people at work come to behave, respond, act or acquiesce. People's responses are a function not just of the determinants of their workplace, but of a whole set of factors and outcomes themselves produced by external contextual and historical forces.

Labour process theory

More recently, interest in the Marxist analysis of employment has centred around the labour process debate rekindled by Harry Braverman's book *Labor and Monopoly Capital* (1974). In short, Braverman outlined a theory of degradation of work which resulted from the continuous decline of skill among the workforce leading to a weakening of bargaining power and a loss of control. He illustrated this process by referring to Taylor's system of scientific management, which, according to Braverman, inevitably led to the continuous reduction in skill levels as work became increasingly reorganised to satisfy the logic of managerial efficiency. Braverman's central contention of inevitable deskilling unleashed a substantial quantity of research to establish the likelihood of such trends. Today, commentators would probably conclude that such 'inevitability' elevates management to a very sophisticated level, and as such reject such an all-embracing account (see Chapter 3). Research suggests that management, and particularly British management, tends to muddle through (Sisson, 1994).

Braverman was therefore far too generous to the capacity of management to 'manage' in a rational fashion. Not only do managers deploy all manner of strategies, not just those that deskill (Friedman, 1977), but, as the complexity of capitalism grows, their choice of options expands. Whether or not the central tenets of his argument are misguided, Braverman's concern for the intersection of management practice and the experience of employment has generated a rich layer of theory, entitled 'labour process theory', and an ever expanding empirical research programme to set against this. For some academics this has also shifted the focal point of research: 'A similar trend can be discerned in the labour process literature where recent interest in management strategy and practices has far outstripped any interest in worker organisation and mobilisation' (Thompson and Ackroyd, 1995, quoted in Kelly, 1998).

Nonetheless, Marxist theory continues to provide a rich source of analysis by making connections between areas of social life excluded from the theories discussed earlier. In a world where work appears less secure for the majority of the workforce and the pressures for performance are increasingly experienced at the level of the individual, it provides a framework for understanding many significant contemporary phenomena which are closely connected to the employment relationship, whether experienced as pressure from the broader context or within the direct experience of the job.

Although Marxist analysis can include a variety of positions (see Gospel and Palmer, 1993: 25), it clearly emphasises the employment relationship and sets it within a discussion of the current stage of capitalist development. Unlike the earlier theories, it draws on a discussion of the fundamental processes of capitalist development which, though changed in form, continues to shape the employment relationship.

As we indicated at the outset of this chapter, for many the insights derived from this theory do not appear to fit comfortably within the world of HRM, high-performance teams, business process re-engineering or many of the other latest management practices and fads. And yet we would contend that its capacity to look beyond an immediate problem and relate this to historical antecedents and contextual factors provides a richness of explanation that holds the potential for a more comprehensive understanding of the issue under discussion.

Although this approach remedies many of the earlier criticisms, it too has its limitations, many of which reside in the concentration on the 'structure' of capitalism, which fails to address some of the inbuilt assumptions about those structures. With the 'economic' base of society influencing the direction and shape of the economic system, it is often hard to see the connections between this level of analysis and the changing experiences of those within the employment relationship. For instance, the fact that half the workforce is composed of women and that their experience of modern work is very different from that of men requires more than an explanation that relies upon male views of male structures and processes. Feminist critiques of the workplace have therefore grown to represent a significant body of knowledge, and in many cases have spent a considerable effort in trying to develop new theories that provide important insights into the employment relationship which for so long has implied men at work.

Marxist theory emerged to explain the problems associated with the growth and development of capitalism. Unlike the other theories, it does not believe in a consensus based upon shared interests. Classes in society exist in opposition to one another. In employment relations, this is represented by the opposing interests of labour and management. Conflict is therefore endemic in the workplace and is hidden only by active programmes of obscuring the realities of gross inequalities of power, control and reward. Once again, employees are called upon to be 'team players' and develop 'a strong sense of loyalty', reflecting the constant process of obscuring the real/experienced conditions of employment.

Turning back to the case study in Exhibit 1.1, we can say that adopting a Marxist analysis would lead to concentration on the permanent antagonism between classes which can come to be represented in the workplace, where conflict in industrial relations is considered endemic. However, although employees hold the potential to oppose employers' interests, they are constrained by the fortunes of economic performance, which in the case of railways since privatisation, have become locked into internal competition. Now, with the pressures to sustain profitability, labour is seen as an area for major cost-cutting.

A Marxist interpretation would therefore begin with an understanding of the changing nature of the railway industry under privatisation and seek to explain the attempt to remove power from organised labour by the last Conservative government. As the *Financial Times* of 4 January 2002 put it: 'Breaking up the power of the main railway unions – the RMT and Aslef – was a significant factor in the Conservative government's privatisation of the railways in the mid 1990's' (for further details see Baldry and Ellison, 2000).

If Marxist theory set out to explain the workings of the capitalist system, it did so at a time when ideas about equality between men and women were only in their formative stages. In this sense the analysis missed the subtleties of the divisions which existed within that system. With so many changes in the nature and composition of employment, feminist theories have done much to expose the inequalities between men and women at work.

Feminist theory

Feminist theory, like many other critical theories, emerged towards the end of the nineteenth century to confront the deteriorating condition in which the majority of women found themselves. As the features of modern capitalism crystallised in the form of large-scale industry and the creation of an urban workforce, women were increasingly located in areas of work that were badly paid, related to definitions of their domestic role and for the most part blocked any chance of achieving a full career to senior positions. With women excluded from the vote and considered inferior to men, the early feminist movement provided a different account of the situation confronting the majority of women (Rowbotham, 1974).

Today, women comprise nearly 50 per cent of the workforce, but when we come to look at the study of employee relations there still appears to be a reluctance to account adequately for women's position in the employment relationship. As Linda Dickens (1989) notes in a special issue of the *Industrial Relations Journal* devoted to feminist analysis:

> The predominant focus of industrial relations academic study, and of related disciplines, had tended to neglect the fact and nature of 'women's work', giving the impression that industrial relations academics were either gender-blind or, like industrial relations practitioners, held the view that 'if it's only women, it doesn't matter that much'.

This 'rediscovery' of women raises important questions about the understanding of women in the workforce and in particular the employment relationship. As Dickens says:

> The question arises, then, whether this rediscovery of women as a potential valuable resource for the 1990s heralds the end of their disadvantaged position in employment. It is a 'rediscovery' of women in that women have been discovered before in times of male labour shortage, as in wartime. This observation must immediately engender some caution, given the achievements of that time.

These two extracts raise several important points for us:

■ If academic theories of industrial relations have only recently acknowledged the contribution of feminist analysis, we need to outline those that can act as a corrective to this shortcoming.
■ If women now make up nearly half the workforce, the implications of the different feminist theories will hold considerable significance for explaining how women understand their position in the employment relationship and the wider labour market.
■ The existence of a variety of feminist theories has important consequences for the selection of appropriate policies to deal with the organisation of women's work.
■ Finally, we need to be able to establish an understanding of the general nature of feminist theories to distinguish them from industrial relations theory.

Features of feminist theories

Feminist theory starts from the premise that if you wish to understand how women and men behave in the workplace, the analysis must commence with a description of capitalism which is informed by a discussion of the role of patriarchy. In other words, the overriding feature of modern society is the existence of a set of arrangements that have been designed by men with the effect of constantly defining women in an inferior position. Feminist theory therefore sets out to reveal the true nature of this form of domination of men over women, and to provide policy options for overcoming the various forms of domination. Each particular variant of feminist theory will emphasise its particular explanation of this dominance and indicate the favoured path of action to help resolve it (Calas and Smircich, 1996).

Patriarchy and gender are central terms in all feminist theories. The former means an arrangement of society and its institutions to reflect men's interests, while the latter indicates that ideas of behaviour attached to biological sex are a product of socialisation and therefore change over time and reflect different political systems and cultures.

Like Marxist theory, the intention of feminist theory is not just to contribute to academic developments, but also to provide understanding, which can inform policy design and implementation.

Feminist theory and employee relations

Although it is hard to see examples of feminist theories within traditional industrial relations, such theories have clearly come to influence research and debate in the area (Dickens, 1989). Looking through publications like the *British Journal of Industrial Relations*, it is apparent that articles devoted to women's work or by those claiming to adopt a feminist analysis are infrequent. This becomes all the more surprising when the majority of projections for job growth in the UK suggest that female employment will be favoured.

The justification for including feminist theories within a discussion of theories within employee relations appears incontrovertible.

Different theories, different policies

In a short section such as this it is impossible to reflect the range and subtleties of all the different theories. Our intention therefore is to outline three of the main feminist theories and establish their contribution to the understanding of the employment relationship.

Liberal feminism

Liberal feminist theory is probably the oldest analysis, developing out of the period of transition to modern capitalism. Its major concern was to establish that women were equal and not inferior to men. As early industrialisation saw the gulf between men and women at work expand (Rowbotham, 1974), liberal feminists sought to:

- argue for equality between men and women;
- create policies for reform;
- reveal the 'cultural' factors that created sex stereotypes;
- focus on removing barriers to advancement, e.g. more women managers.

The primary goal of this approach is to take the institutions of society as given and devise ways of improving the position of women through reform. This can take a variety of forms, such as equal opportunity policies, affirmative action plans and assertiveness training. In essence, from this viewpoint women as individuals can overcome inequality through the removal of barriers and prejudice through appropriate policies.

Much of the writing in HRM and other management and business practices relies upon this type of analysis, where answers exist and management can take the initiative and respond to the call for greater equality for women (Kanter, 1983).

Some argue that liberal feminism provides a simplistic account which fails to recognise the entrenched nature of inequality between men and women in modern capitalist societies. The radical feminists argue that patriarchy and gender are arrangements that are deeply embedded in our society. To pursue a reformist strategy merely reinforces existing inequalities, albeit in a different guise.

Radical feminism

For the radical feminists, like the Marxist analysis above, the structure of modern capitalist society is patriarchal and no amount of reform will change arrangements when each generation of men reinvents institutions and practices that reconfirm male power and privilege.

Radical feminism has the following core features:

- It believes that women's oppression results from comprehensive and systematic inequalities, which are elements of modern capitalist society.
- Unlike in liberal feminism, therefore, the problems women confront at the workplace are neither individual nor psychological.
- Policies like equal opportunities, although they might carry the prospect of improvement for women in the workforce, do not guarantee it, because the institutions that design and implement policies are themselves integral parts of an unequal capitalist society.
- To overcome men's domination over women in both society and the workplace, fundamental change has to take place to transform unequal and hierarchical institutions, organisations and workplaces, and to replace these with organisations that allow women to regain their true identity.

The goal of radical feminist theory is therefore very much at odds with the 'male' world of work as it is experienced. In a period of transition to this new set of arrangements, women would pursue a policy of separateness and establish ways of organising work to include 'participatory decision-making, a system of rotating leadership, flexible and interactive job designs, an equitable distribution of income and an interpersonal and political accountability' (Koen, quoted in Calas and Smircich, 1996). Examples of this can be seen in cases where women have established separate workplaces and avoided the influence of male working practices.

Such theories have done much to redirect our focus away from the particular and local cases of inequality at work and their persistence in the face of political pressure. Radical feminist theory has revealed the entrenched nature of inequality and sexism in our society. Transforming this situation has been problematical when faced with the enormous weight of existing institutions and assumed 'normal' patterns of work and the relative values attached to the different types of work within the labour market.

Postmodernism

In an attempt to explain how inequality between men and women can be sustained through the 'meanings' attached to our day-to-day lives, the postmodern or post-structuralist feminist theories provide a bewildering array of explanations.

Very briefly, these theories start from the view that the very basis of knowledge upon which we guide our lives is highly problematical; that our assumptions about truth, reality and objective science cannot be taken for granted. How we understand the world around us is very much a product of language, or to use their term, 'discourse'. This discourse contains meanings that reflect assumptions and ideas about the organisation of power in a society (Legge, 1995). The impact of a particular discourse upon individuals has profound effects on how they think about themselves and, for example, how they experience the workplace.

For women this means that, by their very involvement in the use of language, they are drawn into a world of meanings that can reflect and justify their unequal position in the labour market. By concentrating on meanings and an individual's identity, postmodernism does appear to have important things to say about the more recent techniques used to influence and shape behaviour which belong to the world of management and HRM.

As a theory for explaining women at work, postmodernism:

- rejects ideas of scientific objectivity;
- suggests that how an individual behaves is a relative and contradictory process and therefore not easily inferred from conventional research;
- dwells on how the subjective individual establishes meanings through engaging with language, which subsequently shape behaviour.

This analysis might argue, for example, that in the area of 'skills' in the workplace, meanings attached to conventional definitions of skill are not the result of some neutral definitional process. Rather, they are the outcome of men claiming status for their skill hierarchies while attaching negative attributes to female skills. In turn, women can come to 'accept' these negative attributes which over time, it would be argued, have led to women being segregated into the lower levels of the labour market (Cockburn, 1983; Collinson *et al.*, 1990).

How far such a subjectivist account of employee relations will be adopted by mainstream employee relations writers is yet to be established. Postmodernism, as we discuss in the next section, has many critics owing to the features outlined above. Conventional employee relations, whether it assumes a unitary, pluralist, Marxist or systems approach, does have the luxury of sharing in a vocabulary that allows for a fairly straightforward exchange and comparison. Where the very language that we use becomes the focal point of the theoretical analysis, attempts to make comparisons become much more difficult.

Feminist theory and the labour market

Returning to the line of argument offered by Dickens at the beginning of this section, it is hard not to appreciate just how significant the feminist approach has become. With such fundamental inequalities still existing between men and women in the workplace (see Chapters 11 and 12), an analysis that accepts the statistics demonstrating this situation and provides ideas for reform and policy appears to be addressing the problems women confront daily in their workplaces.

The sheer scale of the task as depicted in many of these accounts is therefore plain for all to see. Furthermore, those in positions of power can ascribe virtue to themselves should they choose to support one or several of these reforms as either politicians, administrators or managers. As Cockburn (1989) admits: 'Equal opportunities is widely seen as a tool of management. That has sanitised and contained the struggle for equality.' She goes on to argue for a new approach to equal opportunities that relies far more on the radical feminist approach, which sees women uniting with other groups through becoming active in a political sense and by bringing trade union power behind equal opportunity initiatives. By adopting a very different theoretical position she argues that equal opportunities can be used by women to achieve greater power and influence.

Such an illustration serves to demonstrate the variety of feminist theories in use and indicates that each has an important contribution to make when starting to challenge the conventional theories of employee relations, which continue to rely on accounts of the organisation and management of employment that depict men's work as the norm and structures and practices designed by men as neutral. In addition, it has started to address the role of women in trade unions and the problematic nature of women's representation within the official trade union bureaucracy (Heery and Kelly, 1989; Fosh and Heery, 1990).

If we adopted a feminist analysis of the case study it would very clearly demonstrate that women within the rail industry have experienced considerable inequalities compared with their male counterparts. Women hold more of the junior positions and are used by management precisely because of their gendered characteristics for caring, food preparation and dealing with emotional difficulties.

Depending on which particular theory is adopted, the analyses could lead, for example, to:

- encouraging greater representation at senior levels and assertiveness training (liberal feminist);
- seeking to exclude men from the industry and perhaps setting up an all-female rail company, which would be based on flatter organisation structures, reduced hierarchies of pay and a greater level of participation in decision-making (radical feminist);
- an analysis of the meanings and identity of being a railway employee, perhaps revealing how, through prior socialisation, women come to think of themselves as 'naturally inclined' to those occupations that demand service, caring and the range of tasks associated with the traditional domestic role (postmodernism). In their training, such qualities might be seen to be reinforced through the language used and the codes of practice adopted in the job (Legge, 1995).

If feminist theory has started to extend the remit of employee relations theory then so too has the development of comparative theory. In a period in which so many changes in employment and employment practices are explained by the pressures of increasing international competition, then it would be surprising not to acknowledge the contribution from comparative theories of employee relations.

Comparative theory

> The growing internationalisation of economic and political life is questioning the very basis of a sub-discipline whose conceptual and explanatory frameworks have been, until now, overwhelmingly national. (Clark, 1995)

As Clark argued in reviewing a series of new texts all adopting a comparative approach to this discipline, employee relations has taken longer than many other disciplines to look to comparative research to evaluate developments in British employment.

Not only is British industry being increasingly drawn into international business but firms within Britain are competing with overseas companies with very different employment traditions (Held *et al.*, 2000). In addition, British managers, who reflected a fairly insular approach to business, are increasingly confronted with overseas practice peddled by management consultants as the latest panacea (Bean, 1992; Bamber and Lansbury, 1993). How do we come to know about these practices, whether from Japan, the US, Europe or beyond? Over the years, interest in each of these countries has reflected reports based on overseas research. Some of this research could be said to come from international studies of industrial relations while some comes from truly comparative studies. The former are associated with research looking at international bodies or developments which span a range of countries, such as multinational corporations (MNCs) or the role of the General Agreement on Tariffs and Trade (GATT), while comparative studies of industrial relations seek to analyse specific aspects of the employment relationship between two or more countries (Bean, 1992).

Like any area of comparative studies, comparing factors in one country with those in another can have a series of benefits:

■ It helps to establish the relative significance of particular factors in determining aspects of the employment relationship. For example, assessing the impact of two similar pieces of employment legislation might demonstrate other relevant factors that should be considered. For example, do relatively high labour costs in France really stimulate multinationals like Hoover to move operations to the UK?

■ A comparison generates knowledge about overseas examples that can provide alternative forms for conducting aspects of the employment relationship. Many current management practices are brought into this country by academics and consultants using data and evidence from comparative survey work overseas; for example, the practice of quality assurance teams in Japan has been popularised in the UK. The role of the Organisation for Economic Cooperation and Development (OECD) is a case in point, where comparative data are used to exhort member countries to pursue similar policy options.

■ By understanding the stage of development of another industrial system we can better predict the patterns of management, control and employment. Dore's 1973 study of Japanese and British factory regimes pointed to the late emergence of industrialisation in Japan as an important factor in explaining the different regimes of control in the two countries (Hyman and Ferner, 1994).

■ A clearer understanding of overseas systems and practices can provide a useful resource for those involved in designing social policy or legislation in the area of employment. In the case of Britain, this occurred in 1971 when the Conservative government attempted to introduce a form of employment legislation modelled on a US statute. As it turned out, what was designed to reduce industrial conflict actually achieved the opposite effect owing to the adoption of a piece of legislation designed for one industrial system and transferred to another that was quite different (Bamber and Lansbury, 1993).

■ By comparing factors from one country with those of another, new explanations and theories can emerge that can contribute to the growth of the discipline of employee relations.

Background assumptions

Most of the work conducted under the title of comparative employee relations continues to rely upon a modest use of theory in the quest to generate descriptively interesting and informative accounts of all manner of employment practices in overseas settings. Many of the leading current texts commence with a chapter on theory and then get on with the business of covering a substantial range of countries and all their particular idiosyncrasies related to employment. This approach is quite understandable when the complexity of the issues raised by the theoretical questions start to emerge.

What follows is a brief account of some of these difficult questions, which, although they might be played down at present because of the pressures to understand comparative data, nonetheless come back to haunt us when what we use as bona fide overseas data turns out to be inaccurate or inappropriate.

Theories of comparative employee relations

Convergence theory

If overseas patterns of employee relations are to be compared, then there must exist a series of assumptions about what is being compared. A number of theories raise some interesting questions about the context within which those systems exist.

In the 1960s, Kerr and his colleagues popularised the expression 'convergence'. In their book *Industrialism and Industrial Man*, Kerr et al. (1974) suggested that under the influence of modern technology, national systems of employee relations were being drawn together. The pressures of organising modern workplaces based upon collective bargaining ensured that requirements for education and training unleashed a series of related institutional pressures, which, when combined, had the effect of establishing common patterns of institutional life. These in turn led to pluralistic employee relations systems contributing to a range of democratic societal systems.

This optimistic view of western capitalist countries was informed by the conditions of the time, where the US, in a period of global expansion, sought to see itself as a benign harbinger of modern capitalism. Nobody mentioned the fact that it was the US that so often benefited from the economic expansion by providing the inward investment and a series of trading opportunities. Since that period in the late 1950s, the convergence theory of economic development has gained further credibility by the pressures of globalisation and the development of powerful trading blocs supported by the increasing role of multinational corporations. Perhaps the collapse of the Soviet

Union and the eastern bloc countries and the recent demise of Yugoslavia all provide spectacular examples of the globalising pressures from the capitalist countries. With such powerful evidence it is not difficult to see how authors like Amin and Thrift are able to conclude that we have reached a point where we now have a world economic system (Amin and Thrift, 1994). With the EU playing an ever increasing role in the labour market in the UK, it is not hard to see much of the research related to comparative studies of employee relations 'assuming' an underlying belief in convergence theories.

Development theory

A different, though related, theory, comes from a more critical perspective, which does owe some allegiance to the Marxist theories of economic development. Development theory tends to explain the changes taking place within the economic system as a series of stages that are difficult to avoid. Britain's capitalist growth was based upon a pre-capitalist stage where the formative structures of capitalism were being established. For example, early capitalism in the first half of the nineteenth century is represented by the existence of a system of elaborate rules to shape the behaviour of early workers unused to work and time discipline (Pollard, 1958; Thompson, 1968; Landes, 1972; Bendix, 1974). The Master and Servant Act 1825 encapsulated this 'authoritarian' period during which the 'discipline' of early capitalism was established. As different 'periods' emerge, it is argued, so the character of the entire system becomes modified and a new set of social relations is established in the workplace.

If this is correct, then trying to engage in comparative research will pose some difficult questions, such as whether the two countries being compared are at a similar 'stage' of development (see Figures 1.4 and 1.5). If they are not at a similar stage of

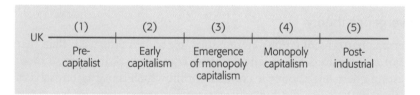

Figure 1.4 **Stages of development**

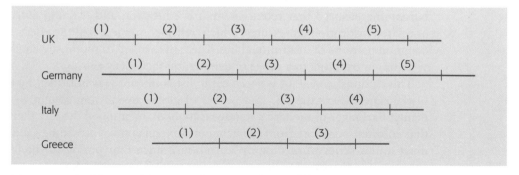

Figure 1.5 **Problems with comparing countries at different stages of economic development**

development, then whether you are studying employment policies, the reasons for unemployment or the different systems for collective bargaining, it is far from comparing like with like. In turn, the range of variables to isolate in the attempt to explain which are the causal variables to account for the particular factor under study becomes impossibly complex.

If we wish to undertake comparative research between the UK and a variety of other countries then we might end up with the situation shown in Figure 1.5. Conducting comparative research could well lead to the stage of economic development being the single most important distinguishing feature between the countries rather than the characteristics of a particular factor. An emphasis on 'stages of development' is therefore an important corrective to those accounts that feel able to descriptively compare the inherent features of a particular aspect of the employment relationship without acknowledging its context.

As Cronin and Schneer (1982) point out:

> It is not unreasonable to argue against comparison altogether. Comparison, after all, presupposes some degree of comparability and thus similarity, and it may well be a mistake to assume that the experience of workers at different times and places is similar. Similarities might, of course, emerge empirically, but the assumption of similarity may pre-empt the discovery of crucial differences.

Internal theory

The final theory in this section may underlie the majority of approaches in this area. It can be referred to as the internal theory of the comparative approach. Quite simply, the approach here is to play down the contextual/historical factors, take the features of the employment relationship and collect data about those features in a variety of different nations. Data verifying the existence and extent of a particular phenomenon are then compared and explained according to some internal logic. For example, problems of poor productivity comparing Polish and French workers might be explained with reference to some set of organisational arrangements or poor levels of motivation within their respective workplaces. Such an account might be the starting point for an explanation but barely moves beyond the surface of the underlying reasons to be found in the context of employment in the two countries.

In one sense this type of comparative theory can act as a first stage in the development of a more rigorous understanding, which will require the insights from the other two comparative theories discussed above. Whatever the level of theoretical sophistication, it is clear that comparative research in the area of employee relations will continue to expand as all the pressures of internationalisation push business to become increasingly global in its design and implementation (Waters, 1995).

In that sense, as the pressures of internationalisation continue to build, it will become increasingly important to recognise the details of divergence to ensure that in areas of employment particular national characteristics are understood for what they are. As Shalev (1980, quoted in Bean, 1992: 8) indicates, however: 'Whatever the ultimate objectives, the fact remains that a good deal of the existing work, although often rich and insightful, has not so far been explicitly theoretical in either its purpose or [its] method.'

As the internationalisation of business grows, so the need to understand overseas systems of employment becomes more urgent. Comparative research in employment relations will inevitably expand as an area of study. However, the theoretical difficulties are substantial, and many researchers and commentators avoid confronting the difficult questions raised in this chapter and settle for descriptive accounts, which do act as a first step to understanding overseas examples but may well lead to false optimism and confidence about our level of comprehension. Perhaps Eaton (2000) has an important observation here when he says, 'It is much better nowadays to think in terms of *international* industrial relations. Yet there remain powerful redoubts of national industrial relations practices, as was pointed out by Muller (1997) in a spirited corrective to the convergence idea.'

For those in search of the latest theorising in the study of employment, postmodernism claims to provide a fundamental break with earlier explanations and emphasises a very different set of factors for explaining the employment relationship.

If we look again at the original case of railways, it is clear that international comparisons are increasingly made and conclusions that Britain's railways are the worst in Europe are often cited. Few such attempts make genuine efforts to research the nature, development and form of industrial relations in the industry in equivalent European countries.

Postmodernism

To conform to the structure adopted so far, we should have entitled this section 'Postmodernist theory', but unlike earlier discussions there is a wide variety of explanations within this domain which claim to represent the true approach to producing a postmodernist explanation. For the study of employee relations, postmodernism has had significant implications, which are perhaps reflected for some in the change in name from industrial relations to employee relations. Before providing a brief review of some of these changes we need to clarify just what is meant by 'postmodernism' for this is closely related to our earlier discussions when identifying the existence of eras, epochs and stages. As other authors have pointed out, not only is postmodernism a theory about the world around us but it also acts as an account of a particular stage in its development (Legge, 1995).

■ Advanced capitalism, eras, epochs or change?

To argue for the existence of a postmodernist era in the case of employee relations is to argue that major transformations in the workplace and the management and experience of employment have occurred. This new era is counterpoised to the pre-existing industrial order, which was known as the Fordist period or the modernist era. The generic feature defining employment in this period was the existence of mass production responding to the needs of mass consumption. During this period, large manufacturing enterprises employing large workforces, often highly unionised, working to set repetitive methods and producing standardised products were the norm. This period, some would argue, lasted 50 years and required great stability to ensure that the mass and scale of the activities were realised and produced the economies of scale necessary for such substantial initial investments.

As well as an account of a particular 'period', it was itself an outcome of a way of understanding and explaining the world of work, which relied on research from the experimental method based on assumptions of positivism. That is to say, the world was 'out there' to be measured and the results to be accumulated to enable those connected to the world of employment to organise work according to the criterion of efficiency and to maximise the use of resources, whether inanimate or animate.

Contrasting modernist and postmodernist theories of employment

If modernist theories looked at the world of work and employment and believed that a scientific method was the appropriate manner for conducting research into employment, what did this mean in practice?

Perhaps the clearest exponent of the modernist theory of employment was Frederick Taylor. Growing up at the turn of the century in the US, Taylor believed that it was quite appropriate to use the methods of the physical sciences to study work. The fact that he called his theory 'scientific management' indicates that he believed that it was based upon objective methods of studying work. If measurement was a straightforward non-problematic procedure in the physical sciences, then it was appropriate for the study of work and employment.

As Baritz (1960) points out so clearly, at this time in the US the success of the physical sciences was such that those trying to study social phenomena, like business, management and employment, were hard pressed to resist what appeared to be answers to difficult questions facing managers and industrialists.

Taylor conducted his research on work organisation and claimed to have discovered a 'science' of work which revealed 'laws' about the nature of work organisation. He was so convinced that he had discovered these laws, akin to the laws of nature, he felt quite justified in suggesting that trade unions, for example, were totally unnecessary. What was the point of discussing work arrangements when he had discovered the 'one best way'? His was a quintessential statement of the modernist theory of work and employment.

That tradition of measuring the details of work continues, so much of the positivist tradition remains within employee relations, albeit in a much more sophisticated form. Accumulating data to obtain an 'accurate' account of employment practices, trends and developments has become a central, if not the most central, concern of the subject. This has been exaggerated over the past decade or so as research resources have become increasingly tied to the production of 'hard data'.

In contrast to this theory, postmodernist theories of work and employment have tended to concern themselves with more subjective dimensions of work. Postmodernist theory involves expressing a concern for language and symbols. This concern for understanding behaviour in the workplace requires an understanding of the creation of the subjective state of mind of that individual. This is in stark contrast to Taylor's 'external' explanation of the worker. To understand the worker, Taylor literally measured the individual with stopwatches, movie cameras and tape measures – the individual worker was a physical object to be understood in terms of his or her external behaviours and actions. The postmodernist explanation starts from a belief that to understand the external actions of individuals requires a method of research that captures the earlier stages of the process of creating meaning. An individual worker acts in a particular way as a result of a combination of ideas, beliefs and values, which are themselves produced by the language, meaning systems and symbols of the world he or she inhabits. To unravel the process by which these subjective factors come to shape the individual worker requires us to understand the language and symbols surrounding that individual.

For those adopting this position, understanding a person's behaviour means studying the language used in the workplace, the culture, rituals, symbols and pattern of communication, all of which influence and shape the individual's behaviour. If these are the variables that determine behaviour, it comes as no surprise that management development and other arms of applied psychology have devoted so much energy to creating languages and techniques with the intention of achieving a role in the motivation and control of the new, subjective, individualised worker (Peters and Waterman, 1982).

This concern for the subjective individual brings us back to the opening comment about the change of name from industrial relations to employee relations. What is implied by the name change is not just a reflection of a different context of employment which includes a labour market dominated by the service sector, a reduction in trade union density, the growth of female employment, the reduction in full-time jobs and the corresponding explosion in part-time and non-standard work, but also the emphasis on individualism implied by the rhetoric of HRM. The insertion of HRM into the world of employment since the early 1980s has, in some minds, confirmed a transformation to a postmodern era and in turn supports its theoretical utility, adopting as it does a concern for culture, symbols, language and an individualised approach to accounting for worker behaviour. In other words, it depicts the worker as a subjective individual (Storey, 1992). Table 1.1 contrasts these two theoretical approaches and emphasises the lack of 'connection' between them.

In the modernist approach, the theory is hard at work generating useful knowledge, which in turn can be utilised for a wide range of policies and actions, whether managerial, organisational or governmental. In the case of postmodernism, knowledge is subjective and hence its application is more problematical owing to the accounts being singular and not necessarily of general application. In other words, unravelling the culture and meaning systems in one particular organisation might well lead to a set of understandings that appear local to that particular organisation.

Table 1.1 Comparing modernism with postmodernism

Modernism	Postmodernism
Adopts a positivistic position:	Adopts a relativist position:
■ Objective measurement possible and necessary	■ Subjective research possible/desirable
■ Research data/knowledge universal	■ Research knowledge relative
■ General laws allow for universal laws	■ Relative nature of knowledge
Restricted use:	
■ Power located in positions of authority and capacity to control	■ Power exercised through relationships/influence and meanings
■ Employee relations knowledge attends to explaining trends and developments for producing appropriate responses	■ Employee relations knowledge to understand how cultural and linguistic variables shape individual behaviour

Source: after Storey (1992)

It does not require a huge leap of logic to appreciate how this depiction of the contemporary worker allows or even encourages an argument in which the function of management becomes enhanced by the perceived need to harness the potential of these 'individualised' and isolated workers. Understood in this light, the role, necessity and performance of management become central to all aspects of organisational performance. The particular form of HRM then comes to supply a set of ideas and practices that perfectly correspond to the requirements of the situation.

What next?

If postmodernism creates a world of workers who are seen as a relative phenomenon, where individuals are both shaped by their environment and surrounding culture and in turn define the world of work according to these meanings, it is difficult to see what overarching theory can unfold to make sense of the overall patterns of employment.

With such relativism built into explanations of individual behaviour, we are left not knowing whether the whole postmodernist project is a further elaboration obscuring the realities of, in this case, the world of work and employment. Maybe there is no 'new' era of postmodernism, post-industrialism; perhaps there has been a failure to understand the subjective individual. Some might suggest that the postmodernist theory has certainly corrected an overconcern with a belief in a hard, measurable world of workers and employment. Yet it has overcorrected this form of positivism and obscured the reality of work and employment. Management function and status have proliferated to the point where they have become an end in themselves, supported by new information technologies and psychological technologies of measurement all aimed at heightening the belief in individualism and hence creating further opportunities for those occupations and professions offering to integrate the mass of atomised individuals into the 'ways of their organisations' (Rose, 1989; Hollway, 1991).

Postmodernism has captured considerable interest from commentators seeking to identify trends in employment. For those in the Conservative government of 1979–97 there was concern to establish the existence of significant changes in the employment relationship and the labour market. The existence of flexibility, deregulation of the labour market, decline in trade union membership and the growth and effectiveness of HRM can all be interpreted as evidence for policies enacted in the early 1980s. Postmodernism's concern for individualism fits neatly into this 'new' world of employment. If we note, however, that like all the other theories it is also trapped in the limitations of its own epoch, we might be left thinking that it fails to recognise many of the abiding features of the employment relationship which continue to shape the experience of work for most of the employed population. As Kelly (1998) puts it: 'There are so many holes in the post-modernist case that there is a genuine puzzle as to why it was ever taken seriously. Its prognosis for the labour movement is not only bleak (that at least would be legitimate point of view), but it is ill-infomed in the extreme.'

Conclusion

Each new theory of employee relations can claim to correct the failure of earlier explanations. Like all accounts dealing with a complex set of variables associated with individual and collective behaviour, however, theories are inevitably partial and represent concerns and interests springing from the period in which they are generated. Academics, consultants and commentators involved in studying employee relations cannot escape the confines of their social context. By understanding something of these different contexts of employment, the theories that are the product of these different periods can be understood as imperfect tools that we must use to try to make sense of the complex area of employment. Hence understanding something of the features of the historical context helps us to make sense of the interpretations located within it.

When Hyman (1994) discusses the issue of theory in industrial relations he recognises the partial and incomplete nature of these theories. In his mind there are three reasons for this poor understanding and treatment by most authors in the field:

- The existence of theory in employee relations is considered important only in as much as it signifies the level of maturity of the discipline.
- If employee relations rests on the substantial achievements of industrial relations research, itself based on the concerns of practising managers, government policymakers and perhaps union leaders, then theory is seen as an 'intellectual sticking plaster', which somehow binds all these disparate 'facts' together.
- Related to the point we alluded to above is the belief that theory is seen as a separate activity from concrete research, that is, it can be developed almost as a *post hoc* device to make sense of the data previously collected.

Understanding, explaining and operationalising theories and perspectives are therefore not straightforward tasks in this emergent discipline, and in this sense they cannot be considered absolute truths or complete systems of explanation that can be regarded as failsafe. Each theory makes sense of some portion of the employment relationship; an understanding of social, political and historical contexts provides us with a set of lenses to make sense of the differing aspects of the employment relationship. With a new set of concerns emerging, including talk of social partnership, minimum wage, works councils and work–life balance and many other developments, the employment relationship is set to change again and those seeking to interpret these developments will no doubt draw upon the theory that accords with their priorities.

Chapter summary

This chapter has discussed a number of theories and frameworks that were developed at a particular historical juncture to explain the employment relationship. As the industrial relations system has changed alongside the vicissitudes of modern capitalism, these explanations have been harnessed to the interests of a number of different groups, ranging from academics of different intellectual persuasions, politicians seeking to impose a particular set of arrangements on the employment relationship, and other parties such as trade unionists, employers or consultants. Each group has seen the employment relationship from its own perspective situated within the particular context of that moment in history. The resulting diversity of interpretations has created a variety of explanations for the same phenomena, a situation that should ensure debate and development of the academic area.

For those studying the employment relationship, an understanding of the existence of these explanations is an important prelude to achieving a degree of realism about the nature of and changes to that relationship. This variety expresses the volatile and uncertain nature of the employment relationship, where employers and employees continue to exchange work for rewards within a dynamic and unstable environment. To appreciate the existence, nature and purpose of the different forms of theories and frameworks, therefore, is to glimpse the realities of how, on the one hand, people construct work and, on the other, they experience that work. In turn, sensing which particular theory makes most sense in understanding a particular problem and the ability to deploy its concepts and insights, is one of the great rewards of studying such a discipline.

Questions

1 Take one of the theories discussed in the chapter and explain how its 'context' helps account for its particular features.

2 Why should unitary theory have emerged towards the end of the nineteenth century?

3 Can you explain the connection between the use of systems theory in the natural sciences and its use in the case of employee relations?

4 What particular features and 'problems' of American society appear to explain the construction of systems theory?

5 Pluralist theory was designed to account for the new institutions of democracy. How is the task of explaining political institutions connected to the world of employee relations?

6 Outline the major flaws in the unitary, systems and pluralist theories.

7 Although a variety of positions exists within the overall project of feminism, outline what you consider to be the common themes adopted by a feminist analysis of the employment relationship.

8 If comparative theory is so useful in understanding overseas examples of employment, why should researchers be wary of the validity of the data they generate?

9 Postmodernism takes account of the individual in the employment relationship. Outline some of the shortcomings of adopting this type of analysis.

Activities

1 Identify a selection of newspapers and, over a few days, see if you can identify one event/incident connected to employment and establish the differing interpretations reflected in each of the newspapers.

2 Outline what you consider to be the purpose of developing theories within the discipline of employee relations.

3 Ask interviewees about their explanations for the rapid growth in remuneration packages over the past five to ten years. Write up your results and compare the different explanations.

4   If theories are a method for organising knowledge and providing a way of making sense of employment, identify which theory you consider is most helpful for explaining the current condition of employee relations.

5   With reference to recent statements in the media, identify a current policy connected with employee relations and locate the competing statements made by the different political parties and representative groups (e.g. the TUC and the Confederation of British Industry). Locate the different positional statements alongside the different theories of employee relations.

6   In the *Financial Times* of 3 March 1997, Andrew Bolger, the employment correspondent, talked about:

the 'startling discrepancy' between the reasons that employees give for absence from work and what managers believe to be the true causes, according to the Industrial Society, the independent training and advisory body. The survey of personnel managers in 327 businesses and organisations found there was general agreement that colds and flu were the prime cause of absence ... the next most frequent reasons given in employees' certification forms were: stomach upsets, headaches, back problems and stress/personal problems. Managers however believed the reasons to be stress/personal problems; sickness of family member/childcare; low morale/boring job; Monday morning blues. The survey said: 'management may hold the key to the problems they themselves identify as causes'. Employers who accommodated working from home, flexible hours and flexible annual leave all enjoyed lower than average absence rates.

Questions

(a) Take one of the theories outlined in this chapter and analyse the prevalence of absenteeism, itemising the factors it would identify as significant for explaining this phenomenon.

(b) Take the unitary theory and provide an explanation of absenteeism followed by a set of policies that might naturally flow from the analysis.

(c) Take each of the theories discussed in the chapter and generate a chart defining the major cause of absenteeism.

7   Reread Exhibit 1.1 on South West Trains and then answer the following questions.

(a) Identify and comment upon the different arguments put forward to explain this strike by the different parties involved in the dispute.

(b) What do you consider to be the central issues over which the different sides of industry are arguing?

(c) How would you describe the different positions and interests of those engaged in this dispute?

(d) Why should the union's sensibilities have been inflamed by the imposition of a pay increase?

(e) Outline some of the presumed changes to employee relations as a consequence of privatisation of the railways, identifying the impact upon management as well as employees.

Useful websites

www.cbi.org.uk **Confederation of British Industry** Britain's 'umbrella' employer's organisation. The site provides information and opportunity for the expression of unified employer 'voice' on Employee Relations and other matters.

www.eiro.eurofound.ie   **European Industrial Relations Observatory On-Line**   Provided by the European Foundation for the Improvement of Living and Working Conditions, it contains substantive information on European developments in industrial relations on an EU, country and sectoral basis.

www.ilo.org   **The International Labour Organization (ILO)**   Database on international work standards and national laws on labour, social security and human rights.

www.incomesdata.co.uk   Up to date intelligence on employment issues, including the economy, labour market and average earnings from Incomes Data Services.

www.labournet.net   A discussion forum for various employment issues.

www.peoplemanagement.co.uk   Online magazine of the Chartered Institute of Personnel and Development, which includes top stories in HR, legal updates, job vacancies etc.

www.statistics.gov.uk   **National Statistics**   This site is the official statistics site for the UK. A wealth of information on the economy with an index that is reasonably navigable.

www.tuc.org.uk   **Trades Union Congress**   Press releases, publications, organisation details, online journals and industrial relations.

References

Adams, R.J. and Meirz, N.M. (eds) (1993) *Industrial Relations Theory its Nature, Scope and Pedagogy.* IMLR Press/Rutgers University and Scarecrow Press, inc Metuchen, NJ and London.

Allen, J. (1992) 'Fordism in modern industry' in Allen, P., Braton, P. and Lewis, P. (eds) *Political and Economic Forms of Modernity.* Milton Keynes: Open University Press.

Amin, A. and Thrift, N. (eds) (1994) *Globalisation, Institutions and Regional Development in France.* Oxford: Oxford University Press.

Armstrong, P., Glynn, N. and Harrison, P. (1991) *Capitalism since 1945.* Oxford: Blackwell.

Bain, G. and Clegg, S. (1974) 'Strategy for industrial relations research in Great Britain', *British Journal of Industrial Relations*, 12(1): 91–113.

Baldry, C. and Ellison, J. (2000) 'Off the rails – worrying trends for worker safety in the rail industry', unpublished paper presented to 18th International Labour Process Conference, University of Strathclyde, Glasgow, April.

Bamber, G. and Lansbury, R. (1993) *International and Comparative Industrial Relations*, 2nd edn. London: Routledge.

Baritz, L. (1960) *The Servants of Power.* New York: Wiley.

Bassett, P. (1987) *Strike Free: New Industrial Relations in Britain.* London: Papermac.

Bean, R. (1992) *Comparative Industrial Relations: An Introduction to Cross-national Perspectives.* London: Routledge.

Beardwell, I. (ed.) (1996) *Contemporary Industrial Relations: A Critical Analysis.* Oxford: Oxford University Press.

Bendix, R. (1974) *Work and Authority in Industry.* Berkeley, CA: University of California Press.

Berger, T. and Luckman, S. (1966) *The Social Construction of Reality: A Treatise in the Sociology of Knowledge.* New York: Doubleday.

Braverman, H. (1974) *Labour and Monopoly Capital: The Degradation of Work in the Twentieth Century.* New York: Monthly Review Press.

Briggs, A. and Saville, J. (1967) *Essays in Labour History.* London: Papermac.

Burawoy, M. (1979) *Manufacturing Consent.* Chicago: University of Chicago Press.

Burawoy, M. (1985) *The Politics of Production.* London: Verso.

Burnham, J. (1957) *The Management Revolution.* Harmondsworth: Penguin.

Calas, M. and Smircich, L. (1996) 'From the women's point of view: feminist approaches to organisation studies' in Clegg, S., Hardy, C. and Nord, W. (eds) *Handbook of Organisation Studies.* London: Sage.

Carey, A. (1980) 'Social science propaganda and democracy' in Boreham, P. and Dow, G. (eds) *Work and the Inequality*, Vol. 2. Basingstoke: Macmillan.

Clark, J. (1995) 'Is there a future for industrial relations?', *Work, Employment and Society*, 9(3): 593–605.

Clawson, D. (1980) *Bureaucracy and the Labour Process: The Transformation of US Industry 1860–1920.* New York: Monthly Review Press.

Clegg, H.A. (1979) *The Changing System of Industrial Relations in Great Britain*. Oxford: Blackwell.

Clegg, S. (1990) *Modern Organisations: Organisation Studies in a Post-modern World*. London: Sage.

Clegg, S. and Dunkerley, D. (1980) *Organisation, Class and Control*. London: Routledge & Kegan Paul.

Cockburn, C. (1983) *Brothers: Male Dominance and Technological Change*. London: Pluto Press.

Cockburn, C. (1989) 'Equal opportunities: the short and long agenda', *Industrial Relations Journal*, 44(1): 213–24.

Collinson, D.L., Knights, D. and Collinson, M. (1990) *Managing to Discriminate*. London: Routledge.

Cronin, J. and Schneer, J. (1982) *Social Conflict and the Political Order in Modern Britain*. London: Croon Helm.

Crouch, C. (1977) *Class Conflict and the Industrial Relations Crisis*. London: Heinemann.

Cyert, R.M. and March, J.G. (1963) *A Behavioural Theory of the Firm*. Englewood Cliffs, NJ: Prentice Hall.

Dahl, R. (1957) 'The concept of power', *Behavioural Science*, 2: 201–15.

Dickens, L. (1989) Editorial 'Women – a rediscovered resource?', *Industrial Relations Journal*, 44(1): 167–75.

Dore, R. (1973) *British Factory – Japanese Factory*. London: Allen & Unwin.

Dos Passos, J. (1952) *USA*. Harmondsworth: Penguin.

Du Gray, P. (1995) *Consumption and Identity at Work*. Milton Keynes: Open University Press.

Dunlop, J.T. (1959) *The Industrial Relations System*. New York: Holt.

Eaton, J. (2000) *Comparative Employment Relations: An Introduction*. Cambridge: Polity Press.

Eldridge, J., Cressey, P. and McInnes, J. (1991) *Industrial Sociology and Economic Crisis*. Hemel Hempstead: Harvester Wheatsheaf.

Farnham, D. and Pimlott, J. (1995) *Understanding Industrial Relations*, 5th edn. London: Cassell.

Fineman, S. (1993) *Emotion in Organisations*. London: Sage.

Fosh, P. and Heery, E. (eds) (1990) *Trade Unions and their Members: Studies in Union Democracy and Organisation*. London: Macmillan.

Fox, A. (1973) 'Industrial relations: a social critique of pluralist ideology' in Child, J. (ed.) *Man and Organisation*. London: Allen & Unwin.

Friedman, A. (1977) *Industry and Labour*. Basingstoke: Macmillan.

Gospel, H. (1992) *Markets, Firms and the Management of Labour in Modern Britain*. Cambridge: Cambridge University Press.

Gospel, H. and Palmer, G. (1993) *British Industrial Relations*, 2nd edn. London: Routledge.

Gourvish, T. (1972) *Mark Huish and the London North Western Railway*. Leicester: Leicester University Press.

Halsey, A.H. (1995) *Change in British Society from 1900 to the Present Day*. Oxford: Oxford University Press.

Hayek, F. (1960) *The Constitution of Liberty*. London: Routledge & Kegan Paul.

Heery, E. and Kelly, J. (1989) 'A cracking job for a woman: a profile of women trade union officers', *Industrial Relations Journal*, 20(3): 192–202.

Held, D., McGrew, A., Goldblatt, D. and Perraton, J. (2000) *Global Transformations: Politics Economics and Culture*. Cambridge: Polity Press.

Hobsbawm, E. (1974) *Industry and Empire*. Harmondsworth: Pelican.

Hofstader, R. (1955) *Social Darwinism in American Thought*. Charlottesville: University of Virginia Press.

Hollway, W. (1991) *Work Psychology and Organisational Behaviour: Managing the Individual at Work*. London: Sage.

Hyman, R. (1989) 'Why industrial relations?' in Hyman, R. (ed.) *The Political Economy of Industrial Relations: Theory and Practice in a Cold Climate*. Basingstoke: Macmillan.

Hyman, R. (1994) 'Theory and industrial relations', *British Journal of Industrial Relations*, 32(2): 165–80.

Hyman, R. and Brough, I. (1975) *Social Values and Industrial Relations*. Oxford: Blackwell.

Hyman, R. and Ferner, A. (1994) *New Frontiers in European Industrial Relations*. Oxford: Blackwell.

Kamin, L. (1976) 'Heredity, intelligence, politics and psychology' in Block, N. and Dworkin, G. (eds) *The IQ Controversy*. New York: Quartet Books.

Kanter, R.M. (1983) *The Change Masters: Corporate Entrepreneurs at Work*. London: Allen & Unwin.

Keenoy, T. (1991) 'The roots of metaphor in the old and new industrial relations', *British Journal of Industrial Relations*, 29(2).

Kelly, J. (1998) *Rethinking Industrial Relations: Mobilisation, Collectivism and Long Waves*. London: Routledge.

Kerr, C., Dunlop, J. and Harbison, F. (1974) *Industrialism and Industrial Man*. Harmondsworth: Penguin.

Kuhn, T. (1970) *The Structure of Scientific Revolutions*, 2nd edn. Chicago: University of Chicago Press.

Landes, D. (1972) *The Unbound Prometheus*. Cambridge: Cambridge University Press.

Laslett, P. (1971) *The World We Have Lost*. London: Methuen.

Legge, K. (1995) *Human Resource Management: Rhetorics and Realities*. London: Macmillan.

Mandel, E. (1978) *Late Capitalism*. London: Verso.

Marchington, M. and Parker, S. (1990) *Changing Patterns of Employee Relations*. Hemel Hempstead: Harvester Wheatsheaf.

McKenna, F. (1980) *The Railway Workers*. London: Faber & Faber.

Palmer, G. (1983) *British Industrial Relations*. London: Unwin Hyman.

Parsons, T. (1952) *The Social System Theory*. London: Tavistock.

Peters, T.J. and Waterman, R.H. (1982) *In Search of Excellence*. New York: Harper & Row.

Philo, G., Beharrell, P. and Hewitt, C. (eds) (1977) *One-dimensional Views: Television and the Control of Information in Trade Unions and Media*. Basingstoke: Macmillan.

Pollard, S. (1958) *The Genesis of Modern Management*. Harmondsworth: Penguin.

Roethlisberger, F.J. and Dickinson, W.J. (1939) *Management and The Worker*. Cambridge, MA: Harvard University Press.

Rose, N. (1989) *Governing the Soul: The Shaping of the Private Self*. London: Routledge.

Rowbotham, S. (1974) *Hidden from History*. Harmondsworth: Penguin.

Salamon, M. (1998) *Industrial Relations: Theory and Practice*, 3rd edn. Englewood Cliffs, NJ: Prentice Hall.

Sewell, G. and Wilkinson, B. (1992) ' "Someone to watch over me": surveillance, discipline and the just-in-time labour process', *Sociology*, 26(2): 271–89.

Silverman, D. (1970) *The Theory of Organisation*. London: Heinemann.

Sisson, K. (1994) *Personnel Management in Britain: A Comprehensive Guide to Theory and Practice*. Oxford: Blackwell.

Storey, J. (1992a) *Management of Human Resources*. Oxford: Blackwell.

Sturdy, A. (1998) *Customer Care in the Consumer Society in Organisations*. London: Macmillan.

Thompson, E.P. (1968) *The Making of the English Working Class*. Harmondsworth: Penguin.

TUC (1997) *Partners for Progress: Next Steps for the New Unionism*. London: TUC.

Undy, R. (1997) Book review, *British Journal of Industrial Relations*, 35(1).

von Bertalanffy, L. (1950) 'The theory of open systems', *Physics and Biology Science*, III: 23–9.

Wolmar, C. (2001) *Broken Rails. How Privatisation Wrecked Britains Railways*. London: Aurum Press.

Waters, M. (1995) *Globalisation*. London: Routledge.

Winchester, D. (1983) 'Industrial relations research in Britain', *British Journal of Industrial Relations*, XX: 100.

Further reading

Beardwell, I. (ed.) (1997) *Contemporary Industrial Relations*. Oxford: Oxford University Press.

Blyton, P. and Turnbull, P. (2000) *The Dynamics of Employee Relations*. Basingstoke: Macmillan.

Hyman, R. (1989) *The Political Economy of Industrial Relations: Theory and Practice in a Cold Climate*. Basingstoke: Macmillan.

Kelly, J. (1998) *Rethinking Industrial Relations: Mobilisation, Collectivism and Long Waves*. London: Routledge.

Rose, E. (2001) *Employment Relations Continuity and Change: Policies and Practices*. Harlow: Prentice Hall.

Chapter 2

Values and their impact on the changing employment relationship

Philip Cox and Ann Parkinson

Learning objectives

By the end of this chapter, readers should be able to:

- understand the influence of social, economic and political factors which contextualise current employee relations;
- understand the impact and implications that values have had and will continue to have in shaping the employment relationship.

Introduction

In writing about people's beliefs and values, all writers draw upon their own interpretations to inform their arguments. In this chapter we are presenting a particular view of the impact of differing values on employee relations for you to use as a framework and we ask you to challenge it in developing your views of what employee relations is and may become in the context of emerging government and EU policies. Exhibit 2.1 is based on probably the largest single downsizing scheme ever undertaken in British industry. It was seen by many professional managers, the industry and the City as an example of better practice in managing the downsizing process, particularly in its capacity to harmonise competing vested interests. It is used to illustrate many of the issues and dimensions that form the subject of this chapter.

In this chapter we seek to explore some of the significant factors that continue to influence changes in employee relations. We revisit the themes and future scenarios which we set out in the first edition of *Employee Relations* and forecast some trends for the early part of the new millennium. As before, the focusing of our vision is facilitated by looking through the lens of values which often attend any significant shifts in relationships at work. By looking at changes in values we hope to plot shifts in thought, motives and behaviours of the significant parties involved in the employment relationship.

We begin by looking at the nature of values in practice through the initial case study, and continue with their influence on behaviour. This is followed by broadly examining changing work values through recent epochs, from the post-war revival in industry underpinned by the work ethic, through the emergent 'get a life' values of 'Generation X', a label used to describe those born in the 1960s and 1970s, which

Exhibit 2.1

Release '92

In April 1992, British Telecom announced that it would be looking for an unprecedented 20,000 volunteers for redundancy as a result of the joint impact on the business of competition, recession, investment in new technology and price regulation. The Release '92 scheme was marketed heavily to all 240,000 employees at every level of the organisation, with almost all individuals being asked by their managers whether they would be interested in leaving the company. The financial package offered was very generous with many add-ons such as outplacement counselling, a training grant and temporary work or consultancy back into the company for a set period depending on the level of the employee. Much of the consultancy work was undertaken for charities in support of BT's pledge to donate 0.5 per cent of its profits to charity.

In devising the terms of the severance payment, one key factor was the third of the stated values, 'we respect each other', and the belief that the company owed its success to the very people it would be encouraging to leave. This was the first big test of the values articulated two years earlier:

- we put our customers first;
- we are professional;
- we respect each other;
- we work as one team;
- we are committed to continuous improvement.

Personnel had to defend the generous terms vigorously against objections from shareholders and some of the newer board members. There was also the recognition that in the midst of a recession there was a potential detrimental impact on society by adding to high levels of unemployment.

In planning the Release '92 scheme, the director of employee relations recognised the need to work closely with the leader of the National Communications Union, building on the collaborative rather than confrontational relationship they had been developing over the years. The focus for the package design was the needs of the individual, and the union response recognised the necessity to downsize and what its members as individuals would accept. There was no industrial action over the loss of some 30,000 jobs, the largest redundancy scheme experienced in the UK.

For many employees, this was the first time they had ever considered that they may not be leaving the company on their retirement. Many felt angry and let down by a company that they thought shared their own values and that had now reneged on the promise of a job for life. Others recognised that the Release '92 package gave them the option to do something different that they had previously not considered or had the financial backing for. The majority of those leaving had joined the company before privatisation and placed a high value on public service, and although they had made the transition to dealing with customers within a private sector framework, a substantial number still felt uncomfortable with the focus on shareholders and profit. By the end of the financial year in March 1993 some 30,000 people had taken advantage of the Release '92 package.

Subsequent smaller schemes attracted a further 85,000 people over the following seven years. The basic financial package stayed broadly the same although without some of the extra incentives and never open to all employees again. By 1994 there was a threat of being forced to accept less favourable terms for particular groups if they were not prepared to leave voluntarily. In less than ten years BT had shrunk its workforce by over 50 per cent by voluntary means.

challenged traditional parental work values of self-sacrifice, to the values of a new generation entering the workforce. Acceptance of authority, cooperative, team players, technology sophisticated, globally oriented, seeking high salaries and career-focused, these New Millennials or Generation Y have grown up in a time of peace and unprecedented prosperity. Often making their own rules, they espouse honesty, directness and integrity and exude self-confidence and independence.

The next section looks at the interplay between the major stakeholders in the drama, with some reflections on the values and behaviours of trade unions in transition, at a time when they continue to struggle for a role that might be perceived as more relevant in a time of steep decline in trade union membership and influence since the 1970s, albeit halted, temporarily. It also looks at employers and employer organisations, which also show a decline in membership (Donaghy, 2001), and the ethical challenges and dilemmas faced in sustaining a capitalist value system in a social democratic political context and challenged by a highly competitive global marketplace.

Finally, consideration is given to the influence of the state with its focus on the political and legal context, encouragement of enterprise, public private partnership (PPP) and the social/employment consequences associated with work–life balance initiatives.

The end of the chapter explores the shift from collectivism to the resurgence of individualism and the growth, from exploitation and coercion to trust, empowerment and employer–employee partnership. We explore the role of the psychological contract in understanding the changing nature of employee relations. In particular we focus on the rise of individualism and the increasing power and choice of individuals to shape their own employment destinies through bypassing traditional collective agreements and the vicarious role of collective representation through trade unions. We also look at the emerging importance of individual employee career choice and preference and the manager–employee relationship. This 'personal contract' which is often implicitly negotiated between an individual employee and the manager often operates in addition to, or in spite of, the formal organisational contract and employer–employee expectations. Based on the findings of our research we explore the significance of this concept and consider the line manager's role as key in both setting and delivering successful employee relations in the workplace and the continuing distal role of trades unions.

Scenario

The 1990s witnessed a transformation in the context and content of employment relations in the UK. Shifts in the labour market, almost as profound as those which heralded the movement of labour from the countryside to the towns during the Industrial Revolution have begun to transform the way in which employers and employees relate (Monks, 1996). Occasions of large-scale, orchestrated, industrial conflicts and confrontation seem much fewer. As the traditional paradigm for conflict resolution passes into history and the degree of reticence to develop alternative approaches which have currency and relevance to the individual increases, any vacuum created may see a growth in spasmodic, loosely organised and coordinated demonstrations by specific interest groups such as the fuel demonstrations of the farmers and road hauliers. Substantial changes have taken place in which historical ideology-based hostiles have been driven by pragmatism, social change and global movements to consider collaboration and partnership in order to survive. Recent literature contains more discussion of the values of trust, commitment, empowerment, shared goals and social partnership between employers and employees. The entrenched attitudes and values of ideology and bigotry often associated with industrial conflict of the 1970s have been cautiously superseded by ones in which unions are having to be more sensitive to business needs and employers somewhat grudgingly tolerating (but certainly less hostile and even valuing) the cooperative role of unions in reforming and delivering changes in the workplace. Driven by the tough conditions in the global marketplace, organisations have begun to recognise the business value of good employee relations and the importance of employee relations management in seeking a competitive edge. Richard Branson suggests that people come first, customers second and shareholders third, and told the Institute of Directors in 1993: 'we know that high standards of service depend upon having staff who are proud of the company. This is why the interests of our people come first . . . in the end the long-term interests of shareholders are actually damaged by giving them superficial short-term priority' (Pfeffer, 1998). Here he recognises that customised quality consciousness and service (customer relations management) alone will not lead to organisational profitability and sustainability unless equal attention is given to employee relations management. It challenges the lip service paid by many organisations to the maxim that 'people are an organisation's most valuable asset' and recognises that there is only so much rationalising, reorganising and downsizing an organisation can do. Painfully, organisations are realising that in the world of the 'knowledge worker', people are its only major asset.

Hence many factors have influenced attitude shifts since the first edition of this book. The context of work has continued to change, its character has changed, where it is done has changed, and the patterns of work itself have shifted. Over 2 million people are employed in call centres, which is more than in car manufacture, coal, shipbuilding, and steel industries combined.

The nature of workers has changed. The rapid rise of 'knowledge' as an organisation's main asset will place such knowledge workers in more powerful positions. The control of intellectual capital (the knowledge, skills, experience and ideas of individuals) and business advantage will lie with individual employees rather than in some form of organisational product or process patented and owned by the business and its shareholders. Such knowledge workers are highly skilled and academically qualified, develop rapidly their knowledge and experience in different areas of business, deal with integrated problems and complexity, and are not daunted by uncertainty and change. Hence if such individuals walk away from an organisation, much of the organisation's 'product' go with them. The power implications of this are profound and the threat to business survival significant. The shift to power in the hands of the workers and away from capital is more of a reality than perhaps it has ever been. Buying commitment and loyalty by throwing rewards at such individuals in the form of 'golden handcuffs' will not be an adequate response, since this is the response of an outmoded paradigm. Handy (2001) suggests that, once awakened to the significance of what they have, individuals will not hand over to organisations their intellectual property for a restricting and limiting contract of employment. They are more likely to want to negotiate a share of the proceeds based on their contribution from their 'intellectual property'. Such individuals take responsibility for their own career, develop their own marketability and employability and will not adhere to the traditional employment relationship. Hence organisations will need to wake up to the reality that 'individualism' in the workplace and not 'collectivism' is likely to be an emerging issue and they will need to develop changes in trade union and management thinking, practices and even paradigms to cope. We illustrate this point later when reviewing the findings of our research.

The rapid development of the global economy since the mid-1990s, business restructuring and re-engineering, shrinking job opportunities in the traditional industries, the impact of technology and the Internet, a significant influx of immigrant labour to cope with skill shortages (in nursing, medicine and IT among others) the impact of increases in size of ethnic minorities, to name but a few areas, have all contributed to employment complexity and the need to change attitudes and behaviour. Individually, each one might be considered significant enough, but their concurrency has created a powerful impact.

The way work is done has undergone a major shift. Less than half the UK workforce has a 'conventional' full-time job. The increased application of flexible working practices has changed for many the format of working life. The diminishing number of full-time jobs, particularly in the traditional industries such as coal, engineering, shipbuilding, iron and steel, the increase in part-time and temporary work, the increasing use of part-time female labour, subcontracting, outsourcing and the rise of short-term fixed contracts have reduced the certainties which once were attached to the old, predictable style of working life. Pearson (1996) states that white male workers under 45 constitute only 22 per cent of the workforce. Hutton (1996) states that only 40 per cent of the 28 million workers are employed full-time, while 30 per cent are self-employed, part-time or casual workers, and 30 per cent are unemployed or working for poverty wages (Hutton, 1996). At least 1 million workers are on fixed-term contracts, with nearly another 1 million working as seasonal or casual employees (Purcell and Purcell, 1999). Portfolio and freelance working has increased rapidly since the late 1990s, not only for professionals but for managers as well. The impact of technology has allowed employees to be globally based. The virtual organisation creates the potential for workers in India, Hong Kong and Taiwan to 'sit' alongside their European colleagues working on projects as efficiently as if they were in the same room. Teleworking has come of age. Many organisations in both the public and private sectors encourage employees to be home-based, using computer technology and the Internet, through which they conduct their work (Barter, 1998). Such organisations have recognised the environmental value and enormous cost savings to be gained by having employees work from home. In a survey conducted by the Institute for Employment Studies it was estimated that almost 10 per cent of employees (2.5 million) work, in some part, from home, and the numbers are rising. Clearly these trends raise questions concerning the nature of the relationship between employers and employees.

Organisations themselves have felt change. Intense competition has forced downsizing and restructuring, leaving many organisations acceptable to the City but undernourished in terms of their knowledge and skills base, as well as violating the long-time relationship with employees (Handy, 1996). Such economic short-termism has resulted in many companies gaining short-term share gains only to discover at their leisure that they have created a massive loss in intellectual capability and competitive edge. The BT case could illustrate this, the company having seen its share value free-fall from £15 per share to less than £4 with little chance of recovery before 2005 (*Financial Times*). The demise, through privatisation, of the large manufacturing and heavy engineering industries – coal, shipbuilding, motor vehicles, construction, steelmaking, gas and electricity – has left a hole in the full-time employment opportunities arena which has been slow to fill. Full-time jobs have often been replaced by low-paid, part-time ones. The continuing rise of the service and financial sectors, with their reliance on part-time working and use of technology, has not filled the vacuum. Young, emergent non-unionised computer and high-tech industries have sprung up with local, individual-based employment approaches.

Yet fundamental to most of these changes of significance has been the impact of economic change, such as the challenge of global competition and the rise of the free market economy with attendant changes to industrial law and the burgeoning progress of technology. In some areas these changes have wrought havoc on employment practices, processes and expectations.

With structural and economic change has come attitude change. Some employers no longer see their responsibility to the employee as anything more than contractual, and a distant one at that (Cannon, 1996). The rise of the mentality that individuals are responsible for the attractiveness of their own employability has left many bemused, worried and incapable of an effective response. The Institute of Personnel and Development survey of 1996 suggests there is growing evidence of employees expressing lower levels of loyalty, commitment and trust towards their employers and uncertainty of their future role and value in their organisations (Guest *et al.*, 1996).

Underpinning many of the changes has been a quiet social revolution. Attitudes to work are changing. The Protestant work ethic has less potency. For young workers particularly, a new ethic has emerged (Cannon, 1996) in which the individual recognises the importance of the present and not the submission of the individual will to the collective. Individuals want value from their lives now, not just dutifully working 'until you pass out' for the benefit of the corporation, as quoted by Hecht of McKinsey Consultants (Hecht, 1997). They are interested in creating a life in which work success does not cost so much and is balanced by quality time for family and non-work interests (*Independent on Sunday*, 20 July 1997).

Middle-aged professionals are following their blue-collar colleagues in downshifting their careers. The stresses and pressures associated with retaining a career are not attractive to all. Family life, personal development and alternative 'careers' are seen as more rewarding and valuable. Downshifting is as evident in the dedicated vocations as it is in other professions. Doctors, consultants and ministers of religion seek to work balanced, often part-time, mixed-role lives as much as their non-vocational and professional counterparts (Cox, 1986; Shaw, 1997).

Also significant are the changing values of the young towards work. Collin (1995) and Coupland (in Cannon, 1996) suggest that through the early 1990s emerged a younger generation which society had failed to engage in the world of work and which became alienated from the traditional values associated with their parents: 'this has a disastrous effect on young people, robbing them of the traditional socialising influences of employment, with its workplace role, values and intergenerational contact' (Collin, 1995). Coupland's characters illustrate the changing expectations the young have of their world. The idea of a career and its purpose was questioned if not perceived as alien to many young people in the 18–30 age group of the time. The attitudes of this Generation X, as it was called, questioned the traditional concepts of work and its role in the life of the individual. The individuals' values differed from those of their parents and were sometimes described by their parents' generation as slackers. Having grown up in a world of one-parent families, unclear gender roles, unemployed middle-class professional fathers and job uncertainty, they did not envy working parents their behaviour of 'presenteeism' (i.e. being first in and last out of an evening, thinking that this will demonstrate organisational commitment and so help them to keep their jobs), neither did they aspire to be top managers who worked excessively long hours, lead out-of-control lives and die young (Cannon, 1996). Their values were based more on seeking interesting work, the learning opportunities it needed to provide, and individual rewards-based contribution, not collective bargaining (Hecht, 1997). They sought to work in organisations in which integrity and honesty were 'behaviours' and not rhetoric which passed with every change of CEO.

The nature of values and their role in understanding changes in employee relations

In analysing the changing nature of relations at work we look through a particular lens; the lens of values that prevail in different parties and how they colour their perceptions of the employee relations context. We take this perspective because of the view that values are the foundation upon which attitudes, motivation and behaviour are based and are at the core of what constitutes a person, or a workgroup. Hence, understanding them can help to explain the nature of the attitudes, actions and codes which shape behaviour. Because they contain interpretations of what is right or wrong, they imply that some behaviours are acceptable while others are not. Consequently, it is inevitable that values held by individuals or groups influence perceptions and often cloud how objective and rational they can be over issues, particularly in times of confrontation and industrial dispute.

In employee relations, different actors and different contexts may have different values. The dynamics that occur between them are often driven by the significant differences in the value systems of each perspective. Describing and understanding these different value systems and their (in)compatibilities and recognising their situational consequences are, in part, what employee relations is all about.

Describing values

Values can be seen as those underlying convictions that are held by individuals or groups. It is a broad, encompassing concept containing a moral flavour of what is right or desirable. Values usually relate to an ideal or standard which guides our conduct and a reference point against which we judge ourselves and which we use to judge others. Rokeach (in Robbins, 1998) defines values as:

> Basic convictions that a specific mode of conduct or end state of existence is personally or socially preferable to an opposite or converse conduct or end state of existence.

Value systems

Individuals or groups have a variety of values, some of which are seen as more important and powerful in determining a position than others. This gives rise to a value system or the ranking of values according to their perceived importance to the individual or group. Different individuals or groups inevitably have different values and value systems. It is understanding these differences between the parties involved in employee relations and developing behaviours that facilitate their compatibility that is the challenge of employee relations.

Values are relatively stable entities. Established and reinforced through the early years of a person's life, they are strongly influenced by parents, social upbringing and wider social and cultural experience. A similar pattern emerges with groups or organisations such as owner-managed businesses or trade unions. Strongly held values that are continually reinforced define a person's or group's value system and become part of the code of behaviour by which they operate. This often gives rise to rituals and procedures which reflect tradition. Hence, traditions tend to reinforce values and values reinforce traditions.

Changing values

Values tend to be stable and enduring entities, and so they tend to change only very slowly. Hence individuals or groups might find it difficult to adjust to demands from or changes to their environment which require significant adjustment to and/or challenge their core values. We return to this aspect when we consider the impact that political, legal and economic change has had upon trade unions and corporations and those groups' difficulties in responding adequately.

Values dominant in the work environment

If we take an epoch perspective it may be possible to plot the changes in the work values of each generation. It is reasonable to assume that the values formed early in life through socialisation will demonstrate themselves in expressed values in the work situation in later years. Hence it may be possible to anticipate the dominant values of individuals according to their age and the era in which they grew up. It suggests that the values of the young employee are likely to be those dominant and reflected by that person when he or she reaches leadership positions later in life. Hence the work ethic values of the young growing up in the 1950s and early 1960s would be expected to be reflected in part by leaders of the 1980s (Thatcherism). Similarly, the existentialist values of the 1970s may be reflected in part by the values of leaders of the late 1990s ('new' Labour).

Hence we can suggest, as other authors have done (Allport *et al.*, 1951; Robbins, 1998) that there are a number of different value systems which define the behaviours of different age groups in the working population. These form the core of Table 2.1.

Group 1 would be the oldest in the work population, whose values reflect dependency on the organisation for security and career opportunity, the importance of honest application and overriding commitment to the organisation, influenced by traditions and moral responsibility, and respectful of power and authority. Very much compliant and

Table 2.1 Dominant values in the post-war workforce

Category	Entered workforce	Approximate age	Individual work values	Organisational work values
1 Protestant work ethic	1945–50s	55–65	Hard work, conservative loyalty to organisation	Command, control, efficiency, compliance, dehumanisation
2 Existentialism	1960s–70s	45–55	Quality of life, non-conforming, seeks autonomy, loyalty to self	Teamwork, quality, respect for individual, involvement
3 Pragmatism	1980s	35–45	Success, achievement, ambition, hard work, loyalty to career	Efficiency, cost reduction
4 Generation X	1990s	25–35	Lifestyle, loyalty to self	Empowerment, organisational learning, self-development
5 Generation Y/ Millennials	2000s	Under 25	Contribution to greater good integrity, challenge hard work, loyalty to relationships	Accept authority, team players, globally oriented lateral careers, social conscience

prone to coercion, these are the individuals who would have difficulty with redundancy and unemployment, feeling betrayed by the system which was supposed to look after them for all their hard effort, loyalty, conformity and compliance.

Group 2 would be more interested in the quality of their lives and would see self-expression, choice and personal freedom as the important aims. Their values would reflect a dislike of materialism, manipulation and control, coercion and compliance. They would be interested in challenging authority, organisational goals and values. Enhancing individual freedom and the best interests of all would be their values.

Group 3 would reflect materialistic goals, giving priority to individual interest, self-achievement, manipulation and commercial exploitation of others and situations. These values thrive upon the promotion of the free market economy and reflect the self-interest values of 'Thatcher's children'. To this group the ends would justify the means, and their ethical stance would be very utilitarian. They are likely to reflect the values of the enterprise economy and free market economic and political values.

Group 4, or Generation X, reflect the values of the young joining organisations in the late 1980s and early 1990s. This generation has brought a significantly changed set of attitudes and values to work. Brought up in a society where single-parent families were on the increase, the loss of lifetime employment and white-collar downsizing common, where parenting was more 'hands off', and suffering from a higher degree of postmodernist angst than their predecessors (Howe and Strauss, 2000), this generation questioned the purpose and role of work in their lives. Their preference was to take control of their lives with an emerging resistance to collectivist values, adherence to organisational normative behaviour, with the requirement to transfer individual rights, freedoms, choices and responsibilities to third parties. The 'job for life' concept, so central to the ethos of the work ethic generation, with its emphasis on organisation career development, was seen as outdated and less relevant.

For Generation X, career means the development of a knowledge and skills portfolio which allows employability. They have many of the values of the existentialists of the 1970s, such as the importance of lifestyle, freedom, meaningful experience, growth and individualism. They too challenge the traditional work ethic by seeking to find meaning and value in life beyond the materialistic. Overeducated and understimulated, their interest is in 'getting a life' which contains a greater balance between work and non-work activity. Many of these young people want a holistic lifestyle, which does not mean working all hours and putting organisational interests above all else. They are not interested in the 'top job', with its living to work mentality (Hecht, 1997): the costs are perceived to be too great. They often appear disillusioned with a world of work which sends their middle-aged fathers home exhausted and 'queuing for a coronary', and their mothers frantic to balance the demands of a career with domestic management. They have more interest in personal growth and development (see Jay's Story below). A survey by Coopers and Lybrand (quoted in Hecht, 1997) found that only 16 per cent of graduates aspired to climb the corporate managerial ladder or wanted a job (power) which involved organising, influencing and motivating other people. Money and status, while important, are secondary to working with talented people, on enjoyable, interesting and varied projects, seeking spiritual meaning and fulfilment in work (see Olivia's Story below).

A further factor of significance is the desire of the talented young to work in organisations which are ethical and which reflect their own personal values. Choice in recruitment and selection based on values and ethics may appear novel, but talent may not gravitate to those organisations that cannot provide young people with a variety of learning experiences which are perceived as relevant and which help to improve their package of skills and experience.

Group 5 , Generation Y or the New Millennials, go further than their Generation X predecessors. Born in times of peace and brought up in a context of economic prosperity and closer parenting, this group is highly confident and assured and does not have the level of angst and uncertainty of the Xers. They have more of a sense of duty and more loyalty to their values (Howe and Strauss, 2000). In fact they tend to be highly self-confident, articulate and communicative, Internet-astute and highly conscious of social and global responsibilities. They enjoy work but do not let it rule their lives, with less expectation of organisation-based careers and the anticipation that multiple career moves are not only expected but desirable. Large organisations are less attractive to such (knowledge) workers, with many anticipating working as entrepreneurs in their own businesses rather than large corporations. Size and growth are often secondary to interesting work, interesting people and a balanced lifestyle (as illustrated by the Occam research explored later in the chapter).

According to a survey by Andersen Consulting, the management consultants, called 'Bringing Girls into Corporate Life', many young women of this group are not impressed by corporate life and do not wish to have organisational careers, or expect or want to be chief executives; rather, they want to spend more of their working time in social service , voluntary organisations or running their own businesses.

Jay's story

Jay, a soft-spoken 25-year-old graduate photographer, denies his generation is arrogant. 'Older photographers tell me how sad it is that we missed out on the eighties – when four-hour lunches and being paid £2,000 a day were the norm – and how much we must be struggling.'

From a young age, Jay heard his father saying that he wished he could do something he enjoyed. 'You need to find a job you will like', Jay was told. His father who used to work in the rag trade, died four years ago at the age of 51 of a heart attack. 'Stress at work killed him', Jay believes.

Jay works long hours because he enjoys it. 'I'm not worried about money as long as I have got enough to stay out of trouble. Recognition from peers is more important than cash.' (Hecht, 1997)

Olivia's story

The case of Olivia, a 30-year-old solicitor for one of the larger City firms in London. Over the past six months she hasn't been home before 10 pm – which gives her just enough time to slob in front of the TV, knock back a bottle of Chardonnay and commiserate with the characters in her favourite soap *This Life*. It's the nearest she gets to a weekly social life. Olivia isn't happy. 'What's the point of earning pots when you haven't got time to spend it?' she says with a sigh.

Stuff the Ferrari, the business lunches at Quags and the weekends in Paris – quality time with friends and family is what upwardly mobile professionals now crave. For Olivia, the comfort £50,000 a year plus 'perks': company car, pension, etc., is, she feels, scant reward for the gruelling routine she endures. Five years ago, she would have been content with a pay rise that matched her commitment. Now, though, she is looking for precisely the opposite – less money in exchange for less responsibility. 'If someone offered me a job for £10,000 or even £15,000 less along with fewer hours I'd take it.' (*The Independent*, 20 July, 1997)

The think-tank Demos (Cannon, 1996) suggests that organisations need to build a new contract with the young in which they provide a varied, reframed work environment, perhaps project-based, where young people can feel that they are doing meaningful, relevant and varied work which enriches their experience rather than the traditional 'apprenticeship time-serving' early experience of photocopying, faxing, answering telephones and making the coffee.

Economic circumstances and organisational actions of the 1990s have reduced significantly the supply of talent available for organisations to remain competitive. Successive governments have allowed knowledge and skill levels not only to recede but also to decline. At the same time the demand for high-level knowledge and skills capability has expanded enormously to the point where their absence threatens organisational survival. Organisations need to rethink their position and ask themselves how they make themselves relevant to young people and how they can provide more meaningful, exciting and challenging work experiences for them. By making work more attractive, organisations build a relationship with their young talent that leads to commercial competitive advantage and survival.

Setting the context: the shift from industrial relations to employee relations

This section looks at some of the contextual factors that have impacted on employee relations during the 1990s. Whereas the major elements have been largely legal and economic, Figure 2.1 illustrates the wider contextual issues that inform the current perspective. The perspectives and values of the central parties involved in the emergence of employee relations – the trade unions, employing organisations and the individual employee – are dealt with in the next three sections.

■ The impact of the state on employee relations since 1980

The Labour years during the 1960s and 1970s saw the rise of trade union power, with its increasing use in the political arena. This was far removed from the original roots of trade unions' purpose as friendly societies, there to help individuals in a welfare capacity

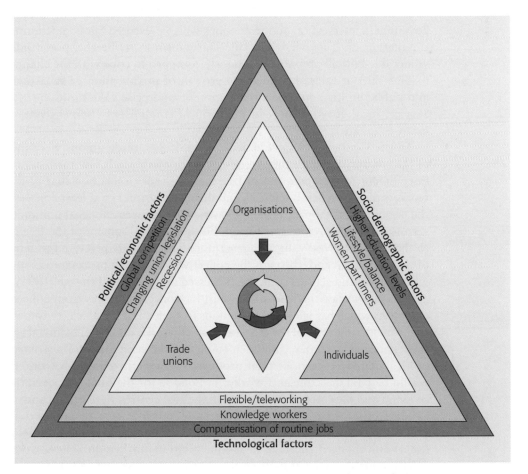

Figure 2.1 **Contextual factors influencing the nature of employee relations**

(Field, 1996). At this time, trade union power reached its height in terms of membership and density, and influenced the 1974–79 Labour government towards employee protection legislation, industrial democracy and the 'social contract' incomes policy.

Characteristic of the Thatcher years in the 1980s was the ideological shift towards the creation of a free market, free enterprise economy in which a rugged entrepreneurial individualism reflected the values of individual innovation and creativity and the potential high rewards associated with it. The major values reflected were those of individualism, defined by Purcell and Gray (Legge, 1995) as 'policies based on belief in the value of the individual and his or her right to advancement and fulfilment at work', individual initiative, energy and drive, self-reliance, acceptance of responsibility, and preparedness to take risks and to own the benefits of the outcomes. In the process, individuals would need to take responsibility for developing their knowledge and skills to deliver the promises of creativity.

The creation of privately owned, commercial enterprises with a Darwinian ethos of success or failure according to how they adapted to the commercial environment was the preferred model of the Conservative government. Its values did not reflect the notion and importance of full employment opportunity for all. Instead, they reflected the ethos in which, as Legge (1995) says, 'firms' survival and growth depend[ed] on [their] "leanness" and "fitness" in dealing with the rigours of the marketplace', without the support of government intervention and restrictions which prevented fair competition and protected the inefficient. This was economic Darwinism at its height, potentially leaving the vulnerable both ill-prepared and poorly equipped to cope with the change.

This shift in values heralded the growth of privatisation of state-owned industries and public utilities, and the introduction of enterprise values into the National Health Service, local government – in the form of compulsory competitive tendering – and many other areas.

To the Conservative government of the 1980s, trade unions were the protagonists of the enterprise culture they were seeking to establish. It saw them as 'an institutional impediment to the operation of free markets (not to mention that of disguising from workers their own best interests)', and therefore harmful or at least unnecessary. Through the use of closed-shop agreements, restrictive practices and legal immunities, they were seen to have the mechanisms for inhibiting the development of the free market central to the Conservatives' values. Furthermore, unions were perceived to fetter the freewill of the individual and, through the collective bargaining process, to control the way in which views and actions could be expressed and presented (Legge, 1995).

This period saw the start of the shift in workplace values from collectivism to individualism which has left the trade unions in some disarray. Collectivism was seen as one of the major inhibitors of the creation of an enterprise economy. National agreements with their national pay rates were seen to distort the economy and restricted the capacity of local employers to price their products at competitive rates. A worker in Newcastle would be paid the same as a worker in London for the same job, even though the cost of living and the costs of production in the two centres were significantly different.

The Conservative government's response to trade union resistance to its free market philosophy was to use its legislative powers. The series of labour laws passed during the 1980s changed the face of labour relations in Britain. The governments of the 1970s ignored unions at their peril: unions were perceived to wield a disproportionate amount of power in industrial relations. Through the 1980s and early 1990s, a series of Acts relating to employment protection and unfair dismissal, collective bargaining, sympathy strikes, secondary picketing, secret balloting for trade union leaders, balloting of membership before industrial action, the closed shop, legal immunity of unions and conditions for union recognition in the workplace did much to change the face of employee relations.

The object of Conservative legislation was not to improve the lot of the individual worker, but to reduce the power of the unions and increase the power of employers. Marginalising the unions would give more flexibility to employers to deal more directly with employees and give them greater power to manipulate workplace practices and processes in favour of their own value systems and business goals without the hindrance of powerful collective interests.

The trade union perspective

The trade union movement inevitably saw the situation differently. Instead of being the political monster that inhibited national economic development and well-being for workers and the 'cager' of the 'captive' individual's right to free expression and dissent, the union movement saw itself as protecting the rights of individuals through the great virtues of solidarity and collectivism. It saw itself as the champion of the weak, actively engaged in confronting and resisting the attempts of greedy, coercive and exploitative employers seeking to maximise shareholder profit at employees' expense.

Although employers might have thrown up their hands in horror at this perspective and descriptions of their values and behaviours, they did not have much of a track record to suggest anything very different. The very reason for trade unions' existence was maltreatment of employees by unscrupulous, exploitative employers. Capitalist values and ethics determined that individuals were just another resource to exploit, and their values gave them the right to do so. The evidence lies in the various organisational and management initiatives taken to increase efficiency and productivity.

The Industrial Revolution saw exploitation on a massive scale. The lack of will to change matters was evident in the values underpinning the *laissez-faire* policies of consecutive governments. The enlightened tried to improve the social, housing, health and educational conditions of the workers, but in the face of those social Darwinists who saw the poor as lazy, dirty, amoral low life. To the employer, the buyer of labour had all the rights whereas the seller of labour had none.

At the turn of the twentieth century, the emergence of Taylorism and the principles of scientific management, to improve efficiency, and Fordism, which valued 'man' as an extension of a machine, simply reinforced the views of trade unions that they were there to protect workers from the excesses of exploitation and coercion.

Even the advent of the human relations school, which emphasised the importance of social factors in the workplace, did little to dissuade organisations from their exploitative and coercive behaviours. The advent of McGregor's Theory Y, in which he espoused the virtues of people at work, and Maslow's attempt to dignify the values of employees, had marginal effect on the endemic values of organisations which still approached employees in an instrumental manner. Using the twin planks of solidarity and collective action, the trade union movement sought to win a greater share of profits for its members and to improve their welfare in the workplace.

■ Historical trade union values

But what values do trade unions represent? Historically, their need to confront the worst abuses of employer exploitation has forced them to be confrontational and to see conflict as a necessary requirement for improving the lot of their members. The diametrically opposed values of capital and labour make conflict inevitable. In fact, it is the clash of opposite value systems which creates the focus for employee relations as a process for managing the tensions and facilitating truce and compromise. For Marxists the position is so categorical that there is no need for employee relations at all, with its attempts to come to a compromise (Blyton and Turnbull, 1998). There is nothing to negotiate about. Collective bargaining and participation should not be entered into since the differences between the two value systems are so profound as to make negotiation futile.

However, it may not be perceived as all bad news. Legge describes this traditional view as 'liberal collectivism', which sees 'group conflict as inevitable and potentially beneficial, if institutionalised through collective bargaining. Management would have a co-ordinating role representing the employer's interests with the trade unions fulfilling the same role for the workforce' (Legge, 1995).

Unions see themselves as protectors of workers who cannot easily help themselves. They are there to provide pay determination through collective bargaining, care and welfare, and national campaigns to influence and lobby on social issues. Their role has been to confront organisational values and strategies which enforce passive compliance through fear of unemployment and to challenge the practices of management which alienate employees by creaming off the fruits of their labours. Their values are enshrined in the rules which govern the codes of behaviour of members. They promote and maintain the values of solidarity through group normative behaviour and have expectations of members that they do not defy the agreed codes of conduct and rules of membership. They discourage the miscreant and aberrant behaviours of those who are perceived to threaten the solidarity and security of the whole. In return for providing 'safety' and protection they require the subsuming of individual will to collective responsibility and action.

Generally, the historical core values of trade unionism have been confrontation through collective action, and solidarity through the use of creative tension and protectionism for union members' jobs for the purpose of keeping wages up and providing better working conditions. These values have been defined and shaped by the traditional values of the coal, docks and steel industries and sustained by their group norms and codes of behaviour. The demise of these industries with their large union memberships, together with downsizing, changing working practices and a loss of 5 million members since 1979, has fragmented the trade union strategy of collectivism and solidarity.

The 1990s have threatened even more the traditional positions and approaches adopted by trade unions. However, David Blunkett (1996) states that the attitudes and the actions of trade unions have to change in the light of changes in the relationship between capital and labour. The impact of the global economy and the shift towards social partnership require the unions to change from their confrontational stance to one of collaboration and partnership with employers and individual employees. Unions may find difficulty in making this transition since their values are deep-rooted and enshrined in their social history and tradition.

The upheavals of the 1980s' legislation and economic recession have combined to transform pay determination. The growth of individualism has shifted the emphasis from collective bargaining, a major plank of trade unionism, to individual determination. In 1975, 90 per cent of pay was determined by collective bargaining, with only 10 per cent determined by the employer. Nowadays, over 60 per cent of pay is determined by the employer, who, based on individual agreement, fixes the rate and invites employees to take it or leave it. Where collective bargaining does happen, the trend is for it to take place at local workplace level rather than nationally. This is an era in which employers expect to get more from their employees for 'paying' less, which the outdated values and strategies of trade unions can do little about.

Just as fundamental a threat to trade unions and their collective values is the trend by employers to marginalise them in the employment setting and to make them less relevant. The rise of management strategies and approaches which build on the new philosophies of human resource management with the emphasis on individual commitment and employee empowerment shifts the emphasis for responsibility directly onto the employee's shoulders. It does not necessitate the intervention of a vicarious intermediary on the part of the individual. The belief that the growth of management education and development throughout the 1990s has encouraged managers to see individuals as people rather than as units of production has further fuelled the trend towards dealing directly with the individual rather than through unions. It gives credence to the view that all good managers should want to deal with their people in a fair and equitable way and now have the training and understanding to do it: laudable values – if only it were the case. For further discussion, see Chapter 5.

The organisational perspective

This section examines the impact of values on the employment relationship within the organisational setting. It discusses how the values of the most influential group have shaped organisations, how values have been used to confer competitive advantage and what impact this has had on how organisations have related to the people within them.

■ Background to thinking in organisations

The shifts in values have reflected how organisations view themselves as well as how organisational theory has developed, which has in turn influenced the development of employee relations practice. Organisations have traditionally taken a functional view of themselves, underpinned by a structure reflecting these divisions, such as operations, finance and marketing. Each division often had its own culture and set of values encouraging an internal focus. The business schools also encouraged functionalism and 'scientific management' by taking a rational/economic approach in the subjects taught to developing managers, rarely taking a holistic view of organisations or teaching 'people skills'. The role of the manager was seen firmly as that of managing the task, rather than managing the people who performed the task.

For over two hundred years, classical management theory has likened organisations to machines, starting from Adam Smith's division of labour, to Fayol and Urwick's view of the task of managers in organisations as planning, organising, command and control. Organisations were designed as if they were machines with a network of interdependent parts, the functional departments further specified by precisely defined jobs. Through hierarchical patterns of authority and command they sought to make organisations into rational systems operating efficiently, seeing people as cogs rather than as human beings. The key values of this era were efficiency and control.

Taylor's model of scientific management took this a step further by analysing and standardising tasks from an engineer's viewpoint, simplifying work so that workers would be 'cheap, easy to train, easy to supervise, easy to replace' (Morgan, 1997). Taylorism can still be seen in organisations, particularly in manufacturing and call centre environments, one hundred years after he presented his first paper on management. As Morgan points out, scientific management worked where there were straightforward repetitive tasks, in a stable environment where people operating the process were compliant and willing to be 'dehumanised'. It worked in a society whose values around work came from the 'Protestant work ethic' tradition, where expectations were no more than the straight exchange of 'a fair day's work for a fair day's pay'. It also worked for a generation who had grown up in a culture, and were steeped in the values, of the military bureaucracy that came with two world wars and national service, used to following commands without question.

Like Taylor, organisations regarded people as a collective entity, part of a machine, numbers on the balance sheet, 'the workforce', to be treated the same way and negotiated with through representatives, not as individuals with their own hopes and opinions. This view was also reflected in the way research into organisations and developing organisational theory was carried out using 'scientific' methods that reduced people to objects through statistics and numbers. To control and efficiency, scientific management added the values of standardisation, compliance, routinisation of tasks and dehumanisation.

The 1960s onwards saw the emergence of a new approach to motivation theory, with McGregor, McClelland, Herzberg and Argyris all demonstrating that motivation was more than just the straight exchange of money for labour. This period also saw the emergence of a new paradigm for thinking about society and therefore organisations, based on the philosophy of Kant and the German Idealists, in 'attempting to understand and explain the social world primarily from the point of view of the actors directly involved in the social process' (Burrell and Morgan, 1979). From this time there was a shift in thinking in the social sciences that started looking at people as individual human beings and thinking of organisations primarily as the people that constitute them.

The importance of values in organisations and in the theory surrounding them is evident in the way the values of influential individuals within shape the organisation. Mangham and Pye suggest that people in organisations draw up their organisation charts to reflect their beliefs and values regarding how they think the world is and how the organisation should be organised to deal with it. They report from their research that 'indeed the sharpest image that remains with us . . . is that of a small group of senior managers seeking to shape events and activities, improvising the music and leading the dance for others to follow' (Mangham and Pye, 1991). The senior managers they researched reinforced their view that their actions were informed by what they valued and influenced how they managed. Those with strong materialistic values were likely to support monetary incentive schemes, whether or not experience revealed greater effort and commitment, demonstrating that they see what they want to see, looking for evidence to support their beliefs, discounting that which questions them. If senior management believed that the workforce were just 'hands' to be controlled, separated from their brains, should it have been a surprise that their employees felt detached, or alienated, often putting considerably more energy into activities outside their work?

Changing organisational values: from control to commitment

It was not until the 1980s that a change of management style and values, based on the thinking of the 1960s, began to emerge visibly in organisations. The post-war years had been characterised by relative stability, a growing economy and full employment. It was in this decade that organisations began to change their view of their workforce from the rational–economic 'factors of production', recognising the workforce as being made up of individuals who had needs beyond pure financial incentives. Organisations found that having the right machinery and technology was no longer enough to be successful. They had to have a motivated, committed workforce to operate them, rather than an interchangeable pool of labour as required by the values of scientific management.

The impact of emerging competition and the focus on marketing

The first of three factors that influenced organisations in changing their traditional ways of thinking in managing their workforce was emerging competition. Western companies had begun to experience the threat of global competition, especially from the Pacific Rim and Japan, and had started to examine the Japanese style of management to understand their success factors. Much evidence was drawn from Japanese industry where high quality and productivity per employee plus successful product/process improvement were seen to be underpinned by employee commitment to company goals and willingness to participate in quality improvement.

Western companies also began to recognise that the other success factor of Japanese companies was their focus on customers. The 1980s saw the development of the concept of total quality in many organisations and the parallel development of the marketing function to drive corporate strategy from customer requirements, rather than from what production was prepared to offer. Inherent in the total quality approach was the understanding of 'internal customers' within the organisation, the recognition of the part people played in achieving corporate objectives, and the need to involve the whole workforce to gain competitive advantage. For those companies engaged in total quality there was an increasing recognition of the need for a change in the values prevalent in the workplace to those of customer service, empowerment, involvement and teamwork.

Valuing excellence

Allied to this, the second influence on values and the need for commitment came out of the 'excellence' literature of the period. Ouchi's *Theory Z*, Peters and Waterman's *In Search of Excellence*, Pascale and Athos' *The Art of Japanese Management*, and Deal and Kennedy's *Corporate Cultures*, all published in 1981 and 1982, set the agenda for commitment. They became standard reading for many managers, and were, as

Campbell *et al.* (1990) put it, the start of a tidal wave of writing on the importance of culture and values. They put the 'soft' factors, which had previously been the domain of the psychologists and organisational development (OD) departments, on the corporate agenda and made them discussable.

This period also saw companies experimenting with different workforce strategies such as AT&T's Quality of Work Life joint venture with the Communication Workers of America, demonstrating how great and productive the contribution of a committed workforce can be. As Ouchi points out, however, long-term relationships, stress on participation, teamwork and consensus decision-making that often characterise the Japanese style were against the conventional values and management practices in the West (Ouchi, 1981). Peters and Waterman, Deal and Kennedy, and Ouchi also found that their 'excellent' companies had a strong code of conduct and values underpinning how they conducted their business.

Creating and changing culture and values for competitive advantage

As managers and directors became formally educated in business through MBA and other qualifications, and management development came to be seen as important as training in technical skills for the workforce, in the boardroom directors began to develop a values-driven framework for their competitive strategy. Writers from Mintzberg and Quinn to Schein have emphasised the role that organisational leaders have in ensuring the organisation has a 'source of identity and core mission', which Schein would argue come from understanding and managing the culture, and articulating the organisation's values (Schein, 1985). This understanding of the 'soft' side of managing organisations was also recognised by the strategic writers such as Quinn *et al.* (1988), who suggested that the key tasks of the leaders of institutions include: the definition of institutional mission and role; the institutional embodiment of purpose; the defence of institutional integrity; and the ordering of internal conflict.

In the study that inspired their book, Deal and Kennedy found that of the 80 companies they surveyed:

- about one-third (25) had clearly articulated beliefs;
- of that third, two-thirds had qualitative beliefs, or values; the remaining one-third had widely understood financially oriented goals;
- all of the 18 companies with qualitative beliefs or strong cultures were outstanding performers and included those cited by Peters and Waterman and by Ouchi.

Organisational culture has been variously described as: 'the way we do things around here' (Deal and Kennedy, 1982); 'patterns of belief or shared meaning, fragmented or integrated, and supported by various operating norms and rituals . . . [exerting] a decisive influence on the overall ability of the organisation to deal with the challenges it faces' (Morgan, 1997) and 'one of the most powerful and stable forces operating in organisations' (Schein, 1996).

Organisational values are core underpinnings which 'serve the normative or moral function of guiding members of the group in how to deal with certain key situations' (Schein, 1985). When the values are internalised by the organisation they become beliefs and assumptions and gradually become automatic and habitual, however, if the values are not based on actual beliefs, they are 'espoused' values only which will predict what people will say, but not how they will react. A company that says that it values teamwork but promotes those who achieve individual objectives at the expense of their colleagues should not be surprised when teamworking breaks down. If an organisation articulates its values it must be consistent, ensuring congruency with strategy and policy to 'resonate with and reinforce the organisation's strategy' (Campbell *et al.*, 1990). One of the dangers that they recognised of not making values explicit was that a company's values were often built on those of the founder members, such as (Bill) Hewlett and (Dave) Packard, Occam (see Exhibit 2.2 later in the chapter) or the senior management team at the time, especially when an organisation was founded. When that group retires and leaves the organisation to professional managers, the fit between the new senior management and the values may be broken, as Hewlett-Packard's recognition of a need to get 'back to the garage' perhaps demonstrates.

In their writings, Deal and Kennedy (1982) and Morgan (1986, 1997) cited well-known examples of values such as: 'IBM means service', 'Excellence in underwriting' (Chubb Insurance) and 'Never kill a new product idea' (3M). Organisations with these strong founding values found it more appropriate to manage their relationship with their employees directly rather than through a third party, hence trade unions failed to be recognised as relevant in these organisations. As the alignment between organisational and employee values became more congruent the need for trade union representation was seen as unnecessary. Organisations wishing to move away from the traditional adversarial industrial relations of the past saw these exemplars as desirable models around which to formulate new practices of values-based employee relations.

A common characteristic of many of these values-based organisations was that they were new start-ups, often in new technology settings where they were not handicapped by the trappings of historical tradition. Organisations with a longer history, coming from an older technology base, would be bound to a greater or lesser extent by the values and beliefs of the past, not always common throughout a large organisation. During this period, many organisations engaged in trying to change their culture formally articulated and published statements of what they thought their values should be. Some examples of value statements are given in Figure 2.2.

Following the insights of the 'excellence' literature, organisations became aware of the significance and symbolic consequences of organisational values, with writers such as Morgan reporting that 'many organisations have started to explore the pattern of culture and subculture that shapes day-to-day action' (Morgan, 1986). He saw this as a positive step towards the recognition of the human nature of organisations and the need to build them around people. Ten years later he reported that the total quality and customer service movements of the time that sought to change managerial and organisational cultures had been largely successful in 'revolutionising and reinventing themselves' through these values. However, for some 70 per cent of organisations these movements became just programmes, failing to shift the dominant culture and mindset and the prevailing political patterns. These would suggest that, for this group, the new values had not been internalised and remained as 'espoused', and the organisations reverted to their traditional values, further reinforced by the downsizing that characterised the 1990s.

Schein (1996) has proposed an explanation for the failure of changing culture and values programmes to take hold. He suggests there are at least three cultures operating within an organisation: 'operators', the line management and workers who make and deliver the products and services; 'engineers', who design and monitor the core technology; and 'executives', who are the senior managers at the top of the organisation. The

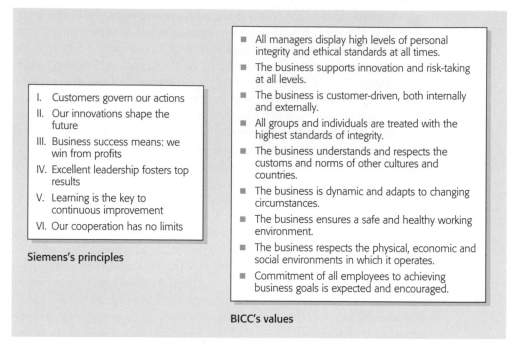

I.   Customers govern our actions
II. Our innovations shape the future
III. Business success means: we win from profits
IV. Excellent leadership fosters top results
V.   Learning is the key to continuous improvement
VI. Our cooperation has no limits

Siemens's principles

- All managers display high levels of personal integrity and ethical standards at all times.
- The business supports innovation and risk-taking at all levels.
- The business is customer-driven, both internally and externally.
- All groups and individuals are treated with the highest standards of integrity.
- The business understands and respects the customs and norms of other cultures and countries.
- The business is dynamic and adapts to changing circumstances.
- The business ensures a safe and healthy working environment.
- The business respects the physical, economic and social environments in which it operates.
- Commitment of all employees to achieving business goals is expected and encouraged.

BICC's values

Figure 2.2 **Organisations' value statements**

executive culture, because of the closeness to the shareholder, only sees the organisation in terms of the 'bottom line'; 'engineers' are focused on improving the technology, seeing people as the factor that operates it and usually abuses it; whereas it is in the 'operating' culture that most of the 'culture and values' change programmes take hold. 'The research findings about the importance of teamwork, collaboration, commitment, and involvement fall on deaf executive ears, because in the executive culture, those are not the important variables to consider' (Schein, 1996).

Culture and values are a key part of defining the company philosophy, which provides the organisation with a framework against which it can assess the extent to which business decisions fit with the company philosophy and provides a mechanism for the defence of its integrity. Peters and Waterman found that their excellent companies all had philosophies that focused on the contribution of people and the need to manage them as adults, without the need to manage them through a third party. The opposite situation is reflected by the thoughts of Argyris (1960), who observed that many organisations took a negative view of human nature, treating people as infants despite motivation theories and recruiting mature, skilled people. Morgan (1997) points out that where the culture is strong 'a distinctive ethos pervades the whole organization: employees exude the characteristics that define the mission or ethos of the whole – e.g. outstanding commitment to service'.

However, most organisations are not made up of a single culture; organisations evolve over time, and even with a strong culture from a visionary founder, as in Mintzberg's (1984) 'missionary' organisation, in time other views will develop. Both Morgan (1997) and Schein (1985) refer to the establishment of the 'counterculture' as different views emerge as the result of changes in the environment the organisation operates in. They also recognise that other 'cultures' prevalent in society and formed from competing value systems such as those rooted in nationality, gender, religion and professional groupings (see Figure 2.1), will impact on the organisation.

Trade unions have also been seen as a counterculture in organisations, with a different value system from that of the organisation. Morgan (1997) suggests that unions owe their existence to the traditional lack of common interests between the organisation and its employees and have their own separate cultural histories which are unique to each union grouping and industry. Unions reflect the view that for a healthy government there should also be strong opposition to keep them in check. However, the evolution of a stakeholder approach recognised a need to balance the wants and values of customers, shareholders, organisation, management, employees, suppliers, government and the community to provide a more strategic view than the traditional confrontation style would allow.

Throughout the focus on quality, customers and 'excellence' during the 1980s, trade unions were increasingly marginalised as organisations experimented with 'soft' HR practices, such as employee involvement and participation, as advocated by the leading writers and consultants and learned from the 'excellent' organisations. This was seen to be supported by the external changes that were happening to the trade union movement.

As trade unions lost their traditional influence over parts of the UK workforce, many organisations were realising that they could also achieve more through the development of an effective relationship with their workforce rather than holding to the more confrontational style of the past. They sought to provide a better service to the workforce in the areas where trade unions had traditionally been strong, such as in communication and providing benefits to employees. Articles such as Walton's 'From control to commitment in the workplace' (Walton, 1985) introduced the concept of commitment to the wider management audience, as the outcome of implementing the strategies advocated by the 'excellence' literature. Commitment was promoted as a means of motivating and controlling employees. Morgan (1997) warns that whereas many organisations attempt to create shared meaning and involve people in the vision and values required to build a unified whole, working for the same ends and mutual benefit, it is also possible to use them manipulatively.

The shift from collectivism to individualism: developing a direct relationship with employees through commitment

The third factor that contributed to the interest in values and commitment was the emergence of the human resources school as motivation was redefined from the perspective of differing individual needs. The changing expectations and educational levels of the workforce on the one hand, and intensified competition on the other, would seem to have made the scientific management model obsolete, with organisational success now deemed to depend on a superior level of performance in the marketplace, which in turn required the commitment of the workforce. One of the factors common to HRM, the success of Japanese companies, and the 'excellence' literature appeared to be the idea of gaining employee commitment through emphasis on mutuality of employer/employee objectives. Epitomised in their model (Figure 2.3), Harvard Business School led the way in HRM, reflecting the changed understanding of the role of personnel or human resource policies in business success, which was taught to a new generation of MBAs and senior executives.

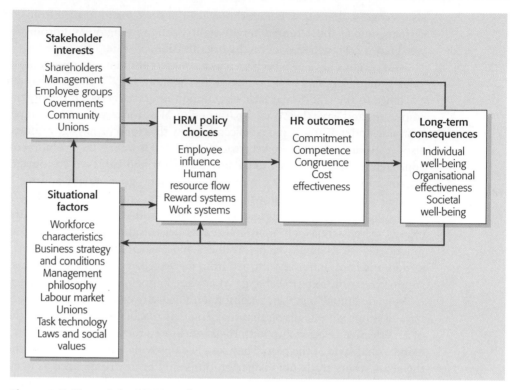

Figure 2.3 Map of the HRM territory

Source: Beer *et al.* (1984) Reprinted with the permission of The Free Press, an imprint of Simon & Schuster Adult Publishing Group, from MANAGING HUMAN ASSETS by M. Beer, B. Spector, P.R. Lawrence, D.Q. Mills, and R.E. Walton. Copyright © 1985 by The Free Press

The change in the role of the personnel reflected the gradual evolution of approaches to management during the twentieth century, based on contemporary understanding of motivation as it moved away from the scientific management model, where workers were viewed as lazy, aimless and mercenary, and willing therefore to tolerate the routinised, specialised jobs of the factory for a price. The realisation that it was necessary to consider the 'whole person' at work, following the Hawthorne studies and a further major phase of research into motivation in the 1960s, led the way to the human resources model. With many departments renaming themselves 'human resources', they took a more strategic role as a support function that enables business strategy rather than the more reactive and detached function that had originally grown out of employee welfare services.

The 'soft' school of HRM

The human resources school recognised that people are motivated by a complex set of factors that are interrelated, including money, need for affiliation or achievement, and the desire for meaningful work. Employees should therefore be looked on as reservoirs of potential talent, and it is management's responsibility to learn how best to tap such resources. The assumptions that come from the research of this period reflect much of what is seen in the West as the Japanese management style: people want to contribute; the more they become involved, the more meaningful work can become; work does not have to be distasteful – hence job enrichment and job design; employees are capable of making significant and rational decisions affecting their work; increased control and completion of meaningful tasks can determine the level of job satisfaction. This philosophy implies a greater degree of participation in decision-making and increased autonomy over task accomplishment and commitment a key outcome.

The 'hard' school of HRM

As organisations were beginning to recognise the value of this philosophy, many senior managers brought up on Taylorism still felt the dilemma of capital's need to control labour while seeking its commitment and cooperation. Until the early 1980s, what was taught in business schools was based on the 'hard' skills of management, concentrating on strategy, structure and systems with their emphasis on the analytical and technical aspects of work. In many organisations with these values, HRM was taken literally, people being seen as a resource to be spent like any other. Decisions were still based on people as numbers on a balance sheet and therefore people were still viewed as a collective.

Walton's article was symptomatic of the shift in thinking and values of a new generation of managers and set out to demonstrate the benefits of a 'commitment' strategy, pointing out that the changing expectations of a better-educated workforce have led to a growing disillusionment with the old-style model of control:

> workers respond best – and most creatively – not when they are tightly controlled by management, placed in narrowly defined jobs, and treated like an unwelcome necessity, but instead, when they are given broader responsibilities, encouraged to contribute, and helped to take satisfaction in their work. (Walton, 1985)

He recognised that a 'commitment' strategy left many questions for the role of trade unions; some organisations sought to derecognise them, while others actively pursued mutual cooperation, in the pursuit of their active support in change.

Results of commitment

The advantages of gaining employee commitment have been perceived to be lower labour turnover, better product quality, greater capacity to innovate and employee flexibility, all leading to the enhanced capability of the firm to achieve competitive advantage. In this, the workgroup is seen as the critical unit, heralding the focus on teamwork (Walton, 1985).

Definition of commitment

The definition of organisational commitment that is most frequently used is that of Porter *et al.* (1974):

> the relative strength of an individual's identification with and involvement in a particular organisation. Conceptually, it can be characterised by at least three factors:
>
> (1) a strong belief in, and acceptance of the organisation's goals and values,
> (2) a willingness to exert considerable effort on behalf of the organisation, and
> (3) a strong desire to maintain membership in the organisation.

Organisations in the 1980s focused on the first two elements of the commitment definition, working on recruiting those who believed in the same goals and values as the organisation, or on organisational change programmes to engender commitment among existing employees, hoping to exchange this for willingness to 'go the extra mile'. The employee relations department often played a key role at a strategic level in working with the board to understand and define the culture and values that were appropriate to the organisation. At an operational level they would develop and implement such programmes as employee involvement and effective internal communications to engender the common belief in organisation goals and values. These programmes also retrieved internal communications as the organisation's prerogative from the trade unions, who had often previously taken on this role owing to poor management capability and skills in this area.

The 1990s: a decade of uncertainty

Where, initially, global competition in the 1980s had encouraged organisations to invest in their employees through such programmes as management development, customer care and total quality management, the intensification of competition and other factors led to recession and mass unemployment at the beginning of the 1990s, often for the same group who had had their expectations raised. The other factors contributing to recession included new technology, privatisation, shareholders demanding greater returns, and the changing societal values enabled by government policy taking away employment protection measures, emasculating the trade unions and reducing unemployment benefits in the UK.

The commitment equation can be seen as what the organisation wanted from the employee, with the exchange from the individual's point of view being in those intangible areas that come from involvement, such as job satisfaction. The recession impacted on many of the 'change programmes' under way in organisations, as many of those with long traditions and corporate memories reverted to their old type, the new values that they had been working on not yet being 'the way we do things around here'.

As companies downsized and restructured, any exchange had become uneven, with organisations no longer wanting people to be committed to remain with the organisation (apart from those with scarce skills), but still wanting their willingness to exert extra effort on its behalf. Employees, on the other hand, faced with being expected to put in more effort, partly to compensate for departed colleagues, without the traditional job security, potentially felt that the organisation's side of the exchange and their commitment to their workforce was missing. Many felt exploited. Organisations in many cases had reverted to their old style of managing but expected their employees to stay with the changes they had started to put in place.

The individual perspective

In order to understand the individual's perspective of the employment relationship, we consider it from two perspectives: the employee–organisation relationship and the employee–union relationship. To inform the former, we view it from the perspective of the changing nature of the psychological contract existing between them. Whereas commitment reflects the organisational aspect of the employment relationship, the wider 'psychological contract' reflects the balance between organisational and employee expectations and has been seen as the key variable in explaining contemporary employment relations (Guest and Conway, 1997). To inform the latter, we view it from the needs of the employee in the context of the changing nature of work and employees' expectations of their trade union.

The employee–organisation relationship

The concept of the psychological contract

The formal contract that employees have with their organisation traditionally covered the tangible aspects of work such as hours to be worked in exchange for pay and benefits, and working conditions. These tangible aspects also formed the area that traditionally was negotiated with the trade union. The psychological contract goes beyond the tangible contract to consider the expectations of the relationship that employees and organisations have of one another. It can be described in two different ways: (1) by the perceived contents and terms of the contract and (2) in how it is formed – the process of contracting. All types of contract, from the formal employment contract to this more psychological one, can be seen to have their roots in exchange theory and reciprocity, where individuals invest or make contributions in return for a particular reward or outcome. Like the concept of organisational commitment (Lydka, 1992; Meyer and Allen, 1997), the psychological contract is also influenced by equity theory, especially where the contract has broken down.

At the centre of the relationship between organisations and their employees is the creation of the conditions that will allow employees to meet their needs and expectations while providing a high level of performance for the organisation. The term 'psychological contract' implies that there is always an unwritten set of expectations operating between the actors of an organisation:

> the actual terms remain implicit; they are not written down anywhere. But the mutual expectations formed between the employee and the employer function like a contract in that if either party fails to meet the expectations, serious consequences will follow – demotivation, turnover, lack of advancement, or termination. (Schein, 1978: 112)

The ways that the organisation demonstrates acceptance of the contract include salary increase, positive performance appraisal, new job assignments, sharing of organisational secrets and promotion. This is in exchange for deciding to remain, a high level of commitment and willingness to accept various kinds of constraints on the part of the employee (Schein, 1978).

Many of these expectations go further than the explicit areas of pay, training and development, and involve the person's sense of dignity and worth, wanting work that is fulfilling and opportunities to develop and grow. Schein suggests that much labour unrest and employee turnover comes from violations of these aspects of the psychological contract dressed up as the explicit, and more acceptable, issues of pay, working hours and conditions which traditionally form the legitimate negotiating agenda.

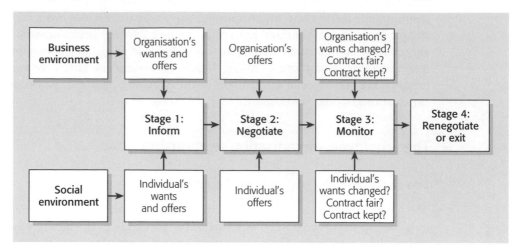

Figure 2.4 **The four stages of psychological contracting**
Source: Herriot and Pemberton (1995)

Herriot's (1995) view of the psychological contract draws on the thoughts of Schein and is focused on the social process of contracting (Figure 2.4). He suggests that it is this aspect that has the most theoretical and practical value as it is only the process that may be similar wherever contracts are made: all of the other aspects are likely to differ as they are made up of the perceptions of individuals. His model builds on Schein's conditions for success.

Rousseau, interested in the content of psychological contracts, starts from the premise that contracts 'are a product of free societies' and that they are underpinned by choice; they arise when people believe themselves to have choice in their dealings with others. She makes the point that having a choice can engender commitment to carry out promises and takes the line of developing a behavioural theory of contracts. Her definition of the psychological contract is 'individual beliefs, shaped by the organisation, regarding terms of an exchange agreement between individuals and their organisation' (Rousseau, 1995: 9).

She emphasises that the individual voluntarily assents to make and accept certain promises as he or she understands them as a key feature of a psychological contract, which involves giving up some measure of freedom. This is similar to Schein's signal of acceptance of the contract through 'willingness to accept various kinds of constraints, delays or undesirable work', although Rousseau warns that:

Contracts are made when we surrender some of our freedom from restrictions in exchange for a similar surrender by another. But by giving up something voluntarily, each gets much more than might be possible otherwise.

Violation of the psychological contract

The recession of the early1990s focused research on what happens when the psychological contract has been violated (Brockner *et al.*, 1992; Parks and Kidder, 1994; Robinson and Rousseau, 1994). As Morrison (1994) explains: 'the issues covered by the contract are emotionally laden, thus, when psychological contracts are not working smoothly, strong feelings are provoked'. As the psychological contract contains many unconscious expectations, many at the heart of an individual's perception of self, any violation strikes at more than disappointed expectations, causing individuals to question beliefs and values about respect, codes of conduct and the integrity of the organisation. The repercussions from broken promises are significant, producing anger and eroding trust between the parties to the employment relationship (Schein, 1978; Robinson and Rousseau, 1994).

The focus on downsizing and restructuring has meant that these contracts have been changed. A formal written contract has to have consent, but with the intangible psychological contract, conditions, not of their choosing, have been imposed on some employees as in the ending of a 'job for life' expectation for older employees. This has led to the situation described by Brockner *et al.* (1992) where layoffs are made and the perception of the fairness in deciding who was to leave and the reasons for leaving affected the commitment of those employees remaining. They found those who had been most committed were the most negatively affected. Their perception of the equity and fairness of decisions on who was to leave had caused those remaining to reassess what they thought of their psychological contract.

The other area that has impacted on the structure of organisations has been the advent of flexible working and issues such as short-term contracts. The extent to which members of the flexible workforce have had a voice in the change of their contracts will also be informed by where they are on Rousseau's continuum between the transactional contract of 'a fair day's work for a fair day's pay', which can now mean short-term, temporary employment, and the relational contract characterised by open-ended relationships and investment from both sides. The transactional contract is closest to the traditional economic exchange, where the terms are tangible, such as money, hours and specific tasks, usually within a specified timescale. The relational contract, on the other hand, is more abstract and concerned with the relationship between the individual and the employing organisation, but has the traditional element of 'a job for life'.

The stark contrast between these two extremes of working can be seen side by side in the case of a regional airport where outsourced service staff have contracts containing phrases such as 'you will be required to be completely flexible in this position . . . work is not guaranteed and will be offered by the company at its discretion depending on the needs of the business', whereas the core airport staff's time includes a volunteering programme where they are encouraged to become involved in local community projects in company time as part of their development.

Multiple perspectives on the psychological contract

These differences can be illustrated by research undertaken with 'knowledge workers' to explore the employment relationship in the 1990s (Parkinson, 1998). The typology that emerged (see Figure 2.5) provides a framework to illustrate the multiplicity of differing perspectives from which the employment relationship can be viewed within a single organisation.

There were at least four different types of perspective on the intangible elements, or informal/psychological contract. The research suggests that the main dimensions that influence people's view of the employment relationship are related to what they are looking for from that relationship, whether that focus is on the purely 'formal' aspects

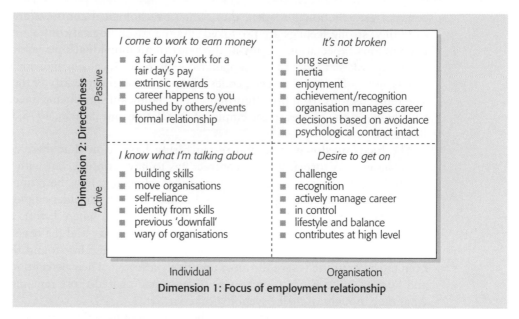

Figure 2.5 **A model of the employment relationship**
Source: Parkinson (1998). © Ann Parkinson 2002

or on looking for a wider involvement in the organisation, which can also be seen as commitment. The second factor that seemed to influence their view of the relationship was how active they were in pursuing their career, which has its roots in the psychological concept of 'locus of control'. The four types were characterised as:

- *I come to work to get money.* This group views the relationship as the traditional basic exchange of 'a fair day's work for a fair day's pay', where motivation is the extrinsic rewards of pay and benefits plus the security of a large organisation. Having 'drifted' into their first job, they would see their career as something that happens to them, allowing themselves to be pushed along by circumstances and other people, often ending up in situations they might not have sought. Outside the formal terms of their employment contract they prefer to keep their relationship with the organisation at a minimum.

- *It's not broken.* This group is looking for achievement, recognition and enjoyment from work, and career decisions happen only when this group feels unable to achieve these things. While everything is going well, there is a feeling of inertia, the psychological contract is intact, the job enjoyable, and the career seems to manage itself. They consciously or unconsciously expect the organisation or their line manager to take responsibility for their career. It is not until something goes wrong, or they are offered an alternative, that they assess the extent to which their psychological contract is being fulfilled.

- *I know what I'm talking about.* Taking their sense of identity from their skills, the members of this group constantly update and develop them, which contributes to their sense of self-reliance. They easily move organisations to pursue their career, several of them having had the confidence to set up on their own at various stages of their careers. However a bad experience previously that was out of their control, such as redundancy, has built a wariness in developing relationships with organisations. Managers saw management as an alternative to using their technical skills, 'something to do when I am not using my core skills'.

■ *Desire to get on.* Looking for challenge and concerned about being recognised for their efforts, the people in this group expect that by contributing and being loyal to the organisation at a high level, they will receive the means to actively manage their career and be in control of their lives. They had a clear idea of what they wanted to do and have recognised the need to plan their careers, not wanting to compromise on lifestyle issues and balancing family life with a career. These people move to take up the next challenge rather than waiting until something goes wrong.

Managers and the psychological contract

These 'types' were generally indistinguishable by age, gender, type of work or length of service, so that getting to know each individual would be essential in order to be able to understand what were their needs of the organisation or how they perceived their obligation in the relationship. A key aspect that emerged was the role of the manager in the informal relationship. Everyone had the same formal, legal contract with the organisation, managed via the personnel department, but their informal, psychological contract was personal, and managed between themselves and their manager as an agent of the organisation, as outlined in Figure 2.6. The quality of that relationship between the manager and employee was an important factor in how the overall employment relationship was viewed. With the delegation of important people management tasks to line managers, the line managers come to represent the organisation in the eyes of the employee. However, managers are also subject to the same factors that colour their

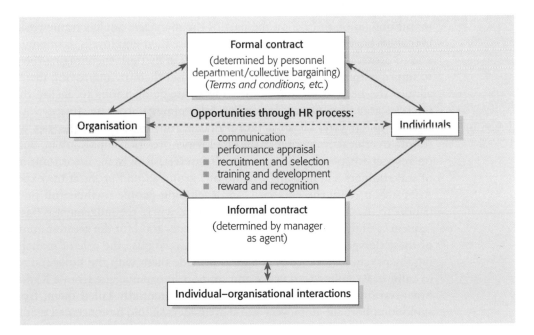

Figure 2.6 Determining the employment relationship
Source: adapted from Parkinson (1999). © Ann Parkinson 2002

view of their relationship with the organisation, leading to a large number of different psychological contracts operating at any one time. Structural changes have meant that the HR function in many organisations manages only the legal, formal side of the employment relationship, while the line manager manages the psychological or informal contract.

Managers in organisations have increasingly had areas such as appraisal, development and recruitment delegated to them that they would traditionally have expected their HR colleagues to handle and for which they have had little preparation or training. For many of them, as well as for others in the organisation, these changes have not been made explicit. These structural changes have also introduced more flexibility into organisations, physically removing managers from their people, either through working in different locations, often in different countries, often from home, or through working at different times especially as the 9 to 5, five-day week becomes less prevalent. Overlaid with a more global workforce, the pressure is on the manager to find a different way of developing a relationship with his or her workforce from that which existed when they sat in the same work area, at the same time of day, with the same people.

Moral obligations and the employment relationship

Understanding the nature of the employment relationship is seen by Soule (1998) as critical to exploring the nature of the moral responsibility of the manager within it. He argues that even at the most basic level where the relationship is seen as little more than a legal structure, to see it as just a fleeting market transaction ignores the theory that firms are all founded on the assumption of some type of stable employment relationship. Soule's premise is that an ethical relationship is built on trust, and in trusting their manager, employees put themselves at risk. Just as the basic mechanistic exchange equation has a fair day's work in exchange for a fair day's pay, the risk must be balanced by a positive moral obligation of care on the part of the manager. Soule's framework suggests that managers have a moral obligation to promote their employees' economic opportunities and to protect them from economic dislocation by both encouraging their development to improve their skills, and thereby protecting them by improving their marketability should the need arise, and influencing strategic decisions to ensure that employees' interests are taken into account when determining corporate strategy.

In a similar way, Legge (1996) proposes four mainstream theories which can contribute to ethical evaluation of the employment relationship: Kantian, with its emphasis on respect for people and against self-interest; Rawlsian, incorporating the concept of stakeholders and insisting that no one group should profit at the expense of others; Aristotelian, with the emphasis on developing people to their full potential to contribute to the community; and utilitarianism, where the judgement is based on the consequences of the action and whether it produces good for the greatest number. From any of these perspectives, organisations need to recognise the role of managers in managing the psychological contract and to provide them with the skills and tools they need to fulfil it. By failing to prepare and support line managers: from a Kantian viewpoint, organisations and the HR profession have potentially failed them; from a Rawlsian standpoint both the employees and shareholders should be concerned that this group may not be able to fulfil this new role; from the Aristotelian perspective, both managers and employees are not fulfilling their potential; even from a utilitarian view, leaving managers thus exposed cannot be to the greatest good of the majority.

It would appear increasingly difficult to view and manage people as the collective of only a few years ago; organisations need to take into account the differing dimensions that make up the individual at work. In order to take into account individuals' needs and expectations, a different approach is required to the organisation's relationship with individuals through their manager, who emerges as the central player in the informal relationship between the organisation and the employee. The manager is the factor that binds the dimensions of the employment relationship model (Figure 2.6) together, suggesting a good relationship may mitigate against harmful effects brought about by external forces. Furthermore, it is how managers model the values of the organisation that will determine whether the individual identifies with the organisation. The above research also suggested that individuals were more likely to stay in an organisation where they felt a fit with their values. This reflects a recent Mori survey which found that 82 per cent of respondents would not work for an organisation whose values they did not believe in (Industrial Society, 2001; Knell, 2000) and is illustrated in the case of Occam (Exhibit 2.2). With the changes in values surrounding work and the increased ability to be treated as an individual and to be in control of their working lives, many people feel that it is no longer appropriate to give away that control to a third party.

In this section we have focused on the change to a more individual-centred approach to the employment relationship but we must also recognise that this is not the individualism that arose out of the 'selfish 80s'. In looking forward to a workplace in which the workforce of the twenty-first century will thrive, it is more complex than taking an individual versus collectivist approach, and reflects the values of a focus on integrity, wanting to contribute to the 'greater good' and working as part of a team. This perhaps can be seen as moving towards a communitarian approach (Etzioni, 1995) and is well

Exhibit 2.2

Occam Direct Marketing – a values based company

Established in 1993 by its two founding directors, this small Somerset company provides a good example of an organisation where values underpin the way people are managed. People are recruited based as much on how they will fit into the ethos of the company as on their skills. The directors are very clear on the culture (Occamness) they want to maintain as the company grows, which they have discussed with everyone:

- a good team spirit
- a strong family feel
- relaxed but professional work environment
- learning from mistakes – not blaming
- enjoying work.

Working for Occam is characterised by working hard but in a conducive setting, where everyone feels part of the Occam family, with no status distinctions or separate offices, and when anyone is under pressure the rest of the team comes to the person's aid to get the job finished. The social aspects are taken seriously: after a particularly busy period all relax together, i.e. they go tank driving or to a health spa; employees get to know new people through lunch dates where a group of people who don't know each other well go out to lunch; there are regular evenings in the pub, fun days, the challenge cup – held until challenged for it on any activity, sporting or otherwise; and lunch breaks are taken with many activities from running or body toning to pumpkin carving. The small size of the organisation and the nature of Occamites has encouraged communication and early raising of issues before major problems arise. The company has a low attrition rate with most people feeling committed to a company that allows them to pursue lifestyle issues rather than a 'career'.

described by Warren (2000) as personalist, which he describes as seeing people in relation to others, where their 'good cannot be had independently of the community but nor can the good of the community be achieved independently of the individual'. This approach recognises the reciprocal nature of the employment relationship in a context that requires the development of trust, open communications and involvement, and reminds organisations that they are working with people rather than 'hands', and teams rather than 'gangs'.

Impact of the psychological contract on traditional employee relations practices

The main activities where trade unions have traditionally been involved in organisations have been collective bargaining over pay and conditions, and communication. It is in these areas that many employee relations departments have expanded from their former industrial relations role during the 1990s.

The recession of the early 1990s, coupled with a cost-cutting focus, has seen many organisations seeking to implement a form of pay for performance scheme focusing on individual performance, rather than a series of increments depending on length of time in a job up to a point where there would be just the payment to keep up with inflation. Many employees had their formal contracts of employment changed either through being 'transferred' to another company following outsourcing, or being offered an individual contract to take them out of collective bargaining. Few of those affected had much choice and, in Herriott and Pemberton's (1995) terms, had little chance to renegotiate their 'psychological contracts'.

The other major area that employee relations departments have retrieved from trade unions has been that of internal communications. Guzzo and Noonan (1994) would see communication between the organisation and its employees as at the heart of determining how the contract is viewed.

The employee–union relationship

The impact of changing work patterns

The world of work has been changing quite significantly since the 1990s. This has produced substantial changes in the way employee relations has developed, as discussed in Chapter 10. The traditional mutual employer–employee relationship has been in demise, driven there by the adoption of flexible working practices, market forces and changes in values. The psychological contract literature confirms this.

The individual relationship with the employer has not been the only relationship to change. The way in which individuals relate to their industrial trade unions has also undergone a significant shift. Much of this shift has come from the need of individuals to adopt different working practices because of the reduction in full-time permanent opportunities, the increase in short-term fixed contracts and part-time working. Much of work has become fragmented and many workers transient. Individuals need to be more mobile and will not stay with the same employer for long periods of time, let alone a lifetime. Hence, the everyday interactions of individuals with their colleagues, which maintain an environment that continually reinforces the values of collectivism and solidarity, loyalties and commitment of individuals to each other, has largely passed. Flexible working practices and their concomitants have encouraged the rise of individualism. No longer do employees identify in the same way with the core values of their industries; no longer do they interact in the same way on a day-to-day basis, sharing common goals or threats so necessary to reinforce group norms and keep behaviours and shared values current.

The large numbers of workers in the dockyards or collieries to provide the mystique, muscle and impact of solidarity are no longer there. The number of organisations employing more than 10,000 workers in the south of England can be counted on one hand (Monks, 1996). Furthermore, industrial trade unions are seen as less relevant and not providing the services individuals need in the current work forum. Hence, members have voted with their feet. Since 1979, trade union membership has fallen by 5 million, with the once mighty Transport and General Workers' Union losing over half its membership.

The shift away from collective pay determination to individually based pay determination has been dramatic. Collective bargaining, the mainstay of trade union activity in the past, was not seen by the bulk of employees as so relevant in the late 1990s. In 1975, 90 per cent of public sector workers had their pay determined by collective bargaining with only 10 per cent determined by the employer. In the 1990s only about 35 per cent of public sector workers had their pay determined by collective bargaining, with 60 per cent by their employers. In the private sector there are hardly any national employer agreements, with less than 25 per cent having their pay determined collectively.

Today, employees are looking for more provision of services which meet their needs. While the traditional role is there for some, most no longer require the range of services that unions have provided in the past.

As individuals have been forced to change their work style and focus, so their needs have shifted. Support based on the best interests of the collective is no longer what the bulk of employees are looking for whereas tailor-made support for individual needs is. Yet this is what the trade unions have found difficult to provide – but they are wrestling with it. It requires a culture change on their part with a significant shift in values to provide services that are seen as relevant and valued by individual members. Part of the difficulty in managing such a change lies with the problem of letting go of those traditional values and beliefs that have underpinned the trade union movement since the Industrial Revolution.

Professional services are needed, such as education, training and career development to make members more employable, contract terms and employment rights, legal support, health and welfare provision, insurance, pensions advice, and health and safety. The new individualism in employment will see employees requiring employment services from trade unions over their working life to help them remain employable and increase their employability.

Chapter summary

Using values as our lens, we have sought to plot the changing nature of employee relations through and beyond the unionised workplace. We have explored the dramatic and dynamic changes in the context within which employee relations are acted out. The impact of the 'radical' political will and ideology of Conservative governments, with resultant legislation (not repealed by Labour), has done much to reduce trade union power to the point where unions are forced to reassess their relevance, function and role. The 1990s saw a shift in power away from the unions, deregulation of the labour market and the promotion of the influence of managerialism with its emphasis on direct (and directing?) negotiations with employees rather than through third-party collective bargaining.

Labour seems in no hurry to return to pre-Conservative policies towards the trade unions. However, Labour's espoused values do show differences from those of its Conservative predecessors. Its rhetoric does emphasise some commitment to restoring some of the rights which workers have lost. By 2002, Labour had committed itself to the European Social Chapter, supported the introduction of a minimum wage agreement, the Working Time Directive, and delivered the Employment Relations Act 1999. This Act gives a union rights of recognition in the workplace if the majority of employees support its introduction and gives individuals the right to union support in cases of grievance or discipline. Yet some argue that Labour's employment proposals are 'minimalist' (Tailby, 1997). There does seem to be some desire to keep unions at a distance and certainly not involve a Labour government in industrial disputes, as evidenced by the National Union of Rail, Maritime and Transport Workers' (RMT) 2002 strike action over train driver and other rail staff pay equivalence. The retention of a flexible labour market approach, not dissimilar from its predecessors', is likely to continue. Where it does seem to differ is in terms of its commitment to employee involvement, consultation in major organisation decisions and the creation of a partnership approach to relations at work. Its policies on unemployment through Welfare to Work are intended to ease the plight of the young and the long-term unemployed, while its emphasis on education and training is intended to help equip individuals with relevant knowledge and skills to make them employable and competitive in a global economy.

Organisations themselves are in transition. Fierce global competition has forced them to develop different forms of flexible work practices, variations in organisational structure, and the increasing use of information technology. It has also forced organisations to reconsider the human factor, with an emerging attitude shift away from seeing employees as a cost to one of valuing individuals for their potential and actual knowledge. Through the strategic use of HRM some organisations recognise that competitive advantage can come from empowering employees rather than controlling them. As Wooldridge (1996) says, managers are building relationships with employees on an adult-to-adult basis rather than the more traditional form of parent to child.

Whereas economic, political and technological factors have had profound impacts on the nature of employee relations, it is in the area of social change and individual expectations that future significance lies. The changing values of young people towards work – values which emphasise individualism, personal control and choice, a demand for interest and variation, self-development and learning, and balanced lifestyle – are likely to influence substantially how employee relations are enacted. If these emergent values inform and shape future organisational attitudes, behaviours and forms of relationships, are we likely to see an even more significant individualising and humanising of the employment relationship in the twenty-first century?

This chapter has sought to explore some of the significant factors that have infuenced the changes in employee relations using changes in work values as our lens to plot the shifts in thought, motives and behaviours of the parties involved in the employment relationship. As the values have changed from the Protestant work ethic of the 1950s and 1960s to the technology sophisticated, globally orientated Millennials now joining the workforce, so has the relationship between organisations and their employees shifted along the collective bargaining to individual contracting continuum.

To values we have set the interaction of the main stakeholders in their historical context to chart the major influences that have contributed to the changing employment relationship. For organisations the impact of technology, globalisation and the knowledge economy have contributed to the recognition of the need to change their relationship with their employees, seeing them as individuals, especially their 'knowledge workers'. For trade unions, the move to individualism together with falling membership and the 1980s employment legislation in the UK, has meant a struggle for a role that might be perceived as more relevant. Through recent research we can see for individuals that understanding their 'psychological contract' provides insights into the increasing significance of the role of the manager and its complexity, as differing values and expectations of work influence the employment relationship.

As organisations have had to evolve so individuals have been forced to change their work style and focus, leaving trade unions at the beginning of a new century facing an uncertain future.

Questions

1 What are the economic, socio-demographic and technological forces that will impact on the differing value sets in organisations?

2 Assume you are a consultant engaged by an organisation of your choice. Advise on the possible consequences on employee relations of a shift in values catalysed by (a) Generation X and (b) Generation Y employees.

3 Does collectivism have a future? What are the factors that determine its relevance?

4 What are the consequences of the shift from 'job for life' to 'get a life' for emergent employee relations practice in organisations?

5 What core values would you predict future trade unions would need to manifest in order to effectively serve members in the twenty-first century?

Activities

1 Using the 'values list' below as a guide, think about which aspects of work are most important to you. What do you value?

Achievement	Advancement	Authority
Challenge	Change	Creativity
Competence	Competition	Cooperation
Developing others	Developing self	Detail
Effectiveness	Ethical practice	Excellence
Excitement	Expertise	Family time
Friendship	Growth	Helping others
High earnings	Honesty	Independence

Influencing others	Intellectual work	Involvement
Job tranquility	Knowledge	Leading
Learning	Location	Loyalty
Making decisions	Managing	Meaningful work
Merit	Money	Openness
Order	Peaceful environment	Power
Precision work	Promotion	Quality of what you do
Reputation	Responsibility	Recognition
Security	Self-respect	Stability
Status	Teamwork	Time freedom
Time at home	Time to do a good job	Travel
Variety	Working alone	Working on leading edge
Working with others	Working under pressure	

Use the space below to write down your top ten values and then spend some time thinking about their relative importance. If you had to give up one, which would it be? What if you had to give up another?

Value	Ranking	Value	Ranking
_____	____	_____	____
_____	____	_____	____
_____	____	_____	____
_____	____	_____	____
_____	____	_____	____

Which value stands out as being the most important to you?

Using whatever approach you like, rank your chosen values from 1 to 10, with 1 being what you value most about work.

2 The following questions relate to the Release '92 case study presented in Exhibit 2.1.

(a) What were the factors that drove Release '92?
(b) What factors might influence people in opting into the scheme?
(c) Why should BT invest so heavily in options such as outplacement and training?
(d) Why do you think there was no industrial action?
(e) What are the implications for later schemes if there are no volunteers left, given the values?
(f) What are the wider implications for the relationship between individuals and their employing organisations?

3 Refer back to the case studies about Jay and Olivia on page 58.

(a) How would you describe Jay's and Olivia's work values?
(b) What might be the implications of such values for (a) their career choices and opportunities, (b) their employers?
(c) To what extent would you see this as the pattern and trend for the future?

Useful websites

www.bitc.org.uk **Business in the Community** A movement of companies across the UK committed to improving their positive impact on society.

www.cipd.co.uk **Chartered Institute of Personnel and Development** Human resource management and human resource development professional association.

www.employment-studies.co.uk **Institute for Employment Studies** The Institute for Employment Studies is an independent, apolitical, international centre of research and consultancy in human resource issues.

www.eoc.org.uk **Equal Opportunities Commission** The EOC is the leading agency working to eliminate sex discrimination in Britain. Apart from news, press releases, etc. there is extensive coverage of policy developments and campaigns, research and statistics, and aspects of the law.

www.gftu.org.uk **General Federation of Trade Unions** A range of services including information, research and education.

www.ilo.org **International Labour Organization (ILO)** Database on international work standards and national laws on labour, social security and human rights.

www.leeds.ac.uk/esrcfutureofwork/output/papers.html **The Future of Work** Series of working papers that touch on the different projected scenarios of the impact of the Internet on working conditions and patterns.

www.nbs.ntu.ac.uk/depts/hrm/hrm_link.htm **General HR links** Useful links to various HR websites from Nottingham Business School.

www.tuc.org.uk **Trades Union Congress** Press releases, publications, organisation details, online journals and industrial relations.

References

Allport, G.W., Vernon, P.E. and Lindzey, G. (1951) *Study of Values*. Boston, MA: Houghton Mifflin.

Argyris, C. (1960) *Understanding Organizational Behaviour*. London: Tavistock.

Barter (1998) *An Examination into the Impact of Teleworking within BGI Transco*, MBA dissertation, University of the West of England.

Beer, M., Spector, B., Lawrence, P.R., Quinn Mills, D. and Walton, R.E. (1984) *Managing Human Assets*. New York: Free Press.

Blunkett, D. (1996) *Analysis*, BBC Radio 4, 15 December.

Blyton, P. and Turnbull, P. (1998) *The Dynamics of Employee Relations*, 2nd edn. Basingstoke: Macmillan.

Brockner, J., Tyler, T. and Cooper-Schneider, R. (1992) 'The influence of prior commitment to an institution on reactions to perceived unfairness: the higher they are, the harder they fall', *Administrative Science Quarterly*, 37: 241–61.

Burrell, G. and Morgan, G. (1979) *Sociological Paradigms and Organisational Analysis*. London: Heinemann.

Campbell, A., Devine, M. and Young, D. (1990) *A Sense of Mission*. London: Economist Books.

Cannon, D. (1996) 'Generation X and the new work ethic', *Proceedings of Future Work Forum*, Henley Management College, June.

Collin, A. (1995) ' "New" individuals for the "New Deal" ', *The New Deal in Employment Conference*, City University Business School, London.

Cox, P.S. (1986) 'Occupational survival', PhD thesis, University of Bath.

Deal, T.E. and Kennedy, A.A. (1982) *Corporate Cultures: The Rites and Rituals of Corporate Life*. Wokingham: Addison-Wesley.

Donaghy, R. (2001) *The Future of Employment Relations.* ESRC Future of Work Seminar Series. Publication 1.

Etzioni, A. (ed.) (1995) *New Communitarian Thinking.* Charlottesville: University Press of Virginia.

Field, F. (1996) *Analysis*, BBC Radio 4, 15 December.

Guest, D.E. and Conway, N. (1997) *Employee Motivation and the Psychological Contract: The Third Annual IPD Survey of the State of the Employment Relationship*, Issues in People Management No. 21. London: Institute of Personnel and Development.

Guest, D.E., Conway, N., Briner, R. and Dickman, M. (1996) *The State of Psychological Contract in Employment.* London: Institute of Personnel and Development.

Guzzo, R.A. and Noonan, K.A. (1994) 'Human resources practices as communications and the psychological contract', *Human Resource Management*, Fall: 447–62.

Handy, C. (1996) *The Empty Raincoat.* London: Arrow.

Handy, C. (2001) *The Elephant and the Flea.* London: Hutchinson.

Hecht, F. (1997) 'A job with life . . . not a job for life', *The Director*, June.

Herriot, P. (1995) 'New dealing', *The New Deal in Employment Conference*, City University Business School, London.

Herriot, P. and Pemberton, C. (1995) 'A new deal for middlemanagers', *People Management*, 15 June.

Howe, N. and Strauss, W. (2000) *Millennials Rising: The Next Generation.* London: Vintage.

Hutton, W. (1996) *Analysis*, BBC Radio 4, 15 December.

Industrial Society (2001) 'Work can only get better', presentation by John Knell to the Future Work Forum, Henley Management College, 21 February.

Knell, J. (2000) 'Most wanted: the quiet birth of the free worker', *Futures Reports*, July.

Legge, K. (1995) *Human Resource Management, Rhetoric and Realities.* Basingstoke: Macmillan.

Legge, K. (1996) 'Morality bound', *People Management*, 19 December.

Lydka, H. (1992) 'Organisational commitment: a longitudinal study of UK graduates', PhD thesis, Henley Management College.

Mangham, I. and Pye, A. (1991) *The Doing of Managing.* Oxford: Basil Blackwell.

Meyer, J. and Allen, N.J. (1997) *Commitment in the Workplace: Theory, Research and Application.* London: Sage.

Mintzberg, H. (1984) 'Power and organization life cycles', *Academy of Management Review*, 9(2): 207–24.

Monks, J. (1996) *Analysis*, BBC Radio 4, 15 December.

Morgan, G. (1986) *Images of Organization.* London: Sage.

Morgan, G. (1997) *Images of Organization*, 2nd edn. London: Sage.

Morrison, D.E. (1994) 'Psychological contracts and change', *Human Resource Management*, Fall: 353–72.

Ouchi, W.G. (1981) *Theory Z: How American Business Can Meet the Japanese Challenge.* Reading, MA: Addison-Wesley.

Parkinson, A. (1998) 'The changing nature of the employment relationship: mapping the subjective terrain of the psychological contract', PhD thesis, Henley Management College.

Parkinson, A. (1999) 'Sustaining constructive relationships across cultural boundaries' in Joynt, P. and Morton, R. (eds) *The Global HR Manager.* London: Institute of Personnel and Development.

Parks, J.M. and Kidder, D.L. (1994) ' "Till death us do part . . .": changing work relationships in the 1990s', *Trends in Organizational Behaviour*, 1: 111–36.

Pascale, R. and Athos, A. (1981) *The Art of Japanese Management.* New York: Simon and Schuster.

Pearson, R. (1996) 'The changing labour market and new patterns of work', *Proceedings of Future Work Forum*, Henley Management College, April.

Pfeffer, J. (1998) *The Human Equation: Building Profits by Putting People First.* Cambridge, MA: Harvard Business School Press.

Peters, T.J. and Waterman, R.H. (1982) *In Search of Excellence: Lessons from America's Best-Run Companies*. New York: Harper & Row.

Porter, L.W., Steers, R.M., Mowday, R.T. and Boulian, P.V. (1974) 'Organizational commitment, job satisfaction and turnover among psychiatric technicians', *Journal of Applied Psychology*, 59: 603–9.

Purcell, K. and Purcell, J. (1999) 'Insourcing, outsourcing and the growth of contingent labour as evidence of flexible employment strategies', in Blanpain, R. (ed.), *Non-standard Work and Industrial Relations*, London: Kluwer Law International.

Quinn, J.B., Mintzberg, H. and James, R.M. (1988) *The Strategy Process: Concepts, Contexts, and Cases*. Englewood Cliffs, NJ: Prentice Hall.

Robbins, S.P. (1998) *Organizational Behavior: Concepts, Controversies and Applications*. Englewood Cliffs, NJ: Prentice Hall.

Robinson, S.L. and Rousseau, D.M. (1994) 'Violating the psychological contract: not the exception but the norm', *Journal of Organizational Behavior*, 15: 245–59.

Rousseau, D.M. (1995) *Psychological Contracts in Organizations: Understanding Written and Unwritten Agreement*. New York: Sage.

Schein, E.H. (1978) *Career Dynamics: Matching Individual and Organizational Needs*. Reading, MA: Addison-Wesley.

Schein, E.H. (1985) *Organizational Culture and Leadership: A Dynamic View*. San Francisco: Jossey-Bass.

Schein, E.H. (1996) 'Culture: the missing concept in organization studies', *Administrative Science Quarterly*, 41: 229–40.

Shaw, M. (1997) 'The Role of Women Methodist Ministers', PhD thesis, University of the West of England.

Soule, E., (1998) 'Trust and managerial responsibility', *Business Ethics Quarterly*, 8(2).

Tailby, S. (1997) 'New Labour, new IR', *Work and Employment*, No. 5, Bristol Business School.

Walton, R.E. (1985) 'From control to commitment in the workplace', *Harvard Business Review*, March/April: 77–84.

Warren, R.C. (2000) 'Putting the person back into human resource management', *Towards a Human Centred Organisation: Third Conference on Ethics and Contemporary Human Resource Management*, Imperial College, January.

Wooldridge, E. (1996) 'The new psychological contract', *Proceedings of Future Work Forum*, Henley Management College, June.

Further reading

Guest, D. (1994) 'Important players in a different game', *People Management*, 26(13), December.

Handy, C. (1997) *The Hungry Spirit*. London: Hutchinson.

Journal of Business Ethics.

Legge, K. (1996) 'Morality bound', *People Management*, 19 December.

Morgan, G. (1997) *Images of Organization*, 2nd edn. London: Sage.

Walton, R.E. (1985) 'From control to commitment in the workplace', *Harvard Business Review*, March/April: 77–84.

Winstanley, D., Woodall, J. and Heery, E. (eds) (1996) 'Business ethics and human resource management', *Personnel Review*, 25(6).

Part Two

The parties in employment

Chapter 3

Management

Graham Hollinshead

Learning objectives

By the end of this chapter, readers should be able to:

- appreciate the contextual influences impinging upon the nature of British management and how management structures in the UK vary from those in some other countries;

- gain insights into the role of management and the calibre and status of British management, as well as current tensions in the managerial role;

- gain an overview of the structure of British industry and commerce, and key developments in organisational form;

- understand, by using selected models and concepts, the influence of market forces on approaches to management;

- discern major styles of employee relations management, identifying and explaining moves towards, and away from, the recognition of trade unions;

- be aware of how the emergence of HRM and recent ideas of partnership between management and trade unions are impacting upon the employment relationship.

Introduction

The changing world of management

The term 'global village' may be overused, yet it is undeniable that global forces now affect virtually every aspect of human activity, including management. This state of affairs is well captured in the following quotation.

Whether you walk the streets of New York or Nairobi, Beijing or Buenos Aires, globalisation has introduced a level of commercial culture which is eerily homogenous. The glittering, air conditioned shopping malls are inter-changeable, the fast food restaurants sell the same high carbohydrate foods with minor concessions to local tastes. Young people drink the same soft drinks, smoke the same cigarettes, wear identical branded clothing and shoes, play the same computer games, watch the same Hollywood films and listen to the same Western pop music. (Ellwood, 2001: 53)

The ubiquity of commercial culture has particular significance in the field of employee relations for a variety of reasons. Firstly, as the notion of tenured employment becomes consigned to the past, the existence and form of work increasingly depends, in a direct sense, on its legitimisation by a body of 'consumers' – consumers including shoppers, clients, citizens, patients, students, passengers as well as, sometimes, fellow employees. Examples of the pervasive nature of 'the market' are manifest. In Britain, the programme of privatisation in the public sector has shifted control of many of the nation's natural assets, including coal, water and electricity, into the hands of shareholders seeking to maximise financial return on personal investment. Similarly, a 'business model' drives organisation and performance in education, health and local government. Meanwhile, in the private sector, adaptation to market contingencies has also been the key to survival. Merely one decade ago the opening of retail outlets on Sundays was regarded by many as an unnecessary incursion into the leisure time of shoppers and assistants alike, but now a trip to the local mall has *become* the Sunday leisure activity for many. And the application of a 'business model' is not confined to domestic examples. The collapse of the Berlin Wall in 1989 signified the demise of communist structures in central and eastern Europe and heralded the achievement of political freedom for citizens of the Soviet bloc. In the sphere of business, this seismic political event represented the prelude for the closure of monolithic and monopolistic conglomerates that had formed the backbone of planned economic management, and their replacement with (frequently western-owned) private enterprises.

Secondly, as multinational corporations straddle national boundaries in order to gain synergies in productive capacity and to maximise international market responsiveness (see Chapter 7), business organisation has become something of melting pot in fusing managerial concepts and techniques from a variety of cultures. Rapid development of information technology has permitted the sub-editing of New York newspapers in Scottish islands, while rival motor manufacturers may assemble common components along a global production line. The following example was used to illustrate a recent television programme on globalisation (Carlton Television, 2001). When a typical US car was investigated to discover whether it had been 'made in America', it was found that nine countries were involved in some aspect of its production or sale. Roughly 30 per cent of the car's value went to South Korea for assembly, 17.5 per cent to Japan for components and advanced technology, 7.5 per cent to Germany for design, 4 per cent to Taiwan and Singapore for minor parts, 2.5 per cent to the UK for marketing and advertising services, and 1.5 per cent to Ireland and Barbados for data processing. Only 37 per cent of the car's marketing value was generated in the US. A consequence of such internationalisation of production has been the global diffusion of ideas of 'best management practice', for example 'lean production', 'total quality management' and 'business process re-engineering'.

Thirdly, the growth of the global economy is associated with a widening gulf between affluence and poverty on an international and domestic basis. Brief statistical examples help to illustrate this point. *Business Week* (2000) magazine reports that, in the US, chief executive officer (CEO) compensation in the 1990s went from 85 times more than what the average blue-collar worker received in 1990 to 470 times that level in 1999. Thomas Frank (2001: 7), drawing on a GE shareholder resolution (1998: 21) found that, in 1997, the former CEO of General Electric was paid some 1,400 times the average wage earned by his blue-collar workers in the US. Moreover, his earnings were 9,571 times the average wage of Mexican industrial workers, who made up an increasing percentage of the GE workforce as production moved over the border. As the *Financial Times* articles in Exhibits 3.1 and 3.2 reveal, the liberalisation of trade is also associated with a dichotomy of terms and conditions *within* national employment systems. It is reported that British chief executives are among the highest paid in the world, while British workers rank among the lowest. Clearly, then, there are few direct links between measures of corporate or national economic performance and overall levels of staff remuneration. Below we investigate major distinguishing features of the deregulated context for business in the UK and attend to the role and position of management.

Exhibit 3.1

Industry chiefs join ranks of very high earners

Chief executives of British manufacturing companies are better rewarded than anywhere except the US, but their workers are the worst-paid in the industrialised world, according to a review of global remuneration published today.

The survey, carried out by the magazine *Management Today*, says chief executives of UK manufacturing companies with sales of more than $500m a year have average remuneration packages worth £509,019, compared with £992,974 in the US.

Their earnings are a third higher than those of counterparts in France, who receive an average of £382,128, and well ahead of Australia (£457,139), Japan (£385,645), Sweden (£311,400) and Germany (£298,223).

By contrast, British manufacturing workers' earnings are put at £20,475, behind all the industrialised countries in the survey. Earnings were 20 per cent higher in France, and more than 50 per cent higher in the US. The findings will increase pressure on ministers to find a way of limiting increases in executive remuneration, which has re-emerged as a political issue following the award of 8m share options to Sir Christopher Gent, chairman of Vodafone.

However, the survey suggests the rate of increase of British chief executives' remuneration packages may have slowed. Earnings are up by 29 per cent since the last survey in 1999, compared with 51 per cent in the US, 73 per cent in Australia, 50 per cent in Japan and 43 per cent in Sweden.

UK earnings appear to be growing faster than in France (20 per cent) and Germany (22 per cent), but this may be a reflection of the weakness of the European single currency against the pound.

In a separate review of directors' remuneration, the survey finds substantial regional differences in the UK. Directors in the south-east are the best paid, with average earnings of £66,900, followed by London (£61,410).

Directors in the north of England earn an average of £61,410, followed by counterparts in Scotland on £61,080, the West Midlands (£60,000), the south-west (£58,920), the eastern counties (£57,840, and Northern Ireland (£55,140). The survey also reports that British accountants are the world's highest earners, with average remuneration of £76,288.

Source: Kevin Brown, *Financial Times*, 26 July 2001. © 2001 The Financial Times Limited

Exhibit 3.2

Workplace deaths show increase of 34%

The number of deaths in workplaces rose by 34 per cent in the past year, the worst figure for industrial accidents for a decade, according to provisional statistics published yesterday by the Health and Safety Commission.

There were 295 fatalities compared with 220 in the previous year, an increase in the rate from 0.8 to 1.1 per 100,000 employees.

Bill Callaghan, HSE chairman, was 'greatly concerned' at the rise in workplace-related deaths due to accidents. 'It goes against the downward trend of recent years.'

The HSE also revealed that as many as 56 per cent of all non-fatal injuries to employees were not reported by employers despite a legal requirement to do so. Only 4 per cent of the self-employed who suffered injuries reported them.

In construction, the fatal injury rate for workers is the highest for 10 years. Death rates are also up in agriculture, the extraction and the utility industries. There has also been a marked rise in fatalities in the services sector and manufacturing.

The statistics came in for scathing criticism from John Monks, Trades Union Congress general secretary. 'These numbers should wipe away any trace of complacency in Britain's boardrooms. Last week we heard about British bosses paying themselves huge bonuses, this week we hear about the price that workers pay in injuries, illness and ultimately death.'

He added that the need for a new Health and Safety Act ot revitalise health and safety, with the recruitment of more inspectors and a new law against corporate killing, could not be starker.

The HSE was at a loss to explain the sudden increase in workplace deaths.

Source: Robert Taylor, *Financial Times*, 31 July 2001. © 2001 The Financial Times Limited

Management in the UK

The interplay of factors outside enterprises at both national and international level over recent decades has served to set management 'free to manage'. The era of Thatcherism commencing in the late 1970s prompted a move away from familiar tripartite forms of decision-making in the sphere of employment and in the broader economic domain, which had involved a process of negotiation and compromise between representatives of organised labour, employers and statutory agencies. Instead, a driving force underlying political and economic transformation since the 1980s has been the conviction that a spirit of entrepreneurialism should be injected into both the private and public sectors of industry in order to promote greater market responsiveness and competitiveness. This shift has been aided and abetted by a set of either deliberately orchestrated or more coincidental developments in the wider society that have served to bolster the position of management. These include:

- changes in the composition of industry, with diminution of the heavier manufacturing sectors in which unions have had their strongholds and growth of the less unionised and less adversarial white-collar sector;
- restrictive legislation in the 1980s and 1990s which made it more difficult for unions and their members to establish autonomous organisation and to take industrial action;

- privatisation of publicly owned utilities, which has involved the replacement of committee structures with business models of management;
- pervasive effects of the agenda of economic deregulation and the prominence of a 'free market' ideology, which implies non-interference from government, or indeed any other external agency, into corporate affairs.

It has been within the climate of economic deregulation that many new ideas surrounding management have proliferated. Notions of human resource management emerged with considerable gusto first in the US, and subsequently in the UK in the early 1980s. These are based on the premise that adept manipulation of personnel policy 'levers' by management, to include the implementation of appropriate measures on employee consultation, job design and staff procurement, development and reward, would be directly linked to competitive advantage. Organisations aspiring towards HRM would frequently aim to gain a full commitment of individuals or teams of employees to the achievement of organisational goals. The approach emphasises the importance of interconnecting the policy aims of personnel management within a guiding strategic framework. More idealistic conceptions of HRM equate high quality employees with high quality products or services, and aim to promote flexibly deployed employees within fluid and adaptable organisational structures.

Desirable though the ideal picture of the employment relationship viewed through the lens of HRM may be, it would hardly be supported by survey evidence examining the climate of employment relations on the shop floor. Cully *et al.* (1999: 275), presenting the results of the most recent Workplace Employee Relations Survey, revealed the following features of working life towards the end of the 1990s: high rates of labour turnover in many workplaces, high rates of disciplinary action taken against employees, and many workplaces where serious injuries or work-related illness had occurred. Although it was found that more employees were satisfied with their jobs than dissatisfied, a high proportion thought management had been poor at involving employees in decisions affecting their working lives. Why, then, do these negative aspects of employment persist in the UK at the beginning of the twenty-first century despite experimentation with modern techniques for the management of people? International comparisons can provide insights into this question.

The international context for British management

Management does not operate in a vacuum. The social, economic and political context for managerial decision-making can determine whether there is a predisposition towards investing in staff, and working with them, or whether there may be an overriding emphasis on cost minimisation, creating the likelihood of adversarial or negative relations. For the purpose of gaining a broader perspective on British management, it is instructive to engage briefly in international comparisons. Taking a broader view reveals that management can assume varied shapes and forms according to the structural facets of the national system in which it exists.

In a comparative, international study of the UK, Germany and France, Christel Lane (1994) uses the notion of industrial order to demonstrate the interdependence of the structure and behaviour in firms on the one hand, and broader social and institutional

Exhibit 3.3

Unions and employers in Germany call for job reform

Germany's employers and trade unions set aside growing differences and called for swifter and more effective steps to create jobs and improve labour market conditions in an unexpected joint statement yesterday. The statement, from the federal employers' association (BDA) and the national trade union confederation (DGB), said agreements since 1999 under the government's Alliance for Jobs programme should be fully implemented. The tripartite, voluntary alliance, created by Chancellor Gerhard Schroder after his election victory in 1998, has been central to government efforts to encourage unions and employers to cooperate on creating jobs and improving labour market flexibility.

There has been concern in recent weeks, however, that worsening economic conditions and growing policy tensions between the three parties may lead to the collapse of the alliance.

Mr Schroder's interest also appears to have waned, especially as his target of cutting unemployment to 3.5m by autumn 2002 has become less realistic. The jobless total rose to 3.85m in June.

Both the BDA and DGB said yesterday's statement, which arose from top-level talks between the heads of the two organisations, was aimed at reviving the alliance and restoring Germany's social partnership tradition.

The communiqué urges member companies and industry-based trade unions to implement fully the alliance agreements on employee rights to improved training and qualifications; on increasing working time flexibility to reduce overtime; and on introducing workplace pension schemes.

The statement also urges the government to introduce measures to prevent the undercutting of wages and social conditions in Germany after the European Union's eastward expansion.

Mr Schroder welcomed the statement, saying it represented 'the recognition by the employers and unions of the modernisation-oriented policies of the Alliance for Jobs'.

In recent weeks, resistance from Mr Schroder to employer proposals to cut unemployment by increasing labour market flexibility and his support for new, union-oriented rules on employee works councils have alienated the BDA. In addition, evidence of slowing economic growth and rising inflation have led to sharp public divisions between unions and employers on expectations for important wage negotiations next spring.

In fact, papering over these divisions appears to have been the unwritten agenda behind yesterday's statement.

The statement does not refer to the negotiations, but it stresses the importance of 'agreements reached' in previous alliance talks. These included commitments to moderate wage settlements to boost employment. Last week Mr Schroder, who fears the effect of high wage increases, publicly reminded trade union leaders that this commitment was still in effect. Peter Klotzke, BDA deputy spokesman said: 'This point [on moderate wage increases] is really what's behind the statement.' For more reports see www.ft.com/europe

Source: Hugh Williamson, Financial Times, 21 July 2001. © 2001 The Financial Times Limited

patterns on the other. Lane argues that the major constituent elements of industrial order are present in all advanced capitalist countries, and include the following institutional complexes:

- *The state* – both as a direct economic rule-maker and as an institution that prominently shapes the rules of other important institutions.
- *The financial system* – linked with the system of education and training, particularly the training of industrial managers and employees.
- *The system of industrial relations* – various intermediate associations, such as trade associations, chambers, etc. which influence the ways in which firms acquire, maintain and coordinate resources.

Specific organisational forms, and the significance attached to each component, will vary from country to country, and yet the effect of the institutional complexes defined is to shape the actors' capacity for action. Lane asserts that, in the UK, a prominent feature is the 'arms' length' distance kept by both the state and the financial system from industry. Harking back to the nation's imperial past, it is argued that the organisation of the City of London and other important financial institutions places demands on management for high, short-term returns on capital. Exacerbated by fear of takeover, this perpetuates a prevalence of financial values at corporate level, and a pre-eminence of accountants in the upper echelons of business. In consequence, underinvestment in capital equipment, particularly technologically advanced products and processes, ensues, as well as neglect of human resources. According to Lane, many training and development decisions have been left to the discretion of managers and needs in this area have frequently been overtaken by pressures to satisfy immediate business objectives. Concern has been expressed about the low level and quality of technical and vocational training in the UK since the 1960s. In contrast, in Germany for example, closer ties have historically existed between the larger financial institutions and firms, with training and other business decisions being given a higher priority through the tripartite deliberations of the social partners (i.e. representatives of management, trade unions and state). This, according to Lane, engenders longer-term perspectives, more cooperative attitudes and a desire to compete on grounds of superior quality and service rather than price. She goes on to assert that, in the UK from the late 1970s onwards, successive Conservative governments attempted to reverse lack of national competitiveness through pursuing radical institutional change. This involved curbing the power of unions and restructuring the system of vocational training under the more complete control of management. Far from engendering a modernised and more forward-looking institutional framework, it is argued that that these changes have, counterproductively, served only to accentuate traditional short-term approaches in the UK and to undervalue investment in skills.

The findings of Lane are corroborated by former journalist Will Hutton in his critique of free market economics in Britain. In his best-selling book *The State We're In* (1996), he argues that British industry is adversely affected by overdemanding targets for profits and time horizons necessary to achieve them. Hutton argues that the British financial system, which is embedded in traditional patterns of political and economic control, serves to perpetuate chronic underinvestment in human and technological capital. He goes on to relate the negative experience of work for many to wider social problems such as quality of child care and urban dereliction. He states:

> Ungoverned British capitalism's lethal demand for some of the highest financial returns in the world has encouraged firms relentlessly to exploit their new freedom to hire and fire. As a result there is a mounting and quite proper sense of crisis spreading across all classes. (Hutton, 1996: xxvii)

Such critiques of the industrial order in the UK would imply that management finds itself preoccupied with coping with immediate financial pressures. In consequence, survival strategies prevail over the establishment of foundations of technological or human proficiency into the longer term. In these circumstances, management itself remains distracted from nurturing professional competence within its own ranks or seriously attending to problems of enhancing real innovative capacity. In the next section we consider the inner workings of British management.

The status and calibre of British management

■ The managerial legacy

Within the domain of British management, those charting the history of its development have commented upon the rudimentary nature of management structures, and, at least until recently, upon low levels of technical and specialist expertise. Some have attributed this to underlying cultural aversions to managerial values. Eric Hobsbawm (1968: 154), a prominent historian, states (and note the masculine terminology which epitomises this male stronghold):

> The aristocratic scale of values, which included amateur status and not apparently trying too hard among the criteria of the 'gentlemen', and inculcated them in the 'public schools' which indoctrinated the sons of the risen middle class, was indeed dominant. Being 'in trade' was indeed an awful social stigma; although 'trade' in this sense meant small-scale shop-keeping much more than any activity in which any really big money, and therefore social acceptance could be gained.

Howard Gospel (1992) finds that in the first half of the twentieth century, at a time when a growing proportion of American, German and Japanese managers were receiving training in applied technical and business subjects, only a small minority of British managers were similarly qualified. 'At the higher reaches of management in large firms the "gentleman amateur" was a common type, while at middle and lower levels the "practical man" who possessed little in the way of formal qualifications remained dominant' (Gospel, 1992: 48). Gospel suggests that management ineptitude at this early, but formative, stage of development served to entrench a pattern whereby management would react opportunistically to market forces, as opposed to formulating internal corporate strategies for the management of labour. He states: 'Thus, in Britain, the invisible hand of the market dominated labour management, and the visible handshake of closer and more lasting relations between employers and employees made only slow progress' (Gospel, 1992: 48).

There is evidence that professionalisation has occurred in recent years, although the legacy of late development is still that underqualified generalists predominate, and those with technical and product quality skills are poorly represented. According to Lane (1989: 95), British managers appeared to be undereducated compared with their continental competitors. Drawing upon a report by the National Economic Development Office (NEDO, 1987: 10), she asserted that British companies have tended to place a greater emphasis on 'pragmatism rather than professionalism' and that personal qualities and background are falsely elevated. Others have argued that the British class structure continued to exert an influence on managerial hierarchies, 'pecking orders' being established through social standing rather than by principles of merit. Martin Joseph (1989: 42), in examining the social background of senior British managers, finds that they are drawn from a narrow class base. He finds, for example, that all of the eighteen governors of the Bank of England in 1982 went either to a public school or to Oxford or Cambridge, or both, and that directors of banks, insurance companies and other financial institutions also come in high proportions from elite educational backgrounds. The implication here is that a self-perpetuating system of elitism exists, in which highly paid, high-status individuals can afford to direct their descendants or relatives into similar occupations. This does not necessarily guarantee that the most able or appropriate people will rise to the top levels of industry and commerce, or that the possession of vital technical, as opposed to social, skills will be fully rewarded. Indeed, Dore (1973: 251) argues that subordinates may resent management on the grounds that authority systems rest upon privilege and 'aristocratic style', this being at the expense of professionalism and efficiency.

Challenges facing management: survival of the fittest?

The picture of British management that is emerging is a lack of sophistication compared with international counterparts. A major feature of the fault-line has been the apparent predisposition towards reliance on external institutions for regulating employment matters, and allowing the exigencies of product and labour markets to prevail over internalised policy formulation. Over the past few decades it has been recognised that global and domestic market pressures are exerting an ever more potent influence not only on managerial activity but also more generally on employment security. This section considers how British managers have fared throughout a time of change and crisis.

Managers and professional workers constitute a significant and growing proportion of the working population, comprising at least one-third of the entire labour market (Wilson, 1993). Yet, as Hendry (1995) points out, managers have been subjected to turbulences caused by severe product market competition and globalisation of production. In the recession of the 1990s, linked with overcapacity in some industrial sectors, it was middle management that bore the brunt of rationalisation and downsizing, with the traditional pyramidal organisational structure becoming bell- or pear-shaped. The problems besetting middle managers have been exacerbated by technological advances that facilitate data capture at lower levels within organisational hierarchies, potentially rendering superfluous the skills and knowledge of managers. This development is well illustrated in the banking and finance sector, where the personal judgement of branch managers on matters such as overdrafts and loans has often given way to spontaneous technological responses to customer enquiries, conveyed to them automatically or by clerical staff.

Privatisation of the former public sector has been particularly extensive in the UK, and it has exposed managers in newly privatised concerns to the pressures of the marketplace and to more rigorous performance criteria. Across both public and private sectors the requirement for customer responsiveness and the assertion of customer rights are stretching conflicting managerial priorities near to breaking point within a cost reduction agenda. A postal survey of around 1,500 managers, across a range of sectors and positions, carried out by Worrall and Cooper (2001) on behalf of the Institute of Management suggests that a range of factors are making the nature of managerial work more complex at the turn of the millennium. These include:

- globalisation;
- a continuing emphasis on controlling costs;
- a rapidly changing technological base;
- legislative change surrounding the workplace;
- growing social pressures in seeking to balance home and work;
- rising demands in the skills needed for effective performance.

Turning to the findings in greater depth, respondents revealed that they had experienced substantial change over the previous year, with redundancies and 'delayering' exercises occurring frequently and considerable attention being given to driving down expenditure. Middle and junior managers commented on changes in their own orientation to work over a three-year period, stating that their sense of loyalty had shifted from their companies to themselves. A number regarded themselves as mercenaries, prepared to shift employment readily if a lucrative offer were forthcoming. A long hours culture was clearly evident, with 91 per cent of respondents working over contract hours and 40 per cent regularly working over 50 hours a week. A culture of 'presenteeism' (social pressure to be seen at work at exceptional times) was firmly established and, somewhat alarmingly, 65 per cent of respondents took the view that overworking was having an adverse effect on their health (14 per cent seriously) while 72 per cent of the sample commented on adverse effects on relationships with partners. Despite the obvious need for skills acquisition in changing circumstances, nearly one-fifth had received no training at all over the previous year. Perhaps the most telling finding was that 56 per cent of junior managers considered their quality of working life had deteriorated over the previous three years, while 45 per cent of chairmen, chief executives and managing directors experienced improvement. Indeed, the report authors state that the hiatus in perceptions at the boardroom door throughout the survey represented a cause for concern. In general, public sector managers displayed a lower level of morale than those in the private sector.

It is clear from the above survey, and other similar investigations (for example, Herriot, 1992) that many of the espoused principles of mutuality between organisational and individual career needs, as encapsulated in the notion of the psychological contract, tend to be illusory. Indeed, the reality of much managerial life would instead seem to be determined by the need for individual survival and material gain in climates of change and uncertainty. Remuneration shows considerable variability according to personal performance criteria for middle and junior ranges, while many directors remained the beneficiaries of ever polarising pay structures as well as comparative job security.

The structuring and restructuring of industry

In this section, a brief, factual overview of the major employment sectors in Britain is presented, in order to detail the organisational contexts in which managers find themselves. Employers in the UK would normally fall into one of three main categories: private businesses, public corporations and public services (Table 3.1). According to the 1998 Workplace Employee Relations Survey (WERS98) (Cully *et al.*, 1999: 19), private businesses account for 72 per cent of all workplaces, and recently there has been a trend towards amalgamation and merger as well as closure. As Bach and Sisson (2000: 23) report, drawing upon WERS98, the UK is now predominantly a service economy, with

Table 3.1 **Types of employer**

Private businesses	Public corporations	Public services	Voluntary bodies
■ Employ over 19 million people	■ Employ around 1 million people	■ Employ around 5 million people	■ Usually small, privately owned organisations providing specialised services to their own members
■ Most common form is registered company (over 1 million)	■ Include nationalised industries and public bodies including the Bank of England, BBC, Royal Mint and UK Atomic Energy Authority	■ Major public services are the NHS (1.2 million employees), education (1.4 million), the civil service (1.1 million), including government agencies, and local authority services (1.5 million), including the police	■ Include professional bodies, trade unions, employers' associations, political pressure groups and worker/producer cooperatives
■ Sector comprises private and public limited companies; this status affects the number of shareholders and whether shares can be issued to the general public	■ Over 30 public corporations were privatised in the 1980s and 1990s		

Source: Farnham and Pimlott (1995: 64)

less than one in five workplaces remaining in the manufacturing sector. This trend has been accompanied by a reduction in average organisational size. By 1998, 16 per cent of workplaces constituted independent private establishments employing fewer than 50 people (Millward *et al.*, 2000: 26). This has caused some consternation among trade unions, traditionally encountering difficulties recruiting members in this sector. A further significant development has been the internationalisation of the UK economy in both private and public sectors. Millward *et al.* (2000: 33), drawing on the WERS series, find the incidence of foreign ownership almost trebled across private sector manufacturing, from 7 per cent of workplaces in 1980, to 19 per cent in 1998. As a further manifestation of the internationalisation of business, a number of large British-owned multinationals, including ICI, GKN, Turner and Newall, Glaxo, BOC, Lonrho, Beecham, and RTZ, now employ more than 50 per cent of their workforce overseas.

It is within this broad picture of organisational evolution, and the apparently ever intensifying need to respond effectively to the pressures of the product market, that the modern M-form or multidivisional company is providing the ideal type for private, and even public, organisations. Purcell and Ahlstrand (1994), on the basis of substantial fieldwork, find that M-form companies dominate the economies on both sides of the Atlantic and that 'at least, for the largest firms, the product division form of organisation is now the dominant form of organisation' (1994: 16). This means that the functional U-form organisation, whose pyramidal hierarchy is the assumed norm for much personnel literature, has been superseded in many respects by this more versatile organisational form (see Table 3.2).

In essence, the M-form set-up has a three-tier structure comprising corporate office, divisions and operating plant. Divisions will normally possess freedom of operation in respect of a particular array of products, and each division will be 'self-contained' with its own executive. The corporate office possesses an extensive set of controls for monitoring and regulating divisional behaviour, and will be responsible for all aspects of business policy and planning, as well as identifying investment priorities. Divisional

Table 3.2 Organisational form and structural typologies

S-form	H-form	U-form	M-form
■ Prevalent in the nineteenth century ■ Small, single plant, single product or product range ■ Owner-controlled, little or no hierarchy ■ Reliance on subcontracting, foreman responsible for labour management control and motivation strategies based on personal, direct and close supervision	■ Often developed through merging of S-forms over time, growing into large multiplant enterprises ■ Holding companies loosely controlled and coordinated constituent plants; small HQ ■ Limited and weak management hierarchies ■ Industrial relations matters determined at plant level, consequently diversity and inconsistency within firms ■ Relied on external support for industrial relations management, from employers' associations ■ Example: British Leyland from the 1950s	■ Growing/merging companies which became unified/centralised ■ Extensive and specialised management hierarchies, duplicated at plant level; larger HQ ■ Formulation of internal, centralised and bureaucratic industrial relations systems and styles, less reliance on employers' associations ■ Examples: (historically) ICI, Ford, Pilkington, the Post Office, British Rail	■ Prevalent in post-Second World War era ■ Multidivisional structures, establishing semi-autonomous divisions usually based on product lines ■ HQ management retains responsibility for strategic decisions and monitoring of lower-level activities, operational decisions left to divisions ■ Deliberately decentralised industrial relations, with various and diverse systems for each division ■ Common in the 1990s; example: Unilever

Source: after Gospel and Palmer (1993: 67–9)

freedom of operation will exist so long as divisions or operating units fulfil corporate needs and expectations.

The strategic advantages of the multidivisional establishment are that product market volatility can be counteracted through switching production from site to site, and that the company itself can gain the upper hand over the marketplace by determining price structures in an oligopolistic or monopolistic manner.

The ability of these organisations to gain market leadership positions also provides them with the resources to take a proactive stance in corporate strategy formulation, and to develop sophisticated human resource policies and practice. The principles of the M-form organisation are applicable to many multinational concerns, as well as to domestic multi-site operations and publicly owned corporations. In keeping with the above, Bach and Sisson (2000: 28) identify three important recent changes in organisational structures, reflecting the revolution in information processing possibilities:

■ A number of major organisations, including ICI and Courtaulds, have redesigned internal organisation into cellular form. Semi-autonomous units are responsible for activities within particular spheres of activity, this associated with the establishment of teamworking.

■ Some budgetary devolution has passed responsibility for managing tasks to the lowest possible unit within the organisation.

■ Internal market principles have been injected into both private and public concerns in order to engender a concept of trade between purchasers and providers within organisational boundaries to encourage accountability, cost effectiveness and to enhance service quality.

Public corporations are managed by government-appointed executives, and include remaining nationalised industries as well as public organisations such as the BBC. The policy of transferring previously nationalised industries into private ownership from the mid-1980s (such as British Telecom, British Airways, British Steel, British Gas and the water supply industry) has meant that erstwhile monopolistic producers are now subject to the rigours of the marketplace, and shareholder interests prevail. Public services employ about 5 million people and include local government, the NHS and the civil service. Funds for these bodies are raised through National Insurance, taxation and local community charges.

The monopolistic position of these organisations, too, has been removed in recent years through the application of internal and external market principles. In a number of instances in the public sector, this has led to forms of organisational restructuring analogous to developments in the private sector. So, for example, an internal market has been created in the NHS through devolving budgets to trusts. Under the provisions of the Local Government Act 1988, certain important local government services, such as refuse collection, street cleaning, school catering, the maintenance of grounds and vehicles, leisure services and sportsfield upkeep, must be put out to tender. In education, local budgeting has been introduced, and institutions are subject to a form of competition for pupils (Hendry, 1995).

The effect of encouraging competition on grounds of cost has been to undermine job security and earnings in the sectors open to subcontracting, as well as contributing to a decline in trade union organisation. Such structural changes have been accompanied by shifts in perceived status, which have tended to be at the expense of professional groups (for example, teachers and doctors). According to Hendry (1995. 45), 'the interests of these professional public employees have been portrayed as being pitched against those of parents, pupils, patients and the public'. Thus a transference of power has occurred from ' "privileged producers" to "sovereign consumers" ' (Keat and Abercrombie 1991: 6). Millward *et al.* (2000: 23) find that, although only a very small number of establishments had moved from public to private ownership between 1990 and 1998, changes of ownership *within* the sector had become common. Around one-fifth of workplaces reported some change of ownership over this period and, of particular note had been the creation of self-managing trusts in the NHS, the reorganisation of local government and the moves to grant-maintained status in higher education.

Approaches to the management of employee relations

■ Introduction: the influence of product markets

The quest for flexible organisational responses to increasingly discriminating and empowered consumers has been pursued with particular gusto in the UK. Here, as we have seen, the protection of statutory regulation of the economy and employment has been progressively removed and large sections of the public sector of industry which previously enjoyed monopoly status are now subject to the rigours of competition from new service providers. Within this climate, some employers have questioned the 'pluralist' articles of faith that have characterised British industrial relations for much of its history. Management may consider that engaging in negotiations and compromises with the representatives of labour will stifle its ability to keep competitors at bay, and a preferred course of action may be to communicate directly with staff. Moreover, the market itself can represent a central catalyst for change in employment practice as standard job definitions, or indeed hours of work, are viewed as being unnecessarily restrictive. Similarly, collectively determined and standardised pay can be questioned in a culture that establishes individual performance as the crucial variable in formulae to determine reward. Although management may have preferred to maintain a degree of detachment from the introduction of potentially unpopular policies, we shall see that, in practice, there are variations in the extent to which corporate management teams possess autonomy in defining the direction of employee relations strategy. As mentioned in earlier sections of this chapter, relatively unsophisticated structures of British management have been associated with a tendency to rely on forces and institutions external to the organisation to determine employment matters. This section examines some notable theoretical contributions towards understanding the links between markets and management strategy in employee relations.

Charting the evolution of British approaches to the management of labour from a historical perspective, Gospel (1992) provides a detailed explanation of the effects of product and labour markets on management systems. It is argued that market transactions are, by their nature, relatively impersonal and short term, but that the insecurities of the marketplace can be superseded by the establishment of firms that comprise longer-term relationships between participants, and which can allocate resources internally in an effective manner. In managing labour, depending on what is economically most advantageous, firms may opt to rely on external regulation of employment matters, they may prefer to internalise responsibility for the management of employment within their own boundaries, or they may decide to combine policies of internalisation and externalisation. The concepts of internalisation and externalisation may be applied to the three broad areas of work organisation, employment relations and management–employee relations (Table 3.3).

As we have seen, a long-standing tradition in the UK has been for employers to rely on external regulation of employment matters. This means that responsibility for many of the operational aspects of employee relations was passed to the external agencies of employers' associations. Such bodies, which frequently acted on behalf of all major employers within industrial sectors, entered into negotiations with industry-level trade union organisations to establish at least minimum terms and conditions across industries. The passing of responsibility for employee relations management to external institutions was accompanied by an acceptance that the short-term inter-actions of both product and labour markets would set the tenor for policy-making in the important areas of recruitment, reward and training. This contrasts with developments in other countries where the focal point for employment strategy formulation has been the level of the corporation. This has accompanied the recognition that

Table 3.3 **Internalisation and externalisation policies applied to three broad areas**

	External strategy	*Internal strategy*
Work organisation (the way work is organised around products and processes)	▪ Reliance on subcontracting	▪ Directly organising own workforce
Employment relations (recruitment arrangements, job tenure and promotion, wage and benefit arrangements)	▪ Poaching or recruiting labour in the market which others have trained ▪ Relying on occupationally oriented apprenticeship arrangements ▪ Making extensive use of state training agencies which train in externally marketable skills ▪ Reliance on external market for labour ▪ Recruiting and laying off as demand changes ▪ Filling higher positions with external as well as internal candidates	▪ Providing own, firm-specific training ▪ More systematically screening and recruiting workers ▪ Aiming to make staff permanent ▪ Developing job ladders and using internal promotion
Management–employee relations (systems of representation, relations with employees and trade unions, and the process of collective bargaining)	▪ Fixing wages according to external market signals ▪ Minimal contracts of employment ▪ Relies on external employers' association to deal with trade unions ▪ Accepts external market criteria for the setting of wages, and the processing of grievances through external procedures	▪ Fixing wages more according to internal administrative procedures than market forces ▪ Developing more extensive fringe benefits, often based on seniority ▪ More elaborate contracts of employment ▪ Aims to promote in-company form of employee representation, e.g. works council or company union ▪ Establishes internal grievance and disputes procedure, even if dealing with 'external' union

Source: after Gospel and Palmer (1993: 55–6)

sustained levels of corporate and national performance could be achieved through investment in, and development of, the skills of internal staff.

In the UK since the mid-1960s, it has been possible to identify moves towards 'internalisation'. The majority of the report of the Donovan Commission (1968) clearly prescribed that company management could assert control over the informality of workplace behaviour through 'grasping the nettle' and initiating more finely tuned and proactive policies and procedures. Such a transition in managerial orientation may, in retrospect, be viewed as an important prelude to the growth of human resource management, which is discussed later. It should be noted, however, that many small concerns still find their survival depends on the interplay of market forces beyond their control, and that broader trends towards subcontracting and part-time working reflect a continuing preference in the UK for the principles of externalisation.

■ Markets and approaches to managing employee relations: investors in people and cost-cutters?

Marchington and Parker (1990), in a study of four unionised multi-plant organisations in the mid-1980s, found that product markets did not exert a homogeneous influence on all organisations. There were differences in the extent to which companies possessed the autonomy and ability to devise employee relations strategies designed to enhance their own competitive advantage. According to these researchers, who themselves warn against overgeneralising from their case results, organisations that possessed monopoly or near-monopoly power and a stable pattern of demand for their products and services tend to enjoy considerable latitude and autonomy in deciding upon employee relations policies. On the other hand, those organisations that are confronted with fierce competition and with a weak market share could well find themselves restricted to cost-minimising strategies in employee relations. If unionism exists in such concerns, it is likely that the tenor of labour relations will be adversarial. Suggesting self-perpetuating virtuous and vicious circles in the linkage between employee relations strategies and product markets, Marchington and Parker argue that the market leaders who opt to *invest* in their human resources are more likely to enjoy a partnership relationship with union(s), if recognised. Closer collaboration between workforce and management is likely to lead to greater reliability of production and quality of output, which will, in turn, bolster the company's market position. In contrast, those concerns that seem destined to engage in cost minimisation, taking a *commodity* view of their workers are more likely to encounter disturbed and poor quality of production, and will inevitably continue to occupy the lower end of the market (see Table 3.4).

Adding a further dimension to the analysis of the influence of the market on the behaviour of employees, it was found that market-based indicators (for example, flow of work) could represent an important piece of ammunition in the armoury of management as it can be used to convey a stark picture of the precariousness of jobs within a highly competitive environment.

Table 3.4 **Types of employment relations policies**

Investment approach	Cost-minimising approach
■ Partnership arrangement with trade union/ employee representatives	■ Adversarial relationship with union(s), non-recognition or derecognition
■ Job security	■ Job insecurity/hiring and firing
■ Longer-term policies	■ Ad hoc/fire-fighting employee relations policies
■ More selectivity in recruitment, higher pay, investment in training	■ Casual approach to recruitment, low pay, little investment in training
■ More sophisticated/two-way communications	■ One-way communication (if any) from management
■ Application of procedures, e.g. discipline	■ Procedures not implemented, 'macho' management

Source: after Marchington and Parker (1990)

In conclusion, these theories suggest that the relationship between markets and management strategy is a complex one. They would imply the possible existence of a 'dual economy', in which market-leading concerns are able to internalise employee relations management processes, embarking on longer-term, investment-oriented approaches, while smaller, more precarious enterprises live with instability and inability to control their own destiny.

Management styles: the dimensions of individualism and collectivism

We can observe contrasting corporate styles towards the management of employment which are conditioned by a plethora of factors such as the market position of the organisation, its size and sector of activity, and the competence of its management. A fundamental question in the field of employee relations is, however, whether the organisation wishes to conduct its affairs by recognising one or more trade unions to represent staff, or whether, for market-based or other more ideological reasons, it wishes to deny the legitimacy of such modes of collective organisation.

In the UK, it appears that orientation towards collectivism has waxed and waned according to macropolitical and economic factors and, notably, the climate set by the government in power. However, at corporate level, what is emerging is that patterns of collectivism and individualism in employment relations comprise a multilayered fabric. Thus, the non-unionised sector comprises not only the notorious Dickensian sweat shops, but also the 'sophisticated' US multinational concern. Even where unions are recognised, the nature and form of recognition can give greater or lesser prominence to union representatives, and there can be large pockets of non-unionism in unionised enterprises, with parallel mechanisms of communication and consultation applied directly to the workplace. In this section an attempt is made to make sense of the range of observable styles of employee relations management by introducing recognised stereotypical classifications, or models.

Drawing upon and elaborating the unitary and pluralistic frames of reference developed by Alan Fox in 1966 (see Chapter 1), Purcell and Sisson (1983) identify five ideal typical styles of managing the employment relationship. Describing style as a guiding set of principles that delineate the boundaries and direction of acceptable management action in dealing with employees which is 'firm specific, ubiquitous and continuous', the following corporate classifications are presented:

- In the *traditional* organisation, labour is viewed as a factor of production, and an authoritarian, often overtly exploitative, attitude is taken towards staff, with employee subordination assumed to be part of the 'natural order' of the employment relationship. Unions are either forcefully opposed or kept at arm's length. Companies associated with this category are likely to be small and owner-managed, or franchised, operating in highly competitive product markets, and placing an emphasis on cost control.
- The *sophisticated human relations* or *paternalistic employer* again is likely to resist unionisation. However, in contrast to the first category, considerable time and expense is invested in engendering high levels of employee commitment to corporate goals and fostering a cooperative and entrepreneurial culture. Recruitment and training policies are finely tuned to ensure the 'right kind' of people are employed, and market rates of pay are exceeded as a disincentive for employees to combine

collectively. Examples of this typology could well be large, single-industry companies (frequently American-owned), with high market share in growth industries. IBM, Hewlett-Packard and Kodak may be fitted into this category.

- The *sophisticated modern (consultative)* operation would accept the union role in specified areas of joint decision-making with the purpose of encouraging employee participation and consent. A 'partnership' is forged between management and unions, and a problem-solving approach characterises interaction between the parties. In common with the second category, a proactive and planned approach is taken to the management of people, with union representatives pivotal in communication processes. Large British- or Japanese-owned single-industry companies, with high market share, operating in process industries could well adopt this style.

- The *sophisticated modern (constitutional)* concern has much in common with the previous category in taking a planned and proactive approach to managing the employment relationship. However, this style places a greater emphasis on the formal regulation and institutionalisation of conflict between the parties, with strong partners negotiating codified agreements at workplace level. This 'legalistic' approach, which clearly delineates areas of managerial prerogative, is quite common in North America, with single industries using mass production, such as Ford, being associated with it. For such companies, product market conditions are likely to be highly competitive and labour costs relatively high.

- The *standard modern (opportunistic)* organisation is in essence pragmatic, with the position of trade unions within the enterprise fluctuating according to their perceived power base. Where labour/product market circumstances, or perhaps employment legislation, bolsters the position of unions, negotiation and consultation are likely to occur. In other circumstances, managerial prerogatives will be reasserted. This approach is typical for conglomerate, multi-product concerns, which allow operating units to react to local circumstances within broad parameters set by senior management. Examples would be heavy manufacturing and engineering companies, such as GKN.

Although ideal types present an oversimplified view of reality, with many organisations in practice possibly straddling a number of these categories, the classifications are useful in helping us to understand why diverse employee relations climates exist in various organisational settings. Clearly, an important explanatory factor in establishing why a particular organisation decides to opt for a sophisticated approach to the management of labour is whether it can afford to invest in its employee relations policies. Thus, the product market position of many small businesses may preclude their paying above-average rates of pay, while this may be an option for larger market leaders. According to Marchington and Wilkinson (1996), organisations selling high-quality products to industrial, as opposed to domestic, consumers in a stable or growing market occupied by a small number of competitors will have greater discretion in establishing an appropriate style than those operating in highly competitive, fashion-oriented and declining markets. However, it is not only product markets that will determine the style of employee relations management that an organisation will adopt. Marchington and Wilkinson (1996) state that there are four further significant sets of factors. First, the *prevalent form of technology* will be significant, with capital-intensive organisations that have phased in new technology, and that have quite technologically independent internal operating units being most able to adopt consultative approaches. Second, the *labour market* will determine factors such as the pool of skills available and traditions of unionisation in the area. Third, *organisational characteristics* relate to the size of the enterprise, its structure in terms particularly of degree of central-isation or decentralisation, and the nature of its ownership. Finally, the *social, legal and political environment*, incorporating factors such as levels of unemployment and employment legislation, will establish the parameters for constraints upon employers and opportunities. It is argued that, together, such factors will serve to influence pre-ferred employee relations styles of management. It is possible, too, that management may find it difficult to harness these various and complex influences, as there are areas of potential irreconcilability within them. An example would be a company that wishes to engage in high quality production but has inadequate supplies of skilled labour available.

Central to Purcell's and Sisson's (1983) distinctions between managerial styles are the dimensions of individualism and collectivism. Individualism concerns 'policies based on the belief in the value of the individual and his or her right to advancement and fulfilment at work', while collectivism is defined as 'a recognition by the management of the collective interests of groups of employees within the decision making process' (Purcell and Gray, 1986: 2). In practice, this is manifested in the existence of structures for collective bargaining or participation, and concerns the degree of legitimacy manage-ment attaches to such structures.

Although constitutionalists, consultors and standard moderns would each mani-fest a form of collectivism, there are clearly differences between them in the degree of legitimacy attached to collective bargaining, and, indeed, the nature of the relationship between management and union representatives. As we have indicated, the consultor emphasises a partnership approach with trade unions, while in other organisations the recognition of trade unions may be grudging, and an adversarial approach evident in negotiations between the parties. Equally, while traditionalists and sophisticated paternalists both resist trade unionism within their enterprises, there would seem to be stark differences in the quality of relationships (at least at a superficial level) between management and employees. Consequently, it would be oversimplistic to argue that collectivism can be directly correlated with more benign 'investment-oriented' man-agements, while individualism is inevitably associated with cost-cutting, authoritarian employers. Considerable debate has surrounded this subject, yet it may be concluded that, within both unionised and non-unionised categories, there is scope for a range of corporate profiles to exist.

In a study that highlights the strategy of M-form concerns which, as previously indicated, are becoming increasingly dominant players in the economic scene, Purcell and Ahlstrand (1994) cast further light upon the dynamics underlying the formulation of employee relations styles and strategies. This organisational form is regarded as an exemplar of internalisation, the authors stating that, for the M-form conglomerate, 'the invisible hand of the market is replaced by the visible hand of corporate office' (1994: 14). Within this structure, it is suggested that employee relations strategies can only be understood in the context of the business in which they operate, and that employee relations decisions are dependent upon, and derivative of, superordinate 'first-order' corporate strategy. Using case study data to observe the evolution of style, it is concluded that the positions of sophisticated paternalism and constitutionalism are being squeezed out by parallel trends towards cost minimisation (associated more with the traditional model) and investment (associated more with the consultative model). This perception has been borne out in the work of other researchers. Marchington (1995: 83), for example, observes that 'employee relations is becoming increasingly bifurcated, not so much between union and non-union organisations, but within each of these broad categories'.

■ Management with or without unions?

There has been considerable debate about the future role of trade unions, with certain commentators on the right of the political spectrum suggesting that unions are part of the 'archaeology' of the British industrial relations landscape. Certainly the climate of the past few decades has not been favourable to trade unions, with intangible, yet commonly observed, shifts in national norms and values away from collectivism and towards the assertion of individual rights and self-interest. More directly, the Thatcher government derecognised unions at GCHQ (recognition rights having been reinstated subsequently by the Labour government), taking a hard line against public sector unions, and progressively undermining trade union rights through its legislative programme. In line with free-market-oriented thinking, the view has been taken, supported by prominent economists (for example, Minford, 1996), that unions represent a monopoly force, artificially inflating market rates of pay, and that they should return to their former role as friendly societies.

According to WERS98 (Millward *et al.*, 2000: 96), union recognition had declined in the UK from 66 per cent of workplaces in 1984 to 47 per cent in 1998. Meanwhile, the proportion or workplaces without unions increased from 27 per cent in 1984 to 47 per cent in 1998. Nevertheless, for many enterprises, particularly large ones, unions remain important participants. Marchington and Wilkinson (1996) suggest a number of reasons for this:

- In larger workplaces, management may regard trade unions as an essential part of the communication process. Rather than deal with each employee individually, or set up direct communication systems with staff, trade unions may provide a channel that is particularly useful in respect of issues associated with pay bargaining and grievance handling. The involvement of unions may also help to legitimise decisions in the eyes of the workforce.
- Unions can assist with providing order and stability in the workplace, especially in persuading employees of the need to use procedures in resolving industrial disputes. If all sides adhere to rules and procedures then this should foster an air of compromise rather than one of aggression and retaliation.
- It is likely that, in some industrial sectors or regions, the need to recognise a union will be virtually inevitable owing to past traditions and current expectations. In these circumstances it may be better for management to select the union it wishes to recognise and the form of desired agreement – for example, a single-union agreement.
- Management may not attach priority to diminishing the role of unions as a corporate objective, and indeed may not be able to achieve this even if it wanted to. Local factors may constrain management and tilt the balance of power in favour of the unions – for example, a skills shortage of a particular grade of labour.

Nevertheless, in a growing number of organisations the perceived advantages of moving towards the derecognition of trade unions have taken precedence over the above factors. It should be noted that derecognition does not always involve complete withdrawal of union rights, but rather some halfway measures. For example, derecognition may occur for particular grades of staff, or in respect of a set of previously negotiable issues (Claydon, 1989). Where there are shifts towards marginalisation of unions, by narrowing the negotiable agenda, typically systems of communication will be introduced by management that bypass unions and are directly channelled towards employees. In observing this phenomenon, Marchington and Parker (1990) quote a food factory manager: 'it's pushing negotiations down to consultation and, consultation down to communication'.

The most straightforward scenario, however, is where an employing organisation decides that it wishes to completely terminate relations with a union or set of unions. In the UK, this has not been a widespread phenomenon. WERS98 (Cully *et al.*, 1999: 92) found that only a small proportion (less than 5 per cent of respondent workplaces) had deliberately removed trade union recognition rights or established alternative channels for representation. More prevalent had been a withering away of membership among the existing workforce and a lack of recruitment as the workforce evolved. A common occurrence, and one that represents a serious challenge for unions, is for newly establishing companies to seldom wish to enter into bargaining arrangements with trade unions.

Where derecognition has occurred, it is commonly associated with changes in corporate ownership, particularly when an enterprise has been passed into overseas (notably American) hands (Beaumont and Harris, 1992). Observation of well-publicised cases, such as Tioxide UK or Unipart, would suggest that derecognition tends to occur when management sees unions as having outlived their usefulness in the wake of the onset of new HRM inspired employment initiatives.

Non-union employee relations

Many studies in industrial relations have concentrated upon unionised environments, and consequently the variations in non-union enterprises seem to have received insufficient academic attention. What is now emerging is that a range of organisational typologies are evident under the banner of non-unionism, which can be more or less favourable to the position of employees within such enterprises.

The 1980s and early 1990s provided a favourable climate for employers who wished to work without trade unions. The industrial relations 'lead' established by successive Conservative governments was one that removed national trade union institutions from the forums of national economic decision-making. It also diminished the position of unions in many reaches of the public sector, and undermined the organisational ability of unions through the enactment of a series of adverse statutes. As well as direct forms of action, the receptiveness of the Thatcher governments towards the entrepreneurial spirit generated by small enterprises as the 'engine room' of the economy proselytised a model which was in essence non-unionist, as did the enthusiastic welcome extended by government to Japanese concerns locating in the UK. Many such transplants were non-union or were placing relations with unions on a radically new footing.

At a corporate level, the union movement has been challenged by the growing influence of overseas policies and practices via multinational concerns opening new sites in new geographical areas. Here it may be difficult for trade unions to gain a foothold, or operating in sectors (for example 'sunrise' industries or services) that have weak traditions of collective awareness and action on the part of employees. The potent North American influence on management thinking and practice in the UK, which is most directly asserted through the operations of the many US-owned multinationals locating on British soil, has in general been detrimental to the interests of trade unions. It is instructive to note that in the US itself, around 85 per cent of the workforce is not unionised. There are well-documented traditions of both hostile (sometimes violent) treatment of union organisers by employers or their agents and 'welfare capitalism'. In respect of the latter strategy, companies such as IBM, Delta Airlines and Motorola have provided employees with an impressive array of terms and conditions and direct channels of communication by way of a deterrent to and intended substitute for trade union organisation. In the US, a growing and lucrative line of consultancy is advising employers on how they may avoid union recognition.

From the trade unions' point of view, it has been difficult to halt the spread of non-unionism owing to a general position of relative weakness. As described elsewhere in this volume, this can be attributed to unions' difficulty in adjusting to factors such as structural changes in employment and an adverse economic and political climate over the 1980s and much of the 1990s. In some enterprises, a vicious circle has been apparent, in which lack of confidence in a union, or apathy, has led to withering away of membership, which in turn has provided the opportunity for *de facto* derecognition (Claydon, 1989).

In seeking to understand the nature of non-union enterprises, it should be pointed out that non-unionism is not necessarily always total, and may take intermediate forms. Some enterprises – for example, in the finance sector – are prepared to allow internal staff associations or consultative committees, but resist what are viewed as external interferences into the business from trade union officials and institutional arrangements. In other organisations, non-unionism may exist for certain groups of staff, e.g. senior management, but not others. In examining the phenomenon of complete non-unionism, however, it should be noted that it is most prevalent in certain regions (notably the south east) and in certain sectors of the economy (for example, in retail and hotels and catering). It is also the case that younger and smaller enterprises are more likely to be non-union (Beaumont, 1990). As suggested by the Purcell and Sisson classification of management styles, the preference for non-unionism may be shared by organisations with apparently contrasting employment management philosophies.

In order to assist understanding the diversity of characteristics and approaches associated with the non-union enterprise, Guest and Hoque (1995) provide a typology. The 'good' employer is likely to be large and a product market leader. Possessing a clear strategy towards the management of its human resources, a range of personnel policies will be adopted to ensure that employee reward packages exceed market rates. Also, employees' behavioural and attitudinal characteristics will be encouraged to comply with company norms and values, and levels of job security and satisfaction will be high. Effective systems will be promoted for the sharing of information and communication. According to Marchington and Wilkinson (1996), the leading food retailers, J. Sainsbury and Safeway, may be placed in this category, having, in recent years, improved their recruitment and induction programmes, placed a greater stress on involvement and communications, and established management development programmes that emphasise open styles of supervision.

Although characterised as 'good', these organisations, which aim to invest in their staff, are certainly not beyond reproach. It would seem that the enlightened approach to the management of people is conditional upon retaining a product market leadership position, and if these organisations fall upon hard times, the continuation of an investment orientation may be subject to question. The example of IBM would seem to illustrate poignantly the contradictions surrounding the 'good' non-union employer. Until the early 1990s the company had provided high levels of job security, commitment to training and development, and much-heralded 'upward' systems of communication, including attitude surveys, 'speak up' and open-door policies. Encountering severe competition in the early 1990s, the company was forced to abandon its plank of policies founded upon notions of job security, and to cut almost one-third of the British workforce. From the employees' point of view, although 'good' non-union organisations provide a set of benefits that may well be in excess of those offered in the more traditional, unionised concern, the workforce is ultimately denied the ability to bring to bear a countervailing and independent influence on management decision-making. The continuation of a relatively protected and favoured employment position for those who are prepared to identify with the 'good' ethos is dependent upon the continued ability and willingness of their employers to maintain a position of enlightened self-interest.

'Bad' and 'ugly' stereotypes refer to the smaller, single-site, more traditional non-union employer. Frequently, these types of organisation would be the satellite providers of the more sophisticated and well-established concerns outlined above. The insecure product market position of these firms and the high level of dependence they have on supplying a few major customers mean that they are particularly susceptible to competition on grounds of cost. In consequence, a premium is placed on flexible deployment of staff, involving high levels of job insecurity. Pay is likely to be low, and formal protection of employment rights through the application of procedures overridden by oppressive, management styles, which are highly personalised in nature, involving arbitrary forms of discrimination and favouritism (Scott et al., 1989). Within such enterprises, the recognition of unions is likely to be viewed as something that will impede their ability to meet the primary goal of short-term survival. It is argued that for many of these concerns, the volatility of their product market position means that, in contrast to more sophisticated organisations, their approach to employment management is reactive and unplanned, inevitability surrounding the necessity to implement flexible practices and cut costs. 'Bad' employers are characterised as those who have little choice but to offer poor terms and conditions, whereas 'ugly' ones deliberately deprive workers of their rights.

'Lucky' organisations are likely to have poorly developed personnel policies and procedures, and pay packages are likely to be scanty. Operating in an opportunistic and pragmatic manner, owners or managers are unlikely to forcefully oppose trade unions, but rather disregard or ignore them as an irrelevance. The prevailing ethos will encapsulate unitary 'team spirit' values, within a paternalistic managerial style. Channels of communication between management and employees are likely to be open.

In examining non-union concerns, there are echoes of the broader bifurcation, or duality, within employment identified earlier. A distinction is apparent between those benefiting from the relatively protected employ of sophisticated market leaders and those working for smaller, market-dependent organisations whose employment is characterised by unfavourable terms and conditions and insecurity.

Reasons given by employers for not recognising trade unions

Organisation	Company comment
Autoglass	'There is no history of unionism within this relatively new industry.'
BP Exploration, Aberdeen	'No employee requests.'
Brightreasons Restaurants	'No formal union in place.'
Bristow Helicopters	'Have never recognised unions.'
British Pregnancy Advisory Services	'Staff have been approached by several unions but have not expressed any interest. Nursing staff do not belong to the RCN.'
Camberley Auto Factors	'No reason. No known union members among employees. No previous applications for recognition – no tradition in the motor trade either, for small branch outlets.'
DuPont Pharma	'Not necessary.'
Eli Lilly & Co. Basingstoke	'Not in line with company philosophy for this site.'
Hashimoto	'Third-party intervention obstructs good communications.'
Hills Pharmacy	'All retail employees covered by JIC for retail pharmacies.'
Kent Training & Enterprise	'As far as we know, no employees are members of a trade union and no Council request has ever been made for representation of this sort.'
Kuwait Oil Co., London	'Only a services office.'
Link House Advertising Periodicals	'Derecognised with effect from 1 January 1994.'
Medelec	'Never been a requirement.'
Norton Healthcare, Harlow	'Don't perceive a need.'
Orbit Valve, Ashchurch	'Greenfield site – management prerogative.'
Pitney Bowes	'We have staff associations.'
Polaroid UK, Dumbarton	'Have own employee representatives elected system with full-time chairperson.'
Private Patients Plan	'So far as I know, no trade union has ever sought recognition.'
Sea Containers Services, London	'Not approached by any trade union.'
Servowarm	'Staff consultative reps at each location covering all types of employment status.'
UCB Group	'This has never been an issue raised by employees and/or the company.'
Wiltshier	'No approaches.'

Source: IRS Employment Trends (1995: 4)

Human resource management and employee relations

In the early to mid 1980s, considerable attention was given to the possibility of a sea change in thinking and practice surrounding the management of employment. The terminology of HRM emerged initially in the US. Here, the climate of entrepreneurialism engendered by the free market economic policies of the Reagan administration, paralleled by the waning union movement and compositional changes in the labour market towards the service sector, provided management with the scope to experiment with new initiatives. The impetus to reconsider the strategic significance of employment practices derived also from the decline in US economic competitiveness relative to Far Eastern economies, and the then 'positive lesson' emerging from Japan of a correlation between the establishment of techniques to engender highly committed employees and strong economic performance. Ideas associated with HRM resonated subsequently in the UK, where an analogous set of contextual political and economic conditions set the scene for enthusiastic debate, among academics and practitioners alike, about the possibilities of reversing what appeared to be long-term economic decline by more spirited and strategic approaches to management. Debates about the definition and character of HRM have been rehearsed at some length elsewhere (see, for example, Storey, 1992 and 2001), but suffice it to say here that there has been considerable ambivalence and even confusion surrounding the concept.

The various definitions of HRM, and prescriptions for employment practice emerging from them, betray conflicting views on the part of their advocates of the ultimate value of the 'human resource' itself. 'Soft' versions of HRM (for example, Guest, 1987) envisage employees to be valued assets, which hold the key to competitive advantage. It is argued that human resource policies, which are oriented towards staff development and involvement, should be formulated in such a way that they deliver 'resourceful humans' (Morris and Burgoyne, 1973). A premium is placed on engendering high levels of employee commitment, adaptability and competence, which is in keeping with high-quality production, and upon establishing direct linkages between human resource policies and broader corporate goals. 'Hard' HRM also stresses the importance of integration between human resource activities and corporate strategy, with human resource systems being used 'to drive the strategic objectives of the organisation' (Fombrun et al., 1984: 37). In contrast to softer conceptions, however, human resources are viewed as being passive and as constituting a business expense along with the other factors of production (land and capital).

Actual areas of policy and practice associated with (softer) conceptions of HRM would, according to Storey (1992), include:

- staff selection as an integrated and key process;
- performance-related pay and single-status conditions for all staff;
- an emphasis on training and adaptive, growing organisations;
- teamwork approaches to job design.

According to the doctrine of HRM, the implementation of these, and related areas of practice, should be custom-made to satisfy the broader goal of obtaining maximum responsiveness to customer requirements, essentially by exhorting staff to work 'beyond contract'. Referring back to our distinctions between internalisation and externalisation, policies associated with softer HRM tend to correlate with an internalised view of the enterprise, an emphasis being placed on those employment policies that augment the indigenous skills base, employee commitment and versatility. This in turn promotes a need for a high level of competence within managerial grades, and the location of key managerial tasks would be with well-equipped general, business or line managers. This clearly points to a pressing management developmental need. By way of contrast, harder HRM retains a reliance on the externalised interplay of market forces.

Has HRM occurred in practice? According to Storey (2001: 10), it is doubtful whether the elements of soft HRM have been linked together into a 'meaningful strategic whole' by the bulk of employers. Nevertheless, there is some suggestion from WERS98 (Cully *et al.*, 1999: 57, 58) that HRM is gaining credibility 'on the ground'. The survey revealed, for instance, that a majority of respondents now formulated a formal HR plan. Around one-third were accredited as Investors in People and formal performance appraisals took place in nearly 80 per cent of workplaces (Storey, 2001: 10). Furthermore, a positive correlation was evident between workplaces employing 'new' management practices and employee involvement schemes and high productivity growth (Cully *et al.*, 1999: 25). Despite these positive signs we should note that, as well as the implementation of HRM practice being piecemeal, major swathes of British industry appear to be relatively untouched by it.

The 'slipperiness' of the HRM concept means that it is difficult to judge how it may be translated into a discernible management style or strategy, and how HRM approaches may impact upon trade unions. Taking softer approaches at face value, a central thrust is the desirability of engendering high levels of employee commitment to organisational goals. This virtue may be achieved through the implementation of communications mechanisms that directly connect management and employees, *not* operating via the intermediary of a third party acting as a representative of the workforce. In this way, employee support can be obtained for preferred managerial courses of action. Direct communications places trade union representatives in an insidious position, as some apparently long-standing goals (for example, staff consultation, improvement of terms and conditions) are realised with active management consent, yet unions themselves may be on the margins of this process. Further, the question may be asked whether dual loyalty is possible on the part of employees, simultaneously to the union and the employer (Guest, 1995). On the other hand, the hard approach may be more likely to directly undermine the union role through marginalisation, non-recognition or derecognition. In seeking to provide understanding of company practice with regard to the interface between industrial relations and HRM, Guest (1995) defines four potential policy options:

- *New realism* – a high emphasis on HRM and industrial relations. This represents a joint approach from management and unions, and emphasises mutuality between the parties. Systems for union representation and direct communications between management and employees may coexist, as has been found from Storey's (1992) survey evidence. Ultimately, however, there are doubts, according to Guest, as to whether robust trade unionism can survive in the context of enthusiastic HRM.
- *Traditional collectivism* – industrial relations without HRM. Here, traditional pluralist industrial relations arrangements are retained, with management negotiating with union representatives across a range of issues. Such a system still exists within large

parts of the public sector. According to recent Workplace Industrial Relations surveys (Millward *et al.*, 1992, 2000), preparedness of management to utilise traditional union channels is dwindling. More encouraging for trade unions was the data from WERS92 pointing to a clear correlation between union recognition and greater wage equality, more disclosure of information, better channels of communication and greater job security than in the case where unions were not recognised.

■ *Individualised HRM* – HRM without industrial relations. As indicated above, there has not been evidence of comprehensive union derecognition in the UK, with traditional bargaining arrangements being systematically supplanted by a new range of policy initiatives. American-owned concerns are most likely to promote a strongly HRM, non-union approach. Such enterprises promote relatively high wages and benefits, sophisticated communications, single-status conditions of employment, employment security related to training provision, and careful screening of potential recruits (Beaumont, 1987).

■ *The black hole* – no HRM or industrial relations. According to Guest, this is becoming a more prevalent option, as the practices of union derecognition and not recognising unions on new sites gather momentum. In non-union environments, as has been suggested above, traditional styles of employment management are gaining ground. Far from establishing strategic connections with corporate objectives, or establishing patterns for employee involvement, these are characterised by opportunistic and unilateral cost-cutting approaches, presenting their employees with bleak and insecure conditions. At best, this would represent a severe strain of hard HRM.

The way forward: a partnership approach?

The Labour government of 2002 has aimed to put into place a 'stakeholder society', implying a revision of the individualist values associated with the previous era of Conservatism and an intention to draw affected interest groups into aspects of decision-making in all walks of national life. In the field of employment, the legislative programme has included provisions to assist in trade union recognition, union representation rights for non-union employees during discipline and grievance procedures, and improved individual rights in areas such as unfair dismissal and parental leave. The overall aim has been to create a legal framework for a new balance in relationships between the representatives of labour and management. Optimism has been apparent in trade union circles that a change in corporate priorities could emerge at organisational level, replacing short-term decisions on investment with organic growth strategies involving employees, customers, suppliers and the local community (Monks, 1998: 173). The case for closer working relationships between the major industrial interest groups has been put forward by some prominent advocates reflecting the more favourable stance taken by the UK government to the European 'social partnership' model (see Chapter 6). The Involvement and Participation Association (IPA) has anticipated greater receptiveness to the fundamental principles it has been advocating for over a century (IPA, 1995), albeit placing a new emphasis on attitudes and culture, rather than previous forms of institutionalised participation or tripartite decision-making (Coupar and Stevens, 1998: 143). The Advisory, Conciliation and Arbitration Service (ACAS), in encouraging labour management partnerships (LMPs), has endorsed the idea that engendering high trust relations between the parties representing labour and management creates an important avenue towards corporate success (ACAS, n.d.).

Organisations as diverse as Blue Circle, Dwr Cymru/Welsh Water, Rhône-Poulenc, Scottish Power, Royal Mail, Baxi, and Granada Service have introduced partnership arrangements. These coexist with time-honoured mechanisms to promote partnership principles, notably as witnessed in the John Lewis Partnership (which is a non-union organisation). The essence of the partnership concept as evident in the more recent initiatives is a commitment towards job security for employees by the organisation, in return for employee agreement to work more flexibly in response to customer requirements . At Welsh Water, for example, major components of the deal struck between the company and its trade unions have included:

- single-status conditions for staff and a unified pay structure with pay determination through a mutually acceptable pay formula;
- the establishment of a single-table representative council with particular projects delegated to issue groups;
- changed working time, involving a reduction in working time with a reorganisation of the working year into a form which is more responsive to customer needs;
- productivity enhancements through flexibility between workgroups, skill enhancements, and delegation of responsibilities previously carried out by supervisors;
- a 'no compulsory redundancy' agreement (Thomas and Wallis, 1998: 163).

It can be seen from the elements of the agreement that partnerships not only concern the substance of the employment relationship, particularly in the fields of pay, deployment and staffing, and job security, but also the mode of interaction between the parties. This purports to emphasise collaboration and trust-building rather than 'old style' adversarial methods. Using terminology originally developed by Walton and McKersie (1965), the partnership approach is based on an *integrative* bargaining ideology, characterised by information-sharing between the parties so that a joint and factually grounded approach is taken towards matters such as pay determination. It is implicit that union representatives (and members) are involved in the corporate machinations surrounding the resolution of employment issues. In contrast, the *distributive* model, which has been used to represent more traditional approaches to bargaining, is characterised by conflict and low trust relationships between the parties in dividing fixed sums.

From the managerial point of view, it is clear that partnership can assist the achievement of overriding corporate objectives, perhaps most notably gaining staff acquiescence to changing conditions of employment in order to promote customer responsiveness. Nevertheless, it is likely to be incumbent upon management to display openness and to be prepared to adopt a participative style. From the perspective of employees, there are ostensibly solid benefits associated with partnership, including the elusive prize of employment security as well as greater predictability in the determination of pay, and possible enhancement in the design of work (Thomas and Wallis, 1998: 163).

Trade unions are likely to be presented with some ambiguity as a result of the onset of partnership arrangements. On one hand, it may be that unions will benefit from moving away from the adversarial postures they are widely believed to have adopted in the past which will enable them to engage with management agendas in a more constructive fashion. This may assist with their winning the endorsement of employers and increased support from members and the public. On the other hand, some comment-ators, for example, Claydon (1998: 181), argue that partnership may represent another 'union Trojan horse'. He cites trade unionists and academics who 'remain sceptical [about] the possibility of genuine partnership on a broad scale and/or who question the desirability of partnership on the grounds that it will render unions less rather than more able to defend and advance workers' interests'. A simplified view of Claydon's argument asserts that unions run the risk of being disenfranchised through the pro-cess of being incorporated into management forums for decision-making, and by being presented with an agenda for discourse which has been primarily determined by man-agement. Thus the sacrifice from the union perspective is the time-honoured and proven ability to forcefully oppose management decisions in areas which are unpalat-able to their membership. That the possibility of partnership does little to advance the position of the employee is argued by Kelly (1998), who finds, for example, that Welsh Water, despite having a partnership deal in place, was more likely to cut staff than its industrial competitors.

Returning to the theoretical perspectives discussed in Chapter 1, it may be asserted that the practice of partnership in the 1990s implies a forfeiting of pluralistic principles in the direction of mutual, yet ultimately unitary, approaches towards the formulation of corporate employment policies. At Welsh Water it is instructive to note that, despite the involvement of trade unions, the stated benefits to the organisation are closely aligned with the HRM paradigm discussed earlier, implying, at face value, a limited shifting of managerial ground. The stated benefits include:

- flexible working arrangements which allow customers to contact the company at their convenience. This has occurred by means of the establishment of a 24-hour call centre;
- improved quality of service, achieved by training work teams and 'empowering' them to take quality initiatives in the running of water and sewage treatment plants;
- cost reductions, created by savings in staffing which have been passed on to the consumer;
- organisational change (which is now, importantly, agreed by employees) necessitat-ing redeployment of labour and working with contractors and temporary staff (Thomas and Wallis, 1998).

In seeking to evaluate the development of partnership at corporate level, we should conclude that there is little evidence that this form of arrangement, although practised by some high-profile exemplars, is widely established across the landscape of the British economy. Indeed, it may be argued that the ability to offer job security as part of a broader package of change measures is scarcely a viable option beyond those organ-isations that possess the resources to invest seriously in their employment policies. It should also be noted that a number of the organisations entering partnership arrange-ments did so at a time of organisational turbulence, sometimes involving staff cuts. In the light of such adverse circumstances for the inception of the arrangement, observers may interpret the coming together of the parties as indicating strong elements of con-venience as well as choice. Trade union involvement in the process of rationalisation and restructuring is not only a legal requirement if redundancies are involved, but can also be of assistance in gaining the commitment of survivors to the management of sub-sequent change. If the reasons for entering into partnership are primarily opportunistic, in keeping with the 'standard modern' model mentioned above, one may question the durability of such arrangements into the longer term.

As mentioned at the outset of this chapter, the management of employee relations occurs within a broader economic, social and political framework. In the UK, the Labour government has introduced further basic protection for individual employees, and for trade unions and their members. Nevertheless, there has been no attempt to dismantle, wholesale, the employment edifice established under the previous Conservative governments. The perpetuation of market forces and deregulation of employment as political incentives for overseas investment fits uneasily with the concept of genuine partnership between labour and capital. In real and international terms, a low skills base, low pay and insecure conditions tend to be concomitants of such macro-level policies.

Chapter summary

Management, in many senses, is an ill-defined and multifaceted actor on the employee relations stage. Much managerial activity is conditioned by the interplay of economic factors above and beyond the level of the enterprise, now against a global backcloth. Moreover, the occupation of management is highly stratified, with a class of chief executive officers being regarded by some as the 'new rulers of the world' (Carlton Television, 2001) while those at the lower end of the corporate ladder endure long hours of work and insecure conditions of employment. In the UK, the position of management itself, and the employment policies it has instigated, have been conditioned by a financial system militating against investment in human capital over the longer term. Despite some evidence that greater sophistication has occurred in the formulation of human resource policies in recent years, there is a clear need for the autonomous actions of employers to be buttressed by statutory support to enhance reserves of organisational talent and promote mechanisms for employee consultation. A more positive and modern approach to the management of employment in the UK would seem to rest upon a review of the political, social and financial circumstances that govern and constrain the managerial task.

Questions

1   How do you view managerial competence in employment relations? How would you improve it?

2   Why are (a) the growth of multinationals and (b) the privatisation of major parts of the public sector important influences on employee relations in the UK?

3   How does a company's market position affect its employment relations policies?

4   What variations exist in types of non-union concern, and how do their employment relations 'climates' vary?

5   How does HRM affect the preparedness of employers to deal with trade unions?

Activities

1 Carry out a PEST (political, economic, social and technical factors) analysis of changes in the context for employment relations in the UK. Locate major styles of employment relations management within this context.

2 Consider Purcell and Sisson's five ideal typical styles of managing the employment relationship, i.e. traditional, sophisticated human relations, sophisticated modern (consultative and constitutional) and standard modern. Relate these to actual organisations with which you are familiar, giving examples of practice that correspond with the stereotypes. Can you identify any recent changes in managerial approaches?

Useful websites

www.cbi.org.uk **Confederation of British Industry** The Confederation of British Industry is Britain's 'umbrella' employer's organisation. The site provides information and opportunity for the expression of unified employer 'voice' on Employee Relations and other matters.

www.dti.gov.uk **Department of Trade and Industry** Provides information and advice from the Department of Trade and Industry to business, employees and consumers on employment and other economic matters.

www.eiro.eurofound.ie **European Industrial Relations Observatory On-Line** Provided by the European Foundation for the Improvement of Living and Working Conditions, contains substantive information on European developments in industrial relations on an EU, country and sectoral basis.

www.emerald-library.com Provides access to a wide range of management journals, reviews and abstracts.

www.employer-employee.com A portal containing miscellaneous, contemporary and entertaining workplace items for the benefit of employers and employees. Contains a special section for small businesses.

www.hrmguide.co.uk A series of linked websites including pages of HRM related articles and features on miscellaneous and contemporary matters.

www.incomesdata.co.uk Up to date intelligence on employment issues, including the economy, labour market and average earnings from Incomes Data Services.

www.peoplemanagement.co.uk Online magazine of the Chartered Institute of Personnel and Development which includes top stories in HR, legal updates, job vacancies etc.

References

ACAS (n.d.) *Time for a Change, Forging Labour–Management Partnerships*, Occasional Paper No. 52. London: ACAS.

Bach, S. and Sisson, K. (eds) (2000) *Personnel Management: A Comprehensive Guide to Theory and Practice*, 3rd edn. Oxford: Blackwell.

Beaumont, P. (1987) *The Decline of Union Organisation*. London: Croom Helm.

Beaumont, P. (1990) *Change in Industrial Relations: The Organisation and its Environment*. London: Routledge.

Beaumont, P.B. and Harris, R.I.D. (1992) 'Double-breasted recognition arrangements in Britain', *International Journal of HRM*, 3(2): 267–83.

Business Week (2000) September.

Carlton Television (2001) Booklet accompanying programme *The New Rulers of the World*, broadcast in July 2001.

Claydon, T. (1989) 'Trade union derecognition in Britain in the 1980s', *British Journal of Industrial Relations*, 27(2).

Claydon, T. (1998) 'Problematising partnership: the prospects for a co-operative bargaining agenda' in Sparrow, P.R. and Marchington, M. (eds) *Human Resources Management: The New Agenda*. London: Financial Times/Pitman Publishing.

Coupar, W. and Stevens, B. (1998) 'Towards a new model of industrial partnership: beyond the "HRM versus industrial relations" argument' in Sparrow, P.R. and Marchington, M. (eds) *Human Resource Management: The New Agenda*. London: Financial Times/Pitman Publishing.

Cully, M., Woodland, S., O'Reilly, A. and Dix, G. (1999) *Britain At Work, As Depicted by the 1998 Workplace Employee Relations Survey*. London: Routledge.

Donovan Commission (1968) *Report of the Royal Commission on Trade Unions and Employers' Associations 1965–68*, Cmnd 3623. London: HMSO.

Dore, R. (1973) *British Factory – Japanese Factory: The Origins of National Diversity in Industrial Relations*. London: Allen & Unwin.

Ellwood, W. (2001) *The No Nonsense Guide to Globalisation*. London: Verso.

Farnham, D. and Pimlott, J. (1995) *Understanding Industrial Relations*. London: Cassell.

Fombrun, C., Tichy, N.M. and Devanna, M.A. (eds) (1984) *Strategic Human Resource Management*. New York: Wiley.

Fox, A. (1966) *Industrial Sociology and Industrial Relations*, Research Paper No. 3, Royal Commission on Trade Unions and Employers' Associations, Cmnd 3623. London: HMSO.

Frank, T. (2001) *One Market Under God: Extreme Capitalism, Market Populism and the End of Economic Democracy*. London: Secker & Warburg.

GE Shareholder Resolution (1998) Reprinted in *A Decade of Excess: The 1990s*, Sixth Annual Compensation Survey London: United for a Fair Economy/Institute for Policy Studies.

Gospel, H. (1992) *Markets, Firms and the Management of Labour in Modern Britain*. Cambridge: Cambridge University Press.

Gospel, H.F. and Palmer, G. (1993) *British Industrial Relations*, 2nd edn. London: Routledge.

Guest, D. (1987) 'Human resource management and industrial relations', *Journal of Management Studies*, 24(5): 503–21.

Guest, D. (1995) 'Trade unions and industrial relations' in Storey, J. (ed.) *Human Resource Management: A Critical Text*. London: Routledge.

Guest, D. and Hoque, K. (1995) 'The good, the bad and the ugly – employment relations in non-union workplaces', *Human Resource Management Journal*, 5(1): 1–14.

Hendry, C. (1995) *Human Resource Management: A Strategic Approach to Employment*. Oxford: Butterworth-Heinemann.

Herriot, P. (1992) *The Career Management Challenge: Balancing Organisational and Individual Needs*. London: Sage.

Hobsbawm, E.J. (1968) *Industry and Empire*. London: Weidenfeld & Nicolson.

Hutton, W. (1996) *The State We're In*. London:Vintage.

IPA (1995) *Towards Industrial Partnership: Putting it into Practice – Rhône Poulenc Staveley Chemicals: A Case Study in Moving to Single Status*. London: Industrial Participation Association.

Joseph, M. (1989) *Sociology for Business: A Practical Approach*. Cambridge: Polity Press.

Keat, R. and Abercrombie, N. (eds) (1991) *Enterprise Culture*. London: Routledge.

Kelly J. (1998) *Rethinking Industrial Relations: Mobilisation, Collectivism and Long Waves*, London: Routledge, in conjunction with company reports presented at a seminar for the Employment Studies Research Unit at the University of the West of England in 1999.

Lane, C. (1989) *Management and Labour in Europe: The Industrial Enterprise in Germany, Britain and France*. Aldershot, VT: Edward Elgar.

Lane, C. (1994) 'Industrial order and the transformation of industrial Britain, Germany and France compared' in Hyman, R. and Ferner, A. (eds) *New Frontiers in European Industrial Relations*. Oxford: Blackwell.

Marchington, M. (1995) 'Employee relations' in Tyson, S. (ed.) *Strategic Prospects for HRM*. London: Institute for Personnel and Development.

Marchington, M. and Parker, P. (1990) *Changing Patterns of Employee Relations*. Hemel Hempstead: Harvester Wheatsheaf.

Marchington, M. and Wilkinson, A. (1996) *Core Personnel and Development*. London: Institute for Personnel and Development.

Millward, N., Stevens, M., Smart, D. and Hawes, W. (1992) *Workplace Industrial Relations in Transition* (ED/ESRC/PSI/ACAS Survey). Aldershot: Dartmouth.

Millward, N., Bryson, A. and Forth, J. (2000) *All Change at Work: British Employment Relations 1980–1998, as portrayed by the Workplace Industrial Relations Survey Series*. London and New York: Routledge.

Minford, P. (1996) *Analysis*, BBC Radio 4, 13 December.

Monks, J. (1998) 'Trade unions, enterprise and the future' in Sparrow, P.R. and Marchington, M. (eds) *Human Resource Management: The New Agenda*. London: Financial Times/Pitman Publishing.

Morris, J. and Burgoyne, J.G. (1973) *Developing Resourceful Managers*. London: Institute of Personnel Management.

NEDO (1987) *Tool Making: A Comparison of UK and West German Companies*, Gauge and Tool Sector Working Party. London: NEDO.

Purcell, J. and Ahlstrand, B. (1994) *Human Resource Management in the Multi-divisional Company*. Oxford: Oxford University Press.

Purcell, J. and Gray, A. (1986) 'Corporate personnel departments and the management of industrial relations: two case studies in the management of ambiguity', *Journal of Management Studies*, 23(2): 205–23.

Purcell, J. and Sisson, K. (1983) 'Strategies and practice in the management of industrial relations', in Bain, G.S. (ed.) *Industrial Relations in Britain*. Oxford: Blackwell.

Scott, M., Roberts, L., Holroyd, G. and Sawbridge, D. (1989) *Management and Industrial Relations in Small Firms*, Department of Employment Research Paper No. 70. London: HMSO.

Storey, J. (1992) *Developments in the Management of Human Resources*. Oxford: Blackwell.

Storey, J. (ed.) (2001) *Human Resource Management: A Critical Text*, 2nd edn. London: Thomson Learning.

Thomas, C. and Wallis, B. (1998) 'Dwr Cymru/Welsh Water: a case study in partnership' in Sparrow, P.R. and Marchington, M. (eds) *Human Resource Management: The New Agenda*. London: Financial Times/Pitman Publishing.

Walton, R. and McKersie, R. (1965) *A Behavioral Theory of Labor Negotiations*. New York: McGraw-Hill.

Wilson, R.A. (1993) *Review of the Economy and Employment 1992/3: Occupational Assessment*. University of Warwick: Institute for Employment Research.

Worrall, L. and Cooper, C. (2001) *The Quality of Working Life: 2000 Survey of Managers' Changing Experiences*. Manchester: UMIST/Institute of Management.

Further reading

Blyton, P. and Turnbull, P. (1998) *The Dynamics of Employee Relations*. Basingstoke: Macmillan, chapters 4 and 9.

Kelly, J. (1998) *Rethinking Industrial Relations: Mobilization, Collectivism and Long Waves*. London: Routledge.

Legge, K. (1995) *Human Resource Management: Rhetorics and Realities*. Basingstoke: Macmillan, chapters 2, 3 and 8.

Salamon, M. (1998) *Industrial Relations Theory and Practice*, 3rd edn. Hemel Hempstead: Prentice Hall, chapter 7.

Storey, J. (ed.) (2001) *Human Resource Management: A Critical Text*, 2nd edn. London: Thomson Learning, chapters 1, 6 and 13.

Chapter 4

Employee representation: trade unions

Jackie Sinclair

Learning objectives

By the end of this chapter, readers should be able to:

- provide a definition of trade unions and employee associations, and trace their early development;
- examine the origins, functions, structure, internal organisation and powers of trade unions;
- examine trends in union membership and explanations for variation;
- analyse the challenges facing trade unions throughout recent decades;
- suggest implications for future developments in trade union fortunes at national and workplace level.

Trade union functions and powers

The trade unions nowadays attract less media attention than they did in the 1960s and 1970s, yet they are a reality in many of Britain's workplaces. In March 2001, there were 206 registered trade unions (plus another 22 which had not sought to be listed by the Certification Officer), with a combined membership in excess of 7 million. Almost half the population of Britain is employed in workplaces where trade unions are recognised for negotiating pay and conditions (Certification Officer, 2001: 8 and *Labour Market Trends*, September 2001: 433). Trade unions are central to employee relations in Britain and other countries. They have never-theless suffered varying fortunes, including a loss of membership and other challenges throughout the 1980s and 1990s, although they appear to have made tentative steps towards recovery since 2000, at least with regards to the decline in membership. Even throughout their troubled periods, they have remained a significant force in the UK, with membership and trade union presence bearing up well in comparison with other western countries such as France and the US. This chapter examines the development of trade unionism, the principles of collective organisation and the fortunes of trade unions in recent years.

■ What trade unions are, and what they do

Trade unions are in essence 'secondary' organisations, since, as Hyman puts it, 'they are associations of workers who are already "organised" by those to whom they sell their labour power and whose actions they are designed to influence' (quoted in Bain, 1983: 61). This characteristic is significant since it is crucial in reaching an understanding of the powers available to trade unions at a particular time, and their ability to be proactive or reactive in response to the various challenges facing them not only in recent years, but throughout their development. The history of the trade union movement is littered with examples of struggles not only against employers over pay and conditions of work, but also against the state, for the right to exist. Such struggles, and resultant victories and defeats, have shaped and been shaped by the political, economic and social context of each particular era, as well as by the circumstances of individual employers or industries. Thus, what trade unions are, is inseparable from what they do.

The most well-known definition of a trade union was coined by the historians Sidney and Beatrice Webb (1920):

> A continuous association of wage earners for the purpose of maintaining or improving the conditions of their working lives.

This conveys two significant features of trade unions: the notion of a collective organisation, and that the composition must be of wage earners – employees rather than owners of enterprises. There are also legal definitions, such as that in the Trade Union and Labour Relations (Consolidation) Act 1992, which similarly conveys the notion of collectivism but does not insist on the organisation being a permanent one. This refers to an organisation, whether permanent or temporary, which consists wholly or mainly of workers of one or more descriptions and is an organisation whose principal purposes include the regulation of relations between workers of those descriptions, and employers or employers' associations.

Both definitions refer to the key functions of a trade union – which, in general terms, denote protection of its members with respect to pay and conditions – and the rules governing the employment relationship. However, such definitions are limited since they fail to capture the complexity and variability of trade unions as organisations. This also has implications for tracing how trade unions developed, and in considering how they are organised democratically.

Defining trade unions and describing their functions are normally subject to a qualitative analysis which utilises the concept of 'unionateness' (Blackburn, 1967). This has been used to try to capture the degree to which the organisation is committed to the broad aims and ideology of the trade union movement, based on the following principles:

- whether the body declares itself a trade union;
- whether it is registered as a trade union;
- whether it is affiliated to the Trades Union Congress (TUC);
- whether it is affiliated to the Labour Party;
- whether it is independent of employers for the purposes of negotiation;

- whether it regards collective bargaining and the protection of the interests of its members, as employees, as a major function;
- whether it is prepared to be militant, using all forms of industrial action which may be effective.

The more of these elements that are embodied by the organisation, the more unionate it is regarded, although not all of these elements are of equal importance for unionateness. There is significant variation among trade unions in Britain and in Europe and elsewhere, particularly as to the means by which they seek to perform their functions, and some demonstrate a high or low degree of unionateness. Some trade unions, for example, have been prepared to take industrial action in pursuit of their members' interests, as in the final element, while others historically have not (e.g. the nurses' union, the Royal College of Nursing, until 1995 when they overturned this policy) or are legally prohibited from doing so (e.g. police). Some do not declare themselves as trade unions as in the first element, but are more akin to professional associations which regulate not only relations with employers but also the professional standards of their members (e.g. some health service professional unions such as the Royal College of Midwives). In other trade unions, collective bargaining may not be paramount. The early craft unions were opposed to it, and favoured unilateral regulation with rates of pay dictated to employers. In recent years, some teachers' unions (e.g. National Association of Schoolmasters/Union of Women Teachers) have abandoned collective bargaining and pursued Pay Review Bodies as a form of pay determination, a method which does not involve face-to-face bargaining with the employer. Nevertheless, a strong presence of other unionate characteristics may be detected among such unions. Some unionate elements may be present in order to retain legal or other protections. For example, all except a small number of staff associations are registered as trade unions, by the Certification Officer, who must be satisfied that a trade union is truly independent of the employer, or other external agencies such as the state, before granting a certificate of independence.

The functions of trade unions focus mainly on their 'bread and butter' role. Unions normally negotiate on behalf of their members for pay and conditions, and an important function is the policing or monitoring of agreements. They seek to prevent employers from imposing arbitrary treatment on their members by negotiating rules that govern the employment relationship, and they represent their members on an individual basis in cases of disciplinary action, potential dismissal or discrimination.

Crouch (1982: 121) outlines the goals of unions as organisations, emphasising the protection of the worker as the vulnerable party within an unequal employment relationship. Such goals, however, are inherently defensive and reactive as opposed to initiating. Even the miners, traditionally viewed as the most militant of trade unions in Britain, in a major dispute prior to the 1926 General Strike were simply engaged in resisting increased working hours and cuts in pay, hence the slogan 'not a penny off the pay, not a second on the day' (Crouch, 1982: 122). This defensiveness has been a source of frustration for some radicals and Marxists, in that working-class movements, in particular the trade unions, have often limited themselves to short-term gains within the wages system.

However, these basic defensive functions are often supplemented by wider objectives; the unionate characteristics refer to affiliation by unions to political bodies or commitment to the labour movement and other social aims. Most larger trade unions affiliate to the umbrella organisation of the trade union movement, the TUC, and this implies some degree of identification with the broader labour movement. Unions such as the National Union of Teachers and the Association of Teachers and Lecturers affiliated late, and one of the largest ten unions, the Royal College of Nursing, is non-affiliated. However, other health services unions have only recently taken up TUC affiliation, such as the Chartered Society of Physiotherapy and the Society of Radiographers. Labour Party affiliation is less widespread among trade unions; by 1992, 30 of the 70 or so TUC-affiliated unions were also affiliated to the Labour Party, while 45 unions maintained a political fund for spending on political objectives, which can include campaigning or lobbying Parliament.

What should unions do?

Defending members' interests is essential, as described above, but priorities will change from time to time in accordance with particular circumstances. A British Social Attitudes Survey conducted among those with a recognised union at their workplace revealed that employees' views on what trade unions should aim to do varied significantly on key issues, in the years 1989 and 1994 (see Table 4.1).

By 1994, more than twice as many wanted their union to protect jobs as wanted them to improve pay, although these were considered of equal importance in the 1989 survey. No doubt influential was that inflation was at a low level during the 1990s whereas job insecurity and unemployment had risen as major concerns.

These various goals, and the priorities of trade unions, are not static as the issues facing the membership will depend on the specific historical context. However, Hyman and Fryer (1975; cf. McIlroy, 1995) point to the institutional goals that trade unions may develop as organisations, and which may from time to time conflict with members' concerns. For example, a fundamental goal will be the survival of the organisation, implying the need to sustain itself through an unfavourable economic or political climate or survive the pressure on resources during a lengthy dispute. Financial stability and efficiency may also be important goals, required to maintain the functioning and day-to-day business of the union, yet these may conflict with the goals of union democracy, or inhibit the members' wish to take strike action, which is often costly to a trade union.

Table 4.1 **Employees' views of what trade unions should try to do, 1989 and 1994**

Unions should...	1989 (%)	1994 (%)
Protect existing jobs	28	37
Improve working conditions	21	20
Improve pay	28	15
Have more say over management's long-term plans	6	14
Reduce pay differences at the workplace	6	4
Work for equal opportunities for women	3	2

Source: *Social Trends* 26 (1996), p. 92

Furthermore, there may be long-term goals that relate not just to the union as an organisation in its own right but also to the broad functions of the labour movement. Trade unions, as part of this movement, always had a commitment to economic, political and social changes, and the advancement of workers, across national boundaries. Hyman (1975: 87) makes this explicit:

> Trade unionists have often proclaimed far more radical aims: the reconstruction of the social order; the abolition of the dominating role of profit; the establishment of workers' control of industry; the reorganisation of the economy to serve directly the needs of the producers and the general members of society; the humanisation of work; the elimination of gross inequalities in standards of living and conditions of life; the transformation of cultural richness from the privilege of a minority to the property of all.

Such aspirations are often reflected in the rulebooks of individual unions, and TUC statements and those of federations of labour.

Unionateness and other employee organisations

Whereas trade unions are the most usual arrangement in which employees combine together, there are other forms of employee organisation. In the UK it has been convention that trade unions are created by the members on behalf of the members (or occasionally through merger) rather than through an external agency such as the state. This in itself is an essential requirement by the Certification Officer, who must be satisfied that an employee organisation is truly independent of employers or other external intervention before it can be registered as a trade union or receive legal protections and immunities under the law. This has had implications for the small number of staff associations evident in the UK. Some are seen as akin to the Japanese 'in house' unions, which typically have been company-sponsored. In Britain these have been limited to the finance or insurance industries, and to white-collar or managerial employees within these sectors; the total membership is not counted separately by the Certification Officer, but up to 2 million people may be members (Gospel and Palmer, 1993: 141). These various employee institutions do not remain unchanging, however. In recent years, employees in the finance sectors appear more 'unionate' as demonstrated by affiliation to the TUC of the Independent Union of Halifax Staff, the NatWest Staff Association and the former Barclays Group staff union, Unifi. These developments, according to Storey, reflect the enormous changes in the industry, namely restructuring and downsizing, and the abandonment of paternalist practices by employers (Storey, 1995, cited in Heery, 1997).

An interesting example emerged during the 1990s of a staff association being refused a certificate of independence by the government-appointed Certification Officer. The Conservative government banned existing trade unions at Government Communication Headquarters (GCHQ), at Cheltenham, in 1984. The GCHQ staff federation GCSF applied for a certificate and was refused in 1989 by the Certification Officer, and in 1992 by the employment appeals tribunal, and again in November 1996 by the Certification Officer. This was on the grounds that the GCSF was vulnerable to interference by the employer at GCHQ (Certification Officer, 1996):

- GCSF's freedom to affiliate with other organisations was significantly restricted; it could not merge with another union nor could it recruit voting members from elsewhere to broaden its membership base.
- The withdrawal of employer-provided facilities could produce severe disruption to GCSF's activities.
- GCSF was faced with an effective ban on taking or inducing industrial action.

The ban on independent trade unions at GCHQ was finally lifted in 1997 by the Labour government. Other organisations that have been refused a certificate of independence by the Certification Officer, however, are the Association of Premier League and Football League Referees and Linesmen, and the Clerical Medical Staff Association. Clearly, some important characteristics of unionateness, in particular independence from the employer, are essential to ensure that the union is genuinely able to act on behalf of its members. This is in contrast with 'sweetheart unions' in the US, which were used to prevent the spread of independent unionism, or the company-based Japanese unions, which are often considerably constrained by the employer.

The rationale for collective organisation among employees

Why is it considered important for employees to have an independent body to act on their behalf, to regulate the employment relationship? Why is it important for employees to combine into a collective organisation rather than deal individually with their employer? First, not all workers do join trade unions, and it is worth exploring the reasons for this, prior to considering the rationale for collective organisation.

Crouch (1982: 47) cites a series of reasons why an individual, or a group of employees, should choose not to join in combination to form a trade union. An important feature, both historically and in more recent times, is employer or government hostility. If the costs of joining or forming a trade union may be sackings, imprisonment or deportation to the other side of the world, clearly this is likely to present a major dilemma for many employees, even if others have taken that risk. While trade union organisation became legally permissible, or even encouraged, in European countries, at least from the early part of the twentieth century, their suppression continued in other parts of the world, in newly industrialised or developing countries such as South Korea, Brazil, South Africa and Singapore. Suppression or avoidance of trade union organisation was, and remains, common also in certain regions of the US, such as the south and west, or certain firms such as those associated with Silicon Valley, in high-tech, computer-related industries. Indeed, employer tactics for discouraging union organisation have been categorised by Donald Roy as 'fear stuff, sweet stuff and evil stuff' (cf. Crouch, 1982: 48). In other words, they could be punitive, with employees threatened with dismissal for attempting union organisation; they could be designed to entice workers away from trade unions by offering generous benefits; or they could involve methods of propaganda such as allegations of unions' links to communism, witchcraft, etc.

Legal or employer suppression of trade unions, therefore, can act as a disincentive for workers to take such a risk, even though many still do. However, even in western countries such as Britain, where the climate was more favourable to union organisation at least in many industries after the Second World War, groups of employees or individuals still can be reluctant to join. Where there is no statutory obligation on employers to recognise a trade union, the employees still rely on employers' willingness to recognise and bargain with unions.

In other instances the trade unions themselves may have done little to attract the membership of groups that have traditionally been hard to organise, such as young people, part-time women workers, or employees in industries such as hotels and catering. On the other hand, unions could historically, in some industries, ensure through a pre- or post-entry closed shop, that only members of a particular trade union could be employed in a particular occupation, hence increasing the likelihood of an individual or group taking up membership.

Apart from these structural factors, which may inhibit the formation or spread of trade unionism, or encourage them, there are still individuals who choose not to join a trade union, even if membership is widespread at their organisation. This can be for a number of reasons such as ideological opposition to trade unions, or even indifference or a failure to appreciate any discernible benefits. However, a further explanation relates to the so-called freerider, who does not join, simply because he or she receives the benefits of union membership regardless of whether he or she actually joins. The individual need not pay a subscription to the trade union, because on a rational calculation, the employer negotiates a pay increase with the trade union, but this is awarded to all employees within a particular company. Such individuals are often presented as harmlessly exercising their individual freedom not to join or contribute to a trade union if they do not wish to. This is to miss the point, however, since only through collective voice can most individuals receive protection in the first place. As discussed below, union strength and solidarity are based on cohesion and a claim to represent at least a significant proportion of workers in a particular grouping. Their strength relies on numbers, and their ability to organise on a collective basis; this is qualitatively as well as quantitatively different from being simply a collection of individuals. It is this notion, whether conscious or unconscious, which informs the impetus for collective organisation.

Many writers (Hyman, 1975; Crouch, 1982; McIlroy, 1995) have as their starting point the disadvantage of the individual worker when facing his or her employer, owing to the imbalance of power in the employment relationship. This hinges on the nature of employment under capitalism: the employee has simply his or her labour to sell in return for wages, whereas the employer has the advantage of ownership of the business, or the enterprise, and the capital which is invested within it. Colin Crouch investigates this rationale, the drive to combine, which is derived from attempting to redress the balance (Crouch, 1982: 45):

> Is it rational for workers to combine together in unions at all? The simplest answer is to point to the weakness of the isolated individual worker in his relations with his employer. While the labour contract pretends to be an even-handed relationship between two equal partners, this is purely a legal fiction. The individual employee is always precisely that, an individual man or woman; but the 'individual employer' is probably a company, including among its employees those working on problems of how to control labour and keep its costs down . . . Combination appears as a rational strategy for workers because it offers the chance of reducing, though never of overcoming, this inequality.

By forming combinations, the individual has the protection of the whole group of workers, who, by acting collectively, can limit the employer's ability, for example, to offer very low rates of pay. They can threaten to withdraw their labour unless certain conditions improve, and they can exert some control over the labour market which is available to employers, by controlling entry to a trade or profession through apprenticeship or training requirements. The ability to do these things depends on a variety of factors, which hinge on the power relations between management and trade unions in a given situation. However, the general imbalance between workers and management is not just based on the position of the former in relation to the latter. It is the nature of capitalism, in which employers have to struggle to retain competitiveness, by keeping up with ever changing market demands and processes such as new production methods. In this struggle, management is under pressure to alter the 'wage–effort' bargain in their favour, by intensifying the pace of work, through, for example, the use of machinery, or increasing the length of time that workers spend at work. Indeed, jobs are threatened by changes in technology and market conditions from time to time. Such conditions are always in a state of flux, and the factors that influence unions' and employers' powers will include the nature of the labour market and product market, the legislative climate, i.e. whether state policy encourages or undermines trade unions and collective bargaining, and the union membership itself, its cohesion and the degree of solidarity among the workforce (Coates, 1983: 60).

There exists, therefore, an 'invisible frontier' of control in every workplace (Hyman, 1975: 26) whereby a power struggle takes place on a continual basis. The notion of power in the workplace means 'the ability of an individual or group to control his [or her] physical and social environment; and, as part of this process, the ability to influence the decisions which are taken and are not taken by others' (Hyman, 1975: 26). Yet how are these powers specifically manifest in the workplace? What are the limits of these powers?

Trade union power

The combination of employees within a trade union forms the basis for protecting the individual via collective action. However, this act of combining does not in itself guarantee that they will have the ability to resist the actions of employers. This depends on their power as an organisation. There is much myth and legend concerning the power of trade unions, particularly during the 1960s and 1970s. For example, Jack Jones, leader of the Transport and General Workers' Union (TGWU), was in 1975 described by opinion polls to be 'the most powerful man in Britain' (McIlroy, 1995: 188). Certainly, union leaders wielded some political influence during the years of so-called corporatist governance. Just prior to this period, however, trade unionists such as the 'Shrewsbury Pickets' received harsh penal sentences from the courts. The power of ordinary union members, and of shop stewards or workplace representatives, some of whom did have considerable leverage in some key industries, was in fact variable. Claims that trade unions, as a single monolithic body, had powers in excess of those of capital were at best exaggerated and any analysis needs to account for varying circumstances for different groups of workers.

Coates (1983) insists that an analysis of union power should be considered in a wider context, posing the question, just how does the power of the trade unions compare with that of the owners of capital and the machinery of the state, such as the courts or police, and which is supported by the prevalent ideology perpetuated by the media?

Despite the enormous constraints imposed on unions' powers and activities, it was conventional wisdom, at least until recent years, that unions 'have too much power' both in terms of the industrial setting and politically. In the case of the former, the power was apparently illustrated by their ability to call strike action, halt production and retain rigid work practices. Yet Coates argues that it was only the high visibility of strikes, picket lines, etc. which fed this notion. Decisions by the owners of capital are taken privately without the high profile that often accompanies union demands – such as resorting to picket lines or strikes. This high visibility is often seen as a measure of power, rather than as a lack of it.

In the case of political powers, the trade unions have traditionally given priority to industrial rather than political methods to exert their influence, by contrast with continental movements where working-class political parties preceded the development of trade unions. British trade unions sought limited influence over government policy, except for periods of 'corporatism' during the 1960s and 1970s when they were represented, along with employers' organisations and state representatives, on tripartite bodies such as the National Economic Development Office. Historically, they have been suspicious of state involvement, relying instead on the system of voluntarism. Although the trade unions set up and continue to fund the Labour Party, there was traditionally a rigid separation between political and industrial activities, a demarcation which Hyman criticised since the two cannot easily be separated (Hyman, 1975: 147). Flanders also argued that whereas overambitious political aims may damage the unity of a trade union, since the membership will have diverse political views, some minimal political interest must exist, to ensure the unions have some legal protections or influence on national policies (Flanders, 1970: 27). A measure of state support for the basic right to exist and organise is seen as essential for unions if they are to receive any meaningful power when facing employers.

Coates concedes that, once recognised by an employer, union powers do exist over a range of limited issues such as working conditions, wages, or the speed of work, but these are negative powers to inhibit those of employers or to jointly negotiate over these issues. Negotiation does not extend to the location of factories, levels of investment, the size of the labour force or other strategic decisions (Coates, 1983: 67). Coates, therefore, is critical of the traditional measures of union power, based on their participation on workplace or state bodies, or even by their effects, which have not been to redistribute wealth or challenge the fundamentals of the economic and social structure. The measures should be based on 'unions' place in the whole structure of social, economic, cultural and political relationships in the society' (Coates, 1983: 75).

Furthermore, not all unions are equal in powers and strength, but much will depend on the strategic importance of the members for the industry or the economy as a whole, or their immediate powers *vis-à-vis* employers such as the perishability of the product. For example, newspaper printers traditionally relied on their power to stop production of newspapers, which obviously must be sold each day, to gain leverage over their employers. Other groups may have the ability to cause damage to the economy (e.g. transport workers) or risk to human life (e.g. emergency services) should they withdraw their labour, but the sensitivity of such action for the 'public interest' has meant that unions are reluctant to take industrial action. Indeed, governments have sought to exercise more legalistic controls in terms of disputes in this area, for example by banning the armed forces and police from taking strike action or forming trade unions.

There are various indicators of trade union power which can provide an idea of the prevailing climate, at national or international and workplace levels. These are:

- union membership in its totality, and membership density, i.e. the proportion of members out of the potential membership and a willingness to act collectively;
- the general economic and business climate, e.g. level of unemployment/employment, product market conditions prevailing in an industry;
- the labour market position of the workers in terms of skills, disposability, ability to disrupt production or services;
- the general political and legal climate which is more or less favourably disposed to encouraging or supporting trade unions, and the level of political influence they might have with regard to political policies;
- the legitimacy offered by employers to trade unions, and their willingness to recognise and negotiate with unions;
- the degree of union activity and facilities at workplace level, e.g. the number, proportions or activities of shop stewards or workplace representatives.

Some of these influences have produced a less favourable environment for the trade unions generally from the 1980s, although, in historical terms, unions faced a harsh climate, with state and employer resistance, from their earliest formation.

Trade union development and structure

■ Early developments

The formation of employee-based institutions to advance the interests of groups of workers with particular marketable skills originated as far back as feudal times, when guilds, organised around the preservation and protection of skilled journeymen and masters had a fair degree of power in relation to the regulation of apprenticeships, pay and the rules covering work methods, including preventing the dilution of skills. The trade unions developed during the early part of the eighteenth century, and were known as friendly societies. Their function was to provide mutual insurance and other benefits such as sickness and unemployment benefit, for those members who made contributions. In the case of trade unions in their more recognisable form and exclusively based on employee organisation, the Webbs (1920) trace their development from the eighteenth and nineteenth centuries, when the state and employers were united in their opposition to combinations of workmen. The Combination Acts 1799 and 1800 outlawed trade unions until the repeal of these laws in 1824 and 1825, but similar laws were applied on the continent. Even with the lifting of an outright ban, however, employers were still able to victimise trade unionists or dismiss workers who were members or activists in trade unions. Those trade unions that emerged first and managed to retain a foothold were those where the members had skills that were rare or valuable to the employer, compared with general labourers' unions, whose members would have been more easily replaced by their employers.

The earliest unions, in Britain as well as in other European countries, were the craft-based bodies based on small-scale enterprises at local level, typically in engineering but also in carpentry, printing and textiles. The source of their strength was the control of external and internal labour markets, through the imposition of the closed shop, or compulsory union membership, the control of apprenticeships, and rules and regulations related to their skills and craft. These bodies continued to provide social insurance benefits such as unemployment and death benefits. Unilateral insistence on rates of pay was preferred to collective bargaining, and was locally based, with employers who refused to comply being boycotted; eventually leading to employers themselves becoming organised into employers' associations. By the 1850s the craft unions became organised on a national basis and were to become known as new model unions, with the Amalgamated Engineering Union (AEU) as the classic model union. Full-time officers were employed, and administrative procedures and processes set up. These unions remained 'elite' bodies, excluding women and unskilled labourers from membership, and were politically conservative. It was their exclusive characteristics which led to their being known as the aristocrats of labour. Their success depended in part on their continuing ability to maintain the unions' coverage on a sectional basis, across different industries, although it was equally dependent on employers' demand for their skills and labour. These controls have been whittled away in many crafts, owing to changes in the craft occupations themselves, including the impact of technology, which have served to undermine the workers' monopoly on expertise (Gospel and Palmer, 1993: 122). Gospel and Palmer maintain the craft unions' powers were no match for those of the 'ancient professions' of law or medicine, whose professional bodies have wide-ranging powers often backed by law (Gospel and Palmer, 1993: 122).

It was partly in response to the elitism of the new model unions that the unskilled, general labourers and others began to set up their own organisations whose strength was based on numbers rather than specific skills, and whose aim was to pursue collective bargaining with employers. It was later, during the 1880s when economic conditions were more favourable for workers, that organisation of unskilled labourers, and particularly women, was successful in some areas, often following strike action against exploitative conditions and starvation wages. The famous match girls' strike by women and girls at the Bryant and May factory in 1888 was followed by action by London dockers and gas workers. Successful organisation around issues of casualisation – whereby workers turned up at the dockside in the hope of a day's work – and low pay meant that large groups of unskilled workers now made some impact. These unions became the forerunners of the large, general unions such as the Transport and General Workers' Union and the GMB, which remain highly significant and sizeable unions.

Union classification

Most continental unions tend to be influenced by political and/or religious affiliations. For example, the Catholic church has played a role in the formation of trade unions in Italy, but so too did socialist or communist movements. Religious affiliation is also significant in the Netherlands, whereas the 16 German unions are industry-based (Hollinshead and Leat, 1995: 99).

In the UK, the classification of unions normally refers to job territories, but is a complex process and often unsystematic, being constantly undermined by changes in skills and technology, with distinctions gradually becoming less relevant as occupational boundaries have blurred – for example, between blue-collar or manual work, and white-collar work. In general terms, however, they included the following categories:

- Craft unions, organising a particular trade or skill, e.g. Amalgamated Engineering and Electrical Union, Royal College of Nursing. Entry would be restricted, and homogeneous membership based on qualifications and training.
- Industrial and occupational unions, organising in a specific industry, e.g. National Union of Mineworkers, National Union of Railway, Maritime and Transport Workers. These would often cover numerous grades within an industry and have less restricted entry than the craft unions. Such forms of organisation developed partly in response to the realisation that the formation of one large union of working-class organisation would in all probability not be realised or sustainable.
- General unions, organising across numerous industries, such as the Transport and General Workers' Union. Their original source of membership was unskilled groups who were not organised elsewhere. No restricted entry would operate, subject to inter-union regulations on poaching of members.

While these classifications are useful to the extent that they denote the origins of the trade unions' formation and character, the characteristics have altered over time. The notion of solidarity with other groups of workers has historically brought trade unions together in alliances or federations; for example, the Triple Alliance of miners, railway and transport workers that was formed in 1914.

Furthermore, union structure was complicated by the emergence of white-collar and public sector unions after the First World War, and their rapid growth after the Second World War when the expansion of public services meant that trade unions such as the National and Local Government Officers' Association (NALGO) and the large civil service unions became increasingly important. In 2002, the largest British union is Unison which represents some 1.3 million members in the public sector, having overtaken the Transport and General Workers' Union. Privatisation of many public sector industries and the tendering of jobs such as school cleaning to private sector companies have affected the membership profile and numbers of the public sector unions.

H.A. Turner, during the 1960s, distinguished between 'open' and 'closed' unions rather than craft or general unions, and this serves as a useful reminder that shifts in union structure are not specific to recent years (McIlroy, 1995). Their degree of openness or closedness represented, to some extent, a deliberate strategy for recruitment and consolidating the powers of the membership. The open unions tended to be expansionist, aiming to increase the range of members and expand recruitment into new areas, whereas closed unions concentrated on the expansion of job controls, status and wages for groups of workers within demarcated areas of skill. McIlroy notes that the current trend is towards openness, while the category of closed unionism is in decline as unions adapt their chosen strategies periodically (McIlroy, 1995: 13). In relation to changes in occupational structure, trade union classifications have been reshaped owing to the disappearance of some unions and the creation of new ones, often through merger. The total number of trade unions has gradually declined, from 453 in 1979, to 206 by the year 2001, according to the Certification Officer's listings. Craft trade unions such as Slade and the NGA merged during the 1980s to form the Graphical, Paper and Media Union, and the engineers merged with the electricians in

Table 4.2 Membership of top ten unions in 2000/1

Top ten unions	Membership[a] (000s)
Unison	1,272
Amicus	1,132[b]
Transport and General Workers' Union	872
GMB	694
Royal College of Nursing of the UK	326
Union of Shop, Distributive and Allied Workers	310
National Union of Teachers	295
Communication Workers' Union	281
National Association of Schoolmasters / Union of Women Teachers	252
Graphical, Paper and Media Union	201

[a] Figures rounded to nearest 1,000
[b] Union formed in January 2002
Source: Annual Report of the Certification Officer (2001: 62); TUC Directory (2002: 33)

1992 to form the Amalgamated Engineering and Electrical Union. The pace of mergers accelerated from the 1980s in what McIlroy describes as merger mania, with 149 mergers taking place between 1980 and 1991. An outcome of this was the increase in the size of unions, although many do remain small, with some 63 per cent having fewer than 2,500 members.

Two forms of merger can be used legally. One is a transfer of engagement, normally involving an absorption of one organisation by another – for example, the transfer of the Scottish Health Visitors' Association to the existing public sector union Unison in 1996. The other involves amalgamation, which usually produces a new organisation. In the twelve months to March 2001, ten such mergers of trade unions took place. The merger of Manufacturing, Science and Finance (MSF) and the Amalgamated Engineering and Electrical Union (AEEU), to form Britain's second largest union, Amicus, has been completed. Table 4.2 shows Britain's major unions by the year 2000, and illustrates how white-collar and public sector unions are now in the top positions. The largest ten unions combined account for 72 per cent of all union membership (*Labour Market Trends*, September 2001).

Multi-unionism in Britain

The evolution of the British trade union movement has resulted in a complex structure in which unions often compete for members based around the same or similar job territories, and within the same industries and workplaces. This is in contrast to the German structure of union organisation along industry lines, or the Japanese 'in-house' single unions.

Although Britain has seen a decline in the number of unions, there is still a much larger number than exist in most other European countries. It is not simply a matter of a large number of unions at national level, however, many workplaces have a multi-union presence with different unions representing different grades of staff within the various bargaining units. Millward *et al.* (1992: 77) make the point that 'compared with most other European countries the number is enormous and the sheer complexity of negotiating arrangements in Britain is almost incomprehensible to Europeans'. In the public sector, multi-unionism is common; teachers in England and Wales, for example, have four trade unions representing classroom teachers and two for headteachers, although the majority of teachers are members of one of the three largest teacher unions. Union presence, however, is no guarantee of union recognition, and 8 per cent of workplaces with more than 25 employees were found to have a union presence but no recognition (Cully *et al.*, 1999: 92).

Table 4.3 illustrates that, in 1998, almost half of all workplaces had no trade union present. In the remainder, 30 per cent of establishments had two or more unions present, with around one-quarter of unionised establishments having four or more unions present.

Multi-unionism has often been seen as problematical by employers, although McIlroy notes that such criticisms are in essence managerialist (Hyman, cf. McIlroy, 1995: 20). Employers in a small number of new plants on greenfield sites have sought to reduce multi-unionism through the pursuit of 'single-union agreements' or failing that, 'single-table bargaining' whereby the trade unions are dealt with on one joint committee to negotiate one agreement. These arrangements have become more common; e.g. in over half the unionised workplaces in retail, wholesale, financial services and other community services, there was a single union agreement (Cully *et al.*, 1999: 94). From the trade union point of view, inter-union conflict can undermine bargaining tactics and solidarity, or encourage competition and divisions within an industry. In 1990, around one-quarter of workplace representatives who reported that there were groups with members in more than one union said there was some active inter-union competition, although this was not prevalent where multi-unionism was already established (Millward *et al.*, 1992: 85). It is common for the various trade unions to work together and coordinate their efforts and bargaining tactics where multi-unionism exists at national or local level. The structure of British trade unions and their forms of workplace organisation, which is ever changing and complex, has seen a reduction in smaller bodies, an increased blurring of the distinctiveness of occupational groupings, and occasional inter-union rivalries.

Table 4.3 **Percentage of workplaces[a] that recognise one or more trade unions**

No. of unions present	Percentage of all workplaces	Percentage of unionised workplaces
0	47	
1	23	43
2	10	19
3	8	15
4	4	8
5	5	9
6 or more	3	6

[a] All workplaces with 25 or more employees
Source: Cully *et al.* (1999: 91)

National and international trade union bodies

■ The Trades Union Congress

The Trades Union Congress (TUC), established in 1868, represents the political arm of the trade union movement, existing as a loose affiliation of member unions. It was formed to give trade unions a political voice and an organisation whereby unions could debate the affairs of the trade union movement as a whole. Its functions are administrative, providing a range of services such as shop steward training, and political, in terms of its pressure group activity. Mediation in inter-union disputes and involvement in strikes are occasional functions. The TUC has a near monopoly of representation, with high levels of union affiliation at over 80 per cent of trade unionists (McIlroy, 1995: 45). In terms of representation, the TUC elects the General Council of approximately 40 members to run its affairs and carry out policy between each annual congress. Membership is related to the size of the affiliated unions, the largest being entitled to six seats. There are special provisions or conferences for groups that have been traditionally under-represented within the trade union movement – for example, reserved seats for women on the General Council, an annual women's TUC conference as well as a black workers' conference. There is some geographical organisation. Scotland has its own TUC, as does Wales, and eight regional councils exist. At local area level, the 435 trades councils operate on the basis of affiliation by local union branches, to provide a focal point for unions within a particular area.

The main functions of the TUC are fourfold:

- As a regulator of trade unions in terms of inter-union conflicts. Traditionally this activity was governed by the Bridlington Agreement of 1939 whereby adjudication between unions was conducted.
- Service provision for affiliates, particularly in the areas of education and research but also financial and legal services.
- As the spokesperson of the trade union movement as a whole, particularly in representations with governments and in seeking to influence economic or employment policies.
- As a spokesperson for affiliates in the international arena, for example within the European Union or solidarity links with trade unionists in other countries.

From time to time attempts have been made to provide a stronger role for the TUC, for example, in the coordination of trade unions or in major disputes with employers. The TUC remains politically weak and fragmented, however, in comparison with its equivalent in the Republic of Ireland (the Irish Congress of Trade Unions) and with some continental European bodies. This is particularly so since the TUC's marginalisation by Conservative governments throughout the 1980s. While it did have a significant role at times during the 1970s, on various tripartite bodies such as those set up under the National Economic Development Office, the TUC was criticised for supporting pay restraint in return for 'walking the corridors of power'. In addition, difficulties for a more interventionist role by the TUC are presented by individual trade unions who still value autonomy, and few disciplinary measures can be imposed on a dissenter. The ultimate sanction of expulsion is rarely used, although the electricians' union, the EETPU, was expelled in 1988 over the poaching of union members during agreements with employers over single-union deals on greenfield sites. The weaknesses of the TUC were exposed after the 1979 general election when the Conservative government adopted a hostile stance towards trade unions. Criticisms of the TUC as ineffectual were furthered by its inability to resist anti-union laws introduced throughout the 1980s. More specific criticisms came over the lack of vigorous support for the miners during the strike over pit closures in 1984/5, and over the dockers' lock-out on Merseyside during the late 1990s.

In order to counter criticisms and to stem the tide of union decline, the TUC underwent a relaunch during 1994, when a series of task groups and internal reforms was designed to make the TUC more representative of labour as a whole (rather than just trade unionists) and which emphasised regeneration and establishing alliances with community-based or other campaign groups. In 1996 the theme 'New Unionism – Organising for Growth' was launched, which argued for successful organising and campaigning, and the task group agreed to the development of an Organisers' Academy based on the 'organising model' utilised in the US and Australia and which contrasts with the 'servicing' role associated with 'business unionism'. Part of its purpose was to develop arrangements for recruiting and training young organisers who reflect the gender and racial diversity among potential members, which unions hoped to attract. Its success is evaluated by Heery *et al.*, who note a number of problems in the Academy's operation, including non-participation by some large, significant unions, and other tensions between trainees and sponsors. On the other hand, trainees, targeting more than 600 employing organisations, directly recruited in excess of 7,500 new union members, and indirectly (through campaigning) a further 18,000 (Heery *et al.*, 2000: 410).

In the period up to and since the election of a Labour government in 1997, the TUC expressed a desire to develop a 'social partnership' arrangement with the government. John Monks, the general secretary, hoped to develop a 'social dialogue' with the Confederation of British Industry, on matters such as the influence of European Union rules, and he hoped that 'the problems of competitiveness' for Britain would be up for discussion (*Financial Times*, 22 May 1997). This approach confirmed the TUC's desire to be seen to distance itself from the associations of the 1970s, and the adversarial attitude long associated with British trade unionism. Its statement on the future direction for trade unionism in Britain, in the anticipation of an election victory for Labour, had the following as its preamble:

> Just as the nation needs a new Government committed to fairness, so we need a New Unionism so that unions and employers can work together in partnership to make Britain's industries and services more efficient and competitive and to protect people at work. The TUC does not simply look to government for action; it works with unions and employers for the common good. (TUC, 1997)

Just how far such a partnership approach at national level, along Irish or continental lines, could be adopted appears limited. It has not attracted enthusiasm from management, and some trade unions may also be lukewarm, bearing in mind the dominance of the voluntarist approach, the memory of corporatism in the 1970s, the subsequent deregulation of employee and trade union rights, the shift towards increasingly managerial prerogatives which has characterised the recent period, and the continued emphasis by employers and the Labour government on deregulation and flexible labour markets.

Prime Minister Tony Blair has continued to promote Britain's position as one of US-style 'unregulated capitalism' with lesser state intervention. In so far as TUC leaders have been consulted, this has been on an ad hoc basis rather than through the range of tripartite bodies the TUC had hoped for (McIlroy, 2000). McIlroy notes that of 70 advisory bodies and task forces set up by the Labour government on issues such as competition, European monetary policy and training, only 31 places were occupied by trade unionists, compared with more than 350 occupied by business people (McIlroy, 2000: 5). The setting up of the Low Pay Commission to make recommendations on the new minimum wage was the nearest the TUC came to a formal tripartite body.

With regard to other policies which weakened trade unions during the Conservatives' term in office, the TUC had pressed for a reform of legislation restricting industrial action and a strengthening of workers' rights by adherence to the Maastricht Treaty's Social Chapter provisions. The government did sign up to the Social Chapter, and EU directives on works councils, parental leave and working time were subsequently extended to cover British workers. However, these were introduced in such a way that minimal rights were extended to employees. For example, the TUC led a legal challenge to the government over the attempt to restrict entitlement to parental leave to parents of children born after December 1999 when the directive became law. John Monks has also sought to warn the government of the dangers of opposing consultative and information-sharing works councils into EU companies employing more than 50 workers (*Financial Times*, 29 October 1999). Domestically, while Labour did introduce new employment rights, including a procedure to pursue union recognition, extended 'family-friendly' and maternity rights, and the minimum wage, the programme remained one which 'restricts' and 'regulates' trade unions and industrial action, promoting 'cooperative' forms of trade unionism whereby unions are confined to the individual enterprise (Smith and Morton, 2001: 120–1). Critics suggest that such changes as have been introduced bestow very few rights upon employees or trade unions as collective entities and autonomous bodies. For example, Smith and Morton argue that the long-awaited statutory recognition procedure for union recognition is complex, and allows *employers* to have a major voice in the determination of bargaining units, while restricting collective bargaining to pay, hours and conditions rather than the wider scope of the 'wage–effort bargain' available in the earlier draft and in previous legislation (Smith and Morton, 2001: 125).

In addition, there has been growing concern about the impact on public sector employees (and the public) of privatisation. More serious protests emerged, following Labour's re-election in 2001, over proposals to increase the role of private sector provision into core public services, under the Private Finance Initiative (PFI). Among the largest unions, Unison, which represents public sector workers, decided to review its links with the Labour Party, and the GMB slashed its funding of the Labour Party by £1 million in protest.

■ International bodies

There are several federations of labour organised on an international basis, to which national union bodies normally affiliate. These appeared during the nineteenth century and had much the same rationale as nationally based confederations: that is, their functions included exchanging information, prevention of strike-breaking by employers, and other solidarity measures. Organisations of miners and printers affiliated to their own international bodies in the late 1880s and the first international working men's association was established under the auspices of Karl Marx (Gospel and Palmer, 1993: 152). Currently, the main international confederation for western countries is the International Confederation of Free Trade Unions (ICFTU), with membership in over 100 countries. It was formed in 1949 following a split from the World Federation of Trade Unions, which became dominated by the former communist bloc of the Soviet Union and east European countries, although its affiliates included European communist-led union confederations in Italy and France (Bridgford and Stirling, 1994: 91). Since the demise of the communist bloc, the ICFTU has been the predominant organisation at international level, although some smaller organisations also exist, such as the World Confederation of Labour (WCL) which has a religious base. The Commonwealth Trade Union Council aims to provide assistance to trade unions in 40 Commonwealth countries, covering some 25 million workers (McIlroy, 1995: 51). A recent development has been the formation of the Union Network International (UNI) which held its first congress in August 2001. Covering an estimated 15 million union members from 140 countries, the UNI, like the ICFTU argues the case for minimal labour standards and protection for workers in developing and developed countries alike, in the light of the effects of the global trading system. At the UNI launch, General Secretary Philippe Jennings made reference in his press release, to the recent protests against the G7 leaders:

> The lesson of Seattle and Genoa must be: more dialogue. People and not only multinationals, must perceive the advantages of globalisation, and this should be a key goal of the negotiators of the European Union. (Agence Europe, 22 August 2001)

The International Labour Organisation (ILO) was founded as a United Nations agency in 1919, formed because of a recognition by nation states that the fair treatment of labour was significant in terms of preventing social unrest. To this end, the prevention of gross exploitation of employees was a broad aim, but other objectives exist alongside this, as the ILO recognised that social reforms such as the elimination of child labour, would have a likely impact on production costs to employers (Hollinshead and Leat, 1995: 292). The ILO attempts to put its 'wish list' into practice through two instruments: conventions, which are legally binding, and recommendations, which nation states may ratify and adopt into their own domestic law. ILO standards exist in many areas related to the protection of workers – for example, equality of treatment and equal opportunity, freedom of workers to associate, conditions of work such as health and safety, and the protection of young workers.

At a European level, the European Trade Union Confederation (ETUC) was formed in 1972 and has 74 affiliated national union confederations representing some 60 million employees. Its functions include research and education but its main role is as one of the Social Partners at EU level, representing its affiliated membership in talks with the employer bodies UNICE and CEEP, and in relation to the social dialogue on various committees and other bodies. Its powers, however, do not extend to collective bargaining, and severe obstacles appear likely to prevent the prospect of transnational bargaining, not least employer opposition voiced by the Confederation of British Industry (CBI), and the tendency in Britain for the location of bargaining to be moving downwards rather than upwards (McIlroy, 1995: 340). Yet, the free mobility of capital and the influence of multinational companies, across the EU as well as worldwide, may make these developments appear more urgent to the trade union side.

Growing numbers of trade unions are taking a proactive stance in mobilising across global frontiers. Links between trade unions have been set up and maintained across national borders. For example, the AEEU has established links with the German metalworkers, and meetings and contacts are maintained by unions in similar industries across Europe. However, the prospect of transnational mergers seems some way off, in part due to the British unions' acceptance of inferior conditions in the competition for jobs (McIlroy, 1995: 341).

Trade union internal organisation and democracy

Internal organisation

Typically, British unions are formally organised geographically: the most basic unit is the branch, which may cover the membership in a particular town or district. Alternatively, the branch may operate at the workplace (or the chapel, as it is known in some industries such as print and journalism) and all members are generally entitled to attend and participate in branch business, usually electing a committee to administer the branch. The next tier of organisation is often a regional or divisional committee, attended by members or delegates who are elected by members of the branch. The key decision-making body of most trade unions at national level is the national executive committee (NEC), its responsibility for making policy decisions between annual or biennial conferences normally making it the supreme decision-making and policy-forming body of a trade union (Figure 4.1).

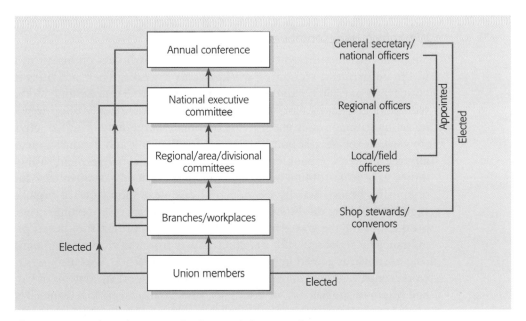

Figure 4.1 **Trade union organisation and democratic structure**

The NECs and principal officers must be elected by postal ballot of individual members, at least every five years, since legislation during the 1980s overrode the unions' own rules on electing their officers. Prior to this, officers could be elected at branch level, or by ballot at annual conference. The principal officers of the union, whose role is to execute policy and administer the affairs of the union, report to the NEC. Of the paid officials, the general secretary would normally be the most senior officer and, since the legal reforms of the 1980s, must be elected by postal ballot. Full-time officials are appointed and salaried, and have often started as lay activists or shop stewards. The full-time officers handle negotiations, grievances, disputes and advice on employment rights, and often deal with union recruitment as well. Specialist local officers may be employed from time to time, such as field officers with responsibility for recruitment drives, or for providing advice or services to membership in various geographical locations. Other salaried staff of a trade union may include legal staff, researchers, equality officers, press or publicity officers and education or training officers, and support staff such as clerks and administrators.

The ratio of full-time officers to members was traditionally low compared to that in continental unions, with one employed for every 3,800 members during the 1960s (McIlroy, 1995: 39) and since then fluctuating only in line with declining or rising membership levels.

It is evident that unions need considerable resources to run their affairs, and the larger unions have assets comparable with those of a small business, derived overwhelmingly from membership subscriptions. Unison had a total income in excess of £110 million for 1999 whereas that for the TGWU, the largest general union, was over £72 million (Certification Officer, 2001: 62). However, considerable expenditure is required to service the membership; despite mergers, which have accelerated in recent years in part for financial reasons, and economies made in personnel and administration during the 1990s, 'overall unions are poorer in the 1990s than they were in the 1950s' (McIlroy, 1995: 45).

Workplace representatives

Shop stewards are the workplace representatives who act on behalf of their members in the department, section or workplace as a whole. Their activities include negotiations over pay and conditions, resolving disputes and representing individual members who have grievances with management. Joint committees of shop stewards can be set up on multi-union sites in order to coordinate bargaining or other activities. The shop steward, as the nearest point of contact for the rank and file union members, is normally the first to communicate on their behalf with management, although stewards' duties vary from routine administration and collection of members' subscriptions, to organising branch activity or industrial disputes. Shop steward organisation became significant during the First World War; the priority of government was to maximise production for the war effort, and this involved curbing the spread of shop steward militancy by seeking to shift bargaining away from the workplace to national level. The role of stewards gained impetus after the Second World War also, when stewards and workgroups were able to build on the fragmented 'informal' systems of bargaining, which had begun to supplement, or even undermine, national arrangements. The development of domestic bargaining, conducted between stewards and local management, was largely fragmented and informal, and based on 'custom and practice', enabling stewards to take advantage of local bonus or piecework schemes in order to improve conditions for their membership. Such bargaining was often outside the control not only of full-time union officers, but even of senior management, leading the Royal Commission on Trade Unions and Employers' Associations of 1968 (the Donovan Commission) to conclude that two systems of industrial relations were in operation in Britain, and to recommend that more official and orderly collective bargaining should be instigated to make industry more competitive.

Despite this picture of shop stewards during the post-war period, as an active and relatively autonomous group with the ability to undermine national, multi-employer agreements, this form of domestic bargaining was rare outside certain sectors of manufacturing, engineering and construction. In the public sector and among much of white-collar work, for example, it was virtually non-existent (McIlroy, 1995: 99). Even within those sectors where it was prevalent, the image of shop stewards as militants and troublemakers gained currency in the media and elsewhere, while on the left they were often viewed romantically as standard-bearers of working-class emancipation. Yet their normally mundane duties of collecting members' subscriptions and dealing with day-to-day welfare issues as well as individual and collective grievances, meant that their role served a useful function for management, not least as a channel for their members' discontent (McIlroy, 1995: 103). The Donovan Commission portrayed them as 'lubricants' rather than as 'irritants' and they were to play a key role in the formalisation of agreements in the post-Donovan era of reform. During the 'social contract' period of the 1970s when pay restraint was the *quid pro quo* for an increase in employment rights, the rights extended to shop stewards included office facilities and time off for training. Such facilities have led to accusations of bureaucratisation among shop stewards, undermining their independence and their main function of organising the rank and file members, and of distancing stewards from their members while concentrating on procedures and paper-chasing. Supporters note, however, that significant levels of bureaucracy existed prior to the 1970s, and that shop stewards' activities, including the degree of conflict and accommodation with management, were always variable by industry (McIlroy, 1995). Shop stewards came under considerable pressure during the 1980s owing to a combination of unemployment and periods of recession, declining union membership, hostile legislation, and management pressure for efficiency drives, changed working practices and more individualistic ways of communicating with employees (Terry, 1995). Numerically, workplace representatives have a significant presence, however, union representatives exist in approximately three-quarters of unionised workplaces, although some non-union employee representatives are also found in unionised and non-unionised workplaces alike, having a presence in 12 per cent of all workplaces (Cully *et al.*, 1999: 95). The various EU directives which take effect at company level (such as works councils) allow for non-union representation on these bodies and, as such, denote a further challenge to the view that trade unions are the most appropriate channel for promoting workers' interests. However, the 'representation gap' is at its most stark in non-unionised workplaces, as almost 90 per cent of these have no worker representative at all, particularly in the smallest businesses (Cully *et al.*, 1999). Even where there is union recognition, shop stewards have often been bypassed or marginalised. Indeed, the WERS98 study found that in half of unionised workplaces, no negotiations with union representatives are conducted over pay or non-pay issues; consultation or information-sharing was the option most often chosen by management (Cully *et al.*, 1999: 103). Yet, in many industries and workplaces, shop stewards do have potential and continuing significance as a focus for collective mobilisation of employees (Darlington, 1994).

Problems of 'democratising' trade unions

The image often portrayed of shop stewards as distanced from both full-time officials and indeed the 'moderate' rank and file members, no matter how simplistic has nevertheless been influential in debates on the issue of trade unions' internal organisation and democratic structures. Such debates have by no means been reducible to a left–right ideological split. The original meaning of democracy as rule by the people was realised within the earliest trade unions, which exercised 'primitive democracy' (Clegg, 1972: 95). Indeed, some trade union leaders, among others, believed themselves to be best placed to run the affairs of the union owing to their own expertise, with the ordinary member 'supplementing this work' (Allen, 1957, quoted by McIlroy, 1995: 150). The difficulty of identifying union objectives and functions has been discussed, and it is in part the recognition of trade unions as a campaigning force that has generated controversy over the need for their internal democracy. Yet they are in essence voluntary organisations, such bodies normally enjoying relative freedom from state interference. The TUC has pointed out that unions are 'more democratic than the city, the civil service or the media' (McIlroy, 1995: 145). The expectation is often that trade unions should be democratic because they were created by and for the 'grassroots' membership, albeit with all the associated difficulties of agreement on the nature and function of unions. However, even if the problem of identifying the various goals, both short-term and long-term, is less pressing, there remains the problem of acting upon them, or identifying the mechanisms for realising these goals. Roberto Michels, concerned with the 'problem' of bureaucracy, developed his thesis of the 'iron law of oligarchy' which argued that in any complex organisation, regardless of the so-called democratic machinery or rhetoric, working class organisations would always be subject to domination by the leadership (Crouch, 1982: 161). This was by virtue of its reliance on leaders who have a specialist role and expertise. It is inevitable that control passes to a small elite or oligarchy, who become distanced from the ordinary members by virtue of a more privileged lifestyle. Crouch finds it surprising that Michels could develop a general theory of labour movement democracy based on the experience of the German labour movement prior to the First World War, which existed under an authoritarian regime (Crouch, 1982: 164). Other writers contest the assumption of the iron law as applicable to trade unions since countervailing pressures exist that contest the oligarchic tendency, such as the shop stewards' movement, and members' expectations of democracy (McIlroy, 1995: 156).

Nevertheless, many union members and leaders are aware of the *potential* for oligarchic tendencies that may arise, and they aim to counter them by adopting structures and procedures that militate against them and facilitate control from the bottom up. Debate on union democracy is linked to the relationship between three agencies: the national or regional union leadership who are paid their salaries from union funds and thus indirectly through the membership; the lay activists, delegates or shop stewards, who play an important role in union affairs but in an unpaid capacity; and the so-called ordinary members who pay subscriptions but otherwise have a minimal role in union affairs. Issues of control, participation by membership, and accountability of those in elected or influential positions within trade unions are central to the debate, with claims made by both right- and left-wing commentators that it is union leaders who are out of touch with their members, and who need to be made more accountable to the wider membership. Ambiguities do arise in the different levels of a trade union from what Hyman refers to as the 'two way system of control' by which disciplinary action can be exercised over a member by a union official, who in turn is employed by the membership (Hyman, 1975: 73). This results in a sometimes contradictory relationship in which union officials are subject to very real pressures to exercise control over their members, e.g. during a dispute. Yet they are paid for by the members whom they serve.

How trade unions are judged in terms of democratic credentials depends on which definition or perspective is adopted. Two main models of union democracy are prevalent, and these illustrate how politicians and union leaders have approached the issue. Fairbrother (1983) describes these as the participatory and parliamentary models. The former emphasises membership participation in decision-making. Interaction between the various layers of union government is considered essential, via a process of dialogue, debate, discussion and constant examination of policies and decisions. Maximum participation of the membership is important for control of the leadership, emphasising the latter's accountability to those they serve, and collective interests rather than individual preferences are given priority. By contrast, the parliamentary model focuses on the rights of individual members to elect representatives who will act on their behalf without necessarily consulting them. Participation is periodic, and the views of the membership are made known to the leadership on an individual basis, often through ballot papers. As with a Member of Parliament, discretion in the activities of the union leader is exercised, and structures and voting procedures are established to ensure periodic accountability.

It is crucial that the values and assumptions that are implied in these two models of union democracy are considered. The parliamentary model is favoured by some union leaders and/or members and was also favoured by the Conservative governments of the 1980s. For example, the introduction of individual secret ballots prior to industrial action and for the election of union leaders was central to the Trade Union Act 1984. Such a procedure dispenses with the need for dialogue and continuous involvement by an active membership, but simply voting on a one-off basis is the sum total of membership participation. Critics of this approach argue that the legislation fails to recognise trade unions as cooperative organisations that exist to advance the collective interests of the whole membership; rather, a trade union becomes a collection of aggregate individuals. Collective organisations are formed in order to increase the power of individual employees. Therefore, the adherence to common decisions involving, if necessary, the subordination of individual self-interest is a prerequisite for union effectiveness (Hyman, 1975). Voting at home, in the absence of debate and discussion, is said therefore to make a mockery of union democracy, especially since the influence of the media over how individuals vote can be brought to bear without the counterbalancing influence of union meetings.

Historically, various constraints have been in operation with regard to the activities of union officials. The diversity of the trade unions and the particular characteristics of the membership will influence the propensity of the members to form factions or to participate in union decision-making. For example, occupational homogeneity, where a workforce is concentrated within one industry, tends to facilitate high participation and opposition, since it is not felt that such actions threaten the cohesion of the union.

In Lipset's study of union democracy in 1956, the parliamentary model utilised by the International Typographical Union involved rival groups competing for office via elections. Opposition by factions or parties need not be recognised officially, and these are often not necessarily seeking power so much as ensuring the demands of the grass-roots membership are addressed. A more diverse union membership, covering a wide range of industries, by contrast, such as that of the TGWU, may be characterised by 'popular bossdom', since the emphasis is more often on sectionalism, with the necessity for a strong leader who can hold the union together. In the absence of well-organised opposition, other countervailing tendencies can be seen in unions such as the National Union of Mineworkers and the GMB, whereby decentralised regions or districts have relatively autonomous decision-making powers.

Legislation and reform of union democracy

The Conservative governments of the 1980s introduced legislation to regulate the internal affairs of the trade unions, such as their decision-making mechanisms for elections and for taking industrial action (Table 4.4). Such activities had traditionally been left to the unions themselves, through their own rulebooks and procedures, although, periodically, state intervention in this area would be attempted. The programme of legislation introduced throughout the 1980s and continuing into the 1990s was based on the assumption that unions were run by militant leaders who often manipulated their members into taking strike action against their will, and that legislation which forced unions to ballot individual members for the election of such officers would enable the views of the 'moderate majority' to surface.

Table 4.4 **Legislation on union democracy and internal organisation**

Act	Provisions
Employment Acts 1980 and 1982	Provision of funds for secret ballots
Trade Union Act 1984, amended by Trade Union and Labour Relations (Consolidation) Act 1992	Ballots for election of union officers Ballots for set-up/retention of political funds Ballots prior to industrial action
Employment Acts 1988, 1990 and 1993	Rights for individual 'strike breakers' not to be disciplined by trade union More complex ballot procedures, e.g. independent scrutineers to be appointed Individual member to confirm, every three years, continuation of 'check off' scheme for deduction of union subscriptions by employer
Employment Rights Act 1999	Requirement for triennial renewal of 'check off' scheme abolished; powers of Certification Officer extended to allow members to complain of breaches of administrative or union government functions Changes to law of unfair dismissal for strikers engaged in lawfully organised industrial action

The Trade Union Act 1984, for example, required trade unions to hold secret ballots prior to taking official industrial action; only those directly involved were to be balloted, and a majority had to specify that they wished to take the action. Cautionary wording on the ballot paper should warn the voter, it was specified, that he or she may be in breach of contract by taking industrial action. Further ballots were introduced for the election, at least every five years, of union officers who were to serve on the main executive body of the trade union, and in 1988 this was extended to include all national executive members whether or not they were entitled to vote.

The 1984 Act also required that trade unions hold secret ballots at least every ten years if they wished to set up or retain a 'political fund' which allows the union to spend money on 'political objects', which were also redefined by the Act. The Labour Party receives most of its funding through this source, although the fund can be used for activities such as political campaigns. Several unions, such as NALGO and the CPSA, held such ballots and set up political funds for the first time during the 1980s. All other unions have repeatedly achieved substantial votes in favour of retaining such funds.

Apart from the procedure allowing trade unions to pursue recognition, the Employment Rights Act 1999 left the existing legislation on unions' internal conduct and organisation largely intact. New quasi-judicial powers were granted to the Certification Officer over union members' complaints, however, with respect to their trade union's administrative or governing procedures (Smith and Morton, 2001: 132). With regard to ballots for union elections and industrial action, the trade unions are still bound by that progamme of legislation passed by the Conservative government. The legislation produced real and potential problems for the trade union movement, including, arguably, inability to discipline its own members for breaches of rules such as strike-breaking, but, as with the example of political funds, also presented challenges that were overcome and even used to their advantage.

Strike ballots and negotiations

Assumptions that the views of a silent majority would produce 'moderation' have not been borne out by the experience of union ballots, since the majority of such ballots have produced votes in favour of taking industrial action. ACAS reported that 3,704 separate ballot exercises were conducted by the two independent balloting organisations during 1995, of which 76 per cent were in favour of industrial action (ACAS, 1995: 39). Postal ballots are notorious for producing low turnouts, whereas the highest turnouts generally are those ballots held at the workplace, but these no longer afford trade unions immunity under the law.

Ballots, however, came to be considered part and parcel of negotiations, and often a high number of votes in favour of industrial action brought the employers to the negotiation table. Severe problems occurred, however, with regard to legal manoeuvres over ballots, some of which relate to the burdensome administrative requirements placed upon trade unions. For example, the Civil and Public Servants Association (CPSA) sent ballots to workplace addresses, when the members concerned had not given written authority for their addresses to be used. The Certification Officer, on receiving a complaint, ruled that the legislation had been breached (Certification Officer, 1996: 32). Employers have used the laws on strike ballots to delay or prevent industrial action primarily through the use of injunctions, but in some instances legal constraints were highly significant politically. When the Conservative government, as part of a commitment to the removal of obstacles to the workings of the free market, proposed abolition of the National Dock Labour Scheme in the late 1980s, the legal constraints imposed by the courts prevented the TGWU from calling for a strike in time to save the scheme. The scheme had been introduced in the 1940s in response to the problems of degradation and casualisation in dockland areas (Blyton and Turnbull, 1994: 132).

It is evident that the government and judicial interventions into the internal affairs of unions were problematical in various ways, but, in general, unions have learned to live with the legal provisions, and in some instances use them to their advantage. Whether or not the outcome has been 'to return the unions to their members' is debatable.

■ Union democracy – widening participation and representation

Many trade unions are aware that in terms of participation and representation, there are some areas where they are less than ideal. In particular, women and ethnic minorities have been under-represented in the executive and senior committees of trade unions and among full-time officers. Women were barred from joining the early craft unions (Cockburn, 1991) in Britain and in other countries, and, facing this exclusion, women workers set up their own forms of organisation. Upon acceptance to the movement, women's membership grew significantly in the post-war period, but still their numbers are not reflected in the trade union hierarchy. Although women constituted one-third of trade union members, there were just four female general secretaries of trade unions in 1994, and women were represented on national executive committees in proportion to their numbers in membership in just one-third of trade unions (Ledwith and Colgan, 1996: 152).

Table 4.5 shows the proportions of women in various union posts in comparison to their membership in the largest ten TUC-affiliated unions. Explanations for this under-representation are cited by Colgan and Ledwith (in Ledwith and Colgan, 1996: 155)

Table 4.5 Women in trade unions – the largest TUC affiliates, 1994

	Unison	TGWU	AEEU	GMB	MSF	USDAW	GPMU	UCW	NUT	UCATT
Total membership	1,400,000	958,834	546,000	800,000	552,000	316,491	250,230	180,586	162,192	157,000
Women (%)	68	18	9	37	27	60	17	20	74	2
On NEC (%)	42[a]	5	0	36	24	61	5	20	27	0
At Conference (%)	46[b]	10	8	25	25	42	11	Not known	48	1
TUC delegates (1993) (%)	54	20	6	33	33	12	5	20	35	1
National officers (%)	20	9	11	13	18	19	5	17[c]	16	0
Regional officers (%)	31	7	0	0	12[c]	21[c]	2[b,d]	0[c]	11	0[c]

[a] 1993 figures; the executive elections in 1995 achieved proportionality for women
[b] 1995 figures
[c] 1993 figures
[d] Branches covering geographical areas are roughly the equivalent of regions
Sources: 'Still a long road to equality', Labour Research, Vol. 83(3): 5–7 (1994); SERTUC Women's Rights Committee (1994); Ledwith and Colgan (1996).

as related to women's inequality at work generally, patriarchal attitudes, union rules on office-holding, inconvenient times and locations of union meetings, unequal sharing of domestic responsibilities and lack of child-care provision. It is not just women's lack of representation in the union hierarchy that is recognised by many unions to be problematical, but also that issues of concern to women are largely absent from the bargaining agenda; indeed the priorities of traditional collective bargaining themselves perpetuate women's disadvantage in paid employment (Dickens and Colling, 1990). Women dominate part-time work and are over-represented in smaller workplaces or in jobs with low pay and status which are hard to organise, but trade unions have until recently often neglected to address the specific issues affecting women at the workplace.

Union membership and density figures also show that ethnic minorities are just as likely to join trade unions as whites, despite sometimes racist tendencies within the trade union movement itself, which historically were always challenged by anti-racist campaigners within and outside the movement (Phizacklea and Miles, 1993). In 1991, the election of the first black trade union leader in Britain, Bill Morris of the TGWU, marked a turning point, and the TUC General Council has three seats reserved for black trade unionists (McIlroy, 1995: 179). The TUC recently launched a high-profile campaign against 'institutionalised racism' in the workplace by setting up the Stephen Lawrence Task Group and has regular 'Root Out Racism' newsletters and conferences. At Ford's Dagenham plant during 1999, some 1,300 workers engaged in strike action in protests at alleged racism at the plant. Union leaders approached the president of the company in Detroit over the incidents, which included racial harassment and intimidation by supervisors, for which the company admitted liability in spite of its earlier claims of zero tolerance towards racism (Kirton and Greene, 2000: 161).

As well as addressing workplace issues which may affect black or women workers, individual trade unions have also undertaken a range of measures, again, with the aim of democratising their own organisations. Strategies have had the aims not only of countering racism, sexism, heterosexism and discrimination against people with disabilities, but also of encouraging wider participation in union power structures. Policies since the 1980s include the appointment of equality officers, electoral reform and other organisational changes, facilities for disabled members, and specialist black members' and women members' conferences. Unison was launched specifically with a constitution based on proportional representation within the union's structures, applicable for all groups who had traditionally been under-represented, namely women, black members, disabled members, lesbians and gay men (Colgan and Ledwith, 1996: 169). The bargaining agenda, traditionally biased towards the male, full-time worker, has shifted increasingly towards the 'mainstreaming' of equality, or to 'equality bargaining', i.e. 'the collective negotiation of provisions that are of particular interest or benefit to disadvantaged groups and/or likely to facilitate equality at work' (Kirton and Green, 2000: 162). Findings from a range of studies (e.g. Millward et al., 1992; Colling and Dickens, 1998, cited in Kirton and Green, 2000) note that unions are instrumental in supporting individual cases of discrimination and equal pay for work of equal value claims, and that employees in unionised environments are more likely to be covered by formal job evaluation schemes which tend to reduce bias in pay gradings (Kirton and Greene, 2000: 164). The trade unions have been among the key actors in influencing the equality agenda, but are aware that their ability to continue as influential agents of change in this regard depends upon the successful achievement of membership growth overall. This is particularly the case in sectors that have been traditionally hard to organise, such as parts of the service sector and among other groups of workers whose interests were often neglected.

Trade union membership and density

There are major difficulties in collecting and compiling accurate information on trade union membership. The two main sources for measuring trade union membership in Britain come from the Labour Force Survey (LFS), which collects information from individuals, and the Certification Officer for Trade Unions and Employers' Associations. Each of these has different methods for compiling data, and consequently some inconsistencies can appear in published sources. According to *Labour Market Trends*, which compiles statistics from both these sources, by autumn 2000, trade unions in the UK had a combined membership of 7.3 million members.

Until 1999, trade union membership had continually declined since its peak of 13.3 million in 1979. The recent decline in membership averaged approximately 3 per cent per annum from the late 1980s, stabilising towards the late 1990s (*Labour Market Trends*, February 1997 and September 2001). Table 4.6 demonstrates the decline in union membership of 1.5 million over a ten-year period. However, the recent changes represent an increase of 169,000 members since 1998 (*Labour Market Trends*, September 2001: 433).

Union membership figures overall relate to total numbers who are members, but a more useful figure, that of union 'density', is often used alongside the aggregate figures. Density refers to the percentage of members out of the potential of trade union membership, either of the labour force in total, which includes the unemployed, or of those in employment. Current figures demonstrate that union density for all employees

Table 4.6 **Trade unions: numbers and membership, 1990–2000**

Year	Total membership, end of year (000s)	Percentage change in membership since previous year	Union density for employees (%)
1990	8,835		38.1
1991	8,602	−2.6	37.5
1992	7,956	−7.5	35.8
1993	7,767	−2.4	35.1
1994	7,530	−3.0	33.6
1995	7,309	−2.9	32.1
1996	7,244	−0.9	31.2
1997	7,154	−1.2	30.2
1998	7,152	0.0	29.6
1999	7,257	1.5	29.5
2000	7,321	0.9	29.4
Change since 1990	−1,514		−8.7

Excludes members of the armed forces, unpaid family workers and those on college-based schemes. Density figures for employees only (e.g. excludes self-employed)
Source: LFS data cited in *Labour Market Trends*, September 2001

was 38 per cent in 1990, compared with the peak figure for union density of 55 per cent in 1979 and declining to just over 29 per cent by the year 2000. However, these general figures disguise significant variations according to a range of factors and characteristics of the workplace and workforce. Union density varies significantly by industry, for example, public sector workplaces exhibit higher union density than do those in the private sector. There are also regional variations, with employees in the north of England being more likely to be union members than those in the south. Variations in density are also shown in terms of characteristics of individuals, such as gender, ethnic origin, marital status, and qualifications and status. Among males, union density is almost 30 per cent, compared with 44 per cent in 1989, and among females density is just under 29 per cent, declining from 36 per cent in the same period. This is despite growing female employment during the 1990s. However, women's union membership has not stood still, but has grown significantly among white-collar professional workers, especially public sector unions such as teachers' and nurses' unions. Job-related characteristics, such as whether full-time or part-time, and the size of the workplace, will also show differences in the union density of employees. Table 4.7 shows union density according to the personal characteristics of employees, namely age, ethnic group and qualifications.

Table 4.7 Union density by individual characteristics, 2000[a]

	All (%)	Men (%)	Women (%)
All employees	29	30	29
Age group			
Under 20 years	6	7	4
20–29 years	19	19	20
30–39 years	31	31	31
40–49 years	38	39	37
50 years and over	35	36	33
Ethnic origin			
White	30	30	29
Non-white	25	23	27
Of which			
Black	29	25	33
Indian	25	26	25
Pakistani/Bangladeshi	16	16	–[b]
Other	23	21	25
Highest qualification			
Degree or equivalent	37	30	46
Other higher education	43	32	52
A-level or equivalent	28	32	21
GCSE or equivalent	24	37	22
Other	26	30	22
No qualifications	24	28	21

[a] Includes all employees except those in the armed forces
[b] Base too low to provide reliable estimate
Source: LFS data cited in *Labour Market Trends*, September 2001

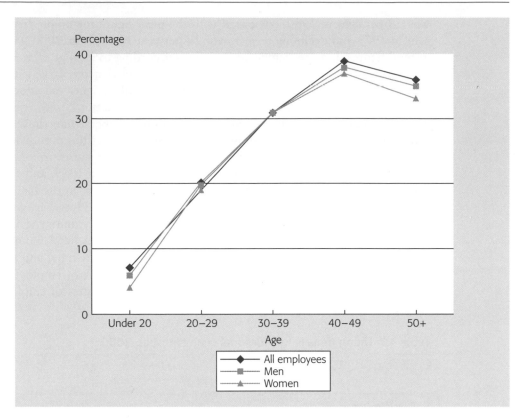

Figure 4.2 **Union density: percentage of each age group, Britain 2000**

Union members are more likely to be in their forties than in their teens, and union density among young people is particularly low, at 6 per cent. Figures 4.2 and 4.3 also illustrate the age profile and the ethnic origin of trade union members. Ethnic minority groups are almost as likely as white employees to belong to trade unions, although there is variation among ethnic groups. Blacks and whites are equally likely to belong to a trade union, with density of 29 per cent for blacks compared with 30 per cent for all whites, although the density figure for black women is higher still at 33 per cent. The converse applies for women of Pakistani or Bangladeshi origin, who are less likely to belong to a trade union than any other ethnic group.

These variations reflect the employment patterns of the different groups, with some groups more likely to work in unionised environments such as the public sector than in small enterprises which are non-unionised, or in self-employment. During the mid-1990s, 51 per cent of employed black women worked in the public sector compared with 31 per cent of employed white women; while 19 per cent of employed Asian women were self-employed compared with 7 per cent of all employed women (Sly, 1995: 251). Such differing labour market experience does feed through to union density figures.

With respect to the qualifications of employees, it can be seen that those with degrees or other higher education qualifications are more likely than any other group to be union members (see Table 4.7). Also notable is that women with higher education qualifications were far more likely to have higher density than men, and the converse for those women whose highest qualifications were A-level or lower.

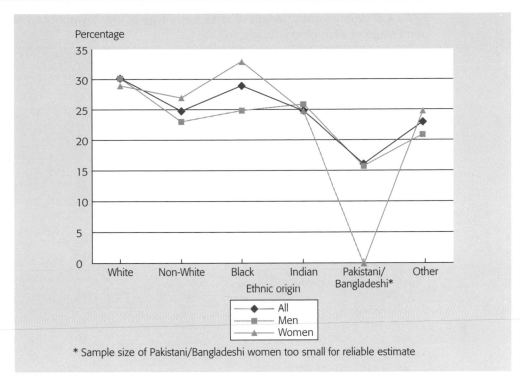

Figure 4.3 **Union density: percentage of each ethnic group, Britain, 2000**

Tables 4.8 and 4.9 illustrate how employment status, type of contract and type of occupational group tend to produce significant variations in union density of employees. For example, part-time workers are less likely to be union members; the predominant pattern of work for women is of part-time employment, and they are more likely than men to work in establishments that have a lower propensity to be unionised, such as small workplaces and private service. It can also be seen that those with supervisory duties have higher density than both those with no managerial duties and those with managerial status.

The density of unionisation in the public sector is three times higher than that in the private sector, as illustrated in Table 4.10. When compared by industry, however, the difference is even more stark. Union density is almost three-quarters of employees in public sector construction compared with just 14 per cent in private sector construction. Taking the broad industry classifications, union density is highest in public administration (59 per cent), education (54 per cent), electricity, gas and water supply at 53 per cent, and lowest in hotels and restaurants with just 5 per cent density, agriculture, forestry and fishing, and wholesale and retail each with 11 per cent density, and real estate and business services with 10 per cent (*Labour Market Trends*, September 2001: 440).

Regional variations reveal that the highest union density is in Wales and north east England, each with 40 per cent of employees in membership, followed by the north west of England, Scotland and Yorkshire and the Humber. The lowest density by region is in the east of England, and the south east with 22 per cent and 23 per cent density, respectively, excluding London which has a density of 25 per cent. Table 4.10

Table 4.8 Union density: length of service and type of employment contract: percentage of each group, Britain, 2000[a]

	All (%)	Full-time (%)	Part-time (%)
All employees	29	32	21
Length of service			
Less than 1 year	12	13	8
1–2 years	18	20	13
2–5 years	22	23	17
5–10 years	33	34	28
10–20 years	45	47	41
20 years or more	60	62	49
Employment status			
Permanent	30	33	22
Temporary	19	20	18
Special working arrangements			
Flexitime	40	44	25
Job sharing	37	–[b]	37
Term-time working	47	74	27
Annualised hours contract	46	49	36
9 day fortnight/4.5 day week	44	45	–[b]
Work mainly in own home	7	–[b]	–[b]
Zero hours contract	16	20	–[b]

[a] Includes all employees except those in the armed forces
[b] Base too low to provide reliable estimate
Source: LFS data cited in *Labour Market Trends*, September 2001

Table 4.9 Union density by occupational group and managerial status of employee: percentage of each group, Britain, 2000

	All (%)	Full-time (%)	Part-time (%)
All employees	29	32	21
Occupational group (SOC90)			
Managers and administrators	19	20	16
Professional	50	51	48
Associate professional/technical	43	40	54
Clerical and secretarial	24	27	20
Craft and related	31	32	–[a]
Personal and protective	28	37	17
Sales	11	11	11
Plant and machine operatives	37	39	18
Other occupations	26	36	17
Managerial status			
Manager	25	26	23
Foreman or supervisor	38	38	36
No managerial duties	29	34	20

[a] Sample size too small for reliable estimate
Source: *Labour Market Trends*, September 2001

Table 4.10 Union density by industry, region and size of workplace, Britain 2000a

	All (%)	Private (%)	Public (%)
All employees	29	19	60
Industry			
Agriculture, forestry and fishing	11	9	_b
Mining and quarrying	33	32	_b
Manufacturing	27	27	58
Electricity, gas and water supply	53	52	_b
Construction	20	14	71
Wholesale and retail trade	11	11	_b
Hotels and restaurants	5	4	40
Transport and communication	42	36	75
Financial intermediation	30	30	_b
Real estate and business services	10	8	51
Public administration	59	24	61
Education	56	26	58
Health	46	17	64
Other activities	23	11	48
Region or country			
England	28	18	59
North east	40	27	70
North west	36	24	65
Yorkshire and Humber	32	20	64
East Midlands	30	20	65
West Midlands	30	21	62
East	22	14	51
London	25	15	56
South east	23	14	50
South west	26	17	54
Wales	40	25	69
Scotland	35	22	65
Workplace size			
Fewer than 25 employees	16	9	51
25 employees or more	36	25	62

[a] Includes all employees, except those in the armed forces
[b] Base too low to provide a reliable estimate
Source: LFS data cited in *Labour Market Trends*, September 2001

also demonstrates that the smaller the workplace, the less likely employees are to be unionised. Among workplaces employing fewer than 25 people, union density is just 16 per cent compared with 36 per cent in those employing more than 25 people. Among smaller workplaces in the public sector, however, density rises to 51 per cent although density is 62 per cent among public sector workplaces employing more than 25 people.

In spite of lower levels of union density than in previous decades, almost half of employees work where there are trade union members at their workplace, and more than one-third of employees have their pay affected by collective agreements. Collective bargaining coverage, however, fell from 70 per cent of employees in 1984 to 54 per cent by 1990, and covered just 41 per cent of employees by 1998 (Cully *et al.*, 1999: 242).

Decline in union membership and density throughout the 1980s and 1990s

Union membership peaked in 1979 with over 13 million members and 55 per cent density, having expanded during the 1960s and 1970s especially with the growth in the public sector and white-collar work. After 1979 this was reversed as union membership declined by 4 million members between 1979 and 1992, although decline was more rapid between 1980 and 1983 (Waddington, 1992: 301). By 1995, approximately 32 per cent of all UK workers were members of trade unions. Density had declined by 20 per cent over the previous seven years, but the rate of decline then slowed from 3 per cent per annum from 1989 to 1 per cent in 1995. Figure 4.4 illustrates recent trends in union membership which continued to decline by 1.5 million, falling in the period 1990 to 2000 by 17 per cent. However, the first two years of the new century saw a recovery for trade union membership, as in two successive years membership increased, reaching 7.9 million by March 2001.

There are several explanations for union membership variation, which is certainly not a recent phenomenon. Rapid growth of union members occurred from the period preceding the First World War until the early 1920s, rising to 8 million, fuelled by wartime production and the large intake of union members among unskilled groups of workers. Decline in membership to 4 million occurred in the 1930s at a time of depression, with numbers being regained, and stabilising at around 9.5 million until the late 1960s. The post-war boom and expansion of the public sector saw a period of exceptional growth in union membership and density until their peak in 1979. It was in the period from the late 1970s until the late 1990s however, that the losses to trade unions were substantial. Explanations have been prolific, but a particular concern is whether this decline is reversible. Most accounts have hinged on such factors

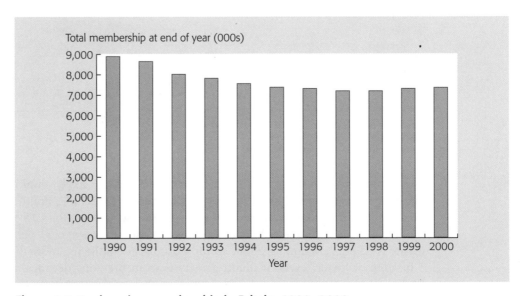

Figure 4.4 **Trade union membership in Britain, 1990–2000**
Source: LFS data cited in *Labour Market Trends*, September 2001

as changing workforce composition, labour laws and other state policies, economic variables affecting levels of inflation, wages and unemployment, and employer and union behaviour.

■ Business cycle

Bain and Elsheikh (1976) produced a model of union growth and decline which suggests a positive effect of rising inflation on union membership levels since workers have an incentive to join in order to protect their standard of living. If rising wages are associated with union membership then this will produce a positive effect on the union. By contrast, a rise in unemployment will threaten union membership overall, since unemployed people have little incentive to remain in membership, and in addition, unions' bargaining power is decreased since management is in a better position to resist their claims. The relatively low inflation of the 1980s and high unemployment may thus have acted as a disincentive to workers to pursue unionisation. The periods of incomes policy of the 1970s, during which time white-collar workers' differentials with manual workers were squeezed, gave the former an incentive to unionise to maintain their living standards. In the 1980s, however, their earnings rose relative to those of manual workers, thus impacting on union recruitment (Waddington, 1992). While 'business cycle' explanations appear credible, such models tend to over-predict levels of unionisation (Waddington and Whitston, 1995: 170).

■ Compositional changes in employment

A massive rise in unemployment, to over 3 million within the Conservative government's first eighteen months of office in the early 1980s, was significant in reducing the highly unionised sectors in the north of England and Scotland, and among male manual workers, who were traditionally heavily unionised. However, the shift in the composition of the workforce, particularly marked from the late 1970s, including changes in gender composition, has had a negative impact on union membership. Employment contracted in those areas where union members were most concentrated, and expanded in areas where they were relatively sparse. The decline in manufacturing employment and rise of service sector employment led to the removal of whole sections of highly unionised workforces employing predominantly males. As discussed above, density among women is traditionally lower than among men, itself a reflection of women's employment in services which unions find difficult to organise, and in part-time enclaves. Where manufacturing plants did open up, new establishments were less likely to be unionised, as were smaller establishments, which also became more numerous (Millward et al., 1992).

Yet there are several reasons for not relying on compositional effects as the main explanatory cause of union decline. The composition of the workforce also underwent significant changes during the 1970s, most of which were disinclined to conditions for union growth, such as a reduction in the manufacturing sector (Waddington and Whitston, 1995: 171). In addition, there is a problem for analysis of disentangling some compositional effects, such as the increase in private services and the increase in female and part-time employment (Waddington and Whitston, 1995: 171).

Legal reforms and state policy

Legal reforms under the Conservatives made it more difficult for unions to organise, to take industrial action or solidarity activities, or to form a closed shop. The reforms were considered by some (e.g. Freeman and Pelletier, 1990) to be the key causes of trade union decline in this period. Other aspects of state policy that have had a negative impact on trade union membership include privatisation of the public sector, such as the water, steel, coal and electricity industries, and competitive tendering for services provided by local government, the NHS and civil service, producing job losses in these highly unionised sectors. The government also withdrew the statutory union recognition procedure, which operated under the auspices of ACAS, and marginalised trade unions at the national level. The withdrawal by the state of such institutional support for trade unionism and collective bargaining has been a major element in weakening them (Purcell, 1993). The state's active encouragement of legislative and other measures designed to create difficulties for the trade union movement served also as an ideological offensive, and encouraged employers to adopt a similar stance.

Policy changes in these areas may have contributed in part to the unions' slight recovery since 2000 with regard to membership, as the Labour government introduced a new procedure by which employees could seek recognition of a union from their employer. Although this procedure has been described as cumbersome, some 470 voluntary agreements between companies and unions, were signed prior to the law taking effect, according to research by Incomes Data Services (*People Management*, 12 July 2001: 6). Clearly, the *prospect* of institutional support for unionisation may have been an important catalyst for some employers and unions to reach such agreements. Nevertheless, employers' responses remain critical in terms of resistance to, or acceptance of, recognition of trade unions for purposes of bargaining and representation of employees.

Employer policies and the 'threat' of HRM

The assertion of managerial prerogative has been manifest in a number of ways, from 'macho management' at British Leyland, P&O and News International during the 1980s, to the less dramatic but gradual reduction in the scope of collective bargaining, and the enforcement of changed working practices reported in the third Workplace Industrial Relations Survey (Millward *et al.*, 1992) and WERS98. Furthermore, where collective bargaining remained, the tendency was a decline in national agreements and towards decentralisation to establishment level, itself often a form of derecognition since shop stewards are denied a platform for the raising of company-level issues (Clark and Winchester, 1994: 713). In both the private and public sectors, management techniques often associated with HRM, such as individual performance-related pay and individual contracts, have emerged. These managerial techniques, although piecemeal and limited in their extent, can be viewed as a threat to the collective traditions of trade unionism in terms of workplace organisation. The thrust of HRM is individualistic, promotes 'flexibility' rather than 'demarcation', and the emphasis is on techniques aimed at eliciting employee commitment to company goals.

Other elements of HRM may be perceived as beneficial for trade union members (e.g. training), yet it is questionable how far such changes have been introduced. The changes that there have been have left largely undisturbed many of the institutions of collective bargaining, and tend to be more widespread in unionised environments than non-union (Millward *et al.*, 1992; Guest, 1995). Cully *et al.* (1999: 110) note that where 'high commitment' practices are introduced by management, these are more likely to be present in workplaces where there is union recognition, although the larger size of such workplaces is also significant here. Such employer-led reforms as have taken place, often viewed as ad hoc rather than strategic, were introduced to assert controls that the political climate afforded them (Sisson and Marginson, 1995: 113). Their impact has been variable on trade unions' ability to organise, bargain on behalf of their members or take effective industrial action.

Commentators have suggested the likelihood that no single causal explanation will suffice, but an interplay of factors will be influential on membership figures over a given period (Metcalf, 1991; Waddington, 1992). The problem, however, is one of weighting the various explanatory factors. Some commentators suggest that it is the cyclical character of economic and political changes which provides a more satisfactory explanation for union decline, rather than the individual factors themselves (Blyton and Turnbull, 1994: 109), and thus membership decline may not be permanent. Furthermore, decline in union membership and density is by no means unique to Britain, and international comparisons suggest that at least some similar conditions are present elsewhere. Economic and compositional forces have also had a negative impact on union membership and density in most industrialised countries (see Table 4.11), most of which have not had the extensive legislative reforms to which British unions have been subject. Indeed, several of the countries saw declining membership while governments were in power which were sympathetic to unions, such as France, Spain and Australia, leading commentators to play down the significance of legislative change in Britain (Brown *et al.*, 1997).

International comparisons

As with all comparative data, caution should be exercised when making international comparisons of union membership and collective bargaining, since methods of collection vary or data quickly become out of date. Estimates published by the OECD on unionisation rates in a range of European countries indicate that Britain's rate is higher than that in Germany, France, the Netherlands and Spain, but lower than that in Austria, Belgium, Ireland, Finland, Norway and Sweden.

Table 4.11 illustrates trade union membership within various countries, including Britain's rank order in terms of density, which has slipped only slightly from ninth to joint tenth place since 1970. Although similar problems have affected European and North American union movements – a decline in union membership and density, weakening of corporatist arrangements, problems of unemployment and casualisation of labour markets – there is still enormous diversity among trade unions in terms of membership, density, bargaining arrangements, and ideological and political attachments. For example, bargaining arrangements for most European countries are at industry level, whereas Denmark and the Netherlands have strong centralised framework agreements and Britain, Spain and Portugal have tended to decentralise bargaining.

Table 4.11 **Trade union membership by country, as a percentage of all employed, 1970–95**[a]

Country	1970 (%)	1980 (%)	1990 (%)	1995 (%)
UK	49 (9th)	53 (9th)	40 (joint 9th)	32 (joint 10th)
Australia	50	48	40	33
Austria	55	51	45	39
Belgium	45	56	51	53
Canada	31	36	36	34
Denmark	62[b]	78	75	78
Finland	51	70	73	79
France	21	17	9	9
Germany	32	34	30	27
Greece	36	37	34	n.a.
Ireland	54	57	48	44
Italy	34	44	34	32
Japan	35	31	25	24
Netherlands	36	32	22	23
New Zealand	41	56	45	22
Norway	50	54	53	53
Portugal	61	61	32	32
Spain	27	25	11	15
Sweden	67	78	82	88
Switzerland	30	31	26	23
US	23	22	16	15

[a] Figures rounded to nearest whole number
[b] Estimated unemployed membership figure excluded
Source: for Australia, Belgium, Canada, Greece, Japan, New Zealand, Portugal, Spain and US: Brown *et al.* (1997); all other statistics from Ebbinghaus and Visser (2000: 63)

■ Employer recognition and non-recognition of trade unions

Despite the major losses in union membership since 1980 and the decline in the coverage of collective bargaining, the significance and extent of union influence on the workplace must not be underestimated. Those companies that do recognise trade unions tend to be large and significant employers. In the mid-1990s, of the top 40 of these companies, employing some 30,000 workers in the UK, 37 recognised trade unions (*Labour Research*, September 1994: 15). Of those that did not, two were in the retail sector which has been difficult for trade unions to penetrate.

However, the decline in unionised workplaces since the mid-1980s is undeniable, and non-union workplaces appear unlikely to provide significant mechanisms for employee representation. WERS98 noted that alternative forms of communication and consultation were more likely to be found in unionised workplaces that in non-union workplaces (Cully *et al.*, 1999: 297). In private sector non-union workplaces with more than 25 employees, just 22 per cent had some form of joint consultative committee for discussion of issues such as health and safety, welfare and working practices (Cully *et al.*, 1999: 244). In unionised workplaces this figure was 32 per cent. Thus the 'representation gap' meant that in significant numbers of workplaces 'managers . . . are content to operate without any means of independent employee voice' (Cully *et al.*, 1999: 109). In spite of the numerous new agreements noted earlier, the failure of trade unions to gain a foothold in new establishments is apparent, and private services, high-tech industries and new manufacturing sites are particularly difficult to penetrate.

Deliberate derecognition of trade unions by management remains unusual but was particularly notable during the 1980s in specific sectors such as newspapers, manufacturing, private shipping, private services and the public sector (Millward *et al.*, 1992: 70). This drop in recognition was patchy across these sectors, being prevalent in small businesses, and in the public sector it was concentrated in two main groupings: the loss of collective bargaining rights for nurses and teachers during the 1980s. This is a little misleading, since the withdrawal of national collective bargaining and its substitution by pay review bodies arguably did not amount to derecognition (Burchill, 1997: 58).

A study conducted by IRS explored the reasons why some employers did not recognise trade unions (*IRS Employment Trends*, 1995: 3). Almost two-thirds of employers in the sample did recognise at least one trade union, but of those who did not, the main reason cited was that they had never been asked to grant recognition. Other reasons cited included the existence of alternative systems of employee representation, that trade unions were not company policy or that management prerogative was the preferred method.

IRS surveyed employers who did recognise trade unions and asked about the perceived advantages and disadvantages of recognising a trade union in the organisation. Among the perceived advantages were that a stable employee relations framework and a structured method of representing employee views were advantageous and that unrepresentative views could be filtered out. Others suggested 'smooth industrial relations' and 'problems are raised before molehills become mountains' (*IRS Employment Trends*, 1995: 9). Guest (1995: 126) cites evidence that trade union recognition is more likely at new establishments where there is already a trade union presence elsewhere in the company, suggesting that 'management accepts, on the basis of experience, that unions have some value'. Perceived disadvantages of recognising trade unions included resistance to change among trade unions, time consuming or slow decision-making and lack of flexibility.

It remains to be seen how the statutory union recognition procedure under the Employment Rights Act 1999 will assist the trade unions in gaining a foothold in difficult sectors in the long term. Even where recognition is granted, there have been occasions when the management, rather than the employees, chooses which union should be recognised following a 'beauty contest'. Such a decision resulted in protests by the Iron and Steel Trades Federation, which claimed to represent half of employees at MFI stores in the North East, after the TGWU was chosen following a 'presentation to senior management' (*Northern Echo*, 10 September 2001, p. 7). Perhaps more worrying for the trade unions is that WERS98 found scepticism among union and non-union members alike, regarding the ability of trade unions to represent their interests effectively. Indeed, union weakness may be evidenced by the fact that, in many workplaces, trade unions were unable to negotiate over pay, conditions and other matters on their members' behalf. This leads Cully *et al.* (1999: 214) to conclude that 'representation is more highly regarded and at its most effective where unions are well organised and, perhaps, have a more legitimate role as a partner in workplace employment relations'.

Trade unions' responses to the challenges of recent decades

There were two main types of response to the problems of loss of membership and employer policies, which were emphasised from the early 1980s. The first centred on business unionism and 'new realism', which was taken up enthusiastically by the then electrical workers' union, the Electrical, Electronic, Telecommunications and Plumbing Union (EETPU) although other unions increasingly adopted the approach. The approach emphasised cooperation with management in accepting 'reality', and is associated with single-union and/or no-strike agreements. Some initiatives in the 1980s and 1990s involved a variation of business unionism, namely the professionalism of union management. Initiatives have included, for example, the use of business planning models involving targets for recruitment and other objectives, appropriate training, including the establishment by the TUC of a National Vocational Qualification (NVQ) for trade union officials, the Organising Academy, and a Cranfield University course for trade union leaders to learn modern management techniques (Heery, 1997). These and other initiatives which resemble a managerial model have become more commonplace but have still caused controversy.

The implication of these measures is that unions are seen as organisations operating in a marketplace to provide potential 'consumers' with a range of services, while union officials persuade them into membership to sell the union's product (Heery, 1997). There has been no shortage of advice for the unions in 'selling themselves' in terms of member services: credit cards, mortgages, Filofaxes and so on. However, there is nothing new about member services: the earliest unions (friendly societies) offered 'mutual' benefits such as insurance and unemployment, sickness and funeral benefits. The emphasis in the context from the 1980s was that individual membership services were to become the *rationale* for joining a trade union, especially for groups of employees who, it is assumed, would have no interest in 'militancy', or collective, solidaristic reasons for joining. The assumptions of a purely individualistic orientation, however, have not been verified, as new members surveyed have been found to have strong instrumental reasons for joining a trade union, such as an expectation that unions would improve their pay and conditions through the means of collective representation (Waddington and Whitston, 1995).

In terms of dealing with employers, 'new realism' has focused on forming new relationships with management, based on mutual goals and cooperation to improve productivity and quality. Examples of this joint approach include those in operation at the Rover car company, Welsh Water, United Distillers and Blue Circle Cement (Tailby and Winchester, 2000: 377). Such deals, in particular the much publicised New Deal at Rover, included a commitment to job security in return for new working practices, although scepticism was expressed in spring 2000 when BMW, the owner of Rover, agreed the sale of the Longbridge car plant with an expectation of significant job losses. Union leaders threatened legal action over the company's failure to consult employees over the transfer of the company and impending redundancies; in spite of the existence at BMW of a European works council, UK-based employees were not represented. John Edmonds, general secretary of the GMB union made the point

> The abiding image that will stick with most people about this whole affair is of the supervisory board meeting in Munich containing German trade unions, discussing the future of a British plant, while British trade unionists are outside the door. (EIRO, 2000: 12)

In some US companies the 'mutual gains' approach has been proclaimed by Kochan as heralding a transformation in industrial relations (Guest, 1995: 119), although evidence for this claim is limited to a small number of firms, primarily in the automobile industry, and where unions are well entrenched. The response of 'new realism' appears to complement the rhetoric of HRM, wherein reference to power relations, the notion of opposing interests, and daily struggles over the 'wage–effort' bargain are generally unacknowledged. Whereas trade union members and officers might not have 'bought into' such ideas, but have at times cooperated in the knowledge that this approach is the best on offer given the climate, it remains to be seen whether real benefits can be delivered. This has not been the only method employed by trade unions to regain lost ground, however. The major alternative approach has been a more 'traditional' collectivist approach, focused on the need to attract new members in the sectors that were hard to penetrate, especially women and young people. A television advertising campaign was launched by the public service union Unison during 1995 which was aimed at young people: 'Using the image of a bear which cannot be shifted by one ant alone, but is moved by an army of ants, Unison is hoping to drive home the traditional trade union message of strength in numbers' (*Guardian*, 12 December 1995, p. 2). The TUC has set out recommendations for trade unions to identify and recruit as many as 8 million members, its own research demonstrating that most non-members have in fact never been approached to join a trade union (TUC press release, 7 September 2001). It suggests launching a new web-based service offering advice and information aimed at groups such as people in casual and insecure employment, or college leavers, the latter being run in conjunction with the National Union of Students.

Campaigns to increase membership in the US, whose trade union membership was also in decline for over 30 years, have encouraged British unions in the belief that decline is not irreversible. Campaigns by the American Federation of Labor and Congress of Industrial Organizations (AFL-CIO) among the low paid and immigrant workers produced a 3 per cent rise in membership over two years, and a more vigorous and militant approach to counter aggressive management and the squeeze on wages (*Guardian*, 11 September 1995, p. 9). A recent high-profile success known as the Justice for Janitors campaign in Silicon Valley demonstrated that, even among the lowest paid and hard to organise groups such as casual workers, part-timers and immigrants, it was possible to increase union membership and campaign for a living wage and health insurance by 'exposing the flagrant gap between rich and poor', and drawing on support from community groups, broadcasters, local politicians and religious leaders (*Unesco Courier*, September 2000, p. 31).

Such developments have not countered the decline of unionisation overall, however, and Guest (1995: 130) summarises the available strategies that trade unions could pursue in Britain:

■ The promotion of a high quality of working life campaign, as part of a more desirable pursuit of a high quality, high productivity environment, in comparison with the low-cost labour market policies at the centre of Conservative policy. This would capitalise on many of the features of European social policy, such as the value of pluralist, partnership structures and employee involvement.
■ The 'friendly society' strategy, which emphasises advice, services and information for members as individuals. This could be valuable at a time of state withdrawal of

benefits, and the increase in grievances over discrimination and unfair dismissal handled by bodies such as ACAS (Guest, 1995: 135).

■ Pursuit of the 'HRM' strategy, which subscribes to the benefits and opportunities that members could avail themselves of at least in soft HRM policies, such as good quality training. Furthermore, unions could push management into fulfilling the rhetoric which promises 'quality', or 'excellence', by insisting on high standards in production, and cooperating with management in the search for competitive advantage, while insisting on their own agenda (such as job security) as part of this strategy.

Guest suggests that these three possible strategies could overlap, and sees no contradiction in trade unions acting both as a collective voice for employees and at the same time as a 'constructive' voice which management may value on behalf of the well-being of the whole enterprise (Guest, 1995: 136). He does, however, acknowledge that such an approach may represent unions' 'best chances of survival', as an alternative to marginalisation promised by the 'black hole' scenario. However, such a strategy would also assume management as well as union acceptance of such a stance, despite British management's general fears that managerial prerogative could be reduced beyond the 'norms' of collective bargaining. Perhaps more importantly, however, such a view suggests some shift in the fundamental attitudes of workers themselves towards collective organisation, their work or their employers (McIlroy, 1995: 399): 'we must not confuse change in the balance of forces between employers and unions with shifts in attitudes to unions or a move towards unitary conceptions on the part of workers'. Certainly, the evidence from WERS98 and elsewhere provides that employees remain dissatisfied over a range of work-related issues including pay and the ability to influence managerial decision-making. Furthermore, where trade unions have the power to make a difference (usually bolstered by high density at the workplace), not only are employees keen to join them but evidence reveals that 'where there was a strong union voice, it was more likely to be welcomed by management than resisted' (Cully *et al.*, 1999: 297). It would appear that union presence in itself is insufficient to make a difference to employees' lives, since that presence does not guarantee joint regulation or significant influence in dealing with employers.

■ The prospects for partnership – threat or lifeline for trade unions?

The TUC has been an advocate of partnership not only at national level but also at the level of the workplace, and the Employment Rights Act 1999 outlined the Labour government's policy towards the promotion of partnership initiatives. The Partnership Fund was developed under the aegis of the Department of Trade and Industry as a mechanism to provide support for training managers and employee representatives, along with other measures for the promotion of workplace partnerships. The context of a new competitive environment and changing economic, social, technological and institutional factors are recognised as having a profound impact on employee relations, and the partnership proposals were seen by proponents as providing an opportunity for companies to adopt a new approach which combines an interest in business efficiency with employees' need for more secure and rewarding employment (Tailby and Winchester, 2000: 375). Based on foundations of mutuality, joint commitment to success, building trust, and informing and consulting staff, the underlying principles with regard to employees are:

- good treatment of employees now and in the future;
- empowerment: creating the opportunity for employee contribution;
- employee rights and benefits;
- employee responsibilities (Knell, 1999: 6).

Such underlying principles and the HRM-style language in which they are expressed are common to proponents of workplace partnership such as the TUC, and the Involvement and Participation Association (IPA) as well as to academic literature aimed at characterising partnership and how the principles translate into practice. Guest and Peccei (1998, cited in Knell, 1999: 6) identify eight main groups of practices associated with an effective partnership approach:

- direct participation by employees in decisions about their own work;
- direct participation by employees in decisions about personal employment issues;
- participation by employee representatives in decisions about employment issues;
- participation by employee representatives in decisions about broader organisational policy issues;
- flexible job design and focus on quality;
- performance management;
- employee share ownership;
- communication, harmonisation and employment security.

Such practices may be described as a menu, whereby organisations have significant discretion over how such policies are configured, and that partnership 'is better thought of as offering a map to guide practice rather than representing a prescriptive model of theory' (Knell, 1999: 8). Furthermore, it can be seen that the rhetoric of HRM is infused into the principles (e.g. 'empowerment', 'flexibility'), while the practices themselves are hardly novel – in fact many aspects (e.g. employee shares, employment security) are common not only to many 'new style' employer–union agreements in particular single-union deals, but also to old style paternalist employers such as the John Lewis Partnership and Cadbury's. The Industrial Society/Department of Trade and Industry reports on several success stories from the Partnership Fund whereby companies such as Leyland Trucks and HP Bulmers had attempted to break out of an 'adversarial' industrial relations climate and embark on building positive relationships and to introduce new working practices and innovations. These reportedly produced beneficial outcomes in terms of improved performance, which were broadly supported by employees (Knell, 1999).

While there is a degree of similarity between the views of proponents, the TUC sets out its priorities in its *Partners for Progress* document, and places a slightly different emphasis on employees' rights to representation and employers' obligations to training to enable the workforce to become 'flexible', or 'efficient'. The components of partnership set out by the TUC are job security; employee voice in the company, including information and consultation; fair financial reward and the recognition that employees have a right to bargain collectively over wages; and investment in training or employee development (Tailby and Winchester, 2000: 376). One major difference between the government, the TUC and the IPA is with regard to unionisation: the TUC insists that only independent trade unions are required for real partnership to work, whereas the IPA regards 'representative structures' as being important (Tailby and Winchester, 2000: 376). The 'best practice' examples identified by the Industrial Society/DTI do include a range of union and non-union organisations. For example, HP Bulmers has an employee council which is 'empowered to discuss matters connected with company policy and decisions that affect the employees' future but not the day to day management of the business' (Knell, 1999: 60). However, evidence indicates that non-union bodies have serious weaknesses with regard to their restricted role, lack of sanctions which are available to unions, marginalisation and difficulty in finding representatives (Lloyd, 2001: 315).

Tailby and Winchester suggest caution with regard to the expectations and presumed benefits of partnership. In terms of its novelty value, for example, many aspects are familiar to the single-union agreements of the mid-1980s (Tailby and Winchester, 2000: 384). However, what is distinctive is the degree of consensus around the principles of partnership compared with the acrimony over 'new realism' which erupted previously. Furthermore, the process of negotiating partnership agreements would appear to offer some novelty with regard to the relatively long-term focus, such as three-year rolling agreements (Tailby and Winchester, 2000: 383). The assumed or reported benefits of partnership need also to be cautiously greeted, since the limited research to date has often relied upon the views of IPA members or winners of the DTI's Partnership at Work Fund, who are themselves more likely to be supporters of the approach. In addition, the agreements have been concluded at times of falling unemployment and shortages of skilled workers (Tailby and Winchester, 2000: 384). From the employees' point of view, employment security clauses are no guarantee against job losses, as the example of Rover (discussed earlier) has borne out, although they may lessen the numbers involved.

The extent to which partnership at the workplace can prove genuinely innovative, and the likelihood of its wider diffusion remains questionable, and will be subject to constraints not only by employers but also by the whole context of competitive conditions, globalised trading and uncertain climate worldwide prior to, but exacerbated by, the events of 11 September 2001.

With regard to British trade unions, there remain the institutional weaknesses for trade unions seeking influence at national level or at the workplace, which many of their EU counterparts do not share.

> In comparison with most EU member states, there is no legal or institutional framework supporting social partnership in Britain. Whilst leaders of the TUC and the CBI may choose to meet more often than a decade ago, their status and role as social partners is very limited and, at industry or sectoral level, trade union and employers' representatives rarely engage in collective bargaining or in institutionalized forms of consultation. Whilst the higher profile attached to national and sectoral social dialogue in the EU may encourage some initiatives in Britain, neither employers associations nor trade unions possess the same degree of legitimacy and organizational experience as many of their continental counterparts for such a role. (Tailby and Winchester, 2000: 385).

Chapter summary

The British trade union movement has certainly faced severe constraints and suffered enormous defeats in the last two decades or so. Yet in many areas, continuity is the order of the day, and non-unionism is far from being widespread in many significant sectors of the economy. Furthermore, recent legislative changes which facilitate union recognition appear to have given grounds for cautious optimism to the trade unions and the TUC, who themselves have instigated organising and recruitment campaigns and have finally seen a small increase in union membership figures and employer–union agreements. Moreover, many similar challenges have been faced by continental European and US trade unions. Yet the political marginalisation and setbacks which continued for two decades have left British trade unions more exposed than their counterparts in France or Germany. With the continuing impact of deregulation and casualisation of the workforce, this situation hardly seems likely to improve the diminishing base of collective bargaining within Britain, let alone across European frontiers. Even where trade unions are recognised, and at the national level, they remain weak compared with many of their European counterparts.

Following the Labour Party's election victory in 1997, trade union members were under no illusion that 'new' Labour would restore their former powers, however exaggerated these powers may have been. Labour in opposition repeatedly stated it would not repeal the anti-union legislation introduced since 1979. In addition, the Labour leader Tony Blair took steps to distance the Labour Party even further from the trade unions which created it. The Labour government has angered many by the stance taken towards public service reform, the level of the minimum wage, and the refusal to embrace more widespread employment rights such as those enjoyed elsewhere in the EU, for example with regard to more generous family-friendly policies. A difference in emphasis compared with the previous Conservative governments can be detected nevertheless. Within its first few weeks of office, the Labour government repealed the ban on trade unions at GCHQ and ended Britain's opt-out of the EU social legislation, the latter action paving the way for new employment rights for atypical workers and in the areas of information and consultation. While Labour appears more 'Euro friendly', in rhetoric at least, than the previous Conservative governments, Prime Minister Tony Blair remains highly sceptical of excessive regulation and wedded to the notion of a 'flexible labour market'.

The second aspect of the Labour government's emphasis relates to the workplace, namely the promotion of 'partnership' between workers and employers. This represents a policy of attempting to move beyond adversarial collective bargaining towards a more cooperative relationship between the parties, in which the emphasis is on mutual gains, with unions actively contributing to modernisation and other initiatives. Some model agreements such as those at Blue Circle and United Distillers are among the rare examples of such an approach, although such companies are hardly representative of British industry. Furthermore, events at Rover during 1999 demonstrated that economic uncertainty, the volatility of specific industries, and the relative weakness of UK workers in respect of employment matters, may make such arrangements difficult to sustain in the long term. The fact that partnership arrangements may be sanctioned without the presence of independent trade unions implies that such weaknesses may become even more entrenched, however. Social partnership agreements at national level, similar to those operating in other EU countries, could have extended the influence of unions over a wider remit of employment and economic policy, although some critics, mindful of the failure to deliver real benefits to ordinary workers during the Social Contract period of the 1970s, may prefer the more ad hoc approach which Labour appears to have adopted.

The trade unions in Britain have some grounds for cautious optimism in respect of their membership numbers and the slightly more favourable climate in which to organise. However, bearing in mind the setbacks of the recent past, the somewhat tentative and partial changes being mooted, and their relative weakness at many workplaces, any wholesale transformation of the trade union movement seems unlikely in the immediate future.

Questions

1   What are the essential features of a trade union and what are its key functions?

2   Outline the factors which may influence whether (a) an individual or (b) a group of employees will join a trade union or not. What are the anticipated benefits of union membership for employees?

3   How is trade union power perceived by different parties, and how can it be measured? Give examples of how state or employer policies have affected union powers in different ways, in Britain and in other parts of the world.

4   What are the principles of democratic organisation behind the two models of union democracy, the parliamentary and participatory models? How necessary is legislative reform of trade unions' internal affairs, and what have trade unions done to increase their own democratic 'credentials'?

5   How significant is trade union membership in Britain in the early 2000s and what factors produce a variation in membership among different parts of the labour force? How can the decline in union membership, and its slight recovery, over the past twenty or so years be explained?

6   What strategies can trade unions embark upon in order to maintain and increase membership levels, and to attract new members from sectors and industries that traditionally have been hard to organise?

Activities

1   You are a London regional trade union officer at a banking and finance union which has been concerned in recent years about fluctuating membership levels. There are currently 3,500 members in your region, who are employed in the major high street banks which recognise trade unions. A further 4,000 would be eligible to join the trade union, however, a small number of these belong to other unions but the majority are not union members even though pay and conditions negotiated on an annual basis with the employers are awarded to all employees except senior managers. The union is concerned that younger entrants to banking are less likely to join the union compared with older employees. Approximately 70 per cent of the employees are female and most work in lower-level, relatively low paid and routine jobs; one-third work part-time. About 10 per cent of the banks' staff are from ethnic minorities, predominantly black and Asian, and they are concentrated into the more junior grades. In the past two years the banks have been closing smaller branches with the consequence that staff have been made redundant; other changes in banking such as new technology and telephone banking, have led to hundreds of job losses in your region.

Along with colleagues, you deal with recruitment of union members, but your responsibilities mainly involve providing information, advice on employment rights, and services for members, and representing members who are subject to discipline or dismissal by the employers.

The union's annual conference has pledged to commit the union to (i) increase membership within the region, and (ii) take more account of workplace issues particularly affecting women, and equality issues. Your task is to devise a strategy for the area, to attract more bank employees into membership.

Questions

(a) Prepare a presentation or written report for the NEC, outlining which policies you would recommend in order to meet these goals, and highlighting issues which may be of particular concern to potential union members.

(b) Design recruitment material aimed at persuading new members to join, and advice and information which can be accessed via the union's website.

2 Discuss the main elements in the new agreement at Cadburys described in Exhibit 4.1. How are they distinguishable from those of 'traditional' management–union agreements? How would the management and trade unions at the company hope to benefit? How likely is it that such deals might become widespread in British industry?

Exhibit 4.1

Choc workers in ground-breaking pay and conditions package

Thousands of Cadbury workers will enjoy new benefits at work after voting for a ground-breaking pay and conditions package, it was revealed today. Union members at the Birmingham-based chocolate giant gave the radical deal, tipped to form the basis for similar agreements in major companies up and down the country, a massive thumbs up.

The two-year wage deal, which will push up salaries by 3.2 per cent this year and by inflation plus 0.5 per cent in the next 12 months, was agreed by 1,522 votes to 387.

A new Cadbury: Clearly the Best document, which contains a host of progressive family-friendly benefits and partnership arrangements with the unions, was passed by a two-to-one total.

And controversial measures to axe weekly wages and replace them with monthly payments were also pushed through on a third poll by the same margin.

The majorities were secured after the proposals on Cadbury: Clearly the Best and monthly pay were comprehensively rejected by the workforce in March and fresh negotiations started to rework the package.

Cadbury bosses wanted the agreement, which swept aside a mass of old, individual agreements at each of the company's plants in Bournville, Bristol and Chirk in North Wales in favour of a unified set of benefits and allowances.

They also wanted to shake up the way the company dealt with trade unions to put the relationship on a partnership basis rather than one of confrontation. Workers will now be able to enjoy family-friendly benefits which are better than the state minimum in all cases, including maternity pay for 18 weeks at normal wages and paid paternity leave for a week.

John Jordan, Transport & General Workers' Union regional organiser, said 'This is ground-breaking in terms of family-friendly policies and is being closed viewed by the whole of the T&G, possibly this will set a blueprint for many other such deals.' Keith Dennis, Cadbury director of personnel, said 'We recognised that things had got to change and there needed to be a contemporary arrangement. This is a new beginning.'

Source: Chris Morley, *Evening Mail*, 30 July 2001

Useful websites

www.dti.gov.uk/er/emar   **Department of Trade and Industry**   Government department with some responsibility for trade union and employment affairs. Website contains trade union membership statistics and details of research projects, publications, trade union and collective rights, European employment directives, and workplace partnership schemes.

www.etuc.org   **European Trades Union Confederation**   Aims, activities and events related to the ETUC, member organisations, trade unions and workers at European level.

www.eurofound.ie   **European Foundation for the Improvement of Living and Working Conditions,** (main centre based in Dublin, Republic of Ireland)   Independent body of the EU created to assist the formulation of future policy on social and work-related matters. Research/publications on developments at EU level, by country and sector, on a range of work-related issues including pay, working time, law, equality, labour costs, pay and collective bargaining.

www.lrd.org.uk   **Labour Research Department**   Independent research body publishing booklets and magazine/information for trade unionists on a range of employment issues such as law, pay and bargaining, disputes, union news, international campaigns, equality and racism.

www.tgwu.org.uk   www.gmb.org.uk   www.unison.org.uk   **Individual Trade Unions** Many individual trade unions have their own websites containing information for members, details on joining the union, youth section, rights at work, research, publications, union officers, news, campaigns and educational issues.

www.tuc.org.uk   **Trades Union Congress**   Gives details about the TUC's organisation, conferences and regional structure, together with a list of affiliated trade unions and services for members and student information. Events and conferences, policies, publications and details of campaigns on a range of employment issues such as rights at work, equality, partnership, the law at work, and globalisation are also included.

www.union-network.org   **Union Network International**   Contains information on global and regional issues, such as labour rights, trade union activism, campaigns, news and conferences worldwide. Trade union news and developments in specific industrial and professional sectors also.

Acknowledgement

Figures and charts on union membership and density were produced by Geraldine O'Brien at University College Dublin, whose assistance is greatly appreciated.

References

ACAS (1995) *Annual Report 1995*. London: ACAS.

Bain, G.S. (1983) *Industrial Relations in Britain*. Oxford: Blackwell.

Bain, G.S. and Elsheikh, F. (1976). *Union Growth and the Business Cycle*. Oxford: Blackwell.

Blackburn, R.M. (1967) *Union Character and Social Class*. London: Batsford.

Blyton, P. and Turnbull, P. (1994) *The Dynamics of Employee Relations*. Basingstoke: Macmillan.

Bridgford, J. and Stirling, J. (1994) *Employee Relations in Europe*. Oxford: Blackwell.

Brown, W., Deakin, S. and Ryan, P. (1997) 'The effect of British industrial relations legislation 1979–97', *National Institute Economic Review*, 161: 69–83.

Burchill, F. (1997) *Labour Relations*. London: Macmillan.

Certification Officer (1996) *Annual Report of the Certification Officer*. London: HMSO.

Certification Officer (2001) *Annual Report of the Certification Officer*. London: HMSO.

Clark, J. and Winchester, D. (1994) 'Management and trade unions' in Sisson, K. (ed.) *Personnel Management: A Comprehensive Guide to Theory and Practice in Britain*. Oxford: Blackwell.

Clegg, H. (1972) *The System of Industrial Relations in Great Britain*. Oxford: Blackwell.

Coates, D. (1983) 'The question of trade union power' in Coates, D. and Johnston, G. (eds) *Socialist Arguments*. Oxford: Martin Robertson: 55–79.

Cockburn, C. (1991) *Brothers: Male Dominance and Technological Change*. London: Pluto Press.

Colgan, F. and Ledwith, S. (1996) 'Sisters organising – women and their trade unions' in Ledwith, S. and Colgan, F. (eds) *Women in Organisations: Challenging Gender Politics*. Basingstoke: Macmillan.

Crouch, C. (1982) *Trade Unions: The Logic of Collective Action*. Glasgow: Fontana.

Cully, M. and Woodland, S. (1996) 'Trade union membership and recognition: an analysis of data from the 1995 Labour Force Survey', *Labour Market Trends*, May.

Cully, M., Woodland, S., O'Reilly, A. and Dix, G. (1999) *Britain at Work, As Depicted by the 1998 Workplace Employee Relations Survey*, London: Routlege.

Daly, M. (1994) 'Women and trade unions' in Nevin, D. (ed.) *Trade Union Century*. Dublin: Mercier.

Darlington, R. (1994) *The Dynamics of Workplace Unionism: Shop Steward Organization in Three Merseyside Plants*, London: Mansell.

Dickens, L. and Colling, T. (1990) 'Why equality won't appear on the bargaining agenda', *Personnel Management*, April.

Ebbinghaus, B. and Visser, J. (2000) *The Societies of Europe: Trade Unions in Western Europe since 1945*. London: Macmillan Reference Ltd.

EIRO (2000) 'BMW Sells Rover and Land Rover', *European Industrial Relations Observatory Update 4*. Dublin: European Foundation for the Improvement of Living and Working Conditions.

Fairbrother, P. (1983) *The Politics of Union Ballots*. London: WEA.

Farnham, D. and Pimlott, J. (1995) *Understanding Industrial Relations*. London: Cassell.

Flanders, A. (1970) *Management and Unions*. London: Faber & Faber.

Freeman, R.B. and Pelletier, J. (1990) 'The impact of industrial relations legislation on British union density', *British Journal of Industrial Relations*, 28(2): 141–64.

Gospel, H.F. and Palmer, G. (1993) *British Industrial Relations*. London: Routledge.

Guest, D. (1995) 'Human resource management, trade unions and industrial relations' in Storey, J. (ed.) *Human Resource Management: A Critical Text*. London: Routledge.

Heery, E. (1997) 'Annual review article 1996', *British Journal of Industrial Relations*, 35(1): 87–109.

Heery, E., Simms, M., Delbridge, R., Salmon, J. and Simpson, D. (2000) 'The TUC's Organising Academy: an assessment', *Industrial Relations Journal*, 31(5): 400–15.

HMSO (1996) *Social Trends 26*: 92.

HMSO (2001) *Annual Report of the Certification Officer*: 62.

Hollinshead, G. and Leat, M. (1995) *Human Resource Management: An International and Comparative Perspective*. London: Financial Times/Pitman Publishing.

Hyman, R. (1975) *Industrial Relations: A Marxist Introduction*. London: Macmillan.

Hyman, R. and Fryer, R.H. (1975) 'Trade unions: sociology and political economy' in McKinlay, J. (ed.) *Processing People*. New York: Holt, Rinehart & Winston.

IRS Employment Trends (1995) 'Employee representation arrangements 1: the trade unions', no. 586 (June): 3–9.

Kirton, G. and Greene, A-M. (2000) *The Dynamics of Managing Diversity: A Critical Approach*. Oxford: Butterworth-Heinemann.

Knell, J. (1999) *Partnership at Work*, Employment Relations Research Series No. 7. London: Industrial Society/DTI.

Labour Research Department (1994) 'Still a long road to equality', *Labour Research*, 83(3): 5–7.

Ledwith, S. and Colgan, F. (eds) (1996) *Women in Organisations: Challenging Gender Politics*. Basingstoke: Macmillan.

Lloyd, C. (2001) 'What do employee councils do? The impact of non-union forms of representation on trade union organisation', *Industrial Relations Journal*, 32(4): 313–27.

McIlroy, J. (1995) *Trade Unions in Britain Today*. Manchester: Manchester University Press.

McIlroy, J. (2000) 'The new politics of pressure – the Trades Union Congress and new Labour in government', *Industrial Relations Journal*, 31(1): 2–16.

Metcalf, D. (1991) 'British unions: dissolution or resurgence?', *Oxford Review of Economic Policy*, 7(1): 18–32.

Millward, N., Stevens, M., Smart, D. and Hawes, W.R. (1992) *Workplace Industrial Relations in Transition*. Aldershot: Dartmouth.

Phizacklea, A. and Miles, R. (1993) 'The British trade union movement and racism' in Braham, P. Rattansi, A. and Skellington, R. (eds) *Racism and Antiracism: Inequalities, Opportunities and Policies*. London: Sage/Oxford University Press.

Purcell, J. (1993) 'The end of institutional industrial relations', *Political Quarterly*, 64(1): 6–23.

SERTUC (1994) 'Women's Special. Women in unions: still too few at the top', *Labour Research*, March.

SERTUC Women's Rights Committee (1994) *Struggling for Equality – A Survey of Women and their Unions*. London: Southern and Eastern Region TUC.

Sisson, K. and Marginson, P. (1995) 'Management: systems, structures and strategy' in Edwards, P.K. (ed.) *Industrial Relations, Theory and Practice in Britain*. Oxford: Blackwell.

Sly, F. (1995) 'Ethnic groups and the labour market: analyses from the spring 1994 Labour Force Survey', *Employment Gazette*, June.

Smith, P. and Morton, G. (2001) 'New Labour's reform of Britain's employment law: the devil is not only in the detail but in the values and policy too', *British Journal of Industrial Relations*, 39(1): 119–38.

Tailby, S., and Winchester, D. (2000). 'Management and trade unions: towards social partnership?' in Bach, S. and Sisson, K. (eds) *Personnel Management: A Comprehensive Guide to Theory and Practice*, 3rd edn. Oxford: Blackwell.

Terry, M. (1995) 'Trade unions: shop stewards and the workplace', in Edwards, P.K. (ed.) *Industrial Relations, Theory and Practice in Britain*. Oxford: Blackwell.

TUC (1997) *Partners for Progress: Next Steps for the New Unionism*. London: TUC.

TUC (2002) *TUC Directory*. London: TUC.

Waddington, J. (1992) 'Trade union membership in Britain, 1980–1987: unemployment and restructuring', *British Journal of Industrial Relations*, 30(2): 287–324.

Waddington, J. and Whitston, C. (1995) 'Trade unions: growth, structure and policy' in Edwards, P.K. (ed.) *Industrial Relations, Theory and Practice in Britain*. Oxford: Blackwell.

Webb, S. and Webb, B. (1920) *The History of Trade Unionism*. London: Longman.

Chapter 5

The state

Mike Salamon

Learning objectives

By the end of this chapter, readers should be able to:

- identify the differences between 'state' and 'government';
- explain the importance of the government in determining the nature of a country's employee relations system;
- explain the extent to which the government is free or constrained in the development of policies and strategies towards employee relations and the labour market;
- identify the differences between *laissez-faire* and corporatist political ideologies and their effect on national systems of employee relations;
- understand government strategies relating to:
  - (a) managing unemployment, promoting labour flexibility and regulating wage levels;
  - (b) promoting social justice within the employment relationship; and
  - (c) regulating industrial conflict.

Introduction

Government policies and strategies play a major, if not fundamental, role in shaping, directing and regulating the social structures and interactions which make up any society. Indeed, they have been an important factor in 'defining' social problems and 'setting the agenda' for national debates about employee relations (Winchester, 1983: 105). However, no government in a democratic society is 'omnipotent and omnicompetent' (Marsh, 1992: 239). The direction and scope of government policies may be constrained within the political mechanism by other political parties and 'pressure' groups or in the wider society by the actions of individuals and groups. The potential transient nature of governments within democratic societies, together with differences in ideology between contending political parties, creates a constant capacity for change in policies and strategies towards employee relations. Furthermore, the existence of a range of state 'agencies' (including the judicial system)

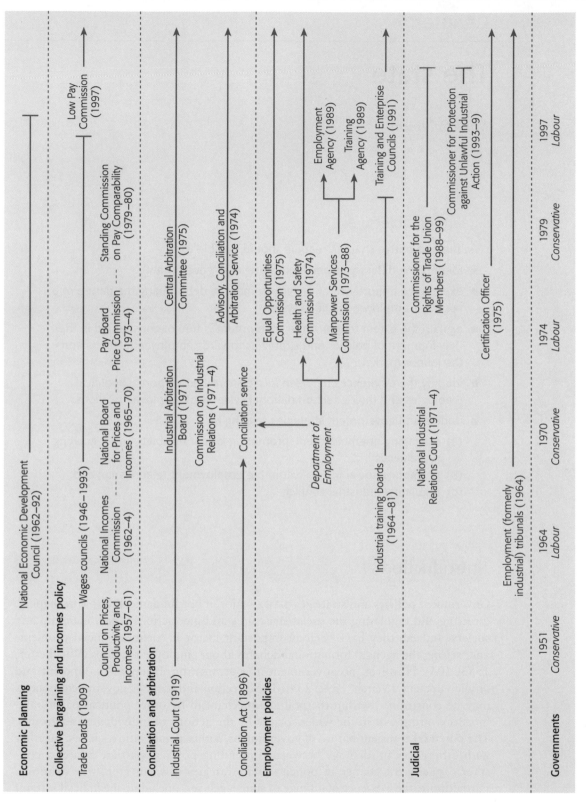

Figure 5.1 State agencies in the UK

responsible for the implementation and enforcement of the government's policies and decisions (see Figure 5.1) raises two important issues:

- the extent to which any such agency may become almost a permanent feature of the system (transcending changes in government) or is of limited duration and closely associated with a specific short-term government policy or decision;
- the extent to which the agency is constrained to support the government or is able to act independently and place a check on the exercise of governmental authority.

The importance of the government's influence on employee relations can be seen in three main areas. First, it is the 'third' (and, at times, the most important) actor in the employee relations system (Poole, 1986: 99) which, by virtue of its unique role as the lawmaker in society, has the power and authority to 'change the rules of the system' (Crouch, 1982: 146). Legislation provides a society-wide enforceable framework of rights and responsibilities, which reflects the government's subjective value judgements regarding such concepts as fairness and equity, power and authority and individualism and collectivism within the employment relationship. Secondly, governments may control, directly or indirectly, a wide variety of organisations within the 'public' sector: ranging from government departments (responsible for the provision of public services such as health, education, police, fire, prisons, etc.), through public utility corporations (communications, transport, coal, electricity, gas, water, etc.), to state-owned commercial organisations which compete with private sector organisations (aircraft and car manufacture, steel production, banking, etc.). The precise extent and mix of organisations within the public sector vary from country to country and over time, and are dependent on the ideological beliefs of the political party in power. The importance of the public sector in influencing employee relations comes not only from its size (as a proportion of the national workforce) but also from its potential to demonstrate a government-preferred 'model' of employee relations. Thirdly, the government's policies and strategies on economic and social matters are significant influences on the general environment within which management, employees and unions (both private and public sector) have to conduct their relationships.

The diversity of national employee relations systems can be explained, at least in part, by differences in underlying political ideology and consequent variations in the nature and extent of government intervention in economic or social issues (Waarden, 1995: 110). Certainly, the economic development of most South East Asian countries (such as Korea, Singapore and Taiwan) appears to have been based on a unitary corporatist 'political economy' approach – including government restriction or control of trade unions in order not to jeopardise the economic development process and, in particular, to secure and maintain inward foreign investment (Bean, 1994: 218). Singapore's institutionalised 'symbiotic' relationship between the ruling political party and trade unions since the early 1960s has made the two almost indistinguishable (Leggett, 1993: 101) and, coupled with the existence of a National Wages Council, has eliminated collective bargaining as a 'political tool' (Beng and Chew, 1995: 83). Similarly, in Taiwan (Lee, 1995) and South Korea (Park and Lee, 1995) governments have, among other measures, prohibited unions from undertaking political activities, allowed the government to veto candidates for union elections and restricted the capacity of unions to undertake strike action. These moves have been aimed as much at ensuring that unions did not provide a focus for political challenge to the government as at achieving economic progress. However, the success of economic growth itself created pressure for political and industrial relations reform in the 1980s and, indeed, the Korean government's attempt to reintroduce union controls in 1991 was defeated by a revitalised union movement.

In marked contrast, the post-capitalist pluralistic approach in the older industrialised countries (the UK, Europe, the US, Canada and Australia) regards both the organisation and society as being multi-structured and potentially competitive in terms of groupings, leadership, authority and loyalty and, therefore, accepts the expression of divergent and opposing views as rational, inevitable and legitimate.

The UK since 1960: a case study in changing government philosophy

In 1960 Kahn-Freund stated that there was 'no major country in the world in which the law has played a less significant role in the shaping of [employee relations] than in Great Britain' (1960: 44). However, this ignored the fundamental importance of early legislation – the Trade Union Act 1871, the Trade Disputes Act 1906 and the Trade Union Act 1913 – which reflected a shift in political ideology from the 'liberal individualists of 1830' to the 'democratic socialists of 1905' (Griffith, 1990). It freed trade unions from the nineteenth-century socio-economic legal doctrines of 'restraint of trade' and 'conspiracy', thereby allowing them to organise, undertake industrial action and participate in wider political activities without the constant threat of being outlaws. Without such legalisation, trade unions would not have been able to develop in the UK. However, the content of the employment relationship itself (terms and conditions of employment) remained to be determined primarily through 'free voluntary collective bargaining' between management and unions (i.e. without state intervention).

The 1960s and 1970s were a period of apparent 'consensus politics'. Both Conservative and Labour governments adopted an interventionist (corporatist) approach, based on Keynesian policies aimed at managing the demand side of the economy, to support their commitment to the maintenance of full employment and the welfare state. Trade union and employer representatives were involved in discussions with government on a wide range of economic and social issues through the National Economic Development Council (NEDC), established in 1962 by a Conservative government. The tripartite formula was maintained in the establishment of a number of state agencies in the 1970s concerned with implementing government strategies: first, the Manpower Services Commission (MSC) in 1973 under a Conservative government and then the Health and Safety Commission (HSC) and Advisory, Conciliation and Arbitration Service (ACAS) in 1974 under a Labour government (see Figure 5.1). The role of the MSC and HSC, together with the Equal Opportunities Commission, was to promote the government's positive employment policies and complemented the work already started with the creation of industrial training boards (ITBs) in 1964.

However, this emphasis on tripartite cooperation did not preclude the use of statutory, as well as voluntary, policies to regulate incomes, and the period saw a number of short-lived state agencies charged with implementing and regulating these policies. Nor did it prevent government concern for the impact of industrial action. In 1969, despite the Donovan Commission report (1968) advocating voluntary reform rather than legislative control, the Labour government felt it necessary to propose changes to the law that would 'help to control the destructive expression of industrial conflict' (White Paper, 1969: 5). The government did not proceed because of pressure from trade unions and the TUC's offer of a voluntary undertaking to press for moderation in trade unions' demands. Nevertheless, a change of government resulted in the Conservative's Industrial Relations Act 1971, which tried to balance some positive gains for trade unions (including statutory recognition procedure and rights to disclosure of information) with bringing them under greater statutory regulation and public accountability. It also sought to establish a system of specialised labour courts and agencies by not only extending the role of industrial tribunals (which existed under earlier 1960s legislation) but also creating a new National Industrial Relations Court and Commission on Industrial Relations (neither of which survived the demise of the government). The legislation provoked such hostility and active resistance by trade unions and members alike that, despite the imprisonment of shop stewards, fines against trade unions and sequestration of their funds for non-payment of the fines, the legislation soon became unworkable.

The subsequent Labour government (1974–9) reconfirmed positive state support for trade unions as part of its 'social contract'. The Industrial Relations Act was repealed – apart from the provisions relating to unfair dismissal and statutory recognition procedure – and the Employment Protection Act 1975 not only provided additional individual employee protection rights (particularly in respect of maternity) but also confirmed union rights to disclosure of information, redundancy consultation, time off for trade union activities, etc. Similarly, the terms of reference set for the Bullock Committee on industrial democracy quite clearly stated that there was a 'need for a radical extension of industrial democracy in the control of companies by means of representation on boards of directors' and pre-empted 'the essential role of trade union organisations in this process' (Bullock Committee, 1977: v).

However, Marsh believes that the 1960s and 1970s were an 'exceptional' period in respect of the unions' political role and involvement with government (1992: 240). Certainly, the effect of the Conservative government's strategy based on a free market *laissez-faire* ideology, developed under Thatcher during the 1980s and continued into the 1990s, was to remove, or at least significantly reduce, direct government economic planning and to rely on market forces, monetarism and unemployment to enhance Britain's international economic competitiveness. It sought to create employment opportunities, increase labour flexibility and emphasise individualism through deregulating employment. The series of substantial pieces of legislation passed between 1980 and 1993 curtailed trade union power and allowed management to re-exert its prerogative. In particular, these Acts restricted substantially the boundary of lawful industrial action, introduced stricter legal requirements for the conduct of industrial action and undermined the unions' organising abilities (most importantly, by abolishing the statutory recognition procedure). Despite union resistance (once again including major disputes and court cases resulting in unions being fined for contempt of court and having their funds sequestrated), the continuing re-election of a Conservative government meant that there was little prospect of the legislation being changed. Certainly, economic conditions (recession and international competition) coupled with employment restructuring (particularly the decline in manufacturing) provided the conditions for the government to exert its authority and ensure union compliance (Marsh, 1992).

At the same time, the government confronted unions in the public sector in its role as employer (telecommunications 1983; National Coal Board 1984/5; GCHQ 1984; teachers 1987) and no longer regarded trade unions as 'joint managers' of the industrial and economic system but rather as a major impediment to its strategy for economic change. It played down the role of the NEDC (finally disbanding it in 1992), reduced the tripartite basis of managing the MSC and ACAS and devolved the implementation of training policies from the centralised ITBs and MSC to local business-led Training and Enterprise Councils (TECs). Wages councils (the only statutory support for collective bargaining in a number of poorly organised and low-paid industries) were first restricted (in 1986) and then abolished (in 1993) as part of the government's strategy to 'price people back into jobs' and, at the same time, the duty 'to promote collective bargaining' was removed from ACAS's terms of reference. Furthermore, throughout the period, the government sought to limit the effects of EU directives on the UK and even 'opted out' of the Social Chapter of the Maastrict Treaty. However, the government did feel it appropriate to create new state agencies to provide support and assistance to individuals seeking to take legal actions against trade unions – the Commissioner for the Rights of Trade Union Members (in 1988) and the Commissioner for Protection Against Unlawful Industrial Action (in 1993).

The experience of the UK during the 1980s demonstrates how a change in the dominant political ideology within a society can produce a substantial shift in its employee relations system. The Thatcherite policies and strategies towards employee relations were driven by an overriding objective of subordinating employee relations to economic reform and development, a strategy very similar to that of the governments of the 'tiger economies' of South East Asia.

The position changed to some extent, but not fundamentally, with the election of Labour in 1997 (and its subsequent re-election in 2001). Despite an overwhelming majority, Labour has not repealed the Conservative legislation and remains committed to 'labour market flexibility'. However, it has sought to project an employee relations approach based on the concepts of 'social partnership' and 'fairness at work'. The government's first actions were to sign up to the EU Social Chapter (Treaty of Amsterdam, 1997), introduce legislation to establish a Low Pay Commission and national minimum wage (National Minimum Wage Act 1998) and, perhaps most symbolic, restore union recognition and representation rights at GCHQ and compensate those who had been sacked for refusing to give up their union membership. The subsequent Employment Relations Act 1999 gave some support to trade unionism by reintroducing a statutory union recognition procedure, constraining management's ability to dismiss lawful strikers and giving employees a right to be accompanied by a union representative or fellow employee at disciplinary or grievance hearings with management. In 2001, the Labour government announced improvements in maternity and parental leave rights, although it stopped short of giving parents a legal right to work flexible hours – only a right for some parents 'to have a request for changed hours seriously considered'. Furthermore, it finally acceded to pressure within the EU and accepted a directive on establishing a statutory right to employee information and consultation within organisations. Perhaps most significantly, the Labour government has recognised the need to reinvolve trade unions through regular 'semi-official' meetings (Maguire, 2001b) and by inviting the TUC to join a permanent TUC–CBI productivity group (somewhat reminiscent of the initiatives of the 1960s).

Government approaches to employee relations

Economic factors, directly or indirectly, appear to dominate government thinking, policies and strategies. In recent years, governments in the UK and Europe have become particularly concerned not only with creating the 'right' conditions for economic restructuring and growth in the face of greater international competition, but also with the increasing costs of tackling social issues (such as unemployment, retirement and the provision of education and health services). Government strategies appear to centre on three main elements of the operation of the labour market: the level of employment, the nature of the employment relationship and the distribution of economic rewards (Poole, 1986: 102). However, the extent, direction and manner of the desired control will differ depending on the political ideology of the government and the relative importance it attaches to social as well as economic objectives (that is, the type of society it wishes to create or, at least, encourage). For example:

- To what extent should the government accept responsibility and take action not only for securing economic development and creating jobs but also for mitigating the social costs of unemployment and economic change?
- What constitutes a fair basis for labour competition (both between organisations and between countries) and how far should employees be protected by legislation against exploitation?
- How far should employees and trade unions be able to exert their collective power through the use of industrial action?
- To what extent should management decisions and actions within the organisation be required to be subject to the consent, or at least influence, of its employees?
- Should governments regulate wages, through a national minimum wage and incomes policy, not only to control levels of pay for the benefit of economic growth but also to ensure fairness and the maintenance of a reasonable standard of living for employees?

Government autonomy

The inextricable link between economics and politics is reflected in the use of the phrase 'industrialised capitalist democracy' to describe countries like the UK. The question that arises from this is, how does a democratic government fit within the capitalist economic system? The essence of democracy appears to rest on two elements. First, significant differences of view exist among the population regarding the nature of the desired society and/or the policies that should be pursued to create or encourage the development of that society. Second, processes exist within the society which allow for the expression of these different ideologies and sectional interests (political parties) and provide the means to implement the desired policies through the authority and power of government (obtaining popular support in elections). In the UK, this difference of ideology and sectional interest has, at least in the past, been expressed through the Conservative Party (supporting capital's interests) and the Labour Party (supporting workers' interests), whereas in Europe it has been expressed primarily through Christian Democratic, Social Democratic and Communist parties.

However, many people believe that the 'national interest' should prevail over sectional ideological interests once a political party becomes the government. In employee relations, this leads to an expectation that the government remains 'neutral' (favours neither management nor trade unions) and protects individuals and the wider society from any abuse of power by either interest group. However, within any democratic society, there will always be significant differences of view about the causes and solutions of most economic and social issues and, consequently, no universal consensus of what is the national interest. All government strategies and policies, therefore, inevitably reflect the government's particular ideological base.

In a similar way, both Hyman (1975: 125) and Blyton and Turnbull (1994: 139) have argued that the political system, irrespective of which political party is in power, must support the maintenance of the capitalist interest. The needs of 'capitalism' for confidence in economic and social stability restrict any radical initiatives in economic or labour policies: government needs capital more than capital needs government. Indeed, Hyman argues that from a Marxist perspective even government non-intervention is, in effect, support for capitalism by not challenging the unequal balance of power between employer and employee which is inherent in the capitalist economic and legal relationships. Even if governments have not in the past always been 'a captive of class forces, economic forces or the capitalist mode of production' (Beaumont, 1992: 17), there is little doubt that it is now increasingly possible for the power of capitalism to constrain or negate any individual government's strategy, as a consequence of the current liberalisation of world trade and the increasing dominance of multinational global organisations (which owe no allegiance to any particular country).

While there is little doubt that the UK Conservative government's legislative strategy after 1979 was 'a key instrument facilitating labour-market restructuring' (Dickens and Hall, 1995: 256), it is more difficult to be certain whether this change in policy direction is evidence of government autonomy, the pursuit of a sectional managerial interest or the inherent demand of the capitalist system under the guise of national interest. Perhaps more significantly, the Labour Party leadership felt it necessary to move away from its traditional base as a 'worker's' party (that is, remove the perception that it represents a sectional interest) and be seen to have the support of the business community in order to make it more electable. Certainly, after being elected in 1997, it maintained a significant degree of continuity with the previous Conservative governments' approach and did not seek to introduce radically different economic, fiscal and labour policies. However, trade unions have also begun to question their traditional relationship with the Labour Party: one political commentator noted that 'unions have come not so much to support a Labour government as to tolerate it' (Younge, 2001b), while another noted that 'the call for disaffiliation [from the Labour Party] is being heard ever more loudly in unions' (Maguire, 2001a). Certainly, despite substantial increases in expenditure on the public service sector (an area of employment where trade unionism remains very strong), the Labour government has also challenged trade unions and others about maintaining an ideological divide between 'public' and 'private' organisations and has been keen to encourage public/private partnerships in both the funding and delivery of public services.

Differences in government strategies, seen both within and between countries, result from different priorities and approaches to the main areas of concern in the labour

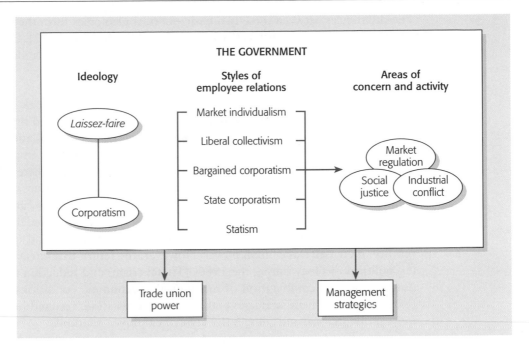

Figure 5.2 **Government and employee relations**

market (regulation, justice and conflict), and these are a reflection of differences in the underlying political ideology (see Figure 5.2).

Political ideology and forms of employee relations

Two basic, but very different, political ideologies may be identified. First, the *laissez-faire* (free market) ideology regards 'free' competition for goods, services and labour within the economic system as the prime basis for regulating society. Not only the work relationship but also the acquisition and provision of 'social' services, such as education and health, are seen as primarily contractual 'economic' matters with an emphasis on the individual being responsible for his or her own well-being, rather than being provided for by the state. The role of government is primarily one of minimising regulation and distortions in the operation of the 'marketplace'. The organisation and collective power of labour, through trade unions, is certainly regarded as a distortion of the normal market mechanism.

Second, the *corporatist* (interventionist) ideology regards economic and social aspects of life as interrelated parts of a whole and a proper matter for political influence and regulation – therefore, the different segments of society should be incorporated into the process of government (particularly 'capital' and 'labour'). It believes that government should accept responsibility, through interventionist regulation, for both protecting individuals from the social problems arising from the operation of capitalism and improving their quality of life. There is concern for ensuring not only that the operation of the economic system is constrained by the need for 'social justice' but also that the governmental process involves consent through mechanisms of social partnership.

The differences between these two basic political ideologies form the foundation of a typology of employee relations (Crouch, 1977, 1982; Strinati, 1982). Different styles of national employee relations result from differences in the governing ideology relative to the power position of trade unions.

- *Market individualism*: *laissez-faire* governing ideology and weak trade unions. Employees are relatively unorganised and individually subordinated by the competitive control mechanisms of the 'market'. Government policy and legislation are directed towards protecting capital's 'property rights' rather than protecting employees against any excesses of managerial prerogative and exploitation. Certainly there is little, if any, support for the role of trade unions. The determination of the nature of the employment relationship is largely in the hands of management and may, at best, be little more than paternalistic. This style of employee relations predominated during the UK's industrialisation until legislation and economic conditions, around the turn of the century, increased trade union power. However, the return to a *laissez-faire* governing political ideology during the 1980s (Thatcherism) and reduction in trade union power, due to a combination of unfavourable economic conditions, new human resource management strategies and restrictive legislation, resulted in a return to a more individualised and competitive style of employee relations.

- *Liberal collectivism*: broadly *laissez-faire* governing ideology but having to accommodate the increasing power of trade unions. Employees are no longer simply individuals but are recognised as having some collective entity and strength. However, trade unions are restricted to an 'economic' role in negotiating basic terms and conditions of employment, while management maintains its decision-making prerogative in the non-economic aspects of the employment relationship. In seeking to maintain a degree of a 'free market' system, the government may intervene to ensure a power balance between management and trade unions. The concepts of 'pluralism' and 'voluntarism' associated with this approach have been important elements of UK employee relations during much of the twentieth century.

- *Bargained corporatism*: corporatist governing ideology and strong independent trade unions. The employment relationship is based on the development of a bipartite 'social partnership' between management and unions at the organisation level and a tripartite relationship between the social partners and government at the national level. It becomes an integrated responsibility, determined at both organisational and society levels. The government is prepared to involve trade unions and management in determining government strategy, not only on employment issues but also on more general economic and social issues, in return for their cooperation in maintaining stability in employee relations to support the achievement of that strategy. This style of employee relations has been a characteristic of Sweden, Germany and the Netherlands (which have had long periods of Social Democratic government) and the underlying principle in the EU's approach to employee relations. This approach may be subdivided (Taylor, 1989: 97) between, at its simplest level, management and unions being consulted frequently by government and, a more advanced form, the formal institutionalisation of the relationship within a broader consensus-based framework of government policy formulation and administration. The UK adopted a partial 'bargained corporatist' style of employee relations in the late 1970s, with the 'social contract' between the Labour government and trade unions.

- *State corporatism*: corporatist governing ideology (often involving a long-term dominant or even single political party) and politically subordinated trade unions. Control over the employment relationship is exercised through the political system rather than economic free-market forces. While this style was the foundation of employee relations in the former communist countries of eastern Europe, it can also be seen in the government's strategy for economic development in some of the 'tiger economies' of South East Asia. Singapore's 'symbiotic' relationship between the government, which has ruled continuously since independence in 1959, and the National Trade Union Congress (NTUC) includes cross-organisational leadership between trade unions and the political party, union exposition and exhortation of national economic development needs to its members and the government's use of legislation to deregister unions which challenge the NTUC or its policies.
- *Statism*: corporatist governing ideology and industrially weak unions. In this style of employee relations, the government redresses the industrial power imbalance between employer and employee by establishing a framework of legislated terms and conditions of employment for all employees. Consequently, trade union activities become more focused on a political as opposed to an industrial role.

It has been suggested that only the extremes can produce stable employee relations – where labour is subordinated either by 'free market' forces within the economic system or by agencies supporting government strategies within the political system (Crouch, 1995: 231). Significantly, perhaps, the UK and other European countries have been largely characterised by 'liberal collectivism' or 'bargained corporatism' styles of employee relations.

The labour market

There are two interrelated areas in the operation of the 'labour market'. The first relates to the price mechanism (wages). The level and relative distribution of pay is influenced by a variety of factors such as, on the employees' side, income expectations and the development of collective power to pursue these expectations, and, on the management side, labour costs and productivity. The second area is concerned with the level and structure of employment (the characteristics of the supply and demand for labour). This is affected not only by the general level of economic activity within organisations or the economy but also by shifts in the economic and industrial structures, technological development and changes in the participation rates within the working population. There have been substantial changes affecting the older industrialised countries since the 1970s (Fevre, 1992: 2–9). These changes include:

- global redistribution of economic activity and jobs away from these countries and towards Asia, eastern Europe and other developing economies;
- increased labour supply through greater female participation in the labour force;
- changes in industrial and employment structures – away from manufacturing and towards service industries; away from manual to non-manual jobs;
- technological developments generally requiring fewer, but more technically skilled, people;
- continuing long-term relatively high levels of unemployment, and employment coming to be seen, by both employees and employers, as more temporary and transient.

The primary concern of all governments is to ensure that the operation of the labour market supports, rather than hinders, economic change and development – in particular, that it promotes labour efficiency and minimises labour unit costs to underpin international competitiveness. A second potential focus of government concern is to mitigate the social and political consequences of economic change (in particular, unemployment). The manner in which a government seeks to 'regulate' the labour market, and the relative importance it attaches to the two areas of concern, will depend to a large measure on its underlying political ideology. Whereas in some countries (for example, Japan, Germany, Sweden and Singapore) the government has been prepared to intervene directly in the working of labour market mechanisms, in other countries (such as the UK and the US) the governments have encouraged management to accept responsibility for the operation of the labour market (deregulation). This is indicative of a 'basic division . . . between those approaches which see the labour market as an arena of competition between individuals and those which see it as shaped and controlled by collective institutions, pressures and customs' (Claydon, 1994: 75) (see Exhibit 5.1).

Unemployment and labour flexibility

Unemployment is invariably a major focus of government attention. It is useful to identify two main groups of government labour market policies (Schmid *et al.*, 1992): *passive* policies (the provision of financial support to the individual during periods without work – unemployment benefit) and *active* policies (the provision of state funds to aid the unemployed in obtaining a new job – training, mobility allowances or job creation). The operation of these policies raises two important issues:

- How should they be funded – indirectly by society as a whole (through government allocation of funds from general taxation) or directly by those currently in the labour market (through contributions from employers and employees)?
- How should the two policy areas be managed – separately, with active policies being implemented through 'employment', 'trade' or 'education' agencies and passive policies being managed within a broad 'social welfare' agency, or integrated together in one agency?

Periods of recession and high unemployment heighten the potential tension between the two sets of policies. They are faced with reduced funding, whether from a decrease in the government's general 'tax-take' or less coming from direct contributions in the employed sector, at the same time as the costs of both types of policy are likely to increase. Direct contributions, by both employers and employees, are a major 'add-on' labour cost for the organisation and, therefore, any increase in the level of these contributions will increase the organisation's unit labour costs. This has the potential for making organisations more uncompetitive or reducing the number of employees, and thereby further increasing the level of unemployment. The alternative is to reduce the cost of, in particular, the passive policies by reducing the level of benefit or tightening the regulations which determine who is entitled to receive such benefit. Certainly, the increasing and continuing high cost of maintaining an adequate level of unemployment benefit, which in most countries is a legal welfare entitlement, has become a major concern in the older industrialised countries, particularly in the UK and other EU countries.

ILO: plan needed for full employment

In its annual employment report, published today, the ILO [International Labour Organisation] argues a renewed commitment by national governments to the concept of full employment with a sustained annual global rate of more than 3.5 per cent could help to resolve the crisis. The report says that full employment is 'not passé' but 'still feasible and highly desirable'.

'Current levels of unemployment make no economic sense and are neither politically nor socially sustainable', said Mr Michel Hansenne, the ILO's director-general yesterday.

'It is not just heartless but pernicious to assume nothing can be done to remedy unemployment, that so called jobless growth (when a country's gross domestic product grows with no substantial jobs growth) is the best that can be hoped for in an increasingly competitive economy or that current unemployment rates somehow constitute a natural and inevitable outcome of market forces.'

The report seeks to demolish a range of assumptions about world employment. 'It is not true globalisation is an uncontrollable supranational force that has largely usurped national policy autonomy', it says. According to the ILO the nation state is 'still the dominant influence on economic and labour-market outcomes. Global financial markets punish unsound macro-economic policies which are, in any case, undesirable in their own right.' It adds, 'The empirical evidence suggests trade with developing countries and the relocation of industries has been only a minor explanatory factor behind the rise in unemployment and the declining wages of unskilled workers in industrialised countries.'

The report questions the popular view that the world is running out of jobs. 'Much of the "end-of-work" literature rests on unwarranted extrapolations from dramatic episodes of corporate downsizing, ignoring job creation elsewhere in the economy.' The ILO says the employment growth rate has remained 'almost unchanged over the last three-and-a-half decades and has not slowed down significantly since 1973', with the pace of job creation remaining steady in the face of the reduced economic growth rate of the 1970s and 1980s.

Nor does the ILO accept job changes are becoming more frequent and employment more unstable, saying there has been an increase not a decline in the length of job tenure. 'On average, individuals currently employed have been in their jobs for six to 12 years depending on the country and this figure has not been declining', it says. Only in Spain have job moves become increasingly frequent, 'probably because of institutional changes'.

The report doubts whether 'labour market imperfections' are 'either the main or sole cause of the upward drift in European unemployment', although it does not suggest they have had no effect. 'Labour market rigidities have not been increasing over the period of rising unemployment', says the ILO.

It says the main 'underlying' cause of increased unemployment is the slowdown in economic growth since 1974. It also criticises the rise in wage inequality, particularly in the US, UK and New Zealand, which it argues is partly due to the decline in trade union density and decentralisation of collective bargaining.

The report states: 'There is no convincing evidence that it is supply-side constraints, rather than a deficiency in demand that have caused the prolonged period of low growth.' It adds: 'Higher growth is possible provided a sustained period of expansionary policies is supported by credible policies to prevent a resurgence of inflationary wage increases and to overcome the skill shortages that will be generated. Without this the expansionary impulse will indeed be choked off by the reaction of the financial markets.' The ILO calls for a return to co-ordinated pay bargaining, the creation of social pacts between unions and employers, as well as the encouragement of profit-sharing or 'some form of tax-based incomes policy if there are no better alternatives'. It wants more efficient labour market policies with subsidies for low wage employment, training focused on the most disadvantaged, incentives for recruiting long-term jobless and improved benefit transfer programmes linking benefits and work more closely together.

The report says developing countries should also be committed to full employment and it argues this can be achieved by creating more open and competitive economies that benefit fully from expanding trade and investment flows in the global economy. The ILO believes, however, the 'trickle-down effects of market reforms will be weak unless they are accompanied by programmes to strengthen the productive capacity of the poor' through improvements in rural infrastructure, education and health services.

Source: Robert Taylor, *Financial Times*, 26 November 1996.
© 1996 The Financial Times Limited

Political ideology, not surprisingly, appears to be an important factor in determining how governments have sought to respond to this situation (Hollinshead and Leat, 1995: 132). Those with a more corporatist governing ideology have been reluctant to reduce levels of unemployment benefit, which they regard as an important element of the welfare system in protecting the individual's living standards. They have tended to concentrate on supporting organisational training (in order to equip existing employees to adjust to change and, thereby, remain competitive and in employment) and developing state-funded and organised training for those not in employment (particularly the young and unemployed). It is those governments with a more *laissez-faire* ideology which have favoured strategies that reduce benefit levels or increase the restrictions on eligibility. They believe that, by reducing financial support when unemployed, the individual will be more prepared to accept those jobs that are available, even if only temporary, part-time or low-paid. In this way they aim to 'price people back into jobs'. At the same time, responsibility has been placed on management and the individual for ensuring that adequate training takes place, and for its funding.

Certainly, throughout the 1980s and much of the 1990s, the UK government's strategies towards the labour market reflected this latter approach. Claims for unemployment benefit have become subject to much closer scrutiny (particularly, requiring the individual to prove that they are 'actively' seeking work) and the long-term unemployed may be compelled to attend 'training' courses under the threat of losing their benefit if they do not. At the same time, the annual increase in the level of social security benefits generally, including unemployment benefit, has been unlinked from the annual change in average earnings so that the gap between the two has widened (increasing the pressure on an unemployed person to take any work available). Furthermore, the Conservative government consistently resisted the adoption of EU directives intended to establish employment protection rights in respect of 'atypical' workers and working time. It argued that such regulations would inhibit the competitiveness of UK organisations in the international market. Even changes in the retirement age and the abolition of legislation restricting the work of women were presented not so much as measures to support the development of equal opportunities but as measures to increase labour 'flexibility'. The Conservative government also abolished the tripartite and national-based approach of the industrial training boards and Manpower Services Commission and transferred responsibility for training to employer-led industry training organisations (ITOs) and locally based training and enterprise councils (TECs) (Keep and Rainbird, 1995).

There has been some change in direction since the election of the Labour government in 1997. Certainly, it has been prepared to 'sign up' for the Social Chapter and accept the adoption of EU directives on employment rights. However, it appears (like its predecessor) to be arguing within the EU for the adoption of policies which will encourage greater labour flexibility. Perhaps its most important employment strategy has been its New Deal approach to welfare and training, aimed at encouraging people 'off welfare and into work'. Despite strong criticism from within the Labour Party itself and from a variety of pressure groups regarding its changes in benefit regulations for single parents and the disabled, the approach has been described by some commentators as 'qualitatively better than any previous government jobs scheme, offering tailored rather than blanket advice to benefit recipients and helping to instill positive attitudes to work' (Atkinson, 2001). The government claims it has helped over 270,000 people into work, although some economists argue that most of these people would have got work anyway as a result of the healthy economy in the late 1990s. However, the government has announced additional money to target the disabled, those not equipped to enter the labour market, geographic unemployment black spots and areas of long-term skill shortages. At the same time, the government has sought to integrate the two strands of the benefit agency and employment service by introducing a number of 'one-stop' shops.

However, employment and unemployment figures need to be interpreted with caution. On the positive side, the number of people in employment in the UK has increased by some 4 million since the mid-1970s and stands in 2002 at 28.1 million. At the same time, the claimant count (those claiming unemployment benefit) fell below 1 million in 2001 (3 per cent of the working population); its lowest for 25 years and well below the peaks of the mid-1980s (over 3 million) and early-1990s (almost 3 million). However, the number of people claiming incapacity benefit (long-term sickness), rather than unemployment benefit, has quadrupled over the past 20 years to 2 million, while on the wider International Labour Organisation (ILO) measure of unemployment (those looking for work), the level of UK unemployment is 1.5 million (more significantly, perhaps, it rose during the third quarter of 2001 – similar to the 1993 recession). Furthermore, if part-time employees who are 'underemployed' because no full-time work is available are included, the unemployment figure could be as high as 4 million. Thus, talk of a 'return to full-employment' or 'work for all' may be premature.

Incomes policy

While fiscal and monetary policies may allow governments to manage the macro-level impact of incomes on the economy, not all governments seek to regulate directly the pay outcomes of collective bargaining (incomes policy). An incomes policy may serve two functions. First, it may be used as an economic 'weapon', restricting pay increases to reduce pressure on labour costs and prices in periods of inflation or regulating pay increases in periods of economic growth in order to avoid inflation. Second, it may act as a mechanism to promote greater 'social justice' by exerting pressure for the realignment of pay levels between different groups within society.

The use of formal incomes policies was an important feature of the UK's employee relations system throughout most of the 1960s and 1970s. After 1979, however, the Conservative government confined itself to a simple 'self-induced if invisible incomes policy' (McCarthy, 1993: 7) of cash limits on the public sector to reduce government expenditure. Although the primary role of the previous incomes policies was as an economic 'weapon' – to restrict pay increases, reduce labour costs and inflation and, thereby, maintain the UK's international competitiveness – those policies did result in some realignment of pay differentials (particularly, a compression of the pay differences between non-manual and manual employees and between skilled and unskilled employees within the manual group). However, attempts to address specific issues of 'social justice' were not successful. While special emotive groups (such as health service and fire service workers) were sometimes, because of their accepted low-pay position, treated as exceptions and allowed to receive increases above the 'economic' norm, so too were groups (such as miners) who, because of their industrial power, represented a potential direct challenge to the overall acceptance of the incomes policy. Even the 'low pay' incomes policy in 1975, which restricted pay increases to those earning below £8,500 per annum, resulted in only a temporary improvement in the position of the lower paid because their increase was absorbed within subsequent pay negotiations.

One of the most difficult issues with any incomes policy is how to enforce its terms. Without the full and active support of both management and unions, the government must rely on some form of statutory-based state agency. The problem is compounded when, as in the UK, collective bargaining is decentralised and fragmented; inevitably the attention of the regulating agency is directed towards the smaller number of major, centralised, private sector, multi-employer agreements and, of course, negotiations under the direct or indirect control of the government itself. Pay increases above the 'norm' made at the organisational level, whether through collective bargaining or not, may easily escape notice. Furthermore, who should be penalised – the employer, the employees or both? And what form should the penalty take? Certainly, it is better to avoid breaches in the first place.

The only time the UK came close to a voluntary cooperative approach was during the Social Contract (1975–9). However, successive governments in Ireland (Prondzynski, 1992) managed to establish tripartite 'understandings' or 'programmes' on national economic and social strategies linked to incomes policies. It was perhaps most effective in regulating pay during the 1970s with centralised national wage agreements. Similarly, Whitfield (1988) believes that the Australian Accord in the 1980s was successful not only because it linked pay issues with other economic, fiscal and social policies and was endorsed by a specially convened National Economic Summit Conference (comprising representatives of federal and state governments, employers, unions and various social welfare groups), but also because the Australian 'arbitration' system of collective bargaining provided a centralised but flexible way to implement the incomes policy. In Singapore, however, the success of the incomes policy may be attributed more to the 'incorporation' (subordination) of trade unions into the political system (Beng and Chew, 1995). The annual wage guidelines set by the tripartite National Wages Council, established in 1972, are required to reflect the performance of the economy and be consistent with maintaining employment and economic growth and are certainly intended to influence collective bargaining in line with public policy.

UK trade unions have always expressed strong reservations about the operation of a formal incomes policy. They have felt that it marginalises their role in negotiating pay increases for their members: the level of pay increase becomes determined by the incomes policy, not union negotiators, and is likely to be similar across most groups and organisations (irrespective of whether they are unionised or not). Although unions are not prepared to support any statutory pay restraint, they have been in favour of some form of central national discussion of pay and the economy to establish a climate within which negotiations would take place freely. In 1990, for example, the TUC accepted the idea of an arrangement which would coordinate major pay negotiations to take place following a 'public' tripartite discussion of the government's annual Economic Review and linked to the setting of the rate for a national minimum wage (GMB/UCW, 1990). Significantly, the deteriorating relationship between the Labour government and trade unions since 1997 over such issues as privatisation, employment rights and the minimum wage has led the government to agree to regular 'semi-official' meetings between the Prime Minister and union leaders and for the Chancellor of the Exchequer to invite the TUC and CBI to join with the government in regular meetings about improving productivity.

Social justice

The existence and range of employment protection legislation is, perhaps, one of the clearest expressions of a government's concern, or lack of concern, for 'social justice' in the operation of the labour market. The UK substantially strengthened its individual employment protection legislation during the 1960s and 1970s – most importantly, in the areas of discrimination (both race and sex), equal pay, health and safety, dismissal and redundancy. While some additions were made after 1979, Dickens and Hall point out that the 'free market' ideology of the Conservative government regarded such legislation 'not as essential minimum standards but as "burdens on business" (particularly in respect of small employers) which deter the employment of more people' (1995: 257). Hence, the government raised the qualifying period before being able to claim unfair dismissal from six months to two years and resisted the expansion of further employment protection rights resulting from EU directives. Furthermore, a number of the more important developments in individual protection which did take place during the 1980s and 1990s did so only as a result of external pressures to comply with EU regulations – for example, equal pay for work of equal value; equal treatment in access to employment, vocational training and promotion; protection on transfer of the undertaking; and common qualifying periods, as between part-time and full-time employees, before qualifying for protection rights. Indeed, the Conservative government appeared to be more prepared to provide individuals with rights that might be enforced against trade unions than it did to extend enforceable rights against management. Since its election in 1997, the Labour government appears to have been more willing than its predecessor to implement EU directives (for example, on parental leave, working time and employee consultation) within UK legislation.

The establishment of the single European market in 1992, in the midst of increasingly competitive world markets, has heightened rather than diminished the issue of social policy regulation. The objective of EU social policy is to ensure that employees share in the organisational benefits gained from the 'single market'. However, Teague (1993) suggests that it is perhaps easier to achieve 'negative' integration (centring on the abolition of regulations and barriers which might restrict the free movement of goods and capital) than it is to achieve 'positive' integration (including the development of common social strategies to ensure that labour is not exploited). A similar tension exists at the global level between the World Trade Organisation (WTO) (liberalising world trade) and the ILO (seeking to establish and enforce international labour standards). Certainly, two areas of 'social justice' have recently been the focus of UK attention: a national minimum wage and 'labour dumping' resulting from the business decisions of transnational organisations.

■ National minimum wage

Perhaps the most crucial foundation to ensuring 'social justice' in the labour market is the establishment and enforcement of a minimum wage. Despite any disagreement about what should be its actual level, the existence of a national minimum wage is a clear expression of the principle that employees should receive a 'living wage', which would help alleviate extreme poverty. Many countries have a statutory national minimum wage – including the US, which is often regarded as the bastion of free market capitalism – and the UK has been singularly out of step with most other EU countries in not having one.

Until 1993, the UK had only a partial 'minimum wage' mechanism in the form of statutory wages councils in a limited range of industries, albeit encompassing some 2.5 million employees. These industries (principally retail, catering, clothing and agriculture) have a high level of female and part-time labour working in small organisations with low unionisation. The wages councils were tripartite bodies (comprising union and employer representatives plus government-appointed independent members) and there was a separate Wages Inspectorate with responsibility for policing the application of the wages councils' statutory orders (agreements) within these industries. It can be argued that without such government support it would have been difficult for collective bargaining to have been established and maintained on a voluntary basis. However, the councils' role in dealing with the problem of low pay is more debatable: despite policing by the Wages Inspectorate, many employers still paid below the wages council rate and these industries have remained among the lowest paid.

The Conservative government abolished wages councils in 1993. It argued that they 'priced people out of jobs', by maintaining artificially high wage rates and restricting the potential for employment growth, as well as creating an undue administrative burden on both the government and small employers. However, employment levels in these industries did not increase following the abolition of the wages councils, although wage levels remained virtually static (i.e. decreased in real terms) (TUC, 1996). Not surprisingly, the Conservative government was also opposed to any suggestion of introducing a national minimum wage. Not only did it regard the idea as the antithesis of a free market, but it also believed that its introduction would have a knock-on effect in pushing up all pay levels. However, one estimate suggested that such a knock-on effect would be limited to the lower levels of the pay structure and any resulting reduction in the employment level would be small (Bazen and Benhayoun, 1992). At the same time, it was argued, government spending of some £2.4 billion per annum on family credit amounted to 'the taxpayer . . . funding cheap labour' (Hutton, 1995).

One of the first moves by the Labour government elected in 1997 was to introduce a national minimum wage (National Minimum Wage Act 1998), with an independent Low Pay Commission (LPC) to receive evidence and make recommendations to government regarding the level, which should take into account any likely effect on employment, inflation and business competitiveness. In its first year (1999), the government accepted the LPC's recommendation of a basic 'adult' national minimum wage (NMW) of £3.60 per hour. However, it rejected the LPC's recommendations in respect of the 'young person' NMW by reducing it from £3.20 to £3.00 per hour and insisting that it should apply to those aged 18–21 years (i.e. the 'adult' rate would apply only when a person reached 22 years of age). In 2000, the rates were increased by 10p and 20p per hour, respectively.

However, the means by which a NMW is determined are perhaps as important as the level set (Sachdev, 2001). In the US, where there is no automatic mechanism for increasing the NMW, each increase requires a bill to be agreed in Congress and then signed into law by the President. This, it is argued, allows both Democrats and Republicans to demonstrate to their constituents (labour and business respectively) how hard they fight for their interests. France, on the other hand, has an automatic non-political element (linked to both price increase and half the real increase in average earnings), as well as a further possible element determined by government decree. Certainly, in the UK the final decision on the NMW rests with the government, and its political dimension was clearly seen in setting the rate for 2001. In late 2000 the government indicated that it wanted the NMW rate for 2001 (an election year) to reflect the growth in average earnings since the introduction of the NMW in April 1999, because it was not a 'welfare benefit' but an 'income linked to the workplace'. However, the Confederation of British Industry (CBI) felt that the level of the NMW was an 'economic' matter to be determined by the independent LPC, rather than a political decision for the government. Nevertheless, in March 2001 the government quickly announced acceptance of the LPC's recommended 11 per cent increase in the NMW (to £4.10 per hour for 'adults' and £3.50 per hour for 'younger' workers with effect from October 2001 – and with a further 10p per hour for both rates in 2002 'depending on economic conditions'), but still rejected the LPC's recommendation to extend the adult rate to 21 year olds. However, the TUC is still pressing not only for the adult rate to be applied to all those over 21 but also for a minimum rate to be introduced for 16 and 17 year olds (currently not covered by the NMW).

Under the legislation, while an employee may take a claim regarding underpayment to either an employment tribunal or the civil court, the Inland Revenue and Contributions Agency also has a responsibility to oversee the NMW and has the power to issue enforcement notices on underpaying employers or even instigate criminal proceedings. While this process recovered an estimated £4 million for employees in underpaid wages during the first two years of its operation, there has been evidence from Citizens Advice Bureaux of both the emergence of a separate labour market for NMW jobs and employers cutting workers' hours, increasing their workload, removing paid breaks or holiday entitlements and increasing charges for tea/coffee (Hetherington, 2000). However, the government claimed that the narrowing of the pay gap between high- and low-paid in 2000, for the first time since the early 1970s, resulted primarily from the effect of the NMW on the wages of women and part-timers. Furthermore, Kitson and Wilkinson (2000) argue that the introduction of the NMW has had 'no negative effects on employment' and, indeed, 'is beginning to act as a spur to competition and efficiency' with small firms 'responding by adopting new, non-wage forms of competition'.

Social or labour dumping

The term 'social dumping' relates to the transfer of work, by transnational organisations, to take advantage of labour differences between countries: reducing employment in one country, while expanding it in another. The problem has become highlighted as trade barriers have been reduced or removed with the creation of regional 'single' markets (like the EU, ASEAN and NAFTA) and the general liberalisation of world trade through the WTO. The 'labour' element is an important aspect of both organisational and national competitiveness, and significant national variations exist in a number of areas:

- direct labour costs (wage levels reflect differences in the cost and standard of living);
- indirect labour costs (hours of work, holidays, fringe benefits and health and safety provisions);
- social 'add-on' costs (employers' costs associated with social security contributions, dismissals and redundancy);
- use of 'vulnerable' groups (females, children, homeworkers, bonded labour, prison labour, etc.).

Within the EU, the problem of social dumping was graphically illustrated by Hoover in 1993 (EIRR, 1993). The company made an agreement with the AEEU for its Cambuslang (Scotland) site which included not only significant changes in working methods to improve labour efficiency and flexibility but also, and perhaps most importantly, measures to reduce labour costs – in particular, a one-year pay freeze and the recruitment of new employees to be initially on two-year fixed contracts at 15 per cent lower wages than existing employees. Then, three days later and without prior warning, Hoover announced that its factory in Longvic (France) would be closed and its work transferred to Cambuslang. While this would create an extra 400 jobs in Scotland, 600 French employees would lose their jobs. French workers were critical not only of Hoover management but also of the AEEU, which they felt had accepted an 'appalling agreement'. However, the AEEU argued that it was 'in the business of defending its members' and had got 'the best deal it could'.

There appear to be three central questions:

■ What is a 'fair' basis for labour competition?
■ Can governments balance a 'social justice' objective of providing employment protection with an 'economic' objective of facilitating employment creation?
■ Should national self-interest take precedence over international cooperation?

The conflict between the UK, under a Conservative government, and its EU partners over the Social Chapter in the Maastricht Treaty has been described as a 'conflict between the proponents of "solidarity" and "subsidiarity", and between the advocates of lesser rather than greater labour market regulation' (Rhodes, 1993: 298). The dispute had not only an ideological element but also a pragmatic one – for one country to gain a competitive edge over other countries (Towers, 1992). Certainly, trade unions believe that, in the face of competition between national governments to attract or maintain investment and employment by offering lower labour costs, greater labour flexibility and a more compliant workforce, employees are virtually powerless to prevent the 'transfer of unemployment' from one country to another. The solution, in their view, lies in limiting the nature and degree of such competition through more international regulation of employment protection rights, harmonisation of social 'add-on' costs and coordination of national employment promotion programmes. The UK government has been under pressure from both UK trade unions which argue that it is easier and cheaper for international organisations to make employees redundant in the UK than in other EU countries and from protesting workers in other countries when UK companies seek to 'export' these practices.

Social dumping is not confined to relations between EU countries, but has become a matter for concern on a global scale. Whereas many, particularly developing, countries see themselves being dominated by global multinational capitalism, older industrialised countries, particularly in Europe and North America, feel threatened by the nature of employment relations that exist in many of the newly industrialised and industrialising countries. As Younge (2001a) points out, WTO agreements are 'for free trade, not fair trade'. This has led to calls for 'social clauses' (minimum labour standards) to be included as part of any trade agreements between the EU and ASEAN countries and in the WTO. This approach may be seen as simply the most effective way of defining and enforcing the limits of 'fair' labour competition, especially the ability of multinational organisations to take advantage of national fragmentation and engage in social dumping. However, Asian countries certainly regard it as both a form of self-protection – which will restrict their competitiveness and, in turn, their continued economic development – and an unwarranted attempt to impose on them a western style of employee relations. Like the UK government's view of EU regulation, they also see this approach as interfering with their right to determine their own approach to and standards of employee relations.

The other side of the coin from the 'free movement of capital' is the issue of the 'free movement of labour'. However, this is not just an EU problem as it expands to include countries from the former eastern Europe whose citizens will also have the right to work or seek work anywhere within the EU's borders. At the broader international level, issues of economic migration appear to have become inextricably bound up with ethical issues relating to refugee or asylum status. Significantly, a number of UK public service employers in health, social services and education have been actively seeking to recruit qualified staff from overseas (including developing countries) in order to cope with staff shortages.

Industrial conflict

The potential for conflict always exists within any social structure. Whereas the dominant group in the social structure may perceive conflict as a threat to the established order which must be controlled or even suppressed, those who seek to challenge the status quo may regard it as a necessary part of the process of developing a new order. Within a pluralistic perspective, conflict is seen as a means of expressing different interests (which have to be resolved) and, therefore, is a necessary element in maintaining the continuity and stability of the social structure. The use of industrial action within the employee relations system is an explicit, collective expression of both concern and power. It is intended to help secure a more favourable outcome to a negotiation or to resist unacceptable management actions. Its 'power' derives from the capacity to create a situation of temporary disorder within the employment relationship and, by so doing, 'prevents even the most enlightened managerial regime from becoming mere paternalism' (Grunfeld, 1966: 367). However, those who support the *laissez-faire* 'free market' ideology believe such disruption to be an 'intolerable abuse of economic freedom' and 'type of warfare' which allows some groups to make gains at the expense of others (Hutt, 1973: 282–3).

■ Public interest in industrial action

The concepts of national interest and social control are, perhaps, nowhere more intertwined in employee relations than when considering the use of industrial action. The legislation (social control mechanism) which governments create in this area is generally projected as being in the public interest, and therefore if some action is stated to be 'unlawful' then, by implication, it is also morally 'wrong' and people become socialised into accepting it as such (Edwards, 1995: 447). Certainly, the UK approach of granting employees and trade unions 'immunity' from legal action when undertaking 'lawful' industrial action implies that it is a privilege – not granted to other groups in society – rather than a right, and, as such, it may be withdrawn if it is not exercised in a 'responsible' manner (that is, in a manner which is acceptable to the government as the guardian of 'national interest'). Governments determine how wide or narrow is the boundary of what is lawful.

The Conservative government's measures after 1980 increased state control over the use of industrial action. It not only restricted the scope of immunity, by narrowing the boundary of lawful industrial action and tightening the procedural requirements (ballots, independent scrutiny, notifying employers, etc.), but also widened the range of 'interested parties' who can instigate legal action against trade unions to include not just management or even union members but any private citizen who feels he or she might be adversely affected by the industrial action. Furthermore, state support for such individuals was provided through the creation of the Commissioner for Protection Against Unlawful Industrial Action. However, the substantial decline in industrial action seen in the UK during the 1980s and 1990s cannot be attributed solely to this increase in legislated 'social control'. Other countries, which did not change their legislation, also experienced a decline. It would seem that economic factors, such as recession, unemployment and decline in manufacturing employment, might have been more influential than the 'social control' factor (legislation).

While trade unions, as organisations, have been the main focus of legal actions relating to their conduct of industrial action, it is the preparedness of the individual members to withdraw their labour and lose pay which really provides the collective strength of such action. Therefore, the extent to which the state supports a 'right' to strike depends, perhaps, more on whether or not the employee is protected against dismissal than on whether he or she may be sued for damages by management. The concept of immunity may be important in protecting union funds but is largely irrelevant for the individual employee – few employers are prepared to take their own employees to court and secure compensation (damages) which are likely to bankrupt the individual. The more important legal principle, under UK legislation, is that the strike is regarded as a fundamental breach of the contract of employment that justifies management terminating the contract. The introduction of unfair dismissal legislation in 1971 did include the provision that the dismissal of a person undertaking a 'lawful' strike can be considered 'unfair', but only if management dismisses some but not *all* employees engaged in the strike. However, if the industrial action is 'unlawful', management has complete discretion to dismiss whomsoever it chooses – an employee selected in this way cannot take any claim to an employment tribunal.

As part of its 1997 election campaign, the Labour Party announced its intention to amend the law in respect of lawful industrial action, but sought to calm business fears by stating that it did not intend either to prevent employers from dismissing strikers or to compel them to reinstate any who successfully claim unfair dismissal. Consequently, the Employment Relations Act 1999 extended automatic unfair dismissal to include the first eight weeks of 'lawfully organised industrial action'. It could be argued that this might increase management's preparedness to mount legal challenges to the union's conduct of industrial action, because, if successful, it would remove the restriction on their freedom to dismiss. Even after the eight-week period, it may still be unfair to dismiss if a tribunal finds that management has not taken 'all reasonable steps' to resolve the dispute. This involves a significant shift in the tribunal's role: from judging management's equality of treatment among employees, to judging the 'reasonableness' of management's method of handling a dispute and its negotiations.

Another area which has been a focus of attention is whether or not the 'right to strike' should continue to exist in essential services (such as gas, electricity, water and sewerage, health services, teachers, transport, refuse collectors, etc.). The disruption caused to other employers, workers and the general public by industrial action in these services is frequently felt to be unacceptable. Furthermore, in so far as these groups are in the public sector, any industrial action inevitably appears to be 'political' – a challenge to the policy or action of the elected government. The removal of the 'right to strike' in these services is usually linked to the use of some form of automatic arbitration to resolve dispute. Without this, the employees would be powerless and open to management exploitation without any form of redress. However, one side-effect of privatisation has been the removal of many of these services from 'public' responsibility. While a government may wish to constrain the social disruption resulting from strikes in these areas, the management of these private organisations is likely to see any accompanying requirement to accept a process of automatic arbitration, not required of other private sector management, as an unacceptable restriction of its freedom to manage and determine its own terms of employment. Significantly, attempts by some state governments in the US to remove the 'right to strike' in private sector 'essential' services, in return for compulsory arbitration, were held to be contrary to the Taft–Hartley Act 1947 which applied to all non-government employees and which specifically permitted strikes. In both Canada (Beaumont, 1992: 130) and Italy (Bridgford and Stirling, 1994: 150) the governments have sought to mitigate the worst effects of strikes in pubic sector services not by abolishing the 'right to strike', but by requiring employees to maintain a minimum essential level of service during the strike – which has often been the case in the UK, but on a voluntary basis.

Role of the state in dispute settlement

Most governments believe that industrial action, because of its potential disruptive economic and social effects, should be used only as a 'weapon of last resort'. In order to facilitate the maintenance of industrial peace, the government may provide for conciliation and arbitration to be available to the parties at public expense – these services were initially established in the UK under the Conciliation Act 1896 and Industrial Courts Act 1919. The use of such processes is voluntary (i.e. at the discretion of the management and union involved in the dispute). However, during the 1980s, the Conservative government appeared to become less concerned about ensuring the maintenance of industrial peace (perhaps because strikes were becoming less of a threat as they declined in both numbers and working days lost) and, like management, more concerned about the effect arbitration might have on management's freedom and responsibility to manage the organisation. Both viewed arbitration as potentially inducing 'unreasonable' claims and intransigent 'non-negotiation' on the part of unions, in the expectation of obtaining a better settlement from an arbitrator than from management (which, in the public sector, was the government itself or one of its agents), and certainly resulted in decisions being made by an 'outsider' (the arbitrator) rather than by management. Management was encouraged to say 'no' to union requests for arbitration and the union could do nothing, if management adopted an intransigent 'non-negotiable' approach, other than accept or resort to the use of industrial action.

Even in the past, during periods of incomes policy, the government tried, by exhortation or even direct instruction, to regulate the decisions of arbitrators in wage disputes. Such an approach could easily compromise the independence of arbitrators and result in their being perceived as little more than administrators of government policy or 'branded as unpatriotic, irresponsible or deaf' if they took a different view of the 'national interest' (Lowry, 1990: 83). Indeed, it was doubts on the part of both management and union about the continuing impartiality of the Department of Employment's conciliation and arbitration services that led to the creation of ACAS, in 1974, as an autonomous body outside direct ministerial day-to-day control. The determination of ACAS to maintain its independence and not be simply a mechanism for implementing government policy has been borne out not only by its refusal to be an enforcement agent for incomes policy (under the Labour government in the 1970s) but also by its refusal to draw up codes of practice on picketing and the closed shop (during the early days of the Thatcher government) (Mortimer, 1981: 24).

However, the ultimate power of the government to push the employee relations system in the direction it wants, through its ability to 'change the rules of the system', has been demonstrated by the removal of the duty to 'encourage collective bargaining' from ACAS's terms of reference in 1993. Despite ACAS's desire to be independent, impartial and apolitical, the government was able to ensure that its work must be brought in line with government policy. However, ACAS's role in individual conciliation has more than doubled since 1990 with the establishment of new individual legal rights relating to payment of wages and breach of employment contract. Each year about one-third of applications to employment tribunals are resolved through ACAS without needing to go before a tribunal.

The high number of applications for legal redress to individual employment disputes might indicate an increasing individualisation of the contractual relationship and a weakening in the unions' ability to protect members. This is reflected, in part, by the Labour government's according the right to be accompanied by a fellow employee an equal role and status with being accompanied by a union official during any 'serious' disciplinary or grievance meeting with management (Employment Relations Act 1999). At the same time, the extension of individual protective legislation and the increase in the number of applications to employment tribunals (some 167,000 in 2000/1) has led some employers to talk about the development of a 'compensation culture' among dissatisfied employees (see Exhibit 5.2). Significantly, strong union opposition led the Labour government to drop ideas to introduce a £100 administrative charge for applications to tribunals (which unions felt would particularly penalise the low paid) and, as part of its 'routine electronic modernisation' of government activities, to list the names of tribunal applicants on a website (which unions felt unscrupulous employers could easily use to blacklist complainants). However, to encourage the parties to resolve their own problems without recourse to the law, the government has proposed giving tribunals the power to reduce or increase any award by a minimum of 10 per cent and a maximum of 50 per cent if it feels that the employee or employer, respectively, fails to comply with statutory grievance or disciplinary procedures (Employment Bill 2001, Clause 31).

Exhibit 5.2

The jury is out over tribunal reform plan

Dave Harrop, a senior official of the Forum of Private Business, thinks that Patricia Hewitt, the Trade and Industry Secretary, left out a word when she described her plans to reform employment tribunals as 'good for British business'. The missing word, says Mr Harrop, is 'big'. For small businesses, he claims, the package is much less satisfactory. His view is widely shared, although everyone agrees that something needed to be done. The number of applications to tribunals rose 50 per cent in the three years to 2000, making the system one of the key irritants between business and the government. Ministers admit that the system is clogging up, wasting hours of management time.

Ms Hewitt claims her proposals, which form a substantial part of the Employment Bill, published last week, will transform the system by preventing misconceived claims, stopping time-wasting and ending inconsistent judgments.

In effect, she says, it will transfer workplace dispute resolution from the courts back to the office. The government believes applications will fall by up to 30 per cent, or between 30,000 and 40,000.

The Bill gives the Secretary of State powers to make regulations introducing a series of new powers for tribunals. The main problems it identifies, and the new powers it introduces, include:

- Time-wasting – tribunals will be able to award costs against parties because of the way that cases have been conducted and up to £10,000 to compensate parties for preparation time. Tribunals will be able to set a fixed period for conciliation by the Advisory Conciliation and Arbitration Service, preventing negotiations from dragging on until the eve of a hearing. And employees will have to follow a three-stage procedure and exhaust internal company grievance procedures before making an application to a tribunal. About 60 per cent of tribunal applicants are thought to make a claim without the employer knowing there is a dispute – though trade unions argue that in unfair dismissal cases, there is often a little incentive for employees to seek talks. Compensation awards could be varied

by up to 50 per cent where either side has not followed the proper procedures.
- Weak and misconceived cases – rarely used powers to strike out cases or required the applicant to post a £500 deposit before continuing will be strengthened and clarified.
- Inconsistency – the two presidents of the employment tribunals will be given powers to issue practice directions to ensure that cases are conducted in similar ways wherever they are heard. Tribunals will be encouraged to ignore minor procedural failings by employers.

The government's official guidance notes, which accompany the Bill, suggest these measures will cost employers between £46m and £86m in initial costs, and a further £44m to £94m a year in running costs, mainly in setting up and running company dispute resolution schemes.

The benefits to companies are put at between £65m and £90m a year – mainly in reduced costs of handling tribunal cases. The net effect should be that the measures are financially neutral for business as a whole.

But both the costs and the benefits will weigh most heavily on smaller companies because they rarely have specialist personnel managers. This means they stand to lose most in terms of management time needed to establish and run the new procedures and to gain most from a reduction in time spent on tribunal cases and avoiding procedural traps.

The measures were given a broad welcome by business organisations, even though Ms Hewitt dropped draft proposals requiring employees to pay a small charge to file an application. But there is a surprising amount of consensus about the Bill's shortcomings.

'This is a package that is good for big business. Plcs will be able to deal very well with all of this but the three-, five- or seven-person business will find it much more difficult', says Mr Harrop.

Many small companies, he says, do not have formal contracts of employment. Although they will be bound by minimum statutory requirements set

Exhibit 5.2 *continued*

out in the Bill, some will not understand their obligations, providing 'a very shaky basis' for operating the new system.

'There may be some reduction in the number of tribunals that go ahead – but I don't see that small businesses are going to recoup a lot of costs they will have to pay out to conform with all this', he says.

Mike Kelly, personnel manager of GRA, the greyhound racing subsidiary of Wembley plc, says he has substantial doubts about whether the proposals to remove procedural pitfalls and achieve more predictable rulings will have much effect.

'We have had some absolutely horrendous cases where we have been told there was nothing more we could have done to show that we had acted properly in dismissing someone but we were still guilty because it was not clear what was in the minds of management, or some other technical grounds', he says.

'I don't think this is radical enough. Employment tribunals are driven by a compensation culture. We are finding it increasingly difficult to challenge people for poor performance or other things.

'Immediately we say we are concerned about something, people say they will not speak to us until they have spoken to their solicitor. The real problem is that tribunals are a playground for lawyers and that is what has to change.'

William Sargent, chairman of the government's own advisory Small Business Council, says it is clear that ministers have made a 'serious effort' to resolve problems in the system but the jury is out on whether they will succeed.

'The actual judicial part of the process is still a bit of a lottery', he says. 'Lawyers will tell you that even

if the facts are straightforward, the result in court is unpredictable. It would be good if [the tribunals] could now turn their attention to the consistency of the judgment.'

'I am not trying to be churlish about this but I am saying that it needs to be made to work.

Mark Mansell, head of employment law at Allen & Overy, the law firm, says the changes will put new emphasis on procedural fairness. 'A lot of disputes could be resolved or avoided if processes [were] followed', he says.

But others are sceptical, suggesting that the number of tribunal applications could even increase. 'The procedures are too simplistic. We're worried that employers will just go through a sham that won't resolve matters in the hope some issues will drop by the wayside', says Steve Cavalier, a partner at Thompson's, a London firm of solicitors with a core trade union client base. 'It will only reduce the number of tribunal claims if employers engaged in it properly and involve unions.'

Sara Veale of the Trades Union Congress says employers may use the new, abbreviated procedure in place of an existing, more comprehensive code drawn up by ACAS.

'We could end up with claims being held back until the last minute. The onus, therefore, is on the employee to demonstrate things aren't going well.'

The upshot, says Ms Veale, is that the new rules could mean more work, not less, for tribunals. That is a message that neither employers nor ministers will be keen to hear.

Source: Kevin Brown and Christopher Adams, *Financial Times*, 14 November 2001. © 2001 The Financial Times Limited

Chapter summary

This chapter opened by explaining the importance of the government (particularly as the lawmaker and controller of state agencies) in determining the nature of the national system of employee relations and how this has been demonstrated in the radical changes in UK employee relations after 1979.

It is clear that any government's approach to employee relations is determined primarily by its political ideology – either *laissez-faire* (free market) or corporatist (interventionist). It is the differences between these political ideologies, linked to the relative power of trade unions, which explains variations in national systems of employee relations and changes in national systems over time. The differences in ideology affect the way in which governments interpret their role and objectives in the management of the economy and dealing with consequent social issues.

Two areas have dominated government activity in the labour market. First, the problem of unemployment: whether this is best tackled through a positive balance of passive policies (provision of social benefits) and active policies (training) or through reduced employee protection and labour market regulation to induce greater labour flexibility. Second, the extent to which, if any, the government can and should seek to manage the pay side of the labour market through formal incomes policies.

Governments also have a responsibility to promote some level of social justice in employee relations. In addition to individual employment protection legislation, many governments maintain some form of minimum wage below which nobody should be paid. More recently, concern has been expressed about the extent to which deregulation of the labour market (for example, in the UK), or the absence of effective international labour standards, will result in social dumping as multinational organisations seek to take advantage of national differentials in labour costs.

All governments are concerned about expressions of social conflict, not least in employee relations. Whereas some see the expression of such conflict as unacceptably harmful (to be restricted and curtailed by legislative controls), others see it as an inevitable and necessary element of expressing and resolving differences within a dynamic social system. The government's approach to social conflict is clearly demonstrated through the legislative framework it creates (in particular, the extent to which it allows or restricts both the individual's and the unions' use of industrial action) and its approach towards the institutions and processes, particularly arbitration, intended to help in the resolution of disputes.

Questions

1 Explain the importance of the government in determining the nature of employee relations. By what means can governments influence employee relations?

2 What are the differences between the *laissez-faire* (free market) and corporatist (interventionist) ideologies? How do the changes in the UK government approach to employee relations over the past 100 years reflect these differences?

3 Consider the role of an incomes policy and compare the UK's experience with those of other countries. What appear to be the essential ingredients for a successful incomes policy?

4 To what extent, and in what ways, do you believe governments can and should promote 'social justice' in the labour market? In your answer, consider both the national and international dimensions.

5 Should governments restrict 'the right to strike'? If so, why and how; and has the UK government gone too far, far enough or should it go further?

Activity

Electronics (UK) plc is about to undertake a joint venture with Deutsch Electronics GmbH to establish a new manufacturing operation in Indonesia to serve the South East Asian market. In order to comply with Indonesian government requirements, they will have to include a local partner – Indon Electronics Sdn Bdh. The unions in Electronics (UK) plc and the works council at Deutsch GmbH have expressed 'serious reservations' that the development of the new operation may lead to a loss of jobs in the UK and/or Germany and have asked for assurances that the workers in Indonesia will receive comparable terms and conditions of employment to those in Europe. However, Indon Electronics Sdn Bdh, which does not recognise trade unions, believes that this will restrict the successful management and competitiveness of the new operations (certainly in comparison to other local electronics firms).

Questions

1   In groups, consider the issues and arguments which might be put forward by the European management, European unions, Indonesian management and Indonesian workers.

2   As the European human resource director, prepare a report for a forthcoming meeting of the three partner companies which analyses the feasibility and desirability of common labour standards.

Useful websites

www.acas.org.uk   Advisory, Conciliation and Arbitration Service   For information on the role and publications of the principal provider of dispute resolution services in the UK.

www.dti.gov.uk/er/index.htm   Department of Trade and Industry – Employment Relations A government department which, among other areas, has responsibility for dealing with employment relations issues.

www.ilo.org   International Labour Organization (ILO)   Database on international work standards and national laws on labour, social security and human rights.

www.lowpay.gov.uk   Low Pay Commission   A statutory body responsible for monitoring the operation of national minimum wage legislation and reporting to government.

References

Atkinson, M. (2001) 'Work, work, work', *Guardian*, 16 March.

Bazen, S. and Benhayoun, G. (1992) 'Low pay and wage regulation in the European Community', *British Journal of Industrial Relations*, 30(4): 623–38.

Bean, R. (1994) *Comparative Industrial Relations: An Introduction to Cross National Perspectives*, 2nd edn. London: Routledge.

Beaumont, P.B. (1992) *Public Sector Industrial Relations*. London: Routledge.

Beng, C.S. and Chew, R. (1995) 'The development of industrial relations strategy in Singapore' in Verma, A., Kochan, T.A. and Lansbury, R.D. (eds) *Employment Relations in the Growing Asian Economies*. London: Routledge: 62–87.

Blyton, P. and Turnbull, P. (1994) *The Dynamics of Employee Relations*. Basingstoke: Macmillan.

Bridgford, J. and Stirling, J. (1994) *Employee Relations in Europe*. Oxford: Blackwell.

Bullock Committee (1977) *Report of the Committee of Inquiry on Industrial Democracy*. London: HMSO.

Claydon, T. (1994) 'Human resource management and the labour market' in Beardwell, I. and Holden, L. (eds) *Human Resource Management: A Contemporary Perspective*. London: Financial Times/Pitman Publishing.

Crouch, C. (1977) *Class Conflict and the Industrial Relations Crisis*. London: Heinemann.

Crouch, C. (1982) *The Politics of Industrial Relations*, 2nd edn. London: Fontana.

Crouch, C. (1995) 'The state: economic management and incomes policy' in Edwards, P. (ed.) *Industrial Relations: Theory and Practice in Britain*. Oxford: Blackwell.

Dickens, L. and Hall, M. (1995) 'The state: labour law and industrial relations' in Edwards, P. (ed.) *Industrial Relations: Theory and Practice in Britain*. Oxford: Blackwell.

Donovan Commission (1968) *Report of the Royal Commission on Trade Unions and Employers' Associations*. London: HMSO.

Edwards, P. (1995) 'Strikes and industrial conflict' in Edwards, P. (ed.) *Industrial Relations: Theory and Practice in Britain*. Oxford: Blackwell.

EIRR (1993) 'The Hoover affair and social dumping', *European Industrial Relations Review*, 230: 14–20.

Fevre, R. (1992) *The Sociology of Labour Markets*. Englewood Cliffs, NJ: Prentice Hall.

GMB/UCW (1990) *A New Agenda: Bargaining for Prosperity in the 1990s*.

Griffith, J. (1990) 'The collective unfairness of laissez-faire', *Guardian*, 14 June.

Grunfeld, C. (1966) *Modern Trade Union Law*. London: Sweet & Maxwell.

Hetherington, P. (2000) 'Employers "flout spirit" of minimum wage law', *Guardian*, 26 July.

Hollinshead, G. and Leat, M. (1995) *Human Resource Management: An International and Comparative Perspective*. London: Financial Times/Pitman Publishing.

Hutt, W.H. (1973) *The Strike Threat System*. New Rochelle, NY: Arlington House.

Hutton, W. (1995) 'Minimum wage offers maximum return', *Guardian Weekly*, 23 July.

Hyman, R. (1975) *Industrial Relations: A Marxist Introduction*. Basingstoke: Macmillan.

Kahn-Freund, O. (1960) 'Legal framework' in Flanders, A. and Clegg, H.A. (eds) *The System of Industrial Relations in Great Britain*. Oxford: Blackwell.

Keep, E. and Rainbird, H. (1995) 'Training' in Edwards, P. (ed.) *Industrial Relations: Theory and Practice in Britain*. Oxford: Blackwell: 515–42.

Kitson, M. and Wilkinson, F. (2000) 'How paying the minimum raises the stakes', *Guardian*, 25 September.

Labour Party (1997) *Labour's Business Manifesto: Equipping Britain for the Future*. London: Labour Party.

Lee, J.S. (1995) 'Economic development and the evolution of industrial relations in Taiwan, 1950–1993' in Verma, A., Kochan, T.A. and Lansbury, R.D. (eds) *Employment Relations in the Growing Asian Economies*. London: Routledge: 88–118.

Leggett, C. (1993) 'Singapore' in Deery, S.J. and Mitchell, R.J. (eds) *Labour Law and Industrial Relations in Asia*. London: Longman: 96–136.

Lowry, P. (1990) *Employment Disputes and the Third Party*. Basingstoke: Macmillan.

Maguire, K. (2001a) 'It could end in divorce', *Guardian*, 26 June.

Maguire, K. (2001b) 'Blair woos unions with more talks at No. 10', *Guardian*, 3 July.

Marsh, D. (1992) *The New Politics of British Trade Unionism*. Basingstoke: Macmillan.

McCarthy, W. (1993) 'From Donovan until now: Britain's twenty-five years of incomes policy', *Employee Relations*, 15(6): 3–20.

Mortimer, J. (1981) 'ACAS in a changing climate: a force for good IR?', *Personnel Management*, February.

Park, Y. and Lee, M.B. (1995) 'Economic development, globalization, and practices in industrial relations and human resource management in Korea' in Verma, A., Kochan, T.A. and

Lansbury, R.D. (eds) *Employment Relations in the Growing Asian Economies*. London: Routledge: 27–61.

Poole, M. (1986) *Industrial Relations: Origins and Patterns of National Diversity*. London: Routledge & Kegan Paul.

Prondzynski, F. von (1992) 'Ireland: between centralism and the market' in Ferner, A. and Hyman, R. (eds) *Industrial Relations in the New Europe*. Oxford: Blackwell: 69–87.

Rhodes, M. (1993) 'The social dimension after Maastricht: setting a new agenda for the labour market', *International Journal of Comparative Labour Law and Industrial Relations*, Winter.

Sachdev, S. (2001) 'Minimum wage needs bit of French dressing', *Guardian*, 17 July.

Schmid, G., Reissert, B. and Bruche, G. (1992) *Unemployment Insurance and Active Labor Market Policy*. Detroit, MI: Wayne State University Press.

Strinati, D. (1982) *Capitalism, the State and Industrial Relations*. London: Croom Helm.

Taylor, A.J. (1989) *Trade Unions and Politics*. Basingstoke: Macmillan.

Teague, P. (1993) 'Between convergence and divergence: possibilities for a European Community system of labour market regulation', *International Labour Review*, 132(3): 391–406.

Towers, B. (1992) 'Two speed ahead: social Europe and the UK after Maastricht', *Industrial Relations Journal*, 23(2): 83–9.

TUC (1996) *Pay Falling in Former Wages Councils Sectors*, TUC press release, 30 August.

Waarden, F. van (1995) 'Government intervention in industrial relations' in Ruysseveldt, J. van, Huiskamp, R. and Hoof, J. van (eds) *Comparative Industrial and Employment Relations*. London: Sage.

White Paper (1969) *In Place of Strife*. London: HMSO.

White Paper (1998) *Fairness at Work*. London: HMSO.

Whitfield, K. (1988) 'The Australian wage system and its labour market effects', *Industrial Relations*, 27(2): 149–65.

Winchester, D. (1983) 'Industrial relations research in Britain', *British Journal of Industrial Relations*, 22(1): 100–14.

Younge, G. (2001a) 'Penalising the poor', *Guardian*, 19 March.

Younge, G. (2001b) 'Tolerated, at best', *Guardian*, 9 July.

Part Three

International influences and changing regulations

Chapter 6

The European Union

Mike Leat

Learning objectives

By the end of this chapter, readers should be able to:

- distinguish and explain the roles of the major institutions in the EU;
- understand and explain the main legislative processes;
- appreciate the significance of EU treaties and the difficulties experienced in the development of the social dimension;
- understand the initiatives that have been taken to enhance equality of pay and treatment between the sexes and assess their impact;
- explain the significance of some of the initiatives taken in the areas of employee participation and the regulation of working time;
- discuss the arguments for and against, the options and the likelihood of the development of an EU-wide system of employee relations.

Introduction

The views expressed by Commissioner Flynn in Exhibit 6.1 touch upon a number of the issues addressed in this chapter. He seems to be suggesting an EU-wide system of industrial relations as a prerequisite to full European integration and as support to a strong social dimension. He expresses the view that monetary union and the single market are both vulnerable without such a strong social dimension. There is the implication in his views as quoted that development of the EU has so far been unbalanced in favour of the achievement of economic, rather than social, objectives such as the single market and a single currency.

There is, however, a more radical dimension to the views reported and this lies in the suggestion that such an EU-wide system should include trade unions and employers exercising joint power and responsibility. This is a concept that is much closer to that of codetermination, common in some member states, than to any notions of partnership that may be envisaged by Tony Blair's Labour government.

Exhibit 6.1

EU industrial relations call

European Union integration will not be complete without the creation of a Europe-wide industrial relations system in which trade unions and employers exercise joint power and responsibility, according to Mr Padraig Flynn, the European social affairs commissioner.

In a speech today in the Hague, Mr Flynn will argue that future social legislation should come not from governments but through dialogue between the European trade unions and employers. This does not mean creating a 'single, harmonised system of industrial relations to replace the way we do things now in different member states', he argues. But he wants unions and employers to 'make their real views known and to develop their own initiatives'. This, he says, is the way the EU should develop so that there can be 'a better balance between economic and social objectives'.

'Monetary union is knocking loudly at our door. But a Union without a strong social dimension cannot be a Union worthy of the name, and without it, the single market and the Emu [economic and monetary union] will both face an uncertain future.'

Source: Robert Taylor, *Financial Times*, 29 April 1997. © 1997 The Financial Times Limited

Flynn is reported as arguing that future social legislation should be the product of dialogue between the Social Partners (the unions and employers associations). Presumably the reference here is to the Social Protocol procedures, now brought fully within the realm of the treaties, which provide for the Social Partners to reach framework agreements which may then provide the base for legislative intervention at the EU level. However, he takes pains to point out that the intention is not to impose a single harmonised system. It would therefore seem likely that he has in mind a set of minimum legal rights and obligations determined at the EU level which would be given effect at the national level through voluntary agreement and implementation by the Social Partners. This would maintain consistency with the principle of subsidiarity. In the UK this would also be revolutionary since there is no tradition of the Social Partners reaching and voluntarily implementing agreements at this level. Presumably the decline in influence of both Social Partners over the past two decades would have to be reversed for such a system to work. Such arrangements would also pose problems of internal government for the UK peak associations (the TUC and CBI) since they have never had much in the way of power or control over the activities of their members.

There are implications in these views for the power and influence at an EU level of both trade union movements and employers' associations, as well as for the lawmaking institutions and processes. These views, if implemented, would presumably lead to some greater degree of convergence between the different national systems, systems that are largely intact even after forty years of association.

In this chapter we examine most, if not all, of these matters: we look at the decision-making institutions and processes, including those associated with the Social Partners, the need for and nature of a social dimension, the issues of subsidiarity and harmonisation, some of the interventions already initiated by the European Commission and agreed by the Social Partners and the likelihood of an emerging EU model of social protection and employee relations.

■ Outline of the chapter

This chapter falls quite naturally into three main sections:

- In the first we examine the main institutions and decision-making processes of the EU as they impinge upon issues of employee relations.
- In the second section we examine some of the more important articles of the founding treaties and initiatives in recent years to amend them and enhance the social dimension. In this context are included the Social Charter and associated Social Action Programme, the Social Protocol Agreement on Social Policy that was attached to the Maastricht Treaty, and, most recently, the revisions to the EC Treaty agreed at Amsterdam in June 1997, and the Charter of Fundamental Rights. We also examine some of the debates surrounding the role of the EU in this area and the principles that cover EU initiatives and objectives.
- We then concentrate on some of the more important individual interventions and initiatives in the areas of equality, working time and employee participation, such as the European Works Council Directive, and the objectives that they are intended to achieve. As far as possible a chronological approach is adopted. We also briefly examine the prospects for and progress towards the Europeanisation of social protection and employee relations.

■ Background to the EU

The EU started life as the European Economic Community (EEC), with six members (see Table 6.1), later became the European Community, and in 1993 became the European Union after the ratification of the treaty changes agreed at Maastricht in 1991.

Perhaps inevitably there is a tendency to see the EU as an organisation primarily concerned with economic and trading matters, but these were not the only reasons for the formation of the EEC and are not the only justifications for membership and enlargement. Major motivations for the formation of the Community in 1957 also

Table 6.1 **The 15 member states of the EU**

Country	Joining date
Germany	Founder member, 1957
France	Founder member, 1957
Italy	Founder member, 1957
Netherlands	Founder member, 1957
Belgium	Founder member, 1957
Luxembourg	Founder member, 1957
UK	1973
Denmark	1973
Ireland	1973
Greece	1981
Spain	1986
Portugal	1986
Austria	1995
Sweden	1995
Finland	1995

included the desire to prevent war within Europe and to halt the spread of communism. The latter may no longer be the spectre that it once was, but the belief that the EU helps to maintain peace in Europe is still strong. It is argued that both peace and economic well-being are enhanced if countries are joined together in a single market with reciprocal trading and economic interests. This occurs in a community which demonstrably benefits the citizens of the various member states through both the generation of wealth and the operation of a form of welfare capitalism supported by labour law that ensures minimum levels of social protection.

It is important to realise that in the EU the term 'social' encompasses employment and related matters, and therefore when we refer to social policies in the EU we are including those relating to employment and to industrial and employee relations.

The UK's membership of the EU has already had an impact upon the country's domestic system of employee relations. In the main this has been achieved through the acceptance of guiding principles, such as those relating to the imperative of equality of pay and treatment between the sexes, the creation of individual rights, such as the right to equal treatment or to minimum periods of paid holiday, and the imposition of some constraints upon substantive outcomes, such as upon rates of pay in the context of equality between the sexes.

So far there has been relatively little intervention in or interference with the established procedures and processes of collective interaction and conflict resolution in individual member states. Employee representatives and employers have had some rights and obligations imposed upon them with regard to the provision of information and consultation requirements on a limited range of subjects (e.g. collective redundancies, transfers of ownership, and health and safety). However, it may be that the European Works Council (EWC) Directive and the comments of Commissioner Flynn quoted in Exhibit 6.1 are indicative of a greater inclination to seek to impose EU-wide procedural prescriptions.

Membership, institutions and the decision-making processes

The EU in 2002 has 15 member states (Table 6.1). However, it is likely that up to a dozen new members will be admitted in the early years of this century. Applicant countries are Bulgaria, Cyprus, the Czech Republic, Estonia, Hungary, Latvia, Lithuania, Malta, Poland, Romania, Slovakia and Slovenia. In addition, Turkey has been recognised as a candidate for membership.

Aspirant members are required to satisfy a range of conditions prior to membership. These can be separated into the following categories:

- *Political criteria.* Article 6 of the Treaty of the European Union spells these out: 'The Union is founded on the principles of liberty, democracy, respect for human rights and fundamental freedoms and the rule of law.'
- *Economic criteria.* These were spelt out at the Copenhagen Summit in 1993 and can be summarised as the existence of a functioning market economy and the capacity to withstand competitive pressure and market forces within the Union.
- *Additional criteria and obligations of membership.* The Copenhagen European Council indicated that membership requires 'the ability to take on the obligations of membership, including adherence to the aims of political, economic and monetary union'.

At the time of writing it seems as if the first batch of new entrants might be accepted into membership as early as 2004/5.

One of the concerns surrounding enlargement has been related to the need to adjust the institutions and decision-making mechanisms of the Union. The Intergovernmental conference at Nice in December 2000 sought to address these concerns, and the agreements reached are embodied in the draft treaty of Nice which is still to be ratified at the time of writing. The provisional revised arrangements are outlined in the following sections.

Institutions

There are four main EU institutions: the European Commission, hereafter referred to as the Commission, the Council of the European Union (often also known as the Council of Ministers), the European Parliament and the Court of Justice of the European Communities (ECJ). The various and respective roles of these institutions are briefly described below, while Figure 6.1 sets out the relationships between them in simple diagrammatic form.

There are also a number of other institutions within the aegis of the EU that are relevant to the subject matter of this chapter. A number of these are described below, including the Social Partners and the European Foundation for the Improvement of Living and Working Conditions (EFILWC).

The Council of Europe is a completely separate and larger organisation with some 40 nations in membership that has absolutely no connection with the EU other than that the EU member states tend also to be members of the Council of Europe.

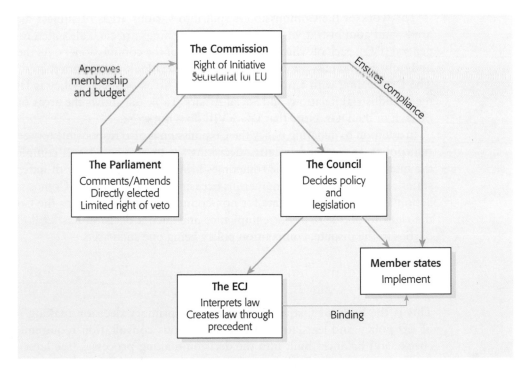

Figure 6.1 **The role and relationships of the major institutions**

The European Commission

The Commission provides the secretariat for the EU and perhaps more importantly has the Right of Initiative with respect to proposals for Union-level policy and legislation, although it must be realised that there are plenty of opportunities for interest groups to lobby the Commission. In many ways it is the institution that sets the agenda for the EU. The term 'Commission' is used to refer both to the organisation as a whole and to the group of commissioners who meet together as the senior internal decision-making forum. It is the latter group that agrees policy and other proposals and initiatives before they go outside to the others for the purposes of consultation and discussion.

The commissioners are nominated by individual member state governments and their appointment is subject to the approval of the European Parliament. The 'big five' member states – Germany, France, Italy, the UK and Spain – all have the right to nominate two commissioners each and the other ten member states each nominate, one producing a Commission with 20 commissioners. Commissioners are supposed to work for and represent the Commission and the EU as a whole and not their home member states.

If the present system were maintained, the imminent accession of the 12 countries currently negotiating membership of the Union would lead to a Commission of 33 members, nearly four times its original size.

The Treaty of Nice limits the Commission to one member per member state, with effect from 2005. A ceiling on the number of commissioners will be imposed once the Union has 27 member states. At that point, the Council will have to take a unanimous decision on the exact number of commissioners (which must be less than 27). The nationality of the commissioners will then be determined by a system of rotation that will be fair to all countries.

The work of the Commission is split into various areas of subject matter or policy areas, and administrative sections. The policy areas are each allocated to a directorate-general (DG), each of which is headed by one of the commissioners. As there are 23 DGs and only 20 commissioners, some commissioners look after more than one policy area. The DG dealing with employment and other areas of social policy is DG V, Employment, Industrial Relations and Social Affairs. Table 6.2 shows the areas of responsibility of each of the DGs. Note that DG XVIII does not exist.

In addition to initiating policy the Commission is also responsible for seeking to ensure that policy and other legislative decisions are implemented and complied with in all the member states. This role sometimes brings it into conflict with individual member states and there have been numerous occasions upon which the Commission has taken action against a member state for non-compliance. In some areas the Commission has the right to decide issues of compliance and such a decision has legal effect upon the parties to the dispute, competition policy being one such area.

The Council of the European Union (the Council of Ministers and the European Council)

This is the body or institution that has the primary decision-making role in respect of EU policy and legislation. There are various consultation requirements and other checks and balances built into the decision-making processes (see later) and in recent years the European Parliament has been granted additional powers in relation to decision-making over a widening range of issues.

Table 6.2 **The areas of responsibility of the 23 DGs**

DG	Area of responsibility
DG I	External Relations (there are also Ia and Ib dealing with particular regions and areas of activity)
DG II	Economic and Financial Affairs
DG III	Industry
DG IV	Competition
DG V	Employment, Industrial Relations and Social Affairs
DG VI	Agriculture
DG VII	Transport
DG VIII	Development
DG IX	Personnel and Administration
DG X	Audiovisual, Information, Communication and Culture
DG XI	Environment, Nuclear Safety and Civil Protection
DG XII	Science, Research and Development
DG XIII	Telecommunications, Information Industries and Innovation
DG XIV	Fisheries
DG XV	Internal Market and Financial Services
DG XVI	Regional Policies and Cohesion
DG XVII	Energy
DG XIX	Budgets
DG XX	Financial Control
DG XXI	Customs and Indirect Taxation
DG XXII	Education, Training and Youth
DG XXIII	Enterprise Policy, Distributive Trades, Tourism and Cooperatives
DG XXIV	Consumer Policy

Membership of the Council varies according to the subject matter under discussion. The object is to have present for decision-making purposes the appropriate govern ment minister from each member state, so that when the Council meets as the Social Affairs Council each member state is represented by the member of government with responsibility at home for the subjects to be discussed. The members of the Council are supported by home country civil servants, who do much of the detailed and pre-paratory work and negotiation. The Council therefore is not a directly elected body and the members are not accountable to any particular constituency of electors; they are accountable to the member state government of which they are a member. The Council is commonly referred to as an intergovernmental body.

The Council traditionally had to make unanimous decisions, in effect giving every member state the ability to block or veto particular proposals. As the size of the Union increased, areas of subject matter have been identified in relation to which decisions can be made by qualified majority voting (QMV). This system means that each member state has a specified number of votes in Council, and these are apportioned roughly in accordance with the size of the country's population (see Table 6.3). Thus, the unified Germany, Italy, France and the UK all have the same and largest number of votes. In total there are 87 votes available and 62 are required in favour of a proposal for it to be adopted via the QMV process. Sometimes reference is made to the 'blocking minority'; this figure is currently 26 Council votes.

Table 6.3 **Qualified majority voting**

Current member states	Votes	Candidate countries	Votes
Belgium	5 (12)	Bulgaria	10
Denmark	3 (7)	Cyprus	4
Germany	10 (29)	Czech Republic	12
Greece	5 (12)	Estonia	4
Spain	8 (27)	Hungary	12
France	10 (29)	Latvia	4
Ireland	3 (7)	Lithuania	7
Italy	10 (29)	Malta	3
Luxembourg	2 (4)	Poland	27
Netherlands	5 (13)	Romania	14
Austria	4 (10)	Slovakia	7
Portugal	5 (12)	Slovenia	4
Finland	3 (7)		
Sweden	4 (10)		
UK	10 (29)		

Figures in brackets for current member states are the proposed votes after 1 January 2005

Impending enlargement of the Union has resulted in amendments to this QMV system being agreed at Nice in December 2000 which do appear to turn a simple mechanism into something appreciably more complex. The new treaty provides for a change in the weighting of votes from 1 January 2005. The number of votes assigned to each member state has been altered and the number to be assigned to the candidate countries when they enter the EU has also been set (see Table 6.3). In future, qualified majority will be obtained:

■ if a decision receives *a specified number of votes* (this threshold will be reviewed in the light of successive accessions);
■ if a decision is approved by *a majority of member states.*

In addition, a member state may ask for confirmation that the qualified majority represents at least 62 per cent of the total population of the Union. If this is found not to be the case, the decision will not be adopted.

The European Parliament

The Parliament has a history of little power and influence despite the fact that it is the only directly elected institution within the EU. Until recently the roles of the Parliament in the formulation of EU policy and the passage of legislation have been limited to lobbying and being one of the bodies that had to be consulted as part of the specified processes. As part of this consultation process the Parliament can put forward amendments, but it has no means of ensuring that the Council accepts them. Consequently it can delay but cannot stop or force change. More recently, and as part of the Maastricht Treaty, the Parliament acquired limited powers of veto on issues put to the Council for adoption in some specified areas of subject matter, including enlargement of the Union. The 1997 Amsterdam Treaty extended these limited powers of veto to include many social policy areas, with further extensions agreed at Nice.

Table 6.4 **Number of MEPs for each country before and after enlargement**

Member states	MEPs	Candidate countries	MEPs
Belgium	25 (22)	Bulgaria	17
Denmark	16 (13)	Cyprus	6
Germany	99 (99)	Czech Republic	20
Greece	25 (22)	Estonia	6
Spain	64 (50)	Hungary	20
France	87 (72)	Latvia	8
Ireland	15 (12)	Lithuania	12
Italy	87 (72)	Malta	5
Luxembourg	6 (6)	Poland	50
Netherlands	31 (25)	Romania	33
Austria	21 (17)	Slovakia	13
Portugal	25 (22)	Slovenia	7
Finland	16 (13)		
Sweden	22 (18)		
UK	87 (72)		

Figures in brackets indicate the future numbers for existing member states

Each of the member states has allotted to it a number of Members of the European Parliament (MEPs). The allocation is intended to be roughly proportional on population grounds, so that the unified Germany, the country with the largest population, has the greatest number of MEPs. The current and future distribution of MEPs by member state is shown in Table 6.4.

The Treaty of Nice limited the number of MEPs to a maximum of 732 and allocated seats between member states and candidate countries with effect from the next elections of 2004. Of course, the candidate countries will not be represented in the European Parliament until they become members of the Union.

Although elected by electors in and on behalf of a particular member state, the MEPs tend to ally themselves in multinational political groupings. They are not sent to the Parliament with a brief to look after the interests of the particular member state from which they come.

The Parliament also has the right to approve the nomination of the Commission and the annual budgets and spending programmes.

The Court of Justice of the European Communities

The ECJ is the final arbiter of European Community/Union law. It is the court of last resort. It tends to deal with two different categories of case:

- Cases that are concerned with matters of EU-level significance, such as a member state alleging that the Council or the Commission has acted improperly or unlawfully, or where the Commission is seeking to ensure that a member state complies with EU legislation, or where one member state is in legal dispute with another. An example of this first category would be the UK government's allegation that the directive adopted on working hours was improperly adopted as a health and safety issue. Cases of this kind could not realistically be processed in the judicial system of one of the member states. These cases are sometimes referred to as direct actions.

■ Cases that commence within individual member states but require the ECJ's final decision on what the law means or how and when it should apply. Examples would include applications by individuals to the UK courts claiming that the UK government had improperly applied the directives on collective redundancies and transfers of undertakings, or that the EU law on equal pay was not being properly applied by a particular employer. Each of these instances starts in the UK courts and eventually reaches the ECJ as the final arbiter.

The ECJ is made up of 15 judges, one from each member state, and 9 advocates-general (A-Gs) drawn from the ranks of academics, judges and lawyers in the member states. Each case that reaches the ECJ is allocated an advocate-general, and he or she is expected to present the Court and the parties with an opinion on the case before it is heard by the Court itself. Rarely are the opinions of A-Gs not followed by the ECJ. The provisions in respect of enlargement of the Union allow for member states each to continue to appoint one judge.

The ECJ must be distinguished from the European Court of Human Rights (ECHR), which is nothing to do with the EU – it has more connection with the Council of Europe than with the EU. The ECHR was established under the European Convention on Human Rights. It has not been uncommon in recent years for members of the UK government and the media to confuse this.

Associated with the ECJ is the Court of First Instance (CFI). This was established by the Single European Act 1986 and was intended to help speed up the judicial process in cases brought by private parties. The scope of the CFI's jurisdiction was extended by the Treaty of Maastricht and now the court can hear cases brought by private parties in all areas or fields. Appeal from the CFI is to the ECJ.

In addition to the four main EU institutions discussed above, there are a number of others that have a particular relevance to the making and implementation of decisions relevant to employee relations. These are the trade union and employers' confederations and associations (known within the EU as the Social Partners) and the European Foundation for the Improvement of Living and Working Conditions (EFILWC).

The Social Partners

At EU level, the Social Partners participate in a process known as the social dialogue, which is discussed in more detail in the final section of this chapter. Presumably these are the organisations that Commissioner Flynn refers to in Exhibit 6.1.

Trade unions

The European Trade Union Confederation (ETUC) is the single representative of the labour movement at EU level. It was formed in 1972/3 and now has in membership all major trade union federations, national and sectoral, in Europe. There have been a number of ex-communist federations that have joined in the years following the break-up of the east European communist bloc, and it is only really since this happened that the ETUC has been able to claim to be truly representative of European labour.

The activities and membership of the confederation are not limited to the member states of the EU and ETUC is the sole significant representative of organised labour across the whole of western Europe. The ETUC represents 58 national trade union centres and confederations from 28 countries, including many of the aspirant member states, and 14 European industry federations. In total these confederations and federations claim more than 53 million members.

However, the ETUC is a massively diverse organisation and it would be wrong to give the impression that there is much cohesion within the movement. The nature and traditions of the many union confederations in membership vary considerably, as do their autonomy and authority in respect of their own membership. Visser and Ebbinghaus (1992) described the ETUC as 'united but fragmented and with little internal cohesion'. There is continuing tension between the national interests and aspirations of member confederations and the objective of cohesion at the EU level. This phenomenon also seems to characterise some of the European Works Councils (EWCs) created subsequent to the directive adopted in 1994.

The organisation has much to thank the EU for, and in particular the Commission, which has been a continuing source of both political and financial support. The importance that the Commission has, over the years, attached to the creation and maintenance of an effective labour movement with a voice and influence at the level of the EU has been considerably beneficial to the ETUC. It is doubtful that the organisation would have been as united and effective as it is (for example, in promoting the Social Dialogue – see later) without such support. One can see this as manifesting the continuing influence of corporatist traditions in much of the EU. This support should not be seen as a purely altruistic approach since it has long been the view of the Commission that an internal market and other dimensions of economic integration would be possible only with the support/acquiescence of European labour.

Turner (1996) takes a relatively optimistic view of the future of the ETUC despite acknowledging that in many respects the development of structures at such a transnational level seems to be at odds with the trends towards the decentralisation of decision-making and collective bargaining. He suggests that the EWC Directive will assist the process of cross-national collaboration within and between labour movements and representatives. While this will initially be at the level of the individual multinational organisation, the structures that now exist within the framework of the ETUC may be both used and reinforced. However, Turner does also point out that the development of an effective labour movement at this EU level needs, in addition to the aforementioned institutional arrangements, transnational rank and file protest.

Below the level of the EU there are a number of international sectoral federations, many of them affiliated to the ETUC, that are active in their respective industries and that often provide the employee representative mechanism for activities at the level of the individual multinational corporation. Examples of these sectoral federations include the European Metalworkers' Federation (EMF), the European Federation of Chemical and Mine Workers Unions (EMCEF) and the International Union of Food Workers (ECF-IUF).

These latter are the organisations that have been in the forefront of negotiating voluntary EWCs in those companies and groups that have them.

Employers' organisations

There are two main employers' organisations operating at the level of the EU:

- the Union of Industrial and Employers' Confederations of Europe (UNICE), which represents primarily private sector employers; and
- the European Centre of Enterprises with Public Participation and of Enterprises of General Economic Interest (CEEP), representing primarily public sector employer interests.

UNICE was formed in the late 1950s and, like the ETUC, represents employers from a much wider constituency than the EU. In 2002, UNICE had 33 national federations in membership representing the interests of employers in 26 countries, including in addition to current member states about half of the aspirant member states.

At the level of the EU, UNICE wants to be influential as an organisation representing a particular interest to the legislators and policy-makers but, unlike the ETUC, it was not keen to become involved with the Commission and ETUC in policy-making as a Social Partner. It is even less keen to become involved in any EU-level bargaining arrangements with the ETUC. This is no doubt due in part to the fact that it does not have a mandate to act in this way, and it and the ETUC do not have compatible structures.

Among its priorities as policies to be pursued, the emphasis is upon international competitiveness, full employment, multilateral trade agreements and minimum regulation. Little specific reference is made to social policies though there are references to the promotion of entrepreneurship and the definition of social policies based on economic realities and structural reforms (lower taxation, more efficient public services and more flexible labour markets) and innovation and lifelong learning. Targeted policies for research, education and training, protection of intellectual property etc. are advocated in order to meet the challenges of the information and learning society.

Membership of CEEP tends to comprise individual employers rather than federations, and the geographical spread of the members of this organisation is much smaller than that of either UNICE or the ETUC, since full membership is open only to organisations from within the EU. As with UNICE, the direction of CEEP's activities are primarily to represent its members' interests to the policy-makers and legislators.

Within the UK the Social Partners at a national level are the Trades Union Congress (TUC) and the Confederation of British Industry (CBI), although they have not traditionally been referred to in these terms. In the past, the TUC with its voluntarist traditions, was very sceptical of the UK's membership of the EU and of the regulatory initiatives taken at an EU level. However, in the latter part of the 1980s and early 1990s the TUC became one of the more avid supporters of the European project, welcoming social protection(s) for its members in the face of successive attempts by UK governments to deregulate and minimise such protection.

The CBI also tended to support the EU concept, although for different reasons – those associated with the prospects for business to be derived from the creation of a single market and, in the 1990s, from monetary union. Both of these UK partners are active members of the appropriate organisations at the level of the EU.

The European Foundation for the Improvement of Living and Working Conditions

The Foundation was established in May 1975 for the primary purposes of contributing to the planning and establishment of better living and working conditions. Its prime activity is to encourage and commission research into appropriate areas of interest and activity and to disseminate the findings. The Foundation houses the centre of the European Industrial Relations Observatory (EIRO) network. The EIRO is charged with the task of producing an annual report on main developments in industrial relations within Europe.

The organisation is managed by an administrative board comprising representatives from and of the Commission, the trade unions, employers and the governments of the member states.

The main focus of the Foundation's work is consistent with the social agenda of the EU:

- promoting better employment;
- extending equal opportunities for men and women;
- managing diversity;
- supporting social inclusion;
- examining the use of time.

Legislative forms and decision-making procedures

The EU can adopt a number of different legislative instruments:

- *Regulations*. These are rare, but once adopted they are applicable directly and generally throughout the EU; they are immediately binding on member states and individuals and do not require any action at member-state level to render them effective. In cases of EU regulations conflicting with national law, the EU regulation takes precedence. The Council can empower the Commission to make regulations.
- *Directives*. A directive is not immediately applicable but requires some action at member-state level to be brought into effect, although this action need not be legislative (implementation can, for example, be through agreement by the Social Partners). Normally a directive specifies an objective to be achieved and the date by which it should be achieved but leaves the means of achievement to the individual member states. Once the implementation date is reached, the directive becomes the law within the EU.
- *Decisions*. These can be made by the Council, and in some instances by the Commission, and once made they are binding on the parties that sought the decision in the first place. They do not automatically have general effect.

There is also a range of non-binding instruments that can be used, such as *recommendations*, *communications* and *opinions*. These are often used when one or more of the institutions wants to exert influence but knows either that there is not sufficient support for the proposal or that the competence to act is lacking.

The consultation procedure

The tradition has in the main been that legislative intervention or action at the level of the EU requires the unanimous support of the member states, and where this is the case the decision-making procedure to be used is called the consultation procedure. This is the least complex of the decision-making procedures and is shown in outline form in Figure 6.2. In the early days of the EU this was the only procedure, and for many years now there has been an assumption that decisions reached using this procedure must be

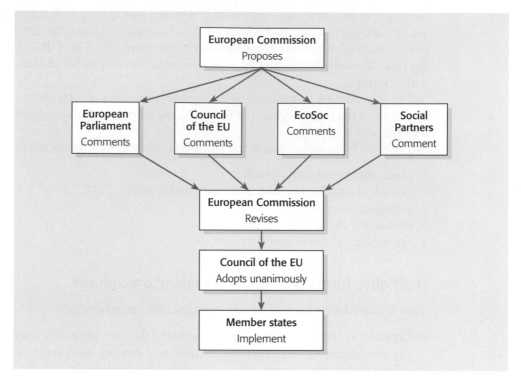

Figure 6.2 **Consultation procedure**

reached unanimously irrespective of whether this was strictly required by the Treaty of Rome. As can be seen quite clearly from the figure, the procedure provides for consultation with a number of forums, but only once, and the Council's decision is final; it may or may not take note of the comments and amendments suggested by these various forums as part of the procedure.

This procedure is necessary in respect of the following areas of social policy: the adoption of provisions to combat discrimination on the grounds of sex, race, ethnic origin, religion or belief, disability, age or sexual orientation (Article 13 EC – and see the later section on equality); strengthening and adding to the rights deriving from EU citizenship (Article 22(2) EC); laying down guidelines for employment policies (Article 128(2) EC); and relating to social security, protection of workers' interests and the conditions of employment of third-country nationals (Article 137(3) EC).

The tradition of unanimity as a prerequisite for legislative action has limited the ability of the EU to progress and change, and the consultation procedure above provides a very limited role for the European Parliament. When, in the mid-1980s, the Council agreed to create the single market by the end of 1992 it was also agreed that the principle of qualified majority voting (QMV) should apply for many of the measures necessary to the creation and effective operation of the market. As a consequence, the Single European Act 1986 included the creation of a new decision-making procedure called the cooperation procedure. This procedure allowed for both majority voting and a more influential role for the Parliament. However, in the arena of social policy this procedure has been superseded by another new procedure called the co-decision procedure.

The co-decision procedure

The co-decision procedure provides for decisions to be reached and legislation adopted via the use of QMV and for a more influential role for the Parliament. This new procedure was of relatively little interest prior to the Amsterdam Treaty revisions of 1997. However, since the Amsterdam agreements, which included a shortening of the procedure (see Figure 6.3), the co-decision procedure denies the Council the right to adopt its common position if efforts to reach agreement with Parliament fail. Under these new proposals a legislative proposal will be deemed to have failed if:

■ the EP rejects it by an absolute majority of component members; or
■ if there is no agreement in conciliation on a joint text (a joint Council–Parliament Conciliation Committee with the Commission also involved as the conciliator).

It is argued that this increases the incentive to reach a compromise as the entire legislative process must otherwise be abandoned. The co-decision procedure has become an important element in the legislative process.

In addition to shortening the procedure and giving the Parliament a more equal role in decision-making, the treaty agreements at Amsterdam extended the scope of the co-decision procedure to a range of areas of social policy and freedom of movement. We have noted above those areas that still require unanimity and the use of the consultation procedure, the rest are now subject to use of the co-decision procedure, including:

■ the ban on discrimination on grounds of nationality (Article 12 EC);
■ measures to bring about freedom of movement (Article 40 EC);
■ measures to ensure social security when exercising the right to move freely (Article 42 EC);
■ directives on freedom of establishment (Articles 44(2) and 47(1) EC);
■ freedom to provide services (Article 55 EC);
■ social policy, including measures to bring about equality of the sexes (Articles 137, 141 and 148 EC);
■ measures to promote education and vocational training (Article 149 EC).

The reference to social policy in Articles 137 to 141 includes specific reference to the EU's competence in relation to the following (see also later section on the Treaty at Amsterdam):

■ improvement of the working environment to protect workers' health and safety;
■ working conditions;
■ the process of informing and consulting of workers;
■ the integration of persons excluded from the labour market;
■ equality between men and women with regard to labour market opportunities and treatment at work;
■ ensuring application of the principle of equal opportunities and equal treatment of men and women in matters of employment and occupation, including the principle of equal pay for equal work or work of equal value.

The protocol or social agreement procedure

This procedure was included in the Maastricht Social Protocol Agreement on Social Policy and was the product of the desire by the Commission and member states other than the UK to increase the social dialogue between the Social Partners at EU level and

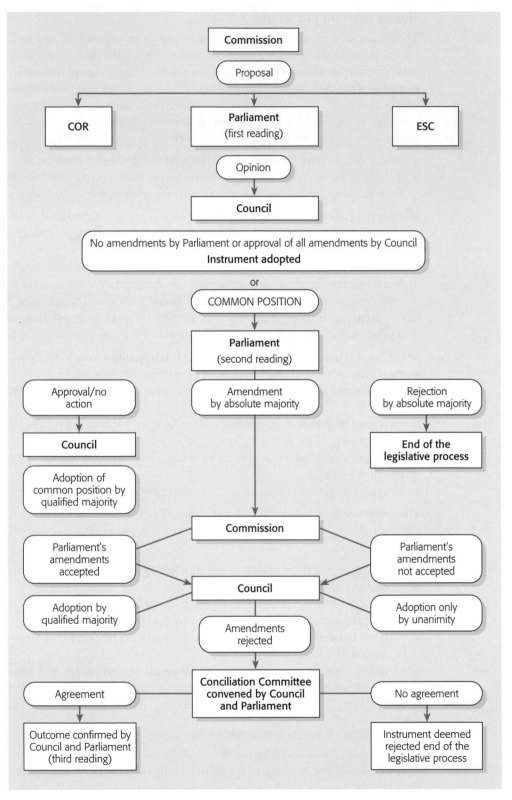

Figure 6.3 **Co-decision procedure**

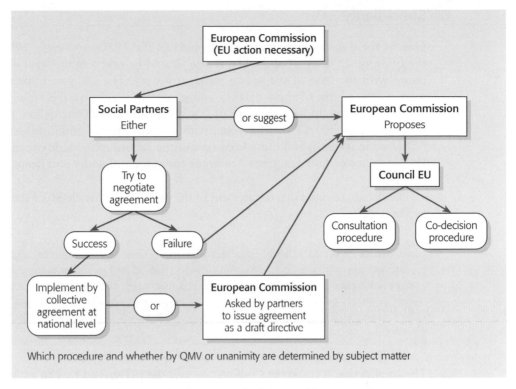

Figure 6.4 **Protocol or social agreement decision-making procedure**

to increase their role in the decision-making process. This was to include giving the Social Partners the opportunity to enter into agreements and contractual relations. The comments of Commissioner Flynn in Exhibit 6.1 are consistent with this intention.

This procedure is depicted in Figure 6.4. As can be seen, the Social Partners can be given the opportunity to reach an agreement between themselves on a proposal for action that has come out of the Commission. If the Social Partners can reach agreement on the content of the proposal they can further agree to seek to give effect to the proposal via collective agreements at national level. Alternatively, having reached agreement on the content of the proposal, they can ask the Commission to process the agreement through the normal consultation or co-decision procedures, as appropriate, depending upon the subject matter.

Generally speaking, the trade unions welcomed this initiative more than did the employers' associations, and the latter have participated somewhat reluctantly. At the time of writing this procedure has been 'completed' on a number of occasions. In the first opportunity given them, the Social Partners were unable to agree the content of proposals that eventually became the EWC Directive. However, since then they have managed to reach framework agreements on a number of issues which they have asked the Commission to propose as a draft directive and which have been given legal effect through the appropriate decision-making procedure. These include:

■ the Directive on Parental Leave (1996/34/EC);
■ the directive on equality between the rights of part-time and full-time workers (1997/81/EC);
■ the directive on fixed-term work (1999/70/EC).

■ Subsidiarity

One of the debates that simmered throughout the 1980s and early 1990s concerned the question of whether and when action should be taken at the level of the EU compared with the level of the nation state (or lower). The UK governments of the time were at the centre of these debates and generally they took the view that action at the EU level should be a measure of last resort and linked the debate to the issue of national sovereignty. Other interests, with perhaps greater ambitions for the creation of EU-wide systems, and those keen on Europe becoming a union much more like the United States of America, tended to argue for more and wider and deeper action at the EU level.

The debate resulted in a restatement of the principle in Article 3b of the Treaty agreed at Maastricht:

> In areas which do not fall within its exclusive competence, the Community shall take action, in accordance with the principle of subsidiarity, only if and in so far as the objectives of the proposed action cannot be achieved by the member states and can therefore, by reason of the scale or effects of the proposed action, be better achieved by the Community. Any action by the Community shall not go beyond what is necessary to achieve the objectives of this Treaty.

The implication is clear: the Commission and the EU should seek to act only when it is clear that the objectives cannot be achieved at the level of each of the member states *and* that they can be better achieved through action at the centre.

The meaning and application of this principle was further developed in the Amsterdam Treaty with a new protocol on subsidiarity which cites three criteria for judging whether the condition above has been fulfilled:

- Does the action have transnational aspects that cannot be satisfactorily regulated by member states?
- Would action by member states or lack of action conflict with the requirements of the Treaty?
- Would action at Community level produce clear benefits?

Social policy initiatives and the social dimension

In the first part of this section we examine some of the background and debates between those reflecting different perspectives, systems and traditions within the various member states, and the relevance of the EU treaties to the development of social policy within the EU.

In the context of the EU, social policy and the social dimension encompass matters that relate to the employment relationship and employee relations as well as to more general areas of social protection. As Commissioner Flynn points out in Exhibit 6.1, his, and presumably the Commission's, view is that without a strong social dimension the EU will not be worthy of the name 'union'.

Nevertheless, the development of the social dimension has been the subject of much debate and disagreement over the years, with different perspectives as to the need for and desirability of action and regulation at the level of the EU.

Generally, social issues and the 'need' for action and regulation have been addressed in the context of the implications of and for economic integration, the creation of the single market and, more recently, monetary union.

It was recognised at the outset by its architects that the market and economic integration process would inevitably create some dislocation of industry and employment and a need for restructuring – that there would be losers as well as winners.

In the main, the debate has been between those who considered that intervention would be necessary in order to cushion these effects and promote restructuring with a more efficient use of labour, and those who took the view that, while integration might have these effects, the market should prevail. Circumstances justifying intervention should be limited to those in which the intervention itself contributed to the process of market integration.

As Hall (1994) explains, the Commission and most of the member states have viewed the social dimension as:

> an important vehicle for securing the support of the European labour movement for the single market project and for enhancing the 'social acceptability' of the consequent economic restructuring . . . the human face of the EC.

This is a debate that has not been resolved and the same perspectives can be seen to inform deliberations within the EU on solutions to the problems of unemployment and international competitiveness. The Commission and the European labour movements have tended to argue the case for the protection of those in employment and the regulation of the labour market to ensure social justice. Employers and other interests have argued the case that economic performance in Europe, including job creation, is undermined by excessive regulation leading to labour market inflexibility.

Contrasts in traditions and systems

We have alluded to the differences between the member states in terms of the traditions of social philosophy and legislative intervention, the latter being significantly influenced by the former. Gold (1993) adopts Teague's (1989) distinction between the social protectionist and the deregulatory perspectives. The social protectionist perspective encompasses the Socialist, Social Democrat and Christian Democrat philosophies, all of which, though to varying degrees and with different priorities, accept the principle of intervention and the need for government to regulate the labour market, insist upon minimum employee rights and promote social justice. This perspective, shared by the majority of the political groups within the EU and also, crucially, by influential groups within the Commission, can be contrasted with that of the UK Conservative governments between 1979 and 1997 and arguably initially that of the Labour government elected in 1997, which has been portrayed as a deregulatory approach. In terms of philosophy or ideology, these UK governments can be characterised as liberal individualist, putting their faith in the market mechanism and individual choice, contract and decision-making as the base for competitiveness and growth.

Hall (1994) and Gold (1993) both seek to locate the regulatory systems in the EU in one of the following three categories:

■ *The Roman–German system.* Here the state plays a crucial role in industrial relations. Gold (1993) follows Due *et al.* (1991) in pointing out that in these systems there is a core of fundamental rights and freedoms guaranteed by the constitution and it is these that constitute the base of national industrial relations. It is common in such systems for there to be quite extensive legal regulation of areas such as working time and the rights of employees to be represented and the mechanisms of that representation. Germany, France, the Netherlands, Belgium and Italy are quoted as being in this category/tradition.

■ *The Anglo-Irish system.* Here the role of the state is more limited and there is a much less extensive set of legislatively created and supported basic rights and protections. Governments in these countries have traditionally left more to the parties themselves and stepped in to regulate and protect only when necessary to defend either the national interest or the interests of certain vulnerable minorities, such as children. In this context, Hall (1994) refers to these systems as voluntarist. Both the UK and Ireland are in this category. In the UK it is arguable that this tradition began to be eroded from the 1960s onwards, and through much of the 1960s and 1970s there was a much greater willingness to intervene and to regulate to provide basic rights and freedoms and to encourage trade unionism and collective bargaining.

■ *The Nordic system.* Prior to the enlargement of the EU in 1995, only Denmark fell into this category, although as Gold (1993) points out, the other Scandinavian countries that were part of this enlargement – Sweden and Finland – also share this tradition. The difference between this system and the Anglo-Irish group is in the degree of emphasis and reliance placed on and in the collective agreement. It is suggested that, in these countries, more emphasis is placed upon the basic agreement freely entered into, usually at national or sectoral level, by both employer and trade union and it is this that provides the central element of the industrial relations system. The state has intervened to regulate only at the request of the parties.

The Commission has traditionally pursued policies and taken initiatives consistent with the Roman–German tradition and there is plenty of recent evidence that this is still the inclination of the directorates with responsibility for social affairs. The debate on unemployment, which has occupied the member states, Commission and other interests substantially since the early 1990s, illustrates these preferences. The Commission has argued that, while it may be desirable to reduce the regulation of the labour market and labour costs, this reduction should not be achieved at the expense of social justice and the weakest and poorest members of the EU (European Commission, 1994). It is also clear that there are other interests within the Commission – for example, those with responsibility for industry and competition policy – that are distancing themselves from the traditions of the Roman–German system of regulation and social protection. Such factions are becoming more willing to countenance deregulation as a necessary response to the pressures of international competition and the need to enhance flexibility in terms of response to the market and labour usage.

Hall (1994) points out that the leading proponent of the view that an extensive EU social policy/dimension would damage competitiveness since it would raise employment costs and reduce labour market flexibility was the UK Conservative government. This was a consistent position after its election in 1979 and was demonstrated by its opposition to a number of individual proposals, in addition to its refusal to adopt the Social Charter or to agree to the Maastricht Treaty until the Social Chapter was removed.

The treaties and social policy

Even at the outset of the creation of the Community in the 1950s, these differences of view can be seen to have contributed to the fudging of the issue of social policy. As Hall (1994) says:

> To date, the evolution of the EC's (Community) social policy role has been uneven and limited. The Treaty of Rome did not establish a clear Community competence in this sphere.

The treaty-based system of law within the EU requires that the founding treaties specifically provide for the relevant authorities and institutions to take the actions envisaged; if the treaties do not do this then action cannot be initiated.

In the early years the absence of such a base does not appear to have posed major problems, partly because there were specific treaty articles covering matters of:

- equal pay between the sexes (Article 119);
- the free movement of labour (Articles 48 and 49);
- assistance with the relocation and retraining of individuals harmed by the integration process as it caused dislocation and restructuring. Article 123 provided the basis for the creation of the European Social Fund (ESF), which has been the main mechanism for achieving improved employment opportunities and enhancing geographic and occupational mobility.

The latter two were both considered essential to the process and objective of integration since failure to take measures to facilitate these aspects might have produced, on the one hand, imperfections in the market-allocating process and, on the other, opposition to and negative impressions of integration.

The absence of specific treaty bases enabling the Commission and the member states to intervene legislatively where necessary on issues of employee rights and the development of a social policy came to the fore for the first time in the mid-1970s. It was the Council agreement to create the single market, embodied in the Single European Act (SEA) 1986, however, that provided a significant impetus to the resolution of this inadequacy in the Treaty of Rome and therefore in the EU.

After the adoption of the SEA the Commission, the labour movements and some member state governments became increasingly concerned about the dangers of 'social dumping'. In this context the term refers to the tendency for multinational companies to locate, and in some instances relocate, their production facilities in those parts of the EU where the labour costs of production and the degree of regulation of the labour market are lowest. The fear was particularly acute in those countries with the most developed labour standards and the correspondingly highest labour costs. Of course, other factors influence location decisions and the counterargument from the direction of economic liberalism suggests that the market mechanism would eventually lead to adjustment and a new equilibrium somewhere between the two opening positions. Putting it bluntly, the fear was that employers would go 'regime shopping' and use the variation in labour costs either to guide their location decisions or to beat down the labour costs and standards in those countries that were most developed.

There are similar concerns in respect of the further enlargement of the EU, as discussed earlier, that investment will be redirected to the aspirant member states where labour costs and living standards are lower. There are also concerns that the higher living standards in the existing member states will encourage a migration of labour from the aspirant member states to those already in membership. The effect of these twin developments could exert pressure of a downward nature on social and living standards throughout the Union as a whole and could lead to greater unemployment in the existing member states. Proponents of a social dimension have not been slow to point this out and to use the threat in support of their argument.

Concerns about social dumping and the absence of an appropriate treaty base for action on social policy led the Commission to propose the adoption by the Council of a statement of minimum social rights. These were contained in the document known as the Social Charter (Exhibit 6.2). By the time the Charter was presented to the Council at its meeting in Strasbourg in December 1989, the Commission had also developed the Social Action Programme (SAP) containing 47 proposals for EU-level action to give effect to many of the minimum rights contained within the Charter.

These Social Charter proposals were acceptable to 11 of the 12 member states, the odd one out being the UK, but because the Charter could only be adopted via unanimity, the UK had an effective veto. Legally, therefore, the Charter had no status and remained only a statement of intent on the part of all member states other than the UK.

The Social Action Programme was devised to give effect to some of the specified Charter rights, but not all of them. Some of the proposals were for legislative intervention in order to put particular rights in place throughout the EU, but many others were either not addressed at all in the action programme or the proposals were of a non-legislative and non-binding nature.

It is neither possible nor necessary in this chapter to explain the full contents of the SAP but it is worth pointing out that there were no proposals in this programme for the legislative imposition of rights for workers in the areas of:

- control or specification of minimum levels of pay;
- imposing or constraining the right of freedom of association (this includes the right to join a trade union or employers' association);
- the right to strike or impose a lock-out;
- imposing or constraining the process and status of collective bargaining and/or co-determination.

It is also worth pointing out that considerable care was taken in both the Charter and the SAP not to impose rights in a manner that was inconsistent with the traditions, practices and laws of the various member states. In other words, there was a general concern to act in a manner consistent with the principle of subsidiarity.

However, the significance of the Social Charter is greater than might be expected given that its adoption was vetoed. It has subsequently formed the base for:

- the draft Social Chapter of the Treaty on European Union at Maastricht in December 1991 which became the base for the Social Protocol and Social Agreement annexed to the treaty; and
- the agreement at Amsterdam in 1997 on a new Treaty Social Chapter, where, in the preamble, it is made clear that the member states remained committed to the principles and fundamental rights contained within it.

Exhibit 6.2

The Social Charter

The rights proposed and incorporated in the Charter fell into 12 main sections:

1 Freedom of movement, including the removal of obstacles arising from the non-recognition of diplomas and equivalent occupational qualifications.
2 Employment and remuneration, including the rights to fair and equitable wages thereby enabling a decent standard of living.
3 Improvement of living and working conditions, with specific reference made to working hours, weekly rest periods and annual leave, temporary, fixed-term and part-time contracts. It is clearly the intention that there should be an upward approximation/harmonisation.
4 Social protection, where the term means adequate and sufficient protection in keeping with the particular situation.
5 Freedom of association and collective bargaining. Both workers and employers should have the right to form and join, or not, associations for the defence of their economic and social interests. The associations should have the right to negotiate and conclude collective agreements and the right to take collective action including strike action. Conciliation, arbitration and mediation should be encouraged and in all cases these rights should be subject to and exercised in accordance with existing national conditions and practice. This section also refers to improvement of the dialogue between the Social Partners at European level.
6 Vocational training. All workers should have the right of access to such training and retraining throughout their working life with particular reference made to the acquisition of new skills in the light of technological developments.
7 Equal treatment for men and women should be assured, and equal opportunities should be developed. Particular mention is made of equality of access to employment, remuneration, working conditions, social protection, education, vocational training and career development. Mention was also made of measures to facilitate both men and women reconciling their work and family lives/obligations.
8 Information, consultation and participation of workers, taking into account the practices in each member state and with particular reference to organisations with establishments or companies in two or more member states. In particular, these rights should apply in cases of technological change having major implications for the workforce in terms of working conditions and/or work organisation, where restructuring or mergers also have an impact upon the employment of workers and in cases of collective redundancy procedures.
9 Health, protection and safety at the workplace. This section refers to satisfactory health and safety conditions in the workplace and harmonisation while improvements are maintained. Specific mention is also made of training, information and consultation.
10 Protection of children and adolescents. They should receive equitable remuneration, be protected from working below a certain age, and particular arrangements should be made to ensure that their development, vocational training and access to employment needs are met. There should also be limits on the duration of such work and their working at night. There should also be an entitlement to initial vocational training upon leaving full-time education.
11 Elderly persons upon retirement should have an entitlement to a decent standard of living.
12 Disabled persons should be entitled to measures aimed at improving their social and professional integration and in particular to vocational training, ergonomics, accessibility and mobility.

At Maastricht in 1991 the UK government refused to agree to a revised treaty that contained the draft Social Chapter. As a consequence of this refusal or effective veto the other member states decided to reach their own agreement which was appended to the Treaty under a device known as a protocol. This particular protocol became known as the Social Protocol Agreement on Social Policy, or Social Agreement. We have already examined the new decision-making procedures involving the Social Partners that were agreed at Maastricht and formed part of the protocol.

Amsterdam, June 1997: Treaty outcomes and amendments

The Social Protocol was repealed and the Social Agreement brought fully into the treaties, Title IX Articles 136 to 145, including the protocol decision-making mechanisms involving the Social Partners described earlier. This has considerably widened the range of social subject matter over which the Community now has competence (Exhibit 6.3).

The ability of the EU to take action on matters of discrimination in future has been greatly enhanced by a new Article 13. This provides the Council acting *unanimously* with the power to take 'appropriate action to combat discrimination based on sex, racial or ethnic origin, religion or belief, disability, age or sexual orientation'.

Within months of this agreement the new Labour government in the UK was expressing its determination to secure EU-wide legislation outlawing discrimination on the grounds of race and ethnic origin, although it has to be admitted that some other member states will have greater difficulty with this proposal. An example is Germany where foreign nationals and those of different ethnic origins are presented already with insurmountable obstacles to obtaining citizenship and thereby the rights to equal treatment that are associated with citizenship. Additionally, they are denied the rights

---

Exhibit 6.3

Amsterdam Treaty agreements

The areas of social policy in which action can now be taken utilising QMV and the co-decision procedure are listed as:

- improvement in particular of the working environment to protect workers' health and safety;
- working conditions;
- the informing and consultation of workers;
- the integration of persons excluded from the labour market;
- equality between men and women with regard to labour market opportunities and treatment at work.

The areas in which unanimity is to apply remain:

- social security and social protection of workers;
- protection of workers where their contract of employment is terminated;
- representation and collective defence of the interests of workers and employers, including co-determination;
- conditions of employment for third-country nationals;
- financial contributions for the promotion of employment and job creation.

As in the past, a range of issues is not addressed at the level of the Union, including: pay (other than between the sexes), the right of association, the right to strike or the right to impose lock-outs.

The Commission and the member states were keen to preserve the right to take positive action in matters relating to the encouragement of equality between the sexes and the Treaty contains also the following paragraph:

With a view to ensuring full equality in practice between men and women in working life, the principle of equal treatment shall not prevent any Member State from maintaining or adopting measures providing for specific advantages in order to make it easier for the *underrepresented sex* [my emphasis] to pursue a vocational activity or to prevent or compensate for disadvantages in professional careers. (Article 141(4) EC)

and protection provided by EU treaties and initiatives since these accrue in the main only to citizens of one of the member states.

The Charter of Fundamental Rights of the European Union

Between the Amsterdam and Nice Intergovernmental conferences in 1997 and 2000 there was much debate about whether the Union should have a legally binding constitution comprising, among other things, a set of fundamental individual rights that would be legally enforceable. Proponents argued that such a set or Charter of Fundamental Rights would be no more than a restatement of existing legal rights. Critics, including the government of the UK, were implacably opposed to giving any such charter legal effect, arguing that it was unnecessary if the rights already existed. It was also argued by opponents of the Charter that it was inconsistent with legal traditions in certain countries and that it was something that individual member state governments could implement separately if they so wished. The outcome of these discussions, the weight of support being in favour, was the proclamation of the Charter at the Nice summit. This is yet another set of rights that must be separated from the Social Charter above, even though many of the Social Charter rights have informed this latest Charter. There is some difference of opinion as to the legal status of the Charter. The UK government has insisted that it has not been incorporated into the legal base of the Union. On the other hand, the Commission and some other member states have argued that individuals will be able to rely on the Charter in cases where they feel that any of their individual rights within it are being challenged by EU laws or decisions by the EU institutions. We must in the future expect the Charter to play a greater role in the determination of difficult legal cases and perhaps gradually for it to inform those decisions and thereby the law through the principles of binding precedent. The 50 rights spelt out in the Charter are grouped into six headings: dignity, freedom, equality, solidarity, citizens' rights and justice. A selective representation of the charter is presented in Exhibit 6.4.

Exhibit 6.4

Charter of Fundamental Rights

Article 5
Prohibition of slavery and forced labour

1 No one shall be held in slavery or servitude.
2 No one shall be required to perform forced or compulsory labour.
3 Trafficking in human beings is prohibited.

Article 12
Freedom of assembly and of association

1 Everyone has the right to freedom of peaceful assembly and to freedom of association at all levels, in particular in political, trade union and civic matters, which implies the right of everyone to form and to join trade unions for the protection of his or her interests.

Article 15
Freedom to choose an occupation and right to engage in work

1 Everyone has the right to engage in work and to pursue a freely chosen or accepted occupation.
2 Every citizen of the Union has the freedom to seek employment, to work, to exercise the right of establishment and to provide services in any Member State.

Exhibit 6.4 *continued*

3 Nationals of third countries who are authorised to work in the territories of the Member States are entitled to working conditions equivalent to those of citizens of the Union.

Article 21
Non-discrimination

1 Any discrimination based on any ground such as sex, race, colour, ethnic or social origin, genetic features, language, religion or belief, political or any other opinion, membership of a national minority, property, birth, disability, age or sexual orientation shall be prohibited.
2 Within the scope of application of the Treaty establishing the European Community and of the Treaty on European Union, and without prejudice to the special provisions of those Treaties, any discrimination on grounds of nationality shall be prohibited.

Article 23
Equality between men and women

Equality between men and women must be ensured in all areas, including employment, work and pay. The principle of equality shall not prevent the maintenance or adoption of measures providing for specific advantages in favour of the under-represented sex.

Article 27
Workers' right to information and consultation within the undertaking

Workers or their representatives must, at the appropriate levels, be guaranteed information and consultation in good time in the cases and under the conditions provided for by Community law and national laws and practices.

Article 28
Right of collective bargaining and action

Workers and employers, or their respective organisations, have, in accordance with Community law and national laws and practices, the right to negotiate and conclude collective agreements at the appropriate levels and, in cases of conflicts of interest, to take collective action to defend their interests, including strike action.

Article 29
Right of access to placement services

Everyone has the right of access to a free placement service.

Article 30
Protection in the event of unjustified dismissal

Every worker has the right to protection against unjustified dismissal, in accordance with Community law and national laws and practices.

Article 31
Fair and just working conditions

1 Every worker has the right to working conditions which respect his or her health, safety and dignity.
2 Every worker has the right to limitation of maximum working hours, to daily and weekly rest periods and to an annual period of paid leave.

Article 32
Prohibition of child labour and protection of young people at work

The employment of children is prohibited. The minimum age of admission to employment may not be lower than the minimum school-leaving age, without prejudice to such rules as may be more favourable to young people and except for limited derogations.

Young people admitted to work must have working conditions appropriate to their age and be protected against economic exploitation and any work likely to harm their safety, health or physical, mental, moral or social development or to interfere with their education.

Article 33
Family and professional life

1 The family shall enjoy legal, economic and social protection.
2 To reconcile family and professional life, everyone shall have the right to protection from dismissal for a reason connected with maternity and the right to paid maternity leave and to parental leave following the birth or adoption of a child.

Policy initiatives: equality, working time and employee participation

It is impossible in a chapter of this size to examine all the individual and specific initiatives that can be argued to impinge upon and to influence employee relations in the UK. Consequently, we have decided to examine those that have arguably had the greatest impact and those that may have similar impact in the future.

In this context we examine initiatives seeking to establish minimum rights for employees in the following areas:

- equality of pay and treatment between the sexes and equality of treatment on grounds such as race, ethnicity, age, disability, religion and belief;
- in respect of the organisation of working time;
- for their representatives to be given information and to be consulted on specific issues such as on the transfer of undertakings, collective redundancies, and health and safety matters and within multinational organisations and the EWC Directive.

Equality

There are various dimensions to the issue of equality between the sexes and distinctions are usually drawn between equality of pay, equality of access to work and equality in terms of treatment at work.

There has been a great deal of debate as to what may be the major causes of this inequality and, given the causes, what might be the best means of seeking to remedy and reduce the extent of the inequality. Evidence that there is inequality is reasonably easy to obtain in areas such as pay and labour force participation but very much more difficult in areas associated with the treatment dimension such as career development, training, promotion opportunities and sexual harassment.

An indication of the scale of inequality is provided by the Commission in its *Annual Report for the year 2000 on Equal Opportunities between Women and Men in the European Union* (European Commission, 2001). In the foreword the following statement is made:

> Much progress has been achieved, but we are still a long way from eradicating the inequalities and injustices that women face as part of their everyday lives: a persistent pay gap of more than 20 per cent; higher unemployment of women and significant under-representation in business as well as in every single political institution in the EU.

They might also have added that the employment of women is far less than for men, currently standing at an average of approximately 52 per cent, some 18 per cent less than for men. The Lisbon Summit in 2000 set an employment rate target for women of 60 per cent by 2010, but as is pointed out in the report, this will be difficult to achieve in an environment where men are paid 20–30 per cent more than women. The gender pay gap in the UK seems to be slightly lower than the EU average. The New Earnings Survey for April 2000 suggests that women's full-time earnings an hour are 82 per cent of men's, a figure consistent with the Labour Force Survey 2000 which found women's pay to be 81.8 per cent of men's. The main reasons for the gap appear to be:

- occupational segregation;
- the unequal impact of family responsibilities;
- direct (unlawful) discrimination.

The Commission has adopted a new framework strategy on gender equality and a five-year gender equality programme, with the priority theme for 2001 being the gender pay gap. The strategy focuses on five objectives, which provide a frame of reference for policy development and to which all Community gender-equality initiatives will be linked:

- equality in economic life;
- equal representation and participation in decision-making;
- equality in social life;
- equality in civil life;
- changing gender roles and overcoming stereotypes.

Much has been achieved in recent years to facilitate the EU's taking action to promote equality between the sexes. The Treaty revisions at Amsterdam have facilitated the mainstreaming of gender equality, with the promotion of equality between women and men being added to the main tasks of the Community as set out in Article 2 of the Treaty. In addition, the Union's competence and ability to take appropriate action of a legislative nature has been enhanced by the inclusion of equality between men and women with regard to labour market opportunities and treatment at work as part of the new Social Chapter and as one of the areas of subject matter where the co-decision procedure can be used. We have already noted the preservation in the treaty agreed at Amsterdam of the right to take positive action.

In addition the new Article 13 in the Treaty provides for the Council to act *unanimously* with the power to take 'appropriate action to combat discrimination based on sex, racial or ethnic origin, religion or belief, disability, age or sexual orientation'.

New directives based on this article have already been adopted (see later) and the Commission is intent upon securing the adoption of a new gender equality directive, based upon this article, in 2002.

This recent flurry of activity can be interpreted both as evidence of a new determination to deal with the issues as well as evidence of the relative failure of the policies pursued and measures taken in the past. In the following sections on pay and treatment we briefly review some of the measures taken earlier before looking at the new Article 13 directives adopted since the Amsterdam Treaty agreement.

Pay

In charting and discussing EU initiatives it should be pointed out firstly that Article 119 of the founding treaty, the Treaty of Rome, provided the right to equality of pay between the sexes. This article has been amended over the years in the light of experience and decisions arrived at by the European Court of Justice. Many judgments were concerned to determine the meaning of pay and whether it included items such as pension contributions and benefits, redundancy payments and various other benefits such as loans and mortgages. The definition in the Treaty is now very wide.

The relevant article is now Article 141 (ex Article 119) of the EC Treaty which states:

1. Each Member State shall ensure that the principle of equal pay for male and female workers for equal work or work of equal value is applied.
2. For the purpose of this Article, 'pay' means the ordinary basic or minimum wage or salary and any other consideration, whether in cash or in kind, which the worker receives directly or indirectly, in respect of his employment, from his employer.
   Equal pay without discrimination based on sex means:
   (a) that pay for the same work at piece rates shall be calculated on the basis of the same unit of measurement;
   (b) that pay for work at time rates shall be the same for the same job.
3. The Council, acting in accordance with the procedure referred to in Article 251, and after consulting the Economic and Social Committee, shall adopt measures to ensure the application of the principle of equal opportunities and equal treatment of men and women in matters of employment and occupation, including the principle of equal pay for equal work or work of equal value.

The original Article 119 and the implementing legislation also failed to adequately define 'equal work', and eventually a directive was adopted in 1975 (75/117) that sought to deal with issues of 'equal work and value'. To all intents and purposes the requirement became that men and women should be paid 'equally for work of equal value'. While this is now encompassed within the Treaty article, there is no attempt at definition as in the case of pay and there are still problems surrounding the question of how to determine both equal work and value. Issues that have arisen over the years include whether the comparable work has to be undertaken at the same time and whether the comparison could be hypothetical.

There have been numerous cases that have determined that the legislation can be appropriately used in instances of indirect as well as direct discrimination.

Indirect discrimination covers circumstances whereby an employer applies policies or practices that in practice disproportionately and adversely affect one sex and that cannot objectively be justified on grounds other than sex. Examples of such indirect discrimination have been found to include payment systems and arrangements that attached pay to the possession of longevity of continuous service, the completion of specified training and an ability to work flexible hours.

The issue of value is just as problematical as that of equal work. The legislation does cover circumstances in which the work of the plaintiff is of greater value than that of the comparator. However, such a finding of greater value cannot then be used to justify the imposition of a rate of pay that is greater than that of the comparator (Murphy and others v An Bord Telecom Eirann).

However, there are a number of other difficulties associated with the concept of value. First, the criterion of value to be used has to be decided, and this can itself concentrate upon either inputs or outputs. For example, the criterion could be:

- the effort, skill and responsibility put into the work;
- the content of the work;
- a measure of the value of the output;
- a mix of these.

Job evaluation and classification schemes tend to be based upon a mix of input and content rather than upon output.

The 1975 Equal Pay Directive (as amended) specifies in Article 1 that job classification systems should be based on the same criteria for men and women and designed so that they exclude any discrimination on grounds of sex. Despite this, there are still many unresolved dilemmas in this area. There have been many criticisms over the years that traditional and existing schemes often did demonstrate a bias in favour of the jobs that were 'male' as opposed to 'female', emphasising more or awarding more points to the characteristics associated with and forming part of the male jobs.

The Commission sought to address some of the remaining problems concerning the meaning, measurement and application of this principle of equal pay for work of equal value via a memorandum (94/6). Pursuant to that it has issued the Code of Practice on the Implementation of Equal Pay for Work of Equal Value for Women and Men (COM (96) 336).

The Commission states that, in particular, the code aims to eliminate sexual discrimination whenever pay structures are based on job classification and evaluation systems, and makes two main proposals:

- that negotiators at all levels should carry out an analysis of the remuneration system and evaluate the data required to detect sexual discrimination in pay structures so that it becomes possible to devise remedies;
- that a plan for follow-up should be drawn up and implemented so that sexual discrimination is eliminated.

Interestingly, the code states quite clearly that the prime responsibility for the avoidance of discrimination rests with the employers. It should also be noted that interventions of this kind are subject to the danger that the greater the degree of the discrimination or wage/earnings gap, the greater may be the employment impact of the interventions directed at narrowing or eliminating that gap. The greater the extent of occupational segregation, the smaller will be the impact of the equal value interventions.

Treatment

The 1975 Equal Pay Directive was followed by the Equal Treatment Directive in 1976 (76/207), which sought to ban discrimination on the grounds of sex in all aspects of employment. The Treaty of Rome did not specifically provide the Community with competence in this area and the directive was adopted utilising an implied competence in the area of equality of treatment between the sexes on the grounds that this constituted a fundamental human right.

The ECJ has also had a role to play in this area of equal treatment, interpreting the legislation and its meaning. An example is in the treatment of the sexes by occupational pension schemes. Case 152/84, Marshall *v* Southampton and South West Hampshire Area Health Authority, was concerned with the application of unequal retirement ages and also with the matter of whether there should be a ceiling on the damages to be awarded in cases of sex discrimination.

In recent times much of this judicial activity has been in connection with issues relating to part-time workers and their rights in comparison with those of full-time workers. A framework agreement on this issue was agreed within the protocol procedures by the Social Partners and given effect in Directive 97/81/EC. Council Directive 98/23/EC extended this directive to the UK.

This agreement and directive have a long history that can be traced back to the Social Charter and subsequent Social Action Programme (SAP). However, the initiative was given impetus by various national and European Court of Justice decisions since early 1994, which have ruled that discrimination between part-time and full-time employees in terms of rights to redundancy payments, rights to join an occupational pension scheme and rights to claim unfair dismissal was indirect sex discrimination. The essence of the grounds upon which these matters can be argued as equality issues rests on the fact that the majority of part-time employees within the EU are female, and therefore to discriminate against these categories of contract or employee is to discriminate indirectly on the grounds of sex. Examples of relevant cases include Vroege ECJ 1994 and Fisscher ECJ 1994.

The main provisions of Directive 97/81 on equality for part-time workers are that:

- those with an employment contract or relationship for less than normal hours compared with a full-time worker should be entitled to equality of treatment on a pro-rata basis, and
- employees should not be discriminated against solely on the grounds that they work part-time rather than full-time.

In addition to enhancing the equality of treatment of part-time workers, this directive is also concerned to facilitate the development of part-time work.

A similar directive with respect to pro-rata equality for people working on fixed-term contracts has also been adopted on the basis of a framework agreement by the Social Partners: Council Directive 1999/70/EC concerning the Framework Agreement on fixed-term work concluded by ETUC, UNICE and CEEP. In this instance, fixed term is defined as follows:

'fixed-term worker' means a person having an employment contract or relationship entered into directly between an employer and a worker where the end of the employment contract or relationship is determined by objective conditions such as reaching a specific date, completing a specific task, or the occurrence of a specific event.

The main purpose of the directive is to ensure that:

In respect of employment conditions, fixed-term workers shall not be treated in a less favourable manner than comparable permanent workers solely because they have a fixed-term contract or relation unless different treatment is justified on objective grounds.

Specific mention is made in the directive that fixed-term workers should (1) have opportunities to be informed of and to apply for permanent positions as they arise, and (2) have access to training opportunities.

In the case of these framework agreements and directives and the directive on parental leave (see below), many of the details were deliberately left for determination at national level.

Another issue on which the Social Partners reached a framework agreement, subsequently adopted as a directive, was that of entitlements to parental leave.

The main provisions of the Directive on Parental Leave (96/34) are:

- that both parents should be entitled to three months' unpaid leave after the birth or adoption of a child, the leave to be taken before the eighth birthday of the child;
- protection from dismissal for asking for parental leave;
- protection of the right to return to work after the leave;
- provision for additional time off in urgent family circumstances such as sickness and accident.

Examples of the details left to determination at national level include what might be an appropriate length of service qualification and the number of days leave that may be reasonable or allowable for the urgent family leave referred to in the agreement.

This directive has not stopped arguments about the value to employees, employers and the government of the provision of paid as opposed to a right to unpaid parental leave. The Commission invited the Social Partners to agree a new set of arrangements relating to the burden of proof in cases of sex discrimination but they declined to do so. Consequently the Council adopted Council Directive 97/80/EC of 15 December 1997 on the burden of proof in cases of discrimination based on sex. The main feature of the directive is contained in Article 4 which states:

Burden of proof

1. Member States shall take such measures as are necessary, in accordance with their national judicial systems, to ensure that, when persons who consider themselves wronged because the principle of equal treatment has not been applied to them establish, before a court or other competent authority, facts from which it may be presumed that there has been direct or indirect discrimination, it shall be for the respondent to prove that there has been no breach of the principle of equal treatment.
2. This Directive shall not prevent Member States from introducing rules of evidence which are more favourable to plaintiffs.

The shift in burden of proof is a change from previous arrangements where it was the responsibility of the plaintiff to establish that there had in fact been a breach of the principle of equal treatment. As noted earlier, this was often very difficult to establish in areas such as promotion, opportunities for training and development etc. Now, once a plaintiff has established facts from which it may be presumed that discrimination occurred, it becomes the responsibility of the respondent to establish their innocence and that there was not a breach of the principle of equal treatment. The expectation was that this change would make it easier for plaintiffs to win disputed cases and indeed that many prospective respondents would not contest cases given the new requirements.

One of the most significant ECJ decisions in recent years was in the Kalanke *v* Freie Hansestadt Bremen case in October 1995. The decision of the ECJ raised considerable doubts about the lawfulness of positive action in favour of one sex in employment and raised the matter of the distinction between positive action and positive discrimination.

The *Land* (state) of Bremen (Germany) was operating a policy of automatically giving priority to women candidates for recruitment and promotion in sectors where they were underrepresented and where a female candidate had the same qualifications as a male candidate. The ECJ found the practice to be in contravention of Article 2(4) of Directive 76/207/EEC (the Directive on Equal Treatment) and found that rules and procedures giving one sex *absolute* and *unconditional* priority go beyond promoting equal treatment or opportunities and overstep the provisions for positive action provided for in Article 2(4). This allowed for action to be taken to remove obstacles to the equal treatment of the sexes as an exception from the main requirement not to discriminate. However, the ECJ found that to *guarantee* women priority went too far.

This decision appeared in the first instance to outlaw the type of *de facto* quota systems that had been the practice in the *Land* of Bremen, and in many other places, and it was this case that prompted the insertion into the treaty agreed at Amsterdam of paragraph 141(4) preserving the right to take positive action.

The Directive on the Protection of Pregnant Workers (92/85) has not been included in this section on equality between the sexes since the directive was adopted as a health and safety measure. In addition, there are some non-binding instruments relevant to issues of equality between the sexes at work and in connection with employment:

- Council Recommendation 92/241, concerned with child care, which among other things encourages the promotion of flexible working as well as a sharing of parental responsibilities.
- Council Resolution on Balanced Participation of Men and Women in Decision-making (95/C168/02).
- A Commission document and a code of practice on the dignity of women and men at work, which seek to address the issue of sexual harassment at work and provide policy guidance to practitioners as well as to member state governments and the Social Partners.

Article 13 directives

One of the apparent inconsistencies in the EU's competence has been in the area of equality. Ever since the original Treaty of Rome in 1957, the Union has had the competence to act in the area of equality between the sexes and on grounds of nationality but not in other areas of equality such as race, ethnicity, age, disability, colour or religion. This was changed by the treaty agreement at Amsterdam in 1997 when the new Article 13 was adopted.

Since then, this new Article has been used to adopt two new directives and the Commission has proposed a third directive using this Article in 2002. The two new directives already adopted are:

- Council Directive 2000/43/EC of 29 June 2000 implementing the principle of equal treatment between persons irrespective of racial or ethnic origin;
- Council Directive 2000/78/EC of 27 November 2000 establishing a general framework for equal treatment in employment and occupation on the grounds of religion or belief, disability, age or sexual orientation.

These two new directives extend the rights of EU citizens not to be discriminated against on a range of new grounds. The adoption of these new directives will also have implications for the policies and practices of employing organisations. The emphasis here is upon the future because there are some years yet before the individual member states have to give effect to the principles and provisions of the new directives. The emphasis of the new measures is on equality of treatment and, as we know from the impact and extent of the earlier measures regarding equality of treatment between the sexes, treatment at the least is likely to extend to include policies and practices in areas such as: employment, recruitment and selection, opportunities for promotion, selection for redundancy or dismissal, treatment in the context of training and development and many other terms and conditions of employment such as retirement policies and practices which may include rights to join a pension scheme and the issue of a compulsory and arbitrary retirement age.

Many countries in the Union are confronted with a future scenario in which the size of the working population is declining, the age of that population is rising and the future costs of maintaining a larger retired population are of concern to governments and other pension providers. In addition, current projections imply that countries within the Union will be so short of labour in 10 or 20 years' time that immigration may well be necessary on a very much larger scale than is the case now. The new provisions, which are likely to result in greater employment opportunities for the older members of the workforce can be seen as paving the way for at least a partial solution to these problems. However, it is important that the second of the directives does provide exclusion in respect of the fixing for occupational social security schemes of ages for admission or entitlement to retirement or invalidity benefits. This would include the fixing under those schemes of different ages for employees or groups or categories of employees as long as this does not result in discrimination on the grounds of sex.

Scope

The scope of the directives differs in so far as the latter limits the coverage of its provisions to occupation and employment (the first four of the bullet points below) whereas the former is extended to include:

- conditions for access to employment including recruitment and selection criteria and conditions and including promotion;
- access to all types and to all levels of vocational guidance and vocational training including practical work experience;
- employment and working conditions, including dismissals and pay;
- membership of and involvement in an organisation of workers or employers;
- social protection, including social security and health care;
- social advantages;
- education;
- access to and supply of goods and services which are available to the public, including housing.

Both directives are also similar in that they encompass both direct and indirect discrimination and use the same definitions of these concepts. We have earlier indicated the difference between direct and indirect discrimination, and the same definition of indirect discrimination is used in these directives. The directives also include harassment as discrimination and this is deemed to occur when an unwanted conduct related to any of the grounds referred to in them has the purpose or effect of violating the dignity of a person and of creating an intimidating, hostile, degrading, humiliating or offensive environment. The directives also make it clear that an instruction to discriminate is deemed to be discrimination.

Genuine occupational requirements and other exceptions

As is the case with existing discrimination legislation in the UK, the directives allow member states to provide for discrimination to be lawful in a number of circumstances which include grounds related to a genuine occupational requirement or qualification. Treatment based on a characteristic covered by the directives shall not constitute discrimination where, by reason of the nature of the particular occupational activities concerned or of the context in which they are carried out, such a characteristic constitutes a genuine and determining occupational requirement, provided that the objective is legitimate and the requirement is proportionate.

The second of the directives allows for lawful differences of treatment on a number of the specific grounds covered by the directive, specifically on grounds of age, religion and disability. In the case of age, the member states may provide that differences of treatment on such grounds should not constitute discrimination in certain specific circumstances such as the setting of special conditions on access to employment and vocational training, employment and occupation, including dismissal and remuneration conditions. Interestingly, there is also provision for member states to allow for the fixing of a maximum age for recruitment which is based on the training requirements of the post in question or the need for a reasonable period of employment before retirement. It has also been noted earlier that member states may provide that the fixing of ages for admission to occupational social security schemes or for entitlement to retirement or invalidity benefits is lawful provided this does not result in discrimination on the grounds of sex. The directive is without prejudice to national provisions laying down retirement ages.

The second directive points out that the provision of measures to accommodate the needs of disabled people at the workplace (for example, adapting premises and equipment, patterns of working time, the distribution of tasks or the provision of training) plays an important role in combating discrimination on grounds of disability. The directive acknowledges that the measures necessary to accommodate the needs of disabled people may impose a disproportionate burden across organisations. In providing for exemptions, the directive stipulates that account should be taken, in particular, of the financial and other costs entailed, the scale and financial resources of the undertaking and the possibility of obtaining public funding or any other assistance.

Positive action

Both directives seek to ensure the lawfulness of what has become known as positive action (see the earlier discussion of the Amsterdam Treaty).

Burden of proof

These new directives also adopt the provisions regarding the burden of proof that have recently been adopted with regard to cases of sex discrimination (see above).

Implementation

In the case of the first directive, member states are required to adopt the laws, regulations and administrative provisions necessary to comply with the directive by 19 July 2003. In the case of the second of the directives the date is 2 December 2003, however, and in order to take account of particular conditions, member states may, if necessary, have an additional period of three years from 2 December 2003, that is to say, a total of six years, to implement the provisions of this directive on age and disability discrimination.

Northern Ireland

In the second of the directives and with specific reference to discrimination on the grounds of religion, the need to promote peace and reconciliation between the major communities in Northern Ireland resulted in the incorporation into this directive of particular provisions allowing differential treatment on the grounds of religion with specific reference to employment in the police force and the teaching profession but only in so far as this is expressly authorised by national legislation.

As has become increasingly common, the directives spell out the objectives to be achieved in terms of minimum rights and standards, and as such can be regarded as providing legislative frameworks within which each member state decides upon the detail to apply within its boundaries.

It has already been mentioned that the provisions with regard to age may encourage the introduction of greater employment opportunities for the more elderly sections of the population of working age and that they may facilitate the introduction of more flexible retirement policies. In the context of demographic developments and trends, such policies are attractive to governments since they provide an opportunity for achieving greater levels of tax receipts and lower public expenditure on social security payments and retirement pensions. There are potential advantages also in meeting the projected labour shortfalls related to demographic projections and they therefore hold out the prospect of assisting the generation of greater economic growth.

Similar advantages may also be derived from the extent to which the other provisions, for example, in the area of race or ethnic origin, also generate greater participation in the labour force and lower unemployment among particular racial groups. However, it must also be acknowledged that evidence from the past 20 years or more does not necessarily encourage optimism in this respect. The existence of similar UK legislation in the areas of race and sex has not prevented the continuation of inequalities in both pay and employment participation rates nor indeed has it eradicated discrimination in employment on these grounds. ACAS details for the year 1999/2000 confirm the receipt of nearly 14,000 applications regarding rights contained within the Equal Pay, Sex Discrimination and Race Relations Acts (see Chapter 8).

Proposal for a new Directive on the equal treatment of men and women as regards access to employment, vocational training and promotion, and working conditions

As noted in the introduction to this section, there are proposals for a new equal treatment directive. At its meeting in June 2001 the Council agreed unanimously an initial position that had then to be processed through the co-decision procedure.

The purpose of the draft directive is to modernise the provisions of the existing text, taking account of the case law of the ECJ, as well as of the two Article 13 directives above.

The intention is that the new directive will eventually add some important provisions to the existing directive including:

- bringing the definitions of direct and indirect discrimination into line with the definitions in the Article 13 directives above;
- recognising sexual harassment as a form of discrimination, again making it consistent with the Article 13 directives;

- reinforcing the protection of women returning to work after maternity leave, providing in particular that women are entitled to return to their job or an equivalent post upon terms and conditions which are no less favourable;
- protecting men on paternity leave so that they have the same rights as mothers on their return to work;
- and (perhaps most controversially) providing for the adoption of positive measures to promote equality between men and women, including single-sex organisations.

It is impossible to know at this stage whether the directive will be adopted in its current form, or indeed whether it will be adopted at all. However, the direction that The Commission wants to go in is clear since these were proposals from the Commission.

The organisation of working time

Directive on the Adaptation of Working Time (93/104)

This directive was adopted in November 1993, to be implemented by November 1996. The directive was adopted as a health and safety matter under Article 118A of the EC Treaty and therefore via the cooperation procedures (QMV).

At the time of introduction, the UK government was unhappy with the nature and content of the directive and managed to secure some significant changes to the original proposals as they went through the legislative process. For example, in securing exceptions for particular occupations and circumstances such as the exemption of trainee doctors, who in the UK regularly work hours considerably in excess of the limits specified in the directive. The UK also managed to ensure that the limits upon working hours could be voluntarily varied subject to the agreement of the parties, whether through individuals agreeing to work longer hours or through the parties agreeing a variation via a collective agreement. Perhaps inconsistently given their resistance, UK delegates did not vote against the directive in the Council; they merely abstained.

The UK government's unease with the directive centred upon two particular issues of more general relevance. The first of these concerns the assertion that the directive was incorrectly adopted as a health and safety issue. This challenge was ruled upon by the ECJ in November 1996 and the Court's judgment affirmed the original decision that the measure was properly introduced.

There are concerns that in forcing the issue the UK government has actually engendered a situation in which, given the relatively liberal interpretation by the ECJ, it may now be easier for the EU to adopt measures on other issues concerning employment utilising the same Treaty article.

The Court cited the World Health Organisation's definition of health (all member states are members of the WHO):

> a state of complete physical, mental and social well being that does not consist only in the absence of illness of infirmity.

From a lay viewpoint it does seem reasonable to suggest that there are health and safety risks to working long hours with insufficient rest periods and breaks, and that night work is likely to have additional health and safety implications.

Secondly, as discussed elsewhere in this chapter, the regulation of working hours, rest periods and entitlement to annual leave ran counter to the ideology of the government and to the voluntarist traditions of the UK. It is understandable that a government, convinced that the key to competitiveness lies in a deregulated and flexible labour market, should object to something it sees as both unnecessary and damaging to competitiveness and therefore to the prospects for growth. Adnett (1996: 262) pointed out that the proposal to limit maximum working hours to an average of 48 per week over a four-month reference period would affect only 3 per cent of the total hours worked in Britain. Eurostat data (1997) showed that average usual full-time hours per week worked in the UK in 1996 exceeded any other member state at 43.9 hours compared with an EU average of 40.3.

The main exceptions cover particular 'problematic' occupations – road, rail, sea or air transport workers as well as managers and trainee doctors – and industries where continuity of production or service is required such as health, the media, postal and telecommunications, emergency and public services, security services and public utilities.

Other provisions of the directive are that workers should have or should receive:

- a minimum of 11 hours' consecutive rest in 24 hours, implying a maximum working day of 13 hours (this can be averaged over a two-week period);
- a minimum of 35 hours' consecutive rest per week in principle to include Sunday (this can be averaged over a two-week period);
- a rest break after six hours' consecutive work;
- four weeks' paid annual leave (three weeks for the first three years of employment) and no payment in lieu (in other words the intention is that the leave should be taken).

The extra provisions covering night workers seek to limit the average length of a night-shift to eight hours in 24, and propose that night workers should have free and regular medical check-ups and the right to transfer to day work on medical grounds.

The main derogation provides that the parties can voluntarily by collective agreement introduce greater flexibility in implementing the directive as long as adequate and appropriate compensatory rest is given (see above).

In practice it seems that the maximum hours element of the directive becomes relevant only in circumstances where an employer is seeking to pressure employees into working in excess of the stipulated maxima against their will and there is the threat of penalty if they refuse.

The feeling in the UK at the time that the directive eventually became applicable – October 1998 – was that the greatest benefit to employees would be in the area of annual paid holiday entitlement. The UK Labour Force Survey 1996 estimated that there were as many as 2.7 million full-time workers with less than four weeks' holiday entitlement per year, with 1.8 million entitled to less than three weeks.

However, official EU data (*Employment in Europe 2000* (2001)) show that, for the UK, annual average hours worked declined by 0.8 per cent in 1998 and by 1.4 per cent in 1999, and there is obviously the possibility that the implementation of the directive into the UK had contributed to this decline. There are many other potential contributory explanations and it is impossible at this stage to say with any certainty what the nature and scale of the impact of the directive has been in the UK.

Discussions within the Union since the adoption of the directive and its eventual implementation in the UK have centred on bringing into the scope of the directive the occupations that were initially exempted or excluded. Two further directives have been adopted subsequently. One deals exclusively with the organisation of working time of seafarers (1999/63/EC), and which interestingly was the product of a sectoral agreement between unions and employers in the industry in Europe, whereas the other (2000/34/EC) is more recent and wide ranging.

This latter directive was adopted after conciliation through the co-decision procedure and relates to workers in all the activities and sectors that were previously excluded. Commission estimates were that, prior to the adoption of this directive, there were up to 5 million workers not protected by the directive.

The main issue concerned doctors in training, and special provisions were agreed regarding the timescale for the implementation of the directive to this group of workers. Member states agreed a timetable of three years for implementation into national law in respect of the other occupations and sectors, four years for doctors in training. However, it was also agreed that there be a transitional period of five years during which the working time of doctors in training would be brought down in stages to a maximum of 48 hours per week on average. Further transitional periods of up to a total of five years were to be available to member states with real difficulties linked to their responsibilities for the organisation and provision of health services and medical care. It is possible, therefore, that the limits on working hours of trainee doctors might not be brought fully into line with all other occupations and sectors until 2014 – 14 years after the adoption of the directive in 2000.

Employee participation

There is a history stretching back to the late 1960s and early 1970s of EU initiatives of various kinds designed to provide legislatively supportable rights for employees and their representative institutions to participate more in the activities and decision-making processes of their employing organisations.

Some of these initiatives have sought to encourage participation across a range of strategic and financial/business issues, and prior to the adoption of the European Works Council directive these initiatives were generally not adopted. Others have been much more targeted, for example in relation to collective redundancies and the transfer of undertakings, and were adopted, as we discuss in this section.

In the main, these initiatives have been concerned to promote participation of a representative and downward communication/consultative nature, although some of the earlier proposals that were not adopted were more ambitious and proposed to introduce schemes consistent with notions of co-management and co-decision.

Many of these participation initiatives can be seen to be rooted in an ideological position that runs counter to the voluntarist tradition of the UK and is even more at odds with the neo-*laissez-faire*, liberal individualist position adopted by governments in the UK since 1979. It is not unrealistic to view the differences between the UK and the other member states on this, as with other issues, as the product/symptoms of a clash of philosophies on how best to regulate a modern capitalist market economy and the desirability and acceptability of particular outcomes.

Commission initiatives can be seen as:

■ an expression of the desire for and belief in a community founded on consensus and harmony with undertones of equity and democracy, participation rights providing a counter to the otherwise unfettered rights of capital;
■ an expression of the belief that providing employees with the right to participate is central to achieving enhancement of the efficiency and competitiveness of the economies of the member states, a means by which competitive advantage can be obtained through the contribution and commitment of the labour force, their knowledge, skill, problem-solving capacity and innovation;
■ a contribution to the enhancement of the quality of working life;
■ a means by which the increasing autonomy and influence of multinational companies might be countered or at least mitigated. The initiatives discussed below have all to some degree been motivated by the perceived power of multinational capital to make decisions in one country that impact upon employees in another.

The motives of the Commission are based on the belief that greater employee participation has the potential to yield benefits for employees, employers, national economies and the economy and social fabric of the EU as a whole.

In the remainder of this section we concentrate upon four particular areas in which initiatives have been taken, i.e. those seeking to:

■ encourage the financial participation of employees in the success of their employing organisations;
■ ensure consultation for employees and/or their representatives in the event of the need for collective redundancies;
■ protect employees' rights and terms and conditions of employment upon the transfers of undertakings;
■ encourage a particular form of participation within Community-scale undertakings.

Financial participation of employees

The Commission has sought to encourage the development of both profit and equity sharing arrangements. In 1992 the Council adopted a non-binding Recommendation 92/443 on Equity Sharing and Financial Participation. This encourages member states to promote such schemes themselves via the creation of sympathetic legal and fiscal environments and regimes, and provides advice on the issues and criteria that those seeking to encourage and introduce such arrangements should consider. More recently the Commission has sought to relaunch the debate on encouraging such schemes with the publication in July 2001 of a staff working paper in which they identify the agenda as:

■ identifying the general principles underpinning national policies;
■ addressing the transnational barriers; these relate in essence to tax, the social and cultural environment, and (differing) social security contributions;
■ establishing a series of Community measures to improve understanding of the different financial participation systems.

In the main, the attraction of these schemes is in the belief, supported by some evidence, that there is an association between employee financial participation and increases in productivity. The Commission in its recent working paper confirm that:

worker participation in company profits is associated with higher productivity levels in every case, regardless of methods, model specification and data used. The development of financial participation schemes is strongly influenced by government action, particularly when tax incentives are made available.

Recent governments in the UK have supported these schemes and provided a favourable tax regime to encourage their take-up.

Collective redundancies

Council Directive 98/59/EC on the approximation of the laws of the member states relating to collective redundancies and consolidating the Directive on Collective Redundancies (75/129 extended by 92/56) seeks to ensure that in the event of specified numbers of redundancies within specified time periods employees and their representatives are given information and consulted in good time and with the intention of reaching an agreement. The consultation should encompass ways and means of avoiding or reducing the number of redundancies contemplated and means of mitigating the effects, for example, through redeployment or retraining.

For the purposes of this directive:

(a) 'collective redundancies' means dismissals effected by an employer for one or more reasons not related to the individual workers concerned where, according to the choice of the Member States, the number of redundancies is:

(i) either, over a period of 30 days:
  – at least 10 in establishments normally employing more than 20 and less than 100 workers,
  – at least 10% of the number of workers in establishments normally employing at least 100 but less than 300 workers,
  – at least 30 in establishments normally employing 300 workers or more,

(ii) or, over a period of 90 days, at least 20, whatever the number of workers normally employed in the establishments in question.

Workers employed on fixed term contracts or for specific projects are excluded from the requirements of the directive.

The information and consultation requirements specify a range of information that the employer should give to the workers' representatives, including:

- the reasons for the projected redundancies;
- the number of categories of workers to be made redundant;
- the number and categories of workers normally employed;
- the period over which the projected redundancies are to be effected;
- the criteria proposed for the selection of the workers to be made redundant;
- the method for calculating any redundancy payments other than those arising out of national legislation and/or practice.

The directive does not define 'workers' representatives' and this is in effect to be determined at national level within the member states and in accordance with their traditions.

The directive also seeks to include decisions that collective redundancies are necessary which are taken not by the direct employer of the workers concerned but by some other undertaking which controls the employing organisation.

By implication, the consultation should take place before the redundancies are to take effect, and the directive specifies that notification of the impending redundancies should be given in writing to the relevant public authority. The redundancies should not take effect until at least 30 days after that written notification. Issues that have arisen over the years with respect to this and earlier directives include:

■ how it is possible to ensure that the parties actually consult with a view to reaching agreement;

■ how consultation at a local level with local management can significantly affect decisions made by a controlling undertaking in another part of the world;

■ the effectiveness of sanctions that can be imposed upon organisations that do not comply with the requirements of the directive – the nature of the judicial process inevitably means that such sanctions are likely to be determined long after the event;

■ large multinational corporations (MNCs) can be very resistant to pressures from particular regimes given that they may well be able to satisfy the requirements of that particular market from sources outside the jurisdiction of the government concerned, given that the movement of capital is relatively easy and MNCs can have a relatively powerful armoury of means of exerting pressure and wielding influence.

Transfers of undertakings

Council Directive 2001/23/EC of 12 March 2001 on the approximation of the laws of the Member States relating to the safeguarding of employees' rights in the event of transfers of undertakings, businesses or parts of undertakings or businesses has replaced earlier directives in this area which were known, perhaps more meaningfully, as the Acquired Rights Directives. The purpose of the directive is primarily to protect employees' rights and terms and conditions of employment on the sale or transfer of the undertaking or business that employs them. As the introduction to the directive puts it:

> Economic trends are bringing in their wake, at both national and Community level, changes in the structure of undertakings, through transfers of undertakings, businesses or parts of undertakings or businesses to other employers as a result of legal transfers or mergers. It is necessary to provide for the protection of employees in the event of a change of employer, in particular, to ensure that their rights are safeguarded.

Over the years there have been numerous debates and court cases concerned to define undertaking. In particular, in the UK, there were debates concerning the question of whether the earlier directives applied to undertakings in the public sector, with successive UK governments arguing for many years in the 1980s and 1990s that they did not. These issues have now at least been partially resolved with and by the following definition of scope in the directive:

> **Article 1**
>
> 1. (a) This Directive shall apply to any transfer of an undertaking, business, or part of an undertaking or business to another employer as a result of a legal transfer or merger.
>   (b) Subject to subparagraph (a) and the following provisions of this Article, there is a transfer within the meaning of this Directive where there is a transfer of an economic entity which retains its identity, meaning an organised grouping of resources which

has the objective of pursuing an economic activity, whether or not that activity is central or ancillary.

(c) This Directive shall apply to public and private undertakings engaged in economic activities whether or not they are operating for gain. An administrative reorganisation of public administrative authorities, or the transfer of administrative functions between public administrative authorities, is not a transfer within the meaning of this Directive.

2. This Directive shall apply where and in so far as the undertaking, business or part of the undertaking or business to be transferred is situated within the territorial scope of the Treaty.

In this instance, unlike the directive(s) considered in the section above, employees are not excluded from the protection of the directive solely because they are working part-time, or are employed on fixed term or temporary contracts of employment. It is the intention of the directive that pension and survivor benefits are protected as are terms and conditions of employment of those currently in employment and who are affected by the transfer.

As part of the strategy for ensuring that these acquired rights are protected, the directive provides employees of both the transferor and transferee affected by the transfer and their representatives with rights to be both informed and consulted on:

- the date or proposed date of the transfer,
- the reasons for the transfer,
- the legal, economic and social implications of the transfer for the employees,
- any measures envisaged in relation to the employees.

The transferor must give such information to the representatives of his employees in good time, before the transfer is carried out.

The transferee must give such information to the representatives of his employees in good time, and in any event before his employees are directly affected by the transfer as regards their conditions of work and employment.

Again, as with the Directive on Collective Redundancies, the consultation should be both in good time before the transfer and with the intention of reaching agreement. Obligations imposed by the directive are to apply irrespective of whether the decision resulting in the transfer is taken by the employer or an undertaking controlling the employer.

Where there are no representatives of the employees affected and this is through no fault of their own, the employees themselves should be given the same information. Employers therefore are not able to circumvent the rights to information simply by virtue of there being no elected employee representatives. One of the weaknesses of the directive may, however, be that it seems that the transferee appears able to avoid consulting with employees of the transferor until after the transfer occurs.

The European Works Council Directive

The EWC Directive, adopted in 1994 for implementation by member states by September 1996, was adopted utilising the Social Agreement annexed to the Maastricht Treaty in the Social Protocol. The Social Partners were given the opportunity to reach a framework agreement but failed. Since the UK was not party to this agreement the directive was not initially applicable to the UK, however, after the election of a Labour government in 1997 the directive was extended to the UK by Directive 97/74/EC.

The directive is aimed only at transnational or Community-scale undertakings and should be viewed as a response to Commission concerns about the power of the multinational to take decisions in one member state that affect employees in others without the employees being involved in the decision-making process.

The intention of the directive is to ensure that all employees in the same Community-scale undertaking/group are both properly and equally informed and consulted about such decisions. The directive was in part a response to the increase in the number and scale of multinational activities and undertakings that accompanied and followed the creation of the single market. It also concerns the ability of MNCs to divert capital investment from one member state to another, and the absence of alternative employee representative arrangements and structures at corporate level.

Further insight into the thinking behind the directive and its perceived advantages can be derived from the statement of Anna Diamantopolou, the responsible commissioner at the time, in welcoming the April/May 2000 report of the Commission into the implementation of the Directive:

Welcoming the report, Employment Commissioner, Anna Diamantopoulou reaffirmed the need to find a new balance that gives employers and managers the flexibility they need to remain competitive while giving workers a sense of security in their work and a stake in the future of the business. In this context mechanisms for proper worker involvement can increase the flexibility of the business environment in which individual firms operate and offer workers the confidence that they will not emerge the losers in the restructuring process.

For the purposes of the directive, 'Community-scale' has two labour force size dimensions. A Community-scale undertaking is one that fulfils both of the following criteria:

- it employs at least 1,000 employees in member states covered by the directive;
- it employs at least 150 in each of two such member states.

Both criteria have to be satisfied and the calculations are to be based on the average labour force over the preceding two years. This is a directive that is consistent with the principle of subsidiarity (see earlier) since it is only at EU level that action could effectively be taken.

The directive applies to companies of any nationality. There is no requirement that the company or undertaking be domiciled in one of the member states, and, once covered by the directive, all of an undertaking's establishments within the member states should be covered by the one procedure.

While the directive contains reference to a model EWC that may in certain circumstances be imposed within an undertaking, this was perceived to be an action of last resort. The directive contains two Articles (6 and 13) which allow for the parties to voluntarily agree arrangements consistent with their own preferences and different national traditions and practices as long as certain minimum requirements are satisfied. Article 13 agreements refer to agreements made between the adoption and implementation of the directive, and Article 6 agreements are those reached voluntarily but after the implementation of the directive (see Exhibit 6.5).

Article 6 process

The responsibility for organising the process of implementation and/or compliance with the directive rests with the central management of the undertaking and may be undertaken at its own initiative or at the request of employees. Employees and their representatives can initiate the process by submitting a written request on behalf of 100 employees in each of at least two member states.

The detail of the directive provides that in such circumstances central management has the responsibility to set up a special negotiating body (SNB) of employee representatives and to convene a meeting with it to 'negotiate in a spirit of co-operation with a view to reaching an agreement' (Article 6.1). The constitution of the SNB should reflect the distribution of the labour force of the undertaking within the EU.

There is a range of possible outcomes of this negotiation process, from a refusal to negotiate, to a failure to agree, to an agreement that is satisfactory to the parties and satisfies the requirements and spirit of the directive.

If the employer refuses to negotiate within six months of an appropriate employee initiative, or in the event of the parties being unable to agree upon voluntary arrangements within three years of the original request for negotiations, the 'subsidiary requirements' included in the annexe to the directive and which specify a particular form of information and consultation arrangement may be imposed. This is sometimes referred to as the 'mandatory model'.

The mandatory model

The main points of the specified/mandatory model of an EWC are:

1 the EWC must have between 3 and 30 members;
2 the EWC should comprise employees of the undertaking or group elected or appointed by them and in accordance with the national legislation or practice;
3 the competence of the EWC should be limited to information and consultation on matters concerning the undertaking or group as a whole or at least establishments or undertakings in two different member states;
4 the composition of the EWC should include at least one member from each member state in which the undertaking or group has an establishment, with the remaining membership determined on proportionate grounds;
5 such an EWC is to be reviewed after four years and the parties may choose to allow it to continue or negotiate an alternative;
6 the EWC has the right to an annual meeting with central management to be informed and consulted on the basis of a written report provided by management and concerned with 'the progress of the business of the Community Scale undertaking or ... group of undertakings and its prospects'.

The subject matter of the meeting is then detailed:

- the structure of the business;
- the economic and financial situation;
- the probable development of the business and of production and sales;
- the situation and probable trend of employment;
- investments and substantial changes concerning the organisation;
- introduction of new working methods or production processes;
- transfers of production;
- mergers, cutbacks or closures of undertakings, establishments or important parts thereof;
- collective redundancies.

Impact of EWC Directive

Nakano (1999) reported that by early 1999 some 540 EWCs had been established, most of them through the Article 13 procedure with only about 100 having been negotiated through the Article 6 procedure. This total represented approximately one-third of all the undertakings that the European Trade Union Institute had estimated exceeded the employment thresholds of the directive, this total being 1,678 companies. Analysed by country of ownership, the four countries with the largest number of companies affected by the directive were: Germany with 395; the US, 298; the UK, 218; and France, 161. Similar figures are given by the Commission in a report of April/May 2000 on the implementation of the directive in which it says: 'With at least 600 agreements over the last five years, it is clearly a success.' The report commends the Social Partners for making so many voluntary agreements and for making the directive

> an essential part of the restructuring process in European companies and of European industry's response to the challenge of globalisation. For the first time in Europe's social and commercial history, we have genuine cross-border information and consultation. What in 1994 looked groundbreaking is becoming increasingly routine inside multinationals. The existing agreements already cover about one-third of all undertakings and about 60 per cent of employees falling under the scope of the Directive.

The Commission therefore perceived the directive to have been a success; an alternative view might hold that some two-thirds of the companies covered by the directive had not agreed the creation of an EWC some six years after its adoption as evidence of relative failure. The number of EWCs established is one criterion for success, yet there are many others that could be applied, for example whether employees through their representatives actually do receive more information and do play a more influential role in decision-making within the undertaking, and whether the EWCs do contribute to greater flexibility and competitiveness.

The Social Partners have raised a number of concerns about the likely impact of the directive. Notably, although trade unions and their officials have generally welcomed the directive they fear they may be marginalised in its implementation – which may embrace predominantly *organisation-based* representation (including non-unionists). Secondly, there has been concern that EWC employee representatives might become isolated both from their own national constituencies and from the wider labour movement, and that they might lack the expertise to understand and meaningfully discuss and challenge the information provided to them. To some extent, whether these fears become well-founded will be dependent upon the interdependence between the EWCs and the unions, for example whether the trade unions at European or sectoral level can effectively support the EWCs with information, expertise and training. Certainly if the EWCs are to be effective and if the influence of the trade unions is to be maintained, the unions will have to demonstrate a degree of transnational cooperation and coherence that has been lacking in the past.

A more optimistic perception of consequences sees the EWC as a catalyst for the development of much greater transnational cooperation and understanding and the development of much more effective networks within the European labour movement. There have also been those who see the EWC as the precursor to the much wider development of European-level collective bargaining within multinational corporations and eventually at sectoral level. Management concerns tend to be related to matters of cost, delay in decision-making, loss of control and fear that confidential information would become part of the public domain thereby damaging the competitive interests of the undertaking. There were also structural concerns that the requirement to consult at the European level was inconsistent with the trend towards decentralisation of operational structures and decision-making. To some extent the position adopted by management is likely to have been coloured by tradition and the regulatory regime of the country of origin. The body of research evidence that is accumulating is as yet insufficient to be able to draw any conclusions as to whether the hopes and fears of the various actors and commentators have been realised. Hyman (2000) reviews much of this evidence and notes that there are examples of management not taking the EWCs seriously, employee representatives not enhancing transnational cooperation but using the information and consultation obtained through participation in the EWC to fight national battles for investment and jobs within the organisation. Alternatively there are more optimistic scenarios in which, despite initial scepticism and lack of trust between employee representatives, this changed over time, and the various employee representatives began to cooperate effectively to their mutual advantage. Hyman concludes that three points seem to deserve emphasis:

- There is enormous diversity of experience rather than a standard model and there is evidence of some national influences and some sector-specific on the form of EWCs.
- As the institutions are evolving, there is learning to be derived for all parties. Some seem to be evolving and becoming more effective in their operation whereas others are not. More research needs to be undertaken to determine why there is such a varied pattern of development.
- An EWC that develops internal cohesion and strategic vision can make an impact; again there is a need for much more research into explanations.

As to whether the EWC is contributing to the development of European-wide collective bargaining within undertakings, there would appear to be very little evidence to support this contention. There will inevitably be instances where, within the EWC, a form of ad hoc bargaining may occur on particular issues, but systematic developments in this direction seem unlikely in the short to medium term.

Proposals for a Directive on Information and Consultation of employees within the National Context

The Commission had initially aimed for adoption of this provision by the end of 2001. However, there have been a number of problems concerning whether any such directive is consistent with the principle of subsidiarity and how prescriptive the directive can be, given the different traditions and practices in member states. It seems likely that the directive will take the form of a framework specifying minimum employee thresholds, levels at which consultation might take place (the company, establishment etc.), and a minimum number of areas of subject matter for employee consultation. In the UK, of course, any such directive will be novel since legal requirements to inform and consult within companies within the national context have been limited to health and safety, collective redundancies and transfers of undertakings. It would seem likely that the directive, if adopted, will require information and consultation on a range of subjects not necessarily any narrower than that required by the EWC.

The Europeanisation of social protection and employee relations

There has been much debate as to whether the social dimension of the EU might lead to a convergence of systems of social protection and employee relations within the EU. To some extent the evidence presented in the preceding sections indicates a gradual extension of the social dimension. This incorporates both the creation of minimum individual rights for employees which are homogeneous across the Union and an emphasis upon the information and consultation of employees and their representatives on a widening range of subject matter in a widening range of organisational contexts. The treaties have also been amended to facilitate the EU taking initiatives on a widening range of social and employment issues. Set against these pressures that are arguably convergent in their direction are others that may be perceived to mitigate these effects. For example, most of the recent initiatives have left many details for resolution at national level and in accordance with national traditions and practices. At the same time there are important areas in which the Union still has no competence or where initiatives would require unanimity such as trade union rights, the right to take strike action, wage regulation and the protection of employees in circumstances of contract termination. In effect, then, there is only limited convergence. Convergence can, of course, be either 'upward' or 'downward' in terms of harmonising employment conditions across Europe. While EU policy seeks to ensure a set of minimum standards, the interests of multinational capital would seem to perpetuate downward pressure through a need to compete by forcing down costs, including labour costs and the costs of social protection. Member state governments with high unemployment can also be tempted by the attractions of deregulation and lower employment costs.

Enlargement of the Union technically should not lead to a weakening of the existing levels of social protection, since the aspirant members have to accept the existing 'acquis communautaire'. However, in reality, there are grave concerns that MNCs will use the lower living standards and labour costs prevailing in the aspirant member countries to export jobs to these countries and to force down labour and social protection costs in the existing member states. It is concerns of this kind which have prompted the Austrian and German governments to ask for restrictions upon inward labour mobility from those countries in eastern Europe on their borders for a period of time after their accession into membership. They are concerned that jobs will be exported and that labour will flood into their countries, thereby exerting downward pressures upon wages and levels of social protection.

There is, then, evidence of an embryonic and very partial EU model of minimum employment rights and procedures relating to employee participation, but with many of the details left to the member states to determine in accordance with national traditions and practices. At the same time there is considerable pressure for a weakening of regulation and social protection in order to facilitate company competitiveness and employment. Both may result in greater convergence within the EU but such convergence is likely to be in opposite directions.

Chapter summary

The EU is an expanding and dynamic organisation of nation states progressing gradually towards different forms of union. So far the emphasis has been upon economic and monetary integration, the creation of single markets in capital, goods and services, and labour, and the creation of a single currency. The social dimension of the EU is relatively underdeveloped in comparison.

The institutions of the EU and the member states are increasingly seeking to take decisions incepting processes that provide the opportunity for majority as opposed to unanimous decisions and involve the Social Partners in the process. Agreements at Amsterdam also seem likely to give greater weight to the views and influence of the European Parliament through the co-decision procedure.

The major achievement of the Amsterdam Treaty revisions may well prove to be the extension of the treaty base for the adoption of policies and other initiatives in the social field.

Until recently the influence of the EU in the social and employment field had been relatively limited, with nation states successfully seeking to preserve their particular traditions and their autonomy. Pan-European regulation has, however, applied in the areas of equality between the sexes, health and safety at work, rights to information and consultation on particular issues, and some freedom of movement of labour. These have been augmented with initiatives geared towards enhancing the rights of workers on atypical contracts, restricting working time, the EWC Directive, a regulation concerning the creation of 'European companies' and the extension of information and consultation requirements to the national context.

Progress towards the Europeanisation of collective bargaining at the level of the multinational corporation would appear to have been limited, although bargaining at the level of the EU through the Social Agreement procedures has yielded a number of framework agreements. The Council has given legal effect to these, and there is some evidence of increased bargaining activity at the sectoral level.

There are clearly interests within the EU that seek further convergence of the social (including employee relations) systems within it. There would appear to have been some procedural progress but enforcement remains a problem. Those efforts that there have been to regulate substantive outcomes (for example, equal pay) have arguably had little impact.

There are clearly a number of different views on both the desirability and prospects of further convergence and upon the direction that it might take. However, there are clear signs that the traditional social protection model that has been a defining characteristic of European systems is under threat.

In conclusion, we may in future witness growing tensions between the central institutions – seeking to maintain the traditional social protection model and emphasising the convergence of procedural systems and the minimum rights of employees and citizens of the EU – and the various member states and constituent companies. The latter may be prone to resist such developments and to assert the need for a more flexible and competitive model in which they are able to dispense with many of these procedural constraints and the rights of employees.

Questions

1   Examine the nature of the social dialogue and the role of the Social Partners. To what extent is it correct to argue that the trade unions can now make the law?

2   Why is it that there are remaining inequalities of pay between men and women and how would you remedy the situation?

3   Consider and discuss the arguments for and against a social dimension to the single market.

4   Explain why the attitudes of the Social Partners in the UK are pro-EU.

5   Discuss how the EWC Directive may provide the opportunity for an extension of collective bargaining at a multinational level.

6   How do you see the Social Chapter agreed at Amsterdam affecting the rights of employees and employers and the balance of power between them?

7   Explain why some member states are concerned about the impact that enlargement of the Union may have upon employment and labour standards in existing member states.

8   Examine and discuss whether the Charter of Fundamental Rights of the European Union proclaimed at the Nice summit in December 2000 seems likely to extend and deepen the social dimension of the Union.

Activity

Examine the two articles in Exhibit 6.6 and briefly identify and discuss how they illustrate different approaches in the two countries to:

(a) the perceived need to regulate the labour market;
(b) the role of the Social Partners;
(c) job creation and the reduction of unemployment;
(d) the balance between work and family life;
(e) approaches to achieving labour flexibility.

Exhibit 6.6

Now there's a four-hour time difference when you cross the Channel

While all eyes are on the 'Will they, won't they?' euro debate, there is another economic change taking place across the Channel that is sending shock waves through the Treasury.

From January 1 last year, all companies in France with more than 20 employees, were obliged to reduce the working week from 38 to 35 hours for all their staff, with the exception of the very top executives;

Exhibit 6.6 *continued*

from January 1 next year, the law will also apply to companies with fewer than 20 employees.

The reduction in working hours was not accompanied by any reduction in salary, and businesses were compensated for any extra costs – such as taking on extra staff – through tax and social security breaks from central government.

The 35-hour week, introduced by the Jospin government, is a method of creating jobs. In 1997, France had one of the highest rates of unemployment in the EU, with 13.8% of the labour force out of work; this year France his one of the highest growth rates in Europe – currently reaching 4% per annum. The CAC-40, its equivalent of the blue-chip FTSE 100, is up 0.5% since the beginning of the year and unemployment has fallen to 8.7%.

'It is the fastest decrease in Europe', said a spokesperson for the French Ministry of Labour. 'The 35-hour week has been a local success; even employers' groups which raised concerns before its introduction have been won over.'

Whether all the job gains can be attributed solely to the 35-hour week is something of a moot point, but the government is too busy basking in the glory to bother with such minor problems.

The French government's triumphalism is all the more understandable given the criticism it had received about the 35-hour week from Britain and other western economies prior to its introduction. 'The received Anglo-Saxon wisdom is that flexible, lightly regulated markets are superior at creating full employment', says Charlove Thorne, senior researcher in futures at the Industrial Society.

'The UK has always resisted attempts to reduce working hours for fear of damaging productivity and competitiveness, so a model that challenges this orthodoxy is extremely threatening.

Loosely speaking, the UK works on the principle of encouraging people back into work by making it so unpleasant to be out of work. The French have taken the opposite approach of tempting people into work by making work a more enjoyable experience.'

To be strictly accurate, the 35-hour week should properly be described as a 1,600-hour year. This means that employees can work more hours during certain periods – say, the pre-Christmas rush – but less at others, and the net effect has been to introduce a hitherto unseen flexibility into the French economy.

Where once the whole of France ground to a standstill in August while people look their holidays *en masse*, now some manufacturing industries are turning over all year round.

Negotiation has been the key to the successful implementation of the 1,600-hour year, 'Social partner dialogue is a hallowed institution in France', says Ms Thorne.

'Every dot and every comma has to be negotiated by management and union. It may be time-consuming and burdensome, but it has allowed every firm to reach its own agreement acceptable to both management and employees.'

Satisfactory agreements have been harder to reach in the public sector, where issues such as productivity are harder to quantify, but by and large most businesses have adapted with little fuss. Marks & Spencer moved over to the 35-hour week in its 18 French stores a year ahead of schedule in 1999, and says that the new working hours had no bearing on its subsequent decision to close its European operation. 'We had to renegotiate some of the terms of employment with our 1,000 staff', says a spokesperson.

'Some paid breaks became unpaid, and we only had to take on 22 full-time equivalent staff to maintain our stores at the same levels.'

One of the effects of the 35-hour week has been that many of the old restrictive working practices have been phased out, and there have been suspicions that employers have used the new regulations to their advantage. 'I think employers have, in some cases, taken the opportunity to load too many tasks on individuals', said Beglasv Versaeud, head of the insurance services sector of the CFDT trades union federation.

Medef, the French equivalent to the CBI, was implacably opposed to the 35-hour week when it was first proposed, but has been rather more muted in its antipathy ever since. Some employers still feel the new regulations limit their flexibility, but overall across both management and workers there

▶

Exhibit 6.6 *continued*

is a growing sense that the 35-hour week may be that rarest of government initiatives: a win–win scenario. Businesses have been able to reorganise their processes to suit their needs and have been compensated for having to take on extra staff, and employees are delighted to have more time off.

Indeed, there is anecdotal evidence that the changes are having a knock-on effect. DIY shops and the leisure industry report higher rates of activity as the French make use of their time off.

Whether everything will be looking quite so rosy next January when the regulations kick in for smaller firms is less certain as generally speaking, they are likely to have less room to manoeuvre. Small firms tend to have lower inefficiencies within their systems, so the 35-hour week is likely to translate more directly into either less productivity or an increased payroll.

The French Ministry of Labour does not appear concerned, though. 'More than 10,000 small businesses have already converted to the 35-hour week', says a spokesperson: 'A lot of smaller enterprises already employ a large number of part-time workers, so these people can work more hours if they want', he adds.

Some economists have voiced concerns that the de facto rise in the minimum wage brought on by the reduction in hours will work against the unemployed and the vulnerable – the very sector the legislation was designed to help.

But the biggest worry is whether the 35-hour week is predicated on bad economics. At present, the tax incentives to employers to compensate for taking on more staff have been funded both by the creation of new indirect social taxes on petrol, cigarettes and alcohol, and through savings on the social security budget. 'When someone comes off benefits and goes back into work', says a government spokesman, 'he or she also starts giving money back to the government through taxes and insurance contributions. We are merely passing on our savings to the employers.'

Source: The Guardian, 11 August 2001.

UK still a nation of workaholics

One in six employees works more than 48 hours a week, according to a report published today which shows that Britain's long-hours culture is becoming more entrenched.

The number of workers putting in more than 48 hours a week stands at almost 4m, an increase of 350,000 since 1992, according to the TUC report, *About Time.*

The rise comes despite the introduction of the European Union's working time directive, which has been law in Britain since 1998. It sets an average 48-hour weekly limit. Britain is the only member state to have a clause allowing individual workers to agree to work longer hours.

'Britain's long-hours culture is a national disgrace', said TUC general secretary John Monks. 'It leads to stress, ill health and family strains.'

Most of those working beyond the 48-hour ceiling are men, according to the study, one in four of them working extra hours. One in 10 men, almost 125m, works more than 55 hours a week, and one in 25 puts in more than 60 hours.

The research also highlights a class divide, with more than half of all managerial and professional employees reporting working extra hours to deal with excessive workloads, while about 70% of skilled and manual workers earn overtime pay.

Mr Monks pointed to the higher productivity rates of other European states, and urged British firms to organise their work more efficiently so that staff could 'work smart' and be more productive in less time.

The TUC says that the EU is likely next year to withdraw Britain's right to maintain a voluntary opt-out from the directive, increasing pressure on employers to cut hours.

Patricia Hewitt, the trade and industry secretary, will promise tomorrow at a conference on the issue that excessive working hours will be cut within five years.

Source: The Guardian, 4 February 2002.

EU directives and other instruments

Code of Practice on the Implementation of Equal Pay for Work of Equal Value for Women and Men (COM (96) 336)

Communication from the Commission of the European Parliament and Council on the Interpretation of the Judgement of the Court of Justice in Kalanje (COM (96) 88)

Community Charter of the Fundamental Social Rights of Workers (The Social Charter) 1989

Council Directive 97/80/EC of 15 December 1997 on the burden of proof in cases of discrimination based on sex

Council Directive 97/81/EC concerning the Framework Agreement on Part-time Work concluded by UNICE, CEEP and the ETUC

Council Directive 98/59/EC on the approximation of the laws of the member states relating to collective redundancies and consolidating the Directive on Collective Redundancies (75/129 extended by 92/56)

Council Directive 1999/70/EC concerning the Framework Agreement on fixed-term work concluded by ETUC, UNICE and CEEP

Council Directive 1999/63/EC concerning the agreement on the organisation of working time of seafarers concluded by the European Community Shipowners Association (ECSA) and the Federation of Transport Workers Unions in the European Union (FST)

Council Directive 2000/34/EC of the European Parliament and the Council of 22 June 2000 amending Council Directive 93/104/EC concerning certain aspects of the organisation of working time to cover sectors and activities excluded from that directive

Council Directive 2000/43/EC of 29 June 2000 implementing the principle of equal treatment between persons irrespective of racial or ethnic origin

Council Directive 2000/78/EC of 27 November 2000 establishing a general framework for equal treatment in employment and occupation on the grounds of religion or belief, disability, age or sexual orientation

Council Directive 2001/23/EC of 12 March 2001 on the approximation of the laws of the member states relating to the safeguarding of employees' rights in the event of transfers of undertakings, businesses or parts of undertakings or businesses

Council Directive 2001/86/EC supplementing the Statute for a European Company with regard to the involvement of employees

Council Recommendation 92/443 on Equity Sharing and Financial Participation. PEPPER I.

Council Recommendation on Childcare (92/241)

Council Resolution on Balanced Participation of Men and Women in Decision-making (95/C168/02)

Directive on the Adaptation of Working Time (93/104)

Directive on Collective Redundancies (75/129 extended by 92/56)

Directive on Equal Treatment: Occupational Social Security (86/378)

Directive on Equal Treatment: Self-employed (86/613)

Directive on Equal Treatment: State Social Security (79/7)

Directive on the Establishment of a European Works Council or a Procedure in Community Scale Undertakings and Community Scale Groups of Undertakings for the Purposes of Informing and Consulting Employees (94/45)

Directive on Parental Leave (96/34). Introduced pursuant to an agreement between the Social Partners in accordance with Article 2.2 of the Social Policy Agreement

Directive on the Protection of Pregnant Workers: The Tenth Daughter Directive (92/85)

Directive on the Transfer of Undertakings (77/187)

Draft Directive on Equal Treatment in Occupational Social Security Schemes (COM (95) 186)

Equal Pay Directive (75/117)

Equal Treatment Directive (76/207)

Green (Consultative) Paper, *Partnership for a New Organisation of Work* (COM (97) 128)
PEPPER II: *Promotion of Participation by Employed Persons in Profits and Enterprise Results (Including Equity Participation) in Member States* (COM (96) 697)
Proposal for a new directive on the equal treatment of men and women as regards access to employment, vocational training and promotion, and working conditions
Proposals for a directive on information and consultation of employees within the national context

Table of cases

Kalanke *v* Freie Hansestadt Bremen, C-450/93 (1995)
Murphy and others *v* An Bord Telecom Eirann (1988)
Vroege *v* NCIV voor Volkhuisvesting BV, C-57/93 (1994)
Fischel *v* Voorhuis Hengelo BV, C-128/93 (1984)
Marshall *v* Southampton and South West Hampshire Area Health Authority, Case 152/84 (1986)

Useful websites

www.etuc.org/en **European Trade Union Confederation** One of the social partners of the European Union, the website provides information on the organisation and its activities, press releases and resolutions.

www.eurofound.ie **European Foundation for the Improvement of Living and Working Conditions** The site provides easy access to a substantial range of research findings undertaken or commissioned by the Foundation.

www.europa.eu.int **European Union On-Line** The website contains news, information about the institutions, an overview, official documents including legislation and the treaties, and it is easy to navigate through it.

www.statistics.gov.uk **National Statistics** This site is the official statistics site for the UK. A wealth of information on the economy with an index that is reasonably navigable.

www.unice.org/unice/Website.nsf/HTML+Pages/UK_index_UK.htm **UNICE** The other main social partner representing employers and business interests. The site provides information about the organisation and its position on a range of EU and other issues.

References

Adnett, N. (1996) *European Labour Markets: Analysis and Policy*. London: Longman.
Due, J., Madsen, J.S. and Jensen, C.S. (1991) 'The social dimension: convergence or diversification of industrial relations in the single European market', *Industrial Relations Journal*, 22(2): 85–102.
European Commission (1994) *White Paper on Social Policy: The Way Forward for the Unions*. Brussels: European Commission.
European Commission (2001) *Annual Report for the year 2000 on Equal Opportunities between Women and Men in the European Union*. Brussels: European Commission.
Gold, M. (1993) 'Overview of the social dimension' in Gold, M. (ed.) *The Social Dimension: Employment Policy in the European Community*. Basingstoke: Macmillan.
Hall, M. (1994) 'Industrial relations and the social dimension' in Hyman, R. and Ferner, A. (eds) *New Frontiers in European Industrial Relations*. Oxford: Blackwell.

Hyman, R. (2000) Editorial, *European Journal of Industrial Relations*, 6(1): 5–7.

Nakano, S. (1999) 'Management views of European works councils: a preliminary survey of Japanese multinationals', *European Journal of Industrial Relations*, 5(3): 307–26.

Teague, P. (1989) *The European Community: The Social Dimension*. London: Kogan Page.

Turner, L. (1996) 'The Europeanisation of labour: structure before action', *European Journal of Industrial Relations*, 2(3): 325–44.

Visser, J. and Ebbinghaus, B. (1992) 'Making the most of diversity? European integration and transnational organisation of labour' in Greenwood, J. Grote, J.R. and Ronit, K. (eds) *Organised Interests and the European Community*. London: Sage: 206–37.

Further reading

Leat, M. (1998) *Human Resource Issues of the European Union*. London: Financial Times/Pitman Publishing.

Chapter 7

Multinationals and employee relations

Mike Leat

Learning objectives

By the end of this chapter, readers should be able to:

- understand the development of modern multinational corporations (MNCs) and the scale of their activity;

- distinguish and compare different models of the MNC;

- discuss the main criticisms of MNCs;

- explain the employee relations difficulties and implications that MNCs may have to deal with as a result of operating in different countries and cultures;

- understand the impact that MNCs may have on national systems;

- analyse the ability of trade unions at national and international level to respond to MNCs;

- understand the need for and role of international organisations in checking the power of MNCs and the difficulties of enforcement;

- discuss the arguments surrounding the insertion of minimum labour standards into free trade agreements;

- understand and discuss the factors influencing the diffusion of employment relations policies and practices in MNCs.

Introduction

This chapter falls into two main parts, the first of which is concerned primarily with establishing the scale of international trade and the significance of the multinational corporation (MNC), some of the characteristics and stages of development of the modern MNC, including the reasons why companies become MNCs, and some of the more influential models or typologies. We also in this first part identify national culture as an important contextual influence and identify some of the more common benefits claimed for, and criticisms made of, MNCs.

In the second part of the chapter the relationship between the MNC and employee relations is examined further. A number of main themes are addressed including:

- the relevance of national contextual differences upon the activities and organisation of MNCs' employee relations policies and practices;
- the impact that MNCs from economically successful countries can have upon employee relations within national systems and indeed internationally, and in this context the phenomenon of 'Japanisation' is discussed;
- the attitudes of MNCs towards trade unions, and the trade union response;
- the role played by some of the supranational regulatory organisations in seeking to influence the employee relations policies and practices of MNCs and the arguments surrounding the issue of minimum labour standards;
- the question of whether and how MNCs diffuse employment relations policies and practices internally across national borders.

The article included in Exhibit 7.1 illustrates a number of the points made in the early part of the chapter concerning the internationalisation of business in the context of a global liberalisation of trade and a massive increase in recent years in the number of companies becoming and operating as MNCs. The article also raises a number of questions which are relevant to issues discussed in the second part of the chapter.

Dyson's decision to relocate manufacture of its bagless vacuum cleaners to Malaysia is presented as a development that was more or less inevitable at some stage, and as an example of a process already prevalent in other industries. The reasons presented for the decision include: the considerably lower labour and other costs in Malaysia (a figure of 30 per cent is referred to); the success of a previous decision to transfer some production there; the quality of the output from that successful experiment; the recognition of the importance of nearness to suppliers; and the need to be globally competitive (and, in particular, to meet demand from the US). Labour costs in Malaysia are £1.50 per hour compared with £4.10 per hour in the UK plant, and while labour market regulation in the UK may be relatively limited, the regulatory regime in Malaysia is considerably less onerous. These represent some of the common reasons for becoming an MNC and investing in manufacturing capacity in the developing world. The reactions to the announcement from government and trade unions illustrate their powerlessness as well as the priority they attach to a national agenda. Dyson refers to consultations with the workforce in the UK but the impression is given that vital decisions have been made already.

The article provides an example of the international division of labour that accompanies the development of global markets. It illustrates how manufacturing and other relatively 'low-tech' functions are exported to developing countries, while high-tech research and development activity is retained, at least for the time being, in the West.

What is a multinational company?

Many terms are used to refer to MNCs including global, transnational and international. Some observers have sought to assign specific meanings to each of these and to distinguish between them. Some of these definitions and distinctions are considered later. In this chapter the term 'multinational' is used generically.

At this stage it is necessary to try to define the MNC, or at least to distinguish it from other organisations that trade internationally, but which do not fall into this category. The simplest of definitions is:

Exhibit 7.1

James Dyson, millionaire inventor and longstanding champion of British manufacturing, faced a barrage of condemnation from the government and unions yesterday after he announced that he plans to shift production of his revolutionary vacuum cleaners to the Far East with the loss of 800 jobs.

The 54-year-old design engineer, who battled sceptical banks and venture capitalists for 15 years to bring his invention to market and subsequently secured a patent infringement ruling against Hoover, has decided that the costs of continuing to produce in Britain have become too great to bear.

The decision, broken to the company's workforce at factory meetings yesterday morning, comes as a serious blow to the north Wiltshire town of Malmesbury where Dyson made its base six years ago and where 8,000 'bagless' vacuum cleaners are produced each day.

The move – which follows a succession of job losses from Britain to lower cost countries in sectors including textiles and motor components – is all the more surprising because of Mr Dyson's frequently expressed support for Britain's fast-eroding manufacturing base.

In an interview with the *Guardian* three years ago the colourful entrepreneur said Britain should be making itself 'a powerful manufacturing nation making wonderful products'. Ironically, given yesterday's announcement, he said that if his company had any sense it would move its production to Taiwan or China but he was holding out against such a move.

Changing circumstances have persuaded the inventor of the dual cyclone bagless cleaner and Contrarotator washing machine to change his mind.

The sudden announcement brought accusations of betrayal from union leaders and caught ministers badly on the hop during a debate at London's Westminster Hall on the loss of jobs in British manufacturing. The trade and industry minister Brian Wilson said it would have been 'useful' for government to have had an opportunity in advance of the announcement to work with the company to see what could be done.

'I would certainly welcome that contact now that the announcement has been made', he said. 'I do believe that there must be room for discussion and I do hope that there are more factors to the calculations of Dyson than the pretty obvious statement of fact that labour is cheaper in Malaysia than it is in Malmesbury.'

Roger Lyons, general secretary of Amicus, Britain's biggest private sector union, accused Dyson of betraying the 800 people whose jobs were being 'shipped' to Malaysia. He called on the Bank of England to cut interest rates again to help beleaguered exporters and safeguard jobs. Peter Booth, national organiser for manufacturing industry at the Transport and General Workers Union, said the Dyson move was 'scandalous'.

The company, which employs 1,800 people at its Wiltshire base, said it had decided on the production switch because of the success of a lower cost manufacturing plant it established in Malaysia two years ago. Impressed by the quality of the cylinder vacuum cleaners being produced in Malaysia it wanted to expand Far Eastern production to supply its existing international markets and meet demand from the US.

'We have tried very very hard to make manufacturing work', Mr Dyson said yesterday. 'It has been very successful, but as we look at the future and the enormous sums we need to plough into the business in order to produce new products and be competitive and continue to grow, we believe this is the way we have to go.'

He said the fact that Britain remained outside the euro was only 'a relatively small factor' in the decision. The driving force was the much lower labour and production costs in the Far East and the fact that the company's suppliers were increasingly based in the region.

Dyson believes the move will enable it to cut production costs by around 30% and plans to plough the resulting savings back into research and development in Britain in a drive to continue to develop new technology products. The company, which chalked up sales of more than £220m in 2000, spends around 10% of turnover on new product development.

Mr Dyson, who yesterday described R and D as the 'heart and soul' of the business, said the decision to cut back the Malmesbury workforce had been a sad and difficult one: 'If it goes ahead, this will be a blow to all those who have put in so much effort.' He dismissed suggestions that the conditional tone of that statement indicated that the company was leaving the door open for a rethink.

'We will be consulting with our workforce over the next few weeks. We don't want to present them with a *fait accompli*, but I have to say that the end decision is fairly inevitable.'

Source: The Guardian, 6 February 2002.

> MNCs are enterprises that in more than one country own or control production or service facilities and activities that add value.

It is the dimension of ownership and control of value-adding activity that sets the MNC apart from the organisation that simply trades internationally or which enters into strategic and international alliances or partnerships which do not involve these elements of ownership and control.

The distinction between organisations that trade internationally and those that fall within the definition of a MNC is demonstrated by Wilkins (1970), who suggests that it is possible to identify four typical stages in the development of American MNCs:

- The US concern sold items abroad through independent agents or, on occasion, filled orders directly from abroad.
- The company appointed a salaried export manager and/or acquired an existing export agency and its contacts. This stage might also involve the appointment of independent agencies in foreign countries to represent the company. The foreign agent would sell on its own account or handle shipments on consignment.
- The company either installed salaried representatives, a sales branch or a distribution subsidiary abroad, or purchased a formerly independent agent located in a foreign country. At this point, for the first time, the company made a foreign investment; *it is only at this point that the company becomes an MNC.*
- A finishing, assembly or manufacturing plant might be built abroad to fill the needs of a foreign market.

This element of ownership or control tends to bring with it the challenge of managing human resources and employee relations in different national contexts and poses for the organisation's management problems associated with international human resource management. International human resource management is commonly defined in terms of the management of human resources *within* MNCs.

In its *World Investment Report 2000*, the United Nations Conference on Trade and Development (UNCTAD) suggests that, of the top 100 MNCs by foreign asset value, 15 employ more than 100,000 people in their foreign operations, the largest number at approximately 260,000 being employed by McDonald's, the fast-food chain (UNCTAD, 2001).

Multinationals and the internationalisation of business

Recent decades have witnessed a significant internationalisation of business and an explosion in the number of companies operating as MNCs. UNCTAD (2001) estimates for the year 2000 suggest more than 63,000 MNCs worldwide, and this compares with 37,000 in its report for 1994. Economies are becoming more financially interdependent, and, as Hodgetts and Luthans (1994) asserted, this interdependence is not unidirectional, from developed to underdeveloped. Industrialised economies are investing in those that are developing, but the developing economies are also investing in those that are already more advanced.

There are a number of different dimensions and components to this internationalisation of business:

- a significant expansion of international trade;
- the liberalisation of trade across national borders through the removal of tariff barriers, the extension of free trade agreements, e.g. the EU and the North Atlantic Free Trade Agreement (NAFTA);
- development of more global product markets and enhanced pressures of international competition;
- the cross-national integration of production within MNCs;
- an expansion in the number and influence of MNCs through joint ventures, cross-national acquisitions and mergers or foreign direct investment (FDI);
- an international division of labour.

This globalisation or internationalisation of business has been greatly enabled by the development and use of new technologies, particularly in the arena of information transfer and communications. Also the increase in the size and extent of free trade agreements incorporating the free movement of capital inevitably facilitates cross-border investment of all kinds.

The term 'globalisation' has become increasingly used to describe both this process of internationalisation and its outcomes. There are numerous definitions of this term and their range is illustrated by those of Ohmae (1990), Walters (1995) and Needle (2000).

Ohmae defines globalisation in terms of the emergence of a borderless world or interlinked economy in which globalised production chains, product markets, corporate structures and financial flows would to all intents and purposes make the nation state and national boundaries irrelevant.

Walters (1995) has a different emphasis:

> A social process in which the constraints of geography on social and cultural arrangements recede and in which people become increasingly aware they are receding.

whereas Needle (2000) proposes:

> Globalisation is a process in which the world appears to be converging economically, politically and culturally.

Undoubtedly, MNCs play an active and influential, some would say dominant, role in driving this process of globalisation and internationalisation.

Ietto-Gillies (1997) suggested that 80 per cent of world trade and all FDI is attributable to MNCs. FDI can take a number of forms, the most significant being the total or partial acquisition of operations in other countries, which may themselves already be operating as MNCs, or the establishment of a completely new operation in another country, commonly known as a greenfield investment, such as that referred to in Exhibit 7.1.

The scale of foreign direct investment

In its *World Investment Report 2001*, UNCTAD reports that global flows of FDI soared by 18 per cent in 2000 to a record $1.3 trillion. The main impetus for this increase is reported to be from cross-border mergers and acquisitions, and UNCTAD notes that there were some 63,000 transnational corporations with 800,000 foreign affiliates, and it is the activities of these transnationals that drive the majority of FDI.

UNCTAD defines a transnational as:

> 'Transnational corporations' comprise parent enterprises and their foreign affiliates: a parent enterprise is defined as one that controls assets of another entity or entities in a country or countries other than its home country, usually by owning a capital stake. An equity capital stake of at least 10% is normally considered as a threshold for the control of assets in this context.

While UNCTAD uses the term 'transnational' as a generic, the essence of the definition, i.e. *control of assets*, varies little from the definition of MNC being used as the generic in this chapter.

As in previous years, in 2000 the ten largest FDI recipients, as well as the ten largest sources of FDI, were developed countries, with one or two exceptions from the developing world (China and Hong Kong). With just over $1 trillion in inflows and a 21 per cent increase in 2000, developed countries remain the prime destination of FDI, accounting for more than three-quarters of global totals. Although flows to developing countries were also up in 2000, to $240 billion, these countries' share of global inflows has fallen over three consecutive years to 19 per cent, the lowest since 1991. Developing countries increased their share of outward flows, from 3 per cent in the early 1980s to 9 per cent in 2000.

The UK and France were the top two FDI source countries, with the US in third place, the total investments being $250 billion, $172 billion and $139 billion, respectively. The top recipient countries were the US, followed by Germany and the UK, and the totals were $281 billion, $176 billion and $130 billion, respectively. Germany was the top recipient country in the EU, owing in large part to VodafoneAirTouch's takeover of Mannesmann – the largest cross-border merger deal in history – and as can be deduced from these figures, the US and Germany were net recipients while the UK and France were net outward investors. From the particular perspective of the EU it must be remembered that significant proportions of these inward and outward totals for EU member states are in respect of intra-EU investments.

UNCTAD also reports that 91 of the world's top 100 non-financial transnational corporations (TNCs), as measured by foreign assets, are headquartered in the US, Japan and the EU. The list was topped by General Electric (US) for the fourth year running, with ExxonMobil Corporation (US) leaping from fifth to second place, Royal Dutch/Shell Group (Netherlands/UK) was in third place, while General Motors (US) had moved from second place down to fourth, and the Ford Motor Company was in fifth place. Others in the top ten were TotalFina SA (France), Toyota Motor Corporation (Japan), DaimlerChrysler AG (Germany), IBM (US) and BP (UK). As is evident from this list, the top ten is dominated are two industrial sectors: motor vehicles and petroleum.

The UK

In a more detailed examination of the UK position in terms of FDI inflows and outflows the Office for National Statistics in its report on foreign direct investment 2000 (Office for National Statistics, 2001) reports that in the year 2000 direct investment abroad by UK companies increased to £167.8 billion, the highest ever recorded figure and an increase of £43.3 billion (35 per cent) on the amount invested in 1999. It reports that the increase in the total for 2000 almost entirely reflected increased flows to Europe: £128.4 billion compared with £38.8 billion in 1999. Flows to all other regions except Australasia decreased during the year.

At the end of 2000 the book value level or stock of direct investment abroad by UK companies stood at £604.6 billion, an increase of £179.9 billion on the level recorded at the end of 1999. The reason that the increase in stock is more than the recorded investment flow reflects the fact that the level estimate takes account of revaluations and movements in exchange rates as well as actual flows of investment.

In 2000, foreign companies invested a record £77.0 billion in UK subsidiary and associate companies, an increase of £22.6 billion from 1999. Investment from Europe increased from £39.4 billion in 1999 to £54.0 billion in 2000 (£51.8 billion from within the EU). Investment from the Americas fell from £17.2 billion in 1999 to £16.3 billion in 2000. France was the largest investor in the UK in 2000 with a total of £31.8 billion, which represented 41 per cent of the total.

At the end of 2000, the stock at book value of direct investment in the UK stood at £291.8 billion, less than 50 per cent of the value of investment abroad. This compared with a figure of £238.3 billion at the end of 1999, an increase of 22 per cent. The US accounted for 34 per cent of the total stock, France 17 per cent and the Netherlands 14 per cent.

In August 1998, Dunn and Bradstreet produced evidence that over 23,300 companies in the UK were at least partially owned by non-UK interests. Approximately one-third of them were offshoots of US organisations, while from within the EU, Dutch, German and French organisations have substantial ownership involvment.

Reasons for investing abroad and locational determinants

Ghertman and Allen (1984) do not cover the full range of forms of overseas investment (for example, the acquisition of a share in an existing company), but they suggest the following reasons why companies decide to establish their own manufacturing or extraction units in foreign countries:

■ In certain industries there are production limits in any one factory. These may be due to the perishability of the product or, for example, its weight and the transportation costs involved. Examples would be in industries such as the production of milk derivatives or liquid gas. It is not advisable to build huge factories in these industries, since the economies of scale in production are not sufficient to offset higher transport or wastage costs. It is far better to set up new factories in the countries where the customers are based. In contrast, in other industries like chemicals or steelmaking, it is possible to make such economies of scale that a large production unit in a single country is justified on the grounds of profitability.

■ Local governments often prefer to have the MNCs invest in their countries rather than export to them. There are benefits in terms of local employment and an outflow of foreign currency can be avoided, resulting in a better trade balance for the host country.

■ Within MNCs, local managements obviously prefer the parent company to set up a manufacturing plant in the host country because this makes the subsidiary more important within the group and at the same time facilitates relations with the host country.

■ Production in only one country leaves the company open to risks of war, nationalisation or confiscation, or vulnerable to increases in duties or the establishment of import quotas or fluctuations in rates of exchange. Similarly, strikes in a single factory could halt sales to several countries at the same time.

Barrell and Pain (1997) take a somewhat different approach and have suggested that cross-border production activity takes place for a number of reasons:

■ Market size.

■ Cost differentials: relatively low production costs (incorporating the impact of real exchange rates) are an incentive.

■ The role played by knowledge-based firm-specific assets. This term refers to assets such as managerial or marketing skills or reputation (including such factors as brand images) and process or product innovations that are firm-specific and may be patented. Barrell and Pain suggest that such assets give economies of scale at the level of the firm rather than at the level of the plant and this may enable single-firm multi-plant operations (some overseas) to show a cost advantage over the alternative of two single-plant firms. They also suggest that innovating companies, in possession of patents, are more likely to invest overseas themselves than to license others in foreign markets to provide the product or service.

■ To improve market access and bypass trade barriers such as those that surround the EU. There are potentially great advantages to the organisation if it sets up a production or service facility within such a free trade area since it gives access to the whole of the new market and avoids the tariffs and other barriers that confront products and services from outside.

In the specific EU context, Barrell and Pain (1997) argue that the fact that the UK is a net outward investor within Europe and elsewhere casts doubt upon the supposed attractiveness of low labour costs and deregulated labour markets. They suggest that once an organisation has decided to invest within the EU in order to obtain the benefits referred to above, then the decisions regarding the precise location of the investment within the EU are influenced by national or regional variables such as:

■ corporate tax burdens;

■ the skills and training, the quality of the labour force;

■ the quality of the infrastructure;

■ language and cultural factors;

■ the cost of labour: the more high-tech the operation, the less do labour costs play a significant part in the investment and location decision.

Individual national regimes and infrastructure are therefore relevant at this stage. Traxler and Woitech (2000) conducted an analysis of the impact of national labour market regimes in western Europe on the investment decisions of US MNCs in the period 1981 to 1992. Their underlying hypothesis was that, given that there are significant differences between these national labour markets in terms both of material labour standards and the extent to which regimes constrain employer prerogative or control, one might expect the MNC to adopt an opportunistic approach and 'regime shop', resulting in investment in those regimes that were beneficial in terms of lower material standards and the least amount of restriction upon managerial prerogative. Their analysis, however, does not support this hypothesis and they conclude that investors neither attributed high priority to labour market regimes in their location or investment decisions, nor did they pursue coherent strategies regarding these regimes. Nevertheless, while other factors such as those mentioned above play an important role in guiding investment decisions, Traxler and Woitech (2000) also comment that internationalisation and the threat of regime shopping can put pressure on regimes' labour standards and upon governments to deregulate in order to compete for investment.

Types of MNC and their approaches to multinational activity

We mentioned earlier that there are a number of different definitions and interpretations of what constitutes an MNC and that different terms are sometimes used. We adopted the term 'MNC' as the generic and a relatively simple definition, but it is important to be aware of at least two of the prominent typologies of forms of MNC and their approaches to the conduct of multinational activity and the attendant responsibilities. These are the models of Perlmutter (1969) and Bartlett and Ghoshal (1989).

■ Perlmutter's typology

Perlmutter (1969) classified a variety of attitudes towards management of increasingly globalised companies, or, in his words, the 'tortuous evolution of the multi-national corporation'. He describes four major approaches to the management of overseas subsidiaries.

Ethnocentric

The values, culture and strategic decisions are determined by the outlook of the parent company, which gives very little power or autonomy to the overseas subsidiaries. Subsidiaries are managed and controlled largely by expatriates or former headquarters staff, and locals have very little input into the way things are carried out in their own country. Lines of communication are often one-way as directives are issued by HQ. The host country subsidiary has a tactical rather than strategic role to play and is dominated by the concerns and culture of the parent company. It is often suggested that this commonly represents the first stage in the development of the MNC and that only after time has elapsed will management at the centre be prepared to move in an alternative direction. Many Japanese and American companies have been accused over the years of trying to introduce employee relations policies and practices that may work at home but that are inconsistent with the traditions of the UK. This approach is sometimes characterised as a belief at the centre of the organisation that the ways of the home country are not only the best but also the only way of proceeding.

Polycentric

Each overseas subsidiary is regarded as an autonomous business unit, controlled and managed by local managers. Key decisions, financial investment and overall strategic goals are still the preserve of HQ and, generally speaking, at this stage, the principal HQ positions are still held by people from the parent company. It is assumed that local managers are most likely to have an understanding of marketing, production and HRM strategies and, indeed, of the requirements of the local regulatory regime. Subsidiaries are therefore allowed a larger measure of autonomy, although there is likely to be strong financial control by the parent company. This approach is much more likely to facilitate the maintenance of policies and practices in the field of employee relations that are consistent with the culture and regulatory regime of the host country. This is discussed further in the following sections.

Regiocentric

Control of both staff and decisions are carried out on a regional or geographical basis, but top positions are still held by nationals of the parent company's country. Regional managers, however, have greater discretionary powers and autonomy, but are constrained by the boundaries of the region in which they operate.

Geocentric

These companies can be described as having the best of all worlds and deploying a mix of both home country and parent company managers in overseas subsidiaries. The exchange of ideas, values, information and working methods is seen as an important activity.

In the last two instances the approach to employee relations is likely to be less conditioned by a particular national culture or regulatory regime, either of the home country or of the host country. National regulatory regimes still have to be complied with where plants and other activities are located, but in such companies one would also expect the development of regional or worldwide approaches, policies and practices.

There have been suggestions that the Perlmutter typology – and, indeed, the following Bartlett and Ghoshal model – can be perceived as stages in the development and maturation of the MNC. However, it is a mistake to take too rigid an approach to the interpretation of these models. As Hendry (1994) says:

> a normally regiocentric or geocentric organisation may adopt an ethnocentric approach on occasion if, for example, it establishes itself in a new country that, for the moment, does not have appropriate skills. More generally, regional units may take on an ethnocentric stance within their own territory.

Edwards et al. (1996) make a similar point in reporting that the stereotypes depicted in the model may be useful as indicators of different approaches and tendencies but should not be regarded as exclusive. In their research they found that MNCs exhibited various of these characteristics simultaneously.

Bartlett and Ghoshal's typology

Bartlett and Ghoshal (1989) categorised MNCs into four main types, each type being determined by how far it had developed over time.

Multinational

Multinationals tend to build a strong local presence in each of the countries in which they invest, and therefore tend towards being decentralised, with local autonomy and little strategic direction from HQ. Spivey and Thomas (1990) described them as decentralised federations in which overseas operations are regarded as a portfolio of largely independent, nationally oriented businesses. They have sometimes been characterised as 'multidomestics'.

Global

Global companies have a more centralised and global approach to markets, and in such firms the HQ would adopt a strong role in determining policy for each of the subsidiaries. Levitt (1983) described conditions wherein markets were crossing boundaries and becoming more like one another as different nationalities developed similar consumer tastes, which contributes to the global perception of markets. As Hendry (1994) argues, these firms require a high degree of integration and need to be managed from a corporate centre.

Porter (1985) described the way in which such global companies could extract economies of scale and scope from worldwide activities and exploit national factor differences. Ford of Europe is said to have typified this kind of operation.

International

This form of MNC has a more federal structure: the centre coordinates rather than imposes or instructs. The suggestion is that as markets become more sophisticated and diffuse, companies depart from the notion that competitive market advantage can be derived by having standardised products and thereby achieving significant economies of scale. These are firms that need to have a high degree of flexibility. Hendry (1994) quotes the different kinds of washing powder (often claimed to be a uniform product) sold in different countries on account of a variance of views held as how best to wash clothes. Different nationalities have different preferences for temperatures and speeds. The variance in pharmaceutical preferences is another example of the trend away from standardisation.

Firms gain competitive advantage not by producing more goods at a cheaper rate, but by being able to apply their knowledge and skills gained worldwide to local circumstances. Such firms can quite easily move resources such as cash into different markets. Hendry (1994) describes their actions as mobilising people, resources of skill and knowledge, on an international scale.

Transnational

This type of company is, in a sense, a response to the difficulties that the previous three forms have in dealing with the increasing complexities of global markets. The stereotypical transnational exhibits more flexible structures than the traditional hierarchy, responsibility is devolved to lower levels and to national teams, knowledge is shared and coordination is achieved through the sharing of values, cooperation and teamwork. These are organisations able to respond to the forces of globalisation, local differentiation and worldwide innovation in technologies and products. Innovation, together with the ability to harness it, is perceived as the primary source of competitive advantage, and innovation is spread throughout the company.

To Bartlett and Ghoshal (1989) this means:

> developing simultaneously the characteristics associated with the MNC, the global firm and the international company – that is, responsiveness to local conditions, efficiency and the ability to handle continuous innovation and learning. Competitive advantage will come from sensing needs in one market, responding with capabilities perhaps developed in a second and diffusing any resulting innovations to markets and facilities around the globe.

They further accept that the transnational company exists more in conceptual form than in actuality and suggest that the transnational represents a new management mentality. Flexibility is a key to managing such forms, and Bartlett and Ghoshal observe that managers seemed to understand very clearly the nature of the strategic challenge but that they had greater difficulty developing and managing the organisational capability to implement the new and more complex global strategies.

Asea Brown Boveri, the electrical engineering firm, is claimed to be one of the very few examples of a transnational company. As Edwards *et al.* (1996) state, the characteristics supposedly include horizontal networking through ad hoc task groups, which then transfer knowledge among the decentralised operating units, each of which enjoys considerable financial autonomy.

The difficulties of finding companies that conform with the transnational stereotype encouraged Edwards *et al.* to distinguish more simply between nationally (includes the Bartlett and Ghoshal multinational) and globally oriented approaches. The research upon which they report, which covered 101 MNCs, 58 UK-owned, led them to conclude that, while there is evidence of globalism, such evidence tends to be more in respect of some aspects of the firm's organisation and activity than others, and that examples of organisations in which globalism dominates are rare. The aspects of the firms where globalism was most common included: the global movement of managers, handing profits over to global headquarters, computerised communications and giving board members global responsibility for a particular function.

One of the implications of this is that we should not be surprised to find firms that operate in a broadly geocentric and transnational manner with respect to some aspects of their activity but nevertheless operate in a polycentric manner when it comes to dealing with employee relations, thereby demonstrating their flexibility and responsiveness to local circumstance, tradition and culture.

MNCs and national cultures

Culture in this context refers to the pattern of values and beliefs that inform attitudes and behaviour and which tend to distinguish one group from another. Hofstede (1991,1994) and Trompenaars (1993) are two researchers who have attempted to distinguish cultures at the national level. Their research has led them to suggest that differences can be detected at this level and that these differences can have significant implications for the following:

- people's attitudes towards work and their employing organisation;
- people's expectations of work and the rewards that they seek;
- whether they regard themselves primarily as individuals or as members of a group;
- their attitudes towards distinct gender roles;
- how they expect to be treated at work;
- their attitudes towards uncertainty and risk;
- their perceptions of appropriate behaviour;
- policies and practices with which they feel comfortable or not;
- what might constitute appropriate managerial styles, organisational forms and structures.

If, as is suggested, these characteristics vary from one country to another, there are significant implications for the management of human resources within MNCs. Moreover, if these resources are to be managed effectively and efficiently there would appear to be a *prima facie* case for the adoption of a polycentric approach: it is this approach that facilitates the adoption of culture-specific policies and practices in particular countries. The ethnocentric approach tends towards ignoring cultural difference, and the regiocentric and geocentric approaches apply at a level above the nation state. The management of human resources within MNCs with such culturally diverse labour forces is often suggested to be the major challenge facing international HRM and it is the perception of national culture as a contingency that lies at the root of the development of the contingency matrix approach to international HRM (see, for example, Luthans *et al.*, 2001).

Many MNCs have been criticised over the years for operating in an ethnocentric manner whereby they seek to impose parent company and country practices in countries in which they may be alien. Ethnocentric organisations tend to take little, if any, notice of local cultures in matters of staffing or employee relations and it may well be that the organisation lays claim to an organisational culture that is reflective of the home country and universal throughout the company. Hewlett-Packard has been an example of such an approach; the 'HP Way' was promulgated throughout the company worldwide but was itself reflective of the culture of southern California and the attitudes and beliefs of the two founders of the company. This concept of culture and the evidence that cultures differ across national boundaries is integral to debates – sometimes referred to as the culture-free versus culture-specific debate – about the feasibility and desireability of seeking to transfer work practices across national boundaries, as for example with Japanisation which is visited in a later section of this chapter.

It is also worth referring back at this point to some of the definitions of globalisation which see it as a process that, among other things, is leading to a convergence of cultures across the world. By implication, if this were to happen then choices between ethnocentric and polycenrtric approaches would not be necessary and the task of international HRM would to some extent become easier with organisations being able realistically to apply the same policies and practices wherever the subsidiaries were located. One of the difficulties which the pursuit of polycentric policies and practices poses for the international HRM manager is the achievement of internal consistency and this would be facilitated in such circumstances.

Where there really are undifferentiated global markets being served by a transnational organisation, and if cultures also do converge, it becomes more realistic to perceive the company operating with a geocentric perspective, developing within a geocentric culture that is not an imitation of any particular national culture, and the attitude towards staffing and employee relations matters is such that country of origin and location have no significance.

The multinational company: a force for good?

In his book *The Real Power Game* (1979), Jack Peel argued:

> Is the multinational an instrument of economic imperialism or a beneficial carrier of advanced management, science and technology? . . . They reflect man's technological ingenuity, the ruthlessness of the board room power game, the inability of national governments to cope adequately with international business problems and the need to relate the profit motive more closely to social responsibility. But to denounce multinationals in general, is as unrealistic as to present them as benign institutions working for the public good. The truth is probably between the two positions. They bring considerable benefits to society but create a plethora of problems. They are a pertinent example of the gap between man's technological brilliance and society's ramshackle social machinery. In a nutshell, multinationals have been trapped by the speed of their own advance. They have far outdistanced their running mates, governments and trade unions, who have to work in a more ponderous, participative – some would say devious – way.

This extract refers to and implies many of the issues surrounding the formulation of an answer to the question posed by the title to this section. Peel suggests that there are different viewpoints and answers and that an honest appraisal is likely to result in a mixed response.

Generally, MNCs are attractive to those countries in which they invest for a number of reasons. It is usually anticipated that the investment will:

- create jobs and thereby improve the working conditions, living standards and prospects of the host country inhabitants;
- assist with the necessary process of industrialisation in developing countries;
- assist the host country's development through the process of technology and knowledge transfer;
- generate tax revenues and foreign exchange receipts for the host country government.

The attitude and approach of the multinational are important here, in that if it adopts an ethnocentric approach, the impact upon employee relations may be greater than if the approach is polycentric. While it seems obvious that the impact of such investment upon employment levels is likely to be beneficial, it is important to be careful in assessing this impact.

The impact of multinational investment upon net employment depends upon the combined effect of three factors:

- Direct job creation. This depends upon both the size and the capital–labour mix in the production process. Highly capital-intensive investment will have relatively poor returns in terms of direct job creation.
- Indirect job creation. This depends upon links with local suppliers and the extent to which the company imports components and other factors of production.
- The Trojan horse or displacement effect of the investment. If the investment merely means that other local producers are forced out of the market then the overall effect upon employment may not be what it first seemed.

FDI that takes the form of a merger with or acquisition of a going concern may have no beneficial impact upon employment at all and, indeed, it may in the long term lead to employment decline as activities and structures are rationalised and reorganised on a European or transnational basis. UNCTAD (2001) estimated that cross-border amalgamations and mergers accounted for the majority of FDI and that the majority of FDI was between and into developed countries.

Within multinational trade alliances and markets, such as the EU, an additional potential complication to these calculations is that investment in one country may have beneficial net effects upon employment there at the expense of employment in one of the other member states. Within the EU there have been instances of this occurring, and the concept referred to as 'social dumping' encapsulates these concerns. One of the major concerns associated with the creation of the single market and the implementation of the principle of freedom of movement of capital and labour was that capital was much more mobile than labour and that consequently capital would be relocated within the market to those areas, regions and countries where the costs of production were lowest. This would result in jobs being created in one area, such as Spain or Portugal where labour and other production costs are relatively low, at the expense of employment levels in places such as Germany and France. The UK, with a government that was keen to create flexible and deregulated labour markets and which saw lower labour costs and enhanced employer prerogative or control as a source of competitive advantage, was seen as a potential beneficiary.

We noted earlier the conclusions of Traxler and Woitech that labour standards and regulatory regimes had not been the prime influences upon US investment into Europe during the 1980s and early 1990s but the authors also noted the potential for MNCs to use the threat of regime shopping to encourage competition between regimes for and in order to keep such investment, particularly when it is job-creating investment.

It has also been noted in Chapter 6 that the prospective enlargement of the EU to the east and south is creating similar fears among the member states at these borders who fear that there will be a displacement of investment into the aspirant member states from those already in membership and that they are seeking restrictions upon inward labour mobility despite the evidence that labour mobility within the EU is low and that there are significant barriers to such mobility.

MNCs have been accused of all sorts of 'crimes', and it is alleged that rather than benefiting the development of the recipient country they actually harm it by:

- causing massive environmental damage through their extraction and exploitation of raw materials and their cynical attitudes towards the land and agriculture;
- distorting and destroying traditional cultures;
- cynically exploiting labour.

The following allegations have also been made:

- While MNCs claim to be investing capital and technology in Third World countries, many extract a large outflow of capital and never relinquish control of their technology.
- They are able to create artificially low profits in high tax countries and high profits in low tax countries by transfer pricing. These techniques can also be used in negotiations with trade unions, whereby a plant may be shown to be 'unprofitable' by the use of creative accounting and a harder bargain may be driven.
- Their great global size enables them to interfere in the political affairs of small host countries.
- Having been attracted to regions or countries offering financial inducements such as investment grants, tax concessions, training grants and cheap labour, it is not unknown for the MNC to uproot and depart when these inducements are no longer available. This phenomenon is known as the runaway firm, and if that firm is the main employer in the region, the whole community suffers when the company withdraws.
- In times of high unemployment national governments are particularly prone to seek to attract MNCs to invest, and this gives the MNC considerable bargaining power to persuade both governments and employees and their representatives to make concessions.
- By dint of widespread and glamorous advertising and promotion, their products often swamp locally produced goods and put local manufacturers out of business.

Allegations concerning the exploitation of labour in the host or undeveloped countries have increased in recent years and there have been a number of exposés of global firms such as Nike, Gap and Adidas. Allegations have been made that the contractors used by these organisations to manufacture their products pay very low wages and that trade unionism is forcefully deterred. It is also alleged that suppliers employ child labour, that employees are subject to harassment and bullying, are compelled to work very long hours and are not allowed breaks, and that the health and safety concerns of the workers are not being addressed. The term 'sweatshop' is often used to describe these operations. An alternative view sometimes expressed is that jobs on these terms are better than no job at all and that while conditions and wage rates may seem poor to us in the West, they are complying with the labour standards and regulations in the countries concerned. It is this kind of behaviour on the part of MNCs and their contractors that encourages the argument that the activities of MNCs should be regulated and that free trade agreements should contain minimum labour standards, much like the social dimension of the EU. We return to this later.

MNCs and national employee relations systems

Whether an MNC is in the very first stages of setting up an overseas subsidiary or (using Bartlett and Ghoshal's model) is at the global stage of internationalisation, one of the problems that it has to confront is managing operations and staff in different cultures and in different national employment relations systems. There is an inevitable relationship between these two. As Schregle (1981) observed:

> A comparative study of industrial relations shows that industrial relations phenomena are a very faithful expression of the society in which they operate, of its characteristic features and of the power relationships between different interest groups. Industrial relations cannot be understood without an understanding of the way in which rules are established and implemented and decisions are made in the society concerned.

This is not the place for a comparative analysis of employee relations systems. There are several texts that do this: for example, Hollinshead and Leat (1995) discuss the systems in a range of different countries and also compare them on a number of important themes, including trade unions, employers, the role of government and the various processes for the resolution of conflict. Nevertheless, it is important to remember that each employment relations system arises from a different history, legal system and socio-political/cultural context.

Dowling and Schuler (1990) emphasise that because employment relations are so diverse across national borders, it is imperative that MNCs employ a polycentric approach when appointing employment relations managers, while Prahalad and Doz (1987) assert that 'the lack of familiarity of MNC managers with local industrial and political conditions has sometimes needlessly worsened conflict that a local firm would have been likely to resolve'.

It is common for MNCs to have to deal with issues arising from national differences. These can pose company-wide problems of consistency of treatment between subsidiaries – for example, on working hours or rates of pay. While internal organisation and arrangements vary considerably from one MNC to another, it is feasible that even in the multidomestic form of MNC, where local autonomy may be high, control/advice from the centre may be prompted by:

- the perceived need to achieve a degree of internal consistency;
- the need to ensure that there is consistency between policies being pursued at a corporate level and those pursued locally.

An example of the latter may be an overseas subsidiary that signs an agreement with a trade union about job security for its members which may then prove an embarrassment to the corporate HQ, which is planning a downsizing or cost-cutting exercise.

The significance of local traditions, customs and knowledge of the national employment relations system, and perhaps in particular the regulatory regime of employment law, has often encouraged MNCs to employ local knowledge and give the role of managing employee relations to a host country national. Japanese MNCs have shown themselves to be adept in this respect, adapting their approach so as to conform with national legislation and tradition but at the same time maintaining the essentials of what might be referred to as the Japanese model of lean production (see next section).

However, there is another dimension to the interaction between MNCs and national systems of employee relations. In a simplistic sense, one can see the foregoing comments and, indeed, much of the discussion in the previous sections as concerned with the impact of national systems upon the MNC and the extent to which the MNC does or does not adapt its approach, policies and practices to these national differences.

The second dimension to this relationship concerns the impact that MNCs themselves might have upon and within national systems. Undoubtedly one of the major employee relations phenomena of the past two decades has been the influence within Europe and the US of Japanese-inspired systems, attitudes and values relating to the design and nature of work and the attitudes and behaviour expected of employees. To some extent this influence can be traced to the activities of Japanese MNCs investing heavily in Europe and the US in the late 1980s and 1990s.

It is easy to overemphasise the scale of this influence and the coherence with which changes have been implemented, but 'Japanisation' cannot be ignored. It would be unrealistic to ascribe the whole of this influence to the presence and example of Japanese MNCs; the demonstrable success of the Japanese economy and the persuasive influence of international organisations such as the International Monetary Fund (IMF) and the Organisation for Economic Cooperation and Development (OECD), academics and management consultants were also influential in encouraging employers in the West to believe that the Japanese had the secret to international competitiveness and profitability.

While the intention here is to concentrate upon Japanisation as the dominant example of the ability of MNCs to influence the nature of a national system, it is not the only example. American and European MNCs can also be seen to have had an impact.

As Edwards et al. (1999) point out, MNCs from economically successful countries have an incentive to export the practices that are considered instrumental to that success to their subsidiaries in other countries, and this will have a wider impact as other organisations perceive these practices as means through which they too can achieve success. Consequently, as Edwards et al. (1999) assert: 'American MNCs were key diffusers of Taylorism . . . Japanese MNCs have been active in diffusing lean production and associated practices designed to secure worker commitment'.

Japanisation: quality, involvement and commitment as competitive advantage

The perceived essence of the Japanese method, the recipe for global success, is an emphasis upon labour, service and product quality, which is to be achieved through a continuous search for improvement that pervades all aspects of the organisation's activity and recognises their interdependence, a system of apparent consensual decision-making and an emphasis upon employee involvement in and commitment to the company.

Organisations within the UK have tried to follow this lead and imitate the success of Japanese organisations with mechanisms such as quality circles and other forms of problem-solving groups and teamworking. The emphasis upon quality has been additionally pursued through various other mechanisms including total quality management (TQM) processes and kaizan or continuous improvement. Just-in-time (JIT) or lean production policies and systems have also been adopted by some organisations and their emphasis upon minimising waste also imposes a concern with quality. All of these have implications for the nature of work and the employment relationship, terms and conditions of employment and the traditions and practice of employee relations.

Some analysts (for example, Eaton, 2000) have suggested that the significance of these Japanese approaches and, in particular, their concern to minimise waste, search for continuous improvement and emphasise quality and flexibility in machine and labour usage, has resulted in a new paradigm or mode of production. This is referred to as 'lean production' and associated in particular with Toyota, which has replaced Fordism as the dominant mode of production in the developed world. In the remainder of this section, attention is given to the nature of the more common of these 'methods and techniques' and to the different views that exist, some positive and some negative, as to their impact upon employees and employee relations.

The quality circle

This – probably the most famous technique associated with Japanisation – became popular in the UK and some other parts of Europe in the 1970s and 1980s. The popularity of this concept in Europe was linked to the perceived need for European manufacturers to compete on the grounds of zero defects. Quality circles are intended to contribute to the process of reducing defects and the need for repair, as well as providing a vehicle through which employees become more valued by, and involved within, the organisation.

Quality circles comprise small numbers of employees (6–10) meeting voluntarily on a regular basis to identify, examine and resolve quality or other operational problems concerned with their own work and immediate environment. Their remit may primarily be to deal with quality problems but they are commonly also expected to devise ways of reducing costs and means for improving the design of work. Groups rarely have the authority to implement their own recommendations and as the problems are resolved there is a danger that there may be a loss of momentum. Experience has also tended to reinforce the view that quality circles need to be both guided and led, and it is quite common for the participants to need training and some access to resources. It is important that management is seen to take note and implement at least some of the recommendations of such groups; the effective continuation of problem-solving groups, whether quality circles or others, tends to depend upon evidence that their work is valued.

The success of quality circles has been the subject of debate over the years. The groups were introduced into hundreds of companies in the UK and some success was claimed in terms of quality improvements, increased job satisfaction and employee involvement.

Much of the criticism of the adoption and application of the concept in Europe has focused upon ambiguity about the true purpose of such schemes, with the view being expressed by some (Batstone and Gourley, 1986: 117–29) that the true purpose of these experiments was not so much to secure improvements in quality and employee involvement as to provide a means by which management was able to circumvent the traditional collective and unionised mechanisms of industrial relations and develop a more individual relationship with employees.

Total quality management

The TQM approach encompasses a number of the techniques typically associated with Japanese organisations. The essence of the approach is a comprehensive and continuous search for improvement – the production of goods and services with zero defects – which involves most employees and knows few boundaries in terms of organisational activity. In many respects it is an approach that seeks to generate a culture of quality throughout the organisation.

The drivers for this attention to TQM are internal and external customers. Internally, customers are the employees involved in the next stage of the process. This may be the next individual or team in the assembly process, or the next person to receive a report or the recipient of advice from a service function internal to the organisation.

The focal point for improvements in quality should be the employees doing the job. A fear of failure should be replaced with a search for failure. If people are blamed for failure, they are unlikely to take risks and unlikely to search for faults and put them right – they are more likely to try to hide them (Marchington and Wilkinson, 1996: 353–4).

The customer-driven nature of such initiatives and programmes and the implications for employees are illustrated in the guiding principles governing a programme initiated within Ford in the UK and quoted by Storey (1992: 57):

- Quality comes first.
- Customers are the focus of everything we do.
- Continuous improvement is essential to our success.
- Employee involvement is our way of life.
- Dealers and suppliers are our partners.
- Integrity is never compromised.

Just-in-time and lean production

The essence of the JIT approach and associated systems is to eliminate waste. At all stages of the production of a good or the provision of a service consideration should be given to minimising the time between a resource being needed and its acquisition and between the production of a good and its purchase or consumption. Thus, systems should be designed which result in the final product being produced just before it is required in the market-place, sub-assemblies being delivered just before final assembly, and bought components being acquired just before they are needed. This enables the company to respond more quickly to market demand and it confirms demand as the driver of the production process.

Carried to its logical conclusion, labour would also be acquired just prior to need, implying a degree of flexibility in labour supply and usage that maybe inconsistent with regulatory frameworks designed to promote security of employment and employment protection (see Chapter 6). Nevertheless, this concept of JIT does give credence and impetus to the models of labour flexibility identified in the 1980s, which distinguish between core and peripheral labour and which have encouraged outsourcing and sub-contracting, part-time working and other forms of atypical contract.

These organisational and technical systems give purchasers considerable power. For example, large companies such as BMW, Ford and British Telecom, which are likely to be the major customer of any supplier of components, can exert great pressure upon the supplier to deliver on time a product of the desired quality.

From an employee relations perspective, these systems can be perceived as placing an emphasis upon trust and responsibility because the relationship between management and employees is one of high dependency. Systems operate without stocks at both ends of the process, and employees are made to be responsible for quality, continuous improvement and the rectification of problems at source. Both TQM and JIT have implied comprehensive change within UK organisations. The emphasis of the former is upon cultural change whereas the latter is more directly concerned with organisational and technical systems.

Incidence and impact of TQM and JIT

There are different sets of views and conclusions about the extent and impact of these comprehensive and culture-changing approaches to the challenge of competitiveness in the global market, which can be seen to be at least partly a product of the influence of Japanese MNCs in Europe.

Legge (1995) summarises the conclusions of many researchers into the impact of these change programmes as evidence of:

- much enthusiasm among managers;
- variable success in implementation;
- the suspicion that in all but a few companies the magnitude of the cultural change and the time over which the enthusiasm and commitment need to be maintained combine to mitigate effective implementation.

There is the suspicion that the notorious short-termism of British business is not suited to these kinds of change programme. As Legge describes it, a lack of stamina is associated with endemic short-termism. An alternative critical view is presented by Parker and Slaughter (1988), who coined the term 'management by stress' to describe the consequences for labour of these initiatives. Teamworking and an emphasis upon zero defects are perceived as mechanisms through which both a culture of blame is introduced rather than eradicated, as the theory proclaims is essential (see earlier), and there is more effective control of the labour resource through peer surveillance.

Nevertheless, the attention that has been paid to this phenomenon of Japanisation and to the notions of quality and flexibility that are integral to it, is in itself reflective of the potential for MNCs to have an impact upon national systems. Indeed, for many working in organisations, the late 1980s and 1990s were characterised by a massively increased emphasis upon quality, even where those responsible seemed unclear as to what quality looks like, and where the drive for quality appeared to apply to everything except the nature of the employment relationship, working life and employee relations.

MNCs and trade unions

The growth, size and spread of MNCs has, for some time, disconcerted unions and their organisation. Not only have MNCs displayed an apparent preference for avoiding union recognition, but also, even where an MNC does recognise a trade union for collective bargaining purposes, there is a variety of strategies which may be adopted in order to counter its influence. One of the disadvantages confronting the trade unions is that the unions tend to be organised nationally. We discuss in subsequent sections the weakness of trade union organisation at an international level.

As Kennedy (1980) and others have pointed out, the MNC may:

- have formidable financial resources, which may enable them to absorb losses in a particular foreign subsidiary that is in dispute with a national union and still show a profit on overall worldwide operations;
- have alternative sources of supply, and this may take the form of an explicit 'dual sourcing' policy to reduce the vulnerability of the corporation to a strike by a national union;
- be able temporarily to move production to facilities in other countries, and there is also the permanent threat of closure of facilities in a particular country or region – what has come to be known as the exit option;
- be able to hide from the unions by having a remote corporate HQ so that it is actually physically difficult for the trade union to find and deal with the real decision-makers in the company;

- have the capacity to stage an 'investment strike' whereby the MNC refuses to invest any additional funds in a plant, thus ensuring that the plant will become obsolete and economically uncompetitive, which can be used as a threat to achieve compliance;
- be able to exert considerable pressures upon governments to regulate or deregulate in their favour especially when there are jobs to be lost or gained as a result of the MNC decision;
- use one or more of the above to persuade the union into competitive or concession bargaining whereby material labour standards or labour flexibilities in terms of working practices are conceded in return for promises of job security, possibly in competition with employees in a subsidiary in another country.

The ability of the MNC to use these strategies depends in part upon the structure of the organisation and the extent to which production is integrated. For example, if the structure is that of a multidomestic it might be relatively easy to source demand in the national market concerned from another country. If, however, the union represents employees who are the sole producers of a particular component in what is a European or global production chain then the power of the union is that much greater, and the ability of the MNC to counter the threat proportionately reduced. MNCs are influential in that they may export work from developed to developing economies. Sometimes they may transfer work from one of their own plants in the developed world to another with much lower costs in a developing economy where trade unionism is little established. Alternatively, they may contract out work previously undertaken in the developed world to contractors in developing countries. Examples would include a Japanese MNC shifting the production of low-tech, high volume television sets from one of its plants in the UK to a newly acquired plant in eastern Europe. A US MNC fashion clothes retailer may decide to contract the manufacture and assembly of its garments to companies in Cambodia and Indonesia rather than to contractors in the UK or US.

MNC attitudes towards trade unionism

Dowling and Schuler (1990) asserted that an MNC's initial attitude and ideology is an important factor in consolidating its position regarding trade unions and employee relations. Notably, trade unionism seems to be an alien concept to many US MNCs, and trade union density in the US is much lower than in most European countries (not including France). In earlier research, Hamill (1983) investigated the employee relations practices of 84 US-owned and 50 UK-owned MNCs operating in three different industries in the UK and concluded that the US MNCs were less likely to recognise trades unions. Edwards et al.'s (1996) research included 101 MNCs of which 58 were UK-owned and 43 foreign-owned. and among their conclusions were:

- the prospects for trade union recognition appear to diminish as globalism advances – over half of the UK and just under half of the European respondents asserted that it was their general policy to avoid bargaining with trade unions;
- where companies were organised on multidomestic lines, 40 per cent avoided unions, whereas the figure for those companies dominated by global organisation rose to 63 per cent;
- avoiding unions seemed to be associated with a strategic emphasis upon market penetration and the existence of advanced organisational systems of management development, a mechanism through which contacts and culture can be reinforced;

■ the avoidance of trade unions was something that many of the companies would choose to do but it was not of sufficient importance in most of the companies that they would base location decisions on this factor alone;

■ if national governments or the EU strengthen the rights of labour and trade unions, it is unlikely to cause an immediate flight of capital from the country or region concerned.

The influence of trade unions on MNCs

Dowling and Schuler (1990) suggested that trade unions may have the ability to constrain the choices of MNCs in three main ways:

■ by influencing wage levels;
■ by limiting employment level variation;
■ by hindering global integration.

They suggested that labour costs, although decreasing in significance, still play a major part in determining cost competitiveness, though the impact is likely to be greater in 'low-tech' operations where labour costs as a proportion of total costs are likely to be the greatest. However, any influence that unions do have on wage levels is potentially significant and may influence employment levels. Dowling and Schuler (1990) further state that the ability of unions to restrict hours of work and patterns of employment may have a more serious effect on profitability than spiralling labour costs.

Trade unions in Europe have traditionally had significant input into the political process, and national regulatory systems are inevitably the product of interaction at this political level. Many countries have legislation that specifies a minimum wage or that prohibits redundancies or changes in working practices unless the company can show that structural conditions make these labour losses unavoidable. Often such procedures are long and drawn out and involve the employer in high redundancy costs. Payments for involuntary redundancy in some countries can be substantial, especially when compared with levels in the US.

Dowling and Schuler (1990) observed that 'many MNCs make a conscious decision not to integrate and rationalise their operations to the most effective degree, because to do so could cause industrial and political problems'. They use as an example Prahalad and Doz's (1987) description of General Motors' sub-optimisation of integration. The latter alleged that, in the early 1980s, GM made substantial investments in Germany (matching its new investments in Austria and Spain) at the demand of the German Metalworkers Union (IG Metal – one of the largest industrial unions in the western world) in order to foster good labour relations in Germany. They conclude:

> Union influence thus not only delays the rationalisation and integration of MNC's manufacturing networks and increases the cost of such adjustments (not so much in the visible severance payments and 'golden handshake' provisions as through economic losses incurred in the meantime), but also, at least in such industries as automobiles, permanently reduces the efficiency of the integrated MNC network. Therefore, treating labour relations as incidental and relegating them to the specialists in the various countries is inappropriate. In the same way as government policies need to be integrated into strategic choices, so do labour relations. (Prahalad and Doz, 1987)

However, recent developments that have enhanced the power and influence of MNCs and diminished the power of both the trade union movement (see, for example, the developing international division of labour above) and national governments to control and limit their activities cast serious doubts upon the abilities of trade unions to continue to influence the objectives and activities of MNCs in the ways and to the extent that is suggested in these earlier studies. The research findings of Edwards *et al.* (1996) would tend to confirm that the influence of the unions upon MNCs diminishes the more the MNCs move along the road of global integration and adopt a global orientation.

Ietto-Gillies (1997) argues that transnational corporations derive power from their multinational interests, which they can wield against uninationals, governments, labour organisations and consumers, and that there is a need to try to reverse this trend and give countervailing power to these other players. Governments should use their control over the quality of both the physical infrastructure and the labour force as bargaining weapons to give support to those players that do not themselves have transnational power.

Trade union responses

At a fairly early stage it became apparent that effective opposition to the power of the MNC demanded cooperation and organisation from the worldwide trade union movement. However, this has not proved to be an easy objective to achieve.

Study of trade union movements in different countries demonstrates the diversity of trade unions: their membership bases, their structures, their objectives and orientations, and their political affiliations differ substantially both within and between countries. (See Hollinshead and Leat (1995) for a comparison of trade union movements in a number of countries on these and other criteria.)

There are many countries in which various union factions and confederations exist and in which effective cooperation on a national scale has been largely unattainable (France and Italy are examples of this in Europe), let alone cooperation on an international scale. In some respects the decline of communism as practised in the Soviet bloc has helped the process of integration and cooperation in the past decade as confederations that viewed the communists as their political and ideological allies have been forced to reappraise their objectives and organisation.

It is also important to bear in mind that when dealing with MNCs, unions may have conflicting national interests. When one country is suffering an economic downturn, trade union officials may put national interests – the interests of their own constituency – before those of international worker solidarity. An example of this occurred in the early 1970s, when the Ford Motor Company, exasperated by the labour climate in its UK plants, decided to make no further investment in them. The media at the time hinted darkly that Ford was about to pull out of the UK and make further investments in the Netherlands. The UK unions were highly critical of Ford but the unions in the Netherlands made no attempt to express solidarity with them. In fact, they expressed full support for the Netherlands businesspeople trying to woo Ford away from the UK. It therefore seems that, while leaders may appreciate the imperative of effective international organisation to combat the power of the MNC, individual members of national unions and confederations are predominantly concerned with their own interests and the interests of their colleagues at national and local levels.

The primacy of national interests is also demonstrated in the following interview in which the German IG Metall leader at Ford, Wilfred Kuckelkorn, indicates that there are still significant difficulties facing joint union action. Kuckelkorn says:

'We want the British unions to win a 35-hour week and they will get practical solidarity from Germany, including overtime bans and working to rule.' But with another breath Kuckelkorn rejects out of hand any thought of joint European collective bargaining with Ford: 'the national unions cannot accept European negotiations. If you take away the power of the national unions they will go down.' (Milne, 1991)

There is relatively little evidence of change in this respect and a number of studies (Hyman, 1999; Hancke, 2000; Traxler and Woitech, 2000) point out that trade unions, especially within Europe, continue to adopt essentially national or local strategies, indeed that they often collude with governments in the pursuit of competitive strategies to attract or retain investment.

Attempts are being made to consolidate international trade union links and to mount worldwide campaigns against global capitalism, but the lack of coherence and coordination does provide MNCs with the opportunity to continue to engage in strategies which in effect pit unions and their members in one country against those in another and to engage in competitive and concession bargaining. In addition to creating discord between trade unionists across national boundaries these strategies can also be used to drive down material labour standards.

Nevertheless, there have been instances over the years of spontaneous and ad hoc international trade union solidarity and activity against particular multinationals. An example of this latter form of cooperation was in 1997 over the decision of Renault to close one of its more productive plants in Belgium in favour of the retention of plants in France. This was made worse by the revelation that the company was seeking grants and other forms of assistance from both the Spanish government and the European Commission to build a new plant in Spain. The controversy occasioned marches and demonstrations of support involving union members and delegations from Belgium, France, Germany, Italy, Spain, the UK, the Netherlands, Portugal, Greece and Austria, but to no avail. Renault demonstrated the power of the MNC to exercise its autonomy and ignore the views of the international trade union movement as represented and also to ignore the requirements of the EU directive that provides employee representatives with rights to prior consultation in the event of collective redundancies.

International trade union organisation

International trade union organisations exist at the global, regional and sectoral levels and there has been a great deal of debate over the years as to how these might best be organised and coordinated. One of the continuing obstacles to such coordination in pursuit of effective action at an international level remains the predominance of the movement's national orientations. The international confederations and organisations that do exist are made up of national unions and union confederations.

■ Global organisations

On a global level, transnational union organisations have tended to be aligned with political and ideological interests. That is to say, in the West, the International Confederation of Free Trade Unions (ICFTU) emerged, with its counterpart in the Communist bloc being the World Federation of Trade Unions (WFTU). There is also a smaller Christian-based World Confederation of Labour (WCL).

The ICFTU has been the most influential of these organisations and this has been perpetuated by the impact upon the WFTU of the break-up of the Soviet bloc. The ICFTU was set up in 1949 and has 221 affiliated organisations in 148 countries and territories on all five continents, with a membership of 156 million. It maintains close links with the European Trade Union Confederation (ETUC) (which includes all ICFTU European affiliates) and the international trade secretariats, which link together national unions from a particular trade or industry at international level. It is a confederation of national trade union centres and confederations, each of which links together the trade unions of that particular country. The ICFTU cooperates closely with the International Labour Organisation (ILO) and has contacts with the International Monetary Fund, the World Bank and the World Trade Organisation (WTO).

Traditionally the ICFTU has been concerned with such issues as:

- the respect and defence of trade union and workers' rights, perhaps particularly in the developing world;
- the eradication of forced and child labour;
- the promotion of equal rights for working women;
- the environment;
- education programmes for trade unionists all over the world;
- encouraging the organisation of young workers.

In recent years the ICFTU has become particularly concerned with the impact of globalisation and the activities of MNCs on labour, and has been campaigning with other organisations to ensure that core labour standards expressed as a workers' rights clause are included in trade agreements brokered by organisations such as the WTO.

At the four-yearly conference in South Africa in 2000 and in a document addressing the future of the trade union movement, there was fairly trenchant criticism of the impact of globalisation and justification of the role of free trade unions:

> Our vision is vastly different to the limitless free-for-all and destructive exploitation, which characterise the era of globalisation directed by the unbridled greed and power of the free market. The rights of working people to express their solidarity and advance their interests have been subjected to relentless attack and erosion, as power has been concentrated in the hands of a privileged few. Yet workers around the world continue to fight for their rights, often against tremendous odds. The free trade union movement remains the most powerful democratic and representative global force for social justice and democracy. (ICFTU, 2000)

The ICFTU expresses its concern that the globalisation of the world economy through increased trade and foreign investment by MNCs is exacerbating income inequality and undermining democratic decision-making by national governments and argues that discrimination and gross exploitation at the workplace in violation of fundamental workers' rights have increasingly become part of global commerce. Often the victims are young and unorganised female workers in export-processing zones which advertise the absence of trade union rights to attract investment.

The organisation is aware that there have been criticisms of the failure of the international trade union movement to effectively combat the activities of the MNCs. It stresses the role to be played by the International Trade Secretariats at sector level (see below) and within individual MNCs, and the need for the trade unions to cooperate within MNCs to ensure a dialogue with management at the highest corporate level.

It feels that there is a growing awareness and concern among consumers, and particularly the young, about the working conditions of the people who make the products they buy, and that this concern can be tapped into in order to encourage MNCs to take these matters seriously. As was noted earlier, there have been a number of exposés concerning precisely these issues and the activities of companies such as Nike and Gap.

International trade secretariats

In some industrial sectors there is a long history of attempts to build international links and organisation. In 1864, the first International Workingmen's Association brought together in London a mix of socialists and trade unionists. The 1890s saw international organisations founded by industrial sectors, such as dockers, steelworkers, miners, engineers and garment workers. By 1914, 28 international bodies (latterly known as international trade secretariats) were in operation.

One of the long-term goals of each international trade secretariat is to achieve transnational bargaining with each of the MNCs in its industry. The elements of the programme are:

- research and information;
- organisation of a company conference;
- establishment of a company council;
- company-wide union and management discussion;
- coordinated bargaining.

However, attempts by the international trade secretariats to become the basis for international collective bargaining have been largely unsuccessful although some have established world company councils to link together trade unionists in different branches of MNCs. As noted above, these sectoral bodies are seen as the instrument through which greater cooperation between trade unions in sectors and MNCs can be mobilised and through which the currently largely unrestricted power of the MNC night be mitigated for the benefit of the labour which they employ.

Within the EU there are examples of social dialogue at sectoral level. Some have argued that the European Works Council Directive of 1994 will provide the necessary opportunity for these secretariats to gain a foothold in many MNCs that have previously been able to resist them. This is discussed in more detail in Chapter 6.

European Trade Union Confederation

The most influential international trade union organisation within Europe is the ETUC. Membership is not confined to federations from member states of the EU and currently the ETUC represents 58 national trade union centres from 28 countries and 14 European industry federations with a total represented membership exceeding 53 million.

The ETUC has long been accustomed to lobbying on a wide variety of issues within the EU such as: gender equality, employee participation, protection of employees' rights in the event of plant closure or transfer of ownership, and health and safety at work, as well as broader issues of social and macroeconomic policy.

However, the ETUC is a diverse organisation and it would be wrong to give the impression that there is much cohesion within the movement. The size, nature, traditions and interests of the many union confederations and unions in membership vary considerably, as do their autonomy and authority in respect of their own membership.

The European Commission has designated the ETUC as the representative Social Partner of European employees and it is in this role that the ETUC is likely to have its greatest impact upon the regulatory environment for both MNCs and employees in Europe. The treaties agreed at Maastricht in 1991 and at Amsterdam in 1997 provide an extension of the role and the influence of the Social Partners, in particular via the Social Protocol procedures. As a Social Partner, more detail is given on the ETUC in Chapter 6 on the European Union.

International regulation and control of MNCs

The first major code of conduct regarding the operation of MNCs was established by the International Chambers of Commerce in 1972, mostly in response to the fears expressed by developing countries. The code incorporated recommendations that:

- host countries adopt a policy of collaboration rather than control, local shareholders should be encouraged and there should be no restrictions on the repatriation of capital, on loans and dividends, or on royalties for technology;
- MNCs should inform the host country of their plans, so that they can fit into the development objectives of the host country, try to choose local partners and offer them a share in the equity of their subsidiaries, volunteer information about their profits and be aware that sources of local financing may give priority to indigenous industrials;
- MNCs should also use local labour and give priority to local suppliers, above all, in the developing countries.

It should be stressed that the code is not compulsory and is solely a question of recommendations for the governments of the countries and the companies involved. There are further recommendations applying to double taxation, repatriation of dividends and proposed guarantees against non-commercial, administrative and political risks.

Guidelines that deal more directly with employee relations issues are those posited by the OECD in 1975. The recommendations of the guidelines cover six categories:

- disclosure of information;
- competition;
- financing;
- taxation;
- science and technology;
- employment and industrial relations.

As with the code established by the International Chamber of Commerce, the OECD code is a series of non-obligatory recommendations, but it has, in fact, taken on an obligatory character through the Committee on International Investment and Multinational Enterprises (IME), an organisation made up of representatives of the governments of the OECD member countries. The trade unions cannot refer a complaint to the Committee (IME) directly; they must go through representatives of their country serving on the Committee. The opinion expressed by the Committee is not necessarily followed by the country seeking clarification and therefore the Committee is not seen as a court which judges the actions of the MNCs.

A good example of the work of the IME, occurring on 30 March 1977, concerned a dispute brought about by the actions of the American multinational Raytheon. Its Belgian subsidiary, Badger, was unprofitable and Raytheon decided to close it down. As Belgian redundancy payments are among the highest in the world, the local Raytheon management baulked at the prospect of paying redundancy payments to some 250 workers as the subsidiary was technically bankrupt. The Belgian government and unions felt that the onus for the redundancy payments lay with the American parent Raytheon and that it should make the payments. The case was referred to the IME, and although its recommendations were somewhat ambiguous, the American parent eventually made the redundancy payments. In this particular case it is reasonable to assume that the OECD's code of conduct was used to pressurise the multinational to act in the way it did.

In 1994, Volkswagen AG (VW) carried out restructuring at its Belgian subsidiary in order to make it more competitive. Although this incurred the immediate loss of around 2,000 jobs with a further 850 job losses to come, production was maintained at pre-restructuring levels. The fact that production was not affected caused the remaining workforce to resist fiercely the increase in the rhythm of work needed to maintain production levels. The result was a series of strikes. During the negotiations between the unions and management in Belgium, VW's HQ in Germany announced that all production lost by the strikes (around 1,000 cars a day) would be transferred from Belgium to VW production units elsewhere in Europe.

The Belgian unions argued that the action taken by VW's HQ breached the OECD's 1976 Declaration on Investment and Multinational Enterprises, which states that companies should not threaten to transfer all or part of their operations from one country to another in order to influence negotiations (including disputes). This is an example of the difficulties facing employees and management of an MNC subsidiary, when the unions, on the one hand, are under strong pressure from a disaffected workforce and the management, on the other, is under strong pressure from HQ to increase competitiveness and productivity in order to retain current allocated production levels.

International Labour Organisation

Established in 1919, the ILO became a part of the United Nations, which itself emerged from the League of Nations (see chapter 18 of Hollinshead and Leat (1995) for a detailed account of the origin, development and initiatives of the ILO). The ILO has been influential in setting world standards in health and safety and in industrial relations and issued a code in 1977 that was concerned with the social policy of MNCs. This code was amended in 2000 and gives guidance to both member state governments and individual MNCs on issues including:

- employment, including equality of opportunity and treatment and the promotion and security of employment;
- training;
- working conditions, including wages and benefits, minimum working age and health and safety;
- industrial relations, including freedom of association, collective bargaining, consultation and dealing with grievances and disputes.

Most recently, attention has tended to centre on regulation through the insertion of minimum labour standards into international arrangements and agreements allowing trade liberalisation, such as those associated with the WTO, NAFTA and membership of the EU. It was noted above in the section on the ICFTU that this is perceived as a prime objective for ensuring that labour is not cynically exploited by MNCs in the pursuit of competitive advantage in the global marketplace. Those in favour of regulation, in addition to the concern that labour should be treated with decency and respect, argue that labour standards in the developed world can only be maintained if workers in developing countries are protected in order to avoid an international downward spiral of cost-cutting. It is also posited that if the international trade system already has rules in respect of intellectual property rights, market access and subsidies, then why should these not be matched in the sphere of labour and environmental standards?

The labour standards that are envisaged in this context tend to centre on the protection of certain fundamental human rights at work and are reflected in the ILO's core labour conventions. The ILO has identified eight conventions (nos 29, 87, 98, 100, 105, 111, 138 and 182) which it considers to be fundamental not just in the preservation of human rights and dignity at work but also as prerequisites for further action in improving both individual and collective conditions of work. These conventions are concerned with:

- the rights of employees to organise and to join free trade unions in order to protect their interests;
- the freedom of these unions to engage in collective bargaining on terms and conditions of employment without public interference;
- the freedom of employees from forced or compulsory labour and the abolition of such labour;
- the freedom of workers from discrimination and their entitlement to equality of treatment and remuneration irrespective of race, colour, sex, religion, and political opinion;
- the banning of child labour below compulsory school-leaving age;
- the banning of slavery and child prostitution;
- the right of workers to enjoy occupational health and safety.

However, means for the effective policing and enforcement of any such rights or minimum standards are lacking. Membership of the ILO is voluntary and agreeing to abide by such conventions is also voluntary. Even where governments agree to abide by a convention but then breach it, there is very little that the ILO and its members can do by way of redress. Effective policing and regulation of the affairs of individual MNCs is a complex and fraught process. Associations of countries in free trade arrangements (such as in the EU) may have some success if they have the ability to damage the MNC financially, for example, by refusing entry, and thereby imposing tariff barriers upon the MNCs products and services, or denying tax benefits. Alternatively, legislation can ensure MNC non-compliance leads to court action and the possibility of the imposition of substantial fines. Even in this latter instance, pressure to comply is diminished by the longevity of the legal process. The inevitable conclusion is that, for the foreseeable future, effective regulation of the employment and HRM policies of MNCs will be left to the efforts of individual governments and their respective legal codes and national level trade union organisation. As we have seen, MNCs have a powerful array of weapons to exert pressure upon both governments and trade unions in any one country. Unfortunately the evidence suggests that, in the final analysis, governments and national trade union organisation have pursued national strategies, even within the EU.

Employee relations policies and practices within MNCs

Much research has been concerned with the question of centralisation/decentralisation of decision-making within the MNC. As an adjunct to this, there has been consideration of whether the MNC HQ seeks to control the activities of the subsidiaries or whether the subsidiaries are allowed a degree of autonomy. An early study was by Hamill (1984), who interviewed 30 personnel directors from MNCs in the UK. The following factors were important in determining the extent to which the parent company intervened in or sought to control employment relations at a local level:

■ The degree of inter-subsidiary product integration. A high degree of integration was found to be the most important factor leading to the centralisation of the labour relations function within the MNCs studied.
■ Whether the subsidiary was US-owned or European-owned. US-owned concerns were found to be much more centralised in terms of labour relations decision-making.
■ Whether subsidiaries were well-established indigenous firms acquired by an MNC or greenfield sites set up by an MNC. The former tended to be given much more autonomy over labour relations than the latter.
■ Whether subsidiaries were performing well or poorly. Poor performance tended to be accompanied by increased investment in labour relations. When poor performance was due to labour relations problems, the MNC tended to attempt to introduce parent-country labour relations practices aimed at reducing industrial unrest or increasing productivity.
■ Whether or not the MNC was a significant source of operating or investment funds for the subsidiary. If this was the case, there was increased corporate involvement in labour relations.

Hamill concluded that because US MNCs tended to be more integrated there was more centralisation. He further found greater similarities between UK- and European-owned firms than between UK- and US-owned companies.

As an overall conclusion to his research, Hamill stated that different MNCs adopt different labour relations strategies and that it is the type of MNC under consideration that is important rather than multinationality itself.

In another early comment on MNCs, Bean (1985) suggests that:

■ European MNCs have tended to deal with labour unions at industry level (frequently through employers' associations) rather than at company level. The opposite is more typical for US firms. In America, employers' associations have not played a key role in the industrial relations system, and company-based labour relations policies are the norm.

■ The comparative size of the domestic and overseas markets and activity is a factor that influences the extent to which the parent company seeks to control overseas operations. If domestic sales are large relative to overseas operations (as is the case with many US companies), it is more likely that overseas operations will be regarded by the parent company as an extension of domestic operations. This is not the case for many European MNCs, whose international operations represent the major part of their business. Lack of a large home market is a strong incentive to adapt to host-country institutions and norms. Bean also notes that, in European MNCs, the overseas subsidiaries are considerably larger than the parent company and cites this fact as a possible reason for greater autonomy in employment relations given to European MNC subsidiaries than to US ones.

More recent research has been undertaken in the UK, as reported by Edwards *et al.* (1996). Their research included 101 MNCs of which 58 were UK-owned and 43 foreign-owned. As noted earlier, one of the objectives of the research was to ascertain the extent to which the transnational model is realistic, but other objectives were to investigate the degree to which the MNCs monitored the activities of subsidiaries, the degree of autonomy of the subsidiaries and the implications for the recognition of trade unions. Their conclusions were:

■ The collection and use of data that facilitated central monitoring was associated with a global rather than a national or multidomestic orientation.

■ The use and comparison of labour performance data seemed more important in those MNCs operating in markets for standardised products but where a global orientation was adopted and products were highly specialised, often being made at only one plant, and where it was crucial to be close to the customer.

■ The degree of central coordination was greater than might be apparent, this being achieved through a mix of financial mechanisms, expectations, contacts and culture.

■ There was some central direction of pay policy in over half the firms and this demonstrated a degree of coordination that was greater than the researchers had expected. As a matter of interest, this policy included a policy to pay above the local market rate in only a few companies.

We noted early in this chapter that the pace of capital restructuring through mergers and amalgamations continues to increase (UNCTAD, 2001). This capital restructuring has been accompanied in some instances by organisational restructuring and rationalisation. This is reflected in the development and strengthening of management structures at a European level which serve to integrate the business functions across Europe. As a result, production or marketing strategies are often no longer the province of national subsidiaries but are determined and integrated at a European level even when the unit is a division rather than the whole company. These structural developments are consistent with genuine transnationalism.

In describing this process Marginson and Sisson (1994) refer to the emergence of the Euro-company. They also point out the converse trend towards the decentralisation and devolution of operational responsibility and financial accountability to individual business units and cost and profit centres within the larger transnational or Euro-company.

Marginson and Sisson (1996) argue that there are trends in most companies involving increasing decentralisation to individual business units and at the same time centralisation to the European level. They argue that the greater the degree of devolution to individual business units within national systems the greater are the needs for internal coordination and control and that this is achieved through the tendency towards centralisation at the Euro-company level. The concentration of strategic integration at the level of the company and control of the decentralised operations are both aided by the new communication and information technologies.

These developments have considerable implications for the conduct and structure of industrial relations within the companies. Where there is a centralisation of certain strategic activities to the corporate or Euro-company level, or the creation of Euro-divisions, a potential exists for the development of company-level or division-specific, and therefore transnational or European, employment and industrial relations policies, structures and institutions at this level. Marginson and Sisson (1994) refer to this as the 'strategic potential to establish a pan-European approach to employee and industrial relations management'.

Schulten (1996) adapts Perlmutter's (1969) typology in referring to this as the development of a Eurocentric approach towards industrial relations, and suggests that there is evidence of this emerging in some of these Euro-companies, particularly in the areas of work organisation and working conditions. The emergence of such company- or division-specific structures would tend to undermine existing sectoral or national and multi-employer systems of joint regulation.

However, this tendency towards a centralisation of employee relations policy, strategy and institutions may be accompanied by operational decentralisation. The decentralisation of operational responsibilities and financial accountability referred to above is likely to necessitate the interaction of management and employees and the determination of the terms of the employment relationship at this decentralised level. If the managements of the decentralised units, whether these be specific subsidiaries, divisions or cost or profit centres, are to be responsible for costs and profits they need to be able to control the business or unit's labour and associated costs. They will arguably be unable to do this if major constituents of these costs are determined at a completely different level, whether this be at the level of the Euro-company or the national system. There may be scope even in such circumstances for the diffusion of some policies and practices that do not have significant cost implications.

Transnational companies may not want or need to take part in multi-employer arrangements but they cannot ignore the regulatory systems of the countries in which they have undertakings and whatever that imposes in terms of rights, outcomes and structures. MNCs may try to influence or mitigate the effects of particular national regulatory regimes but, as noted earlier, they are rarely able to ignore them totally.

Nevertheless, the opportunity does exist for many of these companies to go 'regime shopping', meaning that they may decide on the location of their activities on the basis of low employment costs and deregulatory regimes, shifting their resources so as to take advantage of what they perceive as favourable national systems.

This approach is characterised as the 'social dumping' approach (see earlier) and, as Schulten (1996) points out, there are means by which such organisations can press their employees into concession bargaining arrangements through which they encourage competition for work within the company, between locations and groups of employees. This exerts a downward pressure on terms and conditions of employment, and hence costs, as employees compete against each other for the available work. This may be one way to achieve a convergence of industrial relations across national boundaries within the one multinational.

In their study of the European automotive industry, Mueller and Purcell (1992) found that 'management systematically played one subsidiary against another to introduce night-shifts and to extend operating time in capital intensive areas (gear box and engine production, press shops). After the first subsidiary agreed to a relaxation of existing working time regulations, a kind of "domino-effect" was set in motion. Sooner or later, all the other subsidiaries followed the same pattern.' In this situation a phenomenon called information asymmetry occurs. Information is not uniformly available, so local negotiators threatened with social dumping may not be in a position to check the figures of other subsidiaries. The development of the European Works Council (EWC) may change this situation.

Sengenberger (1992) suggests that if each subsidiary bargains away its wages and conditions, there could be a 'negative convergence' in which all subsidiaries are caught in a race to undermine existing social standards with the result that there is a negative convergence of labour relations at a low level of social regulation.

It is for these and similar reasons that the European Commission and some of the member states have been keen to impose regulatory requirements upon the multinationals. The EWC Directive is the first such example, imposing as it does upon the company the requirement that a corporate European-level forum be established which provides employees with the right, through their representatives, to be informed and consulted on a range of issues.

Schulten (1996) does identify another way in which the emergence of these powerful multinational/Euro-companies may lead to a convergence of industrial relations across national boundaries within the organisation, and that is the 'best practice' alternative, whereby the management searches out and implements across the organisation instances and practices that fall into this category. He suggests that this is most likely to occur in organisations that are actively and continuously seeking to improve quality and 'searching for a more productive and innovative production model' such as the lean production model that has arguably replaced Fordism.

Edwards et al. (1999) have extended the above analysis and argue that diffusion within MNCs is the product of a combination of structural factors and internal political processes. They assert that diffusion is not a universal tendency and is promoted or retarded by four structural factors which they identify as significant and which echo much of the earlier research above. The four structural factors are:

- country of origin;
- the degree of production integration;
- the extent to which companies are structured along global lines;
- the nature of the product market.

There is a degree of interaction between these structural influences. For example, the nature of the product market, whether consumer tastes are homogeneous across national borders or competition in the market is international, influences the extent to which it is realistic or desirable to integrate production activities and management structures internationally. It is easier for the company to integrate production internationally, sometimes in product divisions, where consumer tastes are common, and the company is engaged in the manufacture of a product that can be sold across national boundaries. Where the MNC has taken the opportunity provided by such circumstances to structure management internationally the greater is the potential for the MNC to diffuse employment practices throughout the organisation or product-specific division. On the other hand, if consumer tastes differ across national boundaries and competition is national it is more likely that production and management structures will be nation-specific and it will probably be less relevant and more difficult for the organisation to diffuse employment practices.

The research also highlighted the significance of company growth profiles, in that where a company has grown through the creation of greenfield sites rather than through the acquisition of going concerns it is easier to diffuse employment practices.

However, whether or not diffusion actually occurs, even in organisations where the appropriate structural factors are present, it is also dependent upon the strategic choices of the actors within the organisation, the location, use of power and the existence of what Edwards *et al.* (1999) refer to as 'networking within hierarchy'. Edwards *et al.* assert that it is the interaction of both structural and political factors that shape the nature and extent of diffusion or internal convergence with networking, for example, being more likely in highly integrated and cohesive organisations.

Chapter summary

The past two decades have been a period of rapid and great economic integration and expansion in the volume of world trade. Associated with these developments, there has been a considerable increase in the tendency of companies to become MNCs.

There are a number of different models of the MNC and their approaches to issues such as the management of employee relations and in particular in their overseas or foreign subsidiaries. MNCs have to take some note of national regimes and cultures but the way in which they approach this varies. Where MNCs come from economically successful countries they appear to have the potential to export employee relations policies and practices, such as those associated with Japanisation, throughout the world, impacting upon national systems and traditions as they do so. One of the important features of an MNC's approach to employee relations is its attitude towards trade unions. In the main, MNCs seem to prefer to avoid them if they can.

Trade unions themselves appear to have had little effective input upon the development of MNCs and upon their employee relations policies and practices. The unions need to respond at the national and international levels to defend their members against possible effects of social dumping and regime shopping. They also need to operate effectively within the company to ensure a homogeneous response across national boundaries with their fellow trade unionists, in order to combat a possible attrition of labour standards and working conditions and the device known as concession bargaining. So far the trade union response has been insufficiently international and many have pursued nationally competitive strategies seeking employment and employment security, often encouraged by MNC management and national governments.

Regulation of the activities of the MNC is both necessary and difficult. International organisations have tried, but with little impact, most recently attempts seem to have centred upon the insertion of labour standards based upon perceived fundamental human rights in international agreements and arrangements facilitating free trade.

The diffusion of employment relations policies and practices within MNCs seems not to be universal and appears to be the product of an interaction between a range of structural and environmental influences and contingencies as well as the strategic choices of the actors with organisational power.

Questions

1   Discuss whether MNCs at corporate level need to understand the historical and cultural contexts of the employee relations system of the countries in which they operate.

2   What are features of MNCs that trade unionists and employee representatives may find undesirable?

3   Discuss the arguments for and against the need to introduce minimum labour standards into free trade agreements and arrangements.

4   Discuss whether the MNC is now out of reach of national regimes and what options there may be for international regulation.

5   Discuss the assertion that the diffusion of employment relations policies and practices within MNCs is universal.

Activity

Read Exhibit 7.2 and then carry out the following activities.

1   Undertake a SWOT (strengths, weaknesses, opportunities and threats) analysis for each of the main actors referred to, in the exhibit, i.e. the company, the employees and the UK government.

2   Consider the ways in which Exhibit 7.2 illustrates material in the chapter regarding:

    (a) MNC location and investment decisions;
    (b) the weapons at the disposal of the MNC in discussions with governments and trade unions;
    (c) the 'need' for trade unions to organise and respond internationally;
    (d) structural conditions facilitating the diffusion of employee relations policies and practices;
    (e) company and union responses to the pressures of international competition.

Exhibit 7.2

Ford puts on the brakes

The loss of 1,300 jobs in Merseyside is a matter of great regret. So many redundancies in such a depressed region of Britain will be a sad reverse for those who are trying to breathe new life into the Merseyside economy.

It may seem an especially unfair blow to the workers at Ford's Halewood plant, because they have made great efforts in the recent past to reform working practices and become more efficient. But it is important to draw the right conclusions.

New Labour, for example, looked very much like silly old Labour when it laid routine blame on the Conservatives' free market economic policies. It is wrong. Tory economic policies, including the reform of labour markets, have in the past 15 years contributed to a dramatic revival of the British motor industry. Ford is responding mainly to competitive pressures, which have pushed its European operations deep into the red. Stuck with over-capacity, it has decided to concentrate output of the new Escort model, which comes into production next year, in two of the three existing Escort plants – Saarlouis in Germany and Valencia in Spain.

Halewood has lost out mainly because it is a smaller plant which has received considerably less investment in its assembly lines in recent years. (Investment has been concentrated in the transmission plant at the site.) Productivity is therefore somewhat lower, despite the big gains made since the 1970s when Halewood was a by-word for poor industrial relations.

Job cutting

The relative ease with which it is possible to cut jobs in the UK, compared with Germany and Spain, played a part in Ford's decision. Mr Ian McCartney, Labour's employment spokesman, and trade union officials at Halewood have emphasised this fact when suggesting the government is partly to blame for the job cuts.

One can sympathise with the Halewood shop stewards. But Labour should take care with its pro-nouncements. The fact is that Conservative labour-market reforms have contributed a great deal to encouraging foreign car makers to set up plants and invest in Britain. Japanese companies, particularly, could have chosen other EU countries for European plants. They said one reason for picking the UK was its flexible labour market. They did not come intending to sack staff – but they wished to retain the option in case their plans did not work out.

Car output

Existing car makers – including Ford – restructured their businesses to meet the challenge from the east. Employment in the motor industry has fallen by about two-thirds since the 1970s and will almost certainly fall further. But car output last year hit its highest level for 21 years and is rising. Britain makes 12 per cent of the EU's cars, compared with 9 per cent in 1986.

Ford has played a significant part in this revival, investing nearly £3.5bn in the UK in 1990–95, including almost £500m at Halewood. Ford's British plants are a key element of its European network.

It would be wrong to see only the job cuts which resulted from competitive pressures and technological changes in the motor industry. These pressures also created new jobs.

There is no room for complacency, however. While the top British plants can match the best in the world in quality, the industry still has too many second-rate factories. The country is behind others in training those working in motors, as in other industries. It is here that the government can make the biggest contribution to the industry's success – raising the quality of school and university education.

Future reforms in the training of workers will be of little help to Halewood today. But it will be the best guarantee of future jobs at the plant. A slide back to restrictive labour markets would have the opposite effect.

Source: Financial Times, 17 January 1997. © 1997 The Financial Times Limited

Exhibit 7.2 *continued*

Ford and unions agree Halewood jobs deal

Ford yesterday agreed to scale down its plans for job losses at the Halewood plant on Merseyside from 1,300 to 980 in return for union agreement to call off a ballot on industrial action.

The company, which last month raised the threat of closure at Halewood in a drive to staunch massive European losses, assured union leaders that it wanted to keep the plant open after production of the current Escort model ends in 2000. The company also confirmed it would build the next generation of the Transit van at Southampton after 2000. The Transit will require linked investments, in transmissions at Halewood and body stamping at the Dagenham plant in east London.

The company also said Dagenham, rather than Cologne in Germany, would be its main plant in Europe for the next-generation Fiesta, due early in the next decade. An unspecified new investment will be made at Halewood to raise stamping capacity to cope with expansion at Ford's Jaguar subsidiary.

Union leaders committed themselves to working with Ford to strengthen the company's role in car-making in Britain. However, the agreement, reached after two days of talks between union bosses and Mr Jac Nasser, chairman of Ford of Europe, looked like a clear win for the company. Many of the 'new' investment decisions had been expected.

Ford's main concession, apart from cutting the number of redundancies, was the commitment to build a new multi-purpose version of the next-generation Escort to keep the plant alive after 2000.

The company's willingness to back the project appeared largely based on assurances from the government that it would receive satisfactory subsidies. Neither Ford nor the unions indicated the sum sought. However, both sides seemed confident the project would go ahead. Ford said it would produce another vehicle at the plant if it did not.

The reduction in redundancies is being achieved by switching production of the station-wagon version of the Escort to Halewood from late 1998 and prolonging the life of the Escort van, which is already built at the plant, beyond the end of this year. Production of the next-generation Escort car is being concentrated at Ford's plants in Spain and Germany.

Mr Nasser hailed the deal as 'a historic agreement' for Ford, the unions and Britain. It is likely to increase the competition for subsidies as car makers use each new product to lobby governments for aid for factories in sensitive areas.

In Ford's case, the focus may soon switch to Germany, where the company has so far refused to commit itself to building the next-generation Scorpio executive model at Cologne. Demand for the current Scorpio has slumped, prompting local fears that Ford may be tempted to import the successor model from the US.

Source: Haig Simonian, *Financial Times, Weekend*, 8/9 February 1997. © 1997 The Financial Times Limited

Useful websites

www.etuc.org.en   **European Trade Union Confederation**   One of the social partners and the website provides information on the organisation and its activities, press releases and resolutions.

www.icftu.org   **International Confederation of Free Trade Unions**   The largest trade union confederation, this website contains much information on the trade union position on issues such as globalisation, MNC activities, child labour, the need for social protection and pretty much anything else going on in the world likely to impact upon trade union members.

www.ilo.org   **International Labour Organization (ILO)**   Contains a lot of information on member states, labour standards and the activities and interests of the organisation including the social dialogue and social protection.

www.statistics.gov.uk   **National Statistics**   This site is the official statistics site for the UK. A wealth of information on the economy with an index that is reasonably accessible.

www.unctad.org/wir/index.htm   United Nations Conference on Trade and Development
This is the website for the annual *World Investment Report* which provides a wealth of
detailed information on MNCs, FDI and the scale of mergers and amalgamations and cross-
national investment.

References

Barrell, R. and Pain, N. (1997) 'EU: an attractive investment. Being part of the EU is good for FDI
and being out of EMU may be bad', *New Economy*, 4(1): 50–4.

Bartlett, C.A. and Ghoshal, S. (1989) *Managing Across Borders: The Transnational Solution*.
Cambridge, MA: Harvard Business School Press.

Batstone, E. and Gourley, S. (1986) *Unions, Unemployment and Innovation*. Oxford: Blackwell.

Bean, R. (1985) *Comparative Industrial Relations: An Introduction to Cross-national Perspectives*.
New York: St Martin's Press.

Dowling, P. and Schuler, R. (1990) *International Dimensions of Human Resource Management*.
Boston, MA: PWS–Kent.

Eaton, J. (2000) *Comparative Employment Relations*. Cambridge: Polity Press.

Edwards, P., Marginson, P., Armstrong, P. and Purcell, J. (1996) 'Towards the transnational company? The global structure and organisation of multinational firms' in Crompton, R., Gallie, D.
and Purcell, K. (eds) *Changing Forms of Employment*. London: Routledge.

Edwards, T., Rees, C. and Coller, X. (1999) 'Structure, politics and the diffusion of employment
practices in multinationals', *European Journal of Industrial Relations*, 5(3): 286–306.

Ghertman, M. and Allen, M. (1984) *An Introduction to the Multinationals*. Basingstoke: Macmillan.

Hamill, J. (1983) 'The labour relations practices of foreign owned and indigenous firms', *Employee
Relations*, 5(1): 14–16.

Hamill, J. (1984) 'Labour relations decision making within multinational corporations', *Industrial
Relations Journal*, 15(2): 30–4.

Hancke, B. (2000) 'European works councils and the industrial restructuring in the European
motor industry', *European Journal of Industrial Relations*, 6(1): 35–59.

Hendry, C. (1994) *Human Resource Strategies for International Growth*. London: Routledge.

Hodgetts, R.M. and Luthans, F. (1994) *International Management*, 2nd edn. Maidenhead:
McGraw-Hill.

Hofstede, G. (1991) *Cultures and Organisations: Software of the Mind*. New York: McGraw-Hill.

Hofstede, G. (1994) 'The business of international business is culture', *International Business
Review*, 3(1): 1–14.

Hollinshead, G. and Leat, M. (1995) *Human Resource Management: An International and
Comparative Perspective on the Employment Relationship*. London: Financial Times/Pitman
Publishing.

Hyman, R. (1999) 'National industrial relations systems and transnational challenges: an essay
in review', *European Journal of Industrial Relations*, 5(1): 89–110.

ICFTU (2000) *Launching the Millennium Review – the Future of the International Trade Union
Movement*. Brussels: ICFTU: 1.

Ietto-Gillies, G. (1997) 'Working with the big guys: hostility to transnationals must be replaced
by co-operation', *New Economy*, 4(1): 12–16.

Kennedy, T. (1980) *European Labour Relations*. Lexington, MA: Lexington Books.

Legge, K. (1995) *Human Resource Management: Rhetorics and Realities*. Basingstoke: Macmillan.

Levitt, T. (1983) 'The globalisation of markets', *Harvard Business Review*, May/June: 92–102.

Luthans, F., Marsnik, P.A. and Luthans, K.W. (2001) 'A contingency matrix approach to IHRM'
in Albrecht, M.H. (ed.) *International HRM: Managing Diversity in the Workplace*. Oxford:
Blackwell.

Marchington, M. and Wilkinson, A. (1996) *Core Personnel and Development*. London: Institute for Personnel and Development.

Marginson, P. and Sisson, K. (1994) 'The structure of transnational capital in Europe: the emerging Euro-company and its implications for industrial relations' in Hyman, R. and Ferner, A. (eds) *New Frontiers in European Industrial Relations*. Oxford: Blackwell.

Marginson, P. and Sisson, K. (1996) 'Multi-national companies and the future of collective bargaining: a review of the research issues', *European Journal of Industrial Relations*, 2(2): 173–97.

Milne, S. (1991) 'Germany 37, Britain 39', *Guardian*, 25 October.

Mueller, F. and Purcell, J. (1992) 'The Europeanisation of manufacturing and the decentralisation of bargaining: multinational management strategies in the European automobile industry', *International Journal of Human Resource Management*, 3(1): 15–34.

Needle, D. (2000) *Business in Context*, 3rd edn. Walton-on-Thames: Thomson Learning.

Office for National Statistics (2001) *Foreign Direct Investment 2000*. www.britaininfo.org/economy/xq/asp/SarticleType.1/Article_ID.2001/qx/articles_show.htm

Ohmae, K. (1990) *The Borderless World: Power and Strategy in the Interlinked Economy*. New York: Harper.

Parker, M. and Slaughter, J. (1988) *Choosing Sides: Unions and the Team Concept*. Boston, MA: Labour Notes.

Peel, J. (1979) *The Real Power Game*. New York: McGraw-Hill.

Perlmutter, H. (1969) 'The tortuous evolution of the multi-national corporation', *Columbus Journal of World Business*, 4(1): 9–18.

Porter, M.E. (1985) *Competitive Advantage*. New York: Free Press.

Prahalad, C.K. and Doz, Y.L. (1987) *The Multinational Mission*. New York: Free Press.

Schregle, J. (1981) 'Comparative industrial relations: pitfalls and potential', *International Labour Review*, 120(1): 15–30.

Schulten, T. (1996) 'European Works Councils: prospects of a new system of European industrial relations', *European Journal of Industrial Relations*, 2(3): 303–24.

Sengenberger, W. (1990) 'Intensified competition, industrial restructuring and industrial relations', *International Labour Review*, 131(2): 139–54.

Spivey, W. and Thomas, L. (1990) 'Global management themes, problems and research issues', *Human Resource Management*, 29(1): 85–97.

Storey, J. (1992) *Developments in the Management of Human Resources*. Oxford: Blackwell.

Traxler, F. and Woitech, B. (2000) Transnational investment and national labour market regimes: a case of regime shopping', *European Journal of Industrial Relations*, 6(2): 141–59.

Trompenaars, F. (1993) *Riding the Waves of Culture: Understanding Cultural Diversity in Business*. London: Economist Books.

UNCTAD (2001) *World Investment Report 2001. Promoting Linkages*. New York and Geneva: Overview. Internet Edition. http://www.unctad.org/wirOlove.en.pdf

Walters, M. (1995) *Globalisation*. London: Routledge.

Wilkins, M. (1970) *The Emergence of the Multinational Enterprise*. Cambridge: Cambridge University Press.

Chapter 8

Regulating the employment relationship

Brian Willey and Huw Morris

Learning objectives

By the end of this chapter, readers should be able to:

- understand the significance and limitations of the contract of employment as a means of regulation;
- explain the role of collective agreements in setting employment standards;
- describe the contribution of trade unions in representing workers' interests and dealing with conflicts of interest between working people and employers;
- describe the contribution of statute law in establishing various principles on the treatment of working people (e.g. fairness and non-discrimination), and creating (minimum) employment standards;
- understand the role of statute law in attempting to mould the conduct of employment relations by creating procedural duties and minimum procedural standards;
- discuss the influence of social, economic and political objectives on the formulation of both public policy and employment legislation.

Introduction

The conduct of employment relations has, since the late 1970s, been marked by a significant but gradual shift in approach. There are three discernible interlocking elements:

- a decline in voluntarism and collective *laissez-faire* and a growth of legalism;
- a shift in emphasis away from collectivism towards greater focus on the individual employment relationship;
- the creation, under statute law, of minimum employment standards and procedural requirements which increasingly influence corporate human resource policies and practices.

Traditionally, British employment relations was characterised by academic commentators as owing little to employment law. Principally, there were two instruments available for regulating the employment relationship. One – the contract of employment between the individual employee and his or her employer – was based in law; the other was based on the voluntary action of employers and trade unions, i.e. collective agreements negotiated between trade unions and specific employers.

Generally, employers voluntarily agreed to engage in collective bargaining and also determined the scope of collective agreements. Typically, the scope of such agreements would cover pay, overtime and shift premia (where appropriate), hours and holidays. Such collective agreements were (and continue to be) voluntary agreements. They are presumed to have no legal status unless the parties agreed otherwise. However, provisions of collective agreements were (and continue to be) legally enforceable through the individual contract of employment. Provisions relating to that individual employee (e.g. the rate of pay, length of the working week) are incorporated into the individual's contract. Failure of the employer to implement these provisions would be a breach of the individual contract of employment.

The role of collective bargaining as an instrument for setting employment standards was, by the late 1970s, significant. While just over half of the workforce were trade union members, around 70 per cent had their principal terms and conditions of employment determined through a collective agreement. However, over the following two decades, trade union membership and the incidence of union recognition deals (for collective bargaining) diminished. In the early 2000s, around 30 per cent of the workforce are union members and just under half are covered by collective agreements.

While collective agreements are still invariably voluntary agreements and are incorporated into individual contracts of employment, it is now more difficult to characterise British employment relations as a system based entirely on the principles of voluntarism and collective *laissez-faire*. Legislation has intervened in various ways in respect of trade union recognition, the substantive provisions of collective agreements and in regulating trade unions in the organisation of industrial action to pursue their members' interests.

Admittedly, employers still have some freedom to decide whether or not to recognise unions for collective bargaining. However, legislation was introduced in 2000 that created a framework for statutory recognition provided certain conditions were met (see later in this chapter).

Unions were seen, particularly from the 1960s onwards, as requiring some regulation of their activities. While they were voluntary bodies in which working people were, generally, free to associate, they nevertheless carried out activities that could have profound implications for society and the economy. In particular, tensions existed between Conservative and Labour governments about the consequences of collective agreements for inflation, for mobility within the labour market, and for adaptability and change in working practices. Furthermore, the use of industrial action (particularly in large public sector organisations) was regarded as having adverse consequences for the national economy.

In the 1980s and early 1990s, public policy aimed at the decollectivisation of employment relations. Employers were encouraged by the Conservative governments to withdraw from collective bargaining and to individualise their relationships. Unions also became subject to stringent restrictions on their ability to take industrial action. Since 1997, there has been a readjustment of public policy: union recognition for collective bargaining has been promoted. However, there is no return to collective *laissez-faire*. Restrictions on industrial action are in place – although they have been slightly modified – and individual workers can in certain cirumstances be protected from dismissal. Greater flexibility of approach to collective representation is envisaged. So, unions are no longer the single channel of representation for working people. Systems of non-union employee representatives have been enacted under legislation. The government philosophy underpinning employment relations (and echoing the European Union's social policy approach) is the promotion of social partnership.

In its 1998 White Paper *Fairness at Work*, the government aimed to reconcile good employment practice, business interests and an approach to the conduct of employment relations. It stated:

> Within Britain's flexible and efficient labour market, the Government is proposing in this White Paper a framework in which the development of strong partnerships at work can flourish as the best way of improving fairness at work. But the framework it proposes is not just about the application of employment law. It is designed to help develop a culture in all businesses and organisations in which fairness is second nature and underpins competitiveness. Such cultural change will lead in due course to more positive relationships between employers and employees than the letter of the law can ever achieve. (para. 1.8)

As collective bargaining has diminished in significance, particularly in parts of the private sector, there has been a growth in statutory influence over the regulation and conduct of the employment relationship. The origin of such legal standards are found, in large part, in European Community law and, to a lesser extent, in law promoted by the British government. The consequences of such developments are various:

- Direct statutory impositions into the contract of employment (e.g. equality clause under the Equal Pay Act 1970).
- The creation of minimum standards in respect of terms and conditions of employment (e.g. national minimum wage; maternity and parental leave). These allow employers to provide better standards of treatment if they choose.
- The enactment of minimum procedural standards for dealing with employment matters affecting individual working people (e.g. the requirements in the ACAS Code of Practice on Discipline and Grievance Procedures 2000, and the statutory right to be accompanied).
- The enactment of statutory duties on employers to consult (with union or non-union employee representatives) about specific employment relations issues (e.g. health and safety, certain collective redundancies, and transfers of undertakings).
- The requirement that the conduct of employment relations should be infused with certain principles which reflect social values and public policy objectives. Examples include *fairness* as in dismissal legislation; *reasonableness* as in health and safety, disability and dismissal legislation; *avoidance of unjustified discrimination* as in sex, race and disability discrimination law.

Implicit in much of this framework of employment law is an acknowledgement of a tension that exists between the social purposes of legislation and the economic consequences of such regulation. Government seeks to balance the promotion of fairness, non-discrimination and good employment practice while at the same time taking account of employer concern about the cost of compliance. So, for example, the concept of minimum standards is designed to enable employers to provide improved terms and conditions of employment dependent on their economic circumstances. The concept of reasonableness can involve consideration of cost factors as in the Disability Discrimination

Act 1995 where an employer has a duty to make 'a reasonable adjustment' for a person who is disabled. Excessive cost can be part of the employer's defence for not not making an adjustment. Under the Health and Safety at Work Act (HASAWA) 1974, employers have to comply with certain general duties 'as far as is reasonably practicable'.

The overall shifts in voluntary and legal regulation are summarised in Figure 8.1.

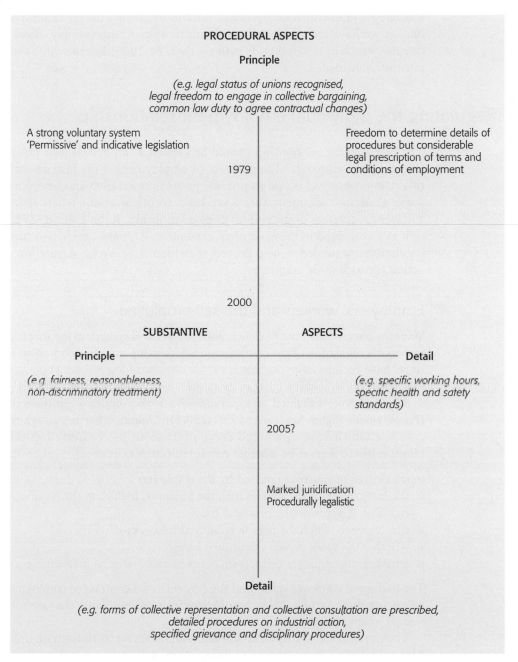

Figure 8.1 **Shifts in voluntary and legal regulation of the employment relationship since 1979**

The dates on Figure 8.1 mark the shifts in the character of British employment relations between the four quadrants. As far as the substantive aspects are concerned, there has been a growing development of the principles indicated. In addition, there has been some movement towards prescribing certain detailed terms and conditions of employment. The process of juridification is the tendency whereby the behaviour employers and unions is determined by reference to legal standards. It is suggested here that this tendency is gradually taking place in Britain. Regarding the procedural aspects, Britain has, as we have indicated, had a voluntarist system. Increasingly, there is evidence of greater detailed prescription. It is likely that, by 2005, Britain will have moved to the position indicated.

Regulating the individual employment relationship

The employment relationship should be viewed as an imbalanced power relationship favouring the employer. The contract of employment is the instrument for regulating this relationship and is said to provide protection for individual employees. However, some academic commentators have been sceptical about whether it does provide sufficient regulation of the employment relationship. Kahn-Freund (1983) has referred to it as a command in the guise of an agreement. Arguably, then, two further sources of regulation are needed to help protect individual employees: statute law and collective action through trade unions.

■ Employees, workers and the self-employed

With the expansion of the flexible labour market and growth in the forms of employment status, the regulation of the employment relationship and the acquisition of employment rights have become more problematical for some working people. These developments are explored here by looking at three categories: employees, workers and the self-employed.

An employee is defined as a person who works under a contract of employment (Employment Rights Act (ERA) 1996 s230(1)). Common law tests have evolved through case law which have elaborated certain factors to be considered in the employment relationship to determine whether employee status exists:

- the degree of control exercised by the employer;
- the integration of the person into the business, including the issue of who bears the risk and, if appropriate, provides tools;
- the extent to which the person is obliged to work;
- whether the work is on a continuing basis;
- whether the employer deducts income tax and National Insurance contributions.

The finding of employee status and the existence of a contract of employment depends on balancing these factors. None is sufficient in itself, but some are essential (e.g. control and payment of wages).

The importance of employee status lies in its access to statutory employment rights. Many (including those relating to unfair dismissal) are restricted to employees.

The law also recognises a further category: a worker. This term embraces those who work under a contract of employment. It also covers a person who works under any contract, whether express or implied and (if it is express) whether oral or in writing, whereby the individual undertakes to do or perform personally any work or services for another party to the contract whose status is not by virtue of the contract that of a client or customer of any profession or business undertaking carried on by the individual. (ERA 1996 s230(3)(b))

In determining whether or not a contract of employment exists, courts refer to the test of 'mutuality of obligation'. This concerns, first, the obligation of the employer to provide work and the employee to perform work, and, secondly, the mutual promises of future performance. Usually, this test is used to decide whether or not a casual worker has a contract of employment. If the second level of obligation is missing, as it may well be for a casual worker, then there is no contract of employment. He or she may, however, be a 'worker'.

Statutory employment protection has begun to encompass this wider group. For example, the National Minimum Wage Act 1998 and the Working Time Regulations 1998 provide entitlements for 'workers'.

A third category of working person is the self-employed. Generally, self-employed people are exempt from statutory employment protection. However, they are covered by, for example, discrimination law and health and safety legislation. The genuinely self-employed (i.e. an independent contractor or those in business on their own account) would, for example, not be integrated into the employer's business; and would not necessarily provide a service personally, and would have no continuing mutuality of obligation. In determining such issues, much would depend on the facts of the particular case. Some individuals can have an ambiguous employment status.

Atypical workers

Atypical or non-standard workers are those who are not full-time permanent employees. They may have different forms of employment status – as part-time, permanent, temporary, on a fixed-term contract, as a job sharer, as a casual worker, as 'bank' staff, as an agency worker, on a zero-hours contract. Whether they enjoy employment protection is dependent on a number of factors:

- Can they establish employee status?
- Do they have any entitlements as a 'worker' under statute law?
- Have they accrued continuity of employment and so entitlement to service related benefits in the employment contract and to service related statutory rights (ERA 1996 ss210–13)?
- Are they covered by specific anti-discrimination law (e.g. the Part-time Workers (Less Favourable Treatment) Regulations 2000; and the provision outlawing discrimination against fixed-term workers)?

The contract of employment

A contract of employment has the following characteristics:

- It is a promise or agreement to offer work and to undertake work.
- It is freely arrived at by the employer and the individual employee.

- It is legally enforceable in the courts and intended to be so.
- It is usually of indefinite duration.
- It involves 'consideration', i.e. something, usually pay, with which the employer buys the promise of the employee to be ready, willing and able to undertake the agreed work.
- It may be in writing, verbally agreed or part verbal and part in writing.
- It need not be signed.

Terms of the contract

A contract of employment comprises express and implied terms. Express terms are likely to cover pay, hours, holidays, overtime and shift rates, notice periods, mobility arrangements, restrictive covenants. They may derive from collective agreements with unions, from management policy or from individual agreements with a particular employee. Information on many express terms will be found in a formal contract or in the statement of initial employment particulars (see below).

Examples of implied terms of the common law of contract are:

- *The duty to obey lawful and reasonable instructions.* This can be an issue in disciplinary action against employees.
- *The duty of mutual trust and confidence.* This can be an issue in harassment and bullying cases when it is alleged that the employer did not provide support for the employee.
- *The duty on the employer to take reasonable care of the employee.* This is supplemented by health and safety legislation (HASAWA 1974).
- *The duty on the employer to pay wages.* This can be an issue when a employee complains to an employment tribunal about unlawful deduction/non-payment of wages (ERA 1996 ss13–14).
- *The duty to promote the employer's business.* This can be an issue when a employer requires the employee to carry out additional tasks within their job description or contractual terms.

Statute law can have an impact, particularly on the express terms. The creation of minimum standards influences the terms of employment that an employer can offer an employee. Also, a statutory imposition, like the equality clause (Equal Pay Act 1970 s1) is deemed to exist in all contracts of employment. This ensures that there should be no sex discrimination between women and men in respect of terms and conditions of employment (including pay).

Information about the contract

Employees are entitled to receive, within eight weeks of starting employment, information about the terms of their contract – the 'statement of initial employment particulars' (ERA 1996 s1). It is not the employee's contract of employment, but it constitutes strong *prima facie* evidence of the contract's terms. It is not conclusive but is said to place a heavy burden on the party who alleges that the real terms are different. The information that should be provided is outlined in Exhibit 8.1.

Statement of initial employment particulars

The following information must be provided in one document.

1 *Names of the employer and the employee*

2 *Date when employment began*
Not necessarily the first day the employee started work: it may be earlier.

3 *Date when continuous employment began*
May include previous employment with that employer, or the consequences of a business transfer, or transfers between companies within a group.

4 *Scale or rate of remuneration, or the method of calculating remuneration*
Together with the right to an itemised pay statement (ERA 1996 s8), employees should be able to check the accuracy of their pay in detail. An employee can complain to an employment tribunal about unauthorised deductions from wages (ERA 1996 ss13–14).

5 *Intervals at which remuneration is paid*
Whether monthly, weekly or at some other interval.

6 *Terms and conditions relating to hours of work (including normal working hours)*
This is affected by the Working Time Regulations 1998 covering maximum working time, rest breaks and rest periods, and the scheduling of shift work.

7 *Terms and conditions relating to holiday entitlements including public holidays and holiday pay*
Enough detail should be provided to enable the employee to calculate the entitlement. The Working Time Regulations 1998 set a minimum paid annual leave entitlement which accrues to employees from the first day of employment.

8 *Job title or brief job description*
Generally, a job description is treated as lawful instructions.

9 *The place of work*
If the employee is required or permitted to work at various places, an indication of this fact and the employer's address(es).

The following information may be provided in instalments, so long as this is done by the end of the second month. It is possible in some cases (*) to cross-refer to other documents if the employee has reasonable access and opportunity to read them.

10 *Terms relating to sickness, injury and sick pay* (*)

11 *Pensions and pension scheme* (*)

12 *Period of notice that each party must give to terminate the contract* (*)
The notice that the employer gives the employee must be the statutory minimum (ERA 1996 s86) or more.

13 *Where employment is temporary*
How long employment is likely to last, or the termination date of a fixed-term contract.

14 *Collective agreements which directly affect terms and conditions*
Where the employer is not party to the collective agreement, the person by whom they are made must be named.

15 *Where employees are sent to work outside the UK for more than one month*:

■ the period of work outside the UK;
■ the currency in which they will be paid;
■ special benefits available while they work abroad;
■ any terms relating to their return.

16 *Disciplinary rules and procedures* (*)
Unless the employer employs fewer than 20 employees (this is likely to change in 2002).

17 *Grievance procedure* (*)

Breach of contract

Failure by the employer to deliver on terms of the contract is a breach of contract. The question of whether any implied terms are breached is decided by a tribunal or court on the facts and circumstances in a particular case. Contract breaches by an employer should normally be raised by the employee(s) through the organisation's grievance procedure (see later section).

Some contractual breaches are so serious that they in effect destroy the contract because the employer fails to deliver on one of the essential terms, for example, the payment of wages, mutual trust and confidence, or the duty to take reasonable care of the employee. Such breaches are repudiatory breaches. The employer's behaviour is such that he or she is in effect indicating an intention not to be bound by the contract. The employee can, then, resign and claim constructive dismissal at an employment tribunal, if the employee has the appropriate qualifying period of service (ERA 1996 s95(1)(c)). For example, an employer's failure to deal with an allegation of workplace bullying is likely to breach the implied term of mutual trust and confidence and also possibly the duty to take reasonable care of the employee. The employee would be claiming at an employment tribunal that this failure was a fundamental breach of the contract.

Breaches of the contract by an employee are likely to be dealt with through the organisation's disciplinary procedure (see later section).

Variation of contract

A contract of employment is agreed at a particular point in time. Business conditions inevitably change, often requiring changes in working practices and in terms and conditions. How, then, can employment contracts be varied lawfully?

It is important to remember that the contract is an agreement, so any change to the terms of the contract can be made only with the consent of the employee(s) concerned. Courts have ruled that unilateral variation by the employer breaches the contract of employment. Consequently, any changes that are proposed by the employer should be discussed with the employees concerned. There should be genuine consultation whereby the employees views are listened to and responded to in a reasoned way. Such consultation may be with union representatives, non-union employee representatives or with individual employees (see later section on consultation). Such consultation, in most cases, can lead to agreement to change, i.e. consensual variation.

However, if there is no agreement to change, then an employer may give due notice to terminate existing contracts of employment and offer new ones which incorporate the changes. Such dismissals could be fair (see later section on dismissal). They could be on the grounds of redundancy or fall into the category of 'some other substantial reason for dismissal' as 'business need'. This approach could result in employment tribunal applications – although whether or not they would be successful would depend on the circumstances.

Changes can be made, particularly to certain working practices, as a result of flexibility built into the contract of employment itself. So, a contract might expressly include a mobility clause or flexible working hours. The implementation of such clauses should, however, not breach the implied term of mutual trust and confidence by, for example, requiring relocation at short notice to another part of the country.

In the context of change, the duty of the employee to obey the employer's lawful and reasonable instructions could be invoked. In a case involving the introduction of technological change, it was ruled that employees could reasonably be expected, after proper training, to adapt to new techniques. Computerisation would result in the jobs remaining 'recognisably the same but done in a different way' (Cresswell and others *v* Board of Inland Revenue [1984] IRLR 190).

Dealing with workplace grievances

Until 2000, there was no single source of guidance, in law, on the handling of individual grievances. That year the ACAS Code of Practice on Disciplinary and Grievance Procedures came into force. It is statutory, and breach of it can be taken into account in a case before an employment tribunal.

In addition to the code, there are five broad aspects of law that have a bearing on the handling of grievances. First, in the statement of initial employment particulars an employer should indicate the person to whom the employee can raise a grievance and any subsequent procedural steps (ERA 1996 ss1–4).

Secondly, it has been affirmed in case law (W.A. Goold *v* McConnell [1995] IRLR 516) that 'there was an implied term of the employee's contracts of employment that the company would reasonably and promptly afford a reasonable opportunity to them to obtain redress of any grievance they might have'. The employer's failure to provide adequate procedural redress was a fundamental breach of the contract.

Thirdly, the failure by an employer to deal with a bullying or harassment complaint would be a breach of mutual trust and confidence and so, a repudiatory breach of the contract of employment. Furthermore, harassment on the basis of sex, race or disability is also direct discrimination for which the employer is liable (see section on discrimination).

Finally, new provisions have been enacted to provide a statutory right to be accompanied in certain grievances (ERA 1999 s10). These provide that where a worker 'is required or invited by his employer to attend a . . . grievance hearing and reasonably requests to be accompanied at the hearing' then he or she may be so. The companion is chosen by the worker and is 'permitted to address the hearing (but not to answer questions on behalf of the worker' and is permitted 'to confer with the worker during the hearing'. The companion may be an employed official of a trade union, a lay union official 'whom the union has reasonably certified in writing as having experience of, or having received training in acting as a worker's companion', or a fellow worker. (Further guidance is in ACAS, 2000: section 3.)

Discipline and dismissal

Statute law has, over the past 30 years, created a framework of standards to limit the power of an employer to act in an arbitrary way when handling disciplinary and dismissal issues. Employees who have 12 months' continuous service have a right to complain of their dismissal to an employment tribunal. If, however, the dismissal is for an automatically unfair reason (see below), there is no qualifying period. If it finds a dismissal unfair, a tribunal may award compensation up to a maximum of £52,600 (2002); and also reinstatement or re-employment. In practice, the median compensation is £2,500; and re-employment is ordered in only 0.3 per cent of hearings (Department of Trade and Industry, 2001).

As a consequence of legal requirements, employers should:

- give reasons for a dismissal (an employee with 12 months' service is entitled to a written statement of reasons – ERA 1996 s92);
- approach disciplinary and dismissal issues reasonably;
- comply with the procedural standards set out in the ACAS Code of Practice on Disciplinary and Grievance Procedures.

The sole or principal reason for a dismissal should be a 'fair reason' (ERA 1996 s98), i.e. on one of the following grounds:

- *Capability or qualifications.* This can include medical capability, although consideration must be given to any implications of the Disability Discrimination Act 1995.
- *Conduct.* This encompasses persistent minor misconduct (e.g. poor attendance) and single acts of gross misconduct (e.g. violence, or drug or alcohol abuse).
- *Redundancy.* In brief, this arises when an employer ceases (or intends to cease) carrying on work that the employee was employed to do either at all or at the place where the employee works (ERA 1996 s139).
- *Statutory restriction.* This covers instances where continued employment in a particular job is rendered impossible because of a statutory restriction (e.g. when an employee who is required to drive is disqualified from driving).
- *Some other substantial reason.* This could cover, for example, the consequence of a criminal conviction for conduct outside work (ACAS, 2000: para. 26; see also earlier section on variation of contract).

In considering a dismissal complaint, an employment tribunal needs to be satisfied about the real reason for the dismissal. In particular, it would decide whether or not it was for an 'automatically unfair' reason. There are many instances in employment protection legislation of unfair reasons. The most notable examples arise under discrimination law. For example, it would be automatically unfair to dismiss an employee if the reason (or principal reason) was sex, pregnancy, race or disability.

When deciding on disciplinary penalties, employers are expected to behave reasonably in the circumstances (ACAS, 2000: para. 16). The code states that 'factors which might be relevant include, the extent to which standards have been breached, precedent, the worker's general record, position, length of service and special circumstances which might make it appropriate to adjust the severity of the penalty'. Taking account of such factors, an employer may choose (as appropriate) from a range of disciplinary penalties: formal oral warning, formal written warning, final written warning or dismissal (with or without notice).

In assessing the fairness of a dismissal, an employment tribunal is required to determine whether 'in the circumstances (including the size and administrative resources of the employer's undertaking)', the employer 'acted reasonably or unreasonably' in treating the reason for dismissal as 'a sufficient reason' (ERA 1996 s98(4)). The employer's view of the appropriateness of dismissal is significant. So, for example, the theft of a single loaf of bread by a shift manager in a bakery was determined to be a fair dismissal. The employer, in the circumstances of the business, was entitled to regard dismissal as a sufficient reason. The decision to dismiss fell within the range of 'reasonable responses' which an employer might adopt.

For handling workplace discipline, the ACAS code recommends that employers have disciplinary rules and a disciplinary procedure. Disciplinary rules would usually cover 'such issues as misconduct, sub-standard performance, harassment or victimisation, misuse of company facilities including computer facilities (e.g. e-mail and the Internet), poor timekeeping and unauthorised absences' (paras 5 and 7).

The essential detailed features of disciplinary procedures are outlined in the code (paras 8–9). A fundamental requirement is that they conform to the principle of natural justice.

> This means workers should be informed in advance of any disciplinary hearing of the allegations that are being made against them together with the supporting evidence and be given the opportunity of challenging the allegations and evidence before decisions are reached. Workers should also be given the rights of appeal against any decisions taken.

In addition, in disciplinary hearings where a formal warning or higher penalty is to be administrered, then, the worker is entitled to be accompanied (see above section on grievance procedures).

Wrongful dismissal

In essence, wrongful dismissal arises where the employer has unlawfully breached the contract of employment by terminating it otherwise than in conformity with its terms. Wrongful dismissal claims can be avoided by giving the employee due notice (or possibly pay in lieu of notice). The statutory minimum notice entitlement for employees increases with length of service (ERA 1996 s86). These claims can be defended if the employer can show that the employee fundamentally breached the contract of employment through, for example, gross misconduct.

An employee alleging wrongful dismissal has six years in which to claim damages for the breach of contract. Damages are to put the employee into the position he or she would have been in had the contract be properly performed. So, wages for the notice period together with lost commission and fringe benefits (including company car) can be claimed. The damages may be reduced to take account of tax and National Insurance contributions and wages earned from a new post in that period. A wrongful dismissal claim, associated with an unfair dismissal application to an employment tribunal, can be linked provided the sum in question is under £25,000 and submitted within three months of the dismissal.

Discrimination, equal opportunities and employment

Social purposes of discrimination law

The development of discrimination law over the past thirty years has been influenced by a number of factors – ethical, social, business and economic:

- social values about fair treatment and social concern about the divisiveness of prejudice and stereotyping (on the grounds of sex, race and disability);
- the increasing promotion of anti-discriminatory policies under EU social policy; and under the European Convention on Human Rights and Fundamental Freedoms 1950 (incorporated into British law under the Human Rights Act 1998);
- social recognition of other discriminatory treatment: on grounds, for example, of age, religion, sexuality, trans-sexual status;
- a recognition that atypical workers in the flexible labour market can experience less favourable treatment (e.g. part-time workers and fixed-term workers);
- the continued 'feminisation' of the labour market;
- the promotion of greater economic participation of under-represented groups;
- growing employer interest in the concept of managing diversity in respect employees and also its relevance for their diverse customer base;
- the ability of businesses to utilise human resources more effectively if their diverse interests and needs are, wherever possible, taken into account.

The grounds for discrimination

Discrimination is about choice. At various stages in the employment relationship choices are made, for example, in recruitment, promotion, access to training and access to benefits. Legislation tries to ensure that such decisions are made against objective criteria. So, for example, the grounds on which a person is refused employment would be capability, experience, education, etc. and not his or her race or sex. Legislation covers the following grounds for fair and unfair discrimination:

Sex discrimination

This covers the treatment of men and women, and also married women. The principal legislation is the Sex Discrimination Act 1975 and the Equal Pay Act 1970. The 1975 Act covers discrimination prior to employment, within employment and in the wider society. The 1970 Act deals with sex discrimination within the terms of contracts of employment. This legislation is founded on the following European Community law:

- Article 141 of the Treaty of Amsterdam, which specifies that there should be equal pay for equal work between the sexes;
- Equal Pay Directive 1975;
- Equal Treatment Directive 1976, which sets out the principle of equal treatment as between men and women.

European discrimination law has been used widely (often through cases in the European Court of Justice) to test women's rights as they increasingly participate in the labour market (see later sections on direct and indirect discrimination).

Race discrimination

This concerns the treatment of people on the grounds of colour, race, nationality or ethnic or national origin. The principal legislation is the Race Relations Act 1976 which also covers applications for employment, conditions within employment and wider social behaviour. It has been supplemented by the Race Relations (Amendment) Act 2000 which covers public authority functions not previously ruled to be unlawful. It also requires public authorities to promote race equality. In 2000, the Council of the European Union adopted a Race Discrimination Directive which will implement the principle of equal treatment between persons irrespective of racial or ethnic origin. The directive is to be implemented throughout the EU by July 2003.

Disability discrimination

The Disability Discrimination Act 1995 defines a disabled person as someone who has a physical or mental impairment which has a substantial and long-term adverse effect on his or her ability to carry out normal day-to-day activities. The employment provisions were implemented from 1996. The exclusion of employees working for small organisations was amended in 1998, reducing the threshold from 20 employees to 15. This exclusion will be rescinded in 2004.

Part-time workers

The Part-time Workers (Less Favourable Treatment) Regulations 2000 implement the 1997 European Directive concerning the Framework Agreement on Part-time Work (97/81/EC). In essence, a part-time worker should not be subject to less favourable treatment than a comparable full-time worker. He or she should receive pro-rata conditions.

Fixed-term workers

The 1999 European directive concerning the Framework Agreement on fixed-term work (1999/70/EC) is to be implemented by July 2002. Its purpose is to apply the principle on non-discrimination to those in fixed-term employment (in comparison with permanent workers) and to establish a framework to prevent abuse arising from the use of successive fixed-term contracts or employment relationships. Regulations are expected to be approved by the UK Parliament in 2002.

Other grounds

There are many other bases on which an employer might discriminate against an employee. In Northern Ireland, the Fair Employment and Treatment Order 1998 outlaws discrimination in employment on grounds of religious belief or political opinion. In 1999, following a ruling in the European Court of Justice, the Sex Discrimination Act was amended to outlaw discrimination on the grounds of trans-sexual status. In 2000, a new discrimination directive was adopted. It requires EU member states to implement domestic legislation outlawing discrimination on grounds of religion and sexuality (by 2003); and age and disability (by 2006) (see Chapter 6).

■ Key provisions in discrimination law

In this section the principal focus will be provisions arising under sex, race and disability discrimination law. The issues considered are: direct and indirect discrimination, objective justification, the duty to make a reasonable adjustments, genuine occupational qualification, victimisation, positive action, vicarious and individual liability, burden of proof, redress and remedies. (There are instances where in the interpretation of particular provisions the Sex Discrimination Act (SDA) and the Race Relations Act (RRA) are treated as a single body of law.)

Direct discrimination

Direct discrimination is less favourable treatment on the grounds of sex, race or disability. It arises, for example, when a woman is treated less favourably than a man (SDA 1976 s1(1)(a)). Courts have developed the *but for* test. The question to be asked is: would the complainant have received the same treatment from the defendant but for his or her sex? (James *v* Eastleigh Borough Council [1990] IRLR 288, HL). Direct sex discrimination has been construed to cover discrimination on the grounds of pregnancy (Dekker *v* Stichting Vormingscentrum [1991] IRLR 27, ECJ) and sexual harassment (Porcelli *v* Strathclyde Regional Council [1986] IRLR 134, Court of Session). As a consequence of the last case, racial harassment would now be considered direct racial discrimination.

Indirect discrimination

Until 2001, indirect discrimination was defined in the following terms under sex discrimination law (SDA 1975 s1(1)(b)). It arose when an employer applies to a woman a condition or requirement, which he would apply equally to a man, but the proportion of women who could comply in practice with the condition or requirement would be considerably smaller than the proportion of men who could comply. The woman in question suffers a detriment because she cannot comply. Examples of conditions or requirements that have been challenged as discriminatory on grounds of sex are age barriers, the requirement to work full-time, mobility conditions and length of continuous service. Each complaint is considered on its own merits to establish whether there was indirect discrimination. For the discrimination to be lawful, the employer must show the condition or requirement to be justifiable, irrespective of the sex of the person to whom it is applied.

Similar provisions exist in the Race Relations Act 1976, whereby a condition or requirement can be challenged as having a disproportionate effect on the ability of one particular racial group to comply in practice, and that the complainant has suffered a detriment. There is no concept of indirect discrimination under the Disability Discrimination Act 1995.

In conformity with new European law, the provisions relating to indirect sex discrimination have been amended under new regulations (SI 2001/2660) since October 2001. The principal change is that the definition of indirect discrimination covers 'a provision, criterion or practice' and the legislation states that this includes 'requirement or condition'. Consequently, the new law appears to be much wider in its coverage. This legislation does not formally change the concept of indirect racial discrimination. However, amendments may be made when the European Race Discrimination Directive 2000 is implemented in 2003.

Objective justification

This is a potential defence for employers when faced by a complaint of indirect sex or racial discrimination. Initially, various unsatisfactory attempts were made by courts to define it. Eventually, the European Court of Justice ruled that the objective standards of justification require that the employer has a real need and that the discriminatory action is necessary and appropriate to achieve that end (Bilka-Kaufhaus GmbH *v* Weber von Hartz [1986] IRLR 317). The court also affirmed the importance of the principle of proportionality in this context.

The duty to make adjustments

This provision arises only under the Disability Discrimination Act (DDA) 1995 (s6). The adjustments are designed to deal with situations where a disabled person is at a substantial disadvantage in comparison with persons who are not disabled. The adjustments must be *reasonable*. So, cost and practicality can be taken into account (s6(4)). Possible adjustments include modifications to equipment, altering working time, or changing the location of work (DDA 1995 s6(3)).

Genuine occupational qualification

Special provisions exist under sex and race discrimination law whereby it is possible to specify, in certain circumstances, that a postholder should be of a particular sex or racial group. Under the Sex Discrimination Act 1975 (s7), the grounds include authenticity, decency or privacy and the provision of personal services. Grounds under the Race Relations Act 1976 (s5) include authenticity and personal services promoting welfare of a particular racial group.

Victimisation

Sex, race and disability discrimination law provides protection against victimisation (SDA 1975 s4; RRA 1976 s2; DDA 1995 s55). Victimisation arises when a person is taking action against discrimination (whether at employment tribunal, giving evidence in such proceedings, or alleging that discrimination has taken place), and has been treated less favourably as a consequence of taking such action.

Positive action

Patterns of sex and race discrimination are historic and deep-seated. The purpose of positive action (SDA 1975 ss47–8; RRA 1976 s37) is to encourage groups that are under-represented in a workforce to apply for particular posts. It encompasses encouragement to apply for jobs and for promotion. It also covers access to training opportunities for under-represented groups.

Vicarious and individual liability

The employer, under sex, race and disability discrimination law, is vicariously liable for the behaviour of an employee, manager or supervisor. For example, under sex discrimination law, anything done by one of these 'in the course of his employment' is treated as being done by the employer as well as by the individual concerned 'whether or not it was done with the employer's knowledge or approval' (SDA 1976 s41(1)). The employer's defence would be to show that 'he took such steps as were reasonably practicable to prevent the employee from doing that (discriminatory) act' (s41(3)). Such steps could include access to an internal grievance procedure, clear and enforcing disciplinary rules about discriminatory conduct, and the implementation of non-discriminatory policies.

Parallel provisions are included in the Race Relations Act 1976 (s32(1)) and the Disability Discrimination Act 1995 (s58(1)). In one race discrimination case, the Court of Appeal ruled that the term 'in the course of employment' should be interpreted broadly in line with 'the natural meaning of those everyday words' (Jones *v* Tower Boot Co. Ltd [1997] IRLR 168. This construction now applies to all discrimination law.

Burden of proof

From October 2001, new regulations (transposing a 1997 European directive) were implemented (SI 2001/2660). In essence, the applicant before an employment tribunal or court must show, on the basis of primary facts, that discrimination has taken place. If the respondent employer fails to provide an adequate explanation for his or her behaviour, then the tribunal shall uphold the complaint drawing the inference that discrimination has taken place. The questionnaire procedure may help establish certain facts in support of an applicant's case. A complainant can serve such a questionnaire on an employer (SDA 1976 s74; RRA 1976 s65; DDA 1995 s56). (The Employment Bill 2001 proposes to extend this procedure to equal pay cases.)

Although this new legislation amends only sex discrimination law, it is likely to be extended as an approach to other discrimination law because it reflects the trends evident in previous case law (King v Great Britain–China Centre [1991] IRLR 513; Zafar v Glasgow City Council [1998] IRLR 36).

Redress and remedies

Applicants for employment, employees, workers and contractors are able to make claims of discriminatory treatment before an employment tribunal. There is no qualifying period of service for those with an employment relationship. Legislation sets out the remedies available to successful complainants (SDA 1975 s65; RRA 1976 s56; DDA 1995 s8) These are a declaration of rights, an award of compensation payable by the employer to the applicant, and recommendations of action that the employer might take in the context of the particular case. The calculation for compensation can include loss of earnings and future earnings and benefits. In addition, an award for injury to feelings may be made. Since 1993, there has been no upper limit on compensation. Median compensation in all discrimination cases is £5,231, and the median injury to feelings figure is £2,500 (Equal Opportunities Review No. 100, 2001).

Collective representation

Traditionally, in British employment relations, unions have been the principal vehicle for employee representation – certainly in collective bargaining. Although some employers did have non-union employee representatives, this was for consultation only. Under employment law, then, unions were the single channel of representation. With the gradual decline of union membership and recognition, a significant representation gap emerged as non-union patterns of employment relations developed. However, there has been a countervailing trend. European social policy measures, under the general promotion of social partnership, have influenced the creation of statutory non-union representation. These measures cover health and safety, collective redundancies, transfers of undertakings, and the development of information and consultation arrangements in certain multinational companies and also at workplace level in specified companies. (The details of these requirements are explored more fully in the later section on the processes of employment relations.) In this section, the general provisions of law relating to unions, union membership, union representatives and employee representatives are considered.

The legal status of unions

Under common law, in the nineteenth century, trade unions were unlawful organisations because they operated in restraint of trade. This doctrine, developed by judges, stated that it was unlawful to place unreasonable obstructions in the way of trade – whether that trade be trade in labour or trade in commodities. In effect, trade union purposes – to regulate the pay and conditions of employment of their members – were contrary to the lawful economic interests of employers.

Towards the end of the nineteenth century, politicians (of both Conservative and Liberal Parties), recognising the economic, social and political importance of the expanding urban working class, decided that, for pragmatic reasons, the legal status of trade unions should be clarified. In 1871, statute law established the legal principles on which present-day trade union law is founded. 'Immunities' were enacted. Parliament created immunity (a form of legal protection) from the doctine of restraint of trade. Consequently, unions are permitted to exist; to seek to regulate, in negotiation with employers, the terms and conditions of employment under which their members work; and to organise, in certain specified circumstances, industrial action. If unions act within this framework of law, then legal proceedings will not be taken against them. The current enactment of union immunities is in the Trade Union and Labour Relations (Consolidation) Act (TULRCA) 1992 (ss10–11).

Independent trade unions

The status of *independent* trade union was introduced in 1974 to discourage unions or staff associations that were under the control or undue influence of employers (TULRCA 1992 ss5–8). It complied with International Labour Organisation Conventions 87 on freedom of association and 98 on the right to organise and collective bargaining. Independence is determined by the Certification Officer who explores various aspects of the union: its history, membership, organisation and structure, finance, negotiating record and whether any facilities are provided by an employer. Independent unions have information and consultation rights in respect of health and safety, collective redundancies and transfers of undertakings. Furthermore they are entitled to obtain information which would be of assistance in collective bargaining.

Trade union membership and the law

The law provides a number of protections for individuals in respect of union membership:

- *Access to union membership.* Individuals have the right not to be excluded from membership by a union, and not to be expelled unless in permitted circumstances (e.g. the conduct of the member) (TULRCA 1992 ss174–7).
- *Access to employment.* It is unlawful for an employer to refuse a person employment because he or she: is not a member of a union, is unwilling to join or resign from a union, or is unwilling to make a contribution to charity (or anyone else) instead of union membership. This means that a job applicant's attitude to union membership is not relevant to recruitment into employment. This legislation, introduced in 1990, effectively outlaws the 'closed shop' (whereby trade union membership is a condition of employment) (TULRCA 1992 ss137–43).

■ *Discriminatory treatment.* It is unlawful to dismiss, threaten to dismiss or take action short of dismissal against an individual in the following circumstances: to prevent or deter the individual from becoming a member of an independent trade union; taking part at an appropriate time in union activities (this does not include industrial action); compelling membership of a particular union. An employee cannot be lawfully selected for redundancy because of union membership or non-membership or for participating in union activities (TULRCA 1992 ss146–67).

■ Trade union democracy and the law

One political debate in the 1970s and 1980s concerned the democratic practice of unions. Legislation enacted by the Conservative government tackled what were perceived to be abuses of power by union leaders and, according to the political rhetoric, 'gave unions back to their members'. The main legal requirements still in force are as follows:

■ A right for members to vote in secret and by post, usually every five years, in elections for the principal executive committee. This includes a right to vote for the union's general secretary and/or general president (TULRCA 1992 ss46–61).
■ A right to participate in a ballot on the establishment or continuance of a political fund. This money can be used for political campaigns (e.g. in favour of or against government economic or social policies), or in support of a particular political party (TULRCA 1992 ss71–81). The Certification Officer reported 38 unions with political funds (Certification Officer, 2001).
■ A range of legal requirements relating to the calling of industrial action (see section below).
■ Greater membership control over union financial affairs. Some of these provisions have existed, in various forms, since the nineteenth century; others are more recent. They include requirements to keep audited accounts; to provide information to members; and to spend money on proper purposes (TULRCA 1992 ss24–45).

■ Trade union representatives and the law

There are three categories of people who may represent members of an independent trade union. First are full-time officers of the trade union, who, usually, are responsible for members who work in a number of organisations in an area or district. These are paid employees of the union and are not covered by the statutory rights outlined in the rest of this section. Secondly, are the workplace officials of the union (often called staff representatives or shop stewards). Thirdly, there are union learning representatives who advise members about their training, education and development needs, often on a one-to-one basis.

Union workplace officials are entitled, where their union is recognised for collective bargaining purposes, to reasonable time off with pay during working hours to carry out certain trade union duties and to undergo relevant training (TULRCA 1992 ss168–9). The duties include: preparing for and participating in negotiations with managers, informing members about the progress of negotiations, involvement in European works councils, and dealing with grievances and disciplinary cases (see earlier section on the right to be accompanied). Pay when undertaking the duties should be what the representative would have earned had he/she been at work or average earnings calculated over a 12-week period. There is a statutory right for time off (only with pay if the employer agrees) for participation in the activities of a union. This would include attendance at conferences organised by the union where an employee might attend as a delegate. Detailed guidance on these rights are set out in the statutory Code of Practice No. 3 on Time off for Trade Union Duties and Activities (ACAS, 1997b).

Union learning representatives currently are not covered by these statutory protections. Under new legislative proposals (Employment Bill 2001), the government aims to include these 3,000 representatives under the existing time-off provisions and to protect them from breaches of their rights.

Non-union employee representatives and the law

In the early 1990s, infraction proceedings brought against the British government, before the European Court of Justice, resulted in a judgment that consultation legislation on redundancies and transfers of undertakings had not been fully implemented (Commission of the European Communities *v* UK [1994] IRLR 392).

One particular shortcoming was the failure to extend the duty to consult to non-union organisations: the right of representation was restricted to recognised independent trade unions. British law was changed and again amended in 1999, so non-union employee representatives now exist under law. There are five circumstances in which it is possible to have such representatives: consultation about health and safety, collective redundancies, transfers of undertakings, in respect of a European works council (in a multinational company that is non-unionised), and where workforce agreements on working time or parental leave are negotiated.

The law on health and safety provides for two principal systems of employee representation: through independent recognised trade unions (Safety Representatives and Safety Committees Regulations 1977), and an employee representative system (Health and Safety (Consultation with Employees) Regulations 1996). The functions of union representatives include investigation of potential hazards and dangerous occurrences, investigating complaints, carrying out specified inspections, and making representations to the employer. The functions of non-union employee representatives are much briefer and identify a range of representational functions. There are protections against victimisation (TULCRA 1992 s146; ERA 1996 s44) and dismissal (ERA 1996 s100).

As far as redundancies and transfers of undertakings are concerned, appropriate employee representatives could be either those already elected by the workforce to consult with the employer, or employee representatives specifically elected to consult about these issues. If a union is recognised for the workforce affected by the redundancies or the transfer, then its representatives must be consulted.

The legislation provides detailed election arrangements for these employee representatives. The employer must ensure that the election is fair. It determines the number of representatives and must make sure that the interests of all affected employees are covered. Also, the employer decides the term of office of the representatives and that candidates for election are employees affected by either the redundancy or the transfer. The voting must be, as far as is reasonably practicable, in secret, and the votes must be accurately counted (TULRCA 1992 ss188–188A; Transfer of Undertaking (Protection of Employment) (TUPE) Regulations 1981 reg. 10A). These representatives are entitled to reasonable time off work with pay to carry out their duties (ERA 1996 ss61–3), and are protected against victimisation and dismissal (ERA 1996 s103).

Broadly similar provisions are indicated for the election and protection of representatives negotiating workforce agreements in respect of working time and parental leave (Working Time Regulations 1998 Schedule 1; Maternity and Parental Leave Regulations 1999 regs 19–20 Schedule 1; ERA 1996 ss45A, 101A).

Finally, under the Transnational Information and Consultation of Employees Regulations 1999, rights are provided for three categories: a member of a special negotiating body or European works council, an information and consultation representative, and a candidate in an election for such positions. There is an entitlement to reasonable time off from work with pay to perform the functions of the post. Pay is determined at the appropriate hourly rate. There is also protection against victimisation and dismissal.

The processes of employment relations

In this section, the two principal collective processes of employment relations are considered: bargaining and consultation. Statute law has increasingly, over the past few years, developed a framework of legal requirements. Some of these initiatives derive from European social policy (in particular the duties to consult) whereas the law on trade union recognition is homegrown.

■ Collective bargaining

Patterns of union membership and recognition are detailed in Chapter 4. These reflect both the consequence of almost two decades of public policy designed to marginalise the trade union movement from any effective participation in employment relations, and also the changes taking place in the British economy, resulting in the structural decline of trade union heartlands (e.g. the manufacturing sector). Clearly, the trade union movement has been concerned to recover its situation and to facilitate membership growth and recognition in new companies and industries. It was successful, to some degree, in gaining the commitment of the incoming Labour government (in 1997) to the principle of statutory recognition for collective bargaining.

Voluntary and statutory recognition arrangements

Traditionally, recognition of a union by an employer for collective bargaining has been a voluntary decision (although there were two periods when a statutory scheme existed: 1971–4 and 1975–80). In June 2000, a new system was enacted. It is operated under the auspices of the Central Arbitration Committee.

In law, there are three broad aspects to this issue: the definitions of collective agreements and collective bargaining; the meaning of recognition; and the process of statutory recognition. 'Collective agreement' means 'any agreement or arrangement made by or on behalf of one or more trade unions and one or more employers or employers' associations' (TULRCA 1992 s178(1)). It relates to one or more of a range of matters (see below). 'Collective bargaining' means negotiations relating to or connected with one or more of these matters. They cover both the substantive and procedural aspects of employment relations (TULRCA 1992 s178(2)):

- terms and conditions of employment;
- engagement or non-engagement, or termination or suspension of employment or the duties of employment of workers;
- allocation of work or the duties of employment between workers;
- matters of discipline;
- a worker's membership or non-membership of a trade union;
- facilities for officials of trade unions (i.e. staff representatives or shop stewards);
- machinery for negotiation and consultation and other procedures (e.g. grievance and discipline), and recognition by the employer of the right of a union to represent workers.

Recognition, in relation to a trade union, is defined as 'recognition of the union by an employer, or two or more associated employers, to any extent, for the purpose of collective bargaining' (TULRCA 1996 s178(3)).

The statutory recognition process

Government aims to promote voluntary recognition agreements between employers and unions. The statutory procedure is for circumstances where such agreement is not possible. Indeed, the Advisory, Conciliation and Arbitration Service (ACAS) commented that, 'overwhelmingly, employers and trade unions have taken a non-confrontational, voluntary approach to reaching agreement on recognition, in preference to using the new statutory powers. This is borne out by the relatively small number of applications (57) that have been made to the Central Arbitration Committee (CAC) to date, as compared to the considerable increase in recognition conciliations dealt with by ACAS (357 between April 2000 and March 2001)' (ACAS Annual Report 2001; CAC Annual Report 2001).

The statutory process covers employers with more than 20 workers. It is a complex process with a number of stages, most which have time limits. The essential elements are as follows:

- *Formal request for recognition.* This is made in writing by an independent union indicating the group of workers for whom recognition is sought (i.e. the bargaining unit). (It is hoped, possibly with assistance from the Trades Union Congress, that competing recognition claims by unions would be resolved beforehand.)
- *Employer's response.* This might take one of three forms: (1) agreement to the union's claim, in which case the statutory recognition process ends; (2) a willingness by the employer to discuss details of the union's request and, possibly with the assistance of ACAS, reach a voluntary agreement; (3) a refusal by the employer, resulting in a union application to the CAC.
- *CAC responsibilities.* There are two initial responsibilities. First, to determine whether the union-proposed bargaining unit is appropriate and if not, to specify an appropriate one. Secondly, to determine whether the union is supported by a majority of employees in the appropriate bargaining unit. This may involve scrutiny of union membership records or arranging an independent secret ballot. Guidance is provided by the Secretary of State for Trade and Industry, in the statutory Code of Practice on Access to Workers during Recognition and Derecognition Ballots (2000).

- *Recognition declared.* A union will be declared, by the CAC, as recognised provided a majority of those voting and 40 per cent of those eligible to vote support recognition. The parties, then, have a negotiation period of 30 days to agree a method by which they will conduct collective bargaining (i.e. a procedural agreement).
- *Failure to agree.* If there is a failure to agree, the CAC must specify the method by which they are to conduct collective bargaining. The Secretary of State for Trade and Industry has issued a model *Method of Conducting Collective Bargaining* which the CAC must take into account when specifying a method. This method will have effect as a legally enforceable contract. If the employer fails to abide by the contract, then a court can order specific performance. Failure to comply with this order can result in contempt of court proceedings.

Supports for collective bargaining

Collective bargaining, whether deriving from a voluntary agreement or as a result of the statutory recognition scheme, cannot exist effectively without some accompanying statutory support. This falls into two categories: disclosure of information, and facilities for representatives.

First is access to relevant information about bargaining issues. An employer who recognises an independent trade union, has a duty to disclose certain information. This relates to the employer's undertaking and without which the union representative would be 'to a material extent impeded in carrying on collective bargaining'. It is information which should be disclosed in accordance with good employment practice (TULRCA 1992 ss181–2). This means that information about pay, conditions of service, staffing, financial indicators, etc. should be provided. There are exemptions covering information that would, for example, be contrary to the interests of national security, was confidential or would cause substantial injury to the employer's undertaking. A statutory code of practice, Disclosure of Information to Trade Unions for Collective Bargaining Purposes (ACAS, 1997a) provides detailed guidance.

Secondly, there is the provision of facilities for representatives. These include statutory provisions for reasonable time off for trade union officials to undertake their duties and relevant training (see earlier section).

The law and collective agreements

There are two aspects to this: the influence of discrimination law on the provisions of collective agreements, and the legal status of such agreements.

Discrimination law, directly and indirectly, affects the content of collective agreements. The Sex Discrimination Act 1986 s6 rules as void any collective agreements that are discriminatory. The equality clause (Equal Pay Act 1970 s1) must also affect the substantive provisions of collective agreements. Likewise, under race discrimination law, it is unlawful for an employer to discriminate against an employee in the terms of employment offered (RRA 1976 s4(2)(a)). By extension, the provisions of a collective agreement which become terms of a contract of employment could also be unlawfully discriminatory. Disability law states that 'any term in a contract of employment or other agreement is void' if it contravenes the employment provisions of the law (DDA 1995 s9(1)). However, the Disability Code of Practice (1996) states that a less favourable contract may be justified if there is 'material and substantial reason' and no reasonable adjustment can be made (para. 5.28).

As far as their legal status, collective agreements are 'conclusively presumed not to have been intended by the parties to be a legally enforceable contract' (TULRCA 1992 s179). They are presumed to be voluntary agreements. If the parties wish them to be legally enforceable, the agreement must be in writing and it should contain a provision stating their intention. It is extremely rare for an employer and union(s) to do this. Both parties prefer the flexibility that a voluntary agreement confers.

Usually, there is only one way in which the substantive terms of a collective agreement have any legal force. This is by incorporation into an individual employee's contract of employment. Those provisions of a collective agreement that are appropriate to the individual (e.g. relating to pay, hours, holidays, etc.) become terms of the contract of employment.

■ Workforce agreements

European social policy emphasises the concept of social partnership between employers and their workforce (see Chapter 6). Collective bargaining is seen as an instrument for implementing certain directives, principally, the Working Time Directive 1993 and the Parental Leave Directive 1996. The first confers flexibility on employers to negotiate certain terms and conditions that are appropriate to their own organisation's circumstances. However, given the considerable shrinkage in union recognition and the reduced coverage of collective bargaining, the British government faced a difficulty in transposing these directives into domestic law and so providing this flexibility. It was resolved with the introduction of the workforce agreement (Working Time Regulations 1998 and Maternity and Parental Leave Regulations 1999). Such an agreement can only be made where there is no collective agreement in force covering a specific group of workers.

A workforce agreement must satisfy a number of conditions:

- It must be in writing.
- It is effective for a specified period not exceeding five years.
- It applies either to all relevant members of the workforce or to a particular group within the workforce.
- It is signed by representatives of the workforce. (If the employer employs 20 or fewer workers, it can be signed by a majority of the relevant workforce.)
- Before the agreement is signed, the employer must provide all the workers to whom it is intended to apply with copies of the text of the agreement.

Under the Working Time Regulations 1998, a workforce agreement (or a union-negotiated collective agreement) can be used to 'modify or exclude the application' of parts of the regulations relating to the following issues: the length of night work, night work involving special hazards, daily rest, the weekly rest period, rest breaks, and the maximum weekly working time (reg. 23).

A workforce agreement under the Maternity and Parental Leave Regulations 1999 can improve upon the key provisions. So, with parental leave, it can specify the notice to be given to the employer, the arrangements to be made for the postponing of the leave, and how the leave should be taken (whether in one-week blocks or on some other basis).

Duties to consult

In recent years, various piecemeal duties to consult have been enacted. Most have derived from European legislation, promoting social dialogue (see Chapter 6). To date, there has been no coherent approach to consultation. However, a proposed new directive on workplace-level information and consultation (adopted by the European Council of Ministers and the European Parliament in March 2002) may provide the basis for future rationalisation (see below). The likely significance of this directive is greater for Britain and Ireland than for other member states which already have works council structures. The long-term consequences for Britain are twofold. First, the need to accommodate the new consultation structures with existing collective bargaining arrangements (where these exist). Secondly, the potential expansion of a collective consultation into non-union organisations.

Defining consultation

It has been shown in many academic studies that consultation is a slippery concept. In some cases, it has been characterised as 'pseudo-consultation', i.e. little more than information disclosure before management makes its own decision. In law, there have been various attempts to define the process. In one case, concerning redundancies in coalmining, Lord Justice Glidewell stated that: 'fair consultation involves giving the body consulted a fair and proper opportunity to understand fully the matters about which it is being consulted and to express its views on those subjects, with the consultor thereafter considering those views properly and genuinely' (R v Britsh Coal Corporation and Secretary of State for Trade and Industry *ex parte* Price [1994] IRLR 72). Such consultation depends on access to relevant information, so the statutory duties to consult have companion provisions relating to information disclosure.

Attempts to promote genuine consultation or social dialogue are found in the existing piecemeal legislation. In respect of collective redundancies and transfers of undertakings, consultation should be 'with a view to reaching agreement' (TULRCA 1992 s188; TUPE Regulations 1981 reg. 10). The TUPE Regulations go further and state that 'the employer shall (a) consider any representations made by the appropriate representatives; and (b) reply to those representations and, if he rejects any of those representations, state his reasons' (reg. 10).

The Directive on Information and Consultation (2002) aims to make consultation meaningful. First, it states that information shall be given 'at such time, in such fashion and with such content' to enable employee representatives to conduct adequate study and, where necessary, prepare for consultation. Secondly, it sees such consultation as:

- enabling employee representatives to meet with the employer and obtaining a response, including reasons for the response, to any opinion the representatives might formulate;
- taking place 'with a view to reaching agreement' on decisions within the scope of the employer's powers.

The Health and Safety at Work Act 1974 specifies certain expectations about the outcomes of the consultation process. It identifies a general duty upon every employer to consult with union or employee representatives, 'with a view to the making and maintenance of arrangements which will enable him and his employees to co-operate effectively in promoting and developing measures to ensure the health and safety at work of the employees and in checking the effectiveness of such measures' (s2(6)).

The European Works Council Directive 1994 describes consultation as 'the exchange of views and the establishment of dialogue between employees' representatives and central management or any more appropriate level of management' (Art. 2). This is reflected in the Transnational Information and Consultation of Employees Regulations 1999.

Against this background, then, the specific legislative provisions are considered.

Health and safety consultation

Consultation is central to health and safety law. In 1977, a system of union-based workplace representatives were appointed specifically to promote a model of work-place-level self-regulation for implementing effective health and safety standards. The representation gap in non-union organisations was plugged in 1996 to ensure full compliance with European law.

The Health and Safety at Work Act 1974 s2(2) sets a general duty on employers 'to provide such information . . . as is necessary to ensure, as far as is reasonably practicable, the health and safety at work of his employees'. There are requirements, under the 1977 and 1996 Regulations to disclose relevant information to union and employee representatives. This would include information on risk assessments and protective measures that could be taken. The Safety and Health of Workers at Work Directive 1989 extends the possibility of consultation from existing work practices to prospective changes. It states that employers shall 'ensure that the planning and introduction of new technologies are the subject of consultation with workers and/or their representatives, as regards the consequences of the choice of equipment, the working conditions and the working environment for the safety and health of workers' (Art. 6(3)(c)).

Consultation on collective redundancies

A duty to consult arises where 'an employer is proposing to dismiss as redundant twenty or more employee at one establishment . . .' (TULRCA 1992 s188(1)). Where the employer is proposing to dismiss 100 or more employees, the consultation should take place at least 90 days before the dismissal and, in other cases, at least 30 days. The employer may claim exemption from the duty to consult if there are 'special circumstances which render it not reasonably practicable for the employer to comply' (s188(7)). An example might be the immediate closure of an organisation. Generally, an employer should take 'all such steps towards compliance' that are reasonably practicable.

The consultation 'shall begin in good time . . . before the first of the dismissals takes effect' (s188(1A)) and should be with a view to reaching agreement with the union or employee representatives. The consultation should include consideration about ways of avoiding the dismissals, reducing the numbers of employees to be dismissed, and reducing the consequences of the dismissals.

The employer must disclose in writing (s188(4)) the following information to employee representatives:

- the reasons for the proposed redundancies;
- the numbers and descriptions of the employees it is proposed to dismiss as redundant;
- the total number of employees of any such description employed by the employer at the establishment in question;
- the proposed method of selecting the employees for redundancy. Employers are increasingly moving away from the last-in first-out principle to one assessing individual employee performance. Any selection criteria must be fair under discrimination law;
- the proposed method of carrying out the dismissals, with due regard to any agreed procedure, including the period over which the dismissals are to take effect;
- the proposed method of calculating any redundancy payments for dismissed employees that are in excess of the statutory minimum.

Transfers of undertakings

The duty on the relevant employers to consult is potentially wide-ranging. A transfer of staff between employers affects two organisations: the transferor (which is shedding the staff) and the transferee (which is acquiring them). So, the duty to consult is placed on both.

The employers of any affected employees must inform representatives 'long enough' before a relevant transfer of the following (reg. 10(2)):

- that the relevant transfer is to take place;
- its approximate timing;
- the reasons for the transfer;
- legal, economic and social implications of the transfer for the affected employees;
- measures which, in connection with the transfer, the employer envisages taking in relation to the affected employees;
- if no measures are envisaged, then that should be indicated;
- information from the transferee about measures (if any) affecting those employees to be transferred.

Among the measures that might be considered are permitted dismissals for 'an economic, technical or organisational reason entailing changes in the workforce of either the transferor or the transferee before or after a relevant transfer' (reg. 8).

Transnational information and consultation

The purpose of the European Works Council (EWC) Directive 1994 (implemented through the Transnational Information and Consultation of Employees Regulations 1999) is to improve the right to information and to promote consultation in specified Community-scale undertakings or groups of undertakings. In essence, this refers to multinational companies (irrespective of national origin) that operate within the EU (and the European Economic Area). A relevant undertaking has a total of a least 1,000 employees within these member states, including at least 150 employees in each of two or more member states (Art. 2).

The issues to be discussed in the EWC or information and consultation procedure include: the economic position of the company, investment plans, product market and sales information, technological change, restructuring, and research and development. The agenda is generally drafted by management. Generally, EWCs meet in plenary session for one day a year.

Workplace information and consultation

In March 2002, the European Council of Ministers adopted a new Directive on Information and Consultation. It is to establish minimum requirements for private and public sector employers. It will cover 'undertakings' with at least 50 employees in one member state (or 'establishments' of at least 20 employees in one member state). It is to be implemented within three years from adoption. Smaller companies will have a further time to comply. In the UK, full implementation will be by March 2008. Companies are required to consult workers on all significant decisions, including restructuring, substantial changes in work organisation and contractual relations, and implications for employment. Also, workers must be informed about the organisation's economic situation. Companies have the right to protect con-fidential information.

Failures to consult

Remedies are available through complaint to an employment tribunal for an employer's failure to consult. Under collective redundancy legislation, if the complaint is well-founded, the tribunal will make a declaration and may also make a protective award (TULRCA 1992 ss189–90). The maximum is 90 days' pay for each affected employee. Pay is set (at February 2002) at £250 per week (ERA 1996 ss220–9). In relation to transfer of undertakings, the tribunal will make a declaration and may award compensation of upto a maximum of thirteen weeks' actual pay (TUPE Regulations 1981 reg. 11).

Different procedures exist for failures under the Transnational Information and Consultation of Employees Regulations 1999. Disputes about the failure of the organisation's central management to establish an information and consultation procedure, or to operate such a procedure appropriately, can be referred to the Employment Appeals Tribunal (EAT). The EAT has the power to order the central management to establish a works council or information and consultation procedure. It also can issue, as appropriate, a penalty notice. The amount of the penalty is up to a maximum of £75,000. The EAT will take into account: the gravity of the failure, the period of time over which the failure occurred, the reason for the failure, the number of employees affected by the failure, and the number of employees of the Community-scale undertaking or the Community-scale group of undertakings in the member states (reg. 22).

The directive on informing and consulting employees requires member states to implement sanctions for non-compliance. It states that adequate administrative or judicial procedures should be available to ensure compliance and that member states should provide for adequate penalties in the case of infringment, which must be 'effective, proportionate and dissuasive'.

Industrial conflict

Individual workers and industrial action

For individual workers, participation in industrial action makes them particularly vulnerable. They may lose pay – certainly if they are on strike – and they may be liable to instant dismissal. There is some limited statutory protection against dismissal but it goes no way towards creating a right to take industrial action. A worker is free to take such action, but he or she must accept certain legal and practical consequences.

Breach of contract

An individual who takes part in industrial action will probably breach his or her contract of employment. A strike – where the employee performs no work – is a repudiatory breach of the employment contract. Until recently, it has been possible for the employer to dismiss strikers instantly – although, for practical reasons, few did so. In 2000, some improved protection against dismissal was enacted (see next section).

Industrial action short of a strike – involving refusal to comply with certain terms of the contract – can, in law, present difficulties. Usually, in these cases, some work is carried out for the employer and the breach of contract is not regarded as fundamental. It is likely to be a refusal to comply with the implied contractual term of obeying lawful and reasonable instructions. In one Court of Appeal case in the early 1970s, involving a work-to-rule by train drivers, Lord Buckley said that, 'I have no hestitation in implying a term into the contract of service that each employee will not, in obeying his lawful instructions, seek to obey them in a wholly unreasonable way . . . I prefer to rest my decision that work to rule is a breach of contract on this ground' (Secretary of State for Employment *v* ASLEF (No. 2) [1972] 2 All ER 949).

A refusal to comply with non-contractual terms might seem a safer form of industrial action for employees. But there are uncertainties. For example, in the 1980s some schoolteachers refused to undertake lunchtime supervision of pupils and to attend out-of-hours meetings. The contract of employment was silent on these issues. However, Mr Justice Scott asserted that, 'it is, in my view, a professional obligation of each teacher to cooperate in running the school during school hours in accordance with the timetable and other administrative regulations or directions from time to time made or given' (Sim *v* Rotherham Metropolitan Borough Council [1986] IRLR 391). Nowadays, the view of most academic commentators is that, with the possible exception of refusals to work voluntary overtime, all forms of industrial action will be a breach of contract.

Employers may impose one of two sanctions in response to industrial action: dismissal of the employee or withholding all or part of the employee's pay.

Dismissal and industrial action

The law on dismissal for participating in industrial action covers three sets of circumstances: where the industrial action is official and protected, where it is official and unprotected, and where it is unofficial and unprotected (TULRCA 1992 ss237–9).

In relation to the first category, legislation (from April 2000) gave employees some protection against dismissal in 'protected industrial action'. Such industrial action has to be lawful. This is determined by reference to the law on trade union immunities (see below). It also has to be officially supported by the union's principal executive committee in accordance with the union's own rulebook.

The protection covers three sets of circumstances:

- Dismissals taking place *during* an eight-week period, starting on the day the employee began to participate in the protected industrial action.

- Dismissals taking place *after* the eight-week period and where the employee had stopped participating in the protected industrial action before the end of the eight-week period.
- Dismissals taking place *after* the eight-week period and the employee continues to take part in the industrial action. However, the employer has not taken 'such procedural steps as would have been reasonable for the purposes of resolving the dispute to which the protected industrial action relates' (TULRCA 1992 s238A(5)). (These procedural steps would be in the appropriate collective agreement between the employer and the union(s) and could include an offer to restart negotiations, or the use of conciliation or mediation services.)

It is automatically unfair to sack an employee for taking part in protected industrial action. A complaint can be made to an employment tribunal with six months of the dismissal, irrespective of the applicant's age or length of service with the employer. If the tribunal finds the dismissal unfair, it can award compensation and also, if the protected industrial action is finished, reinstatement or re-engagement.

Where the industrial action is official and unprotected, the employer has to dismiss all relevant employees and an employment tribunal would not have jurisdiction to hear unfair dismissal claims. The only exception to this is where the employer selectively dismisses certain employees (e.g. union workplace representatives or other leading supporters of the industrial action). These individuals would be eligible to make a complaint. Where the industrial action is *unofficial* (not supported by the union) then there are no protections against selective dismissals.

Pay deduction

For the individual employee, a second important consequence of participation in industrial action is the likelihood of pay deduction. Legislation protecting employees against unlawful pay deduction does not cover such deductions. Employers are entitled to make them (ERA 1996 s14(5))

In the context of a strike, the principle of 'no work, no pay' usually prevails. The situation is, however, more complex in relation to industrial action short of a strike. Here, the issue is whether the employer accepts or rejects the partial performance of the contract of employment.

The issue of 'rejected partial performance' was considered in a Court of Appeal case, Wiluszynski *v* London Borough of Tower Hamlets [1989] ICR 493. Lord Justice Fox set out some important principles:

- Employees cannot pick and choose what work they do under their contract of employment.
- An employee could not refuse to comply with his contract and then demand pay.
- An employer, having told an employee (as a result of his partial performance) that he was not required to attend work and that if he did so it would be on a purely voluntary basis, could not, if he did attend, give him directions to work and at the same time not pay him.

A later Court of Appeal case (British Telecommunications plc *v* Ticehurst [1992] IRLR 219) enhanced an employers' powers. It was stated that two managers could be sent home without pay because they refused to sign an undertaking to work according to their contracts of employment. The court ruled that managers' contracts contained an implied term requiring them to further their employer's interests. Participation in a concerted withdrawal of goodwill was a breach of this term.

There have been instances where employers have accepted partial performance of contracts of employment. The difficulty here, for the employer, is calculating the amount of pay to be deducted for non-performance of particular tasks. Often rough justice prevails. In one case, a schoolteacher refused to accept into his class of thirty-one pupils another five. However, he carried out all his other contracted duties including out-of-school activities. This was ruled to be part-performance of his contract and he suffered a deduction of 5/36 of his salary over the relevant period. The deduction represented 'the notional value of the services not rendered' (Royle *v* Trafford Borough Council [1984] IRLR 184).

Trade unions and industrial action

Breach of contract

When a trade union calls upon its members to take part industrial action, it is, in law, inducing or encouraging a breach of their contracts of employment. In addition, the union is likely to be interfering with commercial contracts between the employer (for whom their members work) and other companies. Under the common law of tort, it is unlawful to induce a breach of contract or interfere with their performance – or to threaten to do this. These are economic torts (or wrongs). Unions are, then, liable for the economic injury caused.

Immunities

Statute law, enacted originally in the nineteenth century, provides some protection for unions from the legal consequences of inducing such breaches of employment and commercial contracts. It is founded on the principle of immunities from action under common law. The scope of these immunities was narrowed during the period of the Thatcher governments (1979–90). At the heart of this protective legislation is 'the golden formula'. So, if the industrial action is 'in contemplation or furtherance of a trade dispute' (TULRCA 1992 s219), it will not form the basis of legal proceedings against the union for breach of contract or threats to breach contracts.

Current law, in effect, specifies a number of questions to that need to be considered.

- *Is there a trade dispute, and has the industrial action been called 'in contemplation or furtherance of that trade dispute'?* A lawful trade dispute must be between workers and their own employer. Secondly, it must be wholly or mainly about employment-related matters (e.g. pay, conditions of employment, jobs, allocation of work, discipline, negotiating machinery) (TULRCA 1992 s244). Secondary (or sympathetic) industrial action, directed against an employer other than the workers' own, is unlawful. However, given the complexity of some corporate structures, it is sometimes difficult to distinguish who is the ultimate employer (i.e. the real decision-maker). The outlawing of secondary action can, in certain circumstances, weaken the effectiveness of industrial action.

■ *Is the trade dispute about trade union membership?* Lawful industrial action is possible on this issue. However, there are certain prohibitions. Such industrial action cannot be used to prevent an employer using non-union labour; to pressurise a contractor, used by the employer of a unionised workforce, to recognise, negotiate with and consult with a union; to pressurise an employer to establish or maintain a 'closed shop' practice; to prevent an employer from dismissing an employee who has been sacked for participating in unofficial industrial action.

■ *Has an individual secret ballot of relevant union members been held to approve the industrial action?* Immunity for the union calling the industrial action is conditional upon approval having been given by a majority of members in a ballot (TULRCA 1992 s226). If there is no approval and the union fails to comply with the detailed prescriptions of the code of practice, the industrial action would be unlawful under the Department of Trade and Industry's Code of Practice on Industrial Action and Notice to Employers (2000).

■ *Is picketing in support of the industrial action lawful?* Picketing is lawful if it is 'in contemplation or furtherance' of a lawful trade dispute and takes place at or near a person's place of work . It must also be for the purpose of peacefully obtaining information or communicating information to persuade another person to work or not to work (TULRCA 1992 s220). Criminal law may be invoked if the pickets commit public order offences. Detailed guidance is provided in the Department of Trade and Industry's Code of Practice on Picketing (1992).

Remedies

Those who are economically 'injured' by unlawful industrial action can take action in the courts. Normally, the injured party would be an employer. The most common course of action is for the employer to seek, in the High Court, an injunction to require the union to stop the unlawful industrial action. It is also possible for an employer to apply for damages. The scale of these is linked to the size of the union. The maximum amount available is £250,000.

Chapter summary

This chapter began by identifying a number of important themes:

■ the balance of power within the employment relationship, which generally favours the employer;
■ the methods for regulating the employment relationship through the contract of employment, statute law and collective agreements;
■ the effectiveness of these methods of regulation.

This summary attempts to assess the contribution that employment law makes to creating some equilibrium in the employment relationship between employer and employee.

On the one hand, it is possible to argue that legislation has introduced some positive provisions. First, the contract of employment, as a regulatory instrument, has been sufficiently and beneficially modified by statute law. What was in essence a contractual relationship built on an economic transaction (i.e. providing work and performing work) has increasingly been clothed in certain social values: fairness, reasonableness and non-discriminatory treatment. Minimum standards have been set for most basic terms and conditions of employment. Minimum procedural standards and requirements are increasingly being specified for the conduct of employment relations.

Secondly, the collective power of employees continues to be enhanced by legislation on consultation and trade union recognition. Thirdly, various statutory agencies have been created with responsibility for overseeing important pieces of employment legislation and ensuring their effective implementation. Among these are the Equal Opportunities Commission, the Commission for Racial Equality, the Disability Rights Commission, the Health and Safety Commission, and the Low Pay Commission. Finally, the employment tribunal system provides a means for individuals to complain about infringements of statutory rights.

On the other hand, it is possible to argue that, despite the accumulation of individual statutory rights, the balance of the employment relationship still favours the employer. Certainly, employer compliance with employment law is variable. Some, mostly larger employers, aim at employment policies and practices that promote standards of good employment practice and may even exceed statutory minimum employment standards. However, at the other extreme, some organisations persist with exploitative and arbitrary employment practices. (Many of these have been recorded in surveys of the National Association of Citizens Advice Bureaux.) In between there are many employers who adopt an approach of minimum compliance.

It might be thought that the right of complaint to employment tribunal provides some safeguard for aggrieved employees. Technically, this may be so. However, there are some limitations:

- a qualifying period of one year's continuous service to claim (for example, unfair dismissal);
- the restriction of some key employment rights (unfair dismissal, maternity and parental leave) to employees;
- the need to have the resources and stamina to take a case through the tribunal process – with or without representation;
- the character of the tribunal process, which has shifted from its orginal conception as an informal, speedy and relatively non-legalistic forum to one that can take considerable time and may be quite legalistic (for example, if the complaint is about discrimination, equal pay or transfers of undertakings);
- the paucity of the likely remedies. Compensation levels are generally low (see earlier sections) and re-employment in unfair dismissal claims is unlikely to be effective.

A realistic overall assessment is that progress is being made in establishing both decent terms and conditions of employment and fair procedures. However, it would be a mistake to see the mere existence of such a body of employment law as evidence of widespread employer compliance.

Questions

1 To what extent does the contract of employment provide protection for an employee?

2 To what extent is discrimination law effective in tackling prejudice and stereotyping in employment, and in promoting equal opportunities in the workplace?

3 How effective is the statutory right on unfair dismissal in achieving its purposes?

4 How effective is the duty to consult which is imposed upon employers in certain specific situations?

5 What are the arguments for and against the recognition of a trade union for collective bargaining?

6 Is it true to say that Britain has a 'right to strike'?

7 Are the procedures to enforce statutory rights, through employment tribunals and statutory agencies (e.g. ACAS and the Equal Opportunities Commission), sufficient to provide redress for individual claimants?

8 What contribution has the social policy of the EU made to British employment law?

Activity

Cashbrokers plc has just lost an employment tribunal case where an ex-employee had alleged sex and race discrimination and unfair constructive dismissal. The circumstances were as follows.

Some weeks after Indira Patel joined the administrative staff of Cashbrokers plc she began to be harassed by another employee in the department, Steve Bradshaw. After she had turned him down for a date, he repeatedly made remarks of a suggestive or sexual nature which she found offensive. Her initial complaint to the departmental manager, Mr Watson, was generally dismissive. He said, 'Don't worry. It's just Steve's way of trying to help you settle in.' However, the harassment continued. When Indira told him to stop it, he made some comment that 'you Asian girls are all the same'.

Indira felt anxious about the situation. There was no system of harassment advisers or any recognised trade union. She was uncertain about whom she could turn to for help. Her friend, Trish, who had worked for the company for three years, said that she should complain to her boss. She told Indira that 'many of the women in the office are fed up with all this laddish behaviour. They think they can say anything they like.' Reluctantly, Indira made a formal complaint to Mr Watson. He said that he needed positive evidence that the harassment was occurring. She produced a copy of an e-mail that Steve had sent her, which contained a sexist and racist joke. Trish also confirmed that she had heard him make an offensive comment to Indira. Mr Watson was satisfied that Indira was telling the truth. Consequently, he moved her temporarily to another administrative department.

After a couple of months, pressure of work was such that Indira had to be moved back to the original department. At the same time, Mr Watson told Steve that the harassment must not recur or he would be given a formal written warning. Shortly afterwards, Steve was promoted to a position as supervisor in the department. He began harassing Indira again – by making comments. On one particular occasion he told her of another forthcoming supervisor vacancy. He said that 'if she played her cards right, he would put in a good word for her to be promoted to supervisor'. She took this to mean that he wanted sexual favours.

Again Indira complained to Mr Watson. He said that he was too busy to deal with the matter and that she should ignore Steve's comments. The ill-feeling between Indira and Steve grew. Eventually, she could stand it no longer and resigned. She complained to an employment tribunal of constructive dismissal and sex and race discrimination.

The employment tribunal found that Indira had been subject to less favourable treatment on the grounds of sex and race. There had been a repudiation of the contract by the employer's failure to take sufficient action to deal with her complaints and this had forced her to resign. The tribunal awarded compensation, made a declaration of Indira's rights and also issued a recommendation that the company should improve its procedures for dealing with harassment claims.

Questions
You are part of a task force of managers and staff from the human resources department. You have been asked to produce a report on the necessary changes. Your report should answer the questions set out below. You should consider your answers in relation to the requirements of employment law, accepted standards of good employment practice, and the needs and interests of the business.

1 Why should an employer concern him or herself about the harassment of an employee?
2 What are the most effective ways to identify whether or not the organisation has a culture of harassment?
3 What might be the consequences of such a culture in relation to the operation of the business?
4 What in-company procedural steps should be available to respond to an allegation of harassment?
5 How should such procedures relate to the grievance procedure within the organisation?
6 What contribution can disciplinary rules and procedures make in dealing with harassment?

Table of statutes and statutory instruments

Statutes

Disability Discrimination Act 1995
Employment Relations Act 1999
Employment Rights Act 1996
Equal Pay Act 1970
Health and Safety at Work Act 1974
Human Rights Act 1998
National Minimum Wage Act 1998
Race Relations Act 1976
Race Relations (Amendment) Act 2000

Sex Discrimination Act 1975
Sex Discrimination Act 1986
Trade Union and Labour Relations (Consolidation) Act 1992

Statutory instruments

Fair Employment and Treatment (Northern Ireland) Order 1998
Health and Safety (Consultation with Employees) Regulations 1996
Maternity and Parental Leave, etc. Regulations 1999
Part-time Workers (Less Favourable Treatment) Regulations 2000
Safety Representatives and Safety Committees Regulations 1977
Sex Discrimination (Indirect Discrimination and Burden of Proof) Regulations 2001
Transfer of Undertaking (Protection of Employment) Regulations 1981
Transnational Information and Consultation of Employees Regulations 1999
Working Time Regulations 1998

Table of European directives

Directive concerning the Framework Agreement on fixed-term work (1999/70/EC)
Directive concerning the Framework Agreement on part-time work (97/81/EC)
Directive implementing the principle of equal treatment between persons irrespective of racial or
    ethnic origin (2000/43/EC)
Directive on Parental Leave (96/34/EC)
Directive on the burden of proof in cases of discrimination based on sex (97/80/EC)
Directive on the Establishment of a European Works Council or a Procedure in Community Scale
    Undertakings and Community Scale Groups of Undertakings for the Purposes of Informing and
    Consulting Employees (94/95)
Employment Directive (2000/78/EC)
Equal Pay Directive (75/117)
Equal Treatment Directive (76/207)
Information and Consultation Directive (2002/14/EC)
Safety and Health of Workers at Work Directive (89/391/EC)

List of cases

Bilka-Kaufhaus GmbH *v* Weber von Hartz [1986] IRLR 317
British Telecommunications plc *v* Ticehurst [1992] IRLR 219
Commission of the European Communities *v* UK [1994] IRLR 392
Cresswell and others *v* Board of Inland Revenue [1984] IRLR 190
Dekker *v* Stichtung Vormingscentrum [1991] IRLR 27
W.A. Goold *v* McConnell [1995] IRLR 516
James *v* Eastleigh Borough Council [1990] IRLR 288
Jones *v* Tower Boot Co. Ltd [1997] IRLR 168
King *v* Great Britain–China Centre [1991] IRLR 513
Porcelli *v* Strathclyde Regional Council [1986] IRLR 134
Price *v* Civil Service Commissioners [1978] IRLR 3
R *v* British Coal Corporation and Secretary of State for Trade and Industry *ex parte* Price [1994]
    IRLR 72
Royle *v* Trafford Borough Council [1984] IRLR 184

Secretary of State for Employment *v* ASLEF (No. 2) [1972] 2 All ER 949
Sim *v* Rotherham Metropolitan Borough Council [1986] IRLR 391
United Bank *v* Akhtar [1989] IRLR 507
Wiluszynski *v* London Borough of Tower Hamlets [1989] ICR 493
Zafar *v* Glasgow City Council [1998] IRLR 36

Useful websites

www.acas.org.uk   **Advisory, Conciliation and Arbitration Service**   For information on the role and publications of the principal provider of dispute resolution services in the UK.

www.cac.gov.uk   **Central Arbitration Committee**   The body responsible for applications by trade unions for trade union recognition and claims relating to the disclosure of information for collective bargaining.

www.cbi.org.uk   **Confederation of British Industry**   The principal representative employers' organisation in the UK, it provides information and undertakes some research.

www.cipd.co.uk   **Chartered Institute of Personnel and Development**   The body responsible for setting standards for the practice of human resource management, undertaking research and providing information about HR practice.

www.cre.org.uk   **Commission for Racial Equality**   A statutory body required to monitor the operation of race relations legislation, provide advice to complainants and to report to Parliament.

www.dfes.gov.uk   **Department for Education and Skills**   A government department which, among other areas, has responsibility for dealing with discrimination and work–life-balance issues.

www.drc-gb.org.uk   **Disability Rights Commission**   A statutory body required to monitor the operation of disability discrimination legislation, to provide advice to complainants and to report to Parliament.

www.dti.gov.uk/er   **Department of Trade and Industry**   A government department which, among other areas, has responsibility for dealing with employment relations issues.

www.eoc.org.uk   **Equal Opportunities Commission**   A statutory body required to monitor the operation of sex discrimination legislation, to provide advice to complainants and to report to Parliament.

www.ets.gov.uk   **Employment Tribunal Service**   The body responsible for overseeing the operation of employment tribunals.

www.europa.eu.int   **European Union**   Provides access to information on the work of the European Commission, the Council of Ministers, the European Parliament, the European Court of Justice and other EU bodies.

www.hse.gov.uk   **Health and Safety Executive**   Responsible for monitoring the operation of health and safety legislation in the UK.

www.inst-mgt.org.uk   **Chartered Management Institute**   Responsible for setting standards in management and management development.

www.iod.com   **Institute of Directors**   The principal representative body of company directors.

www.lowpay.gov.uk   **Low Pay Commission**   A statutory body responsible for monitoring the operation of national minimum wage legislation and reporting to government.

www.tuc.org.uk   **Trades Union Congress**   The principal representative body of trade unions in the UK which provides information and undertakes some research.

References

ACAS (1997a) *Disclosure of Information to Trade Unions for Collective Bargaining Purposes*. London: ACAS.

ACAS (1997b) *Time Off for Trade Union Duties and Activities*. London: ACAS.

ACAS (2000) *Code of Practice on Disciplinary and Grievance Procedures*. London: ACAS.

Certification Officer (2001) Certification Office for Trade Unions and Employers' Associations. *Annual Report of the Certification Officer 2001*. London: HMSO.

Department of Trade and Industry (1992) *Code of Practice on Picketing*. London: The Stationery Office.

Department of Trade and Industry (2000) *Code of Practice on Industrial Action and Notice to Employers*. London: The Stationery Office.

Department of Trade and Industry (2001) *Dispute Resolution in Britain: A Background Paper*. London: DTI.

Kahn-Freund, O. (1983) (Davies, P. and Freedland, M., eds) *Kahn-Freund's Labour and the Law*. 3rd edn. London: Stevens.

Further reading

Arrowsmith, J. and Sisson, K. (2000) 'Managing working time' in Bach, S. and Sisson, K. (eds) *Personnel Management: A Comprehensive Guide to Theory and Practice*, 3rd edn. Oxford: Blackwell.

Auerbach, S. (1990) *Legislating for Conflict*. Oxford: Clarendon Press.

Collins, H. (1992) *Justice in Dismissal*. Oxford: Clarendon Press.

Davies, P. and Freedland, M. (eds) (1983) *Kahn-Freund's Labour and the Law*, 3rd edn. London: Stevens.

Department of Trade and Industry (2002) *Findings from the 1998 Survey of Employment Tribunal Applications*, Employment Relations Research Series No. 13. London: DTI.

Dickens, L. (2000) 'Still wasting resources? Equality in employment' in Bach, S. and Sissons, K. (eds) *Personnel Management: A Comprehensive Guide to Theory and Practice*, 3rd edn. Oxford: Blackwell.

Earnshaw, J., Goodman, J., Harrison, R. and Marchington, M. (1998) *Industrial Tribunals, Workplace Disciplinary Procedures and Employment Practice*, Employment Relations Research Series No. 2. London: DTI.

Edwards, P. (2000) 'Discipline: towards trust and self-discipline?' in Bach, S. and Sissons, K. (eds) *Personnel Management: A Comprehensive Guide to Theory and Practice*, 3rd edn. Oxford: Blackwell.

Ewing, K. (1991) *The Right to Strike*. Oxford: Clarendon Press.

Lewis, D. and Sargeant, M. (2002) *The Essentials of Employment Law*, 7th edn. London: Chartered Institute of Personnel and Development.

Willey, B. (2002) *Employment Law in Context*. Harlow: Prentice Hall.

Statutory codes of practice

Commission for Racial Equality (1983) Code of Practice for the Elimination of Racial Discrimination and the Promotion of Equality of Opportunity in Employment. London: The Stationery Office.

Department for Education and Skills (1996) Code of Practice for the Elimination of Discrimination in the Field of Employment Against Disabled Persons or Persons who have had a Disability. London: The Stationery Office.

Department of Trade and Industry (2000) Code of Practice on Access to Workers during Recognition and Derecognition Ballots. London: The Stationery Office.

Equal Opportunities Commission (1985) Code of Practice on Sex Discrimination, Equal Opportunity Policies, Procedures and Practices in Employment. London: The Stationery Office.

Equal Opportunities Commission (1997) Code of Practice on Equal Pay. London: The Stationery Office.

Part Four

Patterns and practices

Chapter 9

Collective bargaining

Mike Salamon

Learning objectives

By the end of this chapter, readers should be able to:

- identify the continuing importance of the collective bargaining process;
- explain the different functions collective bargaining performs in regulating the conduct of the employment relationship and the different styles of collective bargaining relationship;
- understand recent trends and developments in the structure of collective bargaining institutions (particularly relating to decentralisation);
- appreciate the significance of recent changes in the bargaining relationship (particularly resulting from the introduction of HRM strategies).

Introduction

The Webbs (1902) used the term 'collective bargaining' as part of their categorisation of trade union activities. Trade unions can provide individual members with mutual insurance (monetary benefits to support the individual in the event of sickness, unemployment, industrial action, etc.), so helping them to withstand management impositions. They can, with strong membership and stable organisations, force employers to deal with labour as a collective entity, rather than as isolated individuals, and so secure better terms and conditions of employment (collective bargaining). Furthermore, through the politicisation and influence of the working classes within society, they can seek universal legislative regulation of the labour market and protection of the individual worker (legal enactment). Despite the development of individual employment protection legislation in the UK since the mid-1960s and the decline in trade union membership since the early 1980s, collective bargaining still remains an important, if not dominant, focus of trade union activity – 'what unions do, at least in the UK, is to seek, sign and then administer collective agreements' (Willman, 2001: 113).

The basis of collective bargaining is that 'employees do not negotiate individually, and on their own behalf, but do so collectively through representatives' (Donovan Commission, 1968: 8), resulting in agreements which regulate the employment relationship on a group rather than individual basis. Unlike joint consultation, where management largely controls the process (determines the agenda for discussion and retains the right to decide the final outcome), collective bargaining is founded on the principle of joint regulation. It allows employees (through their representatives) to initiate discussion of issues of concern to them as well as respond to issues raised by management and, most importantly, it requires both sides (employees as well as management) to accept or agree to the outcome. Not surprisingly, management has generally been reluctant to accept collective bargaining or, once accepted, to see its scope extended. Thus, there are two fundamental requirements for effective collective bargaining to take place:

- Employees need to see themselves not simply as individuals but also as part of a group with similar objectives and interests in regulating the employment relationship. However, this feeling has to be given substance through some form of employee organisation (usually by individuals joining an already existing external trade union) which provides the necessary power and representational capacity to undertake joint regulation through collective bargaining with management.

- Management must be prepared not just to accept the existence of the employees' organisation but also to acknowledge its right to represent the interests of employees (grant recognition). This involves accepting some restriction on its authority to make unilateral decisions (managerial prerogative). The extent to which organisational decisions become subject to negotiation and agreement is a reflection of preferred management style, employee/union power and any legislative intervention.

These two requirements are interlinked and both have been subject to considerable pressure in the UK since the beginning of the 1980s. In the first place, trade union membership has declined (due to an unfavourable economic environment, industrial restructuring and changes in management attitude) and this, together with more restrictive legislation, has reduced the ability of trade unions to exert pressure on management to secure favourable outcomes within the collective bargaining process. In the second place, many managements have adopted HRM-based strategies which emphasise the individual nature of the employment relationship and seek to reduce, if not remove, the influence of trade unions on its decision-making. Milner's analysis (1995) of the relationship between union membership levels in the UK and the proportion of employees covered by collective bargaining shows that, at its peak in the mid-1970s when about 50 per cent of employees were members of unions, 85 per cent of employees were covered by 'collective pay-setting institutions' (of which about 8 per cent were covered by statutory wages councils). Thus the benefits of collective bargaining extended well beyond the limits of trade union membership. By the early 1990s, not only had trade union density declined to below 40 per cent but also the gap with the coverage of 'collective pay-setting institutions' had fallen to about 7 per cent, principally because of the decline in multi-employer national collective bargaining arrangements.

The UK Workplace Industrial Relations Surveys (Millward *et al.*, 1992; Cully *et al.*, 1999) confirm that the proportion of employees covered by collective bargaining (in workplaces with more than 25 employees) declined from 83 per cent in 1980 to 41 per cent in 1998. However, as Brown *et al.* show (2000: 615), collective bargaining has not been replaced by individual negotiation but rather by management determination of pay (see Figure 9.1(a)). Nevertheless, collective bargaining remains an important activity. Even in sectors such as construction, manufacturing and financial services about

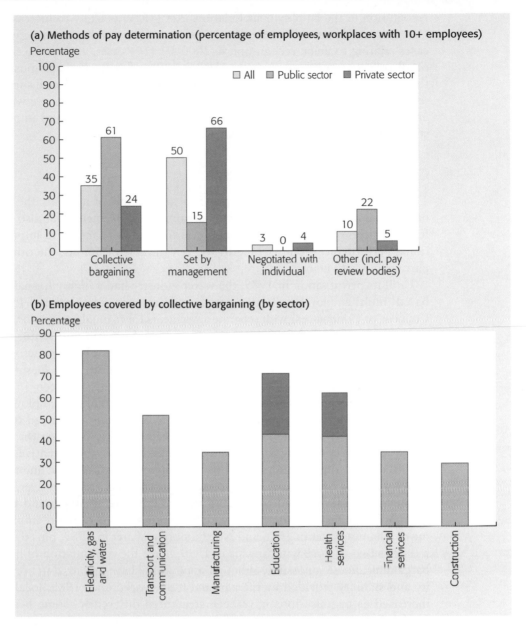

(a) Methods of pay determination (percentage of employees, workplaces with 10+ employees)

(b) Employees covered by collective bargaining (by sector)

Figure 9.1 **Collective bargaining (1998)**

Source: Brown *et al.* (2000: table 1)

one-third of employees are still covered by collective bargaining and the figure rises to 55 per cent in transport and communication, over two-thirds in education and health (if pay determination by pay review bodies, to which trade unions present evidence, are included) and remains at 85 per cent in the recently privatised electricity, gas and water industries (see Figure 9.1(b)). Significantly, the 1998 survey (Cully *et al.*, 1999: 15) identified that almost half of workplaces had union members among their employees and 45 per cent recognised unions. The re-introduction of a statutory right to union recognition in the Employment Relations Act (1999) is likely to increase these levels. Certainly, ACAS recorded a significant increase in the number of collective conciliation cases relating to union recognition in 2000–01 (264 cases, accounting for 22 per cent of all collective conciliation cases) (ACAS, 2001: table 2). Perhaps most importantly, the existence of trade unions in the workplace is still 'associated with superior non-pay terms and conditions compared with organisations where unions are weak or absent' and 'collective bargaining appears to facilitate both access to and improvements on statutory rights' (Brown *et al.*, 2000: 627)

Changes in the water industry

The water industry, in the 1990s, provides an example of not only the abandonment of national multi-employer collective bargaining arrangements but also two quite different strategies at the organisational level to achieve change and improve organisational performance – one seeking to weaken the role of unions, the other working in partnership with unions.

Until its privatisation in 1989, the water industry had a highly formalised 'Whitley-based' multi-employer collective bargaining arrangement (National Joint Industrial Councils or Committees) with separate agreements for manual production workers, craft maintenance workers, non-manual staff and chief officers and senior staff (Ogden, 1993). These provided common pay levels and terms of employment across the industry with joint consultation over other issues at the organisation level. Despite the increasing independence of the individual water organisations, between 1983 (when the statutory National Water Council was replaced by two voluntary employer bodies) and privatisation in 1989, national multi-employer bargaining continued on a voluntary basis – primarily to avoid competitive pay leap-frogging between the organisations – although issues relating to productivity improvements and incentive schemes were devolved to the organisation level. This was supported by the trade unions, whose own policy was for a continuation of uniformity across the industry. However, some regional water authorities wanted to develop their own more strategic and flexible HRM approaches at the organisation level. The withdrawal from multi-employer bargaining of Thames Water in 1986 and Northumbrian Water in 1989, plus the indication of a further two or three withdrawals in 1990, made the continuation of multi-employer bargaining almost impossible, although some would have preferred to keep the uniformity and stability provided by the national framework. Since 1989, local variation has increased as organisations have been structured differently (some being bought by foreign firms or becoming part of wider general utility companies) and have developed different approaches to such issues as single-table bargaining, long-term agreements, performance-related pay, the individual employee–management link (with a reduced role for the trade union) and so on.

Northumbrian Water (IRS, 1992) introduced perhaps the most radical changes in employee relations intended to personalise employee representation (rather than conducting it through a third party – the unions). Having failed to introduce a single-union agreement, management agreed to continue its recognition of the eight existing unions, but only as a joint Confederation of Northumbrian Water Trade Unions (CNWTU) and with the formation of a Northumbrian Water Ltd Employee Association (NWEA) to represent the 17 per cent of employees who were not members of these unions. It also introduced a system of employee councils in each operating area and an overall company council to integrate the processes of communication, consultation and negotiation. The seven company councillors were expected to 'conduct themselves in such a way as to promote harmony and progress of employee relations', and the two representatives of the CNWTU and NWEA, allowed to attend council meetings, were only 'advisers' (although at least one had to be present whenever an 'agreement' was made by the council). Significantly, its first pay negotiation (a three-year deal negotiated in 1991) resulted in endorsement of management's 'final' offer by the council but rejection by the employees in a ballot, followed by an independent review and an increase in management's offer.

Welsh Water (IRS, 1992) adopted what it termed a 'partnership approach' to its reform of collective bargaining arrangements. In moving to single-table bargaining, it introduced a 'representative council' to combine consultation and negotiation with the employee-side representation comprising union full-time officers as well as union lay representatives. Thus the unions' position was not threatened by the change although the National Union of Public Employees (NUPE, now Unison) was derecognised because of its small number of members. Its approach to pay bargaining contained two important features. First, it continued to guarantee that there would be no compulsory redundancies. Secondly, and perhaps more importantly, it developed a pay formula which encompassed not only organisational performance but also changes in the retail price index (which determines its prices) and the results of an independent survey of pay movements in selected Welsh companies. The arrangement also contained a provision either to increase pay or to reduce the next pay increase in the light of the pay survey findings. It is perhaps not surprising that Hyder (the merger of Welsh Water with South Wales Electricity) was cited by the TUC as a case study of good practice which supported its case for union recognition (TUC, 1997).

The process of collective bargaining

Flanders (1968) noted that collective bargaining does not involve the actual sale or hire of labour; it is a rule-making process which determines and regulates, in varying degrees, the terms on which individuals will be employed. However, the importance of collective bargaining is not limited to determining pay and other substantive terms. Its real significance, perhaps, lies in management acceptance of a style of employment relationship which is based on the legitimisation of the expression of the different interests within the organisation (conflict), on joint regulation (constraining the unilateral exercise of managerial authority over employees) and on the principle of employee involvement and influence in a range of organisational decision-making. It is also important to recognise that both the establishment of collective bargaining and the outcome of the bargaining process depend, to a great extent, on the power balance between the two parties (management and the employees collectively). Hence, Flanders (1968) described collective agreements as being 'compromise settlements of power conflicts'. The demonstration of industrial power, through strikes or other types of industrial action, forms an integral part of collective bargaining.

Regulating the employment relationship

Collective bargaining is not the only method for determining and regulating terms of employment and the nature of the employment relationship. They can also be determined unilaterally by management or set by government through legislation. Arguments in favour of the use of collective bargaining generally stem from, on the one hand, a belief in the injustice of unconstrained management discretion (potential employee exploitation) and, on the other, a preference for voluntary arrangements determined by the parties themselves (which allow variability) rather than uniform statutory compulsion. As already indicated, the role of collective bargaining covers more than just negotiating pay increases; Chamberlain and Kuhn (1965) identified three quite different but interrelated functions:

Establishing economic contractual terms

The process is primarily concerned with the distribution of economic wealth through the determination of the substantive terms of the employment contract, such as pay, hours, holidays and other benefits (pension, sick pay, etc.). In the UK, these terms become incorporated into the individual's contract of employment and are, thereby, not only legally enforceable on the employer but also automatically amended whenever the terms of the collective agreement change. It also means that if management terminates the collective agreement, the individual's previous rights cease and become subject to individual negotiation or, more usually, unilateral management determination. Similarly, where so-called fringe benefits become part of the terms of a collective agreement, they cease to be an 'optional' extra to be granted (or not) at the discretion of management but become an integral standard 'right' within the contract of employment.

Constraining managerial power and authority

Many collective agreements are procedural, rather than substantive, in nature. The initial 'recognition' agreement establishes the foundation for all subsequent collective bargaining: it confers legitimacy on the trade union's role and defines those issues which may be subject to joint regulation. Once the union is recognised, further procedural agreements may be negotiated. Some, most obviously the grievance and disciplinary procedures, cover the conduct of the individual employee–manager relationship, whereas others, such as consultation in the event of redundancy, are concerned with the organisational relationship between management and the union. Taken together, procedural agreements provide, in effect, a body of 'constitutional' rules which govern 'managerial', rather than 'economic', relations by constraining the exercise of managerial authority. Such rules seek to balance management's desire for control of labour and the employees' desire for protection against arbitrary management decisions and actions; collective bargaining provides a form of 'government by consent'.

Allowing employee influence in organisational decision-making

The scope of negotiations within the organisation may extend beyond the economic and constitutional functions and allow employees, through their representatives, to influence a wide range of management policies, strategies and decisions which affect their working life. The advantage of collective bargaining, to employees, lies in its implicit assumption

Table 9.1 **Management and union views of control of work issues (% of respondents)**

Work issue	Management		Union	
	Negotiate	Consult	Negotiate	Consult
Grievance handling	24	50	41	36
Health and safety	14	61	22	47
System of payment	13	14	13	8
Equal opportunities	10	40	13	30
Performance appraisal	6	31	10	15
Staffing and manpower planning	5	33	12	20
Employee recruitment and selection	4	20	5	15
Training	3	33	7	29

Source: Brown *et al.* (2000: table 2)

that the output will be a joint *agreement* (in effect requiring the employees' acceptance of management's plans before implementation). The nature of the work, the way it is carried out by employees and the way management assesses their performance have, over the years, been the subject matter of collective bargaining, first through 'productivity' agreements, then 'new technology' agreements and, more recently, 'flexibility' agreements. Employees have been able to influence the design and introduction of new working arrangements by securing agreements on such issues as labour force levels, job flexibility, time flexibility, use of contractors, etc.

The extension of collective bargaining beyond the simple economic and constitutional functions and into wider, more strategic, areas of management decision-making, is indicative of a more cooperative 'management by consent' style of employee relations associated with the wider concepts of 'employee participation' and 'social partnership' within the workplace. However, Brown *et al.* note that even 'where trade unions retain recognition, their influence has become more narrow and consultative' (2000: 626) in many of the non-economic and/or non-contractual areas of organisational regulation ('control of work' issues). Certainly, union representatives appear to think they are 'negotiating' over work control issues more than management (*see* Table 9.1). It is, perhaps, particularly significant that while 41 per cent of union representatives believe they negotiate when handling members' grievances, only 24 per cent of managers believe it involves negotiation, while in the areas other than 'grievance handling' and 'health and safety' less than 50 per cent of managers appear to 'negotiate' or even 'consult'.

The influence of legislation

Collective bargaining in the UK has been relatively unregulated by legislation, despite its importance in changing the character of the employment relationship. Significantly, for a short period under the Industrial Relations Act 1971, the existence of a statutory recognition process (a prerequisite for the development of collective bargaining) did provide both a direct and an indirect pressure on employers to grant recognition and introduce collective bargaining, particularly among non-manual employees in the private sector. Significantly, the 'new' Labour government reinstated a statutory procedure to regulate and support union claims for recognition, as well as giving employees the right to be accompanied by a union representative in 'serious' grievance or disciplinary meetings with management (Employment Relations Act 1999). Furthermore, in addition to the general requirement for employers to allow 'reasonable' time off for representatives of independent recognised unions to carry out their role (including training) (Employment Protection Act 1975), the Labour government has now delineated the specific role of 'union learning representative' within the workplace (Employment Bill 2000), similar to the earlier 'health and safety representatives' (Health & Safety at Work Act 1974). However, even if management does recognise a trade union, it is still free to retain its decision-making prerogative by adopting a non-negotiable ('take it or leave it') stance in any discussions with a trade union. Trade unions must rely on their industrial power to constrain this freedom.

Similarly, collective agreements in the UK are, by their wording and the intention of the parties, not regarded as 'contracts in the legal sense and are not enforceable at law . . . they remain in the realm of undertakings binding in honour' (Mr Justice Lane in Ford v AUEFW and TGWU [1969] 2 QB 303), although its terms are legally enforceable through the individual's contract of employment. The Conservative government of the early 1970s tried to change this position (Industrial Relations Act 1971) – collective agreements were presumed to be legally enforceable between management and union unless they contained a clause to the contrary. Despite this change in the law, virtually all managements accepted union demands for a 'TINALEA' clause – 'This is not a legally enforceable agreement'. Since the subsequent Labour government's Trade Union and Labour Relations Act 1974, a collective agreement is legally enforceable only if it is a written agreement and contains a clause that the parties 'intend the agreement shall be a legally enforceable contract'.

The only direct statutory support in the UK for collective bargaining, introduced in 1909 but repealed in 1993, gave the government power to establish wages councils in low-paid industries where trade unions were too weak to secure collective bargaining on a voluntary basis (primarily in retail, catering, clothing and agriculture). These wages councils included independent members who could, if necessary, carry out a conciliation or arbitration role in any negotiating impasse between the union and employer members. Furthermore, the awards of these wages councils were legally binding on organisations in the designated industries.

However, statutory support for the trade unions' role in collective bargaining has been provided in one important area – disclosure of information. Since the Employment Protection Act 1975, trade unions have had the right to request from management information without which they would be 'materially impeded' in carrying out their collective bargaining role or which would be 'in accordance with good industrial relations practice'. Clearly, access to information is one factor in determining the type of bargaining relationship and, in particular, the balance of power between the two sides. However, obtaining access to management information may not always be to the union's advantage (Hussey and Marsh, 1982), or the union may not have sufficient industrial power to take full advantage of the information it receives (Moore, 1980). More importantly, the legal requirement to disclose information is limited to the *existing* range of issues which are subject to collective bargaining; management is under no legal obligation to provide information to trade unions on those issues which are only subject to consultation (except redundancy). It is, therefore, in management's interests to limit the scope of collective bargaining, thereby restricting the information a union may demand.

Clearly, legislation in respect of collective bargaining can be either negative or positive – it can constrain or support its development. In Malaysia, for example, certain issues are defined as areas of 'managerial prerogative' and excluded from collective bargaining (including the allocation of work, dismissals and redundancy) (Ayadurai, 1993: 84), whereas in Singapore all collective agreements have to be approved by the Industrial Arbitration Court, which is charged with ensuring that the terms of any agreement are 'in the interests of the community and particularly the economy' (Leggett, 1993: 111–12). The US, on the other hand, has had legislation since the 1930s which not only provides a statutory union recognition procedure culminating in a 'representation election' conducted by the National Labor Relations Board (NLRB) but also places a duty on both management and unions to 'bargain in good faith'. The NLRB and courts have also influenced the range of collective bargaining by dividing issues into *mandatory* (bargaining must take place at the request of one party) and *permissive* (both parties must agree to bargaining over the issue). The mandatory group covers a wide range of issues relating to wages, benefits and work-related matters, including work schedules, job security, dismissals, rest breaks, holidays and safety (Mathias and Jackson, 1994).

For almost two decades (1979–97), the Conservative government in the UK was unsupportive of collective bargaining. It not only abolished the statutory recognition procedure (1980) and wages councils (1993), but also substantially reduced the trade unions' ability to exert industrial power within the bargaining process, progressively narrowing the definition of lawful industrial action and increasing the rights of both management and individuals to challenge the actions of unions in the court. In 1993, it also removed the duty 'to encourage collective bargaining' from the terms of reference of the Advisory, Conciliation and Arbitration Service (ACAS). Furthermore, the government appeared to favour a change in the law to 'encourage' employers and unions to agree to legal enforceability of collective agreements (Green Paper, 1991). Unions might then have been legally liable for breach of contract when, in management's view, they did not comply, for example, with a clause to cooperate with management initiatives to improve productivity and flexibility. The government also favoured the removal of the unions' right to information from management – the only major legal underpinning for the collective bargaining process. It is perhaps ironic that it was pressure from the EU which led the Conservative government to undermine the trade union role further, in respect of transfer of undertaking and redundancy, by widening the consultation requirement to 'employee representatives', rather than confining it to representatives of recognised independent trade unions; nevertheless, management also now has to consult 'with a view to seeking agreement to measures to be taken'. Whereas there is no absolute requirement to reach an agreement, management must now, at least in this one area, appear to be 'bargaining in good faith'.

However, the direction of public policy appears to have shifted with the change of government in 1997. Although the Labour government has not relaxed any of the previous government's legislation relating to the exercise of industrial power, it has restored a state-supported recognition procedure. While the TUC sees union recognition as an integral part of building a partnership between management and employees to face competitive pressures (TUC, 1997), the Confederation of British Industry (CBI) wanted training excluded from collective bargaining and a right for individuals to 'opt out' of any union recognition or subsequent collective bargaining and be able to negotiate their own individual contract with management (Taylor, 1997). Although, the introduction of a national minimum wage can be seen as part of the process of *legal enactment* (rather than collective bargaining), it will, for the first time in the UK, provide a national base wage to underpin wage determination through collective bargaining.

Changes in the structural framework

Few countries have a single uniform set of institutional arrangements ('structure') for collective bargaining. In order to understand the varied forms of collective bargaining structure, it is useful to separate multi-employer institutional arrangements (that is, arrangements intended to cover more than one organisation) from single-employer collective bargaining (see Figure 9.2). Multi-employer collective bargaining is usually conducted at the industry or sector level (although it may also exist at a sub-industry or regional level). However, economy-wide arrangements can also be included in this category, even though such arrangements are usually tripartite (involving government) rather than bipartite and may not be collective bargaining in the strict sense, in that they do not necessarily result in formal collective agreements. Any multi-employer bargaining arrangement, at whatever level, has the effect of providing a form of external regulation of the individual organisation, whereas single-employer collective bargaining can be seen as part of an organisation's own internal regulation. However, the two arrangements are not mutually exclusive but may be interrelated to provide a 'layered' structure (that is, the terms of a multi-employer industry agreement may be added to or topped up at the individual organisation level).

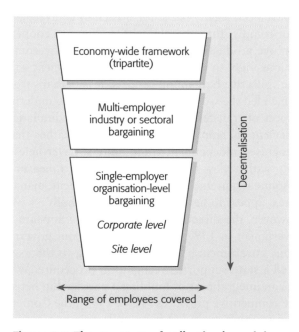

Figure 9.2 **The structure of collective bargaining**

◼ Multi-employer and single-employer arrangements

Economy-wide framework arrangements have been used, for short and long periods, in a variety of countries and are primarily associated with government interventionist strategies to regulate the wage element in the economy. Generally, they make recommendations or provide guidelines for improvements in wages and other terms of employment which are expected to be taken into account by management and unions in negotiations at industry and/or organisational level. The intention is to ensure that, at the macroeconomy level, any improvement in employees' terms and conditions are in line with the country's economic performance. Management gains from a stabilisation of its labour costs and a reduction in competitive bidding-up of wages (whether by powerful trade unions or by organisations themselves). Trade unions gain not only from being able to influence government economic and social policy but also from the uniformity achieved by greater standardisation of improvements across different organisations and groups of employees.

One example of this type of arrangement was the UK's Social Contract (1974–9). This was primarily an accommodation between the Labour government and trade unions (the CBI was not an active party to the arrangement) as an alternative to a government-imposed incomes policy. Since the late 1980s, Ireland has managed to maintain a series of tri-partite 'understandings' or 'agreements', which have included agreed norms for pay increases, variously entitled *Programme for National Recovery* (1987), *Programme for Economic and Social Progress* (1991), *Programme for Competitiveness and Work* (1994), *Partnership 2000 for Inclusion, Employment and Competitiveness* (1996) and *Programme for Prosperity and Fairness* (2000) (Prondzynski, 1998; EIRR, 2001). In Singapore, a permanent tripartite National Wages Council was established by the government in 1972, following increased restrictions on trade unions and collective bargaining, to provide 'authoritative guidelines for annual pay settlements in accordance with prevailing economic conditions' (Leggett, 1993: 100). Centralised agreements, encompassing a 'solidaristic' wage principle based on 'equal pay for equal work', played an important part within Sweden's centralised 'corporatist' approach to industrial relations until the early 1980s (Hammarström, 1993). However, these agreements were implemented and supplemented by further negotiation at the industry and/or organisational level.

The most common form of *multi-employer collective bargaining* in most west European countries is at the industry or sector level. Such agreements are negotiated by national officials of the trade unions and employers' association and apply to all employees, or a stated category of employees (for example, manual process employees, maintenance employees, etc.), of organisations that are members of the employers' association. In some countries (for example, Italy, Belgium, France and Germany) these collective agreements can be extended by legislation to apply to *all* organisations within the particular industry or sector (even those which are neither unionised nor a member of the employers' association). In the UK, even without legislative pressure, organisations have, on a voluntary basis, adopted the terms of the relevant industry agreement (where one existed) in order to ensure that their terms and conditions of employment were in line with other organisations in the industry.

Trade unions in the UK and the rest of Europe have favoured multi-employer industry-level collective bargaining because it promotes fraternalism and solidarity within the workforce, rather than competitive segmentation. It is the embodiment of the principles of 'common rule' and 'rate for the job'. Industry-wide agreements ensure that people doing the same work receive the same terms and conditions of employment, irrespective of differences in their individual performance, the performance of their organisation or local labour market conditions – it limits labour competition based on differential wage levels. At the same time, trade unions are able to 'equalise' their bargaining power within the industry by, in effect, using their strength in some organisations or geographical areas to support those where they are weaker. In some countries, through state support for industry-level bargaining, the level of employees covered by collective bargaining far exceeds the level of union density. For example, in France the level of union density is only 10 per cent whereas collective bargaining coverage is 92 per cent, and in the Netherlands the figures are 26 per cent and 71 per cent respectively (IDS, 1994).

Management has also benefited, certainly in the past, from industry-level collective bargaining. In the early days of the development of trade unions, it provided a means of employer protection against being played off, one against the other, in a series of leap-frogging union claims based on comparisons between organisations. It also helped to prevent 'unfair' competition between organisations in the same industry: the organisation which was outside the industry agreement, and hence able to pay lower wages, was seen as a threat by both trade unions and other organisations. At the same time, industry-level collective bargaining focuses primarily on the economic or market regulation function and, therefore, may be to management's advantage in distancing trade union activity and influence from management strategies at the organisational level. Certainly, in Germany there has been a clear distinction between the economic collective bargaining role of trade unions at the industry or sector level and the work regulation function of works councils at the organisation level (Jacobi et al., 1998).

Single-employer (organisational) bargaining may either be an alternative to multi-employer industry bargaining or exist alongside it as part of a layered set of arrangements. Whereas industry-level bargaining about economic matters, particularly pay, may allow management to limit the trade unions' role and influence over other matters at the workplace, it also has the effect of reducing management's control over wage costs within the organisation. Single-employer bargaining is, by its very nature, specific to the needs of each organisation and conducted by management and trade union representatives from within the organisation. In particular, management is able not only to integrate the regulation of economic and managerial relations, but also to do so within a comprehensive strategic HRM framework that supports business needs. However, it provides a greater opportunity for unions to pursue 'key bargaining' and/or 'leap-frogging' comparability strategies that may result in greater instability in the overall wage determination process.

Certainly, some UK industries, generally characterised by a relatively small number of large (often multinational) organisations, have relied entirely on single-employer bargaining (for example, car manufacturing and oil refining). It is also the predominant structure in some countries. It has been favoured in the US, with its emphasis on a free market capitalism philosophy and its geographically dispersed and segmented labour markets. In Japan, it has been its neo-feudal employment relationship, with its emphasis on a strong internal (organisational) labour market, which has encouraged enterprise-based unions and collective bargaining.

As early as 1968, the Donovan Commission's analysis of UK employee relations identified the existence of a two-tier collective bargaining arrangement in most private manufacturing industries. The formalised system of industry-level agreements provided irreducible uniform minimum levels of pay which were often enhanced by less formalised and fragmented organisation-level bargaining where unions were strong or management was prepared to pay more (for example, because of better organisational performance, to attract better quality employees or to secure employee cooperation in introducing new working arrangements). At that time, the so-called wage drift resulting from organisation-level bargaining over and above national rates was regarded as a significant inflationary factor in the economy which needed to be controlled. National pay rates, rather than being the significant factor in determining pay increases at the organisation level, were primarily a 'safety net' or ratchet mechanism within the pay system. As pay rates at the organisation level increased, so unions were able to safeguard the gain, at least in part, by an upward shift in the national industry minimum (Brown and Terry, 1978).

During the 1970s, reform of organisational collective bargaining focused on increased formalisation as part of management's strategy to regain control. The more recent focus, in the 1980s and 1990s, has been on shifting collective bargaining away from multi-employer arrangements ('decentralisation') as part of a government and management strategy to create a more flexible, responsive labour market. However, it is important to recognise that there is a variety of dimensions to decentralisation. First, it is not always simply a process of abandoning multi-employer in favour of single-employer arrangements but, rather, one of changing the balance between the two levels (IRRR, 1987). The industry agreement can become less of a uniform regulation and more of a framework of common aims or principles within which organisations have freedom to determine their own rules. Secondly, decentralisation may also encompass shifts *within* single-employer bargaining (Deaton and Beaumont, 1980). Organisations may devolve more authority for the determination of terms and conditions of employment to local management within lesser or greater degrees of central corporate coordination. Thirdly, the degree of decentralisation is, in part, a reflection of the nature of the previous arrangements. For example, the first step in decentralisation in Sweden (or any other country which has relied on economy-wide arrangements) has been to shift the focus of collective bargaining to the industry or sector level (EIRR, 1992) – which in the UK is seen as a centralised bargaining level.

Moves away from multi-employer bargaining

The role of multi-employer collective bargaining in the UK has declined substantially during the post-war period. Whereas in 1950 some 60 per cent of employees in the private sector had their pay determined through multi-employer agreements, it had already declined to 35 per cent by 1970 and dropped further to only 10 per cent in 1990, suggesting the abandonment of multi-employer bargaining as even the base for a two-tier arrangement (Brown *et al.*, 1995: table 5.1). In 1998, the 35 per cent of employees whose pay was determined by collective bargaining could be broken down between 15 per cent covered by multi-employer agreements, 13 per cent by single-employer agreements and 7 per cent by workplace agreements (Brown *et al.*, 2000: table 1).

Not surprisingly, a significant number of national multi-employer bargaining arrangements have, for different reasons, ceased to exist in the UK since the early 1980s. The withdrawal of larger organisations was certainly a major factor in the break-up of national bargaining in banking (withdrawal of NatWest Bank), multiple food trade (withdrawal of Tesco and other major supermarket groups) and shipping (withdrawal of Sealink, Cunard and P&O). However, the abolition of multi-employer bargaining among national newspapers and independent television arose primarily from a common management objective, in a highly competitive environment, to take advantage of new computer-based technology to make substantial changes in working arrangements. In the engineering industry, on the other hand, it was the union's own strategy in pursuing organisation-level agreements to secure a shorter working week, following a breakdown in national negotiations, which finally led to the Engineering Employers' Federation abandoning national multi-employer bargaining completely (Blyton, 1992). In other industries, such as the ports and water supply, it was management's desire to establish new organisational cultures, consequent on privatisation, which was the main driving force for abandoning multi-employer bargaining. Even within the remaining multi-employer bargaining in the public sector, the Conservative government encouraged fragmentation and decentralisation through the introduction of executive agencies in the civil service, hospital trusts in the NHS, and locally managed schools (with the authority to determine their own terms and conditions of employment), as well as by supporting local authorities which wished to opt out of national collective bargaining arrangements and establish their own arrangements for determining pay and terms of employment. Finally, the Conservative government abolished the wages councils as part of its strategy to deregulate the labour market. However, for smaller employers there may still be advantages in multi-employer bargaining: for example, new voluntary national multi-employer bargaining arrangements were set up in three industries (licensed clubs, lace finishing, and flax and hemp) even before the abolition of their wages councils in 1993, and the smaller firms in multiple food retailing re-established a multi-employer bargaining arrangement for themselves after the withdrawal of the big supermarket groups.

The catalyst for decentralisation in the UK, and other countries, has been primarily management's desire to optimise its use of labour (achieve greater labour flexibility) to meet the increased threat of international competition. This was supported by the Conservative government during the 1980s and 1990s. It believed that the maintenance of common pay rates through multi-employer bargaining created rigidity in the labour market which did little to reduce inflation and unemployment (Green Paper, 1989). Increased competitiveness could only be achieved, in its view, if pay levels and increases were more related to the profitability or performance of the organisation and local labour market conditions. It has been suggested that, for most managements, decentralisation is an integral part of developing a performance approach within the organisation's management of human resources and enhancing individualism, not simply a mechanism to lower wages or vary them according to local labour market conditions (Jackson et al., 1993; Brown et al., 1995). However, the two elements may not be so easily separated. For example, through creating separate business units, British Airways was able to introduce different (lower) pay and terms of employment for its European operations (centred on Gatwick) and its intercontinental operations (centred on Heathrow) (Colling, 1995).

Changes at the organisational level

The degree to which management seeks uniformity in terms and conditions of employment across the organisation results from a combination of structural factors (the nature of business development, organisation and strategy) and industrial relationship factors (management and union views of the scope and control of bargaining) (Ogden, 1982; Purcell, 1989). Corporate bargaining is more likely to be a feature of organisations which have a relatively integrated production pattern with similarity of work undertaken by employees in different parts of the organisation and central control of finance; devolved bargaining is more likely in diversified organisations with significant variations in production and working arrangements and where the different units compete for investment resources from the centre. Similarly, devolved bargaining at the unit level may allow for greater control of pay in relation to improvements in working methods and performance, whereas corporate-level determination of pay issues may allow management greater freedom at the unit level to make decisions about changes in working methods without having to agree them with trade unions. However, whereas corporate-level bargaining may allow management to set pay negotiations within the wider financial context of the organisation and its goals and plans, it may also create an expectation and opportunity for union representatives to influence these strategic corporate decisions.

However, the apparent devolution of collective bargaining decision-making to unit level does not mean, necessarily, that managers at these levels have complete freedom and discretion to determine pay and terms of employment in their part of the organisation. Most organisations maintain some form of corporate coordination and control over these issues, through formal corporate policies or guidelines, or through regular discussions among the different site managements or with corporate-level management (Marginson *et al.*, 1988; Kinnie, 1990). The 1990 Workplace Industrial Relations Survey identified that 60 per cent of managers involved in establishment-level pay negotiations for manual workers 'consulted' with higher management prior to commencing negotiations (Millward *et al.*, 1992: 234), however, it is not clear which level actually determined management's negotiating mandate.

It is perhaps surprising, given the weakened power of trade unions, that management has not used decentralisation as an opportunity for wide-ranging derecognition of unions. Indeed, successive ACAS annual reports during the 1980s and 1990s have referred to derecognition as being rare. However, two surveys (Claydon, 1989; Gall and McKay, 1994) identified a total of some 400 cases of derecognition up to 1994 but, because of the partial or grade-specific nature of most of the cases, the number of employees was relatively small (about 150,000). Importantly, in the context of decentralisation, Gall and McKay identified that, at least in some NHS trusts, management did not regard the non-granting of recognition for bargaining as derecognition because the unions concerned had not previously had bargaining rights at the organisation level – only at the national 'multi-employer' level. Management's main strategy has been to rationalise and restructure bargaining arrangements at the organisation level in order to overcome the problems of multi-unionism and multiple bargaining units (more complicated negotiation process, inter-union disputes and a reinforcement of differences between groups of employees). Management's primary objective has been to introduce arrangements which facilitate greater intra-organisational consistency, labour flexibility and employee cooperation by introducing single-union agreements and single-table bargaining – which may involve derecognition of some unions in the workplace.

Under a 'single-union agreement' (SUA) management gives one union sole and exclusive recognition rights for most or all employees within the organisation. Bassett (1987) described such agreements as a 'radical' reform of employee relations which offered 'the prospect of stable, consensual industrial relations'. Certainly, many of the agreements include one or more of the following: employee involvement mechanisms (often with a new employee council within which negotiations are conducted with 'employee' rather than 'union' representatives), harmonisation of terms and conditions of employment across the organisation, and the inclusion of a no-strike clause linked to the use of pendulum arbitration to resolve any differences. As a package, these developments support other elements of management's HRM strategies aimed at increasing labour flexibility and employee cooperation (such as teamworking, performance-related pay, training and development, etc.). SUAs were a particular feature of the 1980s, although their number appears to have been limited. Gall (1993) found only 135 such agreements, 15 of which had existed before the 1980s and only 14 of which had been introduced since 1990. This apparent decline in management interest in SUAs can be attributed, in a major part, to the availability of other, perhaps less radical and traumatic, approaches to reforming bargaining arrangements (in particular, single-table bargaining) and the success of other HRM strategies in achieving increased labour flexibility and employee commitment.

The most criticised feature of some SUAs, certainly in terms of their effect on the subsequent bargaining relationship, was management's use of a competitive, so-called beauty contest, approach to selecting which union should be recognised. The winning union had to satisfy management's criteria if it was to gain, and retain, recognition. Indeed, in a greenfield site, the SUA was sometimes concluded before any employees were recruited. As a consequence, the union's *raison d'être* became perceived as one of supporting management strategies and ensuring employee cooperation, rather than one of expressing employee interests and challenging management actions. This process of union incorporation is the complete opposite of unions being formed by and belonging to the employees themselves.

An alternative approach has been the establishment of 'single-table bargaining' (STB) to overcome the long-standing segregation of manual and non-manual employees in most UK organisations (reflected in the use of differentiated terms, such as 'blue collar' and 'white collar' or 'works' and 'staff', and the existence of separate unions, bargaining units, collective agreements and terms and conditions of employment). The introduction of STB involves amalgamating existing organisation-level bargaining units into one, resulting in a single common collective agreement covering both manual and non-manual employees, but retaining multi-union recognition and representation. The concept builds on the practice, in many organisations, of a joint union negotiating committee (JUNC) to bring together several unions representing different segments of manual employees.

A number of factors have led management to consider STB as a way of bridging the gap between manual and non-manual employees (Marginson and Sisson, 1990). First, at a pragmatic level, the existence of a coherent and integrated pay grading system across the organisation provides management with a *prima facie* defence against any legal claim from an employee based on 'equal pay for work of equal value'. Secondly, at a structural level, technological and organisational changes, and the accompanying changes in working arrangements, make it increasingly difficult to distinguish between what is manual and what is non-manual work. Thirdly, at a relationship level, the continuation of differential treatment between these groups is perhaps incompatible with obtaining the involvement and commitment of *all* employees. All of these factors point towards increasing organisational integration and the need for harmonisation and common terms of employment (hours, holidays, sick pay, pensions, etc.) across all groups of employees.

Change in the structure of bargaining arrangements created by the introduction of STB has often been accompanied by changes in the bargaining relationship. Management has used the opportunity to broaden the areas of discussion, beyond pay and conditions, to encompass 'all matters affecting employees at work' (including strategic organisational change and human resource management). In doing so, the processes of informing, consulting and negotiating have become more integrated. While this may allow unions more opportunity to influence a wider range of organisational decision making, management's primary intention is to inculcate a more 'reasonable' and 'responsible' approach on the part of unions. At the same time, drawing unions together into a single negotiating body requires them to reconcile their different, and potentially conflicting, interests *prior* to any single-table negotiation, rather than management coordinating the *outcomes* of multiple negotiations to ensure intra-organisational consistency. The process of reconciliation may be complicated by the form of union representation in STB: if it is pro rata to the unions' membership, then the interests of the larger unions may dominate; but if it is equal representation, then the smaller unions may have undue influence. One approach, adopted in Pilkington Insulation, was to create a dual system composed of the unions' negotiating team, based on equal representation, and an 'advisory' body, based on pro rata representation, which determined the unions' negotiating mandate and ratified agreements (IRS, 1990).

Changes in the bargaining relationship

The process of collective bargaining assumes that there is a continuing interdependent relationship between management and employees and, consequently, that both sides would prefer to resolve their differences on a mutually acceptable basis, rather than end the relationship. However, within this general principle, there are two possible models or styles of collective bargaining relationship: conjunctive or distributive bargaining and cooperative or integrative bargaining (Chamberlain and Kuhn, 1965; Walton and McKersie, 1965).

Conjunctive, or distributive, bargaining

Conjunctive, or distributive, bargaining is generally characterised by:

■ the issue being related to the relative distribution of a limited finite resource (particularly the distribution of money in simple pay bargaining), which creates a win–lose situation (one side's gain is inevitably the other side's loss);
■ although the parties accept that they must achieve some agreement, there is little, if any, positive cooperation between them; the relationship is a competitive one which relies primarily on coercion and bargaining power to determine the outcome.

Cooperative, or integrative, bargaining

Cooperative, or integrative, bargaining is generally characterised by:

- the issue being perceived as a complex problem-solving process (for example, the linking of changes in working arrangements to pay and job security), which has the potential, through the decisions of the two parties, to produce a varying value to the negotiation, so creating a possible win–win situation (both sides achieve a gain);
- although the two parties are pursuing different interests or goals, both parties recognise the need to make concessions to secure a mutually beneficial compromise; the relationship is a cooperative one in which any gain made by one side is dependent on gains being made by the other side as well.

McCarthy and Ellis (1973) argued, at a time of relatively strong unions, that the most effective way for management to obtain employee support for organisational change to meet competitive pressures was through a strategy of 'management by agreement'.

They believed that the development of a cooperative bargaining relationship, which sought to predict and plan for future needs of both management and employees, was preferable to a recriminatory relationship which dwelt on past decisions. However, this requires two fundamental changes. First, management has to accept the extension of employee influence into a wide range of managerial decision-making areas. Secondly, unions have to accept that their role is no longer simply to oppose or challenge 'management' decisions but to be an active party in identifying and resolving organisational problems. Beaumont (1992: 120) noted that, in the public sector, the distributive bargaining relationship increasingly evident in national wage negotiations during the 1970s and 1980s had an adverse spillover effect on the more cooperative relationship associated with the joint consultative arrangements at the organisational level.

As already noted, changes in the structure of collective bargaining inevitably have an effect on the nature of the bargaining relationship. At the same time, the collective bargaining relationship has been affected by a number of HRM developments at the organisational level which have been directed towards enhancing organisational performance, securing employee commitment and strengthening the individual employment relationship.

■ Organisational performance and labour flexibility

The wage–work exchange is at the heart of organisational performance and the collective bargaining process: while management is constantly seeking to improve labour efficiency, employees and unions are seeking to exercise some influence or control over the introduction and form of new working arrangements. Management's drive, in the 1980s and 1990s, for better performance and greater labour flexibility has produced a number of pressures on collective bargaining.

So far as the content of collective bargaining is concerned, Brown et al. (1995) argue that there has been a decrease in the range of issues subject to collective bargaining and that they have become more closely linked to pay (concessionary bargaining) as management seeks to exert greater control over working arrangements. Dunn and Wright (1994) present a more complex picture of the changes during the 1980s.

Procedural provisions (such as recognition, scope of bargaining and union facilities) were in essence unchanged, if not actually expanded. They argue that the *de jure* basis of these provisions made it more difficult for management to repudiate them even when the power balance with unions shifted in their favour. Substantive provisions, on the other hand, changed to reflect greater labour flexibility. In this area, they argue, management has always maintained it has the right to determine and control production, organisational and working arrangements, which are primarily areas of line management concern and control (rather than the HR or personnel specialists, whose role focuses more on the procedural aspects of the employment relationship). However, the way in which greater labour flexibility has been reflected in the substantive provisions of collective agreements appears to have been equally divided between 'general managerial prerogative clauses' and 'more detailed, formal prescription' of the changes – the latter where management perceives a 'continuing problem of imposing the agreement'.

A significant aspect of the drive for greater labour flexibility has been the growth in the so-called atypical or peripheral worker (employees working under a variety of short-term contracts and/or part-time working). The very concepts of 'core' and 'peripheral' employment are based on a separation of employees between those whose employment relationship is relatively secure and determined by the organisation's internal labour market and those whose employment relationship is more tenuous and reflects external labour market conditions (Atkinson, 1984; Atkinson and Meager, 1986). The peripheral workers can act as a buffer which allows management to increase or decrease its labour levels quickly in response to organisational requirements. Peripheral working is not new but, in the past, collective bargaining was directed primarily towards regulating the pay and conditions of permanent full-time employees. Union interest in the organisation's use of peripheral workers surfaced periodically, usually at times of recession, but primarily only to limit their use in order to protect the jobs of full-time permanent employees (the bulk of their membership). Consequently, peripheral workers' terms of employment were often left to management discretion or there was only limited regulation through collective bargaining.

However, the shift in the pattern of employment structures resulting from the increased use of such 'flexible' contracts – particularly, the 6.8 million part-time workers (accounting for 28 per cent of all employees and 45 per cent of female employment) (*Labour Market Trends*, 2000) – must inevitably affect the unions' ability to maintain regulation even within the organisation's internal labour market. The separation of the two groups of employees provides management with a greater opportunity to 'divide and rule'.

Consequently, trade unions are seeking to represent these workers in their own right, rather than collude with management in using them as a protection for full-time permanent employees, and, in so doing, to extend the bargaining agenda to encompass issues which are of direct benefit to such workers (many of whom are women and young people), not least by securing equal rights for them. However, trade unions have not only, at a pragmatic level, to reconcile the potentially conflicting interests of permanent full-time employees and peripheral employees but also, at an ideological level, to oppose the perception of labour segmentation. Management may be reluctant, however, to accept regulation of the pay and conditions of peripheral workers because it will restrict the very freedom and labour flexibility it is seeking.

Even among the 'core' group of permanent full-time employees, there has been a move in some organisations (in both the private and public sectors) to weaken collectivism and enhance individualism. For some groups, particularly managerial and professional employees, this has involved the complete abandonment of the collective basis for determining the employment relationship, often established during the wave of white-collar recognition in the 1970s, and its replacement by 'personal' contracts. For other employees, it may be only a partial personalisation of the contract, such as the introduction of individual performance-related pay. The development of personal contracts has been heralded, from a 'free market' perspective, as a liberation of employees which places 'ordinary workers on a par with directors and senior managers . . . and the end of the "wage slave mentality"' (Mather, quoted in Pickard, 1990: 41), whereas others see it as liberating management, not the employee, by providing management with 'a license to arbitrarily alter pay levels and job content' (*Labour Research*, 1989: 13).

There is no doubt that individualisation of the contractual relationship is the antithesis of collective bargaining. The development of a collective basis to determining the employment relationship was intended to overcome the inherent power disparity between the individual employee and management, and, certainly, there is little evidence to suggest that this power disparity is any less in the 1990s than it was in the 1890s. At the same time, any weakening of the employees' collective power in the area of economic regulation must also weaken their ability to influence management in the areas of managerial relations and organisational decision-making. Significantly, management was often successful in adopting an incremental approach which weakened collective bargaining, perhaps as a prelude to its final abandonment, by offering the inducement of better terms to those individuals who voluntarily accepted 'personal' contracts. However, the Labour government has sought to provide some protection against 'detriment and dismissal' for any employee who refuses to accept a contract different to the terms that would apply under a collective agreement (Employment Relations Act 1999 s17).

An important element in the performance and individualisation process has been the development of performance-related pay – 'unique amongst payments systems in stripping away those collective procedures and institutions which have obscured the essentially individualistic nature of the employment relationship' (Kessler and Purcell, 1992). At the very least, it introduces a personal variable element of pay, under the exclusive control of management, into an otherwise common uniform pay structure. Perhaps more importantly, the process for determining this element of pay is both decentralised and on an individual basis: it is the line manager's assessment of the individual's performance which determines his or her pay increase.

However, performance-related pay is not a form of individual bargaining. The appraisal process is concerned with assessing performance, not negotiating the level of the pay increase: the individual can, at best, only seek to influence the manager's assessment of performance and without the support of a union representative. While unions have been reluctant to cooperate in the introduction of a system that reduces their role in pay determination, they cannot ignore it completely without risking isolation from any potential influence on its operation. They may retain an important collective pay bargaining role in determining general increases in the pay grade bands or even the overall amount of money to be allocated under performance-related pay and, certainly, can seek to ensure fairness and consistency in its application through the joint determination of the procedural aspects of the appraisal process. They may also have a role, in relation to both performance-related pay and personal contracts, in supporting the individual member in their negotiations with management – and for this they need information. This was supported by the Central Arbitration Committee in a decision relating to British Airways when they said that although performance-related pay systems 'severely restrict the role of the trade unions in [traditional] negotiations', they nevertheless required 'more sophisticated monitoring and checking' by unions to ensure fairness (IDS, 1990: 27).

Certainly, a combination of the individualisation of the contract and the development of 'responsible autonomy' forms of work organisation means that 'key areas which were subject to regulation by collective bargaining have been reintegrated into the sphere of management prerogative' (Bacon and Storey, 1993: 15).

Exhibit 9.1

Partnership at Thames Water

In late 1999, following the Office of Water Services (OFWAT) review of charges for 2000 to 2005, the senior management of Thames Water Utilities Ltd (TWUL), which employs about 5,800 people, met representatives of Unison, GMB, AEEU and T&GWU to discuss the situation and enlist the support of the unions in examining ways to reduce costs and increase labour flexibility. It was the unions which suggested developing a 'partnership' approach.

The terms of the final partnership agreement followed extensive discussions in a working party of managers and union representatives and several workshops involving the union representatives and line managers. When the agreement was finally voted on by the employees, only 54 per cent voted but 71 per cent of these voted in favour of the partnership agreement. Following the ballot, working groups were established to examine a number of working issues including shift-pay arrangements, equal opportunities, work–life balance and training.

The partnership agreement contains a number of changes:

■ Some **existing collective agreements** were converted into areas for 'flexible management policies' where management would 'consult' rather than 'negotiate'.

■ **New partnership forums** were established at both TWUL level and business unit level. The TWUL forum comprises an equal number of management and union representatives and has responsibility for *negotiating* changes in terms and conditions, as well as *consulting* on employee-related business strategy and policies and *communicating* wider market and company information. Union full-time officers can attend business unit forums on an *ex officio* basis.

■ The trade unions are recognised by management as the **preferred partners for employee representation** and supported in their drive to recruit in those areas of the organisation where union membership is low.

■ In order to **promote job security** the agreement provides for minimising any period of uncertainty, consulting as early as possible, retraining employees and supporting their transfer to other parts of the organisation and the utilisation of natural turnover, early retirement and voluntary severance before any compulsory redundancy.

Source: 'New partnership channels at Thames Water', *IRS Employment Trends*, 715, November 2000: 6–12.

▶

Exhibit 9.1 *continued*

Terms of the partnership agreement

Partnership principles

The partnership is based on a commitment to respond quickly and effectively to changing business requirements, while, at the same time, making a joint commitment to employment security...

Partnership approach

The partnership aspires to the adoption of the following behaviours...

- **openness** – there should be no hidden agendas and issues should be raised and discussed constructively;
- **solution focused** – discussions should aim to generate solutions and resolve issues quickly;
- **respect** – there should be respect for the valid views and interests of all stakeholders in implementing the partnership;
- **clarity** – where possible, information should be readily available and presented in a format which enables understanding;
- **buy-in** – support for the principles and decisions of the partnership must be visible at all levels; and
- **business focused** – the partnership must keep sight of the need for improvement in the delivery of business performance, and the demands

which that places on employees and managers to respond to change.

Objectives:

- **employment security** – the partnership works together to maximise employment security through delivering business performance;
- **decision-making** – robust decision-making processes for consultation, negotiation and communication. This means, in practice, earlier discussions and sharing confidential information with some representatives, to which others may not have access;
- **communication** – the partnership aims to work quickly and effectively to communicate decisions and progress, to ensure that employees see value in the partnership;
- **representation** – the partnership supports membership of the recognised trade unions, believing that it provides the best way of representing employee views. Where membership of trade unions remains low, alternative arrangements to represent employee views may be implemented; and
- **training** – provision of training in order to achieve the best possible result from the partnership.

Source: 'Thames Water Utilities', *IRS Employment Trends*, 715, November 2000.

■ Developing forms of employee involvement

The focus of management attention has shifted from indirect, representative, power-centred participation through trade unions to direct, task-centred employee involvement. Two elements of recent HRM strategies, aimed at increasing employee involvement and commitment, are particularly important in terms of their potential effect on collective bargaining: the delegation of work-related decision-making to individuals and work-groups, and the creation of employee or works councils.

During the 1970s, employee involvement generally centred on the redesign of the socio-technical system as a means of satisfying employees' needs and improving the quality of their working life. However, since the early 1980s the emphasis has become more managerialist and focused on improving organisational performance. The characteristics of the new approach are embodied in phrases such as 'task ownership', 'empowerment' and 'responsible autonomy'. The underlying principle is that employees, on an individual or group basis, should be given delegated responsibility (and accountability) for the management and performance of their work, rather than being controlled through constant direct supervision. A significant part of the development of semi-autonomous workgroups involves not just organising task allocation and time off among the individual members but, more importantly, determining work targets, maintaining cost and quality controls, coordination of activities with other parts of the organisation, etc.

All of these activities were previously classified as the essential elements of management's role. While in the 1970s managers may have resented such changes as a 'loss of control, threat to their position and authority and anarchy on the shop floor' (Bailey, 1983: 106), developments in the 1980s and 1990s suggest that the process only *appears* to give employees greater control and, in reality, remains 'dominated and restricted by management' (Huiskamp, 1995: 166). The boundaries of the individual's or workgroup's authority, responsibility and autonomy are determined by management and are limited to areas which will increase organisational performance. Management values, interests and objectives become an integral part of each job. As a consequence, it becomes more difficult for employees to identify and justify, even to themselves, the pursuit of interests which are different from those of management. The determination of working arrangements is no longer a management initiative to be negotiated and agreed, on a collective basis, with trade union representatives prior to their implementation (during which process the two distinct interests – management and employees – can be identified and reconciled through compromise). Management is free to determine these issues directly with the individual or small groups of employees.

The development of individual identification with and commitment to management values and goals may be complemented by the creation of company, employee or advisory councils at the collective level. Such councils are intended to change the basis of traditional collective bargaining in two ways. First, all employees are generally afforded the same rights of representation, whether unionised or not, thereby reducing the importance of trade unions within the bargaining process. Secondly, they seek to develop a cooperative, problem-solving style which integrates the joint process of negotiation with the management-controlled processes of information giving and consultation. Similarly, the Conservative government's 'opt out' did not prevent UK organisations from following their EU counterparts in introducing European works councils in the early 1990s; some accepted union involvement in the 'council' and a clear link to established collective bargaining arrangements, while others (some of which recognise trade unions for normal collective bargaining) based their council exclusively on 'employee' representation (EIRR, 1994). Thus, these European consultative bodies may be an alternative forum to traditional collective bargaining or they may lay the foundation for the possible development of transnational collective bargaining.

In most other EU countries there is also a legal requirement for most organisations to have 'works councils', which not only have to be informed and/or consulted by management on general organisation matters (including strategic issues such as investment and rationalisation plans), but also, importantly, have to agree to changes in certain defined labour matters before management may implement the change (for example, working hours and payment systems). However, it is important to recognise that such councils have been developed within a collective bargaining structure which, in effect, contains the unions' role in the more conflictual (distributive) determination of pay and conditions of employment to multi-employer bargaining at the industry or sector level. This has left management free, at the organisational level, to develop a more cooperative problem-solving relationship with employee representatives, through the works council, which focuses on organisational needs. It is not surprising, therefore, that managements find such councils generally supportive of their position and organisational needs and are prepared to persuade employees to accept management plans (Beaumont, 1995: 165). However, decentralisation of collective bargaining will inevitably bring the works councils, most of whose members are already trade unionists, more into the distributive negotiating area of regulating economic relations, with a consequent change in its relationship to management. Significantly, the UK is faced with a similar situation as a result of the Labour government's acceptance of the EU Directive on compulsory management–employee consultation in 2001.

Since its election in 1997, the Labour government has espoused the cause of 'partnership', not least between management, employees and unions at the workplace (*see* Exhibit 9.1). For management, its appears to involve '*redesigning* traditional collective industrial relations' and developing 'a strategy to involve worker representatives in identifying *business problems* and enjoining them in agreed working solutions' (Bacon and Storey, 2000: 415). While partnership agreements commit the parties to the 'needs of the business', they also give unions and employees recognition, job security, information and a say in business decisions. Thus for some within the trade union movement, it represents perhaps the only realistic basis on which to maintain some degree of collective influence in the workplace (TUC, 1999). However, the reality may not always match the principles on which these agreements are supposed to be based. Guest and Peccei examined a number of organisations which were members of the Involvement and Partnership Association and which might, therefore, be expected to display 'best practice' in this field. They found that 'for a group of organisations that might be expected to engage in high trust forms of partnership, the level of direct participation in work decisions and representative participation in wider organisational policy is generally low' and that the agreements seemed to be characterised by a 'constrained mutuality with the balance of advantage, in terms of priciples endorsed and practices in place, leaning clearly towards management' (Guest and Peccei, 2001: 231).

Dispute resolution

Conflict of interest is an inherent part of the employment relationship. It may lead to 'disputes' – management and union unable to resolve their differences – which may sometimes involve the threat or use of industrial action to exert pressure on management (it is an integral part of collective bargaining). Multi-employer collective bargaining mechanisms usually include a disputes procedure to help resolve disputes arising at the organisational level. Consequently, the decline in multi-employer bargaining arrangements has also reduced the availability of such procedures. Alternatively, the parties may seek conciliation or arbitration through ACAS. There is a clear preference, in the UK, for using *conciliation* (which facilitates the two sides reaching their own resolution) rather than *arbitration* (where an independent person adjudicates and makes an award). In 2000–01 ACAS handled 1,226 collective conciliation cases and 545 advisory mediation projects compared to just 62 arbitration and dispute mediation cases (ACAS, 2001: tables 2, 4 and 5). However, it is in the area of arbitration that the most significant development has taken place.

Many UK managers have criticised conventional or 'open' arbitration because they felt that trade unions were able to obtain a better settlement from an 'outsider', who not only has no managerial responsibility for the continuing well-being of the organisation but also has freedom to decide what is a fair and equitable settlement – often a compromise between the union's claim and management's offer. This, it was claimed, produced a potential 'chilling effect' on the conduct of negotiations by inhibiting the exploration of the full range of possible concessions and compromises during the negotiation; either or both sides may keep something in reserve to cover the possibility of an arbitrator 'splitting the difference'.

Consequently, not only has management been more reluctant to accept union requests for arbitration but it has also sought the introduction of 'pendulum' or 'straight choice' arbitration where the arbitrator must find in favour of either the union's claim or management's offer. This approach is not new in UK employee relations (Treble, 1986); most 'disputes of right' require the arbitrator to make a choice between either the union's or management's position. Its application to 'disputes of interest' has been brought over from the US, where it was introduced during the 1950s and 1960s to balance the legal restriction on strike action among essential workers when collective bargaining rights were extended to public sector employees. Its significance for the bargaining relationship is that the win–lose situation in pendulum arbitration provides a 'cost' factor, similar to the use of industrial action, which both sides have to take into account in making their negotiating decisions (Stevens, 1966). However, the 'winner takes all' approach of pendulum arbitration is intended primarily as a deterrent (like the *threat* of industrial action) to induce the parties to bargain 'reasonably' during the negotiation and find their own mutually acceptable solution. Nevertheless, it can be seen to run counter to the principle of seeking a mutually acceptable compromise which underpins the negotiation process (Kessler, 1987). Certainly, pendulum arbitration is not without its problems, particularly where the arbitrator has to deal with a complex, multi-issue dispute or where the positions of neither management nor union appear reasonable (Singh, 1986; Kessler, 1987).

As part of a strategy to reduce the number of employment tribunal cases, the government has proposed (Employment Bill 2001) that failure by either management or employee(s) to comply with minimum statutory procedural standards for dispute resolution (relating to grievances, discipline and dismissal) could result in any tribunal award being increased or reduced by a minimum of 10 per cent and up to 50 per cent.

Chapter summary

This chapter began by showing that collective bargaining continues to have an important role in regulating the terms of the employment relationship. However, as the example of the water industry demonstrated, there have been important changes in both the structures of collective bargaining and the relationship between management and unions.

The importance of collective bargaining lies in redressing the power imbalance between management and the individual employee. It is not just concerned with the economic process of determining pay but, equally importantly, it provides a means of constraining managerial prerogative and allowing employees to influence organisational decision-making. Yet, unlike other countries, there has been little direct legislative support in the UK for collective bargaining.

Multi-employer bargaining, a traditional feature of most European countries, creates standardised terms of employment and stabilises wage competition between organisations. However, a major feature in all industrialised countries has been management's desire to decentralise collective bargaining (and, in some cases in the UK, to rationalise its organisational bargaining arrangements through single-union agreements or single-table bargaining) as part of its HRM strategies to improve international competitiveness through greater labour flexibility. This has been supported, in the UK at least, by the government's strategy to maintain labour market flexibility.

The collective bargaining relationship should not be seen automatically as an adversarial one but may be conducted on a cooperative basis as well. HRM strategies directed towards greater use of peripheral workers and the individualisation of pay and contracts have narrowed the scope of collective bargaining. Similarly, HRM strategies aimed at increased employee opportunities to influence, if not control, their immediate working arrangements and the introduction of employee councils weaken trade union influence within the collective bargaining relationship. More recently the government has sought to encourage the development of 'partnership at the workplace'.

Management has been attracted to the concept of pendulum arbitration because it believes the process will induce unions to act more 'reasonably' in the conduct of collective bargaining.

Questions

1 Why is collective bargaining important? Explain how the different functions of collective bargaining, each in its own way, regulate part of the employment relationship.

2 In what ways do the 'conjunctive or distributive' and 'cooperative or integrative' approaches to the bargaining relationship reflect different views of the interdependence of management and employees? Consider how the use of pendulum arbitration may affect the bargaining relationship.

3 What are the advantages and disadvantages of multi-employer and single-employer collective bargaining structures? Why has management been in favour of decentralisation?

4 In what ways do the different elements of an HRM strategy within the organisation impact on collective bargaining?

Activity

Forest Rural Hospitals will become an NHS trust next year. It has some 2000 employees in two small hospitals (15 miles apart) and five health clinics scattered throughout other parts of the region. Until now its pay and conditions have been determined nationally through the Whitley Council system. It has had three joint consultative committees (medical, administrative and ancillary staff) for some years on which a range of trade unions are represented – BMA, RCN, RCM, Unison, MSF, TGWU, GMB and AEEU.

Questions

1 In two groups (management and union), prepare for a forthcoming meeting to consider (a) whether or not the new trust should establish its own single-employer bargaining arrangements, and (b) what form these might take.

2 As the HR manager chairing this meeting, prepare a report for the board explaining the advantages of single-employer bargaining (and any disadvantages) and analysing the pros and cons of the different forms this might take (including your recommended course of action).

Useful websites

www.dti.gov.uk/partnershipfund **Partnership at Work Fund** Provided by the Department of Trade and Industry to encourage employers, employees and their representatives to work together to solve particular business problems by stressing the importance of communication at all levels.

www.eiro.eurofound.ie **European Industrial Relations Observatory On-Line** Provided by the European Foundation for the Improvement of Living and Working Conditions, it contains substantive information on European developments in industrial relations on an EU, country and sectoral basis.

www.eurofound.ie **European Foundation for the Improvement of Living and Working Conditions** A European Union body set up in 1975 to contribute to the planning and establishment of better living and working conditions.

www.europa.eu.int/index_en.htm **European Union On-Line** Provides access to information on the work of the European Commission, the Council of Ministers, the European Parliament, the European Court of Justice and other EU bodies.

References

ACAS (2001) *Annual Report*. London: ACAS.

Atkinson, J. (1984) *Flexible Manning: The Way Ahead*. London: Institute of Manpower Studies.

Atkinson, J. and Meager, N. (1986) *Changing Working Patterns: How Companies Achieve Flexibility to Meet their Needs*. London: National Economic Development Office.

Ayadurai, D. (1993) 'Malaysia' in Deery, S.J. and Mitchell, R.J. (eds) *Labour Law and Industrial Relations in Asia*. London: Longman: 61–95.

Bacon, N. and Storey, J. (1993) 'Individualization of the employment relationship and the implication for trade unions', *Employee Relations*, 15(1): 5–17.

Bacon, N. and Storey. J. (2000) 'New employee relations strategies in Britain: towards individualisation or partnership?', *British Journal of Industrial Relations*, 38(3): 407–27.

Bailey, J. (1983) *Job Design and Work Organisation*. Englewood Cliffs, NJ: Prentice Hall.

Bassett, P. (1987) *Strike Free: New Industrial Relations in Britain*. Basingstoke: Macmillan.

Beaumont, P.B. (1992) *Public Sector Industrial Relations*. London: Routledge.

Beaumont, P.B. (1995) *The Future of Employment Relations*. London: Sage.

Blyton, P. (1992) 'Flexible times? Recent developments in temporal flexibility', *Industrial Relations Journal*, 23(1): 26–36.

Brown, W. and Terry, M. (1978) 'The changing nature of national wage agreements', *Scottish Journal of Political Economy*, 25(2): 119–34.

Brown, W., Marginson, P. and Walsh, J. (1995) 'Management: pay determination and collective bargaining' in Edwards, P. (ed.) *Industrial Relations: Theory and Practice in Britain*. Oxford: Blackwell: 123–50.

Brown, W., Deakin, S., Nash, D. and Oxenbridge, S. (2000) 'The employment contract: from collective procedures to individual rights', *British Journal of Industrial Relations*, 38(4): 611–29.

Chamberlain, N.W. and Kuhn, J.W. (1965) *Collective Bargaining*. New York: McGraw-Hill.

Claydon, T. (1989) 'Union derecognition in Britain in the 1980s', *British Journal of Industrial Relations*, 27(2): 214–24.

Colling, T. (1995) 'Experiencing turbulence: competition, strategic choice and the management of human resources in British Airways', *Human Resource Management Journal*, 5(5): 18–32.

Cully, M., Woodland, S., O'Reilly, A. and Dix, G. (1999) *Britain at Work: as depicted by the 1998 Workplace Employee Relations Survey*. London: Routledge.

Deaton, D.R. and Beaumont, P.B. (1980) 'The determinants of bargaining structure: some large scale survey evidence for Britain', *British Journal of Industrial Relations*, X(viii): 202–16.

Donovan Commission (1968) *Royal Commission on Trade Unions and Employers' Associations*. London: HMSO.

Dunn, S. and Wright, M. (1994) 'Maintaining the "status quo"? An analysis of the contents of British collective agreements, 1979–1990', *British Journal of Industrial Relations*, 32(1): 23–46.

EIRR (1992) 'The rise and fall of centralised bargaining', *European Industrial Relations Review*, no. 219 (April): 20–2.

EIRR (1994) 'The first UK European works councils', *European Industrial Relations Review*, 251 (December): 20–2.

EIRR (2001) 'Pay adjustment saves national agreement – for now', *European Industrial Relations Review*, 326 (March): 15–17.

Flanders, A. (1968) 'Collective bargaining: a theoretical analysis', *British Journal of Industrial Relations*, VI: 1–26.

Gall, G. (1993) 'What happened to single union deals? A research note', *British Journal of Industrial Relations*, 24(1): 71–5.

Gall, G. and McKay, S. (1994) 'Trade union derecognition in Britain 1988–1994', *British Journal of Industrial Relations*, 32(3): 433–48.

Green Paper (1989) *Employment for the 1990s*. London: HMSO.

Green Paper (1991) *Industrial Relations in the 1990s*. London: HMSO.

Guest, D.E. and Peccei, R. (2001) 'Partnership at work: mutuality and the balance of advantage', *British Journal of Industrial Relations*, 39(2): 207–36.

Hammarström, O. (1993) 'Industrial relations in Sweden' in Bamber, G.J. and Lansbury, R.D. (eds) *International and Comparative Industrial Relations*, 2nd edn. London: Routledge: 197–219.

Huiskamp, R. (1995) 'Industrial democracy, employee participation and operational autonomy' in van Ruysseveldt, J., Huiskamp, R. and van Hoof, J. (eds) *Comparative Industrial and Employment Relations*. London: Sage: 155–72.

Hussey, R. and Marsh, A. (1982) *Disclosure of Information and Employee Reporting*. Aldershot: Gower: 17–33.

IDS (1990) *Incomes Data Services Report*, 570 (June).

IDS (1994) *IDS European Report*, 395 (November).

IRRR (1987) 'Pay bargaining: to centralise or decentralise?', *Industrial Relations Review and Report*, 397 (August): 13.

IRS (1990) 'Single-table bargaining – a survey', *IRS Employment Trends*, 463 (May): 5–11.

IRS (1992) 'Industrial relations developments in the water industry', *IRS Employment Trends*, 516 (July): 6–15.

Jackson, M.P., Leopold, J.W. and Tuck, K. (1993) *Decentralization of Collective Bargaining*. Basingstoke: Macmillan.

Jacobi, O., Keller, B. and Müller-Jentsch, W. (1998) 'Germany: facing new challenges' in Ferner, A. and Hyman, R. (eds) *Changing Industrial Relations in Europe*. Oxford: Blackwell: 190–238.

Kessler, I. and Purcell, J. (1992) 'Performance related pay: objectives and applications', *Human Resource Management Journal*, 2(3): 34–59.

Kessler, S. (1987) 'The swings and roundabouts of pendulum arbitration', *Personnel Management*, December: 40–2.

Kinnie, N. (1990) 'The decentralisation of industrial relations? Recent research considered', *Personnel Review*, 19(3): 28–34.

Labour Market Trends (2000), Table B.11, January.

Labour Research (1989) 'Contract to kill collective action', December: 13–14.

Leggett, C. (1993) 'Singapore' in Deery, S.J. and Mitchell, R.J. (eds) *Labour Law and Industrial Relations in Asia*. London: Longman: 96–136.

Marginson, P. and Sisson, K. (1990) 'Single table talk', *Personnel Management*, May: 46–9.

Marginson, P., Edwards, P.K., Martin, R., Purcell, J. and Sisson, K. (1988) *Beyond the Workplace: Managing Industrial Relations in the Multi-establishment Enterprise*. Oxford: Blackwell.

Mathias, R.L. and Jackson, J.H. (1994) *Human Resource Management*, 7th edn. St Paul, MN: West Publishing, chapters 18 and 19.

McCarthy, W.E.J. and Ellis, N.D. (1973) *Management by Agreement*. London: Hutchinson.

Millward, N., Stevens, M., Smart, D. and Hawes, W.R. (1992) *Workplace Industrial Relations in Transition*. Aldershot: Dartmouth: 217–75.

Milner, S. (1995) 'The coverage of collective pay-setting institutions in Britain, 1985–1990', *British Journal of Industrial Relations*, 33(1): 69–91.

Moore, R. (1980) 'Information to unions: use or abuse?', *Personnel Management*, May: 34.

Ogden, S.G. (1982) 'Bargaining structure and the control of industrial relations', *British Journal of Industrial Relations*, 20(2): 170–85.

Ogden, S. (1993) 'Decline and fall: national bargaining in British Water', *Industrial Relations Journal*, 24(1): 44–58.

Pickard, J. (1990) 'When pay gets personal', *Personnel Management*, July: 41–5.

Prondzynski, F. (1998) 'Ireland: Corporatism revived' in Ferner, A. and Hyman, R. (eds) *Changing Industrial Relations in Europe*. Oxford: Blackwell: 55–73.

Purcell, J. (1989) 'How to manage decentralised bargaining', *Personnel Management*, May: 53–5.

Singh, R. (1986) 'Final offer arbitration in theory and practice', *Industrial Relations Journal*, Winter: 329–38.

Stevens, C. (1966) 'Is compulsory arbitration compatible with bargaining?', *Industrial Relations*, 5(2): 38–52.

Taylor, R. (1997) 'UK unions: employers sense victory on recognition rights', *Financial Times*, 9 December.

Treble, J.G. (1986) 'How new is final offer arbitration?', *Industrial Relations*, 25(1): 92–4.

TUC (1997) *The Business Case for a Union Voice – Take your Partners*. London: Trades Union Congress.

TUC (1999) *Partners for Progress: New Unionism in the Workplace*. London: Trades Union Congress.

Walton, R.E. and McKersie, R.B. (1965) *A Behavioural Theory of Labor Negotiations*. New York: McGraw Hill.

Webb, S. and Webb, B. (1902) *Industrial Democracy*. London: Longman.

White Paper (1998) *Fairness at Work*. London: HMSO.

Willman, P. (2001) 'The viability of trade union organization: a bargaining unit analysis', *British Journal of Industrial Relations*, 39(1): 97–117.

Chapter 10

Employee participation and involvement

Mike Richardson

Learning objectives

By the end of this chapter, readers should be able to:

- distinguish and discern varying interpretations of employee participation and involvement (EPI);
- understand key concepts associated with EPI;
- discuss historical insight into the subject area;
- understand competing and complementary theoretical perspectives;
- identify the most popular forms of EPI and assess the character, level, scale and scope of these forms;
- understand the rationales behind EPI;
- express an informed opinion on the subject utilising case studies to illustrate and illuminate the main theoretical and empirical issues;
- evaluate the strategic approaches of employers and trade unions to EPI.

Introduction

Since 1979, as trade union influence has declined and new employment strategies associated with human resource management have emerged, uncertainties about the future direction of employee relations have brought about a widening interest in employee participation and involvement (EPI). Exhibit 10.1 echoes the enthusiasm emanating from some management (and trade union) quarters at the turn of the century for stakeholder or partnership forms of EPI. It is a useful vignette with which to begin, given the implication that the company in question, Unimerco, is professed to be an exemplar of 'stakeholder capitalism' to be mimicked by those companies and organisations eager to reap rewards from a better industrial relations climate. It is these types of accounts that are often cited as good examples of EPI. In 1989, a glossy government publication, *People and Companies: Employee Involvement in Britain*, profiled similar exemplary illustrations of EPI in order to promote new EPI initiatives. But to acquire a better understanding of EPI a more rigorous examination is required.

Exhibit 10.1

Unimerco

It is not unusual for companies to provide table-tennis tables for their employees' relaxation. But they are usually tucked away in a lounge or sports room, not scattered around the workspace.

At Unimerco, an engineering company based in Sunds, a small town in central Denmark, employees are encouraged to take a break from their duties at the 10 ping-pong tables that stand among the desks and machine tools. The company could be regarded as a model for the type of 'stakeholder capitalism' being scrutinised by business leaders and politicians around the world: it is a company keen on Anglo-American principles of shareholder value, but not at the expense of its workforce. At Unimerco, the theory seems to be working: it has a healthy profits record, has doubled its sales in the past five years and is on course for a further doubling by 2005, mainly through expansion outside Denmark. The company is owned by its employees, who receive a share of the profits every month and are compelled by company statutes to sell their shares if they leave.

As well as the ping-pong tables at the Sunds headquarters, there is a canteen with four cooks and a 24-hour bakery for the 390 employees. All of these employees have a key to the plant and can even accommodate guests; hidden away upstairs are 19 bedrooms kitted out in the manner of a luxury hotel. Kenneth Iverson is Unimerco's managing director and the driving force behind its management principles. It is his philosophy that employee involvement is fundamental to the company's good growth record. 'If you give people good surroundings, they will work better and be more innovative', he says. Another unusual aspect to Unimerco is that the office and factory areas are divided only by a line marked on the floor; employees from different parts of the company are free to intermingle, with the noise from the machinery deadened by special insulating panels in the ceiling. For good measure, the machine tools are painted white instead of the usual green or blue, to create a more restful environment. With expected sales this year of DKr440m (£37m) and 500 employees worldwide, Unimerco is a hybrid of manufacturer and service provider. It divides its business between manufacturing and selling specialised tools for factory machinery, and operating an after-sales service that includes repairs to machinery.

Apart from its staff benefits, Unimerco is run no differently from any other private business, according to Mr Iverson. 'The company is absolutely not to do with socialism', he says.

Mr Iverson is the company's biggest shareholder, holding a 33 per cent stake. Another third is owned by other senior managers, who are solely responsible for running the business, even though they give monthly briefings to staff on trading and are continually looking for new ideas from them. In the past decade, Unimerco has opened offices or small plants in the US, Norway, Sweden and the UK. Non-Danish sales account for 40 per cent of revenues. Unimerco made pre-tax profits of DKr20m last year and Mr Iverson is looking to double this during 2000. In five years, he anticipates that the company could have sales of DKr1bn, only 30 per cent of which would come from Denmark.

According to Mr Iverson, an accountant who has headed Unimerco since 1980, the company's ownership structure encourages its employees to think like small business people. 'We are spreading the ideas of capitalism to the workers, who understand that if you take some money out of one box, there is less left in another box', he says.

The stakeholder principles were introduced by Mr Iverson in 1987. They are based on ideas he picked up while working in Denmark's fishing industry, where boats are traditionally owned jointly by the skipper and crew.

As well as having the profit-sharing plan, the 80 per cent of Unimerco employees who are shareholders see their wages supplemented by an annual dividend. The average non-management employee holds a stake in the company worth a nominal DKr250,000. Yet this stake might be worth substantially more should the shares ever be traded openly.

Palle Rahbek, a machine operator who has worked at Unimerco for 11 years, says the fact that he can stroll across to one of the office workers, for instance to check on shipment details for a

▶

Exhibit 10.1 *continued*

customer, makes it easier to deal with problems. Tom Kjaider, another machine operator, says: 'The atmosphere here is a definite advantage. Compared to a lot of companies, we can have a good dialogue between the different divisions of the business.' Providing this good atmosphere does not come cheap. Unimerco has spent DKr120m in the past two years on new investment at Sunds, including a conference room which doubles as a venue for the employees to watch football matches on a huge television screen. At the flick of a button, the screen glides away to reveal a picture window from which can be seen the large lake immediately outside the building.

It is just one extra feature, according to Mr Iverson, which makes Unimerco a special place in which to work. The logic behind this is obvious: 'I wouldn't like to be a manager in a company and be the only person who was content.'

Source: Peter Marsh, *Financial Times*, 14 January 2001. © 2001 The Financial Times Limited

According to Blyton and Turnbull (1994), EPI has traditionally been the Cinderella of employee relations. But just as Cinderella habitually returns every pantomime season to beguile a new audience of children with fresh interpretations of an old theme, EPI also repeatedly manages to attract a new audience. The form, range, scale and scope of EPI may vary from one generation to the next, but the idea that it can, from the employer's perspective, fulfil a fundamental role in fostering good employee relations as well as improve productivity and profitability has remained. Moreover, the position adopted in the mid-1970s by the Trades Union Congress (TUC), though not without internal dissent, that EPI is progressive for workers in the sense that it advances industrial democracy, is also enjoying something of a renaissance. In the 1990s the TUC sought to renew its influence by campaigning for 'a new "social partnership" approach to industrial relations' (Fernie and Metcalf, 1995: 379) backed by legislation. What it did achieve after the election of Labour in 1997 was government support for partnership via the Partnership at Work Fund, financed with £5 million to be shared among successful bidders over a four-year period. Awards are available of up to 50 per cent of eligible costs of individual projects with a maximum of £50,000 per project. Government's thinking was that:

> By encouraging new partnership activities and helping foster the long term sustainability of existing ones, the fund aims to help the development of a skilled workforce within a flexible and motivated labour market and so stimulate the competitiveness of the UK economy. (DTI, 2001)

Whether or not the employers', TUC's and government's view of EPI coincide, it is pertinent to explore why it has continued to attract advocates from representatives of both capital and labour. Certainly, it does seem appropriate to question why it is that the political system in Britain (and other mature capitalist societies) has managed to accommodate participation by the people, whereas in the workplace this liberal democratic practice has yet to be established.

The first four sections of this chapter serve to acquaint the reader with some of the most significant definitional and theoretical issues necessary to clarify the subject of EPI and provide some explanations that will act as a guide towards understanding important developments in EPI practice. The object is to penetrate the surface appearance of EPI to gain access to more revealing and comprehensive knowledge.

The first section deals with the theoretical origins of EPI in Britain, tracing them from the beginnings of capitalist development when democratic ideas associated with the modern state first began to emerge. The second section undertakes to clarify the meaning of EPI. Definition is important, for to define something one has to explain it and to explain requires clear information about the subject matter. The focus of study then shifts to the theoretical frames of reference commonly used to explain the fundamental nature of the employment relationship. The various theoretical approaches offered provide the current stage on which EPI operates and the basis for its rationale, form and character. Next, the specific theories associated with EPI are investigated that cover shifts in power relations between capital and labour, cyclical patterns of EPI and contingent factors to explain the EPI phenomenon. We then turn to explore empirical information covering four important areas of EPI that in combination with the case studies gives the reader the chance to make the interconnections between theory and practice. A concluding view is then offered and finally a historical case study is given where many of the issues and theories raised in this chapter feature in their empirical form.

Theoretical origins of EPI in Britain

To fully comprehend EPI in its contemporary forms one must be aware of its theoretical roots, as historical and contemporary experiences are closely linked. Hence, it is of value to briefly trace developments associated with EPI from the seventeenth century to the end of the nineteenth century, when large-scale firms and organisations, the forerunners of today's monopoly companies, began to emerge.

In concert with the rise of capitalism in the seventeenth century, rationalist thinkers increasingly challenged the assumption that the existing arrangements concerning the organisation and government of society were 'natural' and immutable. This contributed significantly to the transformation not only in the way Britain was governed but also of the everyday experiences of the population. Philosophers at particular times have made important contributions to political, economic and social reform that have had crucial implications concerning the development of democracy, the employment relationship and EPI practice. This short section serves as a useful introduction to the subject area and provides a basis to further an understanding of contemporary developments in EPI.

Since the seventeenth century, as capitalism began to emerge from the womb of feudalism, differences over the meaning of democracy and who had the 'right' to participate in a democratic process were apparent. The Levellers'[1] demand for increased political democracy did not extend to the lower orders (servants, wage labourers or those on charity) for fear that private property rights might be threatened. The Diggers,[2] on the other hand, did not regard private property as sacrosanct and called for the abolition of wage labour and support for a communist programme (Hill, 1980). But this was only the beginning of the development of liberalism. The conditions of upheaval at this time that gave life to radical movements proved to be only temporary.

Not until the process of industrialisation created a mass working class, and the fusion of economic interests between the new capitalist class and the old aristocracy, did a new wave of radical liberalism come to the fore. John Stuart Mill, nineteenth-century philosopher, economist and Member of Parliament, was convinced that giving democratic rights to the working class would be to give that sector of society a stake in the system and that workers would therefore be less likely to rise up against it. Mill was concerned that workers increasingly viewed their interests as opposite to and in conflict with those of their employers. He analysed movements and ideas that promoted participation and matters of common interest between employers and workers (Mill, 1909). Whereas, like the Levellers, he defended the principle of private property and stressed the advantages of competition, he argued that this mode of production could be sustained and enhanced only if forms of EPI were adopted. One of the nineteenth-century radical experiments in which he took particular interest was 'cooperative production' based on the principles espoused by Robert Owen, mill owner, philanthropist and utopian socialist. Commonly owned self-managed factories, Mill argued, had one economic and moral advantage over the private capitalist: 'the common interest of all the workers in their work' (Mill, 1909: 790). He was convinced that private capitalists could capture some of this advantage by introducing profit-sharing, thereby ostensibly tying the efforts of the individual with the fortunes of the firm while contributing to social justice. From an anti-capitalist perspective, Karl Marx (1973: 288) attacked these profit-sharing schemes as a way of obfuscating the antagonistic relationship between capital and labour.

This initial discussion concerning democracy and the workplace and the merits or otherwise of profit-sharing already implies variance over the question 'what is EPI?' EPI can generate enthusiasm or hostility among participants and arguments among academics concerning its rationale. These reactions often depend on the definition placed on EPI and its linkage with theoretical differences concerning the analysis of industrial relations. Thus, differing definitions of EPI adopted by commentators, whether constrained by set parameters or based on analytical and theoretical disagreements, need to be considered. These definitions can then be associated with particular theoretical approaches to industrial relations in order to see how these inform and account for the interest in and controversy over EPI.

What is EPI?

A useful starting point is to make a distinction between the terms 'participation' and 'involvement'.

■ Participation

Hyman and Mason (1995: 21) classify participation as:

> state initiatives which promote the collective rights of employees to be represented in organisational decision-making, or to the consequence of the efforts of employees themselves to establish collective representation in corporate decisions, possibly in the face of employer resistance.

Collective bargaining, despite its decline in the 1990s, is most commonly associated with this form of participation (see Chapter 9). Other topical participatory schemes such as works councils and worker directors are likely to become increasingly important if, as seems likely, Britain becomes more integrated with Europe (see Chapter 6). These schemes were viewed by Conservative governments as forms of collective bargaining through the back door. There are participatory measures, however, that are outside the ambit of collective bargaining, although these are more generally referred to as forms of industrial democracy.

Workers' cooperatives, where workers themselves own the enterprise and have the right to elect the management team, fall into this category. Also the Guild Socialists, despite campaigning vigorously on a workers' control ticket, particularly between the years 1911 and 1921, supported the joint management of industry by the state and the trade unions with ownership in public hands. Weaker versions of Guild Socialism continued to have some influence in the Labour movement in the 1970s and 1980s (Kelly, 1988). The idea that, despite the negative experiences of post-war nationalisation in this respect (Coates and Topham, 1975), state ownership of key industries and services can provide workers with greater opportunities for participation in major strategic decisions, forms an important part of the industrial policy of the Socialist Labour Party. Even during the 1984–5 miners' strike, the National Union of Mineworkers (NUM) proposed a settlement based on the *Plan for Coal*, a strategy agreed between the National Coal Board, the NUM and the government in 1974, and reaffirmed in 1981, for this state-owned industry, reflecting continuing support for this form of participation (Labour Research, 1984; Freeman, 1986).

However, the push for joint control in state-run enterprises was a feature more associated with the 1970s. Labour's programme for fighting the 1974 general election stated:

> We intend to socialise existing nationalised industries. In consultation with the unions, we shall take steps to make the management of existing nationalised industries more responsible to the workers in the industry and more responsive to their consumers' needs. (Cited in Craig, 1990: 192)

Therefore, this concept of industrial democracy is often associated with the 'them and us' industrial relations environment of the 1970s. While this is still relevant (Kelly, 1988; Kelly and Kelly, 1991), it no longer fits well with either the employers' concept of empowering workers within the new industrial relations order that emerged during the 1980s (Bassett, 1987; Wickins, 1987) or the TUC's idea of social partnership in the 1990s.

What is also absent today, at least in a strongly organised form, is any significant movement advocating workers' control. Although it still has its adherents (in the Basque region of Spain for instance), syndicalism is currently at a low ebb. It is important, however, to know what the syndicalist concept of workers' control is. Syndicalists reject joint control or indeed state ownership of the means of production, arguing that the revolutionary overthrow of the capitalist system can only be achieved by the struggle for workers' control based on direct action through industrially organised unions.

Since 1979, a significant shift from a participatory to an individually based involvement agenda has taken place. Employers have taken the initiative to introduce new or rediscovered schemes that are 'task rather than organisation based' (Hyman and Mason, 1995: 18) as part of a strategy of securing workers' loyalty and commitment to the organisation as well as increasing productivity. This approach is commonly labelled as employee involvement (Guest, 1992; Marchington *et al.*, 1992).

■ Involvement

Changes since 1980 to the national economic, political and legal context in which the employment relationship has operated, as well as the intensification of international competition and the restructuring of the world economy, have been instrumental to employers seeking new or revived ways to achieve a competitive edge. During this period, changes in organisational and job design to increase the effective use of human resources emerged, the implementation of which is associated with more sophisticated techniques of motivation and control of the workforce. Emphasis in many of the organisations that looked to improve labour productivity began to be redirected towards a management strategy promoting the consent and cooperation of the workforce through task-centred and individually focused employee involvement schemes. It should be noted, however, that there is a debate as to whether this strategy has been concerned more with eliminating organised workers' resistance than with the benefits of organisational change (Geary, 1995).

In broad terms, therefore, there is clear division between involvement and participation, although it would be wrong to say that there is no overlap or link between them. It is not unusual to find participation and involvement operating in the same organisation. More often than not, this occurrence results from the pragmatic introduction of the HRM strategy, which fosters involvement schemes as a method of securing employee loyalty and commitment but recognises the organisational reality that existing industrial relations practice cannot always be abolished overnight, if indeed at all (Blyton and Turnbull, 1992).

In short, the meaning of participation is that those employees who have previously been excluded from the organisational decision-making process are actively engaged on a collective basis. Involvement relates to management-initiated policies and practice where empowerment is constrained to operational tasks, rather than organisational decision-making, targeting the individual. This still leaves the level, scale, range and form of participation and involvement to be considered, but these questions are dealt with later in the chapter.

Table 10.1 provides a typology and examples of different types of EPI, although it should be regarded with due caution. Implementation of schemes may vary between organisations. Moreover, often there are fine dividing lines between communication, consultation, involvement and participation, as well as differences in interpretation. Readers should take these factors into account and not use the table in a deterministic fashion. The same applies to Table 10.2, where some basic definitions are provided for guidance as well as the likely directional flow of communication and involvement.

Exhibit 10.2 provides an example of a large public sector organisation attempting to change the 'them and us' relationship that prevailed between management and employees in a situation where interpretations of industrial democracy, participation and involvement play an important part in shaping the attitudes and actions of the prime participants.

Table 10.1 Classification and types of EPI

Classification	Type
Workers' control	Worker self-managed cooperatives
Representative participation	Collective bargaining Worker directors
Representative consultation	Joint industrial councils Joint consultative committees Works councils
Financial participation	Profit-sharing Employee share ownership Unit-wide bonus schemes
Task-based involvement	Quality circles Teamworking Total quality management Suggestion schemes Customer care programmes
Non-representative consultation	Attitude surveys
Communicative involvement	Team briefing Company journal/newspaper Employee reports Videos

Source: adapted from Marchington et al. (1992) and Ramsay (1992)

Table 10.2 Employee involvement: some definitions

Term	Definition
Downward involvement	
House journal/newspaper	A publication produced on a regular and continuing basis by the company for distribution free to staff and other interested parties, which contains information about the organisation and its employees
Team briefing	A regular, structured system to enable top management to cascade throughout the organisation news and developments which are thought to be relevant to particular groups of employees
Upward involvement	
Attitude survey	A questionnaire survey of employees on a one-off or regular basis, which is designed to discover their views about a variety of factors connected with work. It is generally distributed to a sample of employees
Customer care programme	An initiative designed to involve employees in improving relations at the interface between staff and the customer, and to encourage staff to treat customers in a positive way
Quality circle	A small group of employees who meet voluntarily on a regular basis to identify, analyse and solve quality or other operational problems relevant to the organisation
Suggestion scheme	A formal procedure which enables employees to put forward ideas to management for improvements at work, and which provides for a system to reward acceptable suggestions which save money
Total quality management	A systematic process of management in which all employees are expected to see others, both internal and external to the organisation, as customers for their services

Source: Marchington et al. (1992)

Exhibit 10.2

The Royal Mail (Consignia)

The Royal Mail (Consignia) is a state-run industry and has been so throughout its existence. It employs about 120,000 postmen and women, 18,000 of whom are higher-grade employees known as PHGs. The Communication Workers Union (CWU) is the main trade union representing these workers, and union density is high. Since 1992, Royal Mail has operated as nine separate regional divisions. It has been extremely successful, measured in terms of both profitability and service.

Issues/experience related to participation and involvement over the last twenty years

The Post Office was one of a few organisations that experimented with workers' directors following the proposals of the Bullock Committee in 1977. The scheme was dropped soon after the election of a Conservative government in 1979. Although the scheme was ineffectual (Batstone et al., 1983), it did reveal significant differences between management and the union on the interpretation of and desire for industrial democracy. In particular, worker directors were marginalised in the area of organisational decision-making.

Collective bargaining, however, remained central to the conduct of industrial relations throughout the 1980s, but despite a moderate union leadership conflictual relations were a feature of this period. A militant, if rather parochial, CWU membership had an uneasy alliance with its leadership and a strained relationship with Royal Mail managers (Gall, 1995).

Spurred on, after the 1987 general election, by government policy designed to make the public sector more sensitive to consumer needs, the Royal Mail management launched a total quality management (TQM) programme in 1988. Unable to get union agreement, the introduction of teamworking was delayed (Jenkins et al., 1995), although other aspects of the TQM programme proceeded.

In an effort to overcome opposition to teamworking and employee involvement, Royal Mail sought and obtained an agreement with CWU in 1992 that set the parameters to a new industrial relations approach. Partnership was the buzzword, where the union was to be privy to more company information. Moreover, the agreement implied that the union would be involved in strategic matters (Bacon and Storey, 1996), although exactly what this means is unclear. Attempts at privatisation of Royal Mail were successfully defeated through a campaign led by the CWU based on lobbying Conservative MPs rather than mobilising its membership through mass demonstrations and threatened strikes (Gall, 1995).

Frustrated by its inability to gain consent for the introduction of team working, Royal Mail management in 1996 put forward a package of changes to pay and conditions, known as the Employee Agenda. A key feature of this agenda was the introduction of teamworking and the abolition of PHGs (IDS, 1996: no. 714). A UCW membership ballot conducted in May 1996, after talks on the Employee Agenda had collapsed, resulted in favour of industrial action, a decision which, after a summer of disrupted postal services, was reconfirmed in October 1996. Rejection of teamworking carried much weight in the decision to continue the dispute (IDS, 1996: no. 725). Settlement of the dispute was only reached when Royal Mail agreed to separate talks on teamworking from the Employment Agenda package (IDS, 1996: no. 726).

However, in 1997, Post Office workers embarked on another series of stoppages in opposition to the imposition of teamworking. In an effort to replace conflict with cooperation in postal services, the new Labour government, elected in 1997, considered adopting an employee share ownership scheme, a proposal favoured by Royal Mail management, that would give Post Office workers a 49 per cent financial stake in the business. The government spokesperson at the time, Ian McCartney, said he hoped that this would create a climate where Royal Mail employees and managers 'come together with a common approach and a common objective' (The Times, 18 August 1997). However, the frequency of industrial disputes involving postal workers in 2001 reveals that industrial relations problems in this industry have not been resolved. The main fear of postal workers is the continued threat of privatisation. A report commissioned jointly by Royal Mail and CWU in 2001 places blame on both the employer for creating a 'them and us culture' through its autocratic approach and the union for its failure to control unofficial action.

Theoretical approaches to industrial relations

Interpretations of the manner in which participants define, initiate and respond to EPI vary to a large extent, depending upon the theoretical approaches used, although this point should not be exaggerated because participants' views or practice can often be located in more than one approach. The distinctions between the theoretical frames of reference concerning industrial relations have been outlined elsewhere in this book (see Chapter 1). Suffice it here to identify and associate some of the main features from the unitarist, pluralist and radical perspectives informing and shaping the thoughts and actions of the actors in EPI.

Unitarism

Since the emergence in the 1980s of HRM as a serious challenger to the more conventional style of personnel management, unitarism, which during the 1960s and early 1970s seemed to be only of peripheral significance, has regained its status as an important frame of reference. This predominantly managerial oriented perspective, with its individualistic as opposed to collectivist values, now informs HRM thinking on contemporary involvement schemes (Guest, 1989), although the extent of this influence is open to debate. It is worth looking back a couple of decades, however, not only to see how the basic principles of unitarism, despite the apparent dominance of pluralism at the time, still seemed 'natural' to some employers, and indeed employees, in order to stress the continuity of the unitarist perspective, but also to identify some of its main features in practice that are relevant today.

The well-known memorandum of Sir Halford Reddish (1975), the chairman and managing director of the Rugby Portland Cement Co. Ltd, expressing by implication (Farnham and Pimlott, 1995) the principles and values of unitarism, in evidence submitted to the Donovan Commission in 1966 is revealing. The ideology and practice of Reddish and his company in the 1960s mirrors that of some HRM-oriented organisations of the 1980s and 1990s closely associated with involvement schemes. The term 'industrial relations' was deplored by Reddish, who preferred to operate in the human relations tradition, which was strongly influenced by unitarism (Fox, 1975). This approach was based on a hierarchical order, with authority being rooted in a strong leadership. The company did not belong to the pluralist-inclined institution the joint industrial council (JIC) for the cement industry, and notable by its absence in the Reddish memorandum is any mention of trade unions or conflict.

Nevertheless, this company, like other unitarist organisations, recognised the need to furnish its employees with a package concerned with the means to enhance their effectiveness and sustain motivation. Preferably this was to be achieved without trade union involvement, although in some cases this was impracticable (Fox, 1975). Recognition of trade unions does not fit well with the unitarist premise that the interests of all members of the organisation, managers and employees, are locked together in a common purpose. This thinking determined the Rugby Portland Cement Company's behaviour in regard to its employees and is often cited as the mainstay of HRM strategy in organisations such as Hewlett-Packard, Marks and Spencer and IBM in the 1990s (Blyton and Turnbull, 1994). The features identified by Reddish to buttress this approach were chiefly based on effective communication. For instance, important notifications were conveyed to staff via noticeboards before general release; employees were issued with a copy of the directors' report and accounts at the same time as shareholders; each individual plant had a works committee that met monthly; and profit-sharing and employee shareholding schemes were in operation (Reddish, 1975).

While contemporary involvement schemes have much in common with the unitarist-driven practice of Rugby Portland Cement, other factors derived from HRM, such as the strategic connection of involvement schemes with overall business objectives, have added coherence and purpose (Storey, 1992). Critically, however, this has come about as a result of the changed environment of the 1980s and 1990s, a period that has seen the intensification of international competitiveness, an end to the social democratic consensus of the 1960s and 1970s, consistently high levels of unemployment, and diminishing power, influence and membership of trade unions. These elements have brought unitarist thinking back into play. While HRM and many of the accompanying involvement schemes were imported into Britain from Japan via America when the political and economic conditions were ripe in the 1980s, the theoretical support for what is in essence a unitarist approach had long been in place.

Pluralism

The situation described above does not mean that the unitary approach has by any means displaced pluralism as the dominant industrial relations perspective. The situation is more complex, although a full discussion is outside the remit of this chapter. Suffice it to say that pluralism, where conflict is accepted but regulated by collective bargaining (see Chapter 9), has proved fairly resilient. More accurately, derivatives of pluralism have been adept at keeping alive the regulatory role in organisations active in taking up HRM initiatives (Storey, 1992). It is doubtful, though, whether they match up to the generalised description of pluralism outlined by Fox (1975). He defined pluralism as an approach where oppositional interests, recognised as both legitimate and desirable, are kept in check and balance through negotiation based on compromise and underpinned by the principle that neither side seeks to destroy the other.

The management styles identified by Purcell and Sisson (1983) are perhaps more useful in portraying the thoughts and actions of managers concerning industrial relations, particularly in the 1980s and 1990s. Purcell (1987) explains that the unitarist and pluralist frames of reference are rather narrow, restrictive and, most importantly, 'mutually exclusive'. He focuses on the interconnections between individualism and collectivism, arguing that the wide variations found in unitary and pluralist practice often overlap. This may explain why managerially initiated HRM unitarist-influenced employee involvement schemes such as teamworking and TQM have, in a number of cases, been introduced on the basis of agreement through negotiation in situations where trade unions have maintained collective bargaining rights (Monks, 1994). To what extent this 'social partnership' approach has or will affect the pace and direction of managerial practice from collectivised to individualised work relations, and the consequent implications for trade unions, is still not clear (Bacon and Storey, 1993; Taylor, 1997).

■ Radicalism

Radical critiques of EPI influenced by Marxist thinking do vary, although there is little disagreement that EPI must be considered in the context of society as a whole. Workplace relations is only one part of Marx's analysis of the organisation of society. Marxist theory purports that a society's economic base, or mode of production, wields the most power in shaping social, political and religious institutions as well as conditioning ideology to reflect the interests of the dominant class (Hyman, 1975). The dynamic in Marx's analysis is embodied in the relations of production, by which he meant the class structure of society: 'The history of all hitherto existing society is the history of class struggles' (Marx and Engels, 1952: 40). Marx refers to the transition of western civilisation from the stages of primitive communism, slavery and feudalism to capitalism to illustrate his approach to historical change. Marxist theoretical works have subsequently been drawn on as a guide to action: 'The philosophers have only *interpreted* the world, in various ways; the point, however, is to *change* it' (Marx, 1946: 65, italics in original).

Interpretation is the point of departure among those contemporaries influenced by Marxist thought concerning EPI. Their approaches to EPI range from total hostility to enthusiastic support. The argument put forward by those of radical persuasion opposed to EPI schemes of any description is that they serve only to obfuscate the antagonistic relationship between capital and labour and act as a barrier to the development of class consciousness (Kelly, 1988). The gist of this analysis is that EPI schemes legitimise the relationship between capital and labour and 'will bring about the more effective integration of workers into existing economic and social relations rather than produce any alteration in the capitalist system' (Clarke, 1977: 375). By staying aloof from these schemes and adopting an independent defence of their interests, workers can, however, begin to establish the link between conflict at work with the working of the capitalist system in its totality, thus shifting the struggle from the economic to the political sphere.

In contrast, those supporters of radical persuasion for 'encroaching control', popularised by the Guild Socialists (Cole, 1975), believe that EPI schemes should be welcomed provided that inroads into managerial decision-making, whether at task or organisational level, can be demonstrated, the logic being that the workers' position is strengthened *vis-à-vis* the capitalist class. Moreover, under certain conditions workers may be encouraged to intrude further into areas formerly controlled by management, until the time is reached where the strength of the working class is seen as incompatible with the interests of the capitalist class, giving rise to a revolutionary situation.

The problem with this approach is that capital is hardly likely to concede any form of control that threatens its very existence (Kelly, 1988) unless, metaphorically speaking, a gun is held to its head. Conversely, workers are unlikely to reject EPI for what they might see as some distant utopian goals if they see immediate benefits for themselves. Expediency and realism, strongly influenced by the power imbalance between capital and labour in both the particular and general situation, are, more than obligation, the most likely explanations of workers' behaviour (Fox, 1977). This adds weight to the findings of Kelly and Kelly (1991), who found little evidence to support the diminution of 'them and us' attitudes in firms adopting involvement schemes.

Having considered the part played by the main industrial relations perspectives in providing the rationale for and against EPI, we now move on to look at more concrete theoretical explanations of EPI practice that take into account differences in power relationships, cyclical patterns and contingent factors.

Theories of EPI

The impact of power relations and values on the realities of participation

Michael Poole's (1986) study of workers' participation, first published in 1975 when the participation debate in the political and industrial arena was at its height, recognised the importance of advancing a theoretical perspective in revealing the sources that drive developments in the practice of industrial democracy. Poole draws on the theories of Marx, Dahrendorf, Parsons and Weber to assist with building an explanatory framework for the subsequent discussions on management, worker, trade union and state initiatives in relation to industrial democracy.

Poole's central argument is that the form, extent, scope and range of participation in industrial life reflect the basic power processes in society. Thus the advancement of industrial democracy is determined to a large degree by shifts in power relations within society at the national or indeed the international level.

> Participation is viewed as very much the offspring of deeper, *latent* power processes which operate in society and the values about participation which obtain at any given point in time in particular societies and organisations. (Poole, 1986: 14, italics in original)

Poole emphasises that changes in the practice of industrial democracy are more strongly influenced by changes in latent power than the role of values, although both are interrelated in a complex web of cause-and-effect relationships.

The latent power factor of Poole's theoretical perspective rests particularly, though not exclusively, on the Marxist view, expressed here in simple terms: the changes in the social relationships of each class of humans to the means of production (plant, machinery, tools, technology, skills, knowledge and raw materials) are the result of class struggle between those who own or control the means of production and those divorced from ownership and control. The latter, with only their labour power to sell to secure means of subsistence, are thus open to subordination. But this labour power is a vital resource giving rise to the notion of interdependence between capital and labour (Poole, 1986). Unsurprisingly, therefore, the terms 'conflict', 'cooperation', 'compromise' and 'compliance' have all been used to describe continuity and change in social relations, revealing on the one hand the dynamics of latent power and on the other the difficulty of measuring its impact.

The real foundations on which latent power rests, according to Poole, are economic and technological factors along with government action. Economic factors that affect the power relationships between the main participants concerned – workers and management – and shape the character of employee relations are market power, the rate of profit, sales, growth, the degree of industrial concentration and competitive pressures.

Small firms in a competitive market are more likely to look to the short term, prioritise profits and adopt an authoritarian approach to employee relations with little room for EPI. In contrast, large-scale firms or monopolies have long-term objectives and may prioritise growth or sales rather than profits. These firms have much more leeway in the conduct of employee relations (Friedman, 1977) and thus are more likely to recognise unions and favour or even foster participation schemes (Poole, 1986).

Poole, in his theoretical approach, however, was not espousing economic determinism. In his model, values and ideologies of the participant parties concerned also influence the practice of participation, though only within the confines of the framework of latent power discussed above and the existing levels of participation. Moreover, the existing pattern of EPI must also be explained through tracing the historical development of participation. It is through such an examination that EPI has been associated with cyclical trends. Periodic interest in EPI in this theoretical model, according to Poole, is closely linked with heightened industrial unrest. The view that management is more inclined to be attracted to formal participation schemes when its authority seems to be under threat, however, has been developed most fully by Ramsay (1977). Thus we now turn to look at his perspective on the cyclical pattern of worker participation in Britain.

Cycles of participation

Ramsay's contribution looks at phenomena shaping participation chiefly from the macro rather than the micro level. His theoretical rationale is that only through an understanding of the contradictory development of all factors influencing the actions of participants in relation to EPI policy, rather than at the micro level of appearance only, is it possible to advance insights into the nature of EPI.

Ramsay purports that by tracing the history of formal participation schemes over a century or more, a distinctive pattern emerges. In times of heightened class tension, when the challenge to managerial authority from workers and their organisations intensifies, evidence suggests that the amount, scope and extent of formal participation schemes expand. A distinct cyclical pattern can be discerned associating fluctuations in the popularity of management-initiated participation schemes with the ebb and flow of workers' resistance to managerial authority. From this perspective 'participation is thus best understood as a means of attempting to secure labour's compliance' (Ramsay, 1977: 481). But this gives rise to a contradiction. Ramsay, applying a Marxist analysis, reasons that participation is built on the existence of a unity of interests, but the relationship between capital and labour is fundamentally antagonistic. Thus, unsurprisingly, the expected outcome of participation schemes from this perspective should be relative failure. Ramsay argues that this analysis can only be seriously called into question if participation schemes prove dominant and enduring. The evidence he draws on in his original article reveals that participation schemes can be expected to have only a transient existence. There are three main examples:

- 'Triviality' schemes where only non-controversial issues find their way onto the agenda. These schemes deteriorate quickly, handling only 'petty affairs (the "tea, towels and toilets" syndrome)' (Ramsay, 1977: 482). This pattern of events is just as likely an outcome whether the organisation in question is unionised or not. In establishments that recognise unions and employ collective bargaining procedures, other forms of participation have less influence and tend to wither away. In non-union establishments, workers are too weak to make an impact on any matters of substance.

- The case of 'instability'. When serious issues of conflict arise management attempts to resolve them through participation schemes other than collective bargaining and the union recognition this entails. In short, management tries 'to impose a unitary frame of reference' (Ramsay, 1977: 482) on a conflictual situation with the likely outcome of deepening the divisions between management and employees.
- The 'change of committee status', where management integrates collective bargaining with other forms of participation. When participation schemes are introduced to complement collective bargaining they are more likely to last. However, these schemes tend to be peripheral rather than central, hence their influence is minimal.

Ramsay offers a ready explanation for the phenomenon that participation schemes have been and still are attractive to some workers. Both capital and labour see participation in a different light. Management usually introduces participation schemes to facilitate an increase in productivity but often in conditions where its authority is under threat. In so doing it attempts to infuse its employees with a dose of unitary medicine. In this situation, however, employee representatives are more likely to see this as an opening to exert greater influence and advance industrial democracy. Thus, temporarily, participation is compelling to both sides as the contradictory situation between them is not always immediately apparent.

The resurgence of EPI schemes in the 1980s and 1990s has prompted a questioning of Ramsay's theory. Out of an empirical investigation into the motivation and character of these schemes, Ramsay's theoretical perspective on EPI has come under attack. Ackers *et al.* (1992) and Marchington *et al.* (1993) have argued that the 'cycles of control' theory does little to explain the reasons for management's adoption of EPI in the 1990s. Pressure from below since 1979 has evaporated as trade union authority and influences have waned. Ramsay's theoretical model, they argue, puts too much weight on the relations between capital and labour. This has resulted in the relative neglect of examining contingency factors at the micro level – that is, within the company or organisation. It is at this micro level, with a coordinated challenge from below noticeable by its absence, that Ackers *et al.* (1992) locate the main source of new EPI initiatives.

Contingency factors

Thus, according to Ackers *et al.* (1992), it is in response to a multiplicity of contingency factors that EPI in the past twenty years has evolved or been transformed. Responses will vary depending on factors such as the stage of development reached in the business lifecycle, the extent of market pressure, the strategy and structure of organisations, the presence or otherwise of active trade unionism, intermanagerial relations and ideologically driven polices of the state or even employers. As a result, a diversity of experience at company level has emerged, which the detailed, wide-ranging micro-study conducted by the Department of Employment reveals (Marchington *et al.*, 1992).

Marchington *et al.* make use of the wave metaphor to capture these new and disparate developments in EPI. Rather than give support to the idea that EPI schemes follow a recurring historical cyclical pattern driven by the state of play in the power relationships between capital and labour, the 'wave' concept according to Marchington *et al.* is more adaptable and analytically useful. The basic argument emerging from this perspective is that:

> the shape of EI [employee involvement] in organisations varies significantly over time, and can be characterised in terms of wave patterns. These are subject to a range of forces, one of the most important (and frequently overlooked) of which is the career aspirations and mobility of managers, and conflicts between different functions and levels in the organisational hierarchy. (Marchington *et al.*, 1993: 555)

Thus, a fluid, empirically driven enquiry is offered in preference to the rather deterministic theoretical approach adopted by Ramsay.

   To conclude this section, it should be noted that Ramsay (1993: 79) has responded to the critique of his theory by emphasising the importance of considering an empirical micro-analysis in relation to an overarching theoretical standpoint:

> Industrial relations like any other discipline needs theories and facts, debates on method as well as a determination not to draw explanation from the armchair field of vision. Or to put it another way, waves are no substitute for cycles (or vice versa).

The evidence arising out of recent empirical investigations, however, has deepened our understanding of EPI, as Ramsay (1993) has acknowledged, placing the debate concerning theories and motives for EPI centre stage.

EPI in practice

This section focuses on four areas of EPI – communicative involvement, non-representative consultation, task-centred involvement and financial participation – examining some of its most popular forms. It is intended to introduce to readers the practical experiences and consequences of developments in these areas, considering change and continuity, the degree and extent of certain forms of EPI influence, weaknesses in their application and the provisions required for success.

Communicative involvement

House journals

As a downward form of communication the company magazine or newspaper ranks as one of the most popular (Marchington *et al.*, 1992; IRS, 1999). Company magazines have a long history. Lever UK,[3] for instance, first introduced a company journal in 1898 as a means of buttressing its paternalist[4] approach to employee relations. During the twentieth century, to varying degrees, Lever UK has transmitted the culture of paternalism through its company magazine. Moreover, this internal medium has been used as a vehicle to advocate acceptance of work measurement schemes in 1950 and a job evaluation scheme in 1953. More recently, in the early 1990s, the magazine has used its pages to promote flexible working and the harmonisation of working conditions central to the company's Horizon 2000 strategy (Griffiths, 1995).

Clearly, as the Lever UK experience demonstrates, the house journal can be used to reinforce company culture or convey in a favourable light changes required in working practices. However, a continual one-way flow of information may well prove to be counterproductive. Employees can become very cynical if management-initiated information is constantly drip-fed through the medium of its house journal. The question of worker representatives and column space for employees to air their views without undue editorial interference, both considered by Lever UK (Griffiths, 1995), would no doubt give more credence to company magazines by actually involving employees. Some companies encourage this form of involvement but this seems to be the exception rather than the rule.

The most recent trend is for companies to publish the state of their finances in a company report, for internal consumption, with the view that 'opening the books' will improve employee commitment to the organisation (IRS, 1996). This trend, which focuses on industrial economics, implies that the success of the organisation and the well-being of its employees depend on profitability and growth. The idea behind it is that the revealing of financial information to employees is an expression of trust and partnership, fostering the view that it is in the best interests of management and the workforce to pull together in one direction to bring financial and commercial success to the organisation. The problem is that, when a company is doing badly, employees are more likely to think that management is practising 'creative accounting'. When a company is performing well, however, employees might demand a greater share of that prosperity.

Team briefing

Team briefings, according to a survey by the Industrial Society in 1995, are increasing in popularity (IRS, 1996, 1999). In its contemporary form, this system of communication involves line managers disseminating information, approved by top management, to the workforce on a regular basis. This system was promoted by the Industrial Society in the 1980s with a set of objectives in mind: to advance employee commitment, improve efficiency, control the information airways, gain acceptance of change and give more weight to the line manager's role, thus furthering middle management commitment (Marchington, 1989; Ramsay, 1992). The 'team brief' emphasises local issues where middle management and employees can identify their input and, therefore, should be more responsive to change or indeed initiate improvements in work practices themselves.

The weakness associated with team briefings, even when they are informative, well-structured and held on a regular basis, is that management assumes that the interests and concerns of employees concur with those of management. Given this unitary perspective and the buttressing of the middle management role, unsurprisingly, the atmosphere where employees can have an effective say is rather stifling. However, most organisations in recent IRS surveys (1996, 1999) claimed that team briefings allowed communication to flow in both directions. Moreover, these surveys show that team briefings, along with company journals, are the most prevalent form of communication used in the 1990s. This is not proof of their effectiveness, however, as the IRS (1996) survey also reveals that organisations were divided over whether team briefings matched expectations.

■ Non-representative communication

Attitude surveys

An increasing number of organisations are adopting attitude surveys as part of the EPI package, although it should be noted that this practice is not new. Attitude surveys have been in use in Britain since the 1930s when the National Institute of Industrial Psychology first applied them to industry (Townley, 1994). IBM has regularly used opinion surveys to test employees' views on a wide range of issues, including job satisfaction, job specifications and the organisation and management of the company (Bassett, 1987). In the Marchington *et al.* (1992) study, these attitude surveys were conducted in 20 per cent of the 25 organisations that cooperated in their research. In a more recent survey, however, of 49 public and private organisations, almost half recorded the use of attitude surveys (IRS, 1999).

Evidence from the IRS (1996) review and a recent Gallop poll suggest that a significant minority of companies has made major changes based on the findings of these surveys. This point should not be exaggerated, however, as the experience of a single survey in one large organisation, Granada, led it to abandon the project (IRS, 1996). This highlights the problem that, once surveys have been conducted, they become the property of management and the communication process ceases. Action based on attitude surveys is the prerogative of management. The danger in not responding to surveys, however, is that the situations revealed as problematical are likely to be exacerbated by inaction.

Nonetheless, some positive results have been forthcoming. Cussons (UK), the soap manufacturer, for instance, introduced an equal opportunities policy and an awareness training programme aimed at tackling problems of harassment in response to the feelings expressed by the staff in its survey (IRS, 1996). Thus opinions or problems uncovered by surveys can provide an important source of information in the formulation of policy, a point highlighted many years ago by Brown (1954). Brown realised that the disclosure of grievances and tensions in the workforce, which often have a negative impact on performance, helped to avoid misunderstandings but unless followed by positive action was of little value. In short, employees need to see that their views can actually influence decision-making.

The case study in Exhibit 10.3 is mainly based on information taken from two Co-operative Bank plc publications: *Strength in Numbers*, a first report (1997) and *In Touch*, a special edition of the Co-operative Bank customer newsletter (1997). It provides the opportunity to think about EPI in practice using as an example an organisation that claims to still strongly value the cooperative principles on which it was built.

■ Task-centred involvement

Total quality management

While the quest for improved product quality and customer service, to sustain a competitive edge, is not new, globalisation, liberalisation of markets, the pace of change in product markets and technology have all shifted up a gear, demanding a fresh managerial approach (Wilkinson, 1996). Total quality management (TQM) with its customer (internal and external) driven agenda is regarded by some as being able to give companies the edge in this new competitive environment (Juran, 1988, 1991). Moreover, in contrast

Exhibit 10.3

The Co-operative Bank

Employing 4,010 staff in 2001 and profit performance having improved year on year since 1993, the Co-operative Bank's position as one of the leading high street banks looks secure. This success, according to the bank, is the result of the redefining of traditional cooperative values and adapting them to the business environment of the 1990s as introduced in its mission statement of 1988.

What is particularly interesting is that the partnership approach emphasised in the mission statement seems to be in keeping with the TUC's social partnership approach to industrial relations and the Labour government's 'stakeholding' policy. The seven distinct partner groups are: customers, staff and their families, shareholders, suppliers, local communities, society at large, and past and future generations. The partnership approach stresses the importance of the interdependence of the partner groups in creating a dynamic environment healthy for long-term prosperity. According to *Strength in Numbers*, however, the bank places more weight on the contribution of its employees to the attainment of this end:

> It's fair to say that, in terms of ensuring continued success, we depend on nobody more heavily than our staff. (*Strength in Numbers*, 1997, p. 14)

Terry Thomas, the managing director of the Co-operative Bank in 1997, placed great store in the benevolent and paternalist ideas espoused by the nineteenth-century mill owner, Robert Owen. Like Owen, though, Thomas maintained that the building of a partnership approach was not done out of altruism but was a prerequisite to the achievement of a profitable and successful business:

> Many commentators have said that stakeholding is a threat to enhancing shareholder value. They then get lost in a dogmatic argument as to what stakeholding actually is or is not. My lifelong experience as a banker tells me that a combination of the Anglo-Saxon capitalist model with Robert Owen's inclusive approach to a company's key partners, provides this. (*In Touch*, 1997, p. 2)

Owen's scientific approach to managing the workforce rather than his socialism is the predominant factor reflected in the Co-operative Bank's employee relations strategy in the 1990s. The bank's mission statement stresses the importance of involving the partnership as a whole to forge an organisational conscience strong on ethics and with shared values, a common purpose and commitment to success. As part of this strategy the bank has pledged to conduct employee attitude surveys on all aspects of the business:

> We [Co-operative Bank] are committed to carrying out this type of survey on a regular basis to ensure that we remain in touch with the views of our staff in everything we do. (*Strength in Numbers*, 1997, p. 12)

The bank expresses the desire to explore all avenues to help staff to secure job satisfaction. A pilot scheme has been established to provide in-house facilities to study for National Vocational Qualifications as part of a programme to increase the 'employability' of its staff. Schemes such as 'homeworking' where staff are supplied with the necessary equipment to work from home are given as an example of balancing the interests of the organisation and its staff.

To conclude, a few relevant facts taken from an alternative source (Storey, 1995) provide a little more insight and background to events since the relaunching of the Co-operative Bank's partnership approach in 1988. Union membership at the Co-operative Bank was high in the early 1990s at about 90 per cent density. The then Banking, Insurance and Finance Union (BIFU), which represented most of the Co-operative Bank's employees, became increasingly concerned about the introduction of personal contracts and the decline in collective bargaining. Moreover, a staff council was established which BIFU boycotted because it allowed for the representation of non-union as well as union staff. Team briefings were brought into operation at times of crisis, to channel information to staff over the heads of union representatives: this happened when the bank recorded a pre-tax loss of £5,974 million in 1992. The chief executive of the bank warned of the dire consequences if staff voted to take strike action in a ballot organised by BIFU in response to the announcement of a pay freeze in 1991. BIFU did not get a mandate to call for industrial action on that occasion.

More recently, the Co-operative Bank has signed a partnership agreement with the banking union UNIFI, an agreement ratified in a secret ballot of members in 2000. In the same year, Hay Management Consultancy carried out a survey in respect of employment conditions. In general this survey provided positive feedback in respect of personal development, working environment, job security and the bank's cultural and ethical values. Only in regard to pay did staff express deep dissatisfaction, with only 26 per cent registering that they were satisfied.

to many other forms of EPI, TQM's design is such that TQM has the potential to be a permanent and enduring fixture. If this proves to be the case and TQM can be shown to empower workers, then Ramsay's 'cycles of control' theory may indeed require reconsideration (Hill, 1991).

The survey conducted by Marchington *et al.* (1992) revealed that TQM and customer care programmes[5] were indeed popular in that they were operative in 76 per cent of the organisations surveyed. Other surveys published in the same year also point to the expansion of TQM initiatives (Cruise O'Brien and Voss, 1992; Economic Intelligence Unit, 1992). The IRS research (1996), on the other hand, hints at a fall in the popularity of TQM.[6] Only 56 per cent of the respondents in this more recent survey acknowledge the use of TQM and customer care initiatives. Of these, however, we do not know whether TQM has been introduced in full or only in part.

On their own, therefore, these statistics do not suffice. Just what TQM comprises is still unclear. Hill and Wilkinson (1995) in particular, however, have contributed much to clarifying the situation by bringing together the common attributes of TQM across various academic disciplines to provide a generic definition. Thus, it has been made easier to differentiate those organisations consciously moving towards full TQM practice and those mistakenly claiming to be implementing TQM. Investigations have found that some organisations have only selected parts of the TQM package and/or operate TQM at certain levels of the business (IDS, 1990; Cruise O'Brien and Voss, 1992). Moreover, TQM has been found in some cases to be little more than a compilation of old schemes, such as job redesign and quality circles, bolted together (Wilkinson, 1996).

To be successful, TQM has to integrate individual and organisational goals into one unitary objective. To achieve this requires a flatter management structure and commitment from all employees to forge a new quality culture based on continuous improvement (Snape *et al.*, 1995). The problem is, however, that to work successfully TQM has to be driven from the top of the organisation down and it will take several years to become fully established (Hill and Wilkinson, 1995). This does not seem to bode well for employee involvement extending beyond operational task levels or holding employee interest and commitment, given that managers' powers are enhanced first before empowerment trickles downwards.

Snape *et al.* (1995) investigated the difficulty of achieving this aim. The proponents of TQM assume the presence of a unitarist employee relations culture. However, despite fundamental changes in important areas of employee relations, and an increase in managerial authority, over the past 25 years, it is a common error to think that traditional employee relationships no longer have an influential role (Hyman and Mason, 1995). Some evidence of resistance to TQM at the shopfloor level, therefore, should not be surprising (the Royal Mail case study in Exhibit 10.2 is one example). This is in keeping with Ramsay's (1977) and Hyman's (1975) view that capitalist social relations of production are fundamentally antagonistic.

Hill suggests, however, that at the operational level, employees 'have become more involved in issues that were previously the prerogative of management' (Hill, 1991: 565). As he implies later (Hill and Wilkinson, 1995), however, the debate over 'empowerment' and what that means in terms of EPI is yet to be resolved. Contingency factors as much as anything else may explain contrasting views in this debate. No real evidence has surfaced to suggest that TQM will extend employee involvement to the level of organisational decision-making.

As many commentators argue, the role of EPI in TQM programmes is focused on empowering workers at the point of production, and remains detached from the idea of extending EPI into the realms of decision-making in policy areas such as restructuring, investment, acquisitions and so forth (Snape *et al.*, 1995). Proponents of TQM are concerned with motivating 'employees to convert tacit knowledge of the work process into continuous process improvement and innovation' (Cruise O'Brien, 1995: 115). It is easy to see that TQM could end up as redundant in the same way as and for similar reasons to quality circles. Snape *et al.* (1995) imply that this might well be the case unless both EPI is increased and management style and work organisation are radically altered and integrated to attract rather than advocate employee commitment. Cruise O'Brien (1995) echoes this. She argues that a climate of trust is more important to the success of TQM than any problem with design faults. Trust can only be achieved, however, if TQM arrangements do not increase managerial control or incur job losses (Jones, 1997). In today's competitive environment this might not be possible.

Financial participation

Employee financial participation has been the subject of much attention by writers concerned with EPI (Poole, 1986, 1989; Bell and Hanson, 1987; Baddon *et al.*, 1989; Matthews, 1989; Poole and Jenkins, 1990; McLean, 1994; Fernie and Metcalf, 1995; Hyman and Mason, 1995; Knudsen, 1995; Pendleton *et al.*, 1995). Such was the optimism of the Industrial Participation Association (IPA) in 1984 that it concluded an attitude survey on profit sharing and employee shareholding with the prediction that:

> It is not farfetched to think that employee ownership may become as significant a part of employee relations by the turn of the century as unions have been throughout the century. (Bell and Hanson, 1984: 252)

However, the growth of employee share ownership, in which workers have a financial stake in the organisation that employs them, according to Smith (1993), has been due largely to tax incentives and the privatisation programme (where most employee share ownership plans (ESOPs) are to be found) pursued by Conservative governments in the 1980s and 1990s.

It is the distribution of workers' shares that often grabs the headlines. Employee shareholders in Medway Ports, for example, saw the value of their shares increase dramatically after being taken over 18 months after privatisation (*Financial Times*, 23 September 1993, cited in McLean, 1994). Examples such as this, however, are rare. More common, perhaps, are cases such as the flotation of Topps Tiles in June 1997, which made its owners millionaires. In contrast, the 300 employees of Topps stood to gain relatively little. Topps' owners proposed to give their 300 employees 'workers shares equal on average to 7 per cent of basic salary from their own holdings' (*Financial Times*, 28 May 1997). By May 2000, Topps Tiles had more than doubled its workforce to 779 and its share price had increased from the flotation price of 100p to 199½p in October 1997 to 228p in September 2001, but this price represents a 24 per cent fall from the previous year.

However, a full assessment of the stimulus for and impact of financial participation schemes can only be made by looking at past experience. The main reasons put forward for the introduction of such schemes are (1) to secure employee compliance (Baddon *et al.*, 1989; Matthews, 1989), (2) philanthropic or reward for loyalty (Baddon *et al.*, 1989; Matthews, 1989), (3) to weaken the trade union presence and influence and reduce or eliminate the need for collective bargaining, thereby increasing control over workers (Matthews, 1989), and (4) to counteract periods of heightened industrial unrest (Ramsay, 1977). At the macro level, financial participation schemes have been used as part of the overall drive to bring about a shareholding democracy (Copeman *et al.*, 1984).

Historical perspective

Matthews (1989) provides the most comprehensive analysis of profit-sharing in Britain over a long time period. Reaching back to the mid-nineteenth century, he considers the motives for and the effectiveness of profit-sharing up to the late 1980s. He concludes that 'profit-sharing seems to have been consistent with profit-maximizing behaviour by the firm and can be seen largely as a strategy of labour management' (Matthews, 1989: 440). Evidence of political and philanthropic motives was much less convincing. The effectiveness of profit-sharing in Britain over the past century or so, according to Matthews (1989), is weak, though this is based more on a qualitative rather than a quantitative analysis owing to the difficulty of measurement. This could well explain the paradox that profit-sharing is still valued by some employers. The experience of the John Lewis Partnership, with its particular brand of financial participation, deserves to be mentioned here as one of the few examples of employee involvement that has seemingly stood the test of time (see Bradley and Taylor (1992) for a full account). However, although profit-sharing and share ownership schemes have generated considerable interest, they have never become widespread.

Although largely invigorated by tax incentives, the resurgence of interest in financial participation schemes since 1978 has also been associated with other EPI schemes as part of a package aimed at improving the financial performance of organisations (McNabb and Whitfield, 1995) and improving employee attitudinal behaviour (Bell and Hanson, 1984). Moreover, employee share ownership schemes have been examined to see whether evidence of a shift towards increased participation or even industrial democracy exists (Pendleton *et al.*, 1995). With these points in mind we now turn to consider some of the more recent developments concerning financial participation.

Types of financial participation

This section looks at two of the more popular financial participation schemes: profit-sharing and employee share ownership plans (ESOPs).

Profit-sharing

Profit-sharing can be used as a form of monetary discipline on employees if it makes up part of their wage, and is meant as an incentive to work harder. There are some problems with this view, however. Evidence linking individual effort and profit is difficult to determine (Baddon *et al.*, 1989). Profit-sharing can be differentiated from share ownership in that clearly there is no property ownership link, thus commitment to the firm is based on the cash nexus. The end result might be the same, however.

For the employer, profit-sharing offers the advantage of wage flexibility. Labour costs automatically adjust to the firm's economic standing. This means that it is less necessary to lay off labour in times of recession. Consequently, when the economic situation picks up, the workforce and the necessary skills are in place to take immediate advantage of the improved climate (Baddon *et al.*, 1989; McLean, 1994).

At the macro level, according to the Weitzman theory, if profit-sharing is widespread then unemployment will fall without generating inflation (Baddon *et al.*, 1989; McLean, 1994). The hiring of additional workers is relatively cheap in companies operating profit-sharing schemes as the cost is in part shared by other workers, who will in effect take a cut in wages as the profit-based part of their income has to be apportioned to an increased number of workers. The problem is how do you universalise this sort of arrangement to run concurrently (Badden *et al.*, 1989). How low wages will fall in times of depression must also be considered. The other side of the coin, however, is that employees may feel that their jobs are more secure, and in more prosperous times profit-sharing could well be economically advantageous (McLean, 1994).

This form of economic democracy, however, is likely to have a negative impact on EPI, for if workers are involved in the hiring or firing of labour clearly it will be in their economic interests to reduce rather than increase employment levels, making the whole scheme impracticable (Nuti, 1986).

Employee share ownership plans

The ESOP is an American import which works as follows. An ESOP trust is set up to facilitate the execution of all aspects of employee share ownership. It is designed to make loan capital available to employees, expressly to invest in company shares. The appeal to employees is that the future financial benefits, expected to be engendered from the ownership of these shares, should enable them to repay their original loan and accumulate a surplus. The trust acquires loan capital from external sources, for example merchant banks, to purchase company shares, using company assets as collateral. Settlement of loans is achieved through employer donations and contractual repayments from shareholding employees (Cornford, 1990). Of course, these arrangements can vary considerably but the difference between ESOPs and earlier share option schemes, such as approved deferred trust (ADST) and save-as-you-earn (SAYE) schemes, is that they can deliver a comparatively high level of employee share ownership, a possibility that may well have discouraged some employers from adopting ESOPs (Baddon *et al.*, 1989; Hyman and Mason, 1995; Pendleton *et al.*, 1995). Following the March 2000 budget, a new all-employee share ownership plan (AESOP) came into being. Under this new scheme, companies may chose to offer employees two free shares for every one purchased, and employees can buy these 'partnership' shares out of pre-tax salary.

It was the Labour government of 1978 that initiated the revival in financial participation in its Finance Act by allowing tax concessions to firms that made shares (ADSTs) easily available to all of their employees. The Conservative Finance Act of 1980 encouraged full-time employees, subject to service qualifications, to participate in SAYE share option schemes. The Finance Act 1984 offered tax inducements to selected individuals opting to participate in discretionary or executive share schemes. Favoured members of staff were invited to purchase shares at generous rates. In 1989 this principle was extended to cover the whole workforce but has not proved so popular with companies (Hyman and Mason, 1995). For more information on profit-sharing and employee share ownership options in the 1990s see IDS (1998). The Labour government elected in 2001 is hoping that AESOPs will attract greater numbers of employees to take a 'stake' in the company. It sees these 'partnership' shares as a way to build partnership at work.

It is too early to make an assessment of AESOP in relation to its impact on securing greater employee commitment. There is evidence to suggest, however, that ESOPs and profit-sharing have resulted in an attitudinal change by employees from conflictual to more cooperative relationships with employers. Yet, as Poole and Jenkins (1990) highlight, this attitudinal change is only evident in companies that have introduced ESOPs in conjunction with other EPI initiatives – a view endorsed by the TUC (1999). Moreover, Kelly and Kelly's survey concludes that profit-sharing and share ownership have made no real 'difference to underlying "them and us" attitudes among participants' (Kelly and Kelly, 1991: 32). ESOP experience in the UK provides little encouragement to those advocating that this form of financial participation will be instrumental in extending employee participation into the realms of industrial democracy (Pendleton *et al.*, 1995; Trewhitt, 2000). After privatisation, many bus companies introduced ESOPs, raising expectations among employees that by participating in ESOPs they would have a greater opportunity to become involved in their company's decision-making processes. The fact that this did not happen is one reason put forward to explain why only one UK bus company remains wedded to this model. Trewhitt (2000) proposes that the fact that ESOPs did not become firmly established in newly privatised bus companies contributed to the restructuring of the industry through acquisitions and mergers. In the 1990s, 'bus buy-outs have changed ownership structure sooner and at a greater rate than other privatisation buy-outs and buy-outs generally' (Pendleton *et al.*, 1998).

It is worthwhile finishing this section with the observation that 'in an ideal world, employee share schemes reinforce motivation. But when a company is in difficulties they can mean morale is dealt a double blow' (*Financial Times*, 26 May 2001). An apposite remark given the poor performance of world stock markets in 2001.

Chapter summary

While clearly there is not a consensual view of EPI, research findings do reveal that different forms of EPI become prominent at different times for different reasons. In the 1980s and 1990s, EPI was reconstructed by management to restrengthen the competitive power of British companies in a global market and to engender employee commitment by extending workers' influence in task-centred matters (Guest, 1992). Doubts, however, have been expressed about how successful British management has been in changing workers' attitudes (Kelly and Kelly, 1991; Geary, 1994, 1995).

Most forms of EPI in the 1980s and 1990s have empowered workers only at the point of production with respect to work tasks in order to improve productivity and profitability. However, the attraction of task-centred EPI and financial participation is that seemingly direct managerial control techniques could be jettisoned in favour of responsible autonomy (Friedman, 1977), where workers are given more authority and responsibility over operational tasks. Research data from International Survey Research published at the end of 1995 reveals, however, that UK workers are dissatisfied and distrustful of management: 'Motivation and commitment to the company were lower even than in the strife-torn days of the mid-1970s' (*Financial Times*, 12 July 1997). Kelly's (1997) findings also support this view. Furthermore, Kelly also identified research that found employees were becoming increasingly dissatisfied with EPI and thought that the level of involvement in decisions affecting their work was diminishing. This evidence underpins Geary's (1995: 370) view that 'management are more concerned to root out shopfloor challenges to their right to manage than to transform the manner in which work is organised.'

However, despite this increasing scepticism and evidence of workers' resistance to EPI, as illustrated in the Royal Mail case study (Exhibit 10.2), it seems likely that EPI will continue to be an important part of labour management strategy for the foreseeable future. This view is strengthened by the fact that the TUC and the Labour government are seemingly committed to a stakeholding economy that includes the promotion of partnership at work. Moreover, the probability is that British workers will soon have the right to be represented on EWCs (see Chapter 6). Whether this will be enough to win workers' trust and commitment remains to be seen, but unless democracy is extended to the workplace, traditional forms of managerial control, and all the associated problems, are likely to continue.

The final case study (Exhibit 10.4) provides the opportunity to examine EPI experience in one company since its foundation over a century and a half ago. This will facilitate the testing of theoretical perspectives and provide food for thought as to why Mill's (1909) view that workers should have a stake in the system has not yet materialised. A word of warning, however – findings cannot be universalised on the basis of one example.

Exhibit 10.4

DRG FP/Rexam

The difficulty of relating the experience of a company over a long time period is to take account of the changes brought about by takeovers, acquisitions and mergers. This case is no exception. Hence, to trace the history of EPI in DRG FP/Rexam, the firms of ES & A Robinson Ltd (ES&AR) and John Dickinson and Co. Ltd (JD), which merged to form the Dickinson, Robinson Group (DRG) in 1966, are examined. More recent ownership changes have led to the break-up of DRG. The Pembridge Group acquired DRG in 1989 and quickly put into action a restructuring programme that included the dispersal of what were once seen as core sections of the business. Thus, DRG was in effect broken up, destroying most of its character and heritage. Rexam, perhaps, still carries, albeit rather tenuously, the DRG connection. Therefore, aspects of employee relations in Rexam's Bristol operation are transcribed to see if there is

evidence of continuity in respect to EPI. The point here is to trace EPI experience in one organisation over a long period and consider it in the light of contemporary theory and research findings.

ES&AR began trading as a family firm in Bristol in 1844. It expanded rapidly, and by 1885 was employing 600 people. In 1893, ES&AR registered as a limited stock company. Workers' shares, for those aged over 21 and with more than two years' service, were made available at this time. A profit-sharing scheme was introduced in 1912.

By 1918, ES&AR had started a programme of expansion based on acquisitions where ES&AR acted as the parent holding company. Employees in its Bristol factories numbered about 2,000 after the First World War and were well represented by trade unions at the collective bargaining table. After 1918, ES&AR actively participated in its appropriate

Exhibit 10.4 *continued*

employer organisation, which dealt with regional and national negotiations concerning wages and conditions, and was also well represented on the printing industry's joint industrial council (JIC). In 1929 the firm created the new post of personnel manager to deal with an ever increasing workforce. By 1935, the Bristol workforce numbered over 5,000, the majority being young women. Notably, in this year, nine members of the Robinson family held almost one-third of the ordinary share capital, thus the shift towards the separation of ownership from control in ES&AR proceeded very slowly. Its employees held by this time about £75,000 in workers' shares. This sum, however, represented only 4 per cent of the £1,848,000 share capital. Moreover, workers' shares did not carry any voting rights.

In 1919 a new bonus scheme based on 25 per cent of net profits was introduced. In an attempt to break the impact of a national strike in 1922, ES&AR declared that skilled printers belonging to the Typographical Association would lose their profit bonus if they did not return to work, which may well have contributed to the speedy resolution of the strike locally.

For the first time, after the 1926 General Strike, ES&AR introduced a contributory pension scheme for men over 21 and under 52 years, which the firm administered and supported by tendering an annual contribution. This scheme was made a condition of employment and involved the appointment of a trustee from the workforce.

Works committees, as recommended by the Whitley Council, were operational in ES&AR throughout the interwar years, although the craft unions refused to participate. A house journal, first published in 1914, was a regular feature of communication right through to the 1980s. After the merger in 1966, most individual plants also published their own magazines.

In the post-Second-World-War social, economic and political climate, collective bargaining flourished. Low levels of unemployment, increased demand and the reversal of the Trades Dispute Act 1927 assisted in the enhancement of trade union authority. This state of affairs was apparent in ES&AR. JICs still functioned but were hardly ever called upon to resolve problems as, up to 1959, disputes were rare.

But in the national stoppage called by the print unions in 1959 the JIC machinery failed. By 1967, the use of JICs in the printing industry was abandoned. After the 1959 dispute, ES&AR increasingly looked to settling industrial relations problems 'in house'.

JD established a stationery business in Hertfordshire in 1804, and by 1838 had diversified into papermaking. It was the stationery sector that flourished, however, and by 1914 JD employed over 2,500 workers, many of whom were women. In 1886 the firm became a joint stock limited liability company. The pace in the shift from ownership to managerial control, however, is not clear, although there were no family members on the board of directors after 1928.

JD never really warmed to trade unions. Craft workers in the firm joined trade unions at the beginning of the twentieth century but there is no evidence to suggest that they gained recognition rights. During the First World War, however, recognition rights were conceded to craft and non-craft workers. Moreover, JD welcomed the formation of a JIC in the paper industry in 1920. However, fraternisation with this form of industrial relations was short-lived. After the 1926 General Strike, employees were banned from belonging to a trade union. It became a condition of employment for employees to join the Union of the House of Dickinsons, a company union. JD also severed all connections with employers' organisations. Communication was channelled through a house magazine.

In 1920, £50,000 was diverted from company profits to initiate a contributory pension scheme. That same year, employees were also given the opportunity to buy company shares, and by 1933 the number of employee shareholders exceeded 1,400, about 20 per cent of the workforce. After 1926 and the formation of a company union, JD sponsored a new pension scheme to the tune of £100,000. The scheme was contributory, workers paying a levy of 2.5 per cent of their wages topped up by a contribution from the company based on profit levels.

The Union of the House of Dickinson was sustained through the Second World War and continued to influence heavily the relationship between management and employees until the merger with

Exhibit 10.4 *continued*

ES&AR in 1966. In 1946, however, a works committee was set up in one of JD's paper mills to suggest ways of improving efficiency in production areas, and employees were no longer forbidden from joining a trade union.

Following the formation of DRG in 1966, moves were made towards combining the various pension schemes. It was agreed that pensions management should include the consultation and participation of its members. It was not until 1978 that one common pension was achieved. A system was set up to elect employee representatives and trustees who have the power to make decisions on behalf of their members.

By 1981, 70 per cent of the 14,000 people employed by DRG in the UK belonged to a trade union. Collective bargaining was the dominant feature of industrial relations. Increasingly, however, despite national agreements, interpretation had become a matter for in-house negotiation, particularly on issues such as payment for machine extras.

In the 1980s, works councils were introduced in many of DRG's plants. They were not always supported by the trade unions. Other EPI schemes apart from collective bargaining included job evaluation, though only for white-collar workers. In one such scheme the evaluation panel consisted of two employee and two management representatives. Some of the house magazines were under employee rather than management editorship. Suggestion schemes were in operation, which included payment for ideas that were successfully adopted.

By the 1990s, the employment relationship had changed considerably. DRG no longer existed, its constituent parts having been divided among a number of new owners, and trade union representatives were forced into adopting a much more submissive role. Rexam Medical Packaging, which acquired an important segment of the DRG business, identified in 1994 that one of its goals was to achieve 'a total quality approach'. By 1996 it believed it had achieved this. According to the company, training and motivating staff provided the key to this success. New working practices, a flatter management structure and the involvement of staff in resolving work task problems were adopted when a new plant opened in 1992 (Nichols, 1996). However, in January 1997, the *Financial Times* reported that the Rexam packaging group planned to dispose of many of its subsidiaries by 1998, thus putting the credibility of EPI from the perspective of its employees in jeopardy.

Source: Richardson, 1991, 1995

Activities

Reread the Unimerco case study in Exhibit 10.1.

1 How effective do you think Unimerco's EPI programme would be in securing the commitment and motivation of staff in a similar organisation in the UK?

2 The following questions relate to the Royal Mail (Consignia) case study presented in Exhibit 10.2.

   (a) Compare and contrast the 'partnership' approach to employee involvement in Royal Mail with the 'workers' directors' participation experiment.

   (b) To what degree has EPI in Royal Mail been defined and shaped by the fact that it is a state-run industry?

   (c) How mindful was Royal Mail of introducing teamworking into an environment characterised by traditional industrial relations?

3 Answer the following questions with reference to the Co-operative Bank case study presented in Exhibit 10.3.

(a) From the evidence given here, to what extent do you think the Co-operative Bank is committed to an EPI strategy?

(b) Is 'stakeholding' or the 'partnership approach' compatible with EPI?

(c) What would you recommend as a way forward for expanding or improving EPI techniques at the Co-operative Bank?

4 The following questions relate to the DRG/Rexam case study in Exhibit 10.4.

(a) To what extent do you think the DRG/Rexam experience validates either Ramsay's cyclical theory or the contingency model put forward by Ackers *et al.*?

(b) Is it evident that managerial attraction to EPI was a means to weaken trade unionism, substitute trades unionism or provided as an added dimension to participation?

(b) To what extent do you think acquisitions, mergers and job losses weaken EPI objectives?

Notes

1 The Levellers, reflecting the interests of the middle orders, small property holders, artisans, husbandmen and yeomen, agitated for the extension of the suffrage to male householders.

2 The Diggers, a radical religious poltical grouping, believed that private property robbed people of their common rights. God created earth and its life sustaining treasures for all to share equally and not to be exploited by the few to dominate the many.

3 Lever UK started out life as Lever Brothers Ltd, Port Sunlight.

4 Paternalism is a relationship existing between a powerful employer and a weak workforce; a paternalist relationship requires employers' commitment to a clear set of economic and social obligations designed to secure workers' deference.

5 In the survey conducted by Marchington *et al.* (1992) TQM and customer care programmes are classified together.

6 In the IRS (1996) survey TQM and customer care initiatives are classified separately.

Useful websites

www.centre.public.org.uk/news_and_events   Gives links to news items from the Centre for Public Services.

www.dti.gov.uk/er/index.htm   Department of Trade and Industry   A government department which, among other areas, has responsibility for dealing with employment relations issues.

www.eiro.eurofound. ie   European Industrial Relations Observatory On-Line   Provided by the European Foundation for the Improvement of Living and Working Conditions, it contains substantive information on European developments in industrial relations on an EU, country and sectoral basis.

www.europa.eu.int/comm/employment_social/index_en.htm   European Union   Provides access to information on the work of the European Commission, the Council of Ministers, the European Parliament and the European Court of Justice.

www.icftu.org   International Confederation of Free Trade Unions   Links together national unions from a particular trade or industry at international level.

www.ilo.org   International Labour Organization (ILO)   Database on international work standards and national laws on labour, social security and human rights.

www.partnership-at-work.com   **Partnership at Work Fund**   Provided by the Department of Trade and Industry to encourage employers, employees and their representatives to work together to solve particular business problems by stressing the importance of communication at all levels.

www.tuc.org.uk/index.cfm **Trades Union Congress**   Press releases, publications, organisation details, online journals and industrial relations.

References

Ackers, P., Marchington, M., Wilkinson, A. and Goodman, J. (1992) 'The use of cycles? explaining employee involvement in the 1990s', *Industrial Relations Journal*, 23(4): 268–83.

Bacon, N. and Storey, J. (1993) 'Individualization of the employment relationship and the implications for trade unions', *Employee Relations*, 15(1): 5–17.

Bacon, N. and Storey, J. (1996) 'Royal Mail: a new industrial relations framework' in Storey, J. (ed.) *Blackwell Cases in Human Resource and Change Management*. Oxford: Blackwell.

Baddon, L., Hunter, L., Hyman, J., Leopold, J. and Ramsay, H. (1989) *People's Capitalism?* London: Routledge.

Bassett, P. (1987) *Strike Free*. London: Macmillan.

Batstone, E., Ferner, A. and Terry, M. (1983) *Unions on the Board*. Oxford: Blackwell.

Bell, D.W. and Hanson, C.G. (1984) *Profit Sharing and Employee Share-holding Attitude Survey*. London: Industrial Participation Association.

Bell, D.W. and Hanson, C.G. (1987) *Profit Sharing and Profitability*. London: Kogan Page.

Blyton, P. and Turnbull, P. (1992) 'Afterword', in Blyton, P. and Turnbull, P. (eds) *Reassessing Human Resource Management*. London: Sage.

Blyton, P. and Turnbull, P. (1994) *The Dynamics of Employee Relations*. London: Macmillan.

Bradley, K. and Taylor, S. (1992) *Business Performance in the Retail Sector: The Experience of the John Lewis Partnership*. Oxford: Clarendon Press.

Brown, J.A.C. (1954) *The Social Psychology of Industry*. Harmondsworth: Penguin.

Clarke, T. (1977) 'Industrial democracy: the institutionalized suppression of industrial conflict?' in Clarke, T. and Clements, L. (eds) *Trade Unions under Capitalism*. London: Fontana.

Coates, K. and Topham, A. (eds) (1975) *Industrial Democracy and Nationalization*. Nottingham: Spokesman.

Cole, G.D.H. (1975) 'State ownership and control' in Coates, K. and Topham, A. (eds) *Industrial Democracy and Nationalization*. Nottingham: Spokesman.

Copeman, G., Moore, P. and Arrowsmith, C. (1984) *Share Ownership*. Aldershot: Gower.

Cornford, J. (1990) *A Stake in the Company*, Economic Study No. 3. London: Institute for Public Policy Research.

Craig, F.W.S. (1990) *British General Election Manifestos 1959–1987*. Aldershot: Parliamentary Research Services.

Cruise O'Brien, R. (1995) 'Employee involvement in performance improvement: a consideration of tacit knowledge, commitment and trust', *Employee Relations*, 17(3): 1110–20.

Cruise O'Brien, R. and Voss, C. (1992) 'In search of quality', London Business School working paper, London.

DTI (2001) *Partnership at Work Fund*.

Farnham, D. and Pimlott, J. (1995) *Understanding Industrial Relations*, 5th edn. New York: Cassell.

Fernie, S. and Metcalf, D. (1995) 'Participation, contingent pay, representation and workplace performance: evidence from Great Britain', *British Journal of Industrial Relations*, 33(3): 379–415.

Fox, A. (1975) 'Industrial relations: a social critique of pluralist ideology' in Barrett, B., Rhodes, E. and Beishon, J. (eds) *Industrial Relations and the Wider Society*. London: Macmillan.

Fox, A. (1977) 'The myths of pluralism and a radical alternative' in Clarke, T. and Clements, L. (eds) *Trade Unions under Capitalism*. London: Fontana.

Freeman, M. (1986) 'The road to power', *Confrontation*, 1.

Friedman, A.L. (1977) *Industry and Labour*. London: Macmillan.

Gall, G. (1995) 'Return to sender: a commentary on Darlington's analysis of workplace unionism in the Royal Mail in Britain', *Employee Relations*, 17(2): 54–63.

Geary, J.F. (1994) 'Task participation: employees' participation enabled or constrained?' in Sisson, K. (ed.) *Personnel Management*, 2nd edn. Oxford: Blackwell.

Geary, J.F. (1995) 'Work practices: the structure of work' in P. Edwards (ed.), *Industrial Relations*. Oxford: Blackwell.

Griffiths, J. (1995) ' "Give my regards to Uncle Billy . . .": the rites and rituals of company life at Lever Brothers, c.1900–c.1990', *Business History*, 37(4): 25–45.

Guest, D.E. (1989) 'Human resource management: its implications for industrial relations and trade unions', in Storey, J. (ed.) *New Perspectives on Human Resource Management*. London: Routledge.

Guest, D.E. (1992) 'Employee commitment and control' in Hartley, J.F. and Stephenson, G.M. (eds) *Employment Relations*. Oxford: Blackwell.

Hill, C. (1980) *The Century of Revolution*. Walton-on-Thames: Nelson.

Hill, S. (1991) 'Why quality circles failed but total quality management might succeed', *British Journal of Industrial Relations*, 29: 541–68.

Hill, S. and Wilkinson, A. (1995) 'In search of TQM', *Employee Relations*, 17(3): 8–25.

Hyman, J. and Mason, B. (1995) *Managing Employee Involvement and Participation*. London: Sage.

Hyman, R. (1975) *Industrial Relations*. London: Macmillan.

IDS (1990) Report No. 457. London: Incomes Data Services.

IDS (1996) various reports. London: Incomes Data Services.

IDS (1998) Report No. 641. London: Incomes Data Services.

IRS (1996) 'Assessing employee involvement strategies', *Employment Review*, 614: 4–12.

IRS (1999) 'Trends in employee involvement', *Employment Review*, 683: 6–16.

Jenkins, S., Noon, M. and Lucio, M. (1995) 'Negotiating quality: the case of TQM in Royal Mail', *Employee Relations*, 17(3): 87–98.

Jones, O. (1997) 'Changing the balance? Taylorism, TQM and work organisation', *New Technology, Work and Employment*, 12(1): 13–23.

Juran, J.M. (1988) *Juran on Planning for Quality*. New York: Free Press.

Juran, J.M. (1991) 'Strategies for world class quality', *Quality Progress*, March: 81.

Kelly, J. (1988) *Trade Unions and Socialist Politics*. London: Verso.

Kelly, J. (1997) 'The future of trade unionism: injustice, identity and attribution', *Employee Relations*, 19(5): 400–14.

Kelly, J. and Kelly, C. (1991) 'Them and us: social psychology and the new industrial relations', *British Journal of Industrial Relations*, 29(1): 25–48.

Knudsen, H. (1995) *Employee Participation in Europe*. London: Sage.

Labour Research (1984) *The Miners' Case*. London: LRD Publications.

Marchington, M. (1989) 'Employee participation' in Towers, B. (ed.), *A Handbook of Industrial Relations Practice*. London: Kogan Page.

Marchington, M., Goodman, J., Wilkinson, A. and Ackers, P. (1992) *New Developments in Employee Involvement*, Research Series No. 2. Sheffield: Employment Department.

Marchington, M., Wilkinson, A., Ackers, P. and Goodman, J. (1993) 'The influence of managerial relations on waves of employee involvement', *British Journal of Industrial Relations*, 31(4): 553–76.

Marx, K. (1946) 'Theses on Feurbach' in Engels, F. *Ludwig Feurbach and the End of Classical German Philosophy*. Moscow: Progress Publishers.

Marx, K. (1973) *Grundrisse*. New York: Vintage.

Marx, K. and Engels, F. (1952) *Manifesto of the Communist Party*. Moscow: Progress Publishers (reprint of the 1888 translation).

Matthews, D. (1989) 'The British experience of profit-sharing', *Economic History Review*, 2nd series, XLII(4): 439–64.

McLean, H. (1994) *Fair Shares: The Future of Employee Financial Participation in the UK*. London: Institute of Employment Rights.

McNabb, R. and Whitfield, K. (1995) 'Financial participation, employee involvement and financial performance at the workplace', Cardiff Business School Paper, Cardiff.

Mill, J.S. (1909) 'On the probable futurity of the labouring classes' in *Principles of Political Economy*. New Jersey: Kelley (repr. 1976).

Monks, J. (1994) 'The union response to HRM: fraud or opportunity', *Personnel Management*, September.

Nichols, P. (1996) *Work and Employment*. Bristol: University of the West of England.

Nuti, D.M. (1986) *Profit Sharing and Employment: Claims and Overclaims*. Florence: European University Institute.

Pendleton, A., McDonald, J., Robinson, A. and Wilson, N. (1995) 'The impact of employee share ownership plans on employee participation and industrial democracy', *Human Resource Management Journal*, 5(4): 44–60.

Pendleton, A., Wilson, N. and Wright, M. (1998) 'The perception and effects of share ownership: empirical evidence from employee buy-outs', *British Journal of Industrial Relations*, 36(1): 99–123.

Poole, M. (1986) *Towards a New Industrial Democracy*. London: Routledge.

Poole, M. (1989) *The Origins of Economic Democracy: Profit-sharing and Employee-shareholding Schemes*. London: Routledge.

Poole, M. and Jenkins, G. (1990) *The Impact of Economic Democracy: Profit-sharing and Employee-shareholding Schemes*. London: Routledge.

Purcell, J. (1987) 'Mapping management styles in employee relations', *Journal of Management Studies*, 24(5): 533–48.

Purcell, J. and Sisson, K. (1983) 'Strategies and practice in the management of industrial relations' in Bain, G.S. (ed.) *Industrial Relations in Britain*. Oxford: Blackwell.

Ramsay, H. (1977) 'Cycles of control: worker participation in sociological and historical perspective', *Sociology*, 11(3): 481–506.

Ramsay, H. (1992) 'Commitment and involvement' in Towers, B. (ed.) *The Handbook of HRM*. Oxford: Blackwell. (Originally reproduced as *Open Learning MBA Unit 8: Employee Involvement in Management of Human Resources*: University of Strathclyde).

Ramsay, H. (1993) 'Recycled waste? Debating the analysis of worker participation: a response to Ackers *et al.*', *Industrial Relations Journal*, 24(1): 77–80.

Reddish, H. (1975) 'Written memorandum of evidence to the Royal Commission on trades unions and employers' associations' in Barrett, B., Rhodes, E. and Beishon, J. (eds) *Industrial Relations and the Wider Society*. London: Macmillan.

Richardson, M. (1991) 'An examination of industrial relations in the Bristol printing and packaging industry covering the period from the end of the First World War to 1991', dissertation, University of the West of England.

Richardson, M. (1995) 'Industrial relations in the British printing industry between the wars', PhD thesis, University of the West of England.

Smith, G. (1993) 'Employee share schemes in Britain', *Employment Gazette*, April.

Snape, E., Wilkinson, A., Marchington, M. and Redman, T. (1995) 'Managing human resources for TQM: possibilities and pitfalls', *Employee Relations*, 17(3): 42–51.

Storey, J. (1992) 'HRM in action: the truth is out at last', *Personnel Management*, April.

Storey, J. (1995) 'Employment policies and practices in UK clearing banks: an overview', *Human Resource Management Journal*, 5(4): 24–43.

Taylor, R. (1997) 'New Labour, new unionism', *Financial Times*, 5 September.

Townley, B. (1994) 'Communicating with employees' in Sisson, K. (ed.) *Personnel Management*, 2nd edn. Oxford: Blackwell.

Trewhitt, L. (2000) 'Employee buyouts and employee involvement: a case study investigation of employee attitudes', *Industrial Relations Journal*, 31(5): 437–53.

TUC (1999) *Share Ownership and Productivity*. London: Trades Union Congress.

Wickens, P. (1987) *The Road to Nissan*. London: Macmillan.

Wilkinson, A. (1996) 'Three roads to quality' in Storey, J. (ed.) *Blackwell Cases in Human Resource and Change Management*. Oxford: Blackwell.

Further reading

Albert, M. (2000) *Moving Forward: Program for a Participatory Economy*. Edinburgh: AK Press.

Danford, A., Richardson, M. and Upchurch, M. (2002) 'New unionism, organising and partnership: a comparative analysis of union renewal strategies in the public sector', *Capital and Class*, 76.

Hyman, R. (1997) 'The future of employee representation', *British Journal of Industrial Relations*, 35(3): 309–36.

Kelly, J. (1997) 'Industrial relations: looking to the future', *British Journal of Industrial Relations*, 35(3): 393–8.

Lewchuk, W. and Robertson, D. (1997) 'Production without empowerment: work reorganisation from the perspective of motor vehicle workers', *Capital and Class*, 63: 37–64.

McKinlay, A. and Taylor, P. (1996) 'Power, surveillance and resistance: inside the "factory of the future"' in Ackers, P., Smith, C. and Smith, P. (eds) *The New Workplace and Trade Unionism*. London: Routledge.

Waddington, J. and Whitston, C. (1996) 'Empowerment versus intensification: union perspectives of change at the workplace' in Ackers, P., Smith, C. and Smith, P. (eds) *The New Workplace and Trade Unionism*. London: Routledge.

Chapter 11

Pay

Jane Evans

Learning objectives

By the end of this chapter, readers should be able to:

- identify the contemporary contextual factors influencing pay in the workplace;
- examine the functions of pay within the employment relationship;
- consider the implications for pay of changing employee relations frameworks;
- examine the process of pay determination;
- analyse the constituent elements of pay and pay systems.

Introduction

A commonly used term such as 'pay' needs little introduction as to its general meaning but its monosyllabic appeal does disguise a topic of considerable complexity. In this chapter, 'pay' is used to denote the wages, salaries or fees paid by employers in return for the provision of labour. The term includes allowances, overtime and variable elements (such as bonus or performance-related pay) and benefits which have a financial value and are perceived by employees to be linked to their pay (e.g. life assurance, private health care).

This description of pay is reasonably neutral in that it does not anchor itself firmly within any one particular perspective of employee relations. However, in reality, pay is not determined within a vacuum and does introduce questions of employer, employee and union values as well as those of society as a whole. This chapter explores the territory of pay from a number of perspectives but does not seek to be prescriptive in terms of recommending particular approaches to address specific problems.

Pay, as a topic, cannot be addressed in isolation from other aspects of employee relations. For example, there are links with legislation, collective bargaining and discrimination in employment. An understanding of the different theoretical frameworks and of the trends within employee relations is necessary background.

Pay is an enduring and central feature of the relationship between employer and employee that is recognised in this book by its treatment as a separate topic. In particular, this chapter examines:

- the contemporary contextual influences on pay;
- the functions of pay within the employment relationship;
- the implications for pay of changing employee relations frameworks;
- the process of pay determination;
- the constituent elements of pay.

Contemporary contextual factors

A range of factors, including government policy on employment and the economy, the legislative framework, employment trends and labour markets, technological change and societal values, influence pay in the workplace. Increasingly, the UK's membership of the EU and globalisation of markets introduce an international dimension.

Government policy on employment

The change in government in 1997 to a Labour administration after 18 years of Conservatism signalled a new era in employment policy. The original tone for employment reforms was set by a policy document (1996) entitled *Building Prosperity – Flexibility, Efficiency and Fairness at Work*, with the election manifesto targeting areas for reform, two of which are considered here: trade unions and the national minimum wage. Work–life policies moved more visibly onto the Labour government's agenda as it moved through its first term of office.

In terms of pay, trade union reform potentially affects both the climate for pay determination and the role undertaken by the unions. The Labour government stressed from the outset that it did not seek to dismantle all the 'anti-union' laws put in place by the Conservatives, but rather favoured 'partnership not conflict between employers and employees' (election manifesto). Statutory trade union recognition (where a union has over 50 per cent of the workforce as members, within a bargaining unit) was introduced in June 2000 following the Employment Relations Act 1999. Its introduction asserted collective rights of employees that would extend into the area of pay. The Advisory, Conciliation and Arbitration Service comments 'overwhelmingly, employers and trade unions have taken a non-confrontational, voluntary approach to reaching agreement on recognition, in preference to using the new statutory powers' (ACAS, 2001: 8).

The national minimum wage (NMW) was introduced in 1999 to address low pay, reduce the social benefits liability of supplementing the wages of the low paid and to bring the UK into line with other industrialised countries such as the US, Japan and continental Europe. The NMW represents an interventionist approach to pay that asserts an individual statutory right to a minimum level of pay, and is in contrast to the free market views that the Conservative government had espoused and which had been put into practice with the abolition in 1993 of the wages councils for low-pay sectors. The Conservative Party, despite initial hostility to the NMW, withdrew its opposition after its introduction.

The independent Low Pay Commission was established in 1997, charged with advising the government on what the NMW should be. One of the key issues in setting the NMW is its ratio to that of the average wage; the higher the ratio the greater the impact of the minimum wage policy. International comparisons provide differing benchmarks. For example, in the US the minimum wage is approximately one-third of the average wage, whereas in continental Europe it is 50–60 per cent. The government opted for an opening rate of £3.60 per hour, much closer to the US than to the European model. The rate has been adjusted annually to £3.70 (2.8 per cent increase) in October 2000, and to £4.10 (10.8 per cent) in October 2001 (with a scheduled increase to £4.20 in October 2002). ACAS (2001: 9) observes that 'the existence of a national minimum wage appears now to be generally accepted by both trade unions and employers'.

The explanations for patterns of low pay vary. One explanation for such patterns is that these workers have less 'human capital' to offer employers in terms of the education, training and experience that they bring to the labour market. Low pay is therefore intrinsically linked with workers who have low skill levels under such an analysis.

More broadly, low pay has been associated with particular categories of workers, for example with part-time female workers who earn, on average, 60 per cent of the male full-time earnings (New Earnings Survey, 2000). While employment patterns for ethnic minority workers are complex, and may be polarised between the high and low qualified, there is some evidence that there is a concentration in low paid employment of both men and women from ethnic minorities (Kirton and Greene, 2000: 20–5). In evidence to the Low Pay Commission, representatives of female Asian home workers described their 'bleak life . . . a depressing picture of long hours and job insecurity with irregular work . . . pay comes from the incentives of the piece work system' (*Financial Times*, 29 May 1997). Such an example illustrates that a range of factors may contribute to low pay: gender and ethnicity as well as a particular pattern of working (home working). Disabled persons are more likely to find employment in low-skilled or low-status jobs (DfEE, 1997). While there are considerable pitfalls in treating such groups as homogeneous, the underlying trends are relevant in a discussion on low pay. The focus of worker attributes becomes entangled in some ways with the debate on discrimination. 'It is clear that a segmented and segregated labour market exists in Britain. Occupational segregation . . . is linked directly to lower pay, lower status and increased vulnerability of employment' (Kirton and Greene, 2000: 44). For further detail on the discrimination debate, see Chapter 12.

It is also possible to explain patterns of low pay by focusing on the characteristics of establishments where low-paid workers are to be found. McNabb and Whitfield (2000: 586) state that: 'at least some of the factors associated with low pay are institutional in nature and are related to the strategies of employing organizations, the structure of labour and/or product markets and the nature of collective employment relations'. One strategy that organisations can adopt is to minimise costs involving low pay and numerical flexibility, most likely to be present in product markets where price is the main determinant. Low pay is less likely when there is collective representation (McNabb and Whitfield, 2000). Colling (2000: 86) suggests, however, that the NMW provisions may restrict employer strategies that seek to reduce labour costs through contracting or outsourcing, especially in conjunction with the individual rights to representation that may give unions a 'toehold in non-union contracting organisations'. At the same time, contracting strategies allow employers to 'externalise' low pay. By using the 1998 WERS study (see Cully *et al.*, 1998) McNabb and Whitfield complement what they see as the focus on worker attributes taken by the Low Pay Commission (1998) with an emphasis on the employing organisation. Their conclusion is that 'the establishments most likely to pay low wages . . . are single, private sector establishments, in competitive labour markets, which have limited collective industrial relations institutions. Both monitoring and ancillary support should be focused on these' (McNabb and Whitfield, 2000: 605).

The government has taken on board the work–life balance agenda in a number of ways, furthering the debate by publishing a Green Paper *Work and Parents: Competitiveness and Choice in Late 2000*, and entering into round-table discussions with the Trades Union Congress, Confederation of British Industry and Equal Opportunities Commission on flexible working, maternity and paternity provisions. Subsequent legislative measures to help working parents were proposed in 2001 with the Department of Trade and Industry's Work and Parents Task Force recommending that employers should consider seriously requests for shorter hours from parents of children aged under six and of disabled children under 18. Such requests have to be seen against a backdrop of a long-hours culture that appears endemic and widespread in the UK (Arrowsmith and Sisson, 2000: 287–313). The government has instigated reviews into long working hours, responding to concerns about the take-up of entitlements under the Working Time Regulations. Commentators remain divided about the likelihood of change: 'Kicking the long hours culture is not going to be easy' (Arrowsmith and Sisson, 2000: 309). While the detail of the work–life balance debate is outside the scope of this chapter, the issues concerned have a clear impact on terms and conditions in the workplace, and are relevant to employer strategies on pay as well as to employees' aspirations expressed individually and collectively.

Government policy on the economy

The Labour government of 2002 is committed to a market economy that is internationally competitive and strong, with flexible labour markets. There are a number of policy areas relevant to pay that have been evident.

First, the government is keen to hold down public spending and, therefore, has attempted to restrain public sector pay, often in combination with attempts to modernise pay structures, for example in the health services and latterly in terms of reforming police service pay. In practice, the government has faced considerable and continuing challenges. For some groups of public sector workers (such as doctors and dentists, schoolteachers and the armed services), the government needs to take into account the recommendations of independent pay review bodies, the difficulties in attracting and retaining public sector workers, and public opinion (see Exhibit 11.1). At the same time, the administration is mindful of the problems of bitter and long-running public sector pay disputes faced by Labour administrations in the 1970s.

Secondly, the government shares with its predecessors the desire to keep inflation low. Inflation, or the fear of it, has historically driven pay settlements, with the wage–price spiral most evident in the 1960s, 1970s and late 1980s. Employees and unions, anticipating price increases during such periods, sought pay settlements in line with these, sometimes renegotiating several times a year. There has been a period of sustained low inflation. ACAS (2001: 8), in its review of pay settlements for 2000/1 concluded:

Exhibit 11.1

Public sector pay pensions giveaways 'raise expectations'

Ministers are bracing themselves for a battle with nurses and teachers over pay, concerned that generous giveaways to pensioners and hauliers in the pre-Budget report have raised their expectations.

The government is set for a difficult public sector pay round in January after unions submitted bids to pay review bodies for substantial across-the-board increases.

Officials from the big public sector unions said yesterday that while they welcome the extra cash for pensioners, and cuts in vehicle excise duty and petrol tax would benefit their members, the government had sent a message that presenting a case vociferously appeared to work.

'The message from the pre-Budget report is that whoever shouts the loudest gets the most', said one union official. 'That is something our members will bear in mind when the settlement is announced.'

Teachers have requested a double-digit increase to bring their members into line with other graduate groups.

'When the government came to power there was enormous goodwill from teachers. When you look at the balance sheet now after a string of disappointing pay rounds there appear to me more debits than credits for our members. The government is skating on thin ice', said the National Union of Teachers.

Unison, the public service union, requested a substantial pay rise for all members and restructuring of pay scales to help those on the lowest grades.

Officials warned that members in higher education had already rejected their pay offer and were being balloted on industrial action. Local government white collar staff in Scotland were planning a day of action next week.

Nurses, stretched to the limit due to the recruitment crisis, have told the pay review body that an above-inflation pay rise for junior nurses last year helped to attract staff. 'That proves pay works and we want a substantial increase next year too', said the Royal College of Nursing.

Source: Rosemary Bennett, *Financial Times*, 11 November 2000.
© 2000 The Financial Times Limited

Stability in pay settlements which has been a feature of the employment scene for some while now continued this year with pay deals generally coming in at or just above three per cent – very close to the headline inflation rate. Stability in pay settlements couple with a sustained period of low inflation may be the reason why the trend continued to grow for organisations to seek long-term deals, usually tied into an agreement over working practices or conditions.

Thirdly, taxation policies are relevant to pay determination. Direct tax has an impact upon take-home pay and indirect taxation affects household budgets. Employers are wary of changes in corporation tax that influence what they feel they can afford to pay employees. The government's declared policy has been to restrain tax increases, which has arguably contributed towards a stable climate for pay determination, although public pressure to improve public services, especially the NHS, may make it more difficult for the Chancellor to sustain that policy.

■ Legislative framework

Pay is regulated to some extent through legislation. In particular, the Equal Pay Act 1970 (with the Amendment Regulations 1983 and 1996) aims to ensure that men and women are not discriminated against in terms of pay on the grounds of sex. The Employment Rights Act 1996 (formerly the Wages Act 1986) regulates deductions from pay.

The Trade Union Reform and Employment Rights Acts 1993 includes references to itemised pay statements and written particulars of employment. (For more detail on the relevant legislation, see Chapter 8). The thirtieth anniversary of the Equal Pay Act provided a focus for widespread debate on its effectiveness and need for further change. The Equal Pay Task Force (2001) and the Kingsmill Report (2001) proposed a number of reforms, the implications of which are considered later in this chapter in the section on equal pay.

Trends in the labour force and markets

There have been major changes to the UK labour force and job markets since the 1970s. The loss of jobs from the manufacturing sector and the decline in manual employment in the early 1980s was followed a decade later by redundancies of white-collar workers in the service sector. The extent to which these changes represented a radical or permanent shake-up in the labour markets has been open to dispute, for example, the average length of time staff stayed with an employer changed little over the preceding decade (*Social Trends*, 1996). At the same time, employees appeared to feel insecure in the light of downsizing, even if they 'survived' rounds of redundancy and despite a downward trend in unemployment sustained until late 2001. 'The trend has been away from secure tenured employment in the slimmed down anorexic organisation of the 90s' (Redman and Wilkinson, 2001: 317). Employers favour redundancy over pay freezes or cuts (Redman and Wilkinson, 2001: 307). While the longer-term economic impact of the September 11 attacks on the World Trade Centre in New York may be unclear, there was a surge in reported layoffs (notably in the travel industry) in the following months of 2001. At the same time, public sector recruitment remained buoyant (Bank of England, 2001).

The labour force, after declining in the first part of the 1990s, is steadily rising in the early 2000s (mainly owing to demographic changes), with activity rates generally increasing for women and decreasing for men. There are variations between age groups; for example, the proportion of 16–24 year olds in full-time education is increasing, thereby affecting activity rates for this group. At the same time more students are working part-time to fund their studies. Among male workers aged 55–64, activity rates are falling, although less markedly than during the early 1980s. The fall in unemployment may explain why the trend towards early retirement became less marked in the 1990s. Among those who are economically inactive, a small core remain 'discouraged', believing that work is unavailable.

Government social welfare policies influence patterns of participation in the labour force. For example, financial incentives aimed at the jobless or at single parents on benefits seek to encourage the economic participation of these groups.

Technological change

Technological change has had an impact on the skills profile of jobs resulting variously in deskilling, reskilling and skills upgrading. Where such changes occur they have implications for pay levels and pay hierarchies.

The print industry provides an example of the impact of technological change. News International introduced (secretly) in 1986 new technology at a greenfield site

(Wapping), including a 'direct input' system so that journalists could type copy directly into the computer. Previously this work had been done by members of the National Graphical Association (NGA), a craft union recognised by both management and unions as powerful, gaining good pay settlements and working conditions for its members. Journalists who were working for the corporation faced apparently the loss of their jobs and therefore generally agreed to the new system. The secretive imposition of new technology without the negotiated consent of the print unions led to a bitter and prolonged dispute. However, the skills profile of a craft group was irreversibly changed and their powerful position in respect of pay undermined.

Technological change has commonly been associated with greenfield sites and the promise of competitive advantage where there is also the chance for innovation in terms of employee relations/personnel policies and systems. It is not clear to what extent such innovation has happened on greenfield and other sites (McLoughlin and Clark, 1994: 89). There is evidence that advanced manufacturing technology has not been widely introduced within the UK. Innovation in manufacturing has arisen more evidently from cellular production that focuses upon a particular product or component where groups of typically up to 20 workers are expected to be proficient in a range of skills. There have been corresponding changes in payment systems in recognition of workers acquiring new skills (Proctor and Ackroyd, 2000: 228–31). New technology agreements which may be an indicator of employee relations change generally have not been widely adopted in either unionised or non-unionised organisations (Daniel and Millward, 1993).

Pay and the employment relationship

■ The legal function of pay: pay and the contract of employment

In the contract of employment, the employee agrees to provide a personal service for the employer in return for payment; such 'consideration' binds the parties and is therefore at the heart of the contract of employment. The level and nature of the payment is the outcome of negotiations between the parties, who in a legal sense have freely and voluntarily come to an agreement (and seek to update that as long as the contract continues). In reality the negotiations may be governed by collective agreements, restricting the capacity of an employee to reach a purely personal contract, although in theory all contracts of employment are personal and individual. The power relationship between the two parties is unlikely to be strictly equal, so the bargain struck may lead one party to feel coerced.

Brown *et al.* (2000) note that the number of employees who are covered by bargained or statutory collective agreements has substantially declined over the past two decades from 83 per cent in 1980 to 35 per cent in 1998.

> Meanwhile, whether or not backed by collective agreements, employment contracts for most employees have become both highly standardized and formalized . . . Management has achieved a high degree of control over the content of the employment contract, but trade unions still help enforce their members' statutory and other employment right . . . Substantive 'individualization' – the differentiation of contractual terms within the organization has generally not been recognized. (Brown *et al.*, 2000: 626–7)

Employers have not been freed from regulation, rather that the mode of regulation has shifted from collective to individual.

Historically within the UK, the basis of the contract was that of master/servant, so that in consenting to the legal relationship, an employee accepts the status of subordination to the authority of the employer (such legitimate authority being known as the managerial prerogative). Ongoing negotiations between the parties have to be set, therefore, within this context. In matters of pay, the employer can seek to exercise managerial prerogative, for example, in the choice of payment systems.

Pay as a mechanism for fulfilling employer and employee objectives

An understanding of pay depends upon examining further the possible objectives of employers and employees involved in pay determination. There may be areas of common interest but there may be inherent conflict. Differing interpretations of the relationships between the parties are important. For example, a *unitarist* perspective (assuming mutuality of interest between employers and workers) suggests that there need not be conflict between them. A *pluralist* perspective (acknowledging a range of interests) indicates that conflict is possible. A *Marxist* perspective (with a clear divide between capital and labour), argues that conflict is inevitable. (For more detail on these perspectives, see Chapter 1.)

Employee objectives

From an employee's perspective, pay fulfils economic and social objectives. It provides a certain standard of living, enables lifestyle choices to be made and is an indicator of societal status. Individuals' objectives in respect of pay change according to circumstance; for example, security of employment may be valued more highly than the level of pay at certain stages of life.

Employees, therefore, have a mix of objectives, just as employers do. Torrington and Hall (1998: 584–6) identify these as (1) purchasing power, which determines the standard of living, (2) 'felt fairness' about a 'fair rate', (3) rights to a fair 'share' in profits or the nation's wealth, (4) the need to maintain relativities in relation to other workers, (5) the need for recognition, and (6) the need for a suitable composition of pay.

Employer objectives

Pay is a key mechanism by which an employer can persuade individuals to join and stay with the organisation, and make use of their effort and skills in pursuit of organisational objectives. Pay is therefore connected with the attraction, retention and deployment of workers.

Typically, employers have a mix of objectives. Torrington and Hall (1998: 586–9) cite the following: (1) the prestige to be gained from being a 'good payer', (2) the need to be competitive to ensure a sufficient supply of labour, (3) the need for control over workers, (4) the need to motivate and improve the performance of workers, and (5) the need to control costs.

The employer's capacity to attract and retain employees at an affordable cost to the organisation is the result of a mix of variables reflecting the contextual factors discussed earlier in this chapter. It will depend partly on the employment opportunities in the marketplace that are open to potential employees and the relative perceived financial and non-financial merits of the competitors. The potential employee may also make decisions about whether to enter the labour market and whether it is financially viable to withdraw temporarily or permanently, for example during periods of study or to take early retirement.

The employer's ability to use labour to the organisation's benefit through the instrument of pay raises questions of the relative strength of pay as a motivator. While a detailed consideration of motivation theories is outside the scope of this chapter, it is worth noting important principles. Bowey and Thorpe (2000: 97) draw upon a range of motivation theories to advocate an 'eclectic approach', namely employee involvement (in the design of payment systems); the removal of 'demotivators' (barriers to high performance); equity (fairness); reinforcement (encouragement and feedback for employees); relevance of reward (to employees); and goals (clear and of interest to employees). While individual differences, the nature of the work and its context are important variables, Bowey and Thorpe (2000: 96) conclude that the process adopted by management in designing and introducing pay systems is an important determinant of success. Roberts (2001: 530–1) stresses the importance of equity in terms of distributive justice (that reward satisfaction and motivation are influenced by perceived differentials, not absolutes), and of procedural justice (employees must be convinced that the procedure leading to pay outcomes is fair).

■ Pay as a visible manifestation of the psychological contract

The notion of the psychological contract (Schein, 1965) helps explain the centrality of pay in the employment relationship in that it stresses the importance of the unwritten expectations that both parties have. Pay is a visible and tangible manifestation of the value that an employer places upon an employee and confers status. Below this surface statement is a tangled web of mutual expectations with many tensions. When employees talk of equity and fairness, or employers of reasonableness in relation to pay, both parties are alluding more to unwritten expectations than to a legally determined position. If one side believes that the other is frustrating its legitimately held expectation, then a progressive breakdown or breach in the employment relationship will follow. There is some evidence to suggest that breach may be a frequent occurrence (Robinson and Rousseau, 1994). Herriot and Pemberton's (1997) research highlights the importance of negotiating changes in the psychological contract rather than imposing them during periods of organisational restructuring. 'The major issue in analysing and negotiating contracts is not what is being offered by each party so much as what is a fair-exchange deal' (Herriot et al., 1997: 160). In times of job insecurity, it may be dangerous for employers to rely too heavily on employee goodwill derived from a longer-term or relational contract (employee commitment and loyalty in reciprocation for fair pay, training and development, and reasonably secure employment, etc). Employees may well shift their focus to the transactional aspects of the contract, putting more weight on their immediate pay and conditions.

Where unions are involved, there is a triangular arrangement in that the employee has a psychological contract with both the union and the employer. As a union member, the employee has unwritten expectations that the union will not, for example, 'sell out' to the employer. The union expects that its members will support it as required, for example, if it calls for strike action in support of a pay claim, it expects such support to be forthcoming.

Employees' perceptions of fairness are partly determined by their view of how much other employees are paid (often they have imperfect knowledge of what that is). The question of differentials is important, i.e. the maintenance of the gap between their earnings and those of other groups in the organisational hierarchy of pay. Employees also reference their pay by looking at the earnings of groups outside the organisation, making judgements about the fairness (relativity) of their own situation.

The extent of possible breakdown in mutual expectations in relation to pay is reflected within the advisory, conciliation and arbitration work undertaken by ACAS. In 2000/1, approximately 50 per cent of collective conciliation casework, some 13 per cent of advisory mediation work and 44 per cent of arbitration and dispute mediation were attributable to pay and grading issues (ACAS, 2001: 56–8).

The implications for pay of changing employee relations frameworks

■ A new pay order?

In the past couple of decades the UK employee relations landscape and climate have changed, reflecting competitive pressures and the political agendas of both Labour and Conservative governments as well as the perceptions and views of the 'actors'. Corresponding changes have taken place in terms of pay – for example, widespread interest in pay initiatives such as performance-related pay, and the moves away from national collective bargaining. The extent to which these represent a primarily pragmatic response by the 'actors' involved in pay or the emergence of a new pay order is an important question. Both perspectives have their supporters, but the lack of empirical evidence and the difficulties of defining 'old' and 'new' pay are problematical.

The concept of 'new pay', emerging in the US in the late 1980s and early 1990s, is based on what is held to be a distinctive philosophy with a managerialist slant. The terms 'reward management' or 'employee reward' are more commonly used to delineate the departure from traditional pay and the arrival of a new pay order within a UK context. Armstrong (1999) in marking out the territory of employee reward argues for an underlying pay philosophy based on contribution and competence rather than just compensation for attending work. The link between business and reward strategy is seen as critical to the development and success of the latter.

The new pay order appears to fit more comfortably within HRM than in traditional employee relations approaches. It is important, therefore, to place debates on pay within the broader framework of employee relations changes.

■ Pluralism/unitarism; collectivism/individualism

There are a number of possible dimensions on which changes in employee relations can be mapped. Attempts to construct thematic classification systems that describe end states associated with 'traditional' employee relations or HRM as a distinctive employment approach often touch on common themes. Such systems draw attention to the multidimensional aspects of change along a continuum.

Among the common themes are those of pluralism/unitarism and collectivism/individualism. Storey (1992), for example, in identifying 27 points of difference between 'industrial relations and personnel' and 'HRM', described the nature of relations as pluralist in the former, with conflict institutionalised, and unitarist in the latter, with conflict de-emphasised. Another dimension of labour management in the same model associates collective bargaining contracts with industrial relations, and personnel and individual contracts with HRM. The very use of the term 'collective bargaining' in respect of pay suggests a pluralist framework in which collective bargaining provides the mechanisms for a failure to agree and institutionalises the scope for conflict. The decline in membership of trade unions and the restrictive climate they had faced under the Conservative government as well as a resurgence of the managerial prerogative arguably undermined the traditional pluralist framework for pay.

The stated commitment of the Labour government to collective bargaining through compulsory trade union recognition may strengthen the pluralist foundations for pay. At the same time the government has called for a 'stakeholder economy' and a 'partnership' approach to employee relations. It has made it clear to the unions in urging modernisation that it does not want to return to the confrontational climate faced by the Labour administration in the 1970s.

The TUC's official response is broadly supportive although there is unease about this policy among some trade unionists for whom it represents an unacceptable compromise brought about by their weakened industrial position. The TUC general secretary has reflected, 'There is no alternative to capitalism that I can see but are we to have the US model with few rights for workers, the authoritarian model of the East Asian tiger economies, or the European model of social partnership? . . . For small countries like ours, I think it is the only model' (*People Management*, 11 September 1997: 29). 'I believe that trade-unions should aim for partnership style agreements. It makes for an agenda where people are not just in trenches but finding ways of growing what the company does, and what they do themselves' (John Monks, quoted in *Sunday Times*, *Business*, 10 February 2002). The CBI's policy seems to be one of cautious support for partnership.

The new pay order espouses the concepts of the stakeholder and employee involvement, identifying unions as one of the stakeholders (Armstrong, 1999). Collective bargaining is accepted, although minimally addressed, within reward management. There is emphasis on varying pay to acknowledge individual or group contribution. Employee involvement is managerially driven and seeks to minimise the risk of conflict. Overall reward management (as a pay orthodoxy) is more unitarist than pluralist and more individualistic than collectivist rather than exclusively one or the other. The rhetoric of 'partnership' and 'stakeholders' is shared by those who support a pluralist framework and as such may be seen as a counterbalance to adopting more extreme positions at either end of the continuum.

In practice it is probable that new order pay coexists with more traditional approaches, including the presence of trade unions. The survey data of WERS98 suggest that 'an active and strong union presence is compatible with the broad suite of high commitment management practices' (Cully *et al.*, 1999: 111).

Business strategy and pay

Another set of possible changes in employee relations relates to the extent to which practices are driven by business or corporate strategy and are integrated horizontally as well as vertically (Marchington and Wilkinson, 1996). Storey (1992) described the initiatives within industrial relations and personnel as 'piecemeal' and those within HRM as 'integrated', and the corporate plan as 'marginal' to the former and 'central' to the latter. The new pay order clearly stakes its claim to be strategically driven (by management) and stresses the integrative processes that link all aspects of pay to performance management. The evidence for explicit pay strategies at the workplace level is limited (Industrial Society, 1997). Such rhetoric does not feature in more traditional approaches to pay. Lewis (2001: 101) suggests that the strategic reward management model is highly deterministic and 'bottom line', and is based upon 'assumptions of rationality and unitarism that disregard the political realities of organisational life'.

'Soft' and 'hard' approaches to pay

The question of strategic intervention by management raises issues of 'soft' and 'hard' HRM (Guest, 1989), where the former aspires to gain employee commitment and encourage resourceful behaviour, and the latter to utilise labour fully. The new pay order seeks to integrate aspects of both, although there are inherent tensions: for example, paying for performance may encourage the full utilisation of labour but it can risk losing the commitment of those who contribute loyally but are average rather than high performers.

Management style, strategy and pay

In practice, HRM and 'traditional' industrial relations and personnel are found in varying forms in different sectors of the economy and types of organisation. The variations may be explained in part by management style and lead to a particular employee relations strategy (a topic discussed in more detail in Chapter 3). For example, the management style matrix proposed by Purcell and Ahlstrand (1994) identifies a number of possible management choices on the dimensions of individualism and collectivism. The former can vary from management's viewing employees as no more than a commodity, through to their recognising them as a resource. The latter ranges from a unitary position, through an adversarial one, to cooperative collectivism. The combination of choices open to management leads to a variety of styles and strategies. Bacon (2001: 194) suggests that 'there are no simple methods to assess the frame of reference held by managers – indeed they usually hold a complex set of ideas rather than falling neatly into a single and possibly over-simplistic frame of reference'. The evidence from WERS98 shows that 54 per cent of managers were neutral about union membership yet 72 per cent preferred to consult directly with employees (Cully et al., 1999: 19). Perhaps British management is inherently pragmatic. The analysis offered below therefore seeks to establish broad themes rather than represent a more narrowly conceived view of management intent and employee/union response.

If management views employees as no more than a commodity and takes a unitary stand (described in Purcell and Ahlstrand's matrix as a 'traditional style'), then the resulting strategy on pay is likely to be driven solely by cost considerations, and any union recognition or involvement in pay determination will be opposed. This approach to employee relations has been labelled 'Bleak House' (Sisson, 1993), and is associated with dictatorial, authoritarian and exploitative management. Bacon (2001: 204) estimates, on the basis of WERS98 data, that about 22 per cent of British workplaces fall into this category. Dundan *et al.* (2001: 433) suggest that this type of model is found within small to medium-sized enterprises. Building upon the 'Bleak House' model, it seems likely that in such circumstances pay represents no more and no less than the acceptable (market) rate for exchange. In low-pay sectors (for example, hotel and catering), those managements adopting this style have had to take on board the NMW and statutory union recognition.

In those situations where management recognises trade unions but adopts an adversarial view, and does not see employees as a resource (described in the matrix as a 'bargained constitutional' style), then it is likely that collective bargaining over pay will be conducted as a battleground with both guerrilla and open hostilities. In a sense this approach to employee relations fits uncomfortably with the government's calls for partnership and is associated with the industrial unrest of the 1970s.

There are some styles, typified by recognising employees as a resource, which are closer in spirit to what might be called HRM approaches. The matrix distinguishes between those managements that take a unitary view and those that take a cooperative collective view (the former style is referred to as *'sophisticated human relations'* and the latter as *'sophisticated consultative'*). The sophisticated human relations style is likely to seek to exclude union participation but will not see cost minimisation as an appropriate way to approach pay. IBM is a good example of this type of company. It discourages unionisation but has prided itself on paying its employees well. The sophisticated consultative style implies that the involvement of unions in pay determination will be welcomed as parties to what may be seen as a problem-solving exercise in 'fair' distribution of the profit. Rover was a typical example of the sophisticated consultative style before events overtook the company. The company was unionised and had made considerable efforts to move from an adversarial collective stance (which characterised employee relations in the car industry in the 1970s) to a more cooperative one.

Where management adopts a paternalistic style (without or without unionisation), then the emphasis is more likely to be on providing a raft of benefits as well as basic pay, and more interest in employee welfare measures. Many large banking institutions traditionally adopted a paternalistic approach. Ackers (2001: 387) suggests that paternalism has been marginalised.

Bacon (2001: 204–5) draws upon WERS98 data to conclude that 'the predominant employee relations style in the British workplace is not to manage both individualism and collectivism, it is to manage neither'. He suggests that approximately 70 per cent of organisations operate with an 'opportunistic mixture of labour management policies'. Some of these may move towards partnership agreements – in which case negotiations over pay could be part of a raft of discussions on job security, 'gainsharing' success and employee rights to be informed, consulted and represented (Bacon, 2001: 202) Other organisations may move towards 'weakening unionism' in which case the implications for pay are less clear. Only 36 per cent of union members surveyed in 1997 indicated that their reason for joining a union was to seek improved pay and conditions (Waddington and Whitson, 1997: 521), suggesting perhaps that unions are less likely to gain a foothold in this type of organisation on this basis alone. However, 72 per cent looked to the union for support with problems – perhaps that will be a more fruitful basis for union recruitment.

Empirical evidence to support the extent or precise direction of change within pay is elusive, just as it is more generally for the emergence of HRM. There has been some survey evidence, for example, the CBI/Hay Management Consultants survey (1996) suggested that many organisations are making or looking to make changes to pay linked with business performance. More generally, writers such as Legge (1995) and Tyson (1995) are unconvinced that there has been the overthrow of one symbolic order (or orthodoxy) by another (i.e. personnel and industrial relations by HRM). A similar argument seems appropriate for pay. The reality may not match the rhetoric (Legge, 1995).

In practice, change is probably taking place but the new pay order may not be so clearly delineated as it is in its theoretical form in the literature. The Pirelli study suggests that employee relations strategies are evolving to find a compromise position between that of traditional personnel and HRM within a UK framework (Clark, 1995).

The process of pay determination

Collective bargaining and unilateral action by management

All organisations need to develop processes and procedures, mechanisms and institutional arrangements to determine how much of the profits in private industry and the cash limits within the public sector is to be allocated to payroll, and how that allocation is to be distributed among employees. Such processes and arrangements may involve joint determination between employers and trade unions resulting in collective agreements (i.e. collective bargaining) or unilateral determination by management subject to any outside intervention, for example via the NMW or pay review bodies (Cully et al., 1999).

The 'actors' and their network of relationships can be complex (see Figure 11.1). Employers, employees and their representatives (trade unions or staff associations) all have their own expectations and objectives. It has been argued that collective bargaining has been a force for conservatism (Rubery, 1997: 341). Employers may be part of an employers' federation and trade unions members of the TUC or involved in multi-union bargaining. The government's role can be direct (as paymaster in the public sector) or indirect through social and economic policy and legislation. If the parties fail to agree, the help of an independent body such as ACAS may be enlisted.

There have been a number of developments in collective bargaining since the 1970s that are particularly relevant to a study of pay in that they contribute to the climate of change.

The decline in multi-employer, industry-wide pay bargaining

This approach to collective bargaining results in nationally set pay rates that may be enhanced through local negotiations at employer or plant level. By the late 1980s a number of companies had withdrawn from multi-employer agreements (for example, in banking) despite union resistance. The tradition of often informal and fragmented workplace bargaining on top of national pay rates within the private sector had arguably led to wage drift and escalating payroll costs.

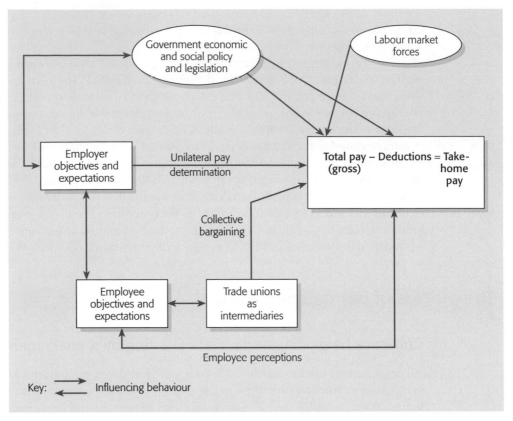

Figure 11.1 **The process of pay determination**

For large, and often diverse companies, management sees single-employer and local pay bargaining as a way of responding flexibly to competitive pressures. Pirelli General, for example, opened a technologically advanced factory on a greenfield site in 1992 in Aberdare, South Wales. The company had withdrawn from multi-employer bargaining in 1987 as part of a break with what it saw to be traditional employee relations patterns. For the new factory, collective bargaining was to be locally conducted and, after considering 'bids' from five unions to represent the workforce, it chose the GMB, with whom it concluded a single-union agreement – a typical development in greenfield unionised sites. The agreement gave local union representatives the right to bargain over pay for the workforce and included a 'no strike' clause with binding arbitration as a final stage in instances of 'non-agreement' (Clark, 1995). Such examples signal the apparent willingness of some employers and trade unions to reach accommodation over pay arrangements in the light of changing economic circumstances.

Decentralisation in the public sector

In the public sector in Britain there has been a long tradition of centralised pay bargaining with complex and complementary sets of arrangements to cover diverse groups of workers. The pay of health service workers, for example, has been negotiated centrally by their various unions through the auspices of the Whitley Council, leading to national agreements for different occupations.

Under the Conservative governments of the 1980s and 1990s, privatisation and other initiatives such as competitive contract tendering and the establishment of health trusts led to some decentralisation and fragmentation over pay negotiations. The dismantling of often long-established procedures has been destabilising. For example, in the privatised electricity industry, Northern Electric plc wanted to pull out of central bargaining and negotiate pay separately for each of the eleven companies it had set up. The unions resisted the proposed changes. Agreement was reached only after conciliation through ACAS (ACAS, 1997: 41–2).

In the National Health Service, the Conservative government had wanted trusts to set pay locally. By 1997, after six years, only 15 per cent of the workforce were on local terms and conditions. Frustrations were evident. The issue of local pay was put on hold and national awards made – for example, by the pay review body for nurses and therapists. The NHS Trust Federation (representing a managerial viewpoint) said in respect of the 1996/7 negotiations, 'Never has so much effort been expended over so little money', and Unison (representing a range of health service employees) judged the process a 'shambles' (*Financial Times*, 12 February 1997).

Single-union deals and single-table bargaining

In both of the above cases the process is streamlined, with only one union negotiating for all employees or, in the case of the latter, unions agreeing on a collective negotiating position. Single-union deals are often associated with greenfield sites and linked with 'no strike' clauses and pendulum arbitration (the use of a third-party arbitrator), as in the case of the Pirelli Aberdare plant discussed above. Unions representing workers in local authorities have agreed to single-table bargaining (this agreement is discussed later in this chapter). Again, these changes apparently signal the willingness of employers and trade unions to seek accommodation to meet current circumstances.

Similar themes of decentralisation, fragmentation and streamlining apply to unilateral management action over pay. The forces for change in collective bargaining apply equally to non-union organisations where the capacity for independent management action is unfettered by union representation. In multidivisional (M-form) companies, where decentralisation and divisionalisation are accompanied by a reduction in central personnel departments, then local managements may find themselves without specialist expert advice.

Decentralisation, fragmentation and streamlining of collective bargaining and unilateral management action over pay may bring problems as well as gains. For example, multi-employer collective bargaining may be cumbersome and slow but it can avoid leap-frogging claims and escalating payroll costs as unions seek to play one employer off against another. Single-table bargaining can be an effective mechanism for combining unions and employer and for focusing on mutual interests, but it may exclude from the agenda (and marginalise, therefore) the 'non-standard workers' less likely to be covered by union representation. Devolved decision-making over pay affords faster and more flexible responses to competitive pressures, however, if such decisions are coupled with the dilution of organisational expertise (typically found in centralised specialist departments), then management action may be misguided. A review of pay processes in public and private sector organisations prompted Murlis to question the 'pay literacy' of some managers: 'We are still living with a generation of senior managers whose appreciation of the influences on pay . . . is far from complete' (Murlis, 1996: 151).

■ Reconciling internal and external pressures on pay

Decisions about pay, whether unilaterally made by management or collectively with unions, need to take into account the requirement for internal equity and fairness as well as the external pressures of the marketplace and of the legislative framework.

Internal equity and fairness

Setting pay hierarchies and structures: job evaluation

In small organisations, senior managers have a personal knowledge of the jobs, the individuals and market rates to set these into some sort of pay hierarchy. It is typically an informal approach with scope for personal negotiation. In larger organisations, the informality and ad hoc methods are less sustainable and employers often seek a more systematic and formal approach to determining the internal relative values of different jobs and roles within the organisation on which a payment system can be based. This judgemental process is called job evaluation, which is a generic term covering a range of different approaches and schemes.

The introduction of job evaluation may be a management-led initiative. Trade unions also seek involvement in job evaluation at the workplace and are likely to be consulted over the process and participate in the subsequent appeals procedure (IRS, 1998).

There are two broad categories of job evaluation scheme: analytical and non-analytical. The difference between the two approaches is that non-analytical schemes make assessments of relative worth by comparing whole jobs, whereas analytical schemes break the job into component parts (known as factors, e.g. skill and know-ledge, mental and physical effort required), using these as the basis for comparison. Commonly, factors are given minimum and maximum numerical values, i.e. points, and weighted to show their relative importance so that jobs can be 'measured' against these and therefore against one another. Schemes which award a numerical score on this basis are referred to as 'points rating'.

Organisations can develop their own analytical or non-analytical evaluation schemes but many use 'off-the-peg' schemes which are marketed by consultants (the most widely used is Hay Management Consultants' scheme). Some schemes are computerised, although human judgement still underpins their design and operation. Organisations may need to make use of several schemes to cover diverse groups, for example, manual and white-collar jobs have traditionally been evaluated separately within local authorities but employers have agreed to move towards a scheme suitable for all employees as part of a single-status deal reached in 1997. It is difficult to establish how widespread job evaluation has become. A review of the recent survey evidence by IRS (1998: 3) concluded that:

> Three quarters of the employers polled used formal job evaluation for at least some jobs . . . there has been no widespread retreat from job evaluation . . . Our research finds very little evidence to suggest that job evaluation is being eclipsed by new devolution of the personnel function to business units and line managers. On the contrary the technique is proving flexible enough to be adapted to such developments in a way that complements them rather than work against them.

Analytical schemes are used by the majority of organisations (IRS, 1998: 5) – these offer protection against equal pay claims. For those critics of job evaluation who had predicted its decline, the continuing interest in its use has been a surprising trend.

The criticisms from academics and practitioners centred on the perception of job evaluation as an inherently bureaucratic system in that it reinforced features associated with bureaucratic structures, such as a strict 'pecking order' and tight job boundaries. It focused exclusively on the job and ignored the contribution of the individual. As a process it was seen as overly elaborate and paraded itself as a science when at best it was systematic. Lawler (1986: 20, 27, 28) led the way with a strong attack on points rating schemes in what he saw as an 'admittedly "biased" article because it focuses on the downside of the point-factor approach'. He concluded that the approach 'reinforced a particular value system . . . once installed it can be terribly captivating . . . but as traditional management is becoming less appropriate, so are point-factor job evaluation approaches'. Elaborate job evaluation schemes that derived their legitimacy from traditional organisations were seen as inappropriate. They seemed incompatible with functional flexibility, less rigid organisational structures, the breaking down of job boundaries and a non-bureaucratic style of management. Decaying job evaluation schemes are seen to lead to what is known as 'grade drift', i.e. pay increases are gained through unjustified upgrading. Such drift leads to escalating pay costs.

The supporters of job evaluation argue that its principles are sound, so even are particular schemes, but that their design needs to reflect the changing climate. Armstrong (1999: 128) argues that: 'Job evaluation processes in fluid and adaptive organisations must therefore be designed and operated flexibly.' For example, in some of the traditional schemes the focus for job comparison was on the tasks associated with a particular job; now the focus has been broadened to take more account of the overall part played by the individual. Some job evaluation schemes have been modified to fit with competence- or skills-based approaches to pay. NatWest Bank, for example, moved to job family modelling. 'This entails building a framework of generic role profiles for a small number of work types within each business which are themselves evaluated using the existing scheme. It then falls to each business to manage the application of jobs to that framework (NatWest spokesperson, in IRS, 1998: 16). Commentators (Murlis and Fitt, 1991: 43) argue strongly that competence- and skills-based approaches do not replace the need for job evaluation and, if so used, risk cost escalation (Pritchard and Murlis, 1992: 22). Job evaluation defines the starting point to which personal payments can be made.

Job evaluation, therefore, despite the criticisms, does seem to satisfy a basic organisational need for internal order, control and equity and, if an analytical approach is used, a defence against equal pay claims. There has been some evidence that organisations are introducing job evaluation in response to change (IRS, 1993: 7). 'However flexible and fast moving an organisation . . . job evaluation provided the essential link between business direction and individual role value' (Murlis and Fitt, 1991: 43). It has been argued that the more devolved and flexible pay systems become, the greater the need for order (IDS 1996: 6).

Complying with Equal Pay legislation
The Equal Pay Act 1970 entitles employees to claim pay equal to that of another employee of the opposite sex in the same establishment if they are doing 'like work' or if the

work that they do is rated as equivalent under a job evaluation scheme. The Equal Pay (Amendment) Regulations 1983 extended this entitlement to include 'work of equal value' and make provision for the designation by ACAS of 'independent experts' to investigate and report to tribunals in respect of equal value claims. The legislation gives employers the right to claim a 'material factor defence' even if the jobs are of equal value. For example, market forces, if objectively justified, may constitute such a defence.

The impact measured crudely in terms of equal pay cases appears limited. ACAS (2001: 69), for example, records that 13 equal value cases were referred to independent experts in 2000/1 and 206 cases in total since the equal value legislation came into force.

There has been some narrowing of the gap between male and female earnings, from 31 per cent to 18 per cent over the period covered by the Equal Pay Act. In the initial period of the legislation (1970–5) the gap closed by nine percentage points. The pace then slowed, narrowing by just two percentage points in the next ten years and by less than six in the last decade (*Bargaining Report*, 1998). The Equal Pay Task Force (2001: 14) has set the objective of eliminating the gender pay gap due to discrimination by 2009.

Union activity in the field of equal pay probably accounts for the recent increase in equal pay claims. Typical bargaining strategy for a number of unions has been to combine equal pay applications to tribunals with intensive bargaining aimed at settling outside the tribunal. (*Bargaining Report*, 1998: 8). The Equal Pay Task Force (2001) advocates a clear role for trade unions (in partnership with employers) in narrowing the pay gap between males and females. The CIPD survey (2001: 3) indicated that the main pressures for change were from trade unions. However it has also been argued that collective bargaining models need to change. A case study of equal pay claims in the electricity supply industry (Gilbert and Secker, 1995: 191–207) concludes that trade union organisation is not sufficient. The necessary conditions appear to be 'real bargaining strength . . . single table centralised pay determination . . . trade-unions recognise inequality . . . members have influence over the pay agenda' (ibid.: 205). The Enderby case (see below) also focuses attention on collective bargaining models in that the speech therapists' pay was subject to a separate bargaining process. The European Court of Justice ruling (1993) was that separate pay bargaining processes could not be used to circumvent the principle of equal pay. Employers and trade unions need to ensure, therefore, comparisons across bargaining groups.

Critics of the legislation argue that the slowness (and costs) of the legal procedures deter applicants (Equal Pay Task Force, 2001: 11). Nearly one in five equal value cases have been in the legal process for more than three years (*Bargaining Report*, 1998: 6). The Conservative government introduced changes in legal procedures in 1996 to try to speed up claims. The subsequent Labour government has indicated its strong support for reforming the equal pay legislation. However, despite some reduction the length of time taken to process claims, the costs and delays are problematical for individuals who pursue claims without union support.

Enderby *v* Frenchay Health Authority and the Secretary of State for Health which started in 1986 is a good example of delays and mounting costs (ET Case no. 8677/86). Dr Enderby is a speech therapist claiming equal pay for work of equal value with clinical psychologists and hospital pharmacists (i.e. the comparators). Speech therapists are mainly female and the psychologists/pharmacists are mainly male. Enderby was followed by claims by other speech therapists. Legal process, following an initial rejection of the claim by the industrial tribunal and including a ruling in 1993 by the European Court of Justice, resulted in the Enderby case (and a selection of the other claims) being referred in 1996 to independent experts. The applicants had union and Equal Opportunities Commission (EOC) support. Enderby and one other case were settled in their favour outside the tribunal. The first cases heard went in favour of the applicants and the rest of the test cases were settled outside the tribunal.

Such set-piece battles receive most publicity among equal pay claims, demonstrating the need for legal and union/EOC support for applicants. The majority of cases referred to independent experts in 1996 (excluding Enderby) involved single applicants and up to three comparators and proceed without such publicity. A majority of equal pay cases are settled outside the tribunal. For example, Unison won £1.2 million for 250 members (*Bargaining Report*, 1998).

The question of gender bias within job evaluation analytical and non-analytical schemes has to be addressed. The latter are not legally sufficient to act as a defence in equal pay claims. Bias can occur in terms of the design of schemes (for example, in the choice and weighting of factors), and their implementation. Such schemes simply reinforce the status quo with its possible inherent inequalities of pay.

Gender bias in job evaluation: some examples of sex bias

Scheme design
- An education factor/sub-factor that relies heavily on qualifications may unfairly discriminate against women (some women's jobs may have had less emphasis on formal qualifications).
- A physical effort factor/sub-factor dealing with lifting and ignoring stamina may disadvantage women (the former is characteristic of some types of male work).

Scheme implementation
- Gender of job holder revealed in job descriptions.
- Evaluation carried out by management only.

Source: Wainwright Trust (1993)

A recent initiative to support the equal pay legislation and encourage best practice in the workplace is the Equal Pay Code (1997). The code requires employers to draw up a policy, review pay and tackle inequality. Importantly, it encourages not just a review of grading (and job evaluation schemes) but a wider scrutiny of the different components of pay, including performance- and competence-based pay. Such a scrutiny has been supported by trade unions. However, survey evidence (CIPD, 2001: 10) indicates that only about 25 per cent of employers make use of the code, although over two-thirds of employers had an equal pay policy.

Pay structures may bring inequity. A Trade Union Research Unit paper (Hastings, 1994: 2) suggests that there needs to be more scrutiny of non-basic pay elements. For example, the trend towards broad banding allows most individuals to be assimilated into new pay structures at current salaries. Women are more likely to be assimilated in the lower ranges so that 'historical discrepancies are perpetuated in a new guise'.

Job evaluation in practice: No-Such Brewery

The brewery has a number of different types of job, including those connected with the brewing and conditioning of beer, its bottling and kegging, and warehousing/despatch.

Management has agreed with the union representing the workers that it will introduce a job evaluation scheme as a basis for pay and grading after union concerns that there are pay inequities between different departments. The personnel department engages a consultant to help with the design of a tailor-made scheme in consultation with the union.

The scheme will be implemented by management using a trained member of the personnel department and a joint management–union panel to evaluate jobs and hear appeals on gradings.

The proposal is to base the scheme on the factors listed below.

Factors for job evaluation scheme

Factor headings	Outline factor description
Knowledge and skill	Formal training; experience; physical ability*
Supervisory responsibility	Responsibility for work of others
Responsibility for product	Responsibility for product or service
Decisions made	Discretion / scope for independent action
Concentration	Mental, auditory and visual attention
Physical effort	Physical / explosive effort
Stamina	Stamina / sustained physical effort
Contacts	Contact with others
Working conditions	Exposure to 'disagreeable' conditions; exposure to hazards*

* Denotes that the factor is further divided into sub-factors

Each factor and sub-factor is divided into a number of defined levels for which a detailed description is given. For example, the sub-factor of 'experience' has three levels which identify the amount of 'on-the-job' experience required by the job holder to perform the job competently. Level 1 is defined as needing up to and including one week's experiential (on-the-job) learning to perform the job to a competent level. Any job in the brewery which falls within that category will be awarded 'level 1' on that sub-factor.

A maximum number of points is set (at the discretion of the consultant) for this scheme. As the factors are seen to be of equal importance or weight, the points are distributed equally between them. A numerical value is thus allocated to each level within every factor and sub-factor.

A job will be scored by deciding the appropriate level in respect of each factor or sub-factor, giving a total numerical value for the job as a whole. For example, a labouring job in the brewery scores highly on the sub-factor of 'physical effort' but less high on 'decisions'.

The scheme is analytical in that it breaks jobs down into component parts, and is described as points rating as it uses a numerical scoring system. It sorts the jobs into a hierarchy.

Setting pay hierarchies and structures: pay structures

Job evaluation, in determining the internal relative worth of jobs, sets a hierarchical framework on which basic pay structures can be pegged. That hierarchy makes explicit the common worth of certain jobs so that they can be grouped for the purposes of pay. In organisations where there is no job evaluation, such groupings are also necessary and are the result of a mix of factors, e.g. management judgement, collective bargaining, historical precedent.

Typically and traditionally, employers separate white-collar and manual employees for pay purposes, recognising further groupings within these. Particular occupations may be grouped into a job family and have their own pay structures. Engineers are an identifiable group with a career structure and a number of possible salary scales/pay grades (Murlis and Fitt, 1991: 40–1). Within such families, benchmark (i.e. representative) jobs provide a reference point for job evaluation and pay. The move towards broad banding (wide ranges of pay) has been associated with families of jobs. However, the trend is not without exceptions. B&Q, the DIY retailer, has moved back from broad banding to spot rates (i.e. a rate for the job) in the interests of pay transparency (IDS, 2001).

Unskilled manual workers are traditionally separated for pay purposes from their skilled colleagues, the latter differentiated by trade or craft. The drive for functional flexibility and technological change have broken down some of the job boundaries between them and led to simplified pay structures.

Sometimes a spot rate is set by management unilaterally or through collective bargaining for all those in a particular grouping. Alternatively, a range of pay (or a number of salary scales) may be attached to a group of jobs, and rules devised to determine where individuals are placed initially within that range and their progression. Such rules will reflect organisational values and pay objectives, e.g. progression may be linked to individual demonstration of competence, skill acquisition, performance or length of service or be linked to career development. The rules also typically reflect external job market pressures, e.g. the range allows employer and employee flexibility when agreeing starting pay. Traditionally, spot rates have been associated with wages, and ranges of pay with salaries, reflecting and reinforcing the divide between white-collar and manual jobs. In collective bargaining the divide may also be evident, with different unions representing the interests of white-collar and blue-collar workers.

There is no set formula for determining the number of pay groupings and the type of salary structure. Armstrong (1999: 217) argues that the structure is linked to the type of organisation and employees. However, certain contemporary trends are discernible. Delayering organisations and functional flexibility have led to the reduction of the number of pay grades in organisations and to the consequent widening of salary bands (called 'broad banding'). Pay progression is no longer, therefore, so clearly linked with hierarchical promotion. Harmonisation has led to the removal of strictly delineated pay groupings for white-collar and manual workers. Organisational restructuring and technological innovation in the workplace have prompted employers to rationalise pay structures and compress pay grades, and unions to accept these.

Executive and senior management jobs are often addressed outside the pay hierarchies and structures of the organisation as a whole. The recent trend has been for a limited number of such jobs, regarded by organisations as key to their success, to receive increasingly high pay. This has widened the gap both with average national earnings and with the pay of others within the organisation itself. In British Airways, for example, the most highly paid executive earns 50 times the average wage, whereas eight years ago it was less than 11 times the average wage. The implications of what has become known as a 'winner takes all' philosophy have yet to be fully assessed. The legitimacy of such high payments has been challenged by governments of different political persuasions and was addressed partially by earlier attempts to force transparency in executive pay

(Greenbury Committee, 1995). In the public sector, pay has been also increasing at a higher rate; the McKintosh review called for an 18 per cent rise in top pay in Scottish local authorities, and more generally six-figure salaries are being paid to chief executives in local government within the British Isles (*Sunday Times*, 14 October 2001). From an employee and trade union perspective, the philosophy raises the fundamental question of internal equity.

External labour market forces

Aligning pay with market values

The preceding sections on equity have examined the processes by which the relative internal worth of jobs is established. All employees, therefore, are located within an internal labour market but they make judgements about the fairness of their pay based on their view of differentials and relativities. Perceptions of external labour markets and prevailing rates of pay shape their expectations.

Changes in labour markets (outlined earlier in the chapter) mean that referencing pay externally is problematical for employers, employees and unions. The sense of job insecurity felt by many workers (and their apparent desire to put security above pay) is likely to hold down their pay demands, at least in the short term. The 'new flexible firm' (Procter and Ackroyd, 2001: 235, 243) suggests that the trend is towards 'insecure, semi-trained, multi-tasked employees competing with subcontracted and alternative suppliers'. In such a model, the 'core' is subject to continuing job insecurity.

Young people in further and higher education have sought the part-time and casual work found in traditional core–peripheral models of employment. Such models offer work for other groups prepared to take less than 'standard' (i.e. 'permanent, nine-to-five' type) employment. Women, increasingly economically active, are more likely than men to be in part-time and temporary jobs. In sectors such as hotels and catering where core–peripheral models are common and union representation of peripheral workers is not widespread, pay has been held at a low level. The NMW aims to address low pay in such sectors but is unlikely to radically change the workers' expectations of pay and conditions given fears about job security and a history of low pay. Hendry (1995: 392–405) argues that the ad hoc pursuit of core–peripheral models has been mostly in those sectors that already had a casualised workforce. The result is that 'such approaches become permanent and institutionalise the disadvantages which accompany part-time and temporary employment. The impact falls especially on women.'

The core–peripheral models of employment are not necessarily associated with low pay. High-tech industries in which the business is project- or contract-based are more likely to rely upon temporary or fixed-term employees who provide the requisite skills to supplement a core workforce. Such employees are highly skilled, with the expectation that their pay is correspondingly enhanced to offset advantages accruing from more permanent employment (e.g. employer pension scheme, support for training).

Job markets are characterised by diversity and change. There are many different job markets operating at the regional, national and international levels, covering a range of occupational groupings. The transferability of skills between occupations and industries is problematical. Skill shortages co-exist with unemployment in line with the decline of certain industries, such as shipbuilding, and the rise of others, such as advanced electronics, with particular shortages in the south east in 2000/1. Torrington and Hall (1998: 603–4) distinguish between those occupations where skills are readily transferable and those that are organisation-specific. Hendry *et al.* (1995: 108–37) note the complexity of labour markets relevant to small and medium-sized companies, concluding that 'small firms may be more vulnerable to the evolution of forces in the external labour market' (1995: 137).

Such diversity and change make it difficult for employers, employees and unions to establish a market rate in practice. The decline in national and multi-employer collective bargaining means that the notion of a going rate set annually in the 'wage (bargaining) rounds' is less clear than it was only a few years ago. Market intelligence will yield, therefore, a range of possible rates within which employers, employees and unions seek a consensus.

A technique called pay benchmarking has become increasingly popular among large companies, particularly in the financial and telecommunications sector, as well as in some government departments. Pay benchmarking (carried out by management consultancies such as Hay Group or Towers Perrin) prepares detailed pay comparisons for a range of jobs. Unions, such as UIFI in the financial services sector, increasingly have to negotiate pay increases on a market-driven rather than inflation-driven basis. Other sources of market pay data include nationally or locally published surveys covering occupations, sectors and particular industries. Employers (and unions) carry out their own surveys or group together to pool intelligence on pay (referred to as 'pay clubs').

In parts of the public sector, external referencing of pay is delegated by government to pay review bodies, which take an independent view of pay for groups such as doctors and dentists, schoolteachers and the armed forces. Identifying occupational groups for comparison in these instances is problematical. However, the occupational groups (and their unions) often seem in little doubt that they are 'falling behind' in terms of pay relative to peers and that their living standards are being eroded.

Aligning pay with international markets

For a limited number of job markets – for example, corporate financiers or corporate executives – pay is referenced internationally. International salary surveys raise issues about the relative purchasing power of personal income, and the taxation and social security charges in different countries. Tokyo, for example, is regularly rated as one of the most expensive cities in which to live, with the cost of living 60 per cent higher than in London, whereas that of Bombay is less than half that of London (Black Horse Relocation Services, 1997). Cost of living is reflected in pay levels, although enhanced payments for expatriate workers may not be sufficient to offset a desire for a particular lifestyle or concern for personal safety.

Taxation and social security deductions vary from country to country, making international comparisons over payroll costs and the take-home value of pay problematical. Tax levels vary considerably – within Europe, for example, average deductions are of the order of 35 per cent in Italy whereas they are just over 25 per cent in Britain (*Sunday Times*, 22 April 2001). Concerns about unemployment levels have prompted government measures to reduce charges and provide incentives to employers to take on new employees. Grants and employment incentives similarly operate in a number of EU countries. Such schemes typically focus on problems pertinent to that country, for example, cushioning unification in Germany. Some problems are common across the EU, for example, youth unemployment (IDS/IPD, 1997).

There are international variations in the composition of pay that make comparisons problematical. For example, the 'welfarism' of Japanese companies means that employee benefits are wide-ranging and hence an important feature. The recent economic difficulties in Japan and the collapse of the 'tiger economies' have meant reductions in company welfarism.

Sparrow (2000: 210–11) stresses the importance of the local institutional context and cultural orientation in reward management. Global approaches to pay need to be tempered with local autonomy.

The constituent elements of pay and pay systems

Introduction: the building blocks of pay

Pay comprises a number of different elements, some 'fixed' and contractual (for example, a weekly wage negotiated as part of the contract of employment) and some 'variable' and at management's discretion (for example, pay linked to individual performance). Total pay consists of basic pay (wages, salaries), additional elements (such as performance pay) and benefits (such as private health care). Some individuals may be paid fees for services. This section considers the architecture of pay.

In building pay structures, the foundations need to be underpinned by the principles of equity, felt fairness, compatibility with organisational objectives and stakeholder expectations, legality and cost-effectiveness. The legal framework is akin to building regulations that set design parameters. The foundations are subject to stresses and strains, such as the tensions between internal equity and external market forces, individualisation and collectivisation of pay, management discretion and contractual obligations, and variable and fixed pay (see Figure 11.2). At the same time, the foundations need to withstand changing organisational paradigms. Architects of pay have to be able to build sufficiently flexible but not 'flimsy' structures – and distinguish between situations in which the structure can be 'shored up' and those circumstances when the foundations have become so unstable that demolition and rebuilding are the only options.

The first level: basic pay – wages, salaries and harmonised pay

Basic pay is time-based payment and is in essence a standardised rate for the job. Wages, salaries and harmonised pay are the terms used to describe that part of pay which the employer contractually agrees to give the employee at regular intervals in return for the provision of a specified number of hours of labour over a given period. These are therefore 'fixed' and contractual.

The terms 'wages' and 'salaries' are significant in that, until fairly recently, these delineated clear boundaries between two different approaches to basic pay. In the workplace there used to be a relatively clear understanding and agreement about the differential use of the terms. Wages were paid weekly, frequently in cash, to manual workers; salaries were paid monthly through cheque or credit transfer to white-collar workers. There was an implicit understanding that salaried employees had a degree of job security and access to other benefits (e.g. pension), whereas 'wage earners' did not enjoy such advantages. These approaches were reflected in explicit and formal

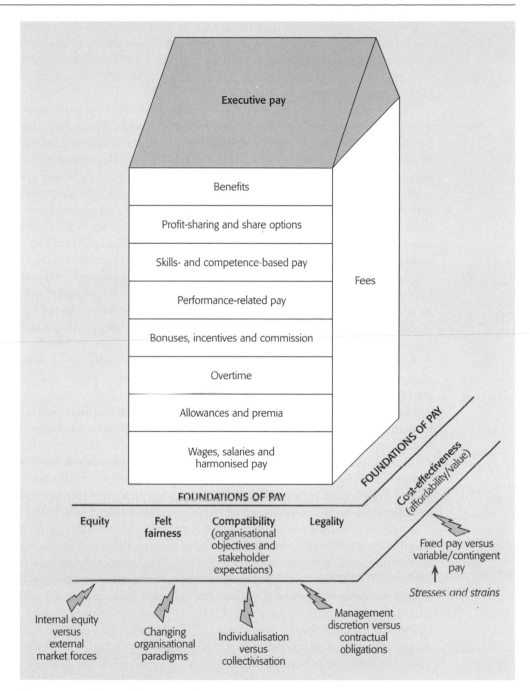

Figure 11.2 **The architecture of pay**

agreements. Salaried staff were quoted an annual amount and typically placed on salary scales that guaranteed regular progression up that scale to a fixed point. Wage earners were more typically paid an hourly rate. It was an inherently class-based system with both explicit and implicit expectations on both sides of the employment and psychological contracts.

Union agreements reinforced the divide. In local authorities, for example, unions representing manual and white-collar workers negotiated different agreements. The move towards harmonising pay and conditions, agreed in 1997, was welcomed by unions and seen by the employers as ending 'second-class treatment' of manual workers (Local Government Management Board, 1997).

The differential use of the terms has become less easy to sustain since the 1980s for a variety of reasons. The Wages Act 1986 repealed the Truck Acts, generally held to be anachronistic statutes from the nineteenth century which had guaranteed payment in the 'coin of the realm', i.e. cash. Employers found themselves therefore no longer statutorily obliged to pay in cash, which was administratively expensive and cumbersome, with evident security risks. Employees were still able to claim payments in cash if that was in their contract of employment. The desire on the part of employers to move away from the weekly ritual of cash payments led in many instances to a collective renegotiation of the employment contract, often with financial incentives offered in return for giving up the residual contractual obligation to be paid in cash weekly. The willingness of employees to be paid by cheque or credit transfer depended on domestic and social habits, e.g. the traditional weekly distribution of the wage packet within the home. At the same time the substitution of those cash payments by cheque or credit transfer assumed a banking facility on the part of employees. Wage payments have therefore been closely linked with class values.

As noted earlier in this chapter, there is arguably endemic job insecurity. A consequence of that has been that the implicit connection of salary with job security has also broken down.

Harmonisation of pay between white-collar and manual workers and moves towards single status (the same treatment for both groups) have signalled a blurring of the traditional divide between wages and salaries as employers have given wage earners access to benefits in line with salaried employees and introduced unified pay systems. Harmonisation fits comfortably within a new pay orthodoxy. It ignores the arbitrary allocation of reward on collective status differences (for example, white-collar or manual) in favour of encouraging more of a stakeholder philosophy.

Single status does not appear to be a widespread initiative, especially in British manufacturing (Hendry, 1995: 354). There may be more pragmatic explanations for harmonisation and single status. The introduction of new technology and the flexible deployment of labour often prompt the employer to simplify and integrate pay systems to replace elaborate but cumbersome pay arrangements built up over the years. Pirelli's new Aberdare plant is a good example (Clark, 1995). Legislation may also have triggered changes. The Single Status Agreement (1997) negotiated for local government workers was partly attributable to the need to avoid equal pay (equal value) claims.

Finally, the divide between white-collar and manual work is no longer clear for a variety of reasons. Technology and automation have altered the content of jobs, downgrading some white-collar jobs and upgrading some manual ones, and requiring common skills of many, especially in pursuit of flexibility. The labels of wage and salary are no longer a clearly recognisable shorthand.

Some writers, for example Torrington and Hall (1998: 591–2), maintain that the employer still treats wage earners and salaried staff differently. Salaried employees still identify more closely with management and 'wage earners see themselves as doing the work that management would never do and which is independent of management apart from the labour-hiring element'. From this perspective, class distinctions and different psychological contracts for the two groups have endured despite changes in the workplace. Druker (2000: 123) concludes that 'status differences between the waged workforce and salaried employees in the UK has not disappeared'.

Adding levels to basic pay

Enhanced payments can be focused on the individual, on the individual as a member of a group (team), and on the individual as a member of the organisation ('corporate citizen'). The permutation will vary from organisation to organisation, but there is an overlap between the three foci (see Figure 11.3). Such payments may be variable and discretionary, or fixed and contractual. The emergence of the new pay orthodoxy suggests that there will be a growth in variable or contingent and discretionary elements linked especially to performance (at the individual, group or organisation level).

The following is a consideration of some of the commonly found additional payments but is not exhaustive. Some of these are attracting particular interest from practitioners and academics, and the discussion is developed here accordingly. In certain circumstances some payments may be consolidated into basic pay.

Allowances

Sometimes referred to as 'premia' or 'plussages', allowances are used by the employer to acknowledge a variety of circumstances, e.g. an allowance for the inconvenience of shift working, or adding extra money for being based in a high-cost area, e.g. the London weighting allowance. Considerable variations exist between industries, for example engineering appears to have widespread shift premia whereas in retail the incidence is low (Arrowsmith and Sisson 1999: 57). The requirement for employees to

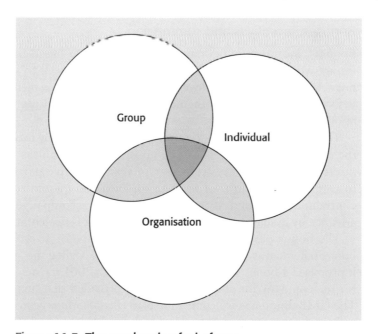

Figure 11.3 **The overlapping foci of pay**

be on call-out is likely to attract an additional payment, or the employer may want to recognise a particular responsibility, e.g. first aiders.

Management may make these allowances contractual and fixed, e.g. London weighting, or discretionary and variable, e.g. payment for accepting one-off individual additional responsibilities, depending upon such circumstances as the perceived relative permanence or frequency of the particular arrangement.

Over time, such allowances can become cumbersome and expensive to administer. In these circumstances management may seek to rationalise and simplify the system, consolidating into the basic wage or salary those allowances that are relatively permanent and frequent.

Overtime

Overtime, with its diverse arrangements, has been an enduring feature of UK payment systems. It is time-based payment linked to basic pay and employment status. Wage earners have traditionally been paid overtime at an enhanced basic rate. Salaried employees, at least at managerial level, have been expected to undertake unpaid overtime (at best with time off in lieu), reflecting different psychological contracts for the two groups.

Employers have historically and typically used overtime as a way of achieving flexibility in working hours. However, it can contribute to rising costs and inefficiency if poorly managed; employees can gain clear advantage by manipulating output or work patterns so that overtime is necessary. Annualised hours (requiring employees to work a total number of hours over a year to be distributed to meet the demands of the industry) may represent a more cost-effective approach. Where overtime is a relatively fixed feature of the working week, then the employee perceives 'take-home' pay inclusive of overtime as the average weekly wage.

Bonuses, incentives and commission

Bonuses, incentive and commission payments are based on output rather than input (hours worked). They are variable payments that seek to increase output by offering financial incentives to employees. A number of such payment systems were in existence before the move towards the new pay orthodoxy and represent an enduring concern about productivity.

The terms 'bonus' and 'incentive' are somewhat loosely used in the workplace although the former typically refers to a lump-sum payment and is normally at management's discretion and will vary from year to year. Incentive payments are normally offered to employees in return for meeting specified and quantified targets; they are typically contractual and fixed in that the targets and accompanying payments are agreed in advance by management and employees or their representatives.

The bonus payments have no standard shape or size. An interesting version of a bonus scheme was introduced into Levi Strauss. Called the 'global success sharing plan', it promised a bonus worth one year's salary in 2001 to each employee who had worked for the company for at least three years, provided that financial targets had been met. The GMB union has welcomed the plan (*People Management*, 7 June 1996).

Bonus schemes that have attracted considerable attention are those paid to City specialists. Companies have been using the promise of bonus payments to retain high-performing staff. During the merger of two Swiss banks, employees were even threatened with the removal of bonus for 'negative behaviour', i.e. succumbing to poaching from other companies (*Financial Times*, 16 December 1997).

Incentive payments have a long and chequered history in employee relations. At shopfloor level, various schemes have been introduced as an addition to basic pay, such as:

- piecework where payment is directly output based;
- work-measured schemes where payment is linked to a standard output rate for an experienced operator set by work measurement techniques;
- linking pay to performance achieved over and above the standard rate set by management.

At the start of the 1990s, piece-rate schemes were still widespread, more so in the public than in the private sector. Such schemes were in decline but still represented a sizeable part of take-home pay for manual workers. The main reasons for the decline have been that such schemes may put speed before quality, discourage initiative, run contrary to flexibility requirements and may have adverse health and safety implications, e.g. repetitive strain injuries caused by sustained operation of particular production processes. Given that quality, initiative and flexibility have been seen as important for achieving competitive advantage, it is not surprising that concern about the efficacy of piece-rate schemes continued throughout the 1990s. At the same time, the new pay order has rejected piece rates as representing too narrow a conception of worker effort (Geary, 1992).

Commission payments are typically associated with sales staff and tied to sales turnover, and may be linked to other forms of employee recognition, such as free holidays. Salespeople may also be paid a bonus or a mix of commission and bonus where the latter takes into account broader aspects of performance rather than just sales targets (Armstrong (1999: 444)). Commission, if poorly managed, can lead to what is described as 'churning', where a salesperson will seek to gain financial advantage by inducing the customer to buy.

Performance-related pay

Individual performance-related pay (IPRP) seeks to reward employees for individual performance, recognising contribution to organisational success by linking pay increases and/or progression within pay scales to meeting performance targets, both quantitative and qualitative. It is, therefore, a broader conception of effort than that found in traditional incentive schemes (Geary, 1992) and fits comfortably within the new pay orthodoxy. From a union perspective, performance-related pay undermines collective intervention in that it focuses on the individual employment relationship. Payments are discretionary and variable, affording management financial flexibility. Torrington and Hall (1998: 625) conclude that performance-related pay 'appears to accord with concepts of distributive justice'. IPRP helps to attract and retain employees, but particular systems and procedures have led to operational difficulties (Kessler and Purcell, 1992).

It is estimated that only one-quarter of firms directly link pay and performance (Industrial Society, 1997). However Kessler (2000: 280–3) suggests that 'reports of the death of IPRP have been greatly exaggerated'. The pendulum swings towards new ideas in pay, and back again when problems emerge.

Team-based pay

The individual focus of performance-related pay has been much criticised in that it runs counter to the team spirit widely heralded as important in many work organisations, and institutionalised in new labels attached to their structures, e.g. team leader. Perhaps it was inevitable that such organisations would seek to link pay to the team ethos. Workgroup norms that govern the behaviour of individuals are developed in such circumstances. Such a payment system is discretionary and variable.

Typically in team-based pay, a bonus pool is allocated to a working group as an incentive, and as a reward in recognition of reaching performance or output targets, or making operational savings. That bonus is then distributed to the group using an agreed formula. An IPD study (Armstrong, 1996) indicates that team pay for white-collar workers is commonly linked to performance, and shopfloor schemes to output or cost savings, a finding that he claims is supported by studies by Industrial Relations Services (IRS, 1995) and the Institute of Employment Studies (Thompson, 1995).

There is little published validation of team-based pay and the evidence is mainly anecdotal. It appears that its use is not widespread (Armstrong, 1999: 349). However, given that team-based pay makes use of financial incentives and links reward to the notion of performance or output or savings, then it seems most probable that research studies on performance-related pay (e.g. Kessler and Purcell, 1992) or on incentives more generally will have some applicability. It may still be problematical to prove a direct link between pay and enhanced performance. There may still be tensions around individual and collective interests. The introduction of team-based pay is probably more linked with cultural and structural issues, and symbolism within an HRM framework (i.e. reinforcing unitarist perspectives, marking out and strengthening work units, and sending messages about the importance of contribution). From a collectivist stance, the same concerns about performance-related pay are applicable to team-based pay.

Skills- and competence-based pay

Skills-based pay

Skills-based pay makes an explicit link between skill acquisition and additional payment. In such systems, employers pay additional specified amounts for demonstrable skill acquisition and/or may link that with pay progression. Skills-based initiatives have been management-led broadly in response to competitive pressures and to demands for quality and functional flexibility. They offer financial flexibility. Such payment systems encourage employees to increase the depth and breadth of their skills. The introduction of National Vocational Qualifications (NVQs) has provided an enabling framework in that it is a convenient peg for skills-based pay. From the collective stance of unions, a national qualification standard reduces the scope for management to exercise its discretion in an arbitrary format. Such systems can, and do, form part of collective agreements. Skills-based pay is, therefore, an example of experimentation but does not neatly fall into the new pay orthodoxy. It is, however, a relatively cooperative approach to pay and appears to recognise that skill acquisition is of mutual benefit to employer and employee. As such, it fits within a stakeholder framework.

It is not surprising that skills-based pay initiatives are found in greenfield sites, such as that of Nissan, or linked with the introduction of new technology, for example in

Pirelli. Initiatives are not restricted to manufacturing, however, and are evident in other sectors, e.g. retailing and local authorities.

Skills-based pay is still quite new, probably explaining why the literature on the subject is often anecdotal. Clark (1995: 233), in his study of the Pirelli plant at Aberdare, notes that the skills-based pay scheme introduced with union agreement had to be overhauled. There was a conflict between employees seeking to gain skills quickly and become fully functionally flexible in pursuit of financial incentives, and the organisational need for skills training to be thorough. Hendry (1995: 214–15) argues that there are inherent problems with the concept of skill itself in the workplace in that managers tend to rely on indirect indicators of skill, e.g. reference to formal qualifications, and emphasise personal qualities when describing skills. It is possible that a failure to resolve such problems may weaken the effectiveness of skills-based pay.

Competence-based pay

Competence-based pay differs from skills-based pay in that it seeks to link pay not just to skills, which can be seen as an input factor in performance, but more broadly to job behaviours and their outcomes. Such a pay system is discretionary and variable, offering the organisation financial flexibility. The emphasis on the individual, the strategic importance of such a pay approach and the link between individual competences and organisational objectives place it within the new pay orthodoxy. It is an increasingly popular pay initiative, so it is important to examine it in more detail.

The term 'competence' has become widespread among academics and practitioners although there have been many debates about its meaning. Definitions of competence include reference to both the characteristics of the individual and the behaviours associated with the job or occupation, although different models will vary the emphasis on one or the other of these elements. The job (or occupation) behaviours may be linked, therefore, to performance levels specified by management in the workplace. Armstrong (1999: 292) broadly defines competence pay as 'a method of paying people for the ability to perform'.

Sparrow (1996: 22) expresses considerable unease about the 'competence' vocabulary that has become widespread in managerial circles in pursuit of the desire for a link between the performance of individuals and strategic management. From an academic perspective, the concept applied in the workplace to HR systems of appraisal and pay is inherently a weak one in that it is not clear what exactly is being measured in competence approaches – inputs, processes or outcomes.

Competence-based pay schemes are typically linked to a competence framework, which may well have been introduced previously in an organisation as a basis for appraisal or recruitment and selection. Such frameworks vary; some may focus on 'core' competences, i.e. those judged by management to be common and central to a given cluster of jobs (e.g. forward thinking for managers); others may focus on a combination of skill areas (e.g. customer focus for sales support staff) and common behaviours (e.g. teamwork). Other frameworks may include specific objectives or targets. Such frameworks need to be derived from a sound and systematic understanding of the jobs in question, i.e. from what is called job analysis, and have to be capable of defining and distinguishing sensitively between levels of job performance, from satisfactory to outstanding. Armstrong (1996: 298) accepts that successful competence-based pay schemes need to meet demanding criteria, including the requirement for 'well researched and analysed competence frameworks'.

The literature has much anecdotal evidence about competence-based pay drawn from both the public and private sectors. There are examples of local authorities that have moved from performance-related pay schemes to competence-based pay for their managers in the hope that the latter will prove more effective in motivating employees. The opportunity itself to experiment with pay systems has largely been seen as a result of the move to local pay bargaining within local government in the context of central government initiatives such as compulsory competitive tendering and review and re-organisation. Commenting on the introduction of competence-based pay schemes in the local government context, Murlis argues that 'good competence based schemes need to be mixed in with PRP [performance-related pay]; I do not see the two as separate' (Thatcher, 1993: 20).

Similar experimentation is reported in the private sector. Sparrow (1996: 27) gives the example of the Automobile Association (AA). The group personnel director has dismantled the reward system that linked competences, performance and labour market considerations in favour of a simpler system. Competences are used for development purposes for the AA's top managers and professionals but pay is linked to labour market information and performance outputs. 'When you talk to managers about competencies, their eyes glaze over . . . competencies . . . are a shorthand way of thinking of people in their roles and looking at key requirements . . . when it comes to performance, there are external environmental factors and political factors and so forth. Competencies are only part of a multi-faceted picture' (Sparrow, 1996: 27).

The newness of the competence-based approaches to pay suggests that it is too early to validate them. Sparrow (1996) urges caution in respect of claims about competence-based pay. He argues that there are four main reasons for concern. First, the performance criteria used to measure competence are often invalidated, based, for example, on appraisal results or the subjective views of senior managers about what constitutes effective performance. Secondly, there is the question of whether all competences should be equally rewarded under a payment scheme regardless of variables such as the length of time required to develop individual competences or how important those competences are to the organisation or in labour market terms. Thirdly, there is the problem of identifying relevant competences during periods of organisational change. Lastly, managers may be biased.

The extent to which Sparrow's note of caution will be heeded is unclear. Armstrong (1999) expresses the view that competence-based pay has been widely endorsed by practitioners. From a collectivist stance there is likely to be the same kind of unease about competence-based pay as there has been about performance-related pay.

Profit-sharing and share options

Profit-sharing and share options are additions to basic pay that are linked to the performance of the company as a whole. Such payments arguably seek to demonstrate a commonality of interest between individual employees and the company as a whole and provide an incentive for the employee to work harder and remain committed to the company. The rhetoric is compatible with partnership approaches (Hyman, 2000: 191–2). In practice, the perceived link between individual effort and company performance may be weak, so it is not clear how powerful profit-sharing is as an incentive. These payments are likely to be variable in line with annual profits, and discretionary, typically based upon a predetermined formula setting minimum levels.

Profit-sharing and share options fit comfortably within the new pay orthodoxy although the payments treat all employees alike. Given that reward management frameworks stress the importance of recognising individual contribution, there is a tension between the even treatment of profit-sharing and share options and the discerning treatment of performance-related pay (Geary, 1992).

Share options have received hostile media coverage in the context of executive pay (especially in the privatised utilities) in instances where it has been felt that executives were able to exercise their share options to their personal financial advantage unconnected with their individual performance. The trend within companies has been to attempt to peg share option entitlement to performance criteria. However, it appears that only about 8 per cent of British firms link executive remuneration to shareholder results (*Sunday Times*, 11 November 2001).

Benefits

The term 'benefits' is used to describe that part of the pay package which can be broadly categorised as either payments in kind (e.g. subsidised meals, social functions) whose 'consumption' is optional, or social welfare provision (e.g. contribution to pension, sick pay above minimum state entitlement, life insurance) which may be deferred until retirement or contingent upon a particular set of circumstances (e.g. ill health). Historically, benefits (sometimes described as fringe benefits or perks) have been seen as tax efficient, and a 'cat and mouse game' is played out between the company's tax advisers and the Inland Revenue to find ways in which benefits could legitimately escape the tax net. (Most benefits are technically classified as part of income by the Inland Revenue and subject to tax.) Benefits are typically contractual and fixed.

The broad categorisation used above disguises the multiplicity of individual benefits that employees may receive. Torrington and Hall (1998: 632) suggest that the benefit element of the pay package has grown significantly within the UK, more so than in other western countries, and is a particular feature of executive pay. They do not quantify the average value of benefits within the pay package but this conclusion suggests that benefits are likely to be a significant part of the total remuneration costs for an employer. It is interesting, therefore, that more attention has not been given by researchers or even practitioners to the effectiveness of benefits packages. Employers may offer benefits generally in line with competitors to attract staff, but the motivational value of those benefits in terms of encouraging particular behaviours receives scant consideration. Performance-related pay, in contrast, represents a far smaller element of take-home pay.

There is some anecdotal evidence that benefits packages as a whole are being more critically considered by employers as opposed to scrutiny being directed on a more ad hoc basis to individual benefits, e.g. the concern expressed by many employers about the rising cost of private health care schemes. The changing nature of the workforce and patterns of employment may explain this change of heart. For example, Hoechst Roussel's merger prompted a review of its benefits (around one-third of its remuneration costs); the reasons cited for change were linked with structural changes in the workforce – more women, more part-timers, less likelihood of long-term employment within the company, less value placed on 'deferred gratification' of longer-term benefits and limited take-up of others. The solution was a move towards flexible benefits (sometimes called cafeteria benefits) in which employees were allowed to choose from a menu to suit individual needs (Crabb, 1995: 40–1).

Exhibit 11.2

Inland Revenue staff to take fresh action on pay

Tens of thousands of Inland Revenue employees will today launch a second round of industrial action in an attempt to win an improved pay settlement.

The Public and Commercial Services Union, which represent most of the Revenue's 70,000 employees, said it would decide next week whether to take stronger action over the size of proposed pay awards to experienced staff.

The action comes at a difficult time for the Revenue, which is updating its pay-as-you-earn records as well as processing self-assessment tax returns ahead of the January filing deadline.

The union said its members were unhappy that the Revenue's proposed settlement of a 4.3 per cent rise in the total pay bill offered too little to long-serving staff.

It said some older members were worried that only 2 per cent of their increase would count towards their final pensionable salary. 'We want to see experience and loyalty rewarded', the union said.

The union said many of its members would work today only between 10am and noon and from 2pm to 4pm – the minimum attendance allowed under the Revenue's flexible working arrangements.

The union, which held a similar day of action last Friday, said it had no proposals for strike action but said its executive would meet on Thursday next week to consider its options. Revenue staff have already approved strike action in a ballot by a majority of almost two to one.

The Revenue said it had no scope to increase its proposed settlement, which would give lower-paid staff rises of up to 7.5 per cent.

'It's a very reasonable pay offer', it said. 'The bottom line is that there is simply no more money available.'

The Revenue, which said it was committed to maintaining its standard of service, has faced criticism this year over its stewardship of personal income tax records.

The department said this summer that it planned to take on 1,250 extra staff to help it fill gaps in more than 8m of its pay-as-you-earn employee tax records.

Source: Michael Peel, *Financial Times*, 7 November 2001.
© 1995–1998 The Financial Times Limited

In the UK the move towards flexible benefits has been cautious despite the publicity that is sometimes attached to individual examples. Schemes offer varying degrees of flexibility, including 'free choice' from a determined list of benefits, 'core-plus' where there is a core of mandatory benefits and some additional choice, and 'modular' where employees select from a range of predetermined packages. The survey evidence suggests that flexible benefits are a factor in attracting and retaining employees and a way of revisiting and giving new value to welfare provisions to meet the needs of a changing labour force (Atherton, 2000; IRS, 2000; IDS Study Plus, 2001).

Benefits packages as a whole have also come under scrutiny owing to harmonisation. One of the traditional features of benefits is that they have been status driven, not just in terms of the divide between wage earners and salaried staff but also within categories of white-collar worker. A survey by the Manufacturing Science and Finance Union (1997) found that there is still a strong 'upstairs/downstairs' culture permeating benefits in the UK. The company car has been one of the most graphic illustrations of this principle of status divide – a sliding scale of makes and models reflected the employee's position in the hierarchy. This particular benefit is also a good example of how individual benefits have been scrutinised in terms of tax effectiveness and policy application (the operation of the policy on company cars is often a source of friction in the workplace).

The treatment of benefits packages in the literature is typically prescriptive and not particularly closely allied with any one school of thought. Historically, benefits were associated with paternalistic employers concerned for the welfare of their employees, but there is little discussion of the development of benefits packages in respect of other management styles. Unions historically saw themselves as providers of benefits; it will be interesting to see whether they will return to this role. If they do, then this may place employee benefits higher on the pay agenda for both employees and employers.

Conclusions

The economic winds of change have blown across both the public and private sectors. Despite more recent economic revival, the chill of remembered recessions has lingered in the workplace. Technological change, in particular that of information technology, has altered radically the nature of work and skills. There has been a shift in political ideology with the Labour administration elected in 1997, and some change in social attitudes to work. It seems improbable that approaches to pay can return to those of the pre-1979 era.

Diversity and experimentation have been the legacy of such changes. Pay initiatives have been introduced although initial enthusiasm is usually tempered by operational realities as well as doubts about efficacy. Trade unions have sometimes been prepared to break with some of the traditions of collective bargaining and support new pay arrangements.

There remain the enduring challenges for all those involved in pay determination. The perennial questions of the nature of the respective roles of government, employers, employees and unions persist. In the workplace the balancing act between external pressures on pay determination and the need for internal equity is as perilous as ever. Experimentation has not provided neat solutions and the pursuit of diversity can sometimes lead to unwieldy pay structures. In practice, pay in the workplace is still driven by expediency and pragmatism.

Chapter summary

This chapter has covered a wide range of pay-related issues that can be summarised as follows:

- Pay is the relatively neutral term used to denote wages, salaries and fees paid to employees in return for labour.
- It is subject to a range of influences, including government policy on the economy and employment, legislation, employment trends and markets, technological change and societal values.
- The Labour government's employment policies include the national minimum wage to address the problems of low pay, and flexible and internationally competitive labour markets.
- Legislation (in particular the Equal Pay Act 1970) has had an impact upon pay in the past two decades.

- Patterns in employment and unemployment and in the labour markets affect the perceptions and expectations of those buying and selling labour.
- Technological change has impacted upon skills profiles of jobs and hence pay levels and hierarchies.
- Pay has a number of functions in the employment relationship, which include a legal function, a mechanism for fulfilling employer, employee and union objectives, a mechanism for control and motivation, and a visible manifestation of the psychological contract.
- A new pay order emerged in the 1990s characterised by a move towards a stakeholder model, a greater emphasis upon unitarist perspectives, individualism and a strategic approach. Changing management styles and employee relations strategies have been reflected in new approaches to pay. The new order of pay is less clearly delineated in practice than in its theoretical form in the literature.
- Pay can be determined through collective bargaining (covering a minority of employees) or through unilateral management action. Pay determination has become more fragmented, decentralised and streamlined since the 1970s. Decisions about pay need to take into account internal equity and external pressures, and job evaluation is one of the ways in which internal equity and fairness can be achieved.
- Pay hierarchies separate groups of workers into pay bands, which are being reduced in number and covering a broader range of pay.
- Equal pay legislation has triggered interest in job evaluation and internal equity issues.
- Pay has to be aligned with external market rates to attract and retain workers.
- International pay comparisons need to take into account the relative purchasing power of personal income, taxation and social security charges in different countries.
- Pay consists of basic wages or salaries or harmonised pay, additions and benefits. The trend is for employers to increase the discretionary and variable elements of pay and to seek to focus pay on individual effort. The 1980s and 1990s were characterised by employers experimenting with payment systems to achieve flexibility and competitiveness. Benefits are an important feature of pay.
- Change, diversity and experimentation have been dominant themes over the last two decades.
- In practice, pay is driven by expediency and pragmatism.

Questions

1 Should a nurse be paid more than a plumber? What factors are likely to govern pay levels for the two occupational groups?

2 How important is pay in attracting graduates to join an organisation, and what kind of pay package are they most likely to want?

3 You are preparing a pay claim on behalf of a union representing craft workers in the building industry. What information do you need and how will you obtain it?

4 High flyers in banking, technology or management now expect the sorts of reward that those in entertainment or sport have received. What are the implications of the 'winner takes all' pay philosophy?

Exhibit 11.3

Police come out in force at parliament to protest against proposed reforms

Thousands of rank-and-file police officers gathered in a protest lobby of parliament yesterday over the government's reform programme.

More than 5,000 off-duty officers dressed in civilian clothes turned up for the biggest public display of protest by the police in nine years.

The officers were objecting to plans proposed by David Blunkett, Home Secretary, to restructure pay and reduce overtime.

A further grievance is a plan to introduce a new generation of quasi-police community support officers.

The government argues that its shake-up of pay and other reforms are needed to make the police more efficient and effective at a time of deepening public fears about the levels of crime.

The Police Federation, which organised the lobby as part of an ongoing campaign, says the pay reforms linked to performance and special skills are divisive and are fuelling a decline in morale within the police force.

It has also accused the government of introducing a two-tier police force, with community support officers being given powers of arrest despite lacking proper training or accountability.

Yesterday, Mr Blunkett had an inconclusive meeting with Fred Broughton, the Police Federation chairman. Both sides indicated that their disagreement would have to go through a long process of conciliation and arbitration.

While their demonstration was conducted peacefully, the mood of the protesters was clearly one of anger and frustration with a Home Secretary they see as confrontational.

Mr Blunkett said he was 'deeply committed' to making conciliation work, 'which means give and take by both sides'.

However, some militant members of the Police Federation are pressing for their organisation to become an affiliated trade union as a first step towards claiming the right to take industrial action. This is currently barred to the police by statute.

Source: Jimmy Burns, *Financial Times*, 14 March 2002.

Activity

Read Exhibit 11.3 and then carry out the following activities.

1 Carry out your own research to identify:
    (a) the process by which national pay levels for police officers are reviewed;
    (b) the current structure of pay for police officers.

2 Examine critically the ways in which pay for police officers can be related to their performance.

3 Identify the types of 'special skills' that the Home Secretary wants to encourage.

4 Investigate the possible role of the Advisory, Conciliation and Arbitration Service in seeking agreement between the Home Secretary and police.

5 Examine critically the implications of introducing regional pay systems for police.

Useful websites

www.acas.org.uk **Advisory, Conciliation and Arbitration Service** Makes reference to employee relations matters, including pay and publishes reports.

www.cbi.org.uk **Confederation of British Industry** Gives regular Human Resources Update that makes reference to pay-related matters and represents its members' interests.

www.cipd.co.uk **Chartered Institute of Personnel and Development** General information on employment including reference to pay related matters, publishes relevant reports and represents its members' interests; membership is required for access.

www.dfes.gov.uk **Department for Education and Skills** Focuses on skills, training, productivity issues and government labour market policy.

www.dti.gov.uk **Department of Trade and Industry** Provides information and advice from the Department of Trade and Industry to business, employees and consumers on employment and other economic matters.

www.eoc.org.uk **Equal Opportunities Commission** Makes reference to equal pay matters and publishes reports and codes.

www.hmso.gov.uk **Her Majesty's Stationery Office** Manages and regulates the use and the licensing of the reuse of all information produced by government which is protected by Crown copyright.

www.incomesdata.co.uk Gives information, publishes reports and surveys on pay matters.

www.kingsmillreview.gov.uk Electronic version of the Kingsmill Report, published by the Cabinet Office.

www.lowpay.gov.uk **Low Pay Commission** Information on low pay issues.

www.tuc.org.uk **Trades Union Congress** Including references to pay related matters and publishes relevant reports.

www.tuc.org.uk/equality/tuc References to Equal Pay Pilot project set up by TUC.

References

ACAS (2001) *Annual Report 2000–2001*. London: HMSO.

ACAS (1997) *Annual Report 1996*. London: HMSO.

Ackers, P. (2001) 'Employment ethics', Chapter 12 in Rodman, T. and Wilkinson, A. (eds) *Contemporary Human Resource Management*. London: Financial Times Prentice Hall.

Armstrong, M. (1996) 'How group efforts can pay dividends', *People Management*, 25 January: 22–6.

Armstrong, M. (1999) *Employee Reward*. London: IPD.

Armstrong, M. and Baron, A. (1995) *The Job Evaluation Handbook*. London: IPD.

Arrowsmith, J. and Sisson, K. (1999) 'Pay and working time: towards organisation based systems', *British Journal of Industrial Relations*, 37(1): 51–75.

Arrowsmith, J. and Sisson, K. (2000) 'Managing working time', Chapter 12 in Bach, S. and Sisson, K. (eds) *Personnel Management: A Comprehensive Guide to Theory and Practice*, 3rd edn. Oxford: Blackwell.

Atherton, P. (2000) 'It's just mind over matter', *Employee Benefits*, No. 37.

Bacon, N. (2001) 'Employee relations', Chapter 7 in Redman, T. and Wilkinson, A. (eds) *Contemporary Human Resource Management*. London: Financial Times Prentice Hall.

Bank of England (2001) *Quarterly Review* (November). London: HMSO.

Bargaining Report (1997) 'Survey, equal value', Report No. 174.

Bargaining Report (1998) 'Surge in equal pay claims', Report No. 185.

Bargaining Report (2000) 'Pay benchmarking challenge to unions', Report No. 206: 11–12.

Bargaining Report (2001) 'Unions still await overall equal pay claim system', Report No. 217: 7–11.

Bawey, A. and Thorpe, R. (2000) 'Motivation and reward', Chapter 5 in Thorpe, R. and Homan, G. (eds) *Strategic Reward Systems*. London: Financial Times Prentice Hall.

Black Horse Relocation Services (1997) *International Best Cities for Business Report*. London: BHRS.

Brown, W., Deakin, S., Nash, D. and Oxenbridge, S. (2000) 'The employment contract: from collective procedures to individual rights', *British Journal of Industrial Relations*, 38(4): 611–29.

CBI/Hay Management Consultants (1996) *Trends in Pay and Benefits Systems*. London: CBI.

CIPD (2001) *Employers and Equal Pay Survey*. London: CIPD.

Clark, J. (1995) *Managing Innovation and Change*. London: Sage.

Colling, T. (2000) 'Personnel management in the extended organization', Chapter 3 in Bach, S. and Sisson, K. (eds) *Personnel Management: A Comprehensive Guide to Theory and Practice*, 3rd edn. Oxford: Blackwell.

Crabb, S. (1995) 'Adding value with better benefits', *Personnel Management*, July: 13.

Cully, M., O'Reilly, A., Millward, N. and Forth, J. (1998) *The 1998 Workplace Employee Relations Survey – DTI, ACAS, ESRC and PSI*. London: HMSO.

Cully, M., Woodland, S., O'Reilly, A. and Dix, G. (1999) *Britain at Work*. London: Routledge.

Daniel, W. and Millward, N. (1993) 'Findings from the Workplace Industrial Relations Surveys' in Clark, J. (ed.) *Human Resource Management and Change*. London: Sage.

DfEE (1997) *Labour Market and Skill Trends 1997/8*. London: DfEE.

Druker, J. (2000) 'Wage systems', Chapter 5 in White, G. and Druker, J. (eds) *Reward Management: A Critical Text*. London: Routledge.

Dundon, T., Grugalis, I. and Wilkinson, A. (2001) 'New management techniques in small and medium sized enterprises', Chapter 14 in Redman, T. and Wilkinson, A. (eds) *Contemporary Human Resource Management*. London: Financial Times Prentice Hall.

Equal Pay Task Force (2001) *Just Pay*. London: EOC.

EOC (1997) *Code of Practice on Equal Pay*. London: EOC.

EOR (1997) '£1 million speech therapists' defence bill', *EOR*, 74 (July/August): 3.

Geary, J. (1992) 'Pay, control and commitment: linking appraisal and reward', *Human Resource Management Journal*, 2(4): 4–22.

Gilbert, K. and Secker, J. (1995) 'Generating equality? Equal pay, decentralisation and the electricity supply industry', *British Journal of Industrial Relations*, 33(2): 191–207.

Greenbury Committee (1995) *Directors' Remuneration: Report of a Study Group Chaired by Sir Richard Greenbury*. London: HMSO.

Guest, D. (1989) 'Personnel and HRM – can you tell the difference?', *Personnel Management*, January.

Hastings, S. (1994) *Identifying Priority Areas in Equal Pay Work*, The Trade Union Research Unit, Discussion Paper No. 45, Ruskin College.

Hay Management Consulting/Sunday Times (1995) *Employment Conditions Abroad, Epic International and Incomes Data Services*. London: Sunday Times/Hay Management Consulting.

Hendry, C. (1995) *Human Resource Management A Strategic Approach to Employment*. Oxford: Butterworth-Heinemann.

Hendry, C., Arthur, M. and Jones, A. (1995) *Strategy through People. Adoption and Learning in the Small–Medium Enterprise*. London: Routledge.

Herriot, P. and Pemberton, C. (1997) 'Facilitating new deals', *Human Resource Journal*, 7(1): 45.

Hyman, J. (2000) 'Financial participation schemes', Chapter 8 in White, G. and Druker, J. (eds) *Reward Management: A Critical Text*. London: Routledge.

IDS (2001) *Case Study: B&Q*, Report No. 833. London: IDS: 18–20.

IDS Study Plus (2001) *Flexible Benefits*. London: IDS.

IDS/IPD (1997) *European Management Guides: Recruitment, Training and Development*. London: IPD.

Industrial Society (1997) 'Survey on PRP', *People Management*, 25 September: 9.

IRS (1993) 'Job evaluation in the 1990s', *Pay and Benefits Bulletin*, October: 4–12.

IRS (1995) 'Key issues in team working', *Employee Development Bulletin*, No. 69, September: 5–15.

IRS (1998) *There is No Value in Job Evaluation*, Report No. 665. London: IRS.

IRS (2000) 'The joy of flex', *Employment Review: Pay and Benefits*, No. 710. London: IRS.

Kessler, I. (2000) 'Remuneration systems', Chapter 11 in Bach, S. and Sisson, K. (eds) *Personnel Management: A Comprehensive Guide to Theory and Practice*, 3rd edn. Oxford: Blackwell.

Kessler, I. and Purcell, J. (1992) 'Performance related pay: objectives and application', *Human Resource Management Journal*, 2(3): 16–33.

Kingsmill, D. (2001) *A Review of Women's Employment and Pay* (Kingsmill Report). London: Cabinet Office.

Kirton, G. and Greene, A-M. (2000) *The Dynamics of Managing Diversity: A Critical Approach*. Oxford: Butterworth Heinemann.

Lawler, E. (1986) 'What's wrong with point factor evaluation?', *Compensation and Benefit Review*, March/April: 20–8.

Legge, K. (1995) *Human Resource Management Rhetoric and Realities*. London: Macmillan.

Lewis, P. (2001) 'Reward management', Chapter 4 in Redman, T. and Wilkinson, A. (eds) *Contemporary Human Resource Management*. London: Financial Times Prentice Hall.

Local Government Management Board (1997) *Single Status: What's It All About?* Background Briefing Paper. London: LGMB.

Low Pay Commission (1998) *The National Minimum Wage: First Report of the Low Pay Commission*. London: HMSO.

Manufacturing, Science and Finance Union (1997) *Study on Status, Perks and Modes of Address*. London: MSFU.

Marchington, N. and Wilkinson, A. (1996) *Core Personnel and Development*. London: IPD.

McLoughlin, I. and Clark, J. (1994) *Technological Change at Work*, 2nd edn. Milton Keynes: Open University Press.

McNabb, R. and Whitfield, K. (2000) ' "Worth so appealingly little": a workplace-level of analysis of low pay', *British Journal of Industrial Relations*, 38(4): 585–609.

Murlis, H. (1996) *Pay at the Crossroads*. London: IPD.

Murlis, H. and Fitt, D. (1991) 'Job evaluation in a changing world', *Personnel Management*, May: 40–3.

New Earnings Survey (2000) London: Office for National Statistics.

Pritchard, D. and Murlis, H. (1992) *Jobs, Roles and People: The New World of Job Evaluation*. London: Nicholas Brealey.

Proctor, S. and Ackroyd, S. (2001) 'Flexibility', Chapter 8 in Redman, T. and Wilkinson, A. (eds) *Contemporary Human Resource Management*. London: Financial Times Prentice Hall.

Purcell, J. and Ahlstrand, B. (1994) *Human Resource Management*. Oxford: Oxford University Press.

Roberts, I. (2001) 'Reward and performance management', Chapter 12 in Beardwell, I. and Holden, L. (eds) *Human Resource Management: A Contemporary Approach*, 3rd edn. London: Financial Times Prentice Hall.

Robinson, S. and Rousseau, D. (1994) 'Violating the psychological contract: not the exception but the norm', *Journal of Organisational Behaviour*, 15: 245–59.

Rubery, J. (1997) 'Wages and the labour market', *British Journal of Industrial Relations*, 35(3): 337–66.

Schein, E. (1965) *Organizational Psychology*. Englewood Cliffs, NJ: Prentice Hall.

Sisson, K. (1993) 'In search of HRM', *British Journal of Industrial Relations*, 31(1): 201–10.

Sparrow, P. (1996) 'Too good to be true', *People Management*, 5 December.

Sparrow, P. (2000) 'International reward management', Chapter 9 in White, G. and Druker, J. (eds) *Reward Management: A Critical Text*. London: Routledge.

Social Trends (1996) London: HMSO.

Storey, J. (1992) *Developments in the Management of Human Resources*. Oxford: Oxford University Press.

Thatcher, M. (1993) 'Rewarding managers for competence', *Personnel Management Plus*, March.

Thompson, M. (1995) *Team Working and Pay*. Brighton: Institute for Employment Studies.

Torrington, D. and Hall, L. (1998) *Personnel Management: HRM in Action*, 4th edn. Hemel Hempstead: Prentice Hall.

Tyson, S. (1995) *Human Resource Management, Towards a General Theory*. London: Financial Times/Pitman Publishing.

Waddington, J. and Whitston, C. (1997) 'Why do people join unions in a period of decline?', *British Journal of Industrial Relations*, 35(4): 515–46.

Wainwright Trust (1993) *Equal Value Training Manual*. London: Wainwright Trust.

Further reading

Traditionally, pay has been addressed in the employee relations literature as part of such topics as collective bargaining, state intervention or public sector pay or in respect of particular areas of interest such as low pay or performance-related pay. In addition to the texts and journal articles referred to in this chapter, readers can pursue specialist interests through a range of sources, examples of which are given here.

Government publications such as *Labour Market Trends*. This provides a regular source of national statistics and discussion as well as a telephone-based information service.

Statutory bodies sponsor and publish research and information. The Equal Opportunities Commission (EOC) and the Commission for Racial Equality (CRE) publish research papers in the field of equal opportunities. ACAS publishes an annual report and individual papers in which pay features in the context of workplace employee relations.

Publications by professional bodies. The Chartered Institute of Personnel and Development sponsors and publishes research on a range of pay issues.

Publications by trade unions and the TUC include survey data and studies as well as discussion documents.

Publications by commercial institutions, for example, Income Data Services, include surveys and studies.

Chapter 12

Discrimination

Sally Howe

Learning objectives

By the end of this chapter, readers should be able to:

- define discrimination and give a picture of the effects of discrimination on employment in the twenty-first century;
- explain why discrimination occurs and consider the psychological, sociological, historical, structural and ethical perspectives;
- understand the more radical approaches to equality management including quotas and affirmative action programmes;
- discuss the managing diversity movement and its impact on discrimination in employment;
- describe the roles and initiative taken by management, trade unions and individuals in promoting equal opportunities in the workplace.

Introduction

Exhibit 12.1 discusses the introduction of the women's Representation Bill which is designed to allow political parties to use all-women shortlists in forthcoming elections. The use of legislation to ensure a balanced representation of men and women in the House of Commons and on local councils is a controversial move which reflects well the complexities and dilemmas of managing diversity and discrimination in the workplace. On the face of it, the House of Commons as a workplace provides no particular restrictive barriers to women, both sexes are free to stand for election, yet of the total number of MPs only a small percentage are women. The Labour Party decided to address this problem by taking positive action to increase the number of women candidates during the 1997 general election by creating all-women shortlists. The policy was interventionist and was challenged by some aspiring male Labour candidates and subsequently ruled to be unlawful. It did result, however, in the election of 101 women MPs in 1997, more than twice the number elected in 1992. At the 2001 general election without all-women shortlists, the number of women Labour MPs dropped to 95. The situation demonstrates well the difficulties inherent in affirmative action, or positive discrimination. Supporters of the policy would point

Exhibit 12.1

All-women shortlist plan for local elections

Political parties will be allowed to use all-women short-lists for local council as well as Westminster elections under legislation to be introduced this autumn.

Ministers plan to have the rules in place before next year's conference season to allow parties to change their selection procedures in time for the next general election.

The decision to include local councils came as some surprise to parties who had been expecting only national elections to be covered.

So far, Labour is the only one of the three main parties to agree to use positive discrimination to boost the number of women MPs.

Iain Duncan Smith, the Tory leader, has said he would like more women MPs but is opposed to positive discrimination. The Liberal Democrats voted against taking action this week. Labour officials say that the issue will be debated at next year's conference and no decision has been taken on what system to adopt. However, ministers say they support all-women shortlists for a target number of available seats rather than other systems. Some opposition from unions is expected. The women's representation Bill is to be introduced to the Commons by Stephen Byers, transport, local government and the regions secretary, and in the Lords by Baroness Morgan, Cabinet Office minister.

Source: Rosemary Bennett, *Financial Times*, 29 September 2001.
© 2001 The Financial Times Limited

to the dramatic increase in women MPs in 1997 and say 'well, it works!' Detractors, such as Iain Duncan Smith, suggest that the policy has not been a success 'because instead of getting people who are high-quality, what we've actually got in is people who haven't really performed as politicians' (Comments during an interview with the website ePolitix.com, in August 2001).

In this chapter the factors that contribute to employment profiles such as that found in the House of Commons are examined. The various explanations and perspectives on discrimination are discussed and the strategies adopted to adjust imbalances evaluated.

The management of discrimination and equal opportunities in the employment relationship is an extremely important subject for organisations and for society in general. Organisations are increasingly being asked to examine their business strategies to ensure that their aims are not simply focused on profitability but also include important issues around managing the expectations of employees and society. Most employees will spend considerable periods of their life in the work environment and are entitled to expect fairness of treatment, some consideration of their need for personal fulfilment, and the provision of a non-threatening work environment.

Increasingly, organisations are also recognising that managing equal opportunities is part of a package of measures that can be used to create effective, committed, high-performance teams of workers. The payback can be measured in both financial and non-financial terms. The ability to manage diversity and utilise all members of the working population is an essential part of creating business advantage.

For the UK, the management of equal opportunities is also an important issue. It is one of the essential elements of a free society which respects basic human rights. It is also necessary in order to prevent the growth of disaffected sections of the community which see no prospect of permanent employment. Politically, opinions on the best way to create this ideal are varied; we examine the free market and social justice approaches in this chapter.

What is discrimination?

The dictionary definition of discrimination is 'to make a distinction'. This is an essential skill in employee relations as all organisations need to be able to make distinctions in areas such as selection, appraisal and reward management. Such distinctions must be based on objective, job-related criteria, however, to be regarded as fair discrimination. Distinctions based on characteristics that are not relevant to the job such as sex, sexual orientation, marital status, colour, nationality, disability or age are considered as unfair forms of discrimination which affect the basic human rights of individuals. The term 'discrimination' will be used to denote unfair methods of creating distinctions in this chapter.

Discrimination can take a variety of forms in any organisation:

- *Individual*, where a member or members of the organisation demonstrate prejudice against another individual often as a result of stereotypical thinking. Examples include: 'women with children are less reliable', 'black people are dirty', or 'older people are slow on the uptake'.
- *Structural*, where the requirements for appointments or promotion have the effect of excluding certain groups or individuals. This may be deliberate or accidental and often results from an over-reliance on levels of experience and qualifications when defining entry into a job.
- *Organisational*, reflecting common assumptions about the type of job certain groups of people are capable of performing. Examples include: 'women are best at secretarial work', 'men are more suited to transport and haulage'.

The consequences of unfair discrimination are many but the most significant include:

- the failure to select/promote the best individual for the job because of restrictions placed on applicants as a result of discriminatory practices;
- the failure to create a balanced workforce containing individuals with a diversity of experience whose creativity and ideas can be utilised by the employer;
- the creation of resentment and poor morale, which undermine team spirit and cooperation.

Discrimination can be examined from a number of perspectives, each contributing some insights into the patterns of labour found in employment today. The main perspectives include:

- A *psychological/sociological perspective*, which examines discrimination as a product of how individuals learn appropriate behaviours for the society in which they live, and how social relationships evolve, particularly between the dominant majority group and minorities.
- A *historical perspective*, which looks at changes in the pattern of discrimination over time and the factors that have contributed to it.
- A *structural/economic perspective*, looking at labour patterns in terms of supply and demand and linking discrimination to the possession of particular attributes.
- A *political/ethical perspective*, looking at discrimination as a basic human right and a fundamental part of a socially responsible nation or workplace.

Each of these perspectives is reviewed briefly to illustrate its contribution to a broader understanding of the nature of discrimination.

The psychological/sociological basis of discrimination

Studies have attempted to evaluate the degree to which discrimination is a learned behaviour or a behaviour that results from certain innate personality traits. Research into child development suggests that many aspects of behaviour are modelled through observation of others and through the process of socialisation. Giddens (1993) defines socialisation as 'the process whereby the helpless infant gradually becomes a self-aware, knowledgeable person, skilled in the ways of the culture into which she or he is born'.

Debates over whether nature (genetic inheritance) or nurture (the way an individual is brought up) is the more important in shaping behaviour have tended to conclude that each is important, but that social learning is an integral part of all human experience. The young child will adopt behaviours as a result of identification with the adults around him or her and will imitate observed behaviours. Important agencies of socialisation include the family, the peer group, educational experiences, and attitudes conveyed by the media. There is a tendency in all human beings to generalise from experience and create stereotypes. Stereotypes are not necessarily formed from malice or ill-will; in many cases they result from a lack of knowledge or concrete experience on which to draw. Stereotyping can, however, lead to prejudice against individuals – holding negative attitudes towards them on the basis of their group membership, rather than on their own merits. The word 'prejudice' comes from the notion of prejudging people as either good or bad before knowing them individually. It is this behaviour that can lead to discrimination.

Other studies have attempted to link prejudice with particular types of personality trait. Hillgard *et al.* (1979) report on investigations into Adolf Hitler's anti-Semitic prejudice in the Second World War and suggest that it can be associated with authoritarian styles of personality. In authoritarian personalities, prejudice may reflect the individual's own insecurities. Highly prejudiced individuals may not be able to face their own weaknesses and may project undesirable traits onto minority groups. This displacement activity involves directing feelings of hostility or anger against individuals or groups who are not the real origin of those anxieties. This leads to scapegoating, or blaming other individuals for the source of one's own troubles. Scapegoating also frequently involves projection, the unconscious attributing to others of one's own desires or characteristics.

Explanations such as the one above do not fully explain widespread prejudice against particular groups in society, however. Other theories develop the idea of social norms – a community's implicit rules specifying the beliefs, attitudes and behaviours appropriate for its members. From particular views of social norms, ethnocentrism may occur – a suspicion of outsiders, combined with a tendency to evaluate the norms of other cultures in terms of one's own culture. Ethnocentrism may also lead to group closure, whereby groups maintain boundaries separating themselves from others. The boundaries are developed and sustained by means of exclusion devices, which sharpen the divisions between one ethnic group and another. Such devices include the limiting or prohibition of intermarriage between the groups, restrictions on social contact and the physical separation of groups from one another in ghettos. In some cases the relationship between groups is one of equal power, but in many cases the dominant group uses closure devices to maintain its privileged position.

Historical trends in attitudes to discrimination

The previous section shows how attitudes to those around us are determined by psychological and sociological behaviours. Social norms are not static, however, they evolve over time and as society changes so do the behaviours considered acceptable or unacceptable. In the twenty-first century, displaying notices saying 'No blacks or Irish' would be considered unacceptable, yet in the 1950s such signs were openly seen on boarding houses. Similarly, to expect a woman to resign from her job if she married would be unthinkable in the UK today, but this still occurred in the civil service in the 1960s.

The factors causing such alterations in social attitudes are complex, but by tracing the historical trends some light can be thrown on the continuing process of change today. We start by examining the development of attitudes towards the roles of men and women in society.

Gender issues

Figure 12.1 shows the distribution of labour in the UK workforce based on age and gender. In 2000, female participation rates in employment continue to outstrip those for men, as it has done since the 1970s. In 1976 there were 9.7 million women participating compared to 12.6 million in 1998, an increase of 30 per cent. Projections show a continuation of this trend, with women expected to account for 46 per cent of the labour force by 2011. The greatest increases in female employment can be seen in the 25–34 age range and particularly in the 45–59 age range. Employment on part-time or flexible contracts continues to be a feature of women's employment. According to the *Labour Force Survey* in autumn 1998, 11 per cent of women of working age in the UK had employment contracts with a flexitime arrangement compared with 8 per cent

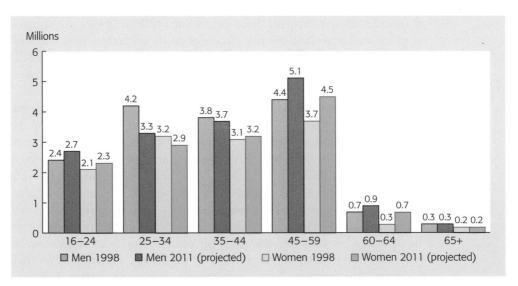

Figure 12.1 **The labour force by age and gender in Britain, 1998–2011**
Source: Office for National Statistics

of men. Term-time working is also popular among women, with 6 per cent of them having this arrangement compared with only 1 per cent of men.

Do these patterns reflect basic biological and physical sex differences between men and women, or are they the result of gender learning and cultural programming? Some researchers have tried to link biological factors with behavioural characteristics, for example, studying the link between males and aggressive behaviour and females and passive behaviour. The evidence for particular types of behaviour being linked to sex is inconclusive; many variations occur. What is evident, however, is that despite the considerable differences found in the respective roles of women and men in different cultures, there is no known instance of a society in which women are more powerful than men. Women are everywhere primarily concerned with childbearing and the mainten-ance of the home, while political and military activities tend to be resoundingly male. This male dominance is usually referred to as patriarchy. The explanation for this con-sistency is linked to the biological fact that women give birth to and nurse children.

Looking at the effects of biological and physical sex differences on employment, have attitudes and practices changed over time? Jobs requiring physical strength, such as mining, agriculture, haulage and building, have traditionally been the preserve of men. Jobs requiring manual dexterity, such as assembly, have been occupied by women. Are these occupational stereotypes biological in origin? Generally, men's body size and weight are greater than women's, making them stronger, but less sensitive to fine movements. This fact has led to many of the occupational stereotypes still seen today. However, although there may be general trends, there are also exceptions, and excluding all women from jobs requiring strength or all men from jobs requiring dexterity is dis-criminatory. What is important is the objective assessment of the relevant factor.

Over time, much physically demanding work has been assisted or replaced by machin-ery. Agriculture and mining today need far less brute strength and use more technology. Haulage companies have computerised loading systems and power-assisted steering and brakes on their lorries, eliminating the need for manual strength. As these changes pro-gress, the biological barrier preventing women entering these jobs becomes less relevant. In the area of child care, also, certain changes have occurred. The growth in the number of childminders and nurseries in the UK demonstrates that more women are choosing to remain in full-time employment after having children rather than withdrawing from the labour force. Overall, women are still disproportionately represented in the part-time labour force, however, suggesting that balancing work and family commitments is still a predominantly female concern. The availability of affordable child care is also one of the main factors limiting women's greater participation in the workforce.

Other factors also impinge on occupational choice, and the evidence suggests that gender learning is a particularly significant factor. Men and women learn what are the socially acceptable jobs to aspire to. Tracing these attitudes back to pre-industrial times, it is interesting to note that there was no clear distinction between the roles of men and women in feudal societies. Family units lived and worked together and roles were adapted to the tasks needed at the time. Even in the early industrial period, craft skills such as spinning and weaving were undertaken by all members of the family. It was only with the arrival of the factory system that it became normal for men to go away from home to work, and women to stay behind and look after the family. The separation of paid factory work from unpaid housework was the most influential factor in determin-ing gender roles from then on. Although there has always been a significant percentage of women in paid employment, in general these jobs were concentrated in assembly work and textile manufacturing, and in domestic service, education and health. Even as late as 1910, more than one-third of all women employed were maids or houseservants. The female workforce was also made up predominantly of single women, who would stop work when they married. The phrase 'a woman's place is in the home' typified attitudes of the time, and to have a working wife was a poor reflection on a man's ability to provide for his family.

What factors came together to change this situation? One significant change was the arrival of reliable birth control methods, which released women from the constant demands of childbearing and rearing. For the first time, a woman could choose the size of her family and be free to pursue other activities outside the home. Another influential factor in changing attitudes was the adaptations caused by the employment shortages during the First and Second World Wars. During the First World War, women carried out many jobs previously regarded as suitable only for men. Welding and other apprentice-trained skills were undertaken by women, as were many aspects of agriculture by land-girls. Women realised that they were capable of undertaking these jobs, and many enjoyed the social contacts and different lifestyles provided by the work environment. Rates of pay for women were invariably set at less than those of men, reflecting the assumption that the work was of lesser value. After the First World War, women were prohibited from carrying on with these roles, and both the government (through the Restoration of Pre-War Practices Act 1919) and trade unions made it clear that women should withdraw their labour in favour of the returning men.

The Second World War saw a repeat of these processes. In 1941, all women aged between 16 and 49 were required to register for work and could be compulsorily directed to full-time civilian labour. By December, women without children could be conscripted into the armed forces. At the end of the Second World War women were again expected to withdraw their labour but were much less ready to relinquish their jobs than before. The previous assumptions about women's capabilities had been broken, and the realisation that child rearing a family could be successfully managed with a job took hold.

As well as the practical consequences of the wars, another influential change factor was the feminist movement. Feminism has many forms but its objectives are to enhance the role of women in society, placing them on an equal footing with men. The early feminists campaigned for political rights. The most well-known group were the suffragists, who achieved the right for women to vote on an equal basis to men in the UK in 1928. After this major achievement, feminism became less evident until the end of the 1960s. The 'swinging sixties' saw many challenges to traditional thought, among which was the rising challenge by women of the male-dominated status quo. In many spheres – legal, economic and social – women questioned why systems were the way they were. Why should women take all the responsibility for child rearing? Why should women be represented in advertisements as either sex objects or slaves? Why should women be paid less than men for the same work? As these issues were debated, the inequities became more apparent to both women and men.

During the 1970s, legal regulation of sex discrimination also helped to establish the principle of equal opportunities for both men and women.

The change in attitudes, as often happens, was not straightforward, however. During the 1980s, feminism faced a counter-revolution from those who believed that women should return to traditional values of marriage and the family. The rises in the divorce rate, number of single-parent families and the incidence juvenile crime have all been blamed on the changes to traditional families. The Conservative Party in the late 1980s and 1990s was particularly fond of expounding 'return to family values' policies.

Faludi (1992) examined the reactions to feminism and in particular the male backlash this has provoked. Feminist ideas have been ridiculed and trivialised and the backlash can be seen to represent a rejection by men of the gains women have made. The 'burn your bra' campaign was seized on by some as a typical example of extremist behaviour by 'women's libbers'.

The 'gender war' mentality of the 1980s has moderated over time into a less confrontational development of the rights of both women and men. Increasingly, in the 1990s it is men who are reassessing the goals set them during gender learning. In the 'masculinity debate' new man reflects on the social expectations of society. Many men are now rejecting the career-focused lifestyle in favour of a more hands-on approach to parenting, and a balance between work and home life. Male redundancy, early retirements and a decline in full-time manual employment have contributed to a society where many more men are outside traditional employment and the 'going out to work' philosophy. Some have found a greater quality of life as a result. These trends have been reflected in various policies at both national level and at organisational level on work–life balance.

Race and ethnicity

Attitudes towards those of different racial or ethnic origins have also changed over time. Today, legislation prohibits any discrimination in employment on the grounds of race or ethnic origin. Nevertheless, a glance at the employment and unemployment statistics makes it clear that some groups in the UK population have a much higher incidence of unemployment than others. The unemployment rate for ethnic minorities in 1998 was more than double that of the white population. Ethnic minorities are also more likely to work in certain occupations such as plant and machinery operatives, and are underrepresented in craft and related occupations, clerical and secretarial occupations and management posts.

This section looks at the history of immigration and the employment of ethnic minorities to attempt to explain the background to these statistics.

A study of attitudes to race and ethnicity can start from the same basis as that of gender. Are there innate, biological differences that distinguish races and their capabilities, or are they shaped by cultural learning or ethnicity?

Attempts to separate human beings into biologically different races have always been fraught with difficulties. For every categorisation produced, exceptions have been found which make the categories of limited value. Genetically, a scientist could not tell by examining a cell whether it had come from a black or a white body. The concept of race is therefore based almost entirely on external physical appearances.

Historically, the UK has always been made up of a variety of ethnic groups. The population in general has French, Scots, Welsh, Irish and Dutch origins. The Irish in the mid-nineteenth century were the largest immigrant group. The Jewish community was established in the seventeenth century and increased substantially as repression drove Jews out of other countries. Dutch immigrants arrived during the Industrial Revolution, as did Chinese immigrants at a later period.

Events at the beginning of the twentieth century were profoundly affected by the First World War. Many men from the colonies fought for the British forces during the war. After it ended, however, discrimination continued, with black troops being excluded from the peace march through London in 1919. Black unemployment in Britain reached record proportions as companies gave priority to white servicemen. The situation was somewhat different after the Second World War. Britain's colonial wealth and industrial dominance had receded considerably between the wars, and after the Second World War the government decided to build wealth at home rather than look for it abroad. Gaps in the labour force were filled by encouraging citizens of the colonies to emigrate to the UK.

In the first two decades after the end of the Second World War, western Europe took in some 11 million workers from abroad (about 5 per cent of the total workforce). Black workers were often faced with hostile colleagues and overt racism in accommodation and employment. Criticisms of the black workers were based on two contradictory opinions: one that blacks disliked work and were here to scrounge on the dole, and the other that blacks were so keen to work, even for low pay, that they took jobs away from British workers and undercut pay rates.

Immigrants tended to gather in areas of low-cost housing, mostly in the inner cities, and establish their own communities to support each other. This in turn led to accusations of insularity and creating ghettos from the white population.

When the employment market changed again in the 1960s and recession resulted from increased competition from the rebuilt economies, government policy altered to limit immigration from the Commonwealth. Enoch Powell headed a movement during this period dedicated to returning black workers 'back home'. The National Front, an openly racist party, was founded in 1966 to further these aims.

During the 1970s, legislation was passed to protect the rights of minority groups in the UK, while at the same time further Immigration Acts tightened up the laws on blacks coming into the country. The recession of the 1970s exacerbated the problems of ethnic minority workers. Rising unemployment hit young blacks hardest of all, and during the 1980s a series of riots took place in many inner cities.

As well as these economic factors, attitudes towards racial discrimination were also affected by civil rights campaigners in both the US and the UK. Martin Luther King led a series of campaigns of active but non-violent resistance to discrimination in the US in the 1950s. King's famous speech stated:

> I have a dream that one day this nation will rise up and live out the true meaning of its creed: 'We hold these truths to be self-evident; that all men are created equal'. I have a dream that one day on the red hills of Georgia the sons of former slaves and the sons of former slave-owners will be able to sit down together at the table of brotherhood. I have a dream that my four little children will one day live in a nation where they will not be judged by the colour of their skin but by the content of their character.

The 'dream' was violently opposed by some whites and King was assassinated in 1968. The Civil Rights Act 1964, which King was instrumental in promoting, established the principle of equality of opportunity for all in the US. During this same period some black activists formed more militant and violent groups such as the Black Panther movement, in reaction to white hostility. The violence of this group eventually caused its collapse towards the end of the 1970s as blacks refocused on more legitimate ways to change society.

Other individuals such as Malcolm X, the son of a white mother and black father, also used their lives to publicise the prejudices faced by minorities. The X was a reference to the practice of slave owners who did not allow black slaves to use a surname.

Collectively, the activities of such individuals raised the profile of black issues and helped to raise public awareness of attitudes to discrimination.

Since that period many other changes have occurred which break down the prejudice between black and white. In South Africa, the system of apartheid was finally removed in 1994, again signalling the right of every individual to be free and self-governing. These changes have been significant, but it will take many more years before ingrained attitudes disappear completely.

The terrorist events of 11 September 2001 have caused a recent increase in racial tension and intolerance, especially against members of the Muslim community in the UK. Lord Dholokia, addressing the Conservative Party conference in September 2001 said: 'We have seen right across Europe and in other parts of the world an upsurge of racism, intolerance, bigotry and narrow nationalism that poses a great threat to the general peace.' He criticised the Conservative government's election campaign against asylum seekers as pandering to bigotry and xenophobia.

It will be a challenge to all organisations and to the UK government to continue the themes of racial harmony and the abandonment of discrimination in the current climate of uncertainty and racial tension.

Age

Historically, attitudes to the effects of age on employment have not been as clearly researched as those of gender and ethnicity. Some factors affecting attitudes to working age can be identified, however, again reflecting social trends. In feudal times, children as young as four or five would have small jobs to perform to assist their family, and in the industrial period children worked extensively in mines, factories and as chimney sweeps, etc. It was not uncommon for children to work 12–14 hour days, and this was not thought inappropriate at the time. Attitudes to child labour changed primarily as a result of increased access to education. Education was not available to all until the late nineteenth century. Compulsory education for all was established in 1870, and the school-leaving age then rose progressively from 10 to 14. Most schools were run by private or church authorities and there was little state regulation.

The world wars, particularly the Second World War, revised attitudes to education. Secondary school education was provided for all by the Education Act 1944, allowing more pupils to stay on after 14. Selective education based on the 11+ system was found to result in only 12 per cent of pupils continuing in education until 17. The comprehensive system, introduced in the late 1960s, removed the selection procedures in most areas of the country. Since then, the proportion of young people staying on in further education has risen. The minimum school leaving age is now 16. *Labour Market and Skill Trends* (DfEE, 2000: 44) reports:

There was a steady growth in the proportion of 16 and 17 year olds receiving some form of education or training between 1985 and 1993 from 66% in 1985 up to a peak of 84% in 1993 and 1994. From 1994 onwards there has been a slight decline in participation down to 81% in 1997, followed by a small rise to 82% in 1998.

In terms of discrimination, young people are often disproportionately represented in the unemployment statistics. Achieving work experience is one of the most difficult problems, with students trapped in a situation where they are not considered for jobs because of a lack of experience, but are unable to gain experience without a job. Various government initiatives such as Youth Training Schemes, Modern Apprenticeships and the Labour Party's New Deal have attempted to help this situation.

At the other end of the age range, demographic changes have affected the numbers of older people in the UK. Historically, older people were perceived as having wisdom, prestige and status in society. More recently, attitudes have changed in favour of the younger age groups, particularly the 25–35 age category. Older workers may now be stereotyped as slow, reluctant to change and less well adapted to the pace of modern life.

Attitudes to retirement have also changed. In the late 1920s, more than half the men over 65 were in paid employment. Retirement was related more to ill-health or physical incapability. Nowadays many individuals wish to retire before the state retirement age, allowing more time for leisure pursuits, or they may wish to move from full-time work to part-time. This trend reflects the improvements in company pension provisions for employees in the UK. Until 1992 the state retirement age was 60 for women and 65 for men. This practice was challenged, resulting in a retirement age of 65 being set for all, with the option of retirement at 60 if so wished. The tendency towards early retirement was also hastened by the recession of the 1980s and 1990s which led many employers to encourage their older staff to take early retirement by providing enhancements to their pension arrangements. This has led to a reduction in the overall age profile in many organisations.

The baby boom generation of the 1960s, together with increased life expectancy, also means that proportionally more people are in the older age ranges in the population and fewer are in the younger bands. By 2011 there will be over 2 million more members of the labour force aged 45 and over.

Campaigns are increasingly focusing attention on age discrimination as a negative feature of employee relations. In 1999 the Code of Practice for Age Diversity in Employment, along with supporting guidance for employers was introduced. The code of practice aims to be a non-statutory, effective measure that will challenge employment practices that unfairly discriminate against employees on the grounds of age. An EU directive approved by member states in autumn 2000 requires governments to introduce laws preventing discrimination on the grounds of age by 2006. The government is currently consulting with all relevant bodies to determine the content of new legislation on age discrimination. Moves could include introducing laws to remove clauses in employment contracts requiring workers to retire at a fixed age, such as 65.

■ Disability

Attitudes to disability have also changed over time. In the Victorian era, both physical and mental disabilities could result in individuals being removed from society and confined in residential homes. The attitude was one of 'out of sight, out of mind' and the idea of integrating the disabled into the community was not considered. The development of more enlightened attitudes in the 1970s saw a reversal of the institutionalisation trend, and a progressive move towards more care in the community. In employment, Leach (1996) notes that:

> The 'social model' and policies of the disabled people's movement have replaced the discredited 'medical model' of disability. Until recently disabled people had been largely politically invisible. They were socially visible only as patients, clients or welfare/charity cases – under the control of medical and other disability-related professionals. The disabled people's movement began fighting for political influence and the right to control both their own lives and their own organisations.

Employment statistics show the difficulties disabled people or those with a long-term illness face in gaining employment. There were over 6.5 million people of working age who reported having a current long-term health problem or disability in the UK in spring 1999, representing about 18 per cent of the total population of working age. People with disabilities have much lower activity rates than people without disabilities. Only 51 per cent of people with disabilities were economically active, compared with 84 per cent of people without disabilities. Unemployment rates for people with disabilities were nearly twice those for people without disabilities. Furthermore, when people with disabilities become unemployed, they are more likely to remain unemployed for longer. Roughly two-fifths of unemployed people with disabilities were long-term unemployed (defined as having been unemployed for a year or more) compared with only around one-quarter of unemployed people without disabilities.

The lack of awareness shown by town planners and architects to the needs of the partially sighted, wheelchair users, etc. has also been exposed.

Health care in the 1990s means that more and more people are being treated and life expectancy is increasing. Modern life brings with it many stress factors, however, and organisations are having to deal with increasing numbers of employees who are suffering from stress exhaustion. Other modern health issues revolve around the ergonomic design of offices and workstations and the effects of VDU work. Disability has to be defined quite broadly to encompass these factors as well as the more obvious areas such as blindness, deafness and physical incapacity.

The introduction of the Disability Discrimination Act (DDA) 1996, made it illegal for firms with 15 employees or more to discriminate against current or prospective staff because of any disability. A few specific categories of employment are exempt: the police, prison officers, fire-fighters, members of the armed forces and those who work on board ships or aircraft, but for most large employers, the law requires them to make 'reasonable adjustments' to working arrangements and environments that place employees with disabilities at a disadvantage to other workers.

The creation of the Disability Rights Commission was intended to give the DDA a higher profile by giving the Act some teeth, although its approach puts conciliation before litigation. Since its establishment, around 4,000 cases citing disability discrimination have come before employment tribunals.

Figure 12.2 shows the results of research conducted by the Chartered Institute of Personnel and Development (CIPD) and Cornell University on the implementation of the employment provisions of the DDA.

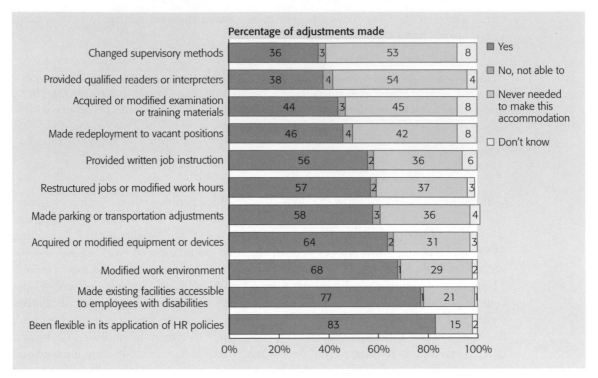

Figure 12.2 Adjustments made by organisations for employees with disabilities
Source: IPD/Cornell University (1999)

All of the areas outlined above have become important in the campaign to provide equality of opportunity for all. Other categories of discrimination are also receiving increased attention. An EU directive approved by member states in October 2000 requires governments to introduce laws preventing discrimination on grounds of sexual orientation and religion by 2003. Organisations are coming under increasing pressure to have policies covering all these areas.

Structural/economic factors affecting discrimination

In addition to the perspectives already considered, discrimination patterns can also be analysed by examining the economic factors affecting the UK labour force and the employment structures that result. This section looks at the position of various groups in the UK economy and examines some of the economic explanations for these patterns.

Economic explanations for discrimination include:

■ human capital theory;
■ segmented labour market theory;
■ reserve army of labour theory.

■ Human capital theory

This economic explanation assumes that labour markets operate in a non-discriminatory fashion, rewarding workers for their productivity. Therefore, if women, ethnic minorities, the disabled or any other group is disadvantaged, this is because they are less productive workers. This assumption cannot be tested easily, because measuring productivity is impossible for many jobs. Researchers therefore examine characteristics that they assume increase productivity such as the skills, experience and commitment that workers bring to their jobs. Workers' skills and experience, according to economists, constitute their 'human capital'. Through education, training and experience, workers invest in their human capital, and these investments make some workers more productive than others. Human capital theorists assume that women's orientation to their families inhibits their investment in themselves and so makes them less productive than men. Equally, the education levels and training possessed by some ethnic minority groups may also disadvantage them in comparison with other groups.

When looking at academic achievements, statistics do suggest that women continue to have fewer qualifications than men. Until recently, however, educational opportunities were different for males and females. Certain subjects on the curriculum such as domestic science and needlework were available only for girls; boys were directed to metalwork and woodwork. Nowadays, such stereotyping has been addressed by the National Curriculum (1989), which provides equal access to all subjects for both gender groups. The evidence from recent studies on equality in education suggests:

> The last two decades have seen tremendous progress in closing the gap between boys and girls in education. Girls have caught up and are doing as well as boys in mathematics and science – which used to be thought of as 'boys' subjects'. Yet it takes a long time to change attitudes about what girls or boys can study at school and beyond. For example, girls still choose secretarial courses, while boys choose to train in areas like engineering and construction. However, women have made major inroads into the professions. Increasing numbers of women study medicine (one third of all doctors are women, as compared with one sixth in 1975), law (1 in 16 solicitors were women in 1975, as compared with nearly half now), architecture and accountancy. Men are also increasingly entering the traditional 'women's' professions of nursing and secretarial work (EOC, 1996).

As educational changes feed through the system, therefore, human capital gender differences should reduce. Other statistics also indicate that more women are continuing into further and higher education than men.

There is considerable variation in the educational attainment of different ethnic groups. Figure 12.3 shows that larger proportions of ethnic minorities than whites had no qualifications in 1998. There were, however, differences between the ethnic minority groups. While 14 per cent of white men and 20 per cent of white women have no qualifications, for Black Africans the respective figures are 8 per cent and 17 per cent. At the other end of the spectrum are the Bangladeshis, with 42 per cent of Bangladeshi men having no qualifications and 55 per cent of Bangladeshi women.

At the other end of the educational spectrum, higher proportions of Black African, Chinese and Indian men are qualified to degree level or hold higher qualifications than white men. Twenty-three per cent of white men of working age had degrees or equivalent qualifications in 1998, compared with 37 per cent of Black African men,

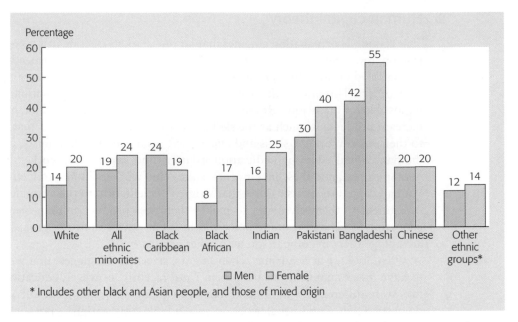

Figure 12.3 Population of working age with no qualifications by ethnic group and gender in Britain, 1998
Source: Labour Force Survey, 1998

29 per cent of Chinese men and 28 per cent of Indian men. For women, nearly one-third of Chinese are qualified to degree standard compared with only 8 per cent of Pakistani and Bangladeshi women.

Segmented labour market theory

This set of economic explanations about the different experiences of work in the UK uses the concept of segmentation in the labour market to explain discrimination. Piore (1975) divided labour markets into two segments: the primary sector, which offers jobs with relatively high wages, good working conditions, chances of advancement, and employment stability, and the secondary sector, which tends to be low paying with poor working conditions, little chance of advancement, high instability and high labour turnover. Barron and Norris (1976), looking specifically at the role of women in employment, also identified a dual labour market pattern with women concentrated in the lower paid, less skilled and more easily disposable sector of the market.

The recent trends in employment towards core and peripheral workers (Atkinson, 1984) have built on this model with an emphasis on the development of a core of highly trained and developed permanent staff supported by peripheral workers and outworkers or contractors. Conditions of employment are often much better for the core group, with peripheral workers considered as more expendable and less worthy of investment. Following through this model, the explanation for disadvantage is that women and members of ethnic minority groups are more likely to be found in the flexible categories of the model than in the core.

Some evidence for this proposition can be found in the Institute for Employment Research projections, which suggested that although employment would grow by approximately 0.8 per cent to the year 2000, the increase would not happen evenly across all sectors. Male employment was projected to rise slightly (around 3 per cent) while female employment would increase more rapidly (an extra 11 per cent). Part-time employment was projected to increase by 22 per cent while full-time employment would decrease by 1 per cent. Self-employment would also increase considerably, by 13 per cent. Married women in particular would show a very low unemployment rate, only 4.6 per cent compared with 11.4 per cent for unmarried women.

These statistics tend to reinforce the idea that labour markets are changing, with more jobs being created in the periphery while core employment is actually reducing. Terms and conditions of employment still favour the reduced number of, predominantly male, core employees at the expense of other categories. The flexible firm model has been criticised, however, as being ill-defined (what exactly is core and what is periphery?) and lacking in actual evidence of its use. The Workplace Industrial Relations Surveys carried out in 1980, 1984 and 1990 showed little evidence of any large-scale increase in the flexible forms of working they examined (part-time, fixed-term contract, freelance and home workers).

Reserve army of labour theory

This theory comes from the writings of Marx, who saw the reserve army as being labour which is only partially employed, sometimes attracted into the labour market but also repelled from it. Reserve army status affects seasonal workers and others whose job security is limited and who can be hired and fired at will. The historical section showed how women were attracted into the labour market during the world wars and then dispensed with again. This type of practice leads to women being categorised as part of the reserve army. Other disadvantaged groups, such as certain ethnic minorities, have also been used in the same way.

At times of labour shortage, employers may be forced to provide measures to encourage women and minorities into the workforce (crèches, term-time-only contracts, targeted recruitment drives, etc.). When the employment situation changes, these measures may be withdrawn, forcing some employees to give up their positions.

During downsizing or redundancy exercises, the selection of those who will be made redundant may also indicate an assumption that women and minorities are a more disposable source of employment.

Statistics to reinforce this pattern produce mixed results. For women, the overall unemployment rate is actually lower than that for men. However, this was almost entirely due to the low unemployment rate of married women. Ethnic minority groups experience much higher levels of unemployment than the white population, however. Table 12.1 illustrates the situation by ethnic group and gender in Britain in 1998.

In combination, these economic theories provide some explanations for the patterns of discrimination found in employment today.

Table 12.1 **Unemployment rates by ethnic group and gender in Britain, 1998**

	Men (%)	Women (%)	All (%)
White	6.5	5.2	5.9
All ethnic minorities	14.0	12.6	13.4
Black Caribbean	14.7	12.1	13.3
Black African	16.0	16.8	16.3
Indian	9.0	9.0	9.0
Pakistani-Bangladeshi	20.2	21.3	20.5
Other ethnic groups[a]	14.2	12.2	14.3

[a] Includes other black and Asian people, and those of mixed origin
Source: *Labour Force Survey*, 1998

Political/ethical issues affecting discrimination

The final perspective on discrimination to be examined is the political and ethical one. Discrimination in the workplace is very much affected by the values and attitudes of the society in which the organisation is located. It would be impossible to detach attitudes to employees at work from the wider social context within which the organisation that employs them exists. As a result, the values and norms held in society generally need to be appreciated so that their impact on the workplace can be evaluated. Values and norms are difficult to identify, however, as no one set of beliefs dominates all members of the society. As a result, what is considered ethical may be very different depending on the groups or cultures being examined.

The relationship between social responsibility and business responsibility is also hotly debated. Elizabeth Vallance (1995) in the introduction to her book *Business Ethics at Work* states:

> business is about making profits and ethics is about being good and, realistically, never the twain shall meet. Being a tough-minded manager implies there's no room for the ethical niceties . . . the currently fashionable talk about the 'social responsibility' of business has been seen by some managers as an attempt to force business to take on the role of government; to protect the environment; to regenerate the inner cities; to deal with everything that is wrong with society, from educational deprivation to racism.

She argues, however, that business ethics are about specific and identifiable moral dilemmas which emerge in the course of business activity and the framework for the logical analysis of such dilemmas. Business ethics are concerned with justice and decency and the production of long-term shareholder value. As such, discrimination issues are very much part of the moral dilemmas that need to be recognised and planned for.

For many employers there is an implied link between ethical standards and long-term business success. In equal opportunities terms, organisations with a reputation for fair and responsible methods of relating to employees should have greater loyalty, commitment and success than those that do not espouse these values. Evidence to support this view is difficult to obtain, as quantifiable measures are hard to identify. There is some evidence from companies who have attempted equal opportunities initiatives that greater business success has resulted. For example, Rank Xerox found in the late 1980s that its efforts to recruit more men into traditionally female jobs and women into male areas paid off not only in terms of correcting a gender imbalance but also in terms of increased response rates and the positive attitudes expressed by applicants about the company (Paddison, 1990).

The other way of evaluating the impact is to consider the cost to the organisation of negative publicity about its business practices. A damaging racism story could well reduce the organisation's ability to attract employees and also affect the response of customers to its products.

Difficulties arise, however, when considering equality of opportunity between different stakeholder groups. Even when considering employees alone, should the organisation provide equal terms and conditions for all or is it acceptable (ethical) to provide enhanced benefits for core workers not enjoyed by those on part-time or temporary contracts? These latter employees may receive far fewer training and development opportunities than their full-time colleagues, and may also be denied the range of employee benefits, including pension entitlements, of others. These considerations have led to a move towards equal treatment for all workers, with legislation being enacted to underpin these rights.

The difficulties of balancing business profitability and success with acceptable and consistent standards of behaviour is, therefore, one of the main challenges of employee relations for the twenty-first century. As globalisation increases and the variety of cultural and ethnic groups in the marketplace expands, the establishment of fundamental rights and the ability to maintain equality of opportunities for all become more and more essential. Some companies, like Levi Strauss, have established global sourcing and operating guidelines. These specify that workers should not be younger than 14 years old (in line with the convention drawn up by the International Labour Organisation), that people should not work more than 60 hours a week, and that workers should be free to join a trade union. Equality of treatment conditions may also form part of this basic package in the near future.

Having examined various perspectives on discrimination, we now look at the different approaches that have been adopted at both state and organisational level to address the problems. The history of each approach can be traced in many cases to assumptions deriving from the perspectives already covered. The main approaches reviewed here are:

- national initiatives and educational programmes;
- more radical approaches such as affirmative action (positive discrimination) programmes;
- the managing diversity approach.

National initiatives and educational programmes

Chapter 8 covers the main legislative approach to equal opportunities and should be read in conjunction with this section. Legislation has played a significant role in the development of national policies on handling unfair discrimination in the workplace.

The Conservative governments in the 1980s and 1990s had a strong preference for educating and influencing organisations by persuasion rather than by legislation. As well as enforcement, one of the other key roles assigned to the Equal Opportunies Commission (EOC) and Commission for Racial Equality (CRE) is the promotion of best practice and the development of education and training initiatives.

Liff (1995) suggests that the codes of practice, procedural approach to managing equal opportunities is based on an attempt to control managerial behaviour by tightly specifying how managers should carry out certain tasks and monitoring, whether they do it or not. Many studies have indicated that managers are very good at evading controls if they wish to. She also comments that such approaches are flawed because they attempt to change behaviour without tackling the underlying prejudicial attitudes that cause it. Discriminatory judgements are often discussed as if they were deliberate actions, yet much research suggests that they are embedded in deep-seated and subtle processes.

Awareness training may help individuals to recognise their own prejudices and the ways in which these affect their judgement. An understanding of these processes might also reduce people's resistance to EU approaches which might otherwise be seen simply as bureaucratic encumbrances. The development of approaches that move further than simply complying with the law are illustrated in Exhibit 12.2.

In evaluating the success of the equal opportunities programme in the health service outlined in Exhibit 12.2, the awareness training was seen as essential to the gaining of commitment to the changes. The systems and procedures were important, but without commitment they would have been left on the shelf, and not implemented further.

◼ National campaigns and special inquiries

Another approach to discrimination involves mobilising support for equality through national campaigns led by a variety of organisations or the commissioning of special enquiries in a specific area of discrimination. A recent example in the area of sex discrimination is the enquiry into equal pay, headed by Denise Kingsmill. Research from the government's women's unit found that the weekly median gross income for women was £125 in 1999/2000, slightly less than half of that for men at £256. The Kingsmill enquiry into equal pay suggests that there may be a case for 'direct intervention' to break down labour market barriers. The report suggests that companies need to dismantle the traditional distinctions between 'male' and 'female' jobs and full- and part-time workers. The most poorly paid were often women working part-time.

The report suggests that the government should lead by example: companies bidding to provide public services should have effective arrangements for identifying and eliminating gender bias in their pay and promotion systems. The government should also review the tax incentives for employers that recruit women who would otherwise by unemployed or on low earnings and train them in occupations in which they are under-represented. Other suggestions include establishing a centre of excellence to commission research on women's employment and pay and to provide practical, market-driven business solutions.

The Department of Trade and Industry (DTI) has responded to the Kingsmill report by committing itself to:

Operating equal opportunities in the health service

The health service typifies many of the discrimination issues in British society as a whole. In post-war Britain, immigrants from the new Commonwealth were encouraged to come to fill the less desirable jobs, many of which were in the NHS's low-paid ancillary service. Many were steered towards harder staff specialities such as geriatrics and mental illness, and into unqualified nursing auxiliary posts. The employment pattern was established, with black and other ethnic minority staff concentrated in the lower-level, poorly paid jobs.

During the 1970s and 1980s, a growing number of tribunal cases showed discriminatory practices embedded in health service procedures. Few health authorities had obtained data on their staff's ethnic origins. In the employment of women, there were also concerns. Women form 75 per cent of the health services' employees, but they too are concentrated in lower-graded, frequently part-time, jobs and are seriously under-represented at senior levels. The introduction of general manager jobs into the NHS has not improved the situation. Only 4 per cent of women hold general manager jobs at district (authority) level and 17 per cent at unit level.

Valerie Amos, the EOC's chief executive in 1990, stated that:

> The NHS expects a lifetime of full-time work, but women's lives are often quite different from that. The NHS still expects the majority of its workforce to conform to the working patterns of the minority of its employees.

Changing demographic patterns and the poor performance of the NHS in retaining staff and attracting returners into the profession led to the need for some serious management thinking on equal opportunities.

The following are the principal measures introduced by the West Midlands region to improve the equality of opportunity for all:

- The production of concise 'how to do it' guides for managers with resource references and case studies based on best practices.
- The publication of *Vacancies Ahead*, a management guide that clearly spelt out the need for a radical change in approach, with staff being valued as an investment rather than a cost to the organisation, and with employment practices that are family-friendly and promote real equality of opportunity, such as flexible working hours, child care and support for careers, career-break and back-to-work schemes and more flexible approaches to career development generally.
- Awareness training for line managers, organised in two stages – first, a one-day workshop to gain commitment, then supporting practical sessions that would help them put plans into practice.
- Management development and training courses to improve the skills of existing staff, particularly those who are under-represented at higher levels.

Source: Parkyn (1991)

- making it easier for women to get information from their employers on potential equal pay problems (equal pay claim questionnaires – mirroring race and sex discrimination claim requirements – are already included in the Employment Bill);
- new reporting requirements for larger companies on how they are managing their 'human capital';
- encouraging private and public organisations to conduct pay reviews;
- spreading best practice through 'fair pay champions' and equal pay awards for industry (to be known as 'Castle awards' after Barbara Castle, the Labour employment minister responsible for developing the Equal Pay Act 1970).

Through these methods, both the government and employers can be persuaded to move towards more fair and appropriate procedures.

More radical approaches: affirmative action (positive discrimination) programmes

Jewson and Mason (1986) suggest that there are two approaches to the management of equal opportunity: (1) the legislative/codes of practice approach, which they describe as liberal, based around equal *treatment*, and (2) the radical approach, which is more concerned with equal *outcomes*. The management of equal outcomes involves a commitment to achieving fair distributions, or quotas, of under-represented groups in the workforce.

Under existing legislation, the establishment of fixed quotas in employment in the UK is not lawful. A previous section mentioned the use of a 3 per cent quota for disabled people in the workforce, and it is this kind of approach which is suggested. The lack of success of the quota approach in disability discrimination was partly because of the lack of enforcement. For a quota system to be effective, the penalties for non-compliance need to be clear.

The US has the longest experience of quota-setting, through the Federal Contract Compliance Requirements, which require organisations to complete statistical returns and targets showing workforce profiles. Where candidates are of equal calibre, the organisation must select an individual from an under-represented group if the targets set have not been fulfilled. For any company employed as a federal contractor or sub-contractor, an affirmative action plan is required which includes goals and timetables. The company is required to give details of the ethnic and gender composition of the workforce. Where there is an under-representation of a particular group, targets are set for the number or proportion of women and/or black people employed. The Office of Federal Contract Compliance Programs (OFCPP) monitors these affirmative action programmes, and a company may be debarred from the federal contractors' list if it does not have a good reason for non-compliance. The system has been endorsed by successive Presidents for over 30 years and has received support from both society at large and the business community.

Studies indicated that the compliance programme had made a difference to improving the employment available to women and minorities. Both groups were found to have greater job opportunities in both quantitative and qualitative terms (IPM/IDS, 1987).

Despite this finding, the UK government considers that contract compliance represents special treatment which cannot be justified. The IPM/IDS investigation suggested that there were two main reasons why contract compliance was opposed:

- *Deregulation*: the burden on business imposed on firms represents an unnecessary constraint on the free operation of the market. Contract compliance entails large workloads on personnel staff for little return in benefits to the firm's personnel practice. Contract compliance procedures are too complex and not related to the contractors' business interests. Irrelevant clauses in contracts give an unfair competitive advantage.
- *Value for money*: freedom to contract ensures fair competition and value for money for the purchasers. Non-commercial clauses have, by definition, nothing to do with value for money and are, therefore, immoral.

Christopher Chope (1987) wrote:

> I do not believe that local authorities should set themselves up as extra statutory enforcement agencies by withholding contracts from those who do not meet what they perceive as minimum requirements for satisfying national legislation – which, after all, properly includes its own provision for regulation and enforcement.

Although UK legislation does not allow a quota approach, it does allow positive discrimination (affirmative action) to address an imbalance in the workforce. Positive discrimination measures include:

- statements in recruitment adverts actively encouraging certain individuals to apply;
- the guarantee of an interview to all applicants of a disadvantaged group;
- targeted recruitment, utilising publications addressed to minority groups (e.g. radio for the blind, black publications in ethnic minority areas, etc.);
- providing special training for women or ethnic minority groups.

Managing diversity

As a consequence of the difficulties discussed above, another approach to managing discrimination has gained ground, particularly in the US. The managing diversity approach takes as its start point the fact that all individuals are different, and that the potential of all members of the working population should be harnessed – no one is excluded, not even white, middle-class males. The differences between an equal opportunities approach and a managing diversity approach are summarised in Table 12.2.

Diversity takes individuals, not groups, as the primary focus of concern. The approach criticises targets and quotas because they emphasise difference. Heilman (1994) concluded that affirmative action helped neither organisations nor individuals. Those people who were perceived to have gained some form of advantage through affirmative action

Table 12.2 **Managing diversity and equal opportunities compared**

Managing diversity	Equal opportunities
Aims to be 'inclusive', focusing on the needs of all individuals in employment	Is focused on the needs of the members of particular groups and so excludes other individuals (women, ethnic minorities, the disabled, etc.)
Recognises that each and every individual is unique in his or her needs and experiences	Treats members of a particular group as if they all shared the same characteristics and experiences
Does not utilise positive action campaigns	Uses special iniatives to focus attention on the issues affecting particular groups
More business-focused	Emphasises the moral, ethical and social issues
More acceptable to line managers	Led predominantly by HRM practitioners

were more likely to have negative evaluations made of them by others, the reason for this being that if someone is good enough to begin with, then they would not need extra assistance. Heilman calls this 'the stigma of incompetence'. She states:

> Our research suggests that, as currently construed, affirmative action policies can thwart rather than promote workplace equality. The stigma associated with affirmative action can fuel rather than debunk stereotypical thinking and prejudiced attitudes.

Other problems with targets include the charge of tokenism, paying lip service to equality without any real commitment.

Managing diversity is more about challenging the traditional attitude of 'this is the way we do things around here', and ensuring that the organisation is positioned to take commercial advantage of social and demographic changes. SmithKline Beecham expresses its approach to diversity as: 'Creating an environment where the potential of the skills and expertise of all our employees is realised through individual people differences being recognised and valued' (Ford, 1996). Ford argues that the more individualistic diversity approach and the group-oriented, equal opportunities approach can coexist happily as two strategies to achieve the same end, namely removal of discrimination. A diversity approach alone may lead to complacency of the 'I already do this' type, but the more positive image created may help disperse the hostility that some equal opportunities programmes have engendered. Ford quotes the case of Rank Xerox, which has combined both approaches in its organisation. The managing director, Bernard Fournier, is quoted as saying:

> Equality and diversity are about creating an environment where everyone is treated equally, whatever their race, religion, sex, colour or any other type of difference. I see differences as a source of enrichment. To be successful we have to be creative and apply diverse perspectives to business problems. Everyone should be able to contribute and should progress in the company in relation to his or her ability.
>
> Today our organisation does not reflect the diversity that exists within the community. This is not a matter of bad will, but rather one of old habits. From an ethics point of view it is clearly the right thing to do. But additionally, to prepare for our future, we need all the best talents, whoever they are. (Ford, 1996)

Rank Xerox believes that a diverse workforce will only add value if it is underpinned by equal treatment. This has prompted positive action initiatives, such as recruitment advertising to encourage applications from groups that are under-represented, support for equal opportunities legislation and an emphasis on the value of the individual. Rank Xerox's own description of itself stresses its work 'valuing equality, promoting diversity'.

Reviewing the outcomes of all the measures discussed above, the management of discrimination has been shown in this chapter to be a multi-level and multi-approach aspect of employee relations. At the level of the organisation, legal requirements and procedural guidelines help to establish systems to minimise discrimination and ensure equal treatment. These systems need to be backed up with a proactive management approach, however, to avoid merely paying lip service to the ideal.

When investigating the reasons why organisations with a stated commitment to equal opportunities did not act more vigorously to implement it, Liff (1995) suggests three possible explanations:

- the relationship between line managers and personnel/HRM specialists;
- the conflicts between equal opportunities and other priorities facing managers;
- resistance from employees.

The relationship between line managers and personnel/HRM specialists tends to mean that responsibility for equal opportunities rests with the latter rather than the former. The personnel/HRM department often has primary responsibility for monitoring and implementing equality initiatives, but in many organisations this function is perceived as advisory only, and not necessarily tuned into business necessity. The status of the function may well affect the importance attached to any initiative of this sort. Personnel has been associated with bureaucratic and inflexible employment systems and procedures; line managers may resist more attempts to burden them with paperwork on monitoring, etc. They may also resent the imposition of recruitment and selection systems designed to positively target under-represented groups. As discussed in the section on quotas and affirmative action, these approaches may sometimes reinforce prejudicial thinking and stereotyping rather than helping.

For this reason, the managing diversity approach may be considered much more valid and acceptable in the eyes of traditional managers. This still begs the question about how the existing inequalities will be addressed. Some campaigners see the approach as a watering-down of the ideals and accuse organisations such as the Equal Opportunities Commission of selling out on their commitment to women and promoting the business case more than the moral issues.

The changing role of specialist and line functions, with more responsibilities being devolved to the line, may either challenge or enhance the focus on eliminating discrimination. If line managers adopt the concepts more effectively, the situation will improve; if the downsizing of personnel/HRM functions leads to a reduced ability to monitor and implement equal opportunities, then the situation may worsen.

Liff's second point is that line managers have multiple priorities and conflicts may arise from the clash of the ideal situation with practical necessity. She uses recruitment and selection as an example of a situation where, ideally, all sources will be explored and all candidates examined against predetermined objective criteria. The cost and the time-consuming nature of these processes may seem quite unacceptable to a line manager who is losing production because he or she is short-staffed, however. A policy of always recruiting externally may be irritating to a manager who believes that a suitable internal candidate already exists. This can lead to a sham exercise where all concerned are dissatisfied with the outcome. As a result of such pressures, line managers may show an ambiguous reaction to equal opportunities, welcoming the theory but resenting the practice.

Employees themselves may also be a factor in resisting equal opportunities initiatives. Those already within the organisation may be hostile to measures that appear to favour other groups. There may even be competition between different sub-groups in the organisation, with those from ethnic minority backgrounds approving of external recruitment, and women (who tend to be concentrated at the lower levels in the organisation) preferring a focus on internal development.

Workgroups may also be more comfortable with a membership formed around like individuals because this gives them a common social structure. Older workers may reject youngsters whom they perceive as different from themselves; women may tease or harass men who join their group. The cultures and traditions of some ethnic minority workers may set them apart from their colleagues. All of these social influences play their part in making complete equality difficult to achieve.

In the wider framework, organisational approaches to equal opportunities have to be set in the context of national and international influences. As discussed before, the UK's ideological differences compared with those of other EU countries have led to some difficulties in this area. When comparing the employment rights in the UK with those of the Netherlands or Belgium, very different management practices emerge. The constitutional underpinning of workers' rights and the government machinery put in place to enforce it provide a different mechanism for equal opportunities development in these countries. The imposition of a minimum wage and other pay and benefits rights have a cost impact, and the realities of managing high levels of social provision at the same time as encouraging economic growth are causing concern in these countries.

The increasing concentration of business into conglomerates and multinationals operating across national boundaries has also focused thinking on how to manage diversity at the same time as trying to ensure parity. The degree of central control over such issues varies between multinationals, with some having a more ethnocentric focus which imposes the values of the parent country, while others have a more polycentric focus, adapting policies to local circumstances. The general points about ethics and social responsibility debated at the beginning of the chapter remain important, however, when considering the relationship between profit and practice.

Looking to the future, it seems that the social trend towards greater tolerance that has already been identified should continue. The greater range of cultures experienced by travel and through the media have removed some of the insularity that characterised particular communities. Education, particularly higher education, also exposes more young people to individuals from other cultures. The interrelationships between nation states mean that it is less easy to turn a blind eye to abuses of human rights, including employment rights. Consumer power is sufficiently well developed and substitute products are nearly always available, so organisations are increasingly aware of the practical consequences of bad publicity.

Nevertheless, discrimination remains, and concern is expressed in some quarters about whether the underlying attitudes have simply been pushed beneath the surface by the current measures. Racial intolerance is still a feature of society, and all sociological studies show that group membership and insiders and outsiders are characteristics that have existed for as long as human societies. It is important that all the parties to the employment relationship keep the issues very much to the forefront and constantly reassess the impacts of particular measures.

The chapter concludes with a look at the role of management, trade unions and individuals in the promotion of equal opportunities.

Management

Within the workplace, managers have the primary responsibility to ensure that working systems provide equality of opportunity for all. As outlined before, codes of practice exist to promote good management practices, but these need to be implemented and enforced. What, then, are the operational realities of managing equal opportunities? In this section we look at the processes of managing in the following areas:

- recruitment and selection;
- induction;
- training and development;
- promotion and appraisal;
- pay and terms and conditions of employment;
- harassment and the handling of grievances;
- discipline, dismissal and redundancy.

Exhibit 12.3

Faces that don't fit

Fat, gay or non-BBC English-speaking – few companies would openly admit to being biased against employees who fall into these groups. But evidence from the Institute for Personnel and Development, which represents personnel staff and provides training, suggests that employers do continue to discriminate for reasons that are often irrelevant to the job.

Discussions with 30 recruitment consultants who are in a good position to gauge employers' true preferences, produced some frank admissions.

Individual interviews conducted by the institute – including the three below – were also revealing.

Accent appears to be of enduring significance. A consultant remarks: 'Accent is important. It communicates background, education and birthplace, and frankly, some backgrounds are more desirable and marketable than others. Off the record, I would advise anyone with a redbrick or industrial accent to upgrade.'

Another says: 'Let's face it – people with Scouse accents sound whiny, and people with Brummie accents sound stupid.'

On weight, one consultant said: 'To put it bluntly, fat people are bad for an organisation's image. We wouldn't put an overgrown tree in the foyer, and we wouldn't let an overgrown person deal with our clients.' Said another: 'I don't think somebody would be rejected solely on that basis, but I would say it creates a bad impression. Being overweight is equated, to some degree, with sloth.'

Geoff Armstrong, the institute's director-general, says the law in certain areas 'can play a significant role in tackling discrimination, but it is not sufficient on its own to change attitudes'. Real change depends on organisations 'taking action voluntarily because they are convinced that managing diversity makes good business sense. Those employers who succeed in recruiting and retaining people from diverse backgrounds will flourish because they can access the innovation and skills to the widest possible pool of talent.'

The institute advises employers to:

- focus on essential and objective job-related criteria when making decisions about people;
- introduce mechanisms to deal with harassment, bullying and intimidating behaviour;
- actively check for and remove unfair biases in systems, procedures and their applications.

Dianah Worman, policy adviser on equal opportunities, says too many judgments are still made on the basis of outdated stereotypes. 'That is bad for the individual concerned, bad for their employer and bad for society.'

Many people never get the chance to fulfil their true potential, she concludes. 'Decisions about people's suitability . . . should only ever be based on merit and ability, not petty prejudice.'

Source: Andrew Bolger, *Financial Times*, 18 December 1996.
© 1996 The Financial Times Limited

■ Recruitment and selection

It is essential that any organisation with a commitment to equality of opportunity thoroughly examines its approach to recruitment and selection. Selection criteria must be based on a detailed analysis of the job to be performed. The development of a person specification is crucial to ensure that all candidates are compared against objective criteria rather than each other. There are a number of established systems of compiling person specifications such as Rodger's seven-point plan and Munro Fraser's five-point plan. Marchington and Wilkinson (1996) have pointed out, however, that:

> Both these sets of personnel specifications are somewhat dated, relating not only to a working environment which was much more stable but also to a social and legal framework where it was considered acceptable to ask questions about an individual's domestic circumstances or private life. Although the broad framework may still be valid, it is now unethical, inappropriate and potentially discriminatory to probe too deeply into some of these areas of the person specification. Moreover, it may not make much business sense either to restrict applications to people with specific educational qualifications or a certain length of experience in an industry or occupation.

When choosing sources of recruitment the organisation should check to ensure that all sections of the community will be reached by the methods. Recruitment by word of mouth has been criticised as potentially discriminatory, particularly if the workforce already has an imbalance which is likely to be perpetuated. Positive action could involve targeting particular groups by placing advertisements in journals that are read by minority groups, or using multimedia including radio to access blind applicants.

The design and content of recruitment advertisements is most important. The content should not indicate any intention to discriminate against particular groups. Many organisations choose to include a statement of commitment to equal opportunities in the advertisement. Visual images should create the right impression. Some advertisements contain photographs of white male employees only – this could send a subliminal message that these are the only type of recruit sought.

When collecting information about candidates, an application form provides a consistent set of data on all candidates. Curricula vitae are less reliable because of individual variations in style and content. Questions asked on an application form should be examined to make sure they do not contain discriminatory assumptions. Educational qualifications should not be structured only on the UK's system, but should allow equivalent qualifications to be recorded from other countries. The requirement to provide employment references may discriminate against those returning to the workforce. The application form should allow the candidate to state non-work experience as well as employment history. Questions about marital status, age or domestic circumstances should be avoided as they are irrelevant to the candidate's ability to perform the job tasks.

Monitoring data should be collected from all applicants. Data should be provided on sex, marital status, disability, age and ethnic origin. This data provides information to show which individuals are applying for the jobs, and whether the progress through interview and final selection is affected by discrimination or not. Without the data, organisations may be entirely unaware that they are discriminating against particular groups.

The categories of ethnic origin for monitoring purposes should use at least the four basic groupings: white, Afro-Caribbean, Asian and 'other'. The CRE recommends the use of the nine categories used in the 1991 census: white, black – African, black – Caribbean, black – other (please specify), Indian, Pakistani, Bangladeshi, Chinese, other (please specify). Where relevant, the organisation may also wish to divide the white category in order to monitor, for example, discrimination against Irish or Greek people. Confusion may arise over nationality and ethnic origin. Over 68 per cent of the ethnic minority population are British, so nationality questions should not be included.

Ideally, the monitoring information should be included on a separate sheet or tear-off section of the application form, and should not be used as part of the selection process at all. It should be reviewed regularly to ensure that bias is not occurring.

When shortlisting, the candidates should be assessed against objective criteria, and the results should be formally recorded to show the reasons why candidates were either accepted or rejected. Staff involved at any stage of the selection process should be well briefed and trained to recognise and minimise bias.

At interview, the interviewers should also have received training in how to conduct a structured selection interview. Questions asked should not be intrusive or impertinent. The interviewer should be seeking factual evidence of ability, not impressions of personality, which can be very unreliable. The EOC provides the following guidance:

> No questions should be based upon assumptions regarding women's roles in the home and the family. There was, perhaps, a time when all such responsibilities were met by women, with men being the sole breadwinners and doing nothing domestically. That situation is no longer true and questions should not be based upon any such assumption.
>
> Questions regarding intentions about marriage and having children are, rightly, regarded as impertinent, are resented and should never be asked.
>
> Any questions, which are asked to find out whether the individual can meet the needs of the job in hours, overtime, mobility, etc, should be asked equally of men and women. (However, it is not necessarily true that asking the same question of both sexes ensures non-discrimination. The use to which the answers are put may still be discriminatory.)

Other selection methods, such as tests, should also be carefully chosen to ensure they do not discriminate unfairly. Tests should be obtained from reputable test agencies or consultancy organisations. Advice should be sought on the suitability of the test for the job under consideration, using a thorough job description as the basis. The tests should be validated, preferably separately for men and women, and for ethnic minority groups. The average scores for each group should be compared to see if there are any marked differences. Where differences are statistically valid, an investigation should be conducted to see if this is due to unfair bias.

Final selection should also compare the candidates against objective criteria. The results of the process should be documented for future reference.

Induction

When preparing for the induction of new employees it is essential that all materials are checked to ensure they are free from bias and do not stereotype employees. All new staff should be welcomed into the workplace and helped to socialise with others. Induction training should be structured to allow for individual variations in pace and learning.

■ Training and development

Access to training should be provided for all employees, and restrictions, such as the need to stay away from home extensively, should be minimised to ensure that access to training is available to all. Training and development materials should be free of bias and use a full cross-section of ages, sexes and races in examples and exercises. All training courses should contain a specific commitment to equal opportunities and evaluation of training should include equal opportunities criteria.

■ Promotion and appraisal

Building equal opportunities into promotion requires much the same discipline as for recruitment and selection. Many organisations seem to have a 'glass ceiling' which prevents women and ethnic minority workers from achieving the top positions in the organisation. Access to promotion should not be based on stereotypical assumptions or prejudice that excludes atypical applicants.

Some organisations have set specific targets for the numbers of women or other under-represented groups in senior management. Action plans can then be formulated to help bring this about.

In appraisal schemes, the criteria adopted should be carefully structured to ensure that the categories used are as far as possible quantifiable and objective. Impressionistic systems that allow greater subjectivity are much more prone to bias.

■ Pay and terms and conditions of employment

This is an important area for discrimination so a variety of systems is needed to ensure fairness in pay and related benefits. The pay system should be based on objective job evaluation methods and the criteria used to value jobs should be examined to ensure that they are not based on discriminatory assumptions. Women's earnings are consistently less than those of men so the basis on which value is calculated should be carefully assessed.

Membership of pension schemes and other related employee benefits should also contain the same conditions for both men and women. Part-time staff should enjoy the same pay and benefits (pro rata) as their full-time colleagues. Holiday entitlement and rest periods should also be built into the contracts of all staff.

The contract of employment itself should contain all the legal requirements, and employers should not issue consecutive fixed-term contracts to avoid the qualifying periods for statutory employment rights. The increasing use of flexible contracts should be examined to see if they disproportionately affect particular groups in the workforce, such as women, young or older workers.

■ Harassment and the handling of grievances

It is important that the organisation states its commitment to the elimination of harassment and indicates that it treats all grievances of this sort seriously. Harassment can be defined as conduct that is unwanted by the recipient or affects the dignity of any individual or group at work. Examples of harassment may include:

- physical contact ranging from unnecessary touching to assault or rape;
- comments, jokes, banter, insults and language related to age, creed, disability, nationality, race, religion, sex, sexual orientation or any other personal characteristic which are offensive to an individual or group;
- offensive or unwanted comments about dress or physical appearance;
- intrusive questions about a person's social or sexual life;
- suggestive remarks or gestures, innuendoes or uninvited propositions for sex;
- racially, sexually or religiously based graffiti or graffiti that is offensive to a group or individual;
- display of pornographic pictures, pin-ups, flags or emblems likely to give offence.

Racial or sexual harassment can be dismissed at times as 'a bit of fun', or 'just a joke'. To the victim, however, the effects of harassment are at best unpleasant and at worst can totally destroy the capacity of the individual to perform the job. Rubenstein (1991) argues:

> A decade ago the consequences of sexual harassment for its recipients were not fully appreciated. Now it is understood that harassment is no joke and that it commonly induces stress, damaging the health of victims. At that time, employers were not aware of the costs to the organisation in failing to prevent sexual harassment. Now there is growing appreciation that the price paid in terms of loss of efficiency, poor morale, absence and labour turnover far outweighs the cost of installing an effective policy to deal with sexual harassment. Back in the early 1980s, employers tended to regard sexual harassment as a personal dispute between employees, of peripheral concern to the organisation. Now it is recognised that sexual harassment damages the working environment and that the responsibility for creating and maintaining a healthy working environment rests on the employer. Not long ago also, for most trade unions, sexual harassment was mainly seen in terms of defending their members accused of a disciplinary offence. Now virtually every major trade union has a clear policy condemning sexual harassment and offers active assistance to its members who have been subjected to it.

Since the Porcelli v Strathclyde Regional Council case [1986] IRLR 134 where the judge stated: 'Sexual harassment is a particularly degrading and unacceptable form of treatment which it must be taken to have been the intention of Parliament to restrain', harassment cases can be brought under the race and sex discrimination legislation. Inciting others to racial hatred is also a totally unacceptable form of behaviour which any employer must eliminate in the most strenuous way. An extension of harassment can also be found in any form of bullying where the perpetrator seeks to gain power over his or her victim. Aggressive management styles which abuse the power of the individual should also be found unacceptable.

In order to eliminate harassment or bullying, the organisation should have a clear policy on such matters. This policy should be in writing and expressly state that all employees have a right to be treated with dignity, and that harassment or bullying at work will not be permitted or condoned. The policy should also state that employees have a right to complain about such behaviour should it occur.

In the first instance, employees should be encouraged to resolve the problem informally. In circumstances where it is too difficult or embarrassing for individuals to do this on their own behalf, they should seek support and ask for an initial approach to be made by a sympathetic friend or confidential counsellor. If an employee wishes to complain formally, the organisation's grievance procedure should be used. Violations of the organisation's policy should be considered a disciplinary offence and the rules should make it clear what will be regarded as inappropriate behaviour at work. The penalties that the offender will be liable to should also be clearly stated.

Discipline, dismissal and redundancy

The organisation's rules on discipline must be carried out uniformly regardless of the sex or race of the individual concerned. As discussed above, discrimination offences should be clearly stated as a disciplinary matter and the individuals concerned should be disciplined according to the policy and procedures of the organisation. Forms of discrimination may also be a gross misconduct offence carrying the penalty of summary or instant dismissal. Racially motivated attacks and severe examples of sexual harassment may be examples of such offences.

In selection for redundancy, the organisation should also consider whether the criteria used unfairly discriminate against a particular section of the workforce. Selecting all part-time staff for redundancy may unfairly discriminate against women, who make up a much larger percentage of such workers. Using age criteria may also unfairly disadvantage older workers. The 'last in, first out' criterion may penalise younger workers.

Trade unions

Unions have a dual responsibility in terms of equal opportunities: first to promote equality in workplace negotiations with employers, and second to ensure that within their own organisations they adopt equal opportunities and anti-racist policies which allow for a fair representation of all workers in union structures.

The historical record of trade unions in equal opportunities has not always been a good one. In many early cases it was clear that unions engaged in activities that were either explicitly racist or showed a complete neglect of race or gender issues. Bygott (1992) reports that the TUC in 1930 passed the following resolution:

> That this congress views with alarm the continued employment of alien and undesirable coloured labour on British ships to the detriment of British seamen and calls upon the government to use all their powers to provide remedial action.

Post-war attempts were made by white trade unionists to restrict black workers to a quota of (generally) 5 per cent of the labour force. It was also understood that the principle of 'last in, first out' at a time of redundancy would not apply if this meant white workers would lose their jobs before blacks.

In the area of sex discrimination unions also have a mixed record. Unions have been found to discriminate against women (notably at local levels) and condone employer discrimination. Part of the explanation for this lies in the historical development of trade unions, which were dominated by men, particularly skilled men. Developments in the 1980s attempted to address women's issues and promote women in unions. The move for this has also been fuelled by concerns caused by declining union membership. Unions have actively sought to develop and advocate policies and negotiation strategies that are likely to attract unorganised or weakly organised workers.

Dickens *et al.* (1988) note that:

> The extent to which union negotiators will experience internal membership pressure for the removal of discrimination/promotion of equal opportunities will depend on the composition of the membership; the identity and priorities of those who are most active within the union and those who hold positions of power within its organisation; and the way in which the negotiating agenda, bargaining objectives and priorities are set.

The Colling and Dickens (1989) study into equality bargaining also looked at the degree to which equality bargaining formed part of the management/union agenda. Three areas were identified for investigation:

- the inclusion of benefits of particular interest/benefit to women, facilitating their full participation in the workforce;
- the equality-aware handling of commonplace bargaining agenda items, such as pay and opportunities;
- an equality dimension to negotiation of change, such as reforming a grading structure or introducing an appraisal scheme.

The findings of their research note in general terms that little evidence was found of an extension of the bargaining agenda as indicated in the first point, little if any sensitivity on the part of most negotiators to equality implications in the handling of commonplace agenda items and only very exceptionally any equality dimension to change. They conclude: 'In short, women, directly or indirectly, were rarely on (or indeed at) the bargaining table'.

When investigating the reasons for the lack of importance attached to equality, the study identified problems with the nature of collective bargaining itself in many organisations. Collective bargaining tended to focus on a narrow bargaining agenda which was stable and unquestioned by the parties involved. This made it difficult to introduce 'new' issues onto the agenda. Collective bargaining was also found to focus almost entirely on increases to pay within existing structures, in other words, on rates of pay. Rarely were more fundamental issues raised about the nature of the pay structures themselves, or the gender disparities that could be found within them. The study notes that:

> We found among negotiators generally an unquestioning acceptance of the existing distribution of jobs and rewards. In particular, the job segregation which underpins a lot of the disadvantage of women was perceived generally by negotiators interviewed as 'natural' or objectively justifiable in terms of workers' preferences, differential skills or the nature of the work involved although, in fact, much of the rationale reflected sexual stereotypes and discriminatory assumptions.

One of the difficulties faced by trade unions in the area of equal opportunities is the degree to which unions should promote the issues of particular sections of their membership, rather than the interests of the membership as a whole. Wrench and Virdee (1996) note that unions debated the question of whether they should concern themselves only with issues common to white and minority ethnic members or should operate special policies relating to the specific interests of minorities. Should they provide equal or special treatment?

Until the end of the 1960s the standard trade union position was exemplified by the TUC view that to institute any special policies would be to discriminate against the white membership. Wrench and Virdee (1996) report Vic Feather, TUC general secretary in 1970, as saying: 'The trade union movement is concerned with a man or woman as a worker. The colour of a man's skin has no relevance whatever to his work'.

Around 1974, changes were detectable at the official trade union level with a recognition that there was a need to move away from a *laissez-faire* attitude towards a more positive role. By 1981, the TUC had produced *Black Workers: A TUC Charter for Equality of Opportunity* and unions were urged to examine their own structures and practices in order to find ways to remove the barriers that prevented black members from reaching union office and decision-making bodies. Seven years later the TUC reissued the charter, and also worked with the Commission for Racial Equality in the production of a code of practice. In recent years the TUC has also lobbied the European Trade Union Confederation to take on board issues of migrants' rights and racial equality.

On sex discrimination, trade unions are also responding and helping to shape attitudes. John Edmonds initiated the 'Winning a Fair Deal' policy at the GMB union in 1986, which confronts issues of discrimination against women in areas covered by GMB collective agreements. A survey by Mason (1994) of 21 unions found that 10 had a national-level committee dealing with race equality issues and nearly two-thirds had taken positive steps such as targeting workplaces, organising conferences for black members and producing recruitment literature in languages other than English. Many unions have also appointed national officers to take responsibility for issues affecting ethnic groups or for women's issues.

Mirza (1995) also reports that the TUC has pledged itself to consulting unions on how improvements can be made, and is urging unions to nominate more black trade unionists to TUC bodies, the Women's Conference and Congress. The TUC has also produced a checklist which suggests strategies that unions are encouraged to pursue at branch, regional and national level.

The difficulties that the union movement has faced in recent years in terms of loss of membership and diminished resources does put in some doubt their ability to pursue equality measures further. Mirza (1995) comments:

> The initial steps that some unions have taken in recent years should be put into perspective against the inaction by a great many more. Any progress that has been made will also quickly recede if unions fail to commit themselves to maintaining, and significantly increasing, the momentum that has been initiated in this area.

Individuals

The employment context of the 1990s puts a high emphasis on the individual in employment as well as organisational groupings. Trade unions and management can promote best practice, but ultimately it is the interpersonal relationships between individuals that determine whether discrimination takes place. Individuals need to be reminded of their own unconscious prejudices and encouraged to 'put themselves in another's shoes'. McEnrue (1993) describes the qualities needed for effective cross-cultural communications as:

- the capacity to accept the relativity of one's own knowledge and perceptions;
- the capacity to be non-judgmental;
- a tolerance of ambiguity;
- the capacity to appreciate and communicate respect for other people's ways, backgrounds, values and beliefs;
- the capacity to demonstrate empathy;
- the capacity to be flexible;
- a willingness to acquire new patterns of behaviour and belief;
- the humility to acknowledge what one does not know.

Kandola and Fullerton (1994) suggest that, on a more individual level, there are things that can be done, including:

- examining your own behaviour styles, attitudes and beliefs;
- considering your own feelings and reactions to people;
- being curious and getting to know others;
- trying to see things from other people's perspectives;
- being honest with others;
- examining your own communication style;
- looking at how flexibly you treat others;
- when leading teams, taking care that all people feel part of the team;
- developing others;
- challenging accepted practices;
- acting as a role model.

Organisations that provide training to help their employees recognise the impact they have on others, and whose culture encourages the qualities listed above, may find that discriminatory tendencies are greatly reduced as a consequence. As Kandola and Fullerton (1994) note in the conclusion to their survey on managing diversity:

> Upon examination it was discovered that the skills necessary to manage diversity are essentially a restatement of an old theme, namely good interpersonal or communication skills. It is these skills that need to be emphasised in training managers in the diversity-oriented organisation. Good managers of diversity are essentially just that – good managers, and good managers are those who deal with employees as individuals rather than expect everyone to be equally motivated and to work in the same way.

Conclusions

The focus of this chapter has been the exploration of the manifestations and causes of discrimination in the employment relationship. Through the various perspectives explored, it is evident that the attitudes that cause discrimination and the practices that accompany it are deep-rooted. The instinct to judge others by the degree to which they are 'like us' provides a powerful impetus to group closure and ethnocentrism. The role a wider society plays in shaping norms of behaviour has also been seen to exert an enormous influence on workplace attitudes. Historically, the jobs available to immigrant groups, particularly post-war, has profoundly affected the employment opportunities and the position of these individuals in the occupational structure of the UK. Traditionally, work patterns, status and pay have been based on a norm of full-time employment. This has had the effect of dividing the labour market along gender lines, to the disadvantage of female employees.

Increasingly, however, since the 1970s, public perceptions of inequality and disadvantage and the government's role in legislation have focused attention on these issues. The riots of the 1970s and early 1980s revealed a degree of anger and desperation in young unemployed and disadvantaged individuals from the inner cities. At the same time, more women, particularly married women, were joining the labour force, and the UK was worried about potential labour shortages caused by the 'demographic time bomb'. Recession moderated the most alarmist predictions and employment shortages were in no way as severe as predicted, but employers and the government began to take a far more active role in examining all sources of labour supply in the market.

Changes to education in the form of a common national curriculum for all, and the setting of performance targets and indicators, have revealed shortcomings in the education provision for some groups. This has been addressed in some cases by the sending in of 'hit squads' to overhaul systems and procedures. The media have also been urged to portray a wider variety of families and work roles to prevent stereotyping and provide effective role models. Positive action programmes have also been run to attract more women into engineering or more men into nursing, for example.

Some change is evident in the types and variety of jobs taken up by women and the increased numbers of women returning immediately to full-time work after childbirth. Likewise, the second and third generations of post-war immigrants may find less resistance to their presence and better job opportunities as the UK adjusts to a multiracial society. A number of high-profile retail recruitment campaigns, such as that at B&Q, have focused attention on the positive attributes of older workers, and younger workers are increasingly encouraged to continue in education or training, thereby enhancing their 'human capital'.

Nevertheless, despite these positive indicators, there is little to be complacent about. Disabled individuals still experience major difficulties in finding meaningful occupation. Too many members of minority ethnic groups still feel marginalised and only comfortable with self-employed status.

Instilling a respect for difference as well as similarity will take more time to filter through to all members of society. The managing diversity movement has attempted to address some of the problems caused by a backlash against positive discrimination programmes. Although in many areas there is still a need to take some form of targeted action to address imbalances, if these measures can be seen to be inclusive, available to all depending on need, rather than exclusive, available to minorities only, they are more likely to be accepted.

Managers and trade unionists have a crucial role in taking anti-discrimination measures forward. It is too easy to have written policies to which lip service is paid rather than wholeheartedly embracing the intentions behind these policies. Involving as diverse a range of individuals as possible in equal opportunities initiatives will also help to ensure that real progress is made.

Chapter summary

This chapter has looked at a particular aspect of the employment relationship – the management of discrimination – and its impact on employee relations practice.

Discrimination is defined as 'making a distinction', but the distinction should be based on fair, not unfair, characteristics. Unfair discrimination may be individual, structural or organisational and be based on many characteristics, including sex, race, disability and age. The consequences of unfair discrimination include poor utilisation of employees and the creation of a resentful and unmotivated workforce.

There are a number of perspectives that can be examined to understand the causes of discrimination. The psychological/sociological perspective examines discrimination as a product of how individuals learn behaviours appropriate to the society in which they live. Socialisation through the influence of the family, peer group, educational experiences and the role models provided by the media help reinforce impressions that can lead to discrimination. Stereotyping is a common way of making judgements about those around you, but it holds dangers if ethnocentrism leads the individual to dismiss those who are not 'like me'. This is thought to be particularly problematical if the individual also has a personality tendency to authoritarianism, which may lead to displacement or scapegoating.

The influence of social norms can also be examined by taking a historical perspective and tracing attitudes to discrimination as they change over time. Gender patterns have altered in this way, with an increasing acceptance of women's role in employment, particularly since the Second World War. The influence of feminism in redefining the status and role of women and the moderating effects of increased technology on jobs which previously had a high need for manual strength have also challenged gender stereotypes. The role expectations of men in society and at work have also been re-evaluated as part of an ongoing debate on masculinity. Historical changes in attitudes to race and ethnicity also show greater attention being paid to these issues. The position of immigrants in the UK, particularly post-war, indicates that occupational stereotyping has occurred, forcing immigrants into low paid, manual labour. The pressures caused by inner-city unemployment led to a series of riots in the UK in the late 1970s and again contributed to a re-evaluation of the position of these groups. The Civil Rights movement in the US, the abandonment of apartheid in South Africa and campaigns by other activists have also contributed to attitude change today.

Age discrimination affects both older and younger workers. The average age of entry into the labour market has been increasing over time. This is linked to the increase in opportunities for further education and to changes to the demographic make-up of the labour force, with fewer young people. Youth unemployment remains a major issue and successive government policies have attempted to address it. At the other end of the age range, early retirement and redundancy have reduced the overall age of the working population in recent years. Those wishing to remain economically active are seen to face many difficulties, with employers regularly using criteria in selection that restrict entrants to the 25–35 age category.

Attitudes to disability, particularly the removal of the 'medical model' of disability, have enhanced the profile of this section of the workforce. The continuance of discrimination and limited employment prospects for those with physical or mental disabilities is still a reality, however. Organisations are also having to broaden their definition of disability to include employees who suffer difficulties from a range of medical or psychological conditions, including stress, while in employment.

Patterns of discrimination can also be examined from an economic and structural perspective. Human capital theory, together with the segmented labour market theory and reserve army of labour theory, provides alternative explanations for the position of particular groups in the occupational structure. When reviewing human capital theory, levels of investment in education and training do show some correlation with the lower employment status of various groups. However, changes are detectable which may moderate these influences over time. The practical difficulties of classifying labour into primary and secondary sectors mean that segmented labour market theory is difficult to evaluate, although an examination of part-time and full-time employment status does indicate that disadvantage is experienced by the former. The reality of the reserve army of labour theory can be examined by looking at the unemployment statistics to see if disadvantaged groups are disproportionately represented. The position of women appears to demonstrate less evidence of reserve army status than that of ethnic minorities, older workers or the disabled.

The final perspective examined was the political/ethical one, which looks at equality of opportunity as a basic human right. The role of employers in providing a working environment which meets the needs of their employees is seen as socially desirable and also 'good for business' in terms of return on investment.

Various measures have been taken to address equality issues in recent years and their success was evaluated. Educational programmes and national initiatives are measures taken to address discrimination. The use of awareness training in revealing prejudice and helping to recognise the points of view of others has been found to be a powerful tool in changing behaviour.

More radical approaches such as affirmative action and quota-setting programmes have also been adopted to force change into the system. The experience of the US, where federal contract compliance clauses have been used to ensure ethnic mix, is ambivalent. On the one hand, the statistics do indicate that more minority applicants are getting jobs. However, the resulting backlash from those excluded has also been a major problem. The UK has not embraced similar practices, feeling that they provide a burden on business and that special treatment cannot be justified. Other forms of positive action such as statements in recruitment adverts encouraging applications from particular groups and targeted recruitment, which utilises publications addressed to minority groups, have been used, however.

The final model of managing equality examined was the more recent 'managing diversity' approach. These programmes aim to be inclusive, not exclusive, and provide measures that could benefit all sections of the workforce. The argument is that employers need a diverse workforce, not a workforce of clones, in order to maintain competitive advantage. Learning how to maximise the potential of all employees was proposed as a significant challenge for all organisations.

When evaluating the impact of all the approaches detailed above, the rate of progress and extent of change is still limited. Factors restricting progress include the difficulties experienced between line managers and HRM specialists. Equality issues are often left to specialists rather than embraced by everybody in the workforce. The conflict between business priorities and equal opportunities priorities is also part of the difficulty, with the recession of the early 1990s forcing managers to adopt a primarily finance-driven model of employment. Finally, the resistance provided by ordinary individuals to such policies can also contribute to the problem.

The chapter ended with an evaluation of the role of managers, trade unions and individuals in the continuing development of fair practices. The role of management in leading the way and ensuring that organisations adopt clear practices and procedures is vital. Policies and procedures need to be effected in the areas of recruitment and selection; induction; training and development; promotion and appraisal; pay and terms and conditions of employment; harassment and the handling of grievances; and discipline, dismissal and redundancy.

The role of trade unions in providing examples of best practice and pressing for equality issues to be included in collective bargaining is also vital. Historically, trade unions were dominated by white, male, full-time employees. The legacy of this traditional membership still causes difficulties when dealing with a more diverse workforce. Union attempts to respond and initiate equal opportunities measures both internally and in the wider sphere of employment need to be developed and continually moved forward.

Each and every employee also has a role to play in minimising prejudice. The qualities needed in order to be responsive to the needs of others are those of an effective communicator; these should be developed and form part of the overall culture of all organisations.

Questions

1 Outline the likely effects on discrimination in the UK if a quota system, like that operated in the US, were set up for all public sector contracts.

2 'The objectives of ethical business management and profit maximisation are incompatible.' Discuss this statement in the context of equal opportunities.

3 Outline the main areas an organisation should examine to ensure that equal opportunities issues have been built into all systems and procedures.

4 'Managing diversity is just another renaming exercise to enhance the image of existing equal opportunities programmes.' Do you agree with this assessment of the managing diversity approach?

5 Recent research suggests that men too face significant amounts of sexual harassment but rarely, if ever, report it. Why do you think this happens and what should be done to address the problem when it occurs?

Activities

1   Investigate the equal opportunities measures taken in your organisation or university/ college. What is the stated position on equal opportunities? Do you feel it is effective in practice? How do the systems compare with the codes of practice available from the Equal Opportunities Commission or Commission for Racial Equality?

2   In the role of an equal opportunities consultant, outline the content and delivery methods to be used on a discrimination awareness training programme for first-line managers.

3   Contact a range of trade unions and ask them for any materials they have available on equal opportunities or discrimination. Review the content and approach taken and compare these with the approach taken by line managers.

4   Interview members of ethnic minority groups and/or women in traditionally male occupations or men in traditionally female occupations. Investigate the difficulties they have faced and how they have overcome them.

5   Review recruitment advertisements from a wide variety of sources to see if they have a commitment to equal opportunities or whether they discriminate or stereotype the applicant either directly or indirectly.

6   Look out for discrimination cases reported at employment tribunals and try to evaluate the issues that led to them being brought.

7   Read the article on family-friendly policies in Exhibit 12.4.

   (a) To what extent do you believe that employers should adopt family-friendly policies as part of their responsibility to the wider society in which they exist?

   (b) How effective do you think the cost–benefit argument is in encouraging employers to make family-friendly provisions?

   (c) What should a family-friendly policy include?

8   Prepare a summary of the position of women in employment in the twenty-first century based on the content of this chapter and the details provided in Exhibit 12.5.

Exhibit 12.4

Battle over family-friendly working

How should employers react to a request by someone coming back from maternity leave to work part-time? What if the request for flexible working comes from a male parent? Or an employee without children?

As a government-appointed taskforce, due to report in November, ponders ways of encouraging 'family-friendly' employment policies, lawyers are warning that this is an issue that already causes frequent problems for business. 'It comes up an enormous amount', says Fraser Younson, head of employment law of McDermott Will & Emery, the law firm. Catherine Prest,

employment partner at Hammond Suddards Edge, another firm, says she deals 'daily' with disputes and queries involving maternity leave and flexible working.

The pressure on employers is likely to increase. A number of changes are in train that will extend parental leave, giving new mothers the right to take up to a year's maternity leave and new fathers the right to two weeks' paid paternity leave from April 2003 (www.dti.gov.uk/er/review.htm).

More fundamental reforms may follow. The taskforce has been asked to look at ways of making it

Exhibit 12.4 *continued*

easier for parents to request flexible working – and to place more responsibility on employers to consider such requests. This may not seem important. Ministers have ruled out changes to the law to compel businesses to allow parents the right to work part-time on demand. Their preferred solution of a 'right' to ask – with no guarantee of what the answer will be – is hardly revolutionary.

But businesses – particularly smaller ones – are concerned about the growing emphasis on employees' rights to flexible working that is reflected by the creation of the taskforce. The British Chambers of Commerce last month claimed that the government was at 'risk of failing in its pledge to mitigate the impact' on small firms of measures in this area.

While employers do not have to accede to all requests for flexible working, they can – and all too often do – break the law by giving unreasonable refusals. 'A blanket refusal to allow anybody to work part-time would be perceived as unlawful', says Ms Prest. 'Even the most Neanderthal employers have moved on that.'

Employers will breach the sex discrimination law – and lay themselves open to potentially unlimited employment tribunal awards – if they set a requirement for a job that women are less likely to be able to comply with than men. Given that women are often the primary carers for small children, a requirement to work full-time can fall into this category.

Employers can defend such claims if they can show that the requirement is justified. But lawyers warn that too few companies undertake the work needed to underpin such a defence.

'There are an awful lot of cases where the employer will say "this is a full-time job and that's it"', says Mr Younson. 'Where the case comes unstuck is that they have never done any analysis or given it a trial.' He warns that 'a reply such as "it's a manager's job and has always been full-time" is never going to work' at a tribunal.

On top of the risk of falling foul of discrimination claims, employees have a right to automatic compensation if they successfully claim unfair dismissal for any reason related to pregnancy or maternity leave.

Elaine Aarons, head of the City employment group at Eversheds, the law firm, says that employers with professional personnel management operations are 'always extremely concerned when dealing with employees coming back from maternity leave – and quite rightly so'.

This concern is likely to be exacerbated when the right to maternity leave is extended to a year. The pace of change in many business sectors, and in technological systems, increases the chances that someone's job description may be inadvertently changed while she/he is away. Ms Prest says that it is 'staggering how often, when someone is on maternity leave, the whole department is reorganised'.

Such reorganisations can trigger legal claims if they are not handled properly. They can also lead to the loss of valuable staff. The drive for greater rights for employees to work flexibly is being complemented by a growing recognition by many companies – particularly bigger ones – that such policies can make commercial sense.

A report last month* highlighted this effect in the City, warning that firms were losing valuable employees because of the macho culture of punishing hours. 'Skills losses to the City, particularly among highly trained senior women, run high and it seems that, in general, little is being done to address the problem', it said.

Many big employers now have flexible working policies that not only reduce the risk of tribunal claims but also often go a long way beyond the minimum legal requirements. But the report warns that the effects of such policies can be undermined by a working culture in which staff feel that their career will be damaged if they do not work full-time.

Andrew McEachern, employee relations manager at Goldman Sachs, the investment bank, a sponsor of the report, says the issue is one that 'many companies are wrestling with – and need to wrestle with'.

Mr McEachern stresses the bottom-line reasons for such concerns: 'Big companies are finding it increasingly difficult to find the talent they need – they need to make sure the people they have stay with them.'

Employment lawyers point out that companies' refusal to contemplate arrangements such as job-sharing and part-time working for relatively senior jobs is often based purely on historical precedent.

'A lot of the reaction is knee-jerk', says Ms Prest. She advocates measures to encourage employers to experiment with flexible working on a trial basis.

'A lot of (the resistence to flexible working) is fear of the unknown', she says. 'My experience is that, as often as not, employers find it's not as bad as they thought.'

Quality of Life in the City, www.parentsatwork.org.uk

Source: Jean Eaglesham, *Financial Times*, 9 July 2001.
© 2001 The Financial Times Limited

Exhibit 12.5

The glass ceiling proves resilient

Not many employers in the western industrialised world would openly discriminate against women in their recruitment and retention strategies. Workplace gender inequalities are the focus of official disapproval. Governments and employer associations as much as trade unions and civil society movements condemn those who seek to treat women in an inferior way to men. But none of this means that gender discrimination is no longer practised. There is depressing evidence to suggest that private sector companies continue to regard women as inherently unequal to men. This week's publication of a wide-ranging, empirically based study by the Geneva-based International Labour Organisation indicates that gender discrimination at work is worsening in many industrialised countries. While women are catching up and overtaking men in their educational attainments and also constituting a growing proportion of the workforce, the gender gap is widening in promotion to chief executive and boardroom posts.

The figures, brought together by the report's author Linda Wirth, are startling. Only 2 per cent of those senior posts in companies are held by women in France and less than 3 per cent in Germany. The proportion is a mere 3.6 per cent in the UK and as low as 1.3 per cent in Australia. Nor are women making any breakthrough in recruitment to the highest echelons of financial services companies although the proportion is increasing in jobs below executive level.

Even in Scandinavia, famed for its progressive attitude and generous, family-friendly policies, women continue to be held back in the private sector.

This gender gap is less apparent in developing countries. The ILO report has found that as many as 40 per cent of employees in administrative and managerial positions in Colombia are women – the same proportion as in Bermuda. In Honduras the proportion is an impressive 47 per cent and in the Philippines 37 per cent.

The problem seems rooted in private sector employers' attitudes. In public services and government employment such gender differences appear less acute. There are more apparent opportunities for promotion of women in the public sector, perhaps

reflecting the determination of states to practise what they preach.

The report examines the range of jobs where women are in demand. It finds few women in senior positions in the so-called line positions that involve revenue-generating responsibilities, usually seen as jobs that lead to executive posts.

In 1999, for example, men still held 93.8 per cent of such line jobs. The pattern was similar in other industrialised countries. Women were more in evidence in personnel management, insurance and pensions management and marketing management. There are still few women employed as managers in research and development and in manufacturing and production.

But while women are often better qualified than men, their average pay is invariably less. In the US, a gap of 16 per cent exists between the earnings of the average male and female manager. The divide is 15 per cent in the UK, 12 per cent in Australia and a massive 35 per cent in Finland.

What is to be done? Linda Wirth thinks the answer lies in the improved educational qualifications of women, leading to an impressive advance into professional and technical jobs.

This will in time erode prejudices that harden custom and practice in companies. She argues that 'gender-sensitive human resource strategies developed by enterprises in recent decades provide the best way through the glass ceiling'. 'Networking, career tracking, mentoring and succession planning that pay particular attention to women can help move them up the ladder', she writes.

Ms Wirth also believes that as women gain more economic power by self-employed business activities and begin to employ others, there will be a 'sweeping aside of gender inequalities in all walks of life in the 21st century'. Perhaps, but it looks like being a protracted struggle. The obstacles to gender inequality will not easily be removed by moral exhortation.

Government policies can help. The enforcement of work–family and work–life programmes and measures to tackle sexual harassment and unequal access to training are important to establishing a framework as

Exhibit 12.5 *continued*

well as a public policy climate where gender discrimination in the workplace becomes unacceptable.

But most hope lies in a recognition by prejudiced employers that affording women the same opportunities as men to advance in their companies by sheer ability and expertise is good for the bottom line. The formation of the 'good' workplace is not a social extra that may cripple competitiveness and inflate costs but a necessary ingredient for business success.

This may not seem so self-evident to men, who often feel threatened and uncomfortable in the face of career women. But it is true. Spreading that message across private sectors everywhere may require a long haul. What Ms Wirth argues wisely is that women at an early stage in their working lives need support – from within and outside the company – to ensure that they gain the experience in a wide range of corporate operations that enables them to win promotion.

Whether this will clear the way past the biggest barrier of all is, however, problematic. Women may wish to bear and rear children and this will require time away from their job. That can upset career progression and many companies do not make it easy for mothers to return to work.

The difficulty may be met by a more enlightened attitude to the provision of childcare, either in the company itself or more widely in society.

But here class differences become apparent. Only in northern Europe does the state provide acceptable and comprehensive provision of childcare that covers more than well-off women. Nannies are for the middle classes. Unless governments and companies together offer women of all incomes civilised childcare, their commitment to gender equality will remain bogus.

In the UK and the US professional women tend to dominate the gender discrimination debate. Ms Wirth reinforces this approach. But we need a strategy everywhere to fight sex inequality for women in low-paid and unskilled jobs as well as for high-flyers.

The word 'class' has been dropped from the modern employment idiom. It should return. The biggest obstacles to piercing the glass ceiling are persistent and intractable class inequalities at the core of modern industrialised societies. When all women are treated equally and not only those with professional qualifications we may see some progress. At present such discrimination is only part of a much wider and more complex problem of class inequality. No amount of modernising rhetoric can spirit away that problem.

Source: Richard Donkin, *Financial Times*, 12 July 2001.
© 2001 The Financial Times Limited

Note

The source of the statistics utilised in the text is *Labour Market and Skill Trends 2000*, DfEE, London. Crown copyright.

Useful websites

www.cre.gov.uk **Commission for Racial Equality** A statutory body required to monitor the operation of race relations legislation, provide advice to complainants and to report to Parliament.

www.disability.gov.uk A site aimed at helping disabled people find out about their civic rights.

www.drc.gb.org.uk **Disability Rights Commission** A statutory body required to monitor the operation of disability discrimination legislation, to provide advice to complainants and to report to Parliament.

www.eoc.org.uk **Equal Opportunities Commission** A statutory body required to monitor the operation of sex discrimination legislation, to provide advice to complainants and to report to Parliament.

www.incomesdata.co.uk Up to date intelligence on employment issues, including the economy, labour market and average earnings from Incomes Data Services.

References

Atkinson, J. (1984) 'Manpower strategies for flexible organizations', *Personnel Management*, August.

Barron, R.D. and Norris, G.M. (1976) 'Sexual divisions and the dual labour market' in Barker, D.L. and Allen, S. (eds) *Dependence and Exploitation in Work and Marriage*. London: Longman.

Bygott, D.W. (1992) *Black in Britain*. Oxford: Oxford University Press.

Chope, C. (1987) in *Contract Compliance: The UK Experience*. London: IPM/IDS.

Colling, T. and Dickens, L. (1989) *Equality Bargaining – Why Not?* London: Equal Opportunities Commission.

DfEE (2000) *Labour Market and Skill Trends 2000*. London: Department for Education and Employment.

Dickens, L., Townley, B. and Winchester, D. (1988) *Tackling Sex Discrimination through Collective Bargaining*. London: Equal Opportunities Commission.

EOC (1986) *Fair and Efficient Selection*. London: Equal Opportunities Commission.

EOC (1996) *Changing Inequalities Between Women and Men: Twenty years of progress (1976–96)*. London: Equal Opportunities Commission.

Faludi, S. (1992) *Backlash: The Undeclared War Against Women*. London: Chatto.

Ford, V. (1996) 'Partnership is the secret of progress', *People Management*, 8 February.

Giddens, A. (1993) *Sociology*, 2nd edn. London: Polity Press.

Heilman, M.E. (1994) 'Affirmative action: some unintended consequences for working women', *Research in Organisational Behaviour*: 16.

Hillgard, E., Atkinson, R.L. and Atkinson, R. (1979) *Introduction to Psychology*, 7th cdn. London: Harcourt Brace Jovanovich.

HMSO (1998) *Labour Force Survey*.

IPD/Cornell University (1999) *Implementation of the Employment Provisions of the Disability Discrimination Act*. London: CIPD.

IPM/IDS (1987) *Contract Compliance: The UK Experience*. London: IPM/IDS.

Jewson, N. and Mason, D. (1986) 'The theory and practice of equal opportunities policies: liberal and radical approaches', *Sociological Review*, 34(2): 307–34.

Kandola, R. and Fullerton, J. (1994) 'Diversity: more than just an empty slogan', *Personnel Management*, November.

Leach, B. (1996) 'Disabled people and the equal opportunities movement' in Hales, G. (ed.) *Beyond Disability*. London: Sage.

Liff, S. (1995) 'Equal opportunities: continuing discrimination in a context of formal equality' in Edwards, P.K. (ed.) *Industrial Relations Theory and Practice in Britain*. Oxford: Blackwell.

Marchington, M. and Wilkinson, A. (1996) *Core Personnel and Development*. London: IPD.

Mason, D. (1994) 'Employment and the labour market', *New Community*, 20(2).

McEnrue, M.P. (1993) 'Managing diversity: Los Angeles before and after the riots', *Organisational Dynamics*, 21(3): 18–29.

Mirza, Q. (1995) *Race Relations in the Workplace*. Institute of Employment Rights pamphlet.

Paddison, L. (1990) 'The targeted approach to recruitment', *Personnel Management*, November.

Parkyn, A. (1991) 'Operating equal opportunities in the health service', *Personnel Management*, August.

Piore, M.J. (1975) 'Notes for a theory of labour market stratification', in Edwards, R., Reich, M. and Gordon, D. (eds) *Labour Market Segmentation*. Lexington, MA: D.C. Heath.

Rubenstein, M. (1991) 'Devising a sexual harassment policy', *Personnel Management*, February.

Vallance, E. (1995) *Business Ethics at Work*. Cambridge: Cambridge University Press.

Wrench, J. and Virdie, S. (1996) 'Organising the unorganised, "Race", poor work and trade unions' in Ackers, P., Smith, C. and Smith, P. (eds) *The New Workplace and Trade Unionism*, London: Routledge.

Chapter 13

Flexibility

Stephanie Tailby

Learning objectives

By the end of this chapter, readers should be able to:

- understand the reasons why labour flexibility became a central theme in public policy, academic and HRM practitioner debates in the 1980s and has remained so subsequently;

- understand the different dimensions of the flexibility debates of the 1980 and, in particular, those generated by theories of a transformation of work; government policies of labour market deregulation; and the policy-oriented model of the flexible firm;

- explain the meaning of the concepts of functional flexibility, numerical flexibility and working-time flexibility;

- evaluate employees' flexibility gains and losses under different forms of teamworking;

- explain the factors that have contributed to the growth of part-time work in the UK, and the forms of flexibility sought or attained by employers through the use of part-time contracts;

- explain the controversies that have surrounded the introduction of the EU Fixed-Term Work Directive and the proposed directive that aims to regulate employers' use of temporary agency staff.

Introduction

Flexibility became a fashionable concept in government, business, media and academic circles from the end of the 1970s. It was applied in prescriptions for change in the organisation and management of work, the construction of working time patterns, and the regulation of pay and employment. Its currency drew sharp criticism. Pollert (1991: xix), for example, decried the 'flexibility fetish' and appealed for the application of 'sharper, more appropriate analytic instruments' in the examination of work and employment restructuring. Other commentators agreed that the concept's coherence attained at an ideological, rather than an analytical, level. Yet many were cautious in predicting any imminent collapse in its appeal (Hyman, 1991) – wisely, as it transpired.

Flexibility is an ambiguous concept. It denotes a quality that, like beauty, is largely in the eye of the beholder. It implies the absence of rigidity, even liberation, from oppressive constraints. Its application to the world of work and employment, however, raises the critical issue of whose interests are at stake? Structures and practices that employers characterise as rigid and inflexible may be a source of security and stability for employees. Exhibit 13.1 illustrates the point. It summarises a dispute that continued in 2001 between Post Office managers and employees at sorting centres around the UK. Immediately at issue were new shift start times and working patterns, although in the background were government initiatives to allow private sector organisations to operate in markets that hitherto had been the preserve of the public corporation. 'Flexible' work practices in this instance threatened for employees a disruption of work and domestic life and an erosion of employment security.

Flexibility remains a prominent and a contentious concept in the practice and analysis of employee relations, for reasons elaborated in this chapter. The discussion is organised in four sections. The first sketches the context in which flexibility became a central theme in government policy, and in management and academic discourse in the 1980s. It distinguishes three discrete but related dimensions of the flexibility debates of the period: theoretical accounts of a 'transformation of work'; government policies of labour market deregulation; and the policy-oriented 'flexible firm' model. The latter

---

Exhibit 13.1

Postal worker strikes spread

Unofficial walkouts by thousands of postal workers spread across the country yesterday in the latest in a series of disputes about the imposition of 'flexible' working practices by Post Office managers, as the publicly owned business faces the threat of private competition.

The Communication Workers' Union, whose leaders met executives from Consignia – the newly named Post Office – to negotiate a return to work, estimated last night that up to 50,000 workers had joined the rolling unofficial stoppages, triggered by industrial action in Watford.

Mail centre and delivery office workers walked out in London, Liverpool, Cardiff, North Wales, Manchester, Preston, Teeside, Maidstone, Stockport and Chester, a spokeswoman for Consignia confirmed yesterday, in a dispute which could delay the delivery of election polling cards.

... The postal stoppages spread after managers tried to divert mail to Liverpool and other sorting centres from strike-bound Watford, where CWU members have been staging official walkouts in protest against new shift patterns, designed to deal with the rapid growth of junk mail.

The union agreed to flexible working in return for higher basic pay last year, but striking London postal workers said yesterday they were not prepared to accept the imposition of a move from 5.25 am to 4 am shift starts, and working patterns which entrenched part-time working.

Postal workers' discontent – which has already lost the Post Office 62,000 days through industrial action in the past year – has been further inflamed by threats from the government-appointed postal regulator, Martin Stanley, to introduce 'serious' private postal competition by the autumn.

Source: Seamus Milne, *The Guardian*, 24 May 2001. © 2002 Guardian Newspapers Limited

delineated an employer's core–periphery employment strategy to attain functional, numerical and financial flexibility – or the ability to adjust swiftly the skills deployed, numbers employed, and wage costs.

The debates on the transformation of work have focused attention on the forms of functional flexibility that employers have sought from 'core' employee groups and the extent to which employees have gained, in terms of skills, job satisfaction or autonomy at work. The issues are explored in the second section of the chapter, which looks at teamwork, and lean production systems.

The third and fourth sections of the chapter are concerned with 'non-standard' employment. The label denotes contractual forms of employment that deviate from the twentieth-century 'norm' (for men) of full-time and open-ended employment. The 'flexible firm' model identified the use of these contractual forms as the means through which employers could attain greater 'numerical flexibility': the ability to adjust the numbers of staff employed to meet fluctuations in the demand for the firm's goods or services. European Union policy and that of the government in the UK have developed, meanwhile, to identify non-standard forms of employment as responsive to employees' interests in attaining a better 'work–life balance' and as the means of widening the labour market participation of formerly 'disadvantaged' groups. In relation to these debates, section three of the chapter examines the growth of part-time employment and the forms of flexibility sought or achieved by employers through the use of part-time contracts. Section four focuses on temporary and agency employment. The chapter summary draws the different themes of the analysis together by addressing the flexibility gains and losses – for firms and for workers – of the past two decades.

The flexibility debates

Employers' interest in labour flexibility is certainly not new or specific to the past two decades. Yet the upsurge of interest in flexibility from the late 1970s does require some contextualisation. Hyman (1991: 261–4) has identified seven relevant elements of change in the 'context, character and conceptualization of work'.

First, the 1970s and 1980s witnessed the 'first sustained and generalized crisis of the Western economies since 1945'. The long post-war boom, a 25-year period of sustained economic growth and relatively high levels of employment, had lost much of its momentum by the 1970s. Instability was exacerbated by 'shocks' such as the oil crises and the deregulation of financial markets. A brief period of economic growth intervened between the recessions of the early 1980s and early 1990s, and large-scale unemployment persisted in many European countries.

Secondly, the 'globalisation' of production and finance was thrust forward by interfirm competition and money market deregulation, and by the creation of regional economic blocs (such as the European single market) which stimulated ownership restructuring and the growth of multinational enterprise. Thirdly, corporations refined their internal control mechanisms. A trend was the devolution of operational policy-making although 'within tightly defined financial controls' (Hyman, 1991: 262). Local managers were empowered, or obliged, to experiment in the area of employee relations, in order to meet tight, centrally defined budget and financial targets.

Fourthly, the contraction of manufacturing employment and expansion of service sector employment, although long-term trends in many countries, accelerated in some. This was notably the case in the UK where the government's monetarist policies accentuated the scale of manufacturing redundancies in the early 1980s. Related to these sectoral shifts were changes in the occupational and gender composition of the workforce that, without innovation in trade unions' strategies, threatened a growth in the 'disorganised' workforce.

A fifth important factor was the political swing to the right in a number of countries. The new agenda 'encompassed a rejection of the "post-war settlement" – the consolidated balance of substantive rights of workers, unions and employers' (Hyman, 1991: 262). Keynesian 'full-employment' commitments were jettisoned, and the deregulation of product and labour markets became principal themes in government policy pronouncements. The Conservative administration in the UK between 1979 and 1997 appeared initially to be the most enthusiastic in its embrace of the neo-liberal agenda. There was a sustained attack on trade union legitimacy, activity and influence in addition to a programme of labour market deregulation that entailed the weakening of the force and coverage of employment protection law.

Sixthly, the development and application of new information and communication technologies provided 'novel opportunities for the reorganization of products, production systems and methods of deployment and control of labour' (Hyman, 1991: 263). As will be seen, some scenarios of the 'transformation of work' highlighted the potential for the application of the new technologies in manufacturing to develop new product market strategies that required for their success a more highly skilled, versatile and empowered workforce. More pessimistic accounts noted the potential for tighter management coordination of workflows and more perfect monitoring of employee performance.

Finally, Japan's rapid economic growth in the 1960s and 1970s and the location of Japanese manufacturing 'transplants' in the US, Europe and especially in the UK in the 1980s, fuelled western interest in 'lean production' and just-in-time inventory control systems. The academic debates on the 'Japanisation' of management techniques in the West paralleled, to a degree, those that were evolving on the application of new production technologies.

Flexibility in work

One inspiration for the interest in flexibility has been the post-Fordist debate. This label can be applied to a set of academic studies that attempt to explain the economic and social dislocation experienced across the industrialised world from the late 1970s in terms of a transition from one distinct phase of capitalist development to a new one (Amin, 1994:1). Informed by a range of theoretical perspectives, these studies do not develop a single, uniform account. They agree that an earlier regime of Fordism was in decay by the 1970s, but differ in their interpretation of the causes of its demise and in their vision of the new regime in the making. The three most influential sets of interpretations are those of the 'regulation approach', pioneered by social scientists in France from the end of the 1970s and informed by a Marxist political economy framework; the 'new production concepts' approach, associated with the work of Kern and Schumann (1989) in Germany; and the 'flexible specialisation' thesis, which was the product of an Anglo-American collaboration (Sabel, 1982; Piore and Sabel, 1984; Sabel and Zeitlin, 1985; Hirst and Zeitlin, 1989). Of the three, the first contributes the most theoretically rigorous and challenging account of the 'crisis of Fordism' and the least optimistic vision of the future for labour in a regime of neo-Fordism. The third gained the widest audience in the UK in the 1980s and is summarised here.

Flexible specialisation

The thesis suggests that alternative 'industrial paradigms' of mass production and flexible specialisation have been available since the nineteenth century. Neither has been destined to dominate, by virtue of technological superiority or economic efficiency. Rather, circumstances have combined at rare moments to present stark choices between the two. The turn of the twentieth century represented the first such 'turning point' or 'industrial divide'; the period since the 1970s has been the second.

The first was 'resolved' in favour of mass production. Epitomised by the moving assembly-line techniques pioneered by Henry Ford at his car plants in the US in the 1920s, mass production technology involved the use of dedicated (single-purpose) machinery and Taylorist forms of work organisation in the manufacture of standardised goods for distribution to large, undifferentiated markets. Economic competition was dominated by the logic of economies of scale under which large firms gained the competitive edge. These pursued volume growth, organised production into long runs of identical parts, and laid out factories to achieve a lineal flow of work between functionally specialised departments (machining, sub-assembly, final assembly, paint and inspection). The social organisation of production resonated with the rigidities of the technical system. The extreme horizontal division of labour deskilled production workers, who were paced by the speed of 'the line'.

Mass production technologies facilitated increases in labour productivity in the decades after the Second World War, and the Keynesian demand-management policies of western governments helped to support the paradigm. According to Piore and Sable (1984), however, its viability had been threatened from the end of the 1960s by the exhaustion of mass markets, 'external shocks' that disrupted the international economy, and an increase in competition from newly developing economies, able to draw on supplies of relatively cheap labour. While these authors admitted that the 'crisis of Fordism' could be resolved in favour of its renewal, they suggested that a shift to a new paradigm of flexible specialisation was the only viable solution.

Their argument, in brief, was that changing consumer tastes and the development of microelectronics production technology had coincided to support the re-emergence, in revitalised form, of nineteenth-century craft production. Flexible specialisation was characterised as the use of general-purpose machinery and skilled, adaptable workers in the manufacture of a wide and changing range of semi-customised goods for specialised niche markets.

Because the new production technologies were easily reprogrammed, they reduced the size of the economic batch. Firms were therefore able to reap economies of scope – the ability to shift cost-efficiently from the production of one good to another – and, with this, exploit the potential of the new market openings for quality, customised goods. As this potential was realised, economies of scale would become less significant as the basis of interfirm competition and small firms would be placed on a more equitable footing with large corporations.

The new product market strategy required far-reaching changes in workforce skills and methods of labour management, amounting to a reversal of the Taylorist and Fordist traditions of the past. Flexible specialisation demanded broadly skilled, adaptable workers who were able to use the new production technologies to engineer a variety of models and semi-customised goods and to switch flexibly between a variety of functions. Mental and manual work were in this way recomposed and tasks were reconstituted into more complete job roles. In short, flexible specialisation was presented as a progressive regime that conferred benefits on firms and workers alike. Jobs were enriched. Employment security was enhanced by virtue of the firm's dependence on employee skills that could not be replaced easily by recruiting from the external labour market. Labour had now to be treated as an asset, rather than as a variable cost, and in order to motivate employees and secure their commitment to enterprise goals, employers were obliged to modify hierarchical control in favour of a more participative approach in employee relations.

The flexible specialisation thesis aroused a good deal of academic interest in the 1980s. Most commentators agreed that it captured some of the features of current developments in manufacturing methods. However, its analysis of these developments and the broader theory of industrial change in which it was embedded were questioned (Williams *et al.*, 1987; Hyman, 1988, 1991). Critics argued that the analysis of economic change focused too narrowly on manufacturing technologies and market structures and that the mass production/flexible specialisation dichotomy was too rigid to capture past and current developments in production systems and labour utilisation. The thesis had little to say about the conditions of work in the expanding service occupations. More specific charges were that:

■ it overstated the dominance of Fordist mass production in the twentieth century;
■ it exaggerated the rigidities of mass production – Henry Ford was exceptional in insisting his customers could have any colour provided it was black;
■ it relied on mainly impressionistic evidence of the break-up of mass markets;
■ it overstated the flexibility of the new production technologies;
■ it underestimated the continuing importance of scale economies.

The purported benefits of flexible specialisation for manufacturing employees were also questioned. Hyman (1988), for example, drew attention to the ways in which the new production and information technologies could be used by managements to direct and monitor more closely employee performance, that is, to reproduce and reinforce hierarchical management control.

■ Flexibility in the labour market

The theoretical debates considered so far have centred on flexibility at work. Flexibility in the labour market has also been a preoccupation since the 1970s, not least because of the political shift to the right in many countries. In the decades after the Second World War, governments in the West adhered broadly to the doctrine of Keynesianism. This legitimated state involvement in the (market) economy by proposing that, through demand-management policies, governments could attain the goals of full employment and price stability. Rising inflation in the 1970s, however, bolstered the challenge of neo-liberalism, the ideology of 'free markets'.

Conservative government policies, 1979–97

The embrace of neo-liberalism was most obvious in the rhetoric and policies of governments in the US and UK, but was by no means confined to these (Hyman, 1991; Gamble, 2001). The Conservative government in the UK in its first term of office (1979–83), set out tight monetary targets and asserted that the control of inflation was to be the priority of macroeconomic policy. Unemployment, which was allowed to rise to over 3 million in the mid-1980s, was characterised as a problem originating in the supply side of the economy. It was argued that institutional 'rigidities' in labour markets had inhibited speedy wage and employment adjustments to changing economic conditions. More specifically, government ministers argued that:

- trade union demands and industry-wide collective agreements preserved wages in excess of market clearing rates, with the result that workers had been priced out of jobs;
- employees' statutory employment protection rights, by limiting employers' freedom to dismiss employees, impeded the reallocation of labour from declining to expanding industries and deterred employers from creating new jobs;
- welfare benefits dampened the incentive for the unemployed to seek work or to accept low-paid jobs.

The government's immediate objective was to erode the bases of trade union influence and to cede to company managers greater freedom in the conduct of industrial relations. This was pursued through a complex set of legislative reforms, enacted on a 'step-by-step' basis, and through reforms of public sector employment (see Chapters 4, 8 and 14). Labour market deregulation became a more prominent theme during the Conservatives' second term of office (1983–7). The reforms pursued included:

- the attenuation of individual employment rights; access to the right to make a claim of unfair dismissal, for example, was restricted, principally by raising the qualifying period of service from six months to two years;
- the elimination of minimum wage protection; the (traditionally weak) wages councils system that had set legally enforceable minimum terms and conditions for workers in some industries was abolished for all but agricultural workers from 1993;
- a reduction in the level and coverage of unemployment benefits.

At the same time, the Conservative government resisted strenuously the extension of EU social and employment legislation, which it viewed as antithetical to the aim of creating a 'competitive, efficient and flexible labour market' (Employment Department, 1994, cited in Beatson, 1995).

Evaluations of the impact of the Conservative government's industrial relations and labour market reforms differ greatly. These are most appropriately considered after empirical studies of employers' work reorganisation initiatives and use of 'flexible' contracts have been reviewed. It is worth noting here, however, that while a relatively early fall in unemployment after the 1990–2 recession was interpreted by some (e.g. Beatson, 1995) as a measure of increased labour market flexibility, authoritative studies continued to show a significant gap between UK labour productivity and that of other G7 (leading) industrial economies (McKinsey, 1998).

Critics of labour market deregulation have interpreted its emphasis on (downward) wage flexibility and the erosion of employment rights as inimical to long-term industry competitiveness, as well as socially iniquitous. In short, it is thought to be counterproduct-ive to the reconstruction of industry and services on the basis of the high quality, high skill, high technology, high productivity 'production model' that is required to secure a competitive edge in the West *vis-à-vis* lower-waged economies. There are various permutations of this argument. For example, proponents of the flexible specialisation thesis argue that the development of such a regime requires state policies that encour-age cooperation among networks of small firms and between firms and their skilled employees. Deregulatory measures that enhance employers' freedom to hire and fire, or to force down wages, as product market conditions dictate, are regarded as at best unhelpful (Hirst and Zeitlin, 1989). Analyses of the configuration of employee relations required to support 'high performance work systems' (discussed later) make similar arguments. Employee commitment is regarded as critical and not easily achieved where there is mistrust in the employer's commitment to a long-term employment relationship (for a summary, see Heery and Salmon, 2000). In other words, the development of flex-ibility in work is argued to require restrictions on employers' ability to adopt alternative routes to profitability, such as the use of a cheap and disposable workforce. However, employers' resistance to such restrictions may be strong. Thus, for many critics of neo-liberalism there is an essential congruity between its ideology and the aspiration of multinational capital not to be confined to any particular (local or national) workforce (e.g. Gamble, 2001).

Labour market policies of Labour since 1997

To what extent have the policies of the Labour government since 1997 diverged from those of the preceding Conservative administration? Again, evaluations differ. Four successive electoral defeats prompted Labour leaders to transform the Party's relations with business and with the trade unions. By the time of the 1997 general election the former were being offered 'partnership' and the latter 'fairness not favours' (McIlroy, 1998). 'New' Labour espoused a 'third way' approach that to some (e.g. Giddens, 1998) promised a shift in UK state policy from neo-liberalism towards a European social market philosophy. Tony Blair defined the 'third way' as 'not laissez-faire nor state con-trol and rigidity; but an active Government role linked to improving the employability of the workforce' (1998, cited in Undy, 1999: 316). This translated, in practice, into a continuing commitment to the control of inflation as the central objective of macro-economic policy, and to labour market flexibility as the route to employment growth. Hence, observers such as McIlroy (1998) concluded that Labour had accepted, in broad terms, the neo-liberal prescription that 'global trends' could be accommodated but not challenged by national governments.

The government's reforms of industrial relations and employment law, as previous chapters have noted, amount to change and continuity with the preceding Conservative administration. New *individual* employment rights have been enacted. These include:

- the statutory minimum floors to hourly earnings established under the National Minimum Wage Act 1998;
- entitlements to rest periods, paid holiday, and not to be required to work over 48 hours a week on average, established by the Working Time Regulations 1998;
- a reduction in the qualifying period of service required for general unfair dismissal protection, from two years to one (from 1999).

A number of the new individual rights have been concerned with the extension of 'family-friendly' policies, or have been labelled as such. Many of these have derived from EU directives that the UK has been obliged to adopt since the Labour government signed up to the Social Chapter in 1997. The provisions include:

- the right to take a reasonable period of time off work to deal with an emergency involving a dependant;
- a right to 13 weeks' (unpaid) parental leave;
- the right for part-time workers to be treated equally with similarly placed full-time workers in the same employment.

The Employment Bill introduced in November 2001 proposes also:

- a right to two week's paid paternity leave for working fathers;
- a right to 26 weeks' paid adoption leave, followed by 26 weeks' unpaid leave;
- an extended right to maternity leave (26 weeks with statutory maternity pay, followed by 26 weeks' unpaid additional maternity leave;
- giving powers to the secretary of state to make regulations implementing the 1999 EU directive on fixed-term work.

New collective employment rights were enacted, including the statutory union recognition procedure introduced as part of the Employment Relations Act 1999. At the same time, however, the Labour government retained much of the Conservative government's industrial relations legislation which had 'aimed to regulate, weaken and democratize the trade unions, in the interests of the Conservatives' wider economic, labour market and political objectives' (Undy, 1999: 326). Evidently the Labour government has a particular conception of the legitimate role of trade unions; the rights and restrictions are designed to encourage a form of unionism that is moderate in its objectives and willing to work 'in partnership' with employers to achieve 'mutual gains'.

Labour's stated aim for its industrial relations and employment law reforms was to promote 'flexibility, efficiency and fairness at work' (DTI, 1998). When the detail of its proposed legislation became known in 1998, the *Financial Times* (21 May) argued that the proposals amounted to the 'biggest extension of rights and trade union opportunities in a quarter of a century'. Yet the content of Labour's legislative programme clearly reflects the tensions in its efforts to balance employment protection with labour market flexibility. The government has been anxious to keep business 'on board'. It has used consultation exercises and tripartite bodies (e.g. the Low Pay Commission) to achieve employers' consent for proposed measures. And it has advertised its commitment to 'light touch' legislation. Thus, while employers have complained about the volume of the legislation, its complexity, or the content of particular measures, trade unions and equal opportunities campaign groups criticised a number of provisions as insufficiently robust. The government has been accused of complying with European proposals in 'a minimalist fashion'. McKay (2001: 294–5) cites the example of its implementation of the EU Part-time Workers (Prevention of Less Favourable Treatment) Directive. The UK regulations were drafted initially to apply only to *employees*, that is those working under a contract of employment. Trade union representatives argued that they should apply to the broader category of *workers* in order to include temporary and agency staff and the self-employed, and meet the requirements of the EU directive. The threat of a legal challenge persuaded government ministers to amend the regulations accordingly.

■ The flexible firm

Different dimensions of the flexibility debates highlighted various forms of labour flexibility required to support enterprise competitiveness, and offered different interpretations of the industry structures and government policies necessary to achieve these. The flexible specialisation thesis urged firms to compete on quality and innovation, rather than on cost alone, and to invest in the development of workers with broad skills who would be interchangeable between work functions and tasks and motivated to contribute their creativity in support of the new product market strategy. The employment practices required to achieve such a degree of worker–management cooperation appeared to be at odds with the neo-liberal emphasis on labour market deregulation and erosion of employees' job protection rights. Yet the flexible firm model (Atkinson, 1984, 1985), which formed a third focus of the UK flexibility debates in the 1980s, suggested that these divergent labour management regimes could be combined within a single enterprise to yield a range of flexibility gains.

The model delineated an enterprise-level response to product market and technological uncertainty that centred on the reorganisation of the firm's internal labour market. The flexible firm segmented its workforce into core and peripheral groups in order to attain functional, numerical and financial flexibility. Core workers were those with key skills, or company-specific skills that were not readily available in the external labour market. Engaged on a full-time and permanent basis, they were trained and rewarded to supply *functional (or task) flexibility*. They were expected to have polyvalent skills that facilitated their allocation and reallocation among a wide range of tasks, and to acquire new competences as changes in technology or markets dictated. The peripheral workforce comprised those with skills that were more generally available in the external labour market and whose terms and conditions, as a result, could be constructed to emphasise the precariousness of their employment. Insecurely, irregularly or indirectly employed, they supplied the *numerical flexibility* that enabled company managers to adjust swiftly the level of labour inputs to meet fluctuations in demand for the organisation's goods or services, and to protect the employment security of the core. The peripheral workforce could include:

- full-time workers who performed relatively routinised tasks which offered few career prospects and were vulnerable to market or technological change;
- workers on 'non-standard' part-time or temporary employment contracts;
- workers who were not employed directly by the company but rather supplied their labour (or were supplied as labour) under a contract for services: subcontractors, self-employed workers and agency temporary staff.

The advantages of a core–periphery strategy for an employing organisation were presumed to be higher productivity from the core workforce; lower wage and non-wage costs from the increased use of peripheral groups; and flexibility in wage costs as the size of the peripheral workforce could be adjusted to meet fluctuations in the demand for the firm's goods or services.

The flexible firm model attracted much interest from managers, academics and journalists in the UK in the 1980s, and from an international audience. Yet much of the academic attention was critical. The model was said to be ideologically charged, in the sense that it appeared to reiterate the neo-liberal preoccupation with labour market flexibility as the source of industry competitiveness (Pollert, 1987). Related criticisms were that it lacked conceptual clarity (Pollert, 1987; Wood, 1989); was ill-supported by empirical evidence (Hunter et al., 1993); and neglected the tensions and new managerial problems to which a core–periphery employment strategy could give rise (Geary, 1992).

Certainly the model's status and purpose were ambiguous. Its proponents argued that it was 'only an analytical tool to help us understand what is going on'. However, they also suggested that firms were adopting the model and that 'this new division of labour' would be 'a permanent feature of the labour market for years to come' (Atkinson and Gregory, 1986: 4, 13). In other words, they presented the flexible firm model as a heuristic device and as a description and an explanation of what was actually taking place (Claydon, 1997), and this confused matters considerably.

The model's key concepts were imprecisely defined and therefore difficult to operationalise. This complicated its use as an analytical device and attempts to 'test' it against empirical evidence. The model suggested various ways in which 'core' and 'peripheral' groups might be identified: on the basis of employment security, contractual status (full-time, part-time, temporary, etc.), skills, tasks, and so on. Each of these and all combinations gave rise to difficulties:

> the identification of the core . . . can easily become circular; core workers have secure employment, and the fact of such employment is used as evidence for the presence of a core. If the core is more clearly defined by both its employment status (and especially its security and legal rights) and its tasks, there is a problem because some groups may have relatively secure employment but not be treated as part of the core of the business; whilst such 'peripheral' workers as part-time women in retailing may be central to the functioning and profitability of the business. (Wood, 1989: 5)

It is worth emphasising that any attempt to evaluate which skills are core is complicated by the fact that:

> 'skill' is socially constructed and also gendered. Thus, skills which are essential to an organisation, but are performed by women, may be socially constructed as semi- or unskilled, and may not be rewarded by the advantages of an internal labour market (by pay, promotion prospects and other non-wage benefits). (Pollert, 1987: 17)

There is therefore the danger of confusing new divisions with an existing, gender-based segmentation of the workforce.

As regards the model's fit with empirical evidence, survey and case study research in the late 1980s and early 1990s tended towards the conclusion that firms pursuing a core–periphery labour utilisation *strategy* were in a small minority (e.g. Hunter et al., 1994). However, Procter et al. (1994) objected that researchers had employed a restrictive notion of management strategy, as top-down, conscious, planned and deliberate, rather than as emergent. The flexible firm model remains influential in the sense that its concepts of core and periphery, numerical and functional flexibility, have been absorbed into 'everyday' practitioner and academic vocabularies. As Kalleberg (2001: 480) suggests, however, research into organisational flexibility has tended to 'proceed along two relatively distinct streams'.

> The majority of studies emphasize the correlates of 'high performance work systems' that are believed to enhance functional or internal flexibility; the other group examines processes of externalization designed to reduce costs and provide organizations with numerical flexibility.

The discussion in this chapter is organised to review in turn each of these separate streams of research, before turning to consider the ways in which functional and numerical flexibility may be pursued simultaneously within an organisation or via its network of relations with other firms.

Functional flexibility

Functional flexibility refers to a firm's ability to allocate and reallocate employees among a wide range of tasks. It is sometimes denoted as *internal* flexibility, to emphasise that the flexibility gains in question are derived from an existing workforce, as distinct from *external* flexibility which conveys the idea of bringing in additional workers and returning them to the external market when work levels fall (i.e. numerical flexibility). The pursuit of internal flexibility, however, can involve changes in the number and timing of working hours (working time, or temporary flexibility) in addition to the reconstruction of employees' job roles (functional flexibility).

Functional flexibility is a broad label and has been applied to a variety of types of change in working practices. These range from some relaxation and reorganisation of job boundaries – as, for example, where production employees are required to take on routine inspection or maintenance tasks – through to multiskilling and the introduction of teamworking. It is these latter forms that are given emphasis in more enthusiastic accounts of functional flexibility, or those that see its development as advantageous both for enterprise competitiveness and for employees who are thought to gain enriched jobs, greater security of employment, a more participative management regime and so on. The terms 'multiskilling' and 'teamworking', however, are often used loosely. Thus, while the former denotes the acquisition of additional skills – for example, where maintenance craftworkers become proficient in electrical as well as mechanical trades (or vice versa) – it is sometimes applied to the simple enlargement of jobs through the addition of further, routinised tasks. Moreover, empirical studies of multiskilling and teamworking 'proper' caution against the view that outcomes for employees are unambiguously positive.

Much of the research in this area has centred on manufacturing industry. This is not because work reorganisation initiatives have been confined to this sector – they have been in evidence in various branches of the private services and in public services. Rather, the manufacturing bias in academic studies of employers' pursuit of functional flexibility is to be explained, in part, by the trajectory of theoretical and practitioner debates. Claims of a 'transformation of work' in late-twentieth-century capitalism centred on work reorganisation initiatives in those industries most closely associated with the Fordist mass manufacturing model and have stimulated further studies and interpretations of the changes effected. Similarly, the 'pervasive ideology of Japanese manufacturing superiority' (Danford, 1998: 410) in the 1980s and 1990s generated much academic interest in the dimensions of a 'Japanese production model', of which functional flexibility and teamworking have been interpreted as among the most significant.

Teamworking

Teamwork has been defined in general terms as 'a group of employees, normally between three and 15 members, who meet regularly in order to work independently on fulfilling a specific task' (Mueller *et al.*, 2000: 1399). At a conceptual level and in practice, however, it can take a great variety of forms. Many studies attempt to classify the forms that have, or are being developed within, a bipolar analytical framework of Swedish and Japanese 'models' of teamworking, or 'socio-technical' and 'Toyotist' teams. There are some difficulties with this approach, but the broad idea is that teamworking in conception and design can involve a significant departure from 'Taylorist' work principles or a reiteration of them.

The notion of socio-technical teams derives from ideas pioneered by researchers at the Tavistock Institute of Human Relations from the 1950s, and that were taken up in experiments with autonomous groupworking at the Kalmar and Uddevalla plants of the Swedish car manufacturer Volvo in the 1960s and 1970s. In the Swedish 'teamwork discourse', the 'emphasis was firmly placed on job-enrichment-orientated teamwork, in particular achieving over time a more ergonomical arrangement of work and a much greater degree of employee sovereignty which, it was hoped, would substantially reduce the strains which workers experienced' (Mueller *et al.*, 2000: 1394). Employees enjoyed 'sufficient freedom to influence such matters as goal formation, performance monitoring, production methods, labour allocation and choice of group leaders' (Danford, 1998: 410). It is against this Swedish model that social scientists have assessed forms of teamwork that, in their design and practice, draw on other traditions and, in particular, the 'Toyotist'.

Interest in teamwork has increased among management scientists in the past fifteen years. And the practice of teamwork has also grown in Europe and in North America: Benders *et al.* (1999, cited in Steijn, 2001) estimate that 36 per cent of workplaces in Europe now use some form of it. An important influence, certainly in the heightened curiosity in teamworking principles, although also in its 'diffusion' as a management practice, has been the 'challenge' of 'lean production', a system pioneered in Japan by Toyota and other large industrial corporations.

Proponents have interpreted lean production variously as a further stage of development beyond mass production (Womack *et al.*, 1990), and as a set of innovations that overcome the limitations of conventional mass production without departing from its basic principles (Wickens, 1993: 85). A central objective is the elimination of 'waste' – that is, human and material resources that are not considered by managers to be contributing continuously at maximum capacity. A key goal is low inventory/minimum 'buffer' stock production, which is pursued through a variety of interrelated practices:

- quick machine set-up times that offset the economies of long production runs and high levels of inventories of work in progress;
- a cellular as opposed to a sequential, production layout: the regrouping of machinery into manufacturing cells which reduces the physical distance between 'workstations' and inhibits the build-up of stocks of parts and work-in-progress inventories;
- the grouping of workers into teams that are assigned problem-solving and quality control responsibilities in addition to production tasks;
- just-in-time production scheduling: the principle that parts and sub-assemblies are produced and delivered for immediate use, at the next stage of production, rather than for stock.

In their influential study, Womack *et al.* (1990: 99) claimed that 'it is the dynamic work team that emerges at the heart of the lean factory'. Team-based work organisation, according to this view, is productive because it upgrades skills and empowers employees, and in this way strengthens their commitment to maintain the continuity of defect-free output, and to contribute their knowledge and skills to the continuous improvement of the production system. Alternative interpretations (e.g. Dohse *et al.*, 1985; Tomaney, 1994) emphasise the similarities with Taylorism. Continuous improvement involves the constant rationalisation of the production system, especially the elimination of 'wasteful' movements, and the standardisation of tasks. Productivity increases are achieved through the enlargement (as opposed to the enrichment) of production workers' jobs and the intensified pace of work achieved through just-in-time scheduling.

Studies of teamworking under the lean production regimes that have been developed in the UK by car manufacturers and firms supplying automotive components to these have tended to concur with the more critical evaluation (Danford, 1998; Delbridge, 1998; Garrahan and Stewart, 1992). Lean production admits adaptation at local level, and if introduced to a brownfield site will be shaped by the established configuration of labour relations. The results of empirical research, however, suggest that:

■ multi-tasking – rather than multi-skilling – is the general theme;
■ traditional, hierarchical forms of managerial supervision are in many instances retained;
■ the elimination of buffers (excess stock, indirect quality inspection personnel), that is intended to accelerate the rate of throughput, results for employees in the experience of an intensified and more stressful pace of work.

Delbridge *et al.* (2000) draw on findings from an international study of management practices of plants in the automotive components industry to examine the distribution of responsibilities for different functions and tasks under lean teamworking. The study embraced 71 plants in nine countries. Delbridge *et al.*'s analysis focuses on the 30 plants that appeared to have the characteristics of 'lean teams'. It highlights three significant sets of findings that add up to the view that these teams are not independent and self-sustaining. First, the technical role of production workers appears to be rather limited. In the plants studied, operators have the principal responsibility for routine quality tasks, but they have not been upskilled to take on significant roles in activities such as maintenance, and do not have significant responsibility for production activities. As Delbridge *et al.* (2000: 1474) suggest, these findings 'question the claim that workers in teams have substantial autonomy and that lean teams are self-managing in any meaningful way'. Secondly, in contradiction to the notion of autonomous group working, the leaders of 'self-managing' teams have the main responsibility for the allocation and pace of work, and for settling grievances, 'implying that the team-leader is the front-line of management'. Thirdly, the roles of 'indirect', specialist occupational groups, have changed, although not always in the ways suggested by popular interpretations of lean production principles. For Delbridge *et al.*, the lack of evidence of upskilling among production workers suggests that the positions of skilled trades, in particular equipment maintenance workers, 'have been consolidated rather than eroded'. On the other hand, they note what 'appears to be a "hollowing out" of the roles of middle managers in the areas of engineering and quality' (2000: 1475), as these functions are transferred to shopfloor teams, or at least to the leaders of these.

Such evaluations have been taken up in the attempts to develop analytical taxonomies of teamworking. Bacon and Blyton (2000) suggest as an alternative to the Swedish–Japanese bipolar taxonomy that of 'high road' and 'low road' teamworking. The inspiration is the burgeoning literature on 'high performance work systems' (HPWS). As Ramsay *et al.* (2000: 502) explain, there has been much discussion among management scholars since the mid-1980s of a 'high road' approach to management, 'in which organizations choose to compete primarily on quality, and rely especially on human resource development and employee contributions to succeed in this'. In a sense, therefore, the debate recasts the themes of the flexible specialisation thesis. While the concept of the HPWS has become prominent in the discussion of high road approaches, it defies definition. Writers using it draw on a range of ideas, including those that have developed from Womack *et al.*'s (1990) study of lean production, and give emphasis to 'high commitment management', or 'high involvement' management, or 'total quality management' (see Wood, 1999, for an overview). The common theme (following Huselid, 1995), nevertheless, is that improvements in organisational performance are achieved through use of innovative HRM practices in particular combinations (or 'bundles') that are mutually reinforcing. Ramsay *et al.* (2000: 502) summarise the strategy prescribed as entailing 'managements ceding a degree of control to employees and introducing a range of progressive methods which increase employee welfare'. The workplace reforms recommended 'generally encompass any changes believed to introduce more flexible workplace practices and to enhance task discretion and responsibility, and usually revolve around the use of teamwork organization' (Godard, 2001: 25).

Bacon and Blyton develop their high road/low road taxonomy as a means of differentiating forms of teamworking and of exploring the links between these forms and outcomes. High road and low road teams are distinguished on the basis of the extent, or scale, of the reorganisation of work practices they represent; the former have more of the practices associated with socio-technical teams (the Swedish model in other taxonomies) and theories that stress participative management through teamworking. High road and low road teams are also distinguished, however, on the basis of the broader employment regimes they represent. This is useful in that it allows analysis of how low road teams 'may also deliver high performance but via a low skill–low wage strategy' (Bacon and Blyton, 2000: 1429). At the same time, however, it highlights the difficulties with bipolar taxonomies. Many analyses of lean production in Japan in the 1980s, for example, note employers' use of relatively high wages (and other internal labour market 'privileges') to secure from core workers cooperation with the continuing rationalisation and standardisation of the production process, in the interests of rising productivity and falling unit costs (Dohse *et al.*, 1985; Sayer, 1986).

Teamworking in the UK

Survey data show that teamworking is increasing its hold on workplaces in the UK, in the service industries and public sector and not simply in manufacturing (Mueller *et al.*, 2000; IDS 2001a). In the national Workplace Employee Relations Survey (WERS), conducted in 1997/8, 83 per cent of managers reported that at least some employees in the largest occupational group worked formally in designated teams, and 65 per cent reported that most employees in this group worked in teams. Cully *et al.*'s analysis of the data, however, suggested that only 35 per cent of workplaces 'operated teams that corresponded approximately to a model of semi-autonomous teamworking' (1999: 42); that is, had teams that had responsibility for a specific product or service *and* allowed team members to jointly decide how work was to be done. Only 3 per cent of workplaces met these criteria and also allowed team members to appoint their own team leaders and, as such, approximated to a model of fully autonomous teamworking.

Other survey and case study evidence provides further insight into the forms of teamworking that have emerged. Ackroyd and Procter's (1998) analysis of work organisation and labour management at the plants of large British-owned manufacturing companies, based on a data archive compiled since 1996, suggests that, among these, teamworking is common, although it is predominantly teamworking of the 'low road' variety. The researchers argue that the arrangements do not depend on high levels of skill or high levels of investment. Rather,

> Output is achieved in part by some reorganization of machinery, but more significantly by a combination of a heavy dependency on the flexible use of relatively unskilled labour and a willingness to utilize external sources of production. The basic arrangement for manufacture is the use of standard technology by means of self-regulating and formally unskilled workers. Production is organized into a number of semi-autonomous segments, which also feature as cost centres. Each of these is periodically and individually assessed in terms of its costs and benefits, and this feature shapes most aspects of management organization and activity, including the control of labour. (Ackroyd and Procter, 1998: 171)

Functional flexibility has been developed, but it is of a particular kind. The erosion of traditional job demarcations, extension of cellular manufacturing and teamworking have allowed an increased use of semi-skilled or unskilled labour because the allocation of groups of employees to groups of machines 'limits the need for all employees to have a broad spectrum of skills' (Ackroyd and Procter, 1998: 174). The emphasis on teamworking, Ackroyd and Procter suggest, follows from its contribution to task coordination and wage cost reduction, 'rather than from any general attachment to the idea as such'. Profitability is maintained not through 'high surveillance management' but rather through regular assessment of the financial contribution of each manufacturing cell and the employment insecurity of production workers. Core employees – that is, those employed directly on full-time contracts – supply numerical as well as functional flexibility. The cellular manufacturing system allows capacity to be 'flexed' to meet demand fluctuations, and units deemed to be underperforming to be displaced by outsourced supplies.

Edwards and Wright's (1996) study of the 'high involvement work system' developed at Alcan's aluminium smelter at Lynemouth shows that 'high road' teamworking is also in evidence. Edwards and Wright report a positive employee response. Workers interviewed cited an increase in the stress and pressure of their work, although also increased job satisfaction, a greater ability to take decisions and better work relations with their colleagues. Three interrelated sets of factors are seen as supporting the success of the new work arrangements:

- the trauma of a recent and major redundancy programme;
- the continuous process technology and pre-existing division of labour which facilitated group work;
- support for the introduction of teamworking.

The plant was virtually 100 per cent unionised, and union involvement in the introduction of change satisfied employees that their interests had been represented. High involvement work systems are intended to deliver high performance, high commitment and high involvement. The success of the arrangements at Lynemouth was reflected in workers' increased job satisfaction (high involvement), improvements in productivity and decreases in overtime, absenteeism and accident rates (high performance). There were signs also of high commitment but expressed largely in terms of employees' greater diligence in the execution of job tasks. Evidence of greater employee identification with the company and its values, or of the emergence of 'high trust' worker–management relations, was thin. Edwards and Wright relate this in part to the continuing uncertainty over the future of the plant in the context of volatile product market conditions.

Productivity, flexibility and partnership

The reassertion of managerial prerogative in the workplace was an objective of the Conservative government's restrictive trade union legislation. The impact of this legislation on economic performance remains a major area of controversy. Commentators such as Crafts (1991) and Metcalf (1989) have argued that by facilitating changes in work organisation and working practices, the government's industrial relations reforms made a major contribution to the upsurge in manufacturing productivity in the 1980s. Nolan (1996), in contrast, finds little evidence of a 'structural transformation' of the supply side of the economy. Highlighting the 'legacy of under-investment – in new technology, plant and people', he suggests that the productivity gains of the 1980s were rooted in three interlinked factors:

> labour shedding; incremental changes in production organisation; and what some analysts have referred to as the 'fear' factor, the central idea being that the threefold increase in unemployment in the early 1980s made employees more likely to acquiesce to new and more intensive (but not necessarily more efficient) work routines. (Nolan, 1996: 116–17)

This assessment suggests that the sources of change offer an insubstantial basis on which to build new 'high trust' production and work regimes (see also Heery and Salmon, 2000: 16–17).

From 1993 to 2001, unemployment in the UK economy was falling but manufacturing employment continued to contract, and accounted for only 14 per cent of all workforce jobs in June 2001. The Labour government since 1997 has championed the need for a 'partnership approach' in company and workplace employee relations on the grounds that this will increase workforce motivation and commitment leading to greater efficiency and productivity gains. The philosophy has been embraced by the TUC and the leaderships of many of the major British unions, and has been elaborated to include, as part of an 'integrative' bargaining agenda, a mutual – management, union and employee - commitment to 'bring together employment security and greater flexibility' (see Chapters 3 and 4).

Knell's (1999) influential study, conducted on behalf of the Department of Trade and Industry, examined 'the conceptual and practical foundations of partnership' among 15 organisations operating across a range of industries and selected because they were thought to have or to be developing a partnership approach. It found that these 'partnership firms' displayed:

> a high rate of innovation and have been successful in introducing new forms of work organisation and in managing the resultant changes. The erosion of hierarchy, the redefinition of roles, increased task discretion, flexible working practices, and the development of semi-autonomous teams were all widespread features of the case study firms. (Knell, 1999: iii)

Moreover, the employees who were interviewed were found to show 'high support for the principles and practices' being adopted by the case study firms. Some of these firms claimed a long-term commitment to a partnership approach (even if they did not label their approach explicitly as such). Others had been prompted by a commercial or financial crisis to engage in a change management programme that gave emphasis to employee or union involvement as the means of securing changes in working practices and performance. At one, Appor Ltd, the early changes, at the beginning of the 1990s, had resulted in a 50 per cent reduction in the size of the workforce (to 39 at the time of the research). Company managers suggested that 'many of those who left were those who didn't want to change – especially those who couldn't cope with the transition from "supervisor" to Coach' (Knell, 1999: 33).

A number of the firms were non-union (four of the nine in manufacturing). The research findings therefore lend some support to the critics of 'partnership' as a trade union renewal strategy. Union moderation may appeal to some employers (for example, those with a unionised workforce or a history of 'adversarial' employment relations), while others pursue partnership in tandem with union exclusion. There are, moreover, the risks for the trade unions of alienating members and potential members through compliance with change management programmes that achieve improvements in organisational performance through 'flexible' work practices that heighten the pace and stress of work for employees (Claydon, 1998).

Part-time work

'Non-standard' employment denotes that which departs in some way from the twentieth century 'standard' of male full-time employment, on an open-ended contract at an employer's place of work. As such, it embraces a wide variety of types of work and contractual forms: part-time work, temporary work, working from or at home, and self-employment, each category of which is heterogeneous. Many of the workers in these forms of employment have fallen outside, or have been covered only partially, by the formal regulations surrounding labour markets – including statutory employment protection rights. Hence workers on non-standard contracts have been discussed as part of the 'insecure workforce' (Felstead and Jewson, 1999: 2), although the actual or felt degree of employment insecurity has been more acute for some than others. The growth in the proportion of the workforce engaged on non-standard contracts has stimulated academic interest in these types of labour contract, as has the trajectory of government labour market policies, and the attention that has been given to policy-oriented models, such as that of the flexible firm.

The flexible firm model identified the use of non-standard labour contracts as a principal source of the numerical flexibility that enabled an employing organisation to match staffing to fluctuations in the demand for its goods or services. Non-standard workers were the 'periphery' and were excluded from the firm's premium employment terms and conditions in order to protect the employment security of the 'core' workforce.

Much of the debate provoked by the flexible firm model centred on the extent to which firms were pursuing a conscious and planned 'core–periphery' employment strategy. New issues for research, however, have since emerged. One influence in the UK has been the Labour government's emphasis, in line with EU employment policy, on the need for employers to make provision for employees' interests in attaining a better balance between work and other interests and commitments. Flexible work arrangements and contractual forms of employment previously denoted as non-standard have been discussed in these terms. Similarly, these have been viewed by public policy-makers as supportive of opportunities for groups previously under-represented in the labour market to become economically active (Purcell, 2000: 130).

This section of the chapter and the next explore particular types of non-standard employment: part-time work and temporary work respectively. They outline the broad trends in the growth of these employment forms, discuss the reasons why people opt for or are relegated to these types of employment, and the reasons why employers use them. The discussion focuses largely on the UK but, where relevant, develops international comparisons.

Definitions of part-time work

In the UK, where the legal regulation of working time has been relatively restricted, there is no statutory definition of standard working hours or part-time work. The Working Time Regulations, introduced in October 1998 to give effect to the EU Working Time Directive, set a maximum limit on the average weekly hours that workers can be required to work by their employer. They do not prescribe 'standard' hours, however, or indeed minimum hours of work. The Part-time Workers (Prevention of Less Favourable Treatment) Regulations enacted in 2000 in compliance with the EU directive, define part-time work in relation to normal full-time hours. In essence, 'a worker whose hours are less than the normal full-time hours at his or her place of work is classified as a part-timer' (IDS, 2001b: 4).

Two main methods of defining part-time work are used in UK government databases: self-assessment and persons not working more than 30 hours a week. The former is used in the quarterly Labour Force Survey (LFS). The 30 hours 'cut-off' has been used in the UK by the Office for National Statistics (ONS) as a guide for participants in employer surveys.

Other definitions nevertheless have applied to employment rights and to social security benefits. UK employment law in the past 'was aimed primarily at work patterns associated with full-time employment' (IDS, 2001b: 4). Part-time employees were excluded from many statutory rights, including the right to claim unfair dismissal, unless they met the qualifying hours thresholds: 'For example, employees had to work at least 16 hours a week for that week to count towards their period of continuous employment (the threshold fell to eight hours after five years' service)' (IDS, 2001b: 4).

Many employers took 16 hours as the threshold at which employees became eligible for company benefits (holiday pay, sick pay, inclusion in company pension schemes and so on). The House of Lords ruled in 1993, however, that UK unfair dismissal and redundancy payments legislation breached EU equality law. The hours thresholds were judged to amount to indirect discrimination against women, who are the more likely to work part-time, and were subsequently removed by the Employment Protection (Part-time Employees) Regulations 1995. The need for a period of continuous employment (reduced from two years to one in 1999) and for employee status, nevertheless remain as obstacles, in particular for temporary and casual workers, many of whom work part-time (Purcell, 2000). Moreover, people who work relatively few hours or whose earnings fall below a specified level are often excluded from the National Insurance system.

On average, part-timers in the UK in 2000 worked 15.6 hours a week, according to LFS data, but there was a wide spread of hours: almost 2 million worked 12 hours or less a week, including more than 1 million who worked 8 hours or fewer (IDS, 2001b: 2). Part-timers' hours, on average, are rather shorter in the UK than in the EU as a whole. The average hours usually worked by male and by female part-timers in the UK in 1996 were 16.2 and 18.0, respectively, compared with EU averages of 19.3 and 19.8 (*Social Trends* 28 (1998): 83). A related factor that has set the UK apart, at least until fairly recently, has been the wide range of working time patterns. In most other European countries, part-time working is 'usually done in the morning, and tends to last at least 20 to 25 hours per week'. In the UK, such regularities have long since disappeared and it 'is hard to discern a typical pattern of part-time work' (Hegewisch, 1996). Thus while particular variants of part-time working have been identified – job-sharing, term-time-only working, Saturday-only working, twilight shifts, zero hours contracts – each forms a small proportion of all part-time employment and may in turn embrace a wide variety of practices.

The growth and composition of the part-time workforce

LFS data show that the number of people in part-time work in the UK rose by approximately 2 million since 1984, to 7.02 million in April/June 2001. The share of total employment (which includes employees, the self-employed, unpaid family workers and people on public subsidy training schemes) taken by those in part-time work has risen from one-fifth (21 per cent) to one-quarter (25 per cent). This expansion of part-time work continues a long-term trend, evident for much of the post-war period, however, and some analyses suggest that the rate of growth of part-time work was most vigorous in the 1960s (Bruegel and Perrons, 1998) or 1970s (Beatson, 1995). Full-time employment fell in the recession of the early 1980s and, among men, only began to recover towards the end of the decade. This context made salient the continuing growth of part-time work. Full-time employment among men and women contracted again in the downturn of the early 1990s and, among men, did not recover to the 1990 level before the end of the decade. Part-time employment grew more or less continuously over the 1990s. The increase in full-time employment after 1993, however, contributed slightly more strongly to the growth in total employment in the period to 2001, and therefore part-time employment's share of the total rose only modestly (see Table 13.1).

Table 13.1 Full-time and part-time employment in the UK, 1992–2001

April–June	All in employment (000s)	Full-time (000s)	Part-time (000s)	Part-time as % all in employment
1992	25,831	19,798	6,033	23.4
1993	25,575	19,489	6,086	23.8
1994	25,778	19,530	6,248	24.2
1995	26,136	19,791	6,345	24.3
1996	26,418	19,880	6,538	24.7
1997	26,982	20,266	6,716	24.9
1998	27,230	20,466	6,764	24.8
1999	27,592	20,747	6,845	24.8
2000	27,926	20,957	6,969	25.0
2001	28,176	21,158	7,018	24.9
Change 1992–2001 (000s)	2,345	1,360	985	
% change 1992–2001	+9.1	+6.9	+16.3	+1.5

Source: LFS (ONS) Historical Supplement

Part-time work has grown in absolute and relative terms across the EU as a whole since 1980. In 2000, part-time jobs formed 18 per cent of total EU employment (European Commission, 2001: 11). However, the growth in part-time working has been distributed unevenly between different member states. Some countries that favoured full-time employment in the early 1980s have continued to do so; part-time work has risen, but not markedly as a share of all in employment. This is notably the case among the southern states of Greece, Italy and Spain (see Table 13.2). In contrast, Denmark, Norway and Sweden had the highest ratios of part-time to all in employment in the early 1980s and in each the share of part-time work has remained fairly constant. Indeed, in the five years to 2000, the share of those employed in part-time jobs increased in all EU countries except Sweden (European Commission, 2001: 19) The Netherlands had the highest proportion of part-time jobs to total employment in 1990 and the proportion continued to rise, from 32 per cent to 40 per cent in 2000. The UK had the fourth highest proportion of part-time employment among EU states in 1990, but has since moved to second place, behind the Netherlands. Across the EU, women form the majority of part-time workers. Those states with an above-average representation of part-time employment tend to be those with the highest rates of female labour market participation. Nevertheless, Finland and Portugal each have a high female activity rate and, in each, full-time employment remains more 'the norm' for women (Rubery and Fagan, 1995; and see Table 13.2).

Part-time work has increased among men in a number of countries, including the UK where it has more than doubled since the early 1980s. This growth was from a low base, however, and part-time work currently accounts for only 9 per cent of male employment in the UK. In contrast, 44 per cent of women in paid employment work part-time and women form 81 per cent of all those in part-time work (Table 13.3).

A majority of men in part-time work in the UK are aged either under 25 years or over 50 years. Around two-fifths of those in the younger age range report their reason for working part-time as being a student or at school (LFS, cited in Sly et al., 1998: 111). The abolition of student grants and the introduction of tuition fees have opened up an

Table 13.2 **Proportion of part-timers in the workforce in EU member states, 1999**

	All (%)	Men (%)	Women (%)
Netherlands	39.4	17.9	68.6
UK	24.8	8.9	44.4
Sweden	23.8	9.4	40.0
Denmark	20.7	9.6	33.9
Germany	19.0	4.9	37.2
Belgium	17.5	4.2	35.8
France	17.2	5.6	31.7
Austria	16.8	4.4	32.6
Ireland	16.7	7.4	30.6
Finland	12.2	7.9	17.0
Portugal	11.0	6.3	16.7
Luxembourg	10.8	1.9	24.6
Spain	8.3	3.0	17.6
Italy	7.9	3.4	15.7
Greece	6.1	3.6	10.1

Source: European Commission (2000, cited in IDS, 2001b: 2)

Table 13.3 **Full-time and part-time employment in the UK by gender, 1992–2001**

April–June	Men in employment			Women in employment		
	Full-time (000s)	Part-time (000s)	Part-time as % all men in employment	Full-time (000s)	Part-time (000s)	Part-time as % of all women in employment
1992	13,351	1,006	7.0	6,473	5,022	43.7
1993	13,096	1,010	7.2	6,393	5,076	44.3
1994	13,121	1,089	7.7	6,408	5,159	44.6
1995	13,286	1,177	8.1	6,506	5,168	44.3
1996	13,324	1,239	8.5	6,556	5,229	44.7
1997	13,586	1,307	8.8	6,679	5,408	44.7
1998	13,741	1,327	9.7	6,725	5,436	44.7
1999	13,843	1,389	9.1	6,904	5,457	44.1
2000	13,995	1,393	9.1	6,962	5,575	44.5
2001	14,108	1,396	9.0	7,050	5,622	44.4
% change 1992–2001	+5.7	+38.8	+2.0	+8.9	+11.9	+0.7

Source: LFS (ONS) Historical Supplement

increasing supply of young people (men and women) available for part-time work, although youth unemployment has also contributed and there are therefore similar trends in several other EU countries (European Commission, 2001). The age distribution of women working part-time in the UK is more even but has a distinct age-related profile.

Female economic activity rates increase with age, and in 1997 peaked at 78 per cent in the 40–49 year range (Sly *et al.*, 1998). LFS data for that year showed that part-time employment was higher among women over 25 years than under, and highest among women in their forties. This distribution, which conforms to the idea of women

Table 13.4 **Labour market and family status of women, UK, summer 2001 (not seasonally adjusted)**

	All women	Women with dependent children (by age of youngest dependent child)					No dependent children	All men
		All						
	16–59	0–18	0–4	5–10	11–15	16–18		
Thousands								
All in employment	12,101	4,791	1,592	1,610	1,187	402	7,310	15,335
Full-time	7,000	1,957	547	609	571	230	5,043	14,102
Part-time	5,099	2,833	1,045	1,000	616	172	2,266	1,230
ILO unemployed	607	231	89	76	75	–	376	956
All economically active	12,708	5,021	1,681	1,685	1,243	412	7,686	16,292
Economically inactive	4,719	2,385	1,306	633	355	91	2,334	2,896
Total	17,427	7,406	2,987	2,318	1,598	503	10,020	19,188
Percentages								
Employment rate (%)	69.4	64.7	53.3	69.4	74.3	80.0	73.0	79.9
Part-time as % all in employment	42.1	59.1	65.6	62.1	51.9	42.8	31.0	8.0
Economic activity rate (%)	72.9	67.8	56.3	72.7	77.8	81.9	76.7	84.9
ILO unemployment rate (%)	4.8	4.6	5.3	4.5	4.5	–	4.9	5.9

Source: LFS, in *Labour Market Trends*, November 2001: 510

returning to (or switching to) work on a part-time basis after childbirth and child rearing, has remained fairly stable over the past 20 to 30 years. What has changed, however, is the age profile of women in full-time employment. Until the 1970s, women under 25 years were the most likely to work full-time. But full-time employment has declined among this group, partly because participation in higher education has risen. At the same time, the incidence of full-time employment among women in the 25–49 age range has increased (Harkness, 1998).

LFS data suggest that women's economic activity rates, their participation in employment and their participation on a full-time or part-time basis are influenced by whether or not they have dependent children and, among those with dependent children, the age of their youngest dependent child (see Table 13.4). Also of relevance among those women with dependent children is whether there is a second parent available to provide child care and/or an income from paid employment. Women with very young children (under five years) are the least likely to be economically active (that is, either in employment or unemployed and seeking work). That said, it is this group that contributed the most rapid increase in the rate of women's labour market participation in the ten years to 1998 (Sly *et al.*, 1998: 80). Financial need, together with improvements in statutory and employers' maternity pay and leave provision, have no doubt contributed to this increase in the number of women who do not quit employment at the time of childbirth, or who return swiftly to employment thereafter. The ability to return to work is nevertheless dependent on the availability of affordable child care. The UK, and also the Netherlands, have been distinguished among EU member states by their relatively poor provision of state-supported child care (Rubery and Fagan, 1995).

■ Industry and occupational distributions of part-time work

Table 13.5 shows the proportion of part-time employment in different sectors and industry groups in the UK. Most industries employ some workers on a part-time basis. It is evident, nevertheless, that part-time employment is concentrated in the service sector, and in particular industries within it. As a proportion of all in employment it is highest in industries with a high density of female employment. In the public sector, over one-third (34.6 per cent) of the workforce in the public administration, education and health industry group work part-time, and the proportion is significantly higher in education and in health (where women account for upwards of 70 per cent of the workforce). Among the private service industries, part-time workers represent over two-fifths of the workforce (41.5 per cent) in distribution, hotels and restaurants, and nearly one-fifth (18.9 per cent) of all workers in the financial services. In manufacturing, in contrast, less than one-tenth of the workforce is part-time. The sectoral recomposition of employment – the decline in manufacturing employment and expansion of service industries – offers part of the explanation for the growth in part-time work, a long-term trend dating from the 1950s. Some service industries have relied 'traditionally' on female and part-time labour. Their relative expansion has contributed to the growth of part-time employment and yet, the proportionate share of part-time employment has increased within a number of these service industries since 1980. Moreover, part-time employment has increased in proportionate terms in some industries that in the past were staffed primarily by full-time employees (e.g. the financial services).

The occupational segregation of women's employment, and of women's part-time employment in particular, is probably more pronounced than its industrial segregation. Hence, as Incomes Data Services reported in 2001: 'Although efforts have been made at European level to extend the breadth of part-time work, those employed on a part-time basis still tend to be in traditionally lower-paid, lower-skilled occupations' (IDS, 2001b: 3).

At the end of 2000, in the UK, part-timers accounted for 55 per cent of staff in selling, 45 per cent in personal and protective services, and 33 per cent in clerical and administrative positions. In contrast, only 5 per cent of workers in craft and related

Table 13.5 Part-time employment, by sector and industry group, 2000

	Percentage of part-timers in sector/industry group
Public sector	30.4
Private sector	23.3
Distribution, hotels and restaurants	41.5
Other services	36.7
Public administration, education and health	34.6
Banking, finance and insurance, etc.	18.9
Agriculture and fishing	16.5
Transport and communications	12.4
Manufacturing	8.2
Construction	6.4
Energy and water	5.4

Source: LFS (2000/1, cited in IDS, 2001b: 3)

positions, 10 per cent in managerial and administrative positions, and 17 per cent of people in professional occupations worked part-time.

The industry and occupational distributions of part-time work provide part of the explanation for part-timers' relatively low average hourly earnings. The gender pay gap has narrowed over the past 30 years, but the improvement has largely been confined to the ratio of female full-time to male full-time average hourly earnings (see Chapter 12). Moreover, an 'intra-gender pay gap' widened in the 1980s and 1990s. The average hourly earnings of female part-time employees were just 75 per cent of female full-time hourly earnings in April 2000, compared with 83 per cent in 1975 (New Earnings Survey data, cited in IDS, 2001b: 3). A partial explanation for this lies in the 'qualifications gap' between women in full-time and those in part-time work and, in relation to this, the skew of their distribution between different occupations.

Women with A-level or above educational qualifications have made some inroads into professional and managerial occupations – where full-time employment is generally the requirement, at least for career progression. The average of female full-time hourly earnings, in consequence, has been raised. Yet, 'qualified' women in full-time jobs often do not attain pay equality with their male colleagues. And women seeking part-time work – whether 'qualified' or not – have often been obliged to accept relatively low-paying jobs that do not provide access to other elements of the reward package offered to full-timers in the same organisation. Data relating to the early 1990s show that around one-third of female part-timers were in fact qualified to A-level or above. A similar proportion had no formal educational qualifications (Harkness, 1998). A significant proportion of the former may be in higher-paid part-time work (for example, in professional occupations in the education or health services). Gallie *et al.*'s (1998) analysis of survey data, however, found that a majority of part-timers reported that they had been recruited to jobs that required no qualifications. In other words, many part-timers are over-qualified for the job roles they fill.

A matter of choice?

The European Commission and the government in the UK have identified part-time work as a means of securing the labour market inclusion of formerly disadvantaged groups, including women with young children and, among these, lone parents. Part-time work has also been highlighted as a means through which employees – men and women – can attain a better work–life balance. Given that many part-time jobs are relatively low grade and low paid, however, it is relevant to ask why people opt for, or are relegated, to them.

The Labour Force Survey asks people in part-time work about their reasons for working part-time. Around four-fifths of women, although only between one-third and two-fifths of men, select the response that they 'did not want a full-time job'. Men are much more likely than women to report that they 'could not find a full-time job'. The exact proportions vary, principally with the state of the labour market. Nevertheless, while in the period 1992–2001 between one-fifth and one-third of men in part-time work gave this reason, it was cited by, at most, one-tenth of women in part-time work. Around one-third of men report being a student or at school as a reason for part-time work, and while the proportion of women giving this reason has risen steadily in recent years, in April/June 2001 it reached only just above one-tenth (*LFS Historical Supplement*). These data have been interpreted as evidence that, among women at least, part-time work is largely voluntary: a matter of choice, rather than of circumstance (e.g. European Commission, 2001). Hakim (1996) has elaborated on this interpretation to suggest there is an increasing polarisation among women. Those working part-time have made the conscious decision to maximise their preference for domestic as opposed to career, paid employment roles. They are 'willing slaves' to lower paid, part-time work, and this is exemplified by their failure to invest in the education and training that would equip them for better paid jobs, with promotion and pay prospects.

Critics argue that such interpretations underplay the influence of class and of gender relations (in the household, and in society more broadly) on women's preferences. Women have been defined and have seen themselves as having principal responsibility for social production, as well as reproduction, in the household and their integration into the 'public' world of the labour market, and paid employment has been structured in this way (Purcell, 2000). Coupled with the inadequacies of state-supported child care, this has meant that employers in the UK have been able to draw on a supply of female labour available and willing to work on part-time terms and conditions. The 'reserves' of labour supply have been supplemented by the rising numbers of students seeking part-time work, to gain work experience or simply to limit their debts. There are larger numbers also of older men who are relegated to part-time work because they cannot find alternative, full-time employment or who opt for it, for example, to 'wind down' from full-time employment prior to or after retirement.

Employers' use of part-time work

In surveys of employers in the UK, the most commonly cited reason for using or creating part-time contracts is to secure greater flexibility (e.g. IDS, 2001b). In the relatively 'tight' labour market context of the late 1990s and first years of the twenty-first century, the retention of skilled staff has also been cited by many employing organisations as a rationale for offering part-time work.

Labour flexibility can be developed in a variety of shapes and forms. Gallie *et al.*'s (1998) analysis of workforce survey data suggests that part-timers are unlikely to contribute greatly to the development of functional flexibility. Many part-time workers remained 'at a severe disadvantage in skill level and skill development' opportunities compared with full-timers in their workplace (Gallie *et al.*, 1998: 159). They were less likely than full-timers to report that they had discretion, in particular to introduce changes on the job.

Some types of part-time contract may be used by employing organisations to secure numerical flexibility, defined as the ease of engaging and dismissing staff in line with workload or product market fluctuations. These would include the 'zero hours' contracts that were used in the 1990s, in particular among large supermarket chains, and under which employees are 'on call' rather than having regular (or indeed, any guaranteed) working hours. Such types of contract illustrate the blurred line, or degree of overlap, between different forms of 'non-standard' work. Zero hours contracts are part-time and temporary and, until recently at least, have generally not been regarded by employers as contracts of employment. Part-time workers in general are more likely than full-timers to be in temporary employment. Yet the majority – Purcell (2000: 120) estimates 60 per cent – are in 'permanent' or, at least, open-ended employment. The hours thresholds that were required by employees to accrue continuous employment and in this way qualify for statutory unfair dismissal protection have been abolished. And since 1999, part-time employees, like full-timers, qualify for such protection after one year's employment. Thus they are, in principle, no more insecure than their full-time colleagues, provided their *employee status* is not in doubt.

A main attraction of part-time contracts for employers is their contribution to working time flexibility, that is the ability to adjust the pattern or timing of staff hours worked over a day, or week, to meet production or sales rhythms. In retailing, as in hotels and catering, it has for long been common for employers to organise shifts of part-timers to meet peak periods of customer trading: lunchtimes, early evening, weekends and so on. The extension of such practices has been encouraged by:

- the availability of information and communications technologies that allow the managers of supermarkets, banks and hospitals, to predict customer flows more accurately;
- investments in new technology, that require intensive use of the capital equipment to 'repay' the costs;
- the deregulation of business trading hours in the 1980s and 1990s.

Large employers in retailing, and in the financial services, now compete in their respective sectors by making their products and services available through a variety of channels (telephone banking, Internet shopping, the conventional high street bank branch) and over extended trading hours. A variety of types of part-time contract has been used to support these competitive strategies and to achieve cost savings. In large retail organisations, part-time employment has become more segmented. Pay and benefits have been improved for some part-timers, who are expected in return to cooperate in the pursuit of working time flexibility, for example, by working new shift patterns or, in some instances, longer hours. Alongside these, a 'periphery' of workers on very short or irregular (zero) hours has been developed (Neathey and Hurstfield, 1995: 206).

The retail banks formerly had well-defined internal labour markets. Pay and career progression to managerial level were the prospects for many (although not all) male entrants, who were recruited from school, trained to acquire 'general banking' skills, and who often remained with the bank for their working life. Many female employees worked full time but most were confined to back-office data processing or front-office customer service roles. Branch closures and redundancies in the 1980s and 1990s, however, have put paid to the idea that banking provides a job for life and have truncated career progression routes. Data processing has been removed from branches and concentrated in establishments that specialise in the work, which has been routinised. Shifts of full-timers and part-timers (employed directly or via an agency) are used to keep the 'machinery' operating virtually around the clock. The bank branches that remain open have been tiered, that is equipped to operate as sales or service-only outlets. The staffing of these, to match customer flows over longer opening hours, has been achieved by amending full-time contracts to include, for example, Saturdays as part of the regular working week, and through the use of a variety of part-time contracts. These include term-time-only contracts (for women) and Saturday-only contracts (for students). Call centres use full-time and part-time staff (agency-recruited or directly employed). The requirement, however, is for regular attendance: term-time-only contracts sometimes are not encouraged as managers believe staff lose their work-speed if they do not practise their 'skills' regularly (Tailby and Harrington, 2002).

The need to meet employees' working hours preferences, and in this way retain skilled and experienced staff, has been cited by a number of employers in recent surveys as a reason for their use of part-time contracts (e.g. IDS, 2001b). This is consistent with the Labour government's claim that work–life balance provision – working hours practices and contractual employment forms that are sensitive to employees' preferences and desires to balance work more effectively with other interests and commitments – yields business benefits as well as employee gains. The Department of Trade and Industry (DTI, 2000) lists work–life balance provision to include, in addition to part-time work:

- *flexitime*, where people can vary the timing of their working hours, although usually outside certain agreed core times;
- *staggered hours*, where employees in a workplace have different start, finish and break times;
- *job-sharing*, where two people carry out the duties of a post that would normally be done by one person;
- *compressed working hours*, which allow people to work their total agreed number of hours over a shorter number of working days;
- *self-rostering*, which gives team members greater control over their work times;
- *annual hours*, systems that organise working time on the basis of the number of hours to be worked over a year rather than a week (usually to fit in with peaks and troughs of work);
- *working at or from home*, for some or all of the time;
- *teleworking*, using a telephone and computer to keep in touch with work;
- *temporary and casual work*;
- *self-employment*, which, as the DTI hints, may involve very long hours of work rather than providing people with greater control over their working hours.

None of these practices is entirely novel and some (in particular, the last two listed) have been often been interpreted as the most 'precarious', or insecure, of all the forms of non-standard work. Many major employers in a range of industries and sectors have embraced the work–life balance agenda and some 'exemplars' have introduced, or have extended to a wider range of staff, access to some or most of the types of provision listed above. The relatively tight labour market of the late 1990s and early 2000s has been an influence, in particular for employers in public services such as education and health where there have been recurrent 'crises' of staff shortages. A strong commitment to become or remain an equal opportunities employer, nonetheless, has been a factor for some organisations. That said, survey data suggest that across all workplaces, provision of flexible working time arrangements is quite limited; part-time work (for women) and shift work for male full-timers remain by far the most common arrangements (Hogarth et al., 2001: 14). In this context, it is relevant to note that studies have shown an upward trend in the proportion of women working full-time who would like to work shorter hours; an increase that is especially marked among women working in professional and managerial jobs. Yet they have also found evidence that 'qualified' women who have moved to a part-time or job-sharing contract after childbirth have experienced a significant downgrading of their conditions and career prospects (Wacjman, 1996, cited in Purcell, 2000).

UK employment legislation has changed since the mid-1990s. Part-time workers have acquired new statutory rights. These include the right to be paid at the statutory national minimum hourly rate, and the right to paid annual leave (introduced as part of the Working Time Regulations, 1998). The Low Pay Commission reported in 2000 that well over 1.5 million workers had benefited from the national minimum wage (NMW); that two-thirds of the beneficiaries were working women; and that two-thirds of these were part-time workers. Part-time workers in the past have been seen as offering employers a relatively cheap source of labour by virtue of their failure to qualify for shift or overtime premia and company benefits. Such discrimination is in principle ruled out by the Part-time Workers (Prevention of Less Favourable Treatment) Regulations that came into force in 2001. These introduce the principle of 'no less favourable treatment' between full-time and part-time workers. McKay (2001: 294) suggests, however, that the 'fact that it is limited to those working under the same type of contract and at the same location narrows the scope for comparison' and may limit the number of part-time workers who will benefit from the regulations.

Temporary work

Temporary employment is 'unequivocally insecure' (Purcell, 2000: 121). This is regardless of whether people choose or are relegated to it. Temporary employment encompasses a range of employment relationships, and its diversity is suggested to an extent by its multiplicity of forms. It includes workers who are engaged directly by an employer either for a fixed term, or on a casual or seasonal basis, or as on-call workers with no regular or guaranteed hours, and staff who are supplied to an employing organisation by a third party recruitment or temporary work agency. Temporary workers are located in a wide range of occupations. Many are recruited to low-grade, low-paid jobs, but there has been growth in temporary employment in the past decade among professionals, managers and technically qualified personnel (TUC, 2001).

▪ Extent and distribution of temporary employment

The LFS provides the principal source of data on the extent of temporary work and allows some assessment of trends. Its reliance on respondents' self-assessment of their employment status, however, may mean that it underestimates the extent of temporary work. Burchell et al.'s (1999) analysis, for example, shows that many workers on fixed-term appointments think they are in permanent employment and report this as their employment status in the LFS. Moreover, the LFS only questions respondents who have identified themselves as employees about the permanency, or otherwise, of their employment. It omits from this questioning the self-employed, a proportion of whom are akin to employees in respects other than the fact that they are engaged by an employing organisation on a 'contract for services' rather than a contract of employment. Burchell et al.'s (1999) analysis suggests that a significant proportion among these 'dependent self-employed' have jobs that are 'chronically insecure'.

Setting these difficulties to one side, it is clear that temporary employment in the UK has increased since the 1980s. In the second half of that decade, temporary employees accounted for a relatively stable 5 to 6 per cent of all employees in employment in the UK. Their numbers rose in the recession of the early 1990s and, according to LFS data, reached a peak of 1.8 million – or 7.8 per cent of all employees in employment – in 1997. The total and proportion have fallen slightly, to 1.7 million and 7 per cent, respectively, in 2001. The aggregate data, however, disguise some important growth trends. Fixed-term contract workers' share of the total of temporary employees rose slightly between 1992 and 1999, to 51 per cent. Seasonal and casual workers' share of the total fell slightly, to around 23 per cent. The proportion of agency temps more than doubled, from 6.6 to 15.5 per cent and has continued to rise.

LFS data show that women currently form a slim majority of all UK temporary employees, and that their share of the total has fallen from 57 per cent in 1992 to 54 per cent in 2001. Yet the gender composition of temporary employment varies with its type. Purcell (2000: 122) notes that men are more likely than women to work on fixed-term contracts, and women are more likely than men to be 'in other, generally more casual categories'.

Among all temporary workers, approximately equal proportions are in full-time and part-time work, but again there are variations by type of temporary employment. Drawing on the 1998 Temporary Employment Survey, IDS (2000: 2) reports that around 70 per cent of seasonal/casual workers are part-time, in contrast to 56 per cent of fixed-term contract workers and 36 per cent of agency workers. The TUC (2001) emphasises that young workers (under 30 years of age) and people from black and ethnic minority groups form significant proportions of the total of temporary employees: 44 per cent and 11 per cent, respectively. Approximately 50 per cent of all temporary agency workers are under 30 years old (TUC, 1999).

Among the different industry groups, the share of temporary to all employees is highest in public administration, education and health. LFS data show that in spring 1999 there were 0.5 million temps, representing 10 per cent of all employees in this public service group which had over half of the UK total of fixed-term contract workers (cited in IDS, 2000: 3). Government reforms of public sector employment have been an influence. Employers in the public sector have been obliged to operate within tight budgets, determined on an annual basis. Those in local government and health were statutorily required in the 1980s and 1990s to open to competitive tender with private sector organisations the provision of specified ancillary services, formerly performed in-house. Best Value has displaced compulsory competitive tendering since 1997 (see Chapter 14), but the pressures on public service organisations to reduce costs (or out-source activities) remain. Temporary workers represented 6.8 per cent of all employees in banking, finance and insurance in 1999 when this industry group accounted for one-third of all temporary agency workers recorded in the LFS. Distribution, hotels and restaurants had roughly one-third of all casual and seasonal workers (IDS, 2000: 2). Four per cent of manufacturing employees were temporary in 1999, but the pro-portion was higher in mechanical engineering and vehicle engineering (Gallie *et al.*, 1998: 173) which may reflect the extension of lean production regimes (*Financial Times*, 1 February 1996).

Temporary work is not the preserve of low-skilled and low-paid groups of workers and, as suggested, its growth has been recorded among professionals, managers and technically qualified employees in the past decade (TUC, 2001). Temporary workers in these occupations are likely to be engaged on fixed-term contracts, although among public service 'professionals', agency temping is increasingly common. Over half of those who are seasonal or casual workers are in craft, personal and protective services, plant and machine operative and other occupations. Over half of the temporary agency workers recorded in the 1998 Temporary Employment Survey were in clerical and secretarial positions (IDS, 2000: 2). A survey of recruitment agencies conducted for the DTI in 1999, however, found that 70 per cent of the temporary workers supplied by these labour market 'intermediaries' were men, and that one-fifth of the male total were classified occupationally as information technology, computing and telecommunications workers (Hotopp, 2000).

Temporary employment has grown across the EU as a whole since the mid-1980s. European Commission figures (cited in McKay, 2001: 291; see also European Commission, 2001) suggest that the proportion of jobs that were temporary contracts rose from 8.3 per cent in 1985 to 13.2 per cent in 2000. Some marked differences are apparent in temporary workers' share of total employment in different countries. Data relating to 1997 range from 6.3 per cent in Belgium to 13.1 per cent in France and 33.6 per cent in Spain (European Commission, 1998, cited in IDS, 2000: 15). Set in this context, the UK appears to have a relatively low incidence of temporary work (although, as will be seen, it has an above-average incidence of temporary agency workers).

Among the factors contributing to the cross-national variations are differences in national employment law. Legislation regulating dismissals and redundancies among 'permanent' employees (i.e. those on open-ended contracts) may provide, to differing degrees, an incentive for employers to create temporary jobs. Most EU countries, however, have legislation that regulates the types of tasks and work that can be constructed as temporary (and in some countries the maximum length of temporary contracts is also prescribed in law). The relatively high share of temporary employment in the Spanish economy has been attributed to the relatively strong 'job protection rights' enjoyed by 'permanent' workers and the introduction in the 1980s of legislation that extended the circumstances in which employers could use temporary contracts. Conversely, the UK's relatively low share of temporary to all employment has been attributed to the relatively weak employment protection that all workers have enjoyed under UK employment law (see, for example, Beatson, 1995).

In the past in the UK there has been no explicit legal distinction between permanent and temporary employees (IDS, 2000: 11). However, the length of continuous employment required to accrue the statutory right to claim unfair dismissal has meant that workers on short contracts have been especially insecure – that is, especially 'disposable', from an employer's point of view. Moreover, up until 1999, employers were able lawfully to require workers on fixed-term contracts to waive their statutory rights to claim unfair dismissal and financial compensation for redundancy. At the time of writing, the law has as yet to be amended to clarify the identity of the employer of temporary agency staff – the agency supplying these workers or the client organisation that uses their labour services. Some among the large agencies (e.g. Manpower) employ some temps directly, but many temporary work agencies do not – they simply act as a third party, placing workers temporarily with 'companies who have no legal employment relationship with them' (TUC, 1999: 9). As a consequence, many temporary agency staff have been unable to qualify for statutory unfair dismissal protection. The employment agency industry in the UK has been much less regulated by legislation than in most EU countries, and the Conservative government abolished the need for firms to obtain a licence to operate in it (see Exhibit 13.2 later in this chapter).

Surveys of employers' use of fixed-term and other directly employed temporary staff suggest that many have offered temporary workers the same basic pay as 'permanent' employees (and, in some instances, higher pay) and access to overtime and shift premium payments, although a significant proportion have not. Some employers have offered temps access to some of the company benefits extended to 'permanent' staff, but among these a number have insisted on a qualifying period of service. Outside the public sector, it has been rare for employers to provide temps with access to company or occupational pension schemes (TUC, 2001; see also IDS, 2000: 7). In short, it would appear that the attraction of temporary contracts for some employers has been the ability to save on pay and/or 'on-costs' as well as to secure gains in numerical flexibility. That said, it is evident that some employing organisations have been willing, or have been obliged, to offer premium rates of pay to secure the services of staff whose skills are in short supply, and who have opted to supply their labour on a temporary basis only.

Employees' preferences

Temporary work is by definition insecure and can involve working alongside 'permanent' colleagues whose terms and conditions are superior. As Gallie *et al.*'s (1998) analysis indicates, for many workers it is likely to mean limited job satisfaction and limited access to the on-the-job training that may be the prerequisite for progression to a 'permanent' appointment. Yet temporary work can offer attractions for some people. For professionals with qualifications and skills that are highly marketable, it may offer autonomy and flexibility and the opportunity to 'play the field' and bid up salaries (TUC, 2001). Students, who form a significant proportion of the temporary workforce, may fall between these two extremes. They may be forced into paid employment by virtue of spiraling debts and the pressure to accept whatever work is available. On the other hand, some may see temporary employment as a means of gaining the work experience that may enhance their subsequent marketability, or as a means of gaining a 'foothold in the door' of a company they would like to work for.

The LFS asks temporary employees about their reasons for having temporary employment. Its findings suggest that, alongside age, sex, ethnic origin, qualifications and occupation, the state of the labour market is an influence on whether workers opt for or are relegated to temporary work. In 1992, when the UK economy was barely recovering from recession, over two-fifths (43 per cent) of male temporary workers reported they were in temporary employment because they could not find a permanent job. By 2001, this proportion had fallen to less than one-third (31 per cent), whereas the proportion who reported that they did not want a permanent job had risen from one-fifth (20 per cent) to over one-quarter (26.3 per cent). Among female temporary employees, the proportion who reported they did not want a permanent job remained more stable, at around one-third, in the first half of the 1990s, although this rose in the second half of the 1990s to a peak of 37 per cent in 2000. The proportion who reported they could not find a secure job fell from a peak of above one-third (37 per cent) in 1994 to less than one-quarter (24 per cent) in 2001. The state of the labour market (the overall availability of employment opportunities) may therefore be taken as an influence on workers' preferences and opportunities. But the trends in the growth of types of temporary work have to be related also to the practices of employing organisations, the growth of the employment agency industry, and developments in UK employment law.

◼ Employers' use of temporary labour

Incomes Data Services (IDS, 2000: 4) distinguish four employers' rationales for using fixed-term and other directly engaged temporary staff. These are:

- covering for the absence of permanent employees;
- coping with fluctuations in workload (often seasonal);
- completing specific projects or specialist projects;
- minimising redundancies where changes to working practices are anticipated.

To the list could be added the objectives of minimising pay or 'on cost' labour charges. It is important to note, however, that in surveys employers often report the disadvantages of using temporary staff (see TUC, 1999, 2001; IDS, 2000). A fairly common perception is that temporary employees are less committed and less reliable than staff whose employment security is not so immediately in doubt.

Employers' use of temporary agency staff has often been analysed from a 'transaction cost' theory perspective associated with the work of Williamson (1975, 1985). The idea is that employers secure administrative cost savings by outsourcing labour recruitment and labour management to an external organisation, in particular where their demand is for relatively small numbers of workers with general (as opposed to company-specific) skills. Yet, in practice, employers have used agency supply for a broader range of reasons; in construction, for example, an objective has been to avoid statutory obligations, such as the provision of sick pay, holiday pay and redundancy pay (TUC, 1999). In addition, the delegation of labour management functions to a third party may create its own difficulties, for example in terms of assuring the quality of labour supply (see Grimshaw *et al.*, 2001).

Employers traditionally have had available a range of means of covering short-term absences among permanent staff (on holiday or on sick leave). In addition to agency supply or use of a short contract, these means include asking permanent staff to work overtime. NHS hospitals have always had to resource a 24-hour, 365 day a year demand for medical and nursing services and many have used a 'bank' of nursing staff who are on call to fill in for staff absences or to meet workload peaks. 'Bank' nurses include not only those who work only on a casual basis, but also those who have a regular, full-time or part-time NHS job and undertake bank nursing as a second job. Until recently, many hospitals treated casual bank staff as akin to staff on zero hours contracts; they were not regarded as employees and were not given access to sick pay, holiday pay, the occupational pension scheme, etc. In short, their use offered the advantages of cheapness and flexibility.

Employers in some industry sectors have traditionally organised staffing to meet seasonal peaks and troughs in the workload; for example, via summer shutdowns in manufacturing plants, or the recruitment of casual and seasonal workers in hotels and catering. Employers in some sectors have become more attentive to the seasonality of trade and to the means of matching staff numbers and expertise to these rhythms. Retail banks, for example, now draw on their (student) supplies of Saturday-only staff to meet the Christmas peak in customer sales-flows in their branch networks.

Since seasonal peaks in workload are regular and recurrent, their staffing can be planned. Similarly, some retail banks use temporary agency workers to meet planned, temporary increases in the volume of customer enquiries generated by the launch of a new product (for example, a new mortgage repayment scheme). Most use agencies as a means of securing sufficient supplies of labour to meet staff turnover in their data processing centres, where the work is routinised, and some of the banks use agencies as a means of 'screening' recruitment to open-ended employment in their call centres. Staff are recruited by an agency and retained as agency staff for a period of weeks before being offered a 'permanent' appointment (or not). Practices vary among the banks, however, and agency recruitment to call centres and branch networks is eschewed by some on the grounds that it is expensive (agencies charge a commission for their services) and does not guarantee the calibre of staff to meet the quality or speed of customer service required. Thus in the 1990s, when banks were downsizing their branch networks, they tended to use fixed-term contract staff rather than temporary agency workers or, indeed, open-ended contracts, to fill vacant positions.

Much attention has been given to the increased use of temporary agency nursing staff in NHS hospitals since the late 1990s. Hospital managers have had to meet rising levels of patient demand for their services, and the more exacting performance targets instituted by government (e.g. to reduce the length of time patients have to wait for treatment). At the same time, they have experienced difficulties in recruiting and retaining staff on regular, open-ended contracts. This reflects an accumulation of staff grievances regarding workloads, pay and the inflexibility of working hours. Bank nursing supplies have proved insufficient to meet the staffing shortages on the wards, and hospital managers have been obliged to rely increasingly on agency supply. Indeed, some temporary work agencies have been adept in recruiting NHS nurses who want additional shifts, and now secure these through an agency rather than through the NHS hospital bank. Able to command high commissions for their services, these agencies have been able to offer nurses regular (additional) work at relatively attractive hourly pay rates, and with some choice as regards their preferred working hours.

■ New rights for temporary staff

The framework of UK employment law has changed since the late 1990s. Temporary workers have made gains, although the law continues to allow discrimination against them in a range of respects. The Employment Relations Act 1999 circumscribed employers' right to oblige fixed-term contract staff to waive their statutory entitlement to unfair dismissal protection, although waiver clauses in respect of redundancy payments are still lawful. The length of service required for unfair dismissal protection has been reduced to a year, rather than abolished, and the requirement of 'employee' status remains. Therefore many workers on short contracts will continue to find it difficult to qualify for this statutory right, as will many of the 'dependent self-employed' and agency staff who are not employed by the agency through which they secure work. All workers are covered by the National Minimum Wage Act 1998 and by the provisions of the Working Time Regulations 1998. The latter initially restricted the right to paid annual leave to workers who had been employed continuously by the same employer for at least 13 weeks. The TUC challenged that this did not fulfil the UK's obligations under the EU Working Time Directive, and the length of service qualification – which discriminated against short-contract and freelance workers – has been abolished. IDS (2000) reports that the legal obligation to pay holiday leave has encouraged some employers to convert temporary jobs into 'permanent' appointments (i.e. because it has restricted the cost-cutting advantage of the former). 'Poor' employers, nevertheless, may find other ways of accommodating the legislation, and the TUC (1999:12) notes that some temporary work agencies have implemented holiday rights by 'leaving take home pay unchanged, but reducing basic pay and adding a notional holiday pay element to the wage packet'.

The European Commission has seen non-standard employment as a means of meeting employers' requirement for greater flexibility and of increasing labour market participation among 'disadvantaged' groups. At the same time, commissioners have acknowledged that labour market deregulation risks fuelling the growth of 'poor quality' jobs that do not contribute to productivity improvements (see, for example, European Commission, 2001). European trade unions have campaigned for higher 'labour standards' – better pay and conditions and stronger employment rights for workers – against European employers' appeals for further labour market deregulation. Some compromises have been reached. The Fixed-term Directive, adopted in June 1999, puts into effect the framework agreement on fixed-term work concluded earlier in that year by the European Trade Union Confederation and the European-level employers' organisations UNICE and CEEP. The directive aims to:

- prevent fixed-term employees from being less favourably treated than similar permanent employees;
- prevent abuses arising from the use of successive fixed-term contracts;
- improve access to training for fixed-term employees;
- ensure fixed-term employees are informed about available permanent jobs.

Member states were required to comply with its provisions by July 2001, but the UK government has made use of the additional year allowed for consultation 'to take account of special difficulties'.

At the beginning of 2002, details were 'leaked' of a draft EU directive that proposes to give temporary agency workers rights to the same remuneration as long-term employees doing comparable jobs. The proposals would cover pay, pensions, holiday and other benefits such as health insurance, interest-free loans, non-discretionary bonuses and share schemes (*Financial Times*, 17 February 2002). Among EU member states, the UK has one of the highest levels of use of temporary agency workers, and agency workers in this country have had fewer rights, *vis-à-vis* 'permanent' staff, than their counterparts elsewhere in Europe. In other words, they stand to gain most from the proposed directive. Whether it will be translated into EU legislation, however, remains to be seen. In the UK, employers' organisations and representatives of the major employment agencies have articulated their strong disapproval, claiming that, if passed, the proposed directive 'could damage the labour market irreparably' (see Exhibit 13.2).

Chapter summary

Labour flexibility has been a central theme in public policy and in academic debates since the 1980s. The concept has been applied in prescriptions for change in the organisation and management of work, the construction of working time patterns, and the regulation of pay and employment. This chapter has explored different dimensions of the 1980s 'flexibility debates' and some of the issues in the restructuring of work and employment that continue to be discussed in the terms established by those debates.

Exhibit 13.2

Fears over flexibility if temps get greater rights

The growing army of 'temps' in the workforce means that a draft Brussels directive giving agency workers greater rights would particularly affect employers in Britain.

As more temps are employed in the UK than in any other European country, the directive could be the most contentious European Union employment reform yet for the government to adopt.

And because Britain accounts for half the European total of agency workers, it could be hard for opponents of the proposals – and worried ministers – to win allies among other member states.

Employers are already arguing that the directive could damage the labour market irreparably.

James Reed, chief executive of Reed, one of the country's biggest recruitment agencies, said the directive was unworkable.

'It is bad news for the economy and for individuals, particularly the disadvantaged. Flexible labour has been a huge asset keeping unemployment at the lowest level in Europe', he said.

Behind Brussels' thinking is a recognition, welcomed by the trade unions, that the secretaries, clerical workers, computing staff, engineers, teachers and nurses employed by agencies do not enjoy the same rights as permanent colleagues.

With agency 'temping' growing fast, employers are able to tap a skilled and flexible labour resource, often at less cost than hiring staff themselves.

The problem is that agency workers can easily be exploited. Sarah Veale, of the Trades Union Congress, said: 'At call centres, it's not uncommon for people to have their contracts terminated and to be re-employed as agency workers on less pay and with fewer rights.'

To discourage substitution and abuse, Brussels wants agency workers to have the same remuneration as longer-term counterparts.

Employers have lobbied the European Commission to get the wording changed. Several commissioners are understood to have voiced concern about the draft and its publication is to be delayed, perhaps until after next month's EU summit in Barcelona.

Ministers are anxious about the directive's impact. Last year, the government reluctantly agreed to include pay and pensions when it implemented legislation giving fixed-term workers equal rights. In part, that decision was to emphasise that remuneration is an area of national discretion.

This time ministers could adopt a similar stance and try to resist including remuneration if the directive demands it.

Some member states, including Spain, France and Italy, already have stringent national legislation restricting the use of agency labour. In Germany and the Netherlands agencies have to reach agreements at a national level with trade unions. In Britain, most workers are not covered by collective agreements of this kind.

The Confederation of British Industry's case is that the directive is incompatible with UK practices and would damage competitiveness. The employers' organisation argues that a temp's relationship is with the agency, so comparisons with long-term staff are inappropriate. Agency work, it adds, is often a route into employment for young people and the long-term unemployed. Temping helps companies fill skills gaps and respond quickly to fluctuating demand.

But the TUC says legislation is needed because the rights of agency temps are weak. They cannot claim unfair dismissal and do not qualify for statutory redundancy. They are unlikely to be allowed to join the company pension scheme.

Requirements for employment agencies to be licensed disappeared under the previous Tory government.

'It is not a picture of non-stop abuse, but there are difficulties with agencies that spring up overnight', said Ms Veale. 'Unless you're caught not paying the minimum wage, you can get away with a lot.'

Source: Christopher Adams, *Financial Times*, 18 February 2002.
© 1995–2002 The Financial Times Limited

The 'flexible specialisation' thesis envisaged that firms and employees would secure mutual gains from the use of new information and communication technologies and 'flexible' forms of work organisation in the manufacture of quality goods for high value-added niche product markets. Government ministers in the UK in the 1980s mirrored their counterparts in the US by urging that industry competitiveness and the invigoration of employment growth required the deregulation of markets – the exposure of firms and, more especially, workers to the discipline of 'free market forces'. The flexible firm model attracted a good deal of academic and practitioner interest. It suggested that employers could use a numerically flexible peripheral workforce to underwrite the employment security of a core employee group whose commitment, flexibility and versatility could be tapped to secure productivity and quality gains.

The model's broad and bipolar categories of core and periphery, comprising skilled and secure full-time workers and those on insecure non-standard contracts respectively, proved overly rigid for the purposes of understanding the range of ways that employers could attain cost savings, productivity increases and other 'flexibility' gains. Ackroyd and Procter's (1998) study of the 'new flexible firm', for example, showed that large British-owned firms, operating in the manufacturing sector in the UK, had been able to cut costs by developing functional flexibility among relatively unskilled workers employed on a full-time basis. The employment security of these workers was threatened constantly by their employer's preparedness to outsource supplies if this contributed further labour cost savings.

It was evident by the early 1990s that certain forms of non-standard employment had become more common in the UK economy as a whole. Part-time work and self-employment increased in relative terms in the 1980s, and in the 1990s there was some growth in temporary employment and a marked increase in temporary agency work. There was clear evidence of the 'diffusion' of new forms of work organisation, although lean production regimes and a number of versions of teamworking were shown to reinforce rather than to depart from Taylorist principles. Yet core employment, if taken to mean relatively secure employment, was not greatly in evidence. Manufacturing and service sector employers met the recession of the early 1990s by downsizing. Journalists and academics drew on anecdotal and survey evidence to report a pervasive sense of job insecurity among most employee groups, including managers and professionals. The increased incidence of work related stress was reported widely in the mid-1990s and, in relation to this, studies highlighted the UK's long-hours work culture.

Statistics showed that average full-time working hours were longer in the UK than in any other EU country. Yet Green's (2001) careful analysis suggests that the principal trend of the 1980s and 1990s was an increasingly uneven distribution of working hours, as between individuals and households. On the eve of the introduction of the Working Time Regulations in 1998, a higher proportion of the workforce was working long hours (in excess of 48 hours a week) in comparison with the position in the late 1970s, and a higher proportion was working short hours (fewer than 20 hours a week). There was an increased polarisation between work-rich and work-less households. In comparison with the late 1970s there were more dual-income households in which the male and female 'heads' each worked full-time. There were also more households in which no one of working age had paid employment.

Since 1997, government labour market policy in the UK has complemented rather than confronted directly that pursued at the level of the European Union, although this is partly because flexibility has become a stronger theme in the latter. The Labour government reiterated its Conservative predecessor's emphasis on the need for 'flexibility and efficiency' in the labour market but elevated 'fairness at work' as a policy goal. It retained much of the 1980s industrial relations legislation although it also enacted new collective employment rights, on the understanding that the trade unions will moderate their objectives and seek a 'partnership' relationship with company managers to secure flexibility and efficiency gains. The government delivered its commitment to enact certain minimum labour standards and has urged employers to attend to employees' aspirations for a better work–life balance. Yet various studies questioned the impact of the Working Time Regulations, which allow employers to secure individual and collective employee opt-outs from the 48-hour maximum working week provisions. And while relatively tight labour market conditions in the five years to 2002 encouraged many employers to extend employees' access to 'flexible' working hours, across all work-places it was part-time work (for women) and shift work (among males in full-time work) that remained the most common non-standard working time patterns.

EU directives that aim to reduce discrimination against workers on non-standard contracts have been proposed and some have been enacted. It remains to be seen how the new legal obligations will influence UK employers' use of the various types of non-standard work. It is evident, however, that the UK's implementation of EU legislation will continue to be shaped by the competing claims of employers and trade unions – for the freedom to use 'flexible' contracts and the obligation not to abuse the labour of workers engaged on them.

Questions

1 Why has the concept of flexibility dominated discussion of work and employment restructuring in the advanced economies in the past two decades?

2 What is meant by the concepts of numerical flexibility, functional flexibility and working time flexibility?

3 Why do researchers analyse teamwork with reference to the 'Swedish model' and the 'Japanese model' of team-based work organisation ?

4 What factors have contributed to the growth of part-time employment in the UK since the 1980s?

5 What types of flexibility do employers seek or attain through the use of part-time contracts?

6 In what respects does temporary work form a heterogeneous employment category?

7 What is meant by 'work–life balance'? How might part-time work assist or undermine your efforts to attain such equilibrium?

Activity

Study the section on temporary work, and Exhibit 13.2 in particular. Imagine you are (a) a senior civil servant in the Department of Trade and Industry in the UK, (b) a trade union official, (c) an employer, (d) a senior manager of a large temporary work agency, and (e) an agency temp. Sketch your response – in each role – to the proposed EU directive on temporary agency workers.

Useful websites

www.dfes.gov.uk **Department for Education and Skills** Focuses on skills, training, productivity issues and government labour market policy.

www.dti.gov.uk/er **Department of Trade and Industry** Covers the work of the Employment Relations Directorate of the DTI, dealing with relations between workers and their employers, including individual and collective rights. Access for details of employment legislation (1998 Working Time Regulations, 1998 National Minimum Wage Act, etc.), research monitoring the impact of the legislation, consultation documents issued prior to the introduction of regulations, etc.

www.eiro.eurofound.ie **European Industrial Relations Observatory On-Line** Website of the European Foundation for the Improvement of Living and Working Conditions. For all 15 European Union member states there are three or four articles each month, as well as some comparative studies. Comprehensive coverage of new UK employment legislation and articles on the conflicting perspectives of the TUC and CBI on regulation and flexibility.

www.eoc.org.uk **Equal Opportunities Commission** The EOC is the leading agency working to eliminate sex discrimination in Britain. Apart from news, press releases, etc. there is extensive coverage of policy developments and campaigns, research and statistics, and aspects of the law.

www.lowpay.gov.uk **Low Pay Commission** Access to reports and publications of the UK Low Pay Commission established by the National Minimum Wage Act 1998 to advise the government about the National Minimum Wage.

www.tuc.org.uk **Trades Union Congress** The TUC's campaign sites focus on working hours, temporary workers, etc. Employment research section includes quarterly labour market briefings.

References

Ackroyd, S. and Procter, S. (1998) 'British manufacturing organization and workplace industrial relations: some attributes of the new flexible firm', *British Journal of Industrial Relations*, 36(2): 163–84.

Amin, A. (1994) 'Post-Fordism: models, fantasies and phantoms of transition' in Amin, A. (ed.) *Post-Fordism: A Reader*. Oxford: Blackwell: 1–39.

Atkinson, J. (1984) 'Manpower strategies for flexible organisations', *Personnel Management*, August: 28–31.

Atkinson, J. (1985) 'Flexibility: planning for the uncertain future', *Manpower Policy and Practice*, 1: 26–9.

Atkinson, J. and Gregory, D. (1986) 'A flexible future: Britain's dual labour market', *Marxism Today*, 30(4): 12–17.

Bacon, N. and Blyton, P. (2000) 'High road and low road teamworking: perceptions of management rationales and organizational and human resource outcomes', *Human Relations*, 53(11): 1425–58.

Beatson, M. (1995) *Labour Market Flexibility*, Employment Department Research Series No. 48. London: Department of Employment.

Bruegel, I. and Perrons, D. (1998) 'Deregulation and women's employment: the diverse experiences of women in Britain', *Feminist Economics*, 4(1): 103–25.

Burchell, B., Deakin, S. and Honey, S. (1999) *The Employment Status of Individuals in Non-standard Employment*, Employment Relations Research Series No. 6. London: Department of Trade and Industry.

Claydon, T. (1997) 'Human resource management and the labour market', in Beardwell, I. and Holden, L. (eds) *Human Resource Management: A Contemporary Perspective*. London: Financial Times/Pitman Publishing: 73–117.

Claydon, T. (1998) 'Problematising partnership: the prospects for a co-operative bargaining agenda' in Sparrow, P. and Marchington, M. (eds) *Human Resource Management: The New Agenda*. London: Financial Times/Pitman Publishing.

Crafts, N. (1991) 'Reversing relative economic decline? The 1980s in historical perspective', *Oxford Review of Economic Policy*, 7(3): 81–98.

Cully, M., Woodland, S., O'Reilly, A. and Dix, G. (1999) *Britain At Work, As Depicted by the 1998 Workplace Employee Relations Survey*. London: Routledge.

Danford, A. (1998) 'Teamworking and labour regulation in the autocomponents industry', *Work, Employment and Society*, 12(3): 409–31.

Delbridge, R. (1998) *Life on the Line in Contemporary Manufacturing*. Oxford: Oxford University Press.

Delbridge, R., Lowe, J. and Oliver, N. (2000) 'Shopfloor responsibilities under lead teamworking', *Human Relations*, 53(11): 1459–80.

Dohse, K., Jurgens, U. and Malsch, T. (1985) 'From "Fordism" to "Toyotism"? The social organization of the labor process in the Japanese automobile industry', *Politics and Society*, 14(2): 115–46.

DTI (Department of Trade and Industry) (1998) *Fairness at Work*, Cm. 3968. London: The Stationery Office.

DTI (2000) *Essential Guide to Work–Life Balance*. www.dti.gov.uk/work-lifebalance

Edwards, P. and Wright, M. (1996) 'Does teamworking work and if so, why?', paper presented at ESRC seminar, the Manchester Series, 'Human Resource Management in Crisis?' Manchester Metropolitan University, 27 September.

European Commission (2000) *Employment in Europe 2000*. Brussels, European Commission, October.

European Commission (2001) *Employment in Europe 2001, Recent Trends and Prospects*. Luxembourg: Office for Official Publications of the European Commission.

Felstead, A. and Jewson, N. (1999) 'Flexible labour and non-standard employment: an agenda of issues' in Felstead, A. and Jewson, N. (eds) *Global Trends in Flexible Labour*. Basingstoke: Macmillan: 1–20.

Gallie, D., White, M., Cheng, Y. and Tomlinson, M. (1998) *Restructuring the Employment Relationship*. Oxford: Clarendon Press.

Gamble, A. (2001) 'Neo-liberalism', *Capital and Class*, 75 (special issue), Autumn: 127–34.

Garrahan, P. and Stewart, P. (1992) *The Nissan Enigma – Flexibility at Work in a Local Economy*. London: Mansell.

Geary, J. (1992) 'Employment flexibility and human resource management: the case of three American electronics plants', *Work, Employment and Society*, 6(2): 251–70.

Giddens, A. (1998) *The Third Way*. Cambridge: Polity Press.

Godard, J. (2001) 'Beyond the high-performance paradigm? An analysis of variation in Canadian managerial perceptions of reform programme effectiveness', *British Journal of Industrial Relations*, 39(1): 25–52.

Green, F. (2001) 'It's been a hard day's night: the concentration and intensification of work in late twentieth century Britain', *British Journal of Industrial Relations*, 39(1): 53–80.

Grimshaw, D., Ward, K.G., Rubery, J. and Beynon, H. (2001) 'Organisations and the transformation of the internal labour market', *Work, Employment and Society*, 15(1): 25–54.

Hakim, C. (1996) *Key Issues in Women's Work: Female Heterogeneity and the Polarisation of Women's Employment*. London: Athlone Press.

Harkness, S. (1998) 'The gender earnings gap: evidence from the UK', *Fiscal Studies*, 17(2): 1–36.

Heery, E. and Salmon, J. (2000) 'The insecurity thesis' in Heery, E. and Salmon, J. (eds) *The Insecure Workforce*. London: Routledge: 1–24.

Hegewisch, A. (1996) 'Part-time working in Europe', *Flexible Working*, May: 14–16.

Hirst, P. and Zeitlin, J. 1989. 'Flexible specialisation and the competitive failure of UK manufacturing', *Political Quarterly*, 60(2): 164–78.

Hogarth, T., Hasluck, C. and Pierre, G. with Winterbotham, M. and Vivian, D. (2001) *Work–Life Balance 2000: Baseline Study of Work–Life Balance Practices in Great Britain*, Summary Report. University of Warwick: Institute for Employment Research and Iff Research.

Hotopp, U. (2000) 'Recruitment agencies in the UK', *Labour Market Trends*, October: 457–63.

Hunter, L., McGregor, A., MacInnes, J. and Sproul, A. (1993) 'The 'flexible firm': strategy and segmentation', *British Journal of Industrial Relations*, 31(3): 383–409.

Huselid, M.A. (1995) 'The impact of human resource management practices on turnover, productivity, and corporate financial performance', *Academy of Management Journal*, 38: 635–72.

Hyman, R. (1988) 'Flexible specialisation: miracle or myth?' in Hyman, R. and Streeck, W. (eds) *New Technology and Industrial Relations*. Oxford: Basil Blackwell.

Hyman, R. (1991). '*Plus ça change?* The theory of production and the production of theory' in Pollert, A. (ed.) *Farewell to Flexibility?* Oxford: Blackwell Business: 261–83.

IDS (2000) *Temporary workers*. IDS Studies Personnel Policy and Practice, 689 (May).

IDS (2001a) *Teamworking*. IDS Studies Personnel policy and practice. December.

IDS (2001b) *Part-time Workers*. IDS Studies Personnel Policy and Practice, 715 (September).

Kalleberg, A. (2001). 'Organizing flexibility: the flexible firm in a new century', *British Journal of Industrial Relations*, 39(4): 479–504.

Kern, H. and Schumann, M. (1989) *Das Ende der Arbeitsteilung?* Munich: Beck.

Knell, J. (1999) *Partnership at Work*, Employment Relations Research Series No. 7. London: Department of Trade and Industry.

McKay, S. (2001). 'Annual review article. Between flexibility and regulation: rights, equality and protection at work', *British Journal of Industrial Relations*, 39(2): 285–304.

McKinsey Global Institute (1998). *Driving Productivity and Growth in the UK Economy*. London: McKinsey.

McIlroy, J. (1998) 'The enduring alliance? Trade unions and the making of new Labour, 1994–1997', *British Journal of Industrial Relations*, 36(4): 537–64.

Metcalf, D. (1989) 'Water notes dry up: the impact of the Donovan proposals and Thatcherism at work on labour productivity in British manufacturing industry', *British Journal of Industrial Relations*, 27(1): 1–31.

Mueller, F., Procter, S. and Buchanan, D. (2000) 'Teamworking in its context(s): antecedents, nature and dimensions', *Human Relations*, 53(11): 1387–424.

Neathey, F. and Hurstfield, J. (1995) *Flexibility in Practice: Women's Employment and Pay in Retail and Finance*, Equal Opportunities Research Discussion Series No. 16. London: Industrial Relations Services.

Nolan, P. (1996) 'Industrial relations and performance since 1945' in Beardwell, I. (ed.) *Contemporary Industrial Relations, A Critical Analysis*. Oxford: Oxford University Press: 99–120.

Piore, M. and Sabel, C. (1984) *The Second Industrial Divide: Possibilities for Prosperity*. New York: Basic Books.

Pollert, A. (1987) 'The "flexible firm": a model in search of reality (or a policy in search of a practice)?', Warwick Papers in Industrial Relations No. 19, Industrial Relations Research Unit, University of Warwick.

Pollert, A. (1991) 'Introduction' in Pollert, A. (ed.) *Farewell to Flexibility?* Oxford: Blackwell Business: xvii–xxxv.

Procter, S.J., Rowlinson, M., McArdle, L., Hassard, J. and Forrester, P. (1994) 'Flexibility, politics and strategy: in defence of the model of the flexible firm', *Work, Employment and Society*, 8(2): 221–42.

Purcell, K. (2000) 'Gendered employment insecurity?' in Heery, E. and Salmon, J. (eds) *The Insecure Workforce*. London: Routledge: 112–39.

Ramsay, H., Scholarios, D. and Harley, B. (2000) 'Employees and high-performance work systems: testing inside the black box', *British Journal of Industrial Relations*, 38(4): 501–32.

Rubery, J. and Fagan, C. (1995) 'Does feminization mean a flexible labour force?' in Hyman, R. and Ferner, A. (eds) *New Frontiers in European Industrial Relations*. Oxford: Basil Blackwell: 140–66.

Sabel, C. (1982) *Work and Politics*. Cambridge: Cambridge University Press.

Sabel, C. and Zeitlin, J. (1985) 'Historical alternatives to mass production: politics, markets and technology in nineteenth century industrialisation', *Past and Present*, 108: 133–76.

Sayer, A. (1986) 'New developments in manufacturing: the just-in-time system', *Capital and Class*, 30: 43–72.

Sly, F., Thair, T. and Risdon, A. (1998) Women in the labour market: results from the spring 1997 Labour Force Survey', *Labour Market Trends*, March.

Steijn, B. (2001) 'Work systems, quality of working life and attitudes of workers: an empirical study towards the effects of team and non-teamwork', *New Technology, Work and Employment*, 16(3): 191–203.

Storey, J., Wilkinson, A., Cressey, P. and Morris, T. (1999) 'Employment relations in UK banking' in Regini, M., Kitay, J. and Baethge, M. (eds) *From Tellers to Sellers*. London: MIT Press: 129–58.

Tailby, S. and Harrington, J. (2002) 'Contingent employment in retail banking', New Understanding of European Work Organisation case study research report (forthcoming).

Tomaney, J. (1994) 'A new paradigm of work organisation and technology?' in Amin, A. (ed.) *Post-Fordism, A Reader*. Oxford: Blackwell: 157–94.

TUC (1999) *Temporary Workers, Permanent Rights*. London: TUC.

TUC (2001) *Permanent Rights for Temporary Workers*. London: TUC.

Undy, R. (1999). 'Annual review article. New Labour's "industrial relations settlement": the third way?', *British Journal of Industrial Relations*, 37(2): 315–36.

Wickens, P. (1993) 'Lean production and beyond: the system, its critics and the future', *Human Resource Management Journal*, 3(4): 75–90.

Williams, K., Cutler, T., Williams, J. and Haslam, C. (1987) 'The end of mass production?', *Economy and Society*, 21(3): 321–54.

Williamson, O. (1975) *Markets and Hierarchies: Analysis and Anti-trust Implications*. New York: Free Press.

Williamson, O. (1985) *The Economic Institutions of Capitalism*. New York: Free Press.

Womack, J., Jones, D. and Roos, D. (1990) *The Machine that Changed the World*. New York: Rawson Associates.

Wood, S. (1989) 'The transformation of work?' in Wood, S. (ed.) *The Transformation of Work? Skill, Flexibility and the Labour Process*. London: Routledge: 1–43.

Wood, S. (1999) 'Getting the measure of the transformed high-performance organization', *British Journal of Industrial Relations*, 37(3): 391–418.

Chapter 14

Public sector employment

Martin Upchurch

Learning objectives

By the end of this chapter, readers should be able to:

- discuss the origins and current composition of public sector employment;
- consider the special features of public sector employee relations and, in relation to this, discuss the concept of model employer;
- examine recent developments and contemporary issues in public sector employee relations, in particular the attempted transition from an industrial relations to an HRM context.

Introduction

Employee relations in the public sector have experienced a major transformation since the 1970s. The reasons for this change are located in a reversal of the state's approach to the public sector, in terms of both the scope and scale of its activity and the relationship it has with the public as a 'provider' of public services. Ideological commitment to market forces combined with a concentration on supply-side economic forces has meant that public spending is no longer been seen by governments as a panacea for economic ills during downward swings of the business cycle. The role of the public sector as a vehicle for boosting demand has been replaced by notions that 'excessive' public spending is harmful to the national economy. Indeed, the Conservative government in the 1980s and into the 1990s was not alone among advanced industrial countries in being openly distrustful of the public sector, and often sought to 'scapegoat' public spending as the cause of economic demise (Ferner, 1994). The consequences for employee relations have been severe, involving restrictions on the growth of the wage bill, a cutback in levels of staffing in the drive for efficiency, and the introduction of new management initiatives designed to reflect financial accountability within a market environment. Two results of this 'wind of change' have been a thorough overhaul of much of the organisational culture and structure of the public services and an increase in industrial disputes, both in absolute terms and in relation to the traditionally more strike-prone private manufacturing sector. The return of Labour to government in 1997 made little difference to this approach, with inherited spending limits being adhered to in the first years of the government's first term. Policies to inject private finance into the public sector are now part of government objectives through various Private Finance Initiatives (PFIs)[1] and public private partnerships (PPPs).

While the size of the public sector as an employer has been reduced with privatisation and contracting out, it nevertheless still employs one-fifth of the UK workforce in total, and so an understanding of developments remains important in its own right. The total employed in public administration and defence, education, and health and social work totalled just under 6 million in 2001. Those directly employed by the state, as Crown civil servants, equalled some 501,000 in 2000. The NHS has more than 1 million employees and is the largest employer in Europe; local government is the largest sector with approximately 2.5 million employees, mainly concentrated in education, social services and the police and fire services. The remaining nationalised industries or public corporations such as the Post Office and Bank of England have less direct control from central government but nevertheless are subject to Parliamentary accountability and restrictions on trading. Total employment in this sector is just over half a million. Finally, 113,000 people work in over 1,000 public bodies or 'quangos' (quasi-autonomous government organisations) which carry out functions at an 'arm's length' to government, but which have some government financial support. Examples of these include the Arts Council and the Health and Safety Commission and Executive.

This chapter begins with an overview of the development of the public sector prior to the onset of change in the mid to late 1970s. The structure of employment within the sector is then described before analysing why change occurred in the 1980s and 1990s. New management initiatives are then outlined as well as the mechanisms for establishing the difficult question of public service pay. A profile of public sector trade unionism is then given together with some analysis of disputes and strikes. Finally, the chapter seeks to address the approach of the Labour government and the agendas for further change in this century.

From 'model employer' to 'winter of discontent'

From the end of the First World War in 1918 through the development of the post-1945 welfare state, successive governments adopted a 'model employer' approach to the public service (Fredman and Morris, 1989). In practice this meant that the government, as employer, should set some example to the private sector in terms of fair treatment of employees and recognition of representation rights in collective bargaining. Fair treatment meant not only the benefits of pay and conditions but also high levels of job security, good (non-contributory and index-linked) pensions and generous sick pay schemes. 'Fair' pay was achieved by the establishment of an elaborate set of 'comparability' mechanisms that sought to assess the skills of public servants with the nearest equivalents in the private sector and to set the resultant pay level in the 'average-to-good' range of the private comparators.[2] The role of trade unions as bargaining partners was also thoroughly institutionalised by the establishment of pay review bodies[3] and councils such as the National Whitley Council for the civil service or the Burnham Committee for teachers, which allowed for formal consultation and negotiation on pay and conditions. Such a recognition of the role of trade unions came as a result of the perceived need to contain and control the growing trade union movement in the immediate aftermath of war. J.H. Whitley, deputy speaker of the House of Commons, had produced his committee report in March 1917, which recommended the establishment of joint councils between employers and employees 'to give opportunities for satisfying the growing demands made by trade unions for a share in industrial control' (quoted in Wigham, 1980). Most public sector unions were naturally quick to campaign for the introduction of the 'Whitley Councils' into the public service. Rules and procedures were also subject to joint consultation and implemented through code books, which allowed for national standards to be maintained (for example, the Pay and Conditions of Service code for the civil service included over 11,500 paragraphs of regulations, from major pay scales down to the comparative obscurity of 'daily pedal cycle allowances'). In cases of dispute, an elaborate procedure of appeals and arbitration was constructed that allowed full trade union representation and staged involvement during the appeal process.

Other reasons for the establishment of this model employer approach were as follows.

First, there was recognition in the inter-war period that a modern industrialised society was becoming more complex and complicated to administer and hence a professional civil and public service was needed as a result. To recruit and retain good staff it was therefore necessary to ensure that pay levels and other conditions of service were 'fair' and comparable with the private sector.

Secondly, the achievement of this comparability and the associated development of an effective internal labour market for professionals within the public service were in themselves difficult to accomplish. Sophisticated machinery (the pay review bodies) were therefore needed to overcome this problem.

Thirdly, it was important to 'legitimise' the process of the establishment of fairness and comparability by the involvement of trade unions within the institutional structures as representatives of staff. Thus, the formalised involvement of trade unions, including the positive official encouragement to all staff to join the appropriate and recognised union, helped the senior management of the public service in the task of maintaining a sense of fairness as well as easing the considerable administrative burden of assessing hundreds of separate pay scales over a huge range of crafts and occupations. To help ease the burden further, the process of comparability was best served by the establishment of strict incremental progress through the pay scales, which recognised seniority of service and could be applied easily if the employee moved jobs within the service or moved to another part of the country.

The concept and practice of model employer thus created a bureaucratic and centralised machinery in which employee relations were conducted, and which gave some concession and advantage to public sector unions and their members. The associated rules and regulations governing the employment relationship consolidated the growing hierarchical organisation structure of large ministries and government agencies bound by statute in their tasks and functions.

Keynesianism and the birth of the welfare state

The concept of the model employer continued through and after the Second World War. The public sector became more important in the atmosphere of post-war reconciliation and reconstruction for two reasons.

First, the fear of a return to the depression years of the 1920s and 1930s had created political space for the adoption of John Maynard Keynes's theories of demand management of the economy. In 1944, the government had published a White Paper arguing the necessity for policies likely to produce 'high and stable levels of employment' in the post-war period, and by the end of the war Keynesian economics had been accepted as orthodoxy by the Treasury. From the 1950s through to the mid-1970s, both Conservative and Labour governments then sought to maintain full employment by a variety of fiscal and monetary measures that ensured a major role for the public sector in boosting domestic demand to avoid recession.

Secondly, the value of public spending as a counter to recession was boosted by the perceived political need to both reconstruct British industry and society and head off social discontent with the creation of a post-war welfare state. The wartime coalition government had produced the Beveridge Plan in 1942, which emerged as a 'new declaration of human rights brought up to date for an industrial society and dealing in plain and vigorous language with some of the most controversial issues in British politics'. After this post-war 'political settlement' the 1945–50 Labour government proceeded to bring in the enabling legislation creating the pillars of the welfare state, together with legislation to nationalise certain industries in an effort to rationalise and modernise. The central aspects of legislation and their practical outcomes can be summarised as follows.

The National Insurance Act 1946 and the National Health Service Act 1946 laid down the principles of universality, which gave equal right of access to a developing range of social benefits and free medical treatment. Such 'rights' as sickness and unemployment benefit were made available to those who had paid their share of National Insurance contributions and were available for a limited period only. The NHS legislation would, of course, mean the building of new hospitals as well as the expansion of general practitioners' workload. The Housing Acts 1946 and 1949 released local authorities from the obligation that they should build accommodation only for the 'working class', but in reality allowed councils to raise money and begin a process of building housing for the masses, first as post-war prefabricated bungalows to house the homeless and later as mass council estates on compulsorily purchased land. The Education Act 1944 formed a fourth pillar of the welfare state and granted free secondary education for all up to the age of 15. The combined effect of the legislation was to massively boost the role and scope of the public sector within the economy, leading to the creation of hundreds of thousands of jobs which included, in particular, new and expanding opportunities for female employment in the so-called caring occupations, such as nursing and teaching. Another important consequence of this post-war expansion was the creation of large numbers of new jobs in lower-paid areas that serviced the public functions of the welfare state (cleaners, porters, junior clerks, etc.). An expanding economy meant that labour shortages were a problem, and so it was necessary to draw not only more women into employment, either as full- or part-time workers, but also, in the 1950s and 1960s, to recruit immigrant labour from the Caribbean and Indian sub-continent. Special recruitment drives took place in the West Indies, for example, to fill new and vacant posts in areas such as public transport and nursing. By 1980, 2.3 million people were employed by central government and just over 3 million by local authorities.

The profile of those employed within the public sector also changed dramatically as a result of the post-war programme of nationalisation. The first organisation to be nationalised was the Bank of England, on 1 March 1946, but this was followed by the nationalisation of civil aviation (1946), coal, cable and wireless (1947), transport and electricity (1948), gas (1949) and iron and steel (1951). By 1961 the nationalised industries and public corporations employed 2.2 million people, and throughout the next two decades, until the era of privatisation, the total employed stabilised around 2 million. All in all, by the end of the 1970s, almost 30 per cent of all employment in the UK was in the public sector.

Employee relations during the period of model employer

Employees in the public sector, especially in the post-war period, enjoyed some distinctly superior terms and conditions compared with their private sector counterparts as a result of the model employer approach. First, their pay was generally set, under the terms of fair comparison, within the average-to-good range of those equivalent jobs in the private sector. While inflation was relatively low (as it was through the 1950s and 1960s), any period of 'catching up', in terms of waiting for the results of comparability exercises, was not an insurmountable problem. In addition to pay, most white-collar civil and public servants also enjoyed the benefits of a good non-contributory pension scheme (the contributions being offset against pay levels) and job security for the more senior grades in return for contractual obligation to accept transfer anywhere within the relevant branch of the public service (enhanced with generous relocation packages). Benefits for junior white-collar grades and industrial grades were less good. Pay was generally low but other conditions of service schemes (pensions, sick pay, etc.) were superior to those found in most of the private sector.

However, public sector employee relations in this period were not without their problems. One particular concern, the role and status of women in the public service, had dogged industrial relations since the 1920s over the two issues of equal pay and the 'marriage bar' (which denied employment to those, such as women teachers, who married). Campaigns were launched by the unions in favour of equal pay in the 1930s but were unsuccessful. Some of the public sector unions restored the campaign after the war but were not supported by the TUC until 1950. It was not until 1955 that the government agreed to gradually introduce equal pay into the public services in stages until full operation in 1961. This, of course, predates the Equal Pay Act 1970, for which women in the private sector had to wait before justice was done.

The campaign to end the marriage bar on married women's employment actually split the trade unions in the immediate post-war period. The Union of Post Office Workers, together with some of the senior grade civil service unions, wanted to keep the bar based on arguments that men were family breadwinners. Others, such as the Civil Service Clerical Association, wanted to abolish it. Similarly, in teaching, the National Association of Schoolmasters (NAS) was in favour of retention while the National Union of Teachers (NUT) and Union of Women Teachers (UWT) favoured abolition. However, the experience of women working in the war and their increased absorption into the labour force clearly made the bar anomalous, leading to eventual abolition by the government in phases during the lifetime of the 1945–50 Labour administration.

Public sector employees have also been restricted in some of the 'rights' to participate in political affairs such as standing for local councillor or parliamentary positions as members of a political party. The rules disallowing open political sympathy, or campaigning or standing in elections, have generally been applied to the more senior grades or those in 'politically sensitive' posts. Political vetting of candidates for some posts (with questions geared at political sympathy or parents' nationality) have also been designed to preserve the alleged neutrality of civil appointments in the public service. The trade unions were also affected by the provisions of the Trades Disputes Act 1927 which, in the aftermath of the defeated General Strike (1926), removed the 'right' of civil service and some other public sector unions to affiliate to either the TUC or the Labour Party. These particular restrictions were repealed after the war.

As the immediate post-war period receded, many of the unions became increasingly aggressive towards government restrictions on pay, particularly as it affected the public sector. Government incomes policy aimed at restricting wage increases was always enforced more rigorously in the public sector (with the government as employer) than it was in the private sector. This, combined with increasing fears of inflation, problems of low pay, and some dissatisfaction with the machinery of pay comparison and its ability to provide compensatory increases, led to the first pay strikes throughout the public sector in the 1970s. Local authority unions conducted their first coordinated national strike over pay in the autumn of 1970 and they were followed by the Union of Post Office Workers, which led its first national strike in 1971 (ending in defeat). In 1973, the civil service also experienced its first national pay strike. Meanwhile, in 1972 and again in 1974 the National Union of Miners went on all-out strike to re-establish their pay position in the 'earnings league' – a reference to their perceived worsening pay in comparison with other manual groups in the private sector. The miners were victorious in both their strikes and caused an election in 1974 after the Conservative prime minister, Edward Heath, threw down the election gauntlet in the aftermath of his attempt to control coal stocks by ordering a 'three-day working week' for all industrial and domestic coal consumers. The resultant victory for the Labour Party did not prevent public sector industrial strife. In 1977, firefighters in the Fire Brigades Union secured a new pay comparison formula after a short all-out strike. Finally, after two years of wage restraint in the public sector under the 1974–9 Labour government, the pay dam finally burst in the 1978/9 'winter of discontent' as NHS and local authority workers conducted a series of all-out and selective strikes designed to restore public sector pay levels to private sector equivalents. A new pay comparability body (the Clegg Commission) was created as part of the settlement of the strikes.

The arrival of militancy in the public sector in the 1970s was also accompanied by internal factional strife in some of the white-collar unions as left-wing 'opposition' groups began to challenge the trade union leaderships' more moderate influence. In unions such as the NUT, the Civil and Public Services Association (civil service clerks), and the local authority white-collar union NALGO, these groups were backed by organisations such as Militant and the Socialist Workers' Party. They were often separate from the more established Communist-Party-led 'broad lefts' within the unions and grew to have some influence as militancy increased generally in the 1970s (see Seifert, 1987; Kelly, 1988).

In summary, with the government as direct or indirect employer and the continuation of the model employer policy, many policy issues covering social affairs, such as equal pay, took place in the public sector in advance of the private sector. The experience of public sector employee relations in the 1970s and the increased tensions over pay meant that the period was very much a 'coming of age' of the unions and their relationship with the government after the more genteel approach of the 1950s and 1960s. It is now necessary to examine the 'wind of change' that swept through the public sector in the aftermath of Margaret Thatcher's Conservative Party election victory in 1979.

Monetarism, Thatcherism and public spending cuts

The crisis of public sector funding can be traced to the onset of economic recession following the oil 'shock' of 1973/4 and the consequent hike in inflation. The new phenomenon of 'stagflation' – rising prices combined with rising unemployment – threw the Labour government (1974–9) into crisis and sounded the death knell of Keynesian economic management. Inflation in 1975 reached 24 per cent and, as the economy slowed and unemployment rose, public spending as a proportion of GDP soared to average 43.7 per cent in the period from 1974 to 1985 (compared to 37.7 per cent in 1970–3). Part of this increase was related to expanded social security payments to cover increased unemployment but part was also the result of the increased wage bill for public sector employees as comparability awards raced to keep up with inflation. In 1976, faced with a balance of payments crisis and increasing national debt, the Labour government was forced to seek a loan from the International Monetary Fund (IMF), which was granted on condition that the Chancellor (Denis Healey) introduced a monetarist economic programme aimed at capping public spending and reducing the public sector borrowing requirement (PSBR). The consequent programme of 'cash limits' for the public sector was designed to control public spending plans of individual departments and ushered in recruitment freezes and a variety of other cost-cutting measures throughout the sector.

■ The period of retrenchment: the 1980s and 1990s

While the 1974–9 Labour government had set in train the reversal of policy towards public sector spending, the incoming Thatcher administration stepped up the attack with extra ideological vigour. The new government's attitude to the public sector was one of hostility as a result not only of monetarist orthodoxy but also of a perceived need to liberate market forces in an effort to boost Britain's competitive position in the world economy. It was argued that the public sector was a burden to the economy in that it did not create wealth and it 'crowded out' investment opportunity that could otherwise be allocated to the profit-making private sector (Bacon and Eltis, 1978). In addition, the public sector unions, and their increasingly powerful influence and militancy, were seen as obstacles to the restructuring of the British state and the introduction of *laissez-faire* market forces. As a consequence, the Thatcher administration embarked on a programme of policy measures designed both to reduce the size of the public sector and to confront the public sector unions and the ever increasing wage bill. The various policy initiatives are listed below.

Privatisation and contracting out

The privatisation programme was launched by the government in the 1980s in line with the 1979 Conservative manifesto commitment. This was to be achieved primarily with the public offer of shares and involved a total of 43 companies by the end of 1996. The share sales had the added advantage of raising revenue for the government and temporarily reducing public sector debt. In 1983–4, for example, over £1 billion was raised, and in 1984–5 over £2 billion. The peak years were 1988–9 (£7.1 billion: BP, gas and steel) and 1992–3 (£8.2 billion: BT and electricity). Programmes of the contracting-out of services to the private sector (involving a tendering process) were confined to a range of services in local authorities, the NHS and the civil service, such as cleaning, rubbish collection and catering. In terms of employee relations, most of the privatisations and contracting out were bitterly opposed by the unions concerned, involving one-day strikes by BT unions against job losses and fears of reduced services (such as the potential loss of rural telephone kiosks), and selective strikes against the loss of jobs and introduction of inferior conditions of service for those areas of work threatened by contracting out (Fairbrother 1996; Foster and Scott 1998). Both privatisation and contracting out also fragmented the collective bargaining framework and reduced the power and influence of public sector unions, particularly in local authorities where workers in key areas of 'industrial muscle', such as refuse collectors, now found themselves working (if they were taken on) in un-unionised and anti-union companies. In many respects this entailed a significant shift in employee relations whereby the pattern began to resemble that of the private sector (Carter and Fairbrother, 1999).

Confrontations with the unions

The system of 'cash limits' on departmental spending engendered a series of confrontations with the unions forced to make a 'choice' between increased pay and job loss (given the restrictive limit on budgets). The increased tensions resulted in an upsurge of industrial disputes in the public sector throughout the 1980s including the civil service (1981 and 1987), hospital and railway workers (1982), social workers (1983), teachers (1985, 1986 and 1987), local authority white-collar staff (1989) and ambulance workers (1989). Apart from the two disputes in 1989, in every case the unions were defeated in their key objectives of either winning pay demands or opposing programmes of public spending cuts. Industrial action against specific programmes of spending cuts was particularly difficult to sustain. The NHS, for example, saw some flashpoints when staff occupied wards that were threatened with closure programmes (Seifert, 1992: chapter 7). The general pattern of defeats for the unions meant that a period of demoralisation set into the ranks of the public sector unions. The government offensive against the unions also included attacks on the 'fair comparison' principle of pay determination. In the civil service the pay comparability machinery for all but senior civil servants was withdrawn and teachers lost their rights to negotiate on pay. These defeats for the unions opened the door for a further erosion of relative pay and enabled the government to achieve more easily some of its objectives in cutting the public sector pay bill. The institutional status of trade unions was also downgraded by employer action to redefine facilities agreements in the civil service, and many local authorities reduced the 'time off' allocated to trade union local representatives to conduct their trade union business. The 'check-off' arrangement, whereby trade union subscriptions were deducted from wage packets automatically by employers, was also withdrawn in many areas of the public service. Finally, the provision that new staff were 'recommended' in the civil service to join the appropriate trade union was dropped by the new Conservative government.

In the nationalised industries, confrontation was just as sharp. British Steel management defeated the unions in an all-out national strike in 1980, and decentralised collective bargaining to business divisions and rationalised jobs throughout the industry in the process (see Blyton and Turnbull, 1998: chapter 7). Most important of all was the defeat of the year-long strike conducted by the National Union of Mineworkers in 1984–5 over the withdrawal of coal price subsidies and the introduction of a pit closure programme. The defeat of the miners, and the consequent authority it placed in the hands of the government, had clear ramifications for trade union 'solidarity' in Britain, and led to some soul searching within the trade union movement. One other point of interest concerning government attacks on the public sector trade unions was the banning in 1984 of trade union membership for 8,000 employees at the Government Central Headquarters (GCHQ) in Cheltenham. For 40 years previously, GCHQ collated signals intelligence worldwide. The ban was imposed by ministerial decree (i.e. without the necessity of a parliamentary vote) by the Foreign Secretary, Sir Geoffrey Howe, on the presumption that intelligence-gathering and trade union membership were incompatible. The banning followed the case of 'spying' for the Soviet Union by an employee at Cheltenham. Civil service unions opposed the ban and alleged that it was instigated by President Reagan in the US as a condition for continuing US financial support for the centre (the US government also proposed the introduction of the polygraph – lie detector – as a test for all new recruits). Fears that the ban might spread to other civil servants in politically sensitive areas were allayed after the general secretary of the TUC, Len Murray, went on television to call a one-day general strike in protest at the ban. With only a few days' notice, more than 1 million people went on strike in response to the TUC's call. One of the first tasks of the incoming Labour government in May 1997 was to reinstate trade union recognition at GCHQ.

It can be seen from the above that the concept of model employer no longer applied under the Conservative governments in the 1980s. The attacks on trade union power and influence, combined with their 'deinstitutionalisation' and redefining of the value of pay comparison, changed the framework of public sector industrial relations. Spending cuts, privatisation and contracting out also reduced the size of the public sector. The net effect of the cuts in the size of the sector are apparent in the fall in the number of those employed. More than 1.9 million jobs were cut between 1981 and 1994 as a result of either privatisation and contracting out (a transfer to the private sector) or spending cuts in remaining public services. Totals employed in the civil service, for example, fell by 20 per cent between 1981 and 1994. The public sector share of employment in the economy has fallen from a high of 30 per cent to just over 20 per cent as a result.

While the institutional role of trade unions had changed and cuts in spending had taken place, the government and public sector employers also attempted to alter management style and techniques. It is to this issue that we now turn (see Exhibit 14.1).

'Marketisation' and new public management

The Conservative government was also concerned to introduce the ethos of 'marketisation' into the public sector as a way of injecting some 'discipline' into decision-making and offering market choice to potential consumers of services. This process of marketisation, typified by the breakdown of units and divisions into cost and/or budget centres, has been accompanied by new levels of financial and administrative accountability for managers and new forms of management practice designed to motivate the workforce in the absence of profit-related market discipline.

Local managers, whether heads of schools, chief nursing officers, governors of penal establishments or commanders of units within the armed forces, are now responsible for offsetting pay increases against productivity and efficiency savings. Headteachers, for example, can now choose between separate items of budget expenditure, such as

Exhibit 14.1

UK public sector strikes and the search for private finance

For those of a nervous disposition, last week's strikes by the UK Post Office and the London Underground might suggest a return to the bad days of the late 1970s. Taken with the likely return of a Labour government, the spectre is all too familiar: chaos in the capital, unburied corpses and rubbish in the streets. Calmer reflection suggests nothing of the kind. Transport and postal strikes catch the nation's attention, but across the economy as a whole, the reality is that strike figures are still the lowest on record. Critics might pose a different question. Recent strike threats in the private sector, such as that by British Airways pilots, have been quietly averted. Why do public sector managers seem so much less adroit in handling disputes?

The answer comes in two parts. First, today's public sector managers often come from the private sector. The Post Office chairman is an ex-director of personnel at Unilever. The head of London Underground was formerly with British Airways. His boss, the chairman of London Transport, comes from Harvard Business School, McKinsey and P&O. The second part of the answer goes to the heart of what the two disputes are about. In both cases, management is trying to change the organisation's culture: to make it less rigid and more capable of change. The ultimate goal, in both cases, is to make the workers think and act more like their private sector counterparts.

Thus, the Post Office is trying to move away from its old hierarchical culture towards a system of teamwork. London Underground is trying to reform structure in which, for instance, holiday rotas are still organised by the workforce rather than the management.

The ultimate driving force in both cases is the same: the need to attract private sector finance. At the extreme, this means privatisation: explicitly advocated by Post Office management and unlikely to be opposed by London Transport. It might seem an odd time for managers to be thinking in those terms. Even in the unlikely event of a Tory election victory, privatising the Post Office, while still a Tory objective, would prove difficult and contentious.

As for London Underground, privatisation has apparently been dropped from the Tory manifesto as being too politically sensitive. For a Labour government, of course, privatisation – under that title, at any rate – would be anathema. But the main issue would remain. The Post Office and London Underground need to invest heavily if they are to carry on doing their jobs. The more they can present themselves in private sector guise, the easier it will be to attract private finance.

In the Post Office's case, this might seem perverse. Investment is certainly needed to keep pace with the rapid development of electronic media and digital information. But in a private sector context, the Post Office would have no trouble at all in raising the money. Its management, after all, would have a good story to tell: a consistent record of profit, strong cash flow and a remarkable level of customer satisfaction. At present, the Post Office is not allowed to borrow, since that would count as government debt. But as a private company, its balance sheet would allow it to borrow well over £1bn without strain.

The case of London Underground is less clear cut. If its accounts were drawn up in private sector fashion, its operating loss might be relatively small. But by comparison with the Post Office, it is hugely capital intensive. This year, it will swallow close to £1bn of taxpayers' money, of which more than half will be spent on the new extension to the Jubilee Line.

Attempts to help out with private finance have so far proved tough going. The £2bn-plus London CrossRail project, providing an underground link between the capital's railway termini, is supposed to contain an element of private funding. But the main burden will fall upon the taxpayer. Unsurprisingly, therefore, the project has been postponed to the next century.

The government's Private Finance Initiative is supposed to help here, but the results so far are not encouraging. The Northern Line of the Underground is being supplied with some £800m worth of new trains through a leasing arrangement with the suppliers, GEC Alsthom. But even that was opposed by the Treasury as being in breach of its rules, as was a plan to lease out some of the automatic barriers at Underground stations. It would be perhaps unfair to single out the Treasury as the culprit. The history of

Exhibit 14.1 *continued*

nationalised industries in the UK has left its scars. In their heyday, investments by nationalised companies too often proved disastrous. An important reason was that since spending was ultimately backed by government, managers lacked the guidance of the market on the balance between risk and opportunity.

Given the context, today's public sector managers might well feel occasionally helpless. Their ownership structure is unsuited to the job they have to do. Their workers, meanwhile, have no incentive to speed the transition to a private sector model, since they have every evidence that it means upheaval and insecurity.

There is a central irony to all this. The City and the financial markets are criticised for being short-termist. In the closing years of the century, the reality

is just the other way round. Governments – not only in the UK – are increasingly weighed down by the fiscal burden of pensions and unemployment. Long-term capital projects are no longer to be thought of, especially by governments which know that proposing taxes to pay for them would spell doom at the polls. The world is therefore reverting to a 19th century model, whereby long-term private savings are channelled by the financial institutions into long-term investments. The problem is not one of a shortage of funds. The question is rather how public sector managers, squeezed between hostile owners and resentful employees, can gain access to the money.

Source: Tony Jackson, *Financial Times*, 12 August 1996. © 1996 The Financial Times Limited

staff requirements, books and equipment, or administrative items (Menter *et al.*, 1997). The principle of 'consumer choice' must again be seen as an attempt to introduce market discipline. Prime Minister John Major's (1991–7) initiative on the Citizen's Charter[4] sought to empower consumers of public services if targets for service provision failed. Parental choice in schooling or penalty clauses for service operators of contracted-out services, such as refuse collection or road sweeping, are examples.

The principal changes can be summarised as follows:

- Reorganisation of the civil service into executive agency status and further decentralisation into non-departmental public bodies (NDPB). Staff remained civil servants in status but the overall head of the agency, the chief executive, could be appointed from either the public or the private sector. Links were maintained with the appropriate government department through a contractual 'framework document'. Pay, conditions of employment and gradings from April 1996 were decentralised to each agency and NDPB. These changes follow the Next Steps policy introduced into the civil service in 1988 designed to break up the civil service into more discrete accounting units.[5]
- Simulation of competition through the purchaser–provider division (commonly called the internal market[6]). Introduced in 1981, this is now apparent in the NHS, NHS trusts and local authorities. NHS trusts, for example, have powers to appoint staff, establish their own conditions of service, and shape their own industrial relations procedures. Within the NHS, the market measures have led to competition between hospitals and their departments for internal 'contracts'. Labour savings have clearly been identified as an aid to competitiveness, and fears over job security have arisen as a result. Employers have often responded to their new powers by challenging working practices, and tightening up on discipline and sickness procedures. The conflict between 'cost-cutting' and quality service provision has also been apparent, and this in particular has led the Labour government in 2002 to rethink the logic of these market reforms within the NHS environment.

■ Within local authorities the ability to raise revenue through local taxation has been curtailed by the 'rate capping' procedure enacted by central government, meaning some spending cuts and service withdrawal as a result. Decentralised and devolved managerial accountability also means that many sections of local government now operate within their own budgets and staffing arrangements. Similar arrangements also exist in the school sector through the local management of schools (LMS) initiative. This substitutes local authority planning in the schools sector in favour of more direct headteacher responsibility combined with parental choice for state school places. The ability of local secondary schools to opt out of local authority financial control and to raise additional monies reinforces this process of consumer 'choice', especially when combined with the publication of school 'league tables' giving results of examination performance.[7] Both the programme of school opt-outs and league tables were initially opposed by the NUT, leading to dispute. The failure of the campaign to prevent the measures led to the NUT withdrawing its opposition.

Management style and technique in the public sector have been much influenced by the emphasis on performance, objectives and targets. This focus reflects the primary change of devolving financial accountability but also mirrors parallel changes in management techniques much associated with HRM or 'Japanisation' in the private sector, as well as competitive costing programmes involving a potential private sector service provider as is the case with Best Value[8] (local authorities) or the Private Finance Initiative (Kerr, 1997). The forms of 'New Public Management' that have evolved have sought to break down the traditional bureaucratic and hierarchical organisation structures that were previously dominant. In addition, this renewed emphasis on rational managerial accountability has acted to allay some of the blame for service cuts from government policy and transfer them to the individual decisions of managers (Winchester and Bach, 1995). In many instances the change has resulted in a downgrading of the traditional importance of negotiated procedures as unions have become de-institutionalised, work has intensified, and collective bargaining has fragmented. Many of the old conditions of service handbooks, which formerly laid down rules and regulations of conduct, working procedures and conditions of service, have been downgraded in importance or abandoned. In some cases, new local agreements have been negotiated with local trade unions, but in other cases, such as in further education colleges, attempts have been made to completely redefine contract terms and impose new ones. Large-scale, long-running disputes with the unions concerned have resulted.

As an alternative management approach, personnel practices have concentrated much more on appraisal systems, the use of direct communication with employees (rather than through trade unions) and on quality initiatives such as total quality programmes or quality circles. Teamworking (particularly in the NHS) has also been emphasised. Such changes have posed considerable problems, either because of trade union opposition or because of the difficulties of assessing 'performance' in the public service when no 'value added' contribution can be identified. What measures of performance, for example, can be applied to nurses when the fate of the sick is dependent on so many other factors than simply the care given by an individual nurse? Similarly, how can the performance of a social worker or teacher be assessed when caseloads or class size are possibly more important variables in performance outcome? Such problems manifested themselves in difficulties for the government's policies. In the NHS, for example, local trust managers have attempted to raise productivity by reducing staff, changing the mix of required skills, extending working time flexibility and casualisation of contracts, and reducing wage costs by reducing overtime premia, sick and holiday pay (Fisher, 1999). The result has been a deterioration in staff–management relations and, in some cases, an increase in trade union activity. Recent research by Marsden and French (2000) also reports the general experience of staff in the public sector when confronted with new forms of performance-related pay (PRP). Among their main findings were that:

- most staff believed that PRP was divisive, undermined morale, caused jealousies and inhibited workplace cooperation;
- most staff believed that PRP had not raised their motivation;
- many believed that line managers used PRP to reward their favourites;
- many line managers believed PRP had reduced staff cooperation with management.

Despite these general misgivings from staff on new pay determination it is in the field of pay that the most important changes have taken place, and it is this area which is now examined.

Pay determination: comparability, indexation and performance

We have already seen how the government, in abandoning the model employer approach, has sought to shift the emphasis away from pay being determined by 'fair comparison' to that of 'affordability'. This shift of emphasis has also corresponded to devolved managerial authority and the perceived need to encourage individual performance and flexibility by using pay as the incentive. Despite these trends, nearly three-quarters of public sector employees still had their pay determined by collective bargaining (Millward *et al.*, 1992), with the remainder attached to some form of indexation or review by a third party. To a large extent this reflects the difficulties of assessing performance of the public servant (as already discussed) as well as the entrenched opposition of trade unions to the break-up of more collectively beneficial systems. A summary of the major sectoral differences is given below.

The civil service

The pay comparability machinery associated with 'Whitleyism' and the model employer was abandoned by the government in 1981 (despite trade union opposition involving a 20-week dispute of selective strikes). In the aftermath of the dispute, the government established an enquiry into civil service pay (the Megaw Report) which concluded with recommendations that maintained 'informed' collective bargaining and which geared pay awards to the priorities of 'recruitment, retention and motivation'. Performance-related pay was introduced shortly afterwards for senior grade staff and the system of 'automatic' yearly incremental progression up long scales was altered to allow for performance-only related 'merit' increases to be reserved at the higher end of the scales for most white-collar grades. The extra flexibility in the system satisfied some management criteria but the unions were successful in retaining automatic incremental progression for at least some part of the pay scale. The agreement was achieved on the basis that the outside pay comparisons would be at the lower end of the 'league table' rather than in the average (median) to good range.

However, the introduction of agency status into the civil service in the 1980s and 1990s led to a fragmentation of paymasters and a devolution of collective bargaining to more discrete areas of work within the service. As a consequence, the determination of the pay scales and the mix of automatic and merit increments have become much more diverse. Pay bands are now commonplace, linked to job-evaluated regrading of skills, tasks and responsibilities. The Treasury, as overall paymaster, retains some control over pay within agencies and has the power to reverse decisions. On the other hand, some civil service departments are likely still to be fully privatised (Amersham International – a scientific establishment formerly part of the civil service – was in fact the first government privatisation) and would consequently be completely outside the scope of public sector pay determination.

The National Health Service

The NHS contains a multitude of occupational grades covered by numerous bargaining units and trade unions. Ten separate Whitley Councils have traditionally acted as forums for negotiations based within the fair comparison remit. In addition, doctors and dentists have been catered for by a review body that, after consultation with all interested parties, has made recommendations on pay and conditions to the government. This highly centralised system has been altered rather than fundamentally challenged in the 1980s and 1990s. Following a lengthy dispute over pay in 1982, the government created two new pay review bodies for nurses and midwives, and employers and government have since sought to influence the outcomes of these reviews by incorporating greater elements of affordability at the expense of comparability. This has resulted in continuing skirmishes between the various unions representing nurses and midwives and the government as ultimate paymaster. In particular, there has been a determined effort to relate nurses' pay to local, rather than national, labour market conditions with proposals for basic increases that could be 'topped up' (or not) by the need to recruit and retain within the local labour market. Despite this, it has been possible to enhance nurses' pay relative to others within the NHS, either by better than average pay awards or by reassessing the grading criteria on which individual nurse's pay is assessed.

The difficulties of localising nurses' pay have been caused not just by opposition from unions but also by the problems of defining a local labour market for nurses, many of whom relate to a *national* occupational labour market and have highly individual personal profiles relating to skills, grade and contractual status. It is for these reasons that 90 per cent of NHS trusts have reverted to national, as opposed to local, pay rates for nurses (*People Management*, 25 September 1997).

One other issue which has clearly upset union negotiators has been the tendency of governments to 'stage' awards of the pay review body and save money by delaying full implementation of any award. This pattern has been repeated by the Labour government in its decision to stage the 1998 award for nurses.

Elsewhere within the NHS, the system of collective bargaining through Whitley Councils continues. The government has been more than willing, however, to utilise its policy of 'cash limits' to suppress pay rises, and in 1989 this policy caused confrontation with ambulance workers, who staged a 'work to rule' in order to secure a pay review index similar to that enjoyed by the emergency services of the police and fire services. While securing a higher pay settlement than previously offered, the ambulance workers failed in their attempt to establish indexation. National agreements for Whitley-related grades have nevertheless shown signs of fragmentation as more discrete elements of local pay linked to 'recruitment and retention' have emerged and managers have begun to exercise power in seeking more flexibility in pay with links to new working arrangements.

Local government

Similar patterns of change are recorded in local authorities, with moves by the individual employers to establish local rates outside of the national collective agreement. The employers (i.e. the management of individual local authorities) are members of separate institutions (representing Scotland or the metropolitan or county councils), which for bargaining purposes has led to some discrepancy of position in key disputes. This was highlighted in 1989 during a dispute with the union representing white-collar staff (NALGO) when the employers failed in their efforts to dismantle and break the national collective agreement and impose more locally based agreements in its place. However, within local authorities there remains much scope for variation in pay that can be engineered through grading agreements struck at local level. Thus, it is perfectly possible for differences in remuneration for skills and occupations to arise between authorities as different interpretations of grading formulas are imposed or negotiated. The evaluation of jobs and skills by formal (and sometimes informal) means has thus been a central issue in local authority employee relations, sometimes with important equal opportunities implications when it can be demonstrated that particular jobs are gender specific (e.g. canteen assistants compared with 'binmen').

More significant changes have taken place within education (see Exhibit 14.2). Further education colleges and the former polytechnics were removed from local authority financial control in the early 1990s, resulting in attempts by the college management and employers' forums to break with the traditional national collective agreements. This led to two national one-day strikes in the former polytechnics in order to preserve national conditions of service. The end settlement led to a revision of contractual obligations for lecturers and the establishment of local agreements within a national 'framework agreement'. National bargaining on pay was preserved, but since the transformation of the former polytechnics into 'new' universities with similar funding arrangements (but dissimilar conditions of work) to the 'old' universities there has been division of opinion between the union representing 'new' staff (NATFHE) and 'old' (Association of University Teachers) as to whether or not lecturers would be better served with national bargaining or a pay review body. The introduction of new contractual arrangements into the further education sector proved much more contentious, leading to a series of national and college-based disputes as lecturers' teaching hours were lengthened and holidays reduced. The bitterness of many of these disputes was compounded by the ability of college principals to award themselves (with governing body approval) large salary increases. To date there remains no agreed outcome to this dispute and in fact, in 1995 and 1996 at least, the sector has recorded in official statistics a significant proportion of 'working days lost' through strikes (see later section).

Exhibit 14.2

Plan to boost pay for top teachers

The government yesterday called for a new salary structure to reward a class of advanced skills teacher it wants to introduce. In advice to the schoolteachers' review body, Mr David Blunkett, education and employment secretary, said he wanted a 'distinct new role' for particular teachers in raising standards by 'supporting and mentoring' trainee and newly qualified teachers.

Mr Blunkett has expressed concern that the only avenue for career advancement for good teachers is to go into administration. He acknowledges that under the present system there is no financial incentive for them to remain in the classroom. In his letter to Mr Tony Vineall, the review body chairman, Mr Blunkett made clear he wanted a tight pay settlement to ensure most of the extra £1bn announced for education in the Budget went to improving standards.

Mr Blunkett is having to reconcile a financial squeeze on education with the government's crusade to raise standards – to be the centrepiece of a 200-clause education Bill in the next parliamentary session. However, he indicated he was amenable to funnelling more money to the new grade of teacher and asked the review body to consider how best to achieve that. 'Skilled and experienced teachers are the key asset of our schools and we need to retain them in the profession', Mr Blunkett said.

Teachers' unions condemned the proposal. Mr Doug McAvoy, general secretary of the National Union of Teachers, called for 'a significant increase' for all teachers. Mr Phil Willis, Liberal Democrat education spokesman, said: 'Increased salaries for advanced skills teachers can help improve schools, but they will only affect a very small proportion of teachers. The government must not allow this to become a case of robbing Peter to pay Paul.'

The review body will make its recommendations on pay for all 400,000 teachers in England and Wales in time for the government to announce the 1998–99 pay round in February. 'We need to ensure those who are in the service for 20–30 years have a career structure', Mr Blunkett said. Plans for the new 'super-teachers', as Mr Blunkett dubs them, were outlined in a government White Paper last month. Mr Blunkett also asked the review body to consider reinforcing headteachers' management role by requiring them to report to governors each year to ensure individual performance did not fall below recognised standards.

Source: John Kampfner, *Financial Times*, 7 August 1997. © 1997 The Financial Times Limited

In secondary and primary education there has been a long history of disagreement between the unions and employers as to the outputs of the Burnham Committee negotiating forum. A series of disputes led eventually to the government deciding to abolish the system of national collective bargaining in 1987 and through the Teachers' Pay and Conditions Act 1987 to enable the Secretary of State to impose pay rates on the teaching service. In 1991 a pay review body was established for teachers with a part remit to establish performance-related pay within schools. However, the introduction of performance systems within schools has been very limited. Schools rely on trust and teamwork between teachers, and few heads are likely to be willing to threaten this by the introduction of potentially divisive merit-based pay. Opposition from the teaching unions would also mean a difficult path would lie ahead in its introduction.

■ Indexation

Both the police and fire service (representing 200,000 employees) have their pay determined by indexed attachment to outside movements in earnings. The police are the one sector of civilian public employment denied by law a 'right' to strike, having lost this right in the aftermath of their strike defeat in 1919. Their indexation formula was established after a campaign organised by the Police Federation (the police union) in 1979, and initially linked annual increases to the increase in the whole economy average earnings. Since 1994 their pay increases have been linked to the median increase in private sector non-manual settlements. Other issues affecting police pay have been the baseline level (again subject to dispute in 1979) and the possibility of the introduction of performance-related pay. The latter issue again raises questions of the efficacy of linking pay to performance in a public service occupation. Firefighters won an indexation system in the aftermath of their dispute with the Labour government in 1977. Their pay is linked to the top quartile of male manual earnings. As mentioned in the previous section, ambulance workers failed in 1989 to secure an indexation system; their case at the time rested on the proposition that they should be considered an equivalent 'emergency' service to the police and fire service. During the life of the 1979–97 Conservative governments it was mooted within government circles that a strike ban should be introduced in the emergency services. However, legislation, although often expected, failed to materialise before the election defeat of May 1997.

The public sector under 'new' Labour

The first two years of the Labour government after 1997 saw little change within the sector. The spending limits of the previous Conservative government were adhered to by the Chancellor. However, new agendas for the public service have since begun to emerge in terms of the government's commitment to modernising government, as expressed in its 1999 White Paper. This White Paper had as its declared objectives to:

- break down barriers between departments and local authorities;
- get the best people for the job – whether public, private or voluntary;
- create a greater say for people in forming policies;
- recognise and reward the best staff;
- tackle the fear of taking risks within the sector.

Examples of new initiatives under these declared objectives are plans to extend the hours by which public services can be accessed. In the NHS, for example, walk-in centres and direct line Internet access have been established. Civil servants are also encouraged to develop cost-cutting initiatives by pooling resources across departments and avoiding duplication, and to adopt a system of peer review to assess progress in achieving the necessary cultural changes within the service. The government also established a series of focus groups and 'peoples' panels' to enact some level of feedback on satisfaction or otherwise with the level and state of public services.

Beyond these cultural and organisational initiatives the government has shown a renewed determination to inject private finance into public service provision either through the PFI (Private Finance Initiative) or PPP (public private partnership) programmes. It is in these areas that controversy has arisen and some confrontation with public service trade unions has occurred. PFI has been aimed especially at hospital provision and is a continuation of the Conservative policies introduced in 1993. No public money is released for major hospital works unless the relevant NHS trust has first drawn up a plan for a private finance initiative within the building programme. Private companies might then build hospitals and let them over a contracted period to the NHS. The Labour government has adopted this programme and announced in 2000 that it was on course for the private funding of public projects worth £20 billion by 2003 (*Financial Times*, 16 March 2000). New arrangements whereby private finance is introduced are to be extended into primary care facilities and social services and in 850 schools (*Guardian*, 17 July 2001). The main public service union, Unison, however, has taken issue with the government over the programme, claiming that private finance initiatives 'are an inefficient means of financing improvements to public services . . . for every £1bn of PFI contracts, the cost to the public purse is £50m per year more than if the public sector could borrow directly' (Unison, 2001). The union also claims that the costs of PFI may then be directly met by cuts in services and in the employment conditions of public service workers. During 2000, a long-running dispute took place at Dudley hospital over such issues. Some parallel union concern has taken place in local authorities whereby the government Best Value initiative (see Boyne, 2000), designed to improve service accountability, has been perceived by some union members as an extension of compulsory competitive tendering.[9] A flashpoint with the PPP initiative was the long-running argument between the government and the newly elected mayor of London, Ken Livingstone, centred on the proposed new funding arrangements for London Underground. The continuation of the privatisation drive also touched one of the last remaining nationalised industries – the Post Office. The overall corporate management body for Royal Mail was renamed Consignia and during 1999 the Postal Services Bill was announced, freeing the Post Office to engage in more commercial undertakings, eventually becoming a government-owned plc. The Post Office has now been transformed into 12 business units with separate profit accountability. Lastly, the government took a decision in October 2001 to revise the arrangements for the privatised Railtrack by introducing parliamentary legislation to turn the company into a not-for-profit organisation without shareholders. In summary, the issue of privatisation proved a contentious one during the second term of the Labour government. Potential confrontation with unions meant that the 2001 Trades Union Congress was likely to be a focal point of union discontent and potential opposition to many of the government's plans. The GMB union, for example, had threatened to withdraw £250,000 annual funding to the Labour Party if its plans were not revised. Other union leaders, such as Sir Ken Jackson, general secretary of the Amalgamated Engineering and Electrical Union (AEEU), have on the other hand been supportive of the government's privatisation agenda. In the event, the key debates at the TUC were curtailed as the 2001 Congress itself was ended before the debate could take place in response to the terrorist attacks on New York and Washington on September 11.

Assessment: employee relations or industrial relations?

No assessment of the public sector is complete without recognition of the fact that the sector stands apart from the private sector in that there has been a continuing relative resilience of trade union membership and density and a higher propensity in recent years for industrial dispute. In 2000, average union density in public administration was 61 per cent, in education was 58 per cent and in health was 64 per cent. This compares with a density rate of 29.4 per cent for all employees in Britain (*Labour Market Trends*, September 2001). Overall union density in the public sector is around three times greater than in the private sector. In terms of industrial disputes during the 1990s, the public sector has consistently provided the most significant proportion of 'working days lost'. Some of the key areas of disputes were as follows:

- 1991 – a strike by council workers over redundancy matters accounted for 102,000 working days lost (13 per cent of the annual total).
- 1992 – a similar strike by council workers accounted for 81,000 working days lost (15 per cent of the 0.5 million total).
- 1993 – a strike by civil servants over market testing, privatisation and cuts in service accounted for 162,000 working days lost (25 per cent) out of 0.6 million days total. The workers involved in this one-day strike accounted for 42 per cent of all workers on strike in 1993.
- 1994 and 1995 – a strike by college lecturers over the introduction of new contracts of employment accounted for 63,000 (22 per cent) of the 0.28 million days lost in 1994 and 39,000 (9 per cent) of the 0.41 million days lost in 1995.
- 1996 – a strike by university staff (all grades) over pay accounted for 111,700 (9 per cent) of the 1.3 million days lost. Sixty-eight per cent of all days lost in this year came as a result of productivity disputes in the London Underground and Royal Mail.
- 1997 – the largest single number of disputes in any sector was in education, which recorded 35 stoppages and 27,900 working days lost. The Royal Mail also recorded another significant number of disputes.
- 2000 – one-quarter of all working days lost were due to ten stoppages in health and social work.

Part of the increasing prominence of the public sector in strike statistics is the result of the decline of *individual* propensity to strike in the private sector (Dickerson and Stewart, 1993). However, the continued propensity of public sector workers both to remain relatively well unionised and to strike, does need some explanation. In addition, the relative resilience of collective bargaining as a form of pay determination and the continued legitimacy of the trade union role in the face of new management techniques need some analysis. In many respects, traditional forms of adversarial bargaining have kept pace in the public sector with employer- and government-driven attempts to inject employee relations techniques designed to 'individualise' and 'de-collectivise' the employment relationship. Some reasons for this lingering 'industrial' rather than 'employee' relations framework are now suggested.

Trade union attachment

Membership of the public-sector-based trade unions grew dramatically in the post-war period alongside the growth of the public sector. However, the growth in density outstripped the growth in membership potential in most areas. For example, union membership in national and local government, education and health increased from 1.46 million in 1948 to 2.25 million in 1968 and 5.76 million in 1979, while density rates increased from nearly 60 per cent to nearly 80 per cent over the same period (Waddington, 1992). Job cuts and privatisation from 1979 on took their toll on membership in these sectors and totals fell to 3.8 million in 1987. Density, however, remained stable at just under 79 per cent before some slippage occurred in the 1990s. The pattern of membership in some of the larger unions can be seen from Table 14.1.

Table 14.1 **Membership of selected public sector trade unions**

Union	1979	1997	2000
GMB (local authority manual grade workers)	967,000	709,708	712,010
CWU (communications)	333,453	273,814	287,732
National and Local Government Officers Association (NALGO)	753,000	na	na
National Union of Public Employees (NUPE)	692,000	na	na
Confederation of Health Service Employees (COHSE)	213,000	na	na
Unison (1993 merger of above three unions)	(1,657,926)[a]	1,300,451	1,272,350
Public and Commercial Services Union (PCS)	(445,329)[b]	265,902	258,278
National Union of Teachers (NUT)	290,740	191,828	201,297
National Association of Schoolmasters/Union of Women Teachers (NAS/UWT)	152,222	172,852	180,682

[a] NALGO, COHSE and NUPE   [b] PCT plus CPSA
Source: Certification Office and TUC annual reports

There exists a mixture of occupational, craft and industrial unions within the sector. For example, in the NHS, manual grades are represented by Unison (the result of a merger in 1993 of NALGO, NUPE and COHSE) or GMB, whereas nurses might join the professionally oriented and non-TUC-affiliated Royal College of Nursing (RCN) or Unison. Staff technicians are generally represented by MSF (Manufacturing, Science and Finance) and maintenance grades by AEEU (Amalgamated Engineering and Electrical Union). In the civil service, unions have historically been split by occupation and grade for white-collar staff in separate unions. However, a series of mergers have created one 'conglomerate' union (PCS) for many other grades, including administrative and executive officers, security officers and Inland Revenue staff. Technical staff can join the IPMS (Institute of Professional Managers and Specialists) while the Association of First Division Civil Servants (FDA) recruits the senior 'mandarin' grades. In primary and secondary education, the major unions are the NUT and the NAS/UWT (and the EIS in Scotland). The NUT has the majority membership in primary schools whereas the NAS/UWT shares membership in the secondary sector. Headteachers can join the National Association of Head Teachers (NAHT). Further education college lecturers and those in the 'new' universities are generally represented by NATFHE (National Association of Teachers in Further and Higher Education) while those in the pre-1992 universities are represented by the Association of University Teachers. Talks on a confederation or merger between these unions is ongoing. Administrative staffs in local authorities, education and the NHS are usually represented by Unison and sometimes MSF (now renamed Amicus, after merging with the AEEU in 2002).

The growth in membership of the public sector unions has given them more weight and influence within the TUC and the trade union movement in general. In the 1970s, the public sector unions gained more seats on the TUC General Council at the expense of some declining private sector and manually based unions. Since its creation by amalgamation in 1993, Unison is now Britain's largest union with over 1.3 million members against the Transport and General Workers' Union's 800,000. The merger of the CPSA and PTC in the civil service into the Public Commercial Service Union (PCS) had been held up in the past because of fears in the junior grade union (CPSA) that their members would be in the same union as their executive grade 'bosses' in the PTC. It is also worth noting that many of these 'public' sector unions also have substantial membership bases in the private sector following privatisation or 'hiving-off' of government departments and nationalised industries.

The relatively high density of membership for many of these unions is partly a legacy of the model employer years when trade unions established strong membership bases aided and abetted by the legitimacy given to them by their institutionalisation in the process of collective bargaining and working procedures.

The fact that managerial grades have also been traditional union members throughout much of the public sector may also have helped to make union membership socially acceptable within the workplace without a 'fear' of victimisation for joining.

The sustained growth of membership throughout the 1960s and 1970s is more complex to explain. White-collar staff in general were drawn into unions during this period at a greater rate than average in all sectors, leading to some debate as to the cause of this new 'white-collar' unionism. Instrumental reasons, linked to the perceived ability of unions to deliver wage increases within a framework of collective bargaining, were undoubtedly important. Further debate surrounds the contention that white-collar staff were becoming more collectivised and identifying themselves as working class within an increasingly large, bureaucratic and 'Taylorised' public sector work environment increasingly typified by automated routine work procedures and the emergence of 'clerical factories' (see Prandy et al. (1982) for a contemporary review of the debates). Public sector unions have exhibited more 'unionateness' in recent years, with the decision of some of the unions to newly affiliate to the TUC or to establish political funds for campaign purposes (although falling short of affiliation to the Labour Party).

In the 1980s and 1990s, individual workloads increased as a result of recruitment freezes, cutbacks and cash limits. The need to monitor service outputs and record information for budgeting purposes has also created extra administrative burdens. More government interference and suppression of wage and salary increases have also occurred. The potential role of trade unions as defenders of terms and conditions has become much more important as a result, and where an attempt has been made to fulfil this role the resultant increase in levels of activism within the unions at local level is likely to have enhanced participation and encouraged membership recruitment and retention (Fairbrother, 1996). Pressures on individual managers to meet financial targets and to provide a public service within strict cash limits have also led to a tightening of discipline over such issues as sickness and unauthorised absence as well as the adoption of a more aggressive management style (Edwards and Whitston, 1991). Workers, in other words, are working harder within the public sector, and if so then a sense of injustice is likely to arise if there is no corresponding revision of the effort-bargain. This again, within the workplace, is likely to increase feelings of 'them and us' and create opportunities for active unions to polarise feelings and cement loyalties towards the trade union case.

Many of the trade unions in the sector have also played a dual role as trade union defenders of terms and conditions and representatives of the 'professional' interests of their members. This has enabled them in many instances to offer a service to their members on training provision and career advice that enhances their appeal. In fact many of these 'professional associations', which are not affiliated to the TUC, have seen significant growth of membership over the 1990s against the general trend (Farnham and Giles, 1995). The Royal College of Nursing, for example, has grown from 134,689 in 1979 to over 360,000 in 2000. Other growing associations include the Secondary Heads Association, the British Association of Occupational Therapists, and the Association of Teachers and Lecturers. In some cases the professionally oriented approach of such associations has meant that they have adopted a 'no strike' policy (e.g. the RCN and Professional Association of Teachers), but in some cases (e.g. the RCN and Royal College of Midwives) this policy has seen some relaxation in the 1990s, reflecting a heightening of industrial relations tension within the public sector.

The final explanatory factor for trade union attachment in the sector has been the common cause established by the unions between the defence of jobs and the defence of service provision. The deleterious effects on service provision caused by spending cuts (hospital ward or library closures, for example) have meant that unions have gained extra legitimacy for their cause in defending both jobs *and* services. The likelihood of some success, however minimal, in resisting closure plans or cutbacks has improved as a result, particularly where it is clearly possible to reverse spending cuts within the local process of political accountability. This added political and social dimension to the role of public sector unions, if effectively deployed, gives the unions an enhanced identity which may well have acted as a spur to membership recruitment and retention.

The choice dilemmas within the sector, between service provision, cost and efficiency, have also set limits to the degree of flexibility that could be expected in terms of employers' strategies to change working practices. It is to these dilemmas that we now turn.

■ Service provision versus cost cutting: a management dilemma

The pressures on managers to continue to provide a public service against the background of public spending cuts have meant that efforts to introduce many aspects of performance incentives and HRM techniques have been dampened. The difficulties of setting targets and performance objectives for individual staff in public services have already been discussed. In particular, the problems of isolating 'value added' in monetary terms are apparent where no test of increased profits or market share can be made. In some cases it will be possible to determine 'outputs' if these relate, for example, to identifiable performance indicators such as increased student numbers in education or decreased empty bed space in hospitals. However, such targets, if pursued uncautiously, may well have deleterious effects on 'quality' of service or level of provision that may have contradictory effects on other performance 'indicators' that are quality related or which relate to customer/client/public satisfaction. Such policy dilemmas are also likely to create some cynicism among employees unless the performance criteria are transparent and seen to have accommodated some of the more difficult policy contradictions.

These problems, combined as they are with an increasingly low-trust working environment inspired by pay restrictions and job cuts, have meant that some newer personnel practices such as appraisal, merit pay or 'quality' programmes have often met with resistance from staff and their unions. Thus, proposals for a teachers' performance appraisal system have created disputes in schools, and in further and higher education continual union resistance meant that new systems in many instances were effectively imposed by college employers (and their developmental value reduced as a result). Within schools, the government finally succeeded in establishing its 'threshold' system of individual performance-related pay. However, morale and productivity have not necessarily been improved. A government commissioned Mori survey in 2001, established as part of the Department of Education and Skills review, found that two-thirds of teachers who had succeeded in obtaining the £2,000 per year performance bonus said it had done little to boost their confidence. For the one in seven teachers who refused to apply, the scheme was reported to be a major factor in any decision to leave the profession (*Times Educational Supplement*, 21 September 2001 – see Exhibit 14.3). Similarly, proposals for quality circles in departments of the civil service in the 1980s were withdrawn after union boycotts amid fears that any emerging proposals would inspire non-negotiable service or job cuts.

Exhibit 14.3

Performance-related pay for teachers

The following case study examines the introduction of performance-related pay for teachers, the union response, and the workings of the scheme in practice.

1 The government's threshold plan

Qualified teachers with a good honours degree and seven years' teaching experience, together with other teachers with nine years' experience, will be able to apply for the scheme. The cash for the threshold payments comes from a separate government fund over and above that reserved for teachers' salaries. Schools will have available in their budgets an extra £2,000 annually for each full-time teacher who crosses the threshold which will be in place until at least March 2002. Teachers applying for the money had to fill in an application form and headteachers then made an assessment drawing on the opinions of senior staff and line managers as appropriate. External assessors would then verify the headteachers' recommendations through a sample. Pay increases would be backdated to September 2000. A successful High Court challenge was made by the unions to certain aspects of the scheme's operation, but eventually the scheme was introduced after some changes were made by the government.

2 The union view

Cash first, details of performance pay later, unions say
Teachers' leaders are to accept the link between pay and pupil progress in an attempt to get threshold cash to members as quickly as possible. Only the National Union of Teachers will press for the controversial link to be dropped, as the government attempts to get the policy on to the

statute book after its High Court defeat. However, a new survey of teachers who applied for the pay rise shows they have little confidence in the standards they must meet to get their extra £2,000-a-year. Only four in 10 believed the eight standards – which include the pay and results link – described good teaching, the Association of Teachers and Lecturers' survey found. Eight out of 10 said filling in the forms had been a 'bad experience', with half believing performance pay would divide staff.

Education Secretary David Blunkett will refer the eight standards to the School Teachers' Review Body, asking it to report back by the end of September. That could mean some teachers get their rise as early as November. All payments will be backdated to September 1.

The NUT this week warned the review body it risked getting into a 'constitutional dispute' over devolution if it accepted responsibility for the standards. The union believes ministers should let standards in Wales be decided by the Welsh Assembly.

Tony Vineall, the review body chairman, is understood to have told the union it was a matter for the government. The NUT denied applying pressure. Most unions fear infuriating members who would have to repeat the time-consuming application process if the standards changed. The ATL found that the 197,000 applicants took an average of 16 hours to fill in the forms. These unions will instead press for changes next year. Once the criteria become part of the review body's remit, they could be debated annually.

Even the NUT, whose action led to the standards being ruled unlawful, is pressing for a quick solution: drop the results link and debate the standards next year. The union's general secretary Doug McAvoy said: 'We oppose payment by results and will continue to do so. What we have done is ensure there is a statutory vehicle open for us to use.' The National Association of Head Teachers and the Secondary Heads Association said any change this year

▶

Exhibit 14.3 *continued*

would be unacceptable to members assessing applications. NAHT general secretary David Hart said: 'There is no way headteachers would go through the process again.'

The National Association of Schoolmasters Union of Women Teachers said there had been plenty of informal consultation over the standards. Deputy general secretary Eamonn O'Kane said repeating the exercise would be 'utterly unacceptable'. (Nicolas Barnard, *Times Educational Supplement*, 8 September 2000)

3   The scheme in practice

■ When the scheme was finally in place, 201,000 teachers, around 80 per cent of those eligible, applied to be assessed for performance-related pay by presenting the appropriate portfolio of evidence and achieving the necessary threshold of performance.

■ If successful, a teacher would receive a salary enhancement of £2,000 for that year.

■ Thirty-seven per cent of the 201,000 applications were from primary teachers, 52 per cent from secondary teachers, 5 per cent from centrally employed local education authority staff, and 4 per cent from special schools.

■ A total of 1,300 schools did not apply i.e. the head-teachers did not enter into the scheme.

■ Men and women applied in equal proportions, but 4.6 per cent of men failed, compared with 2.2 per cent of women.

■ Common failings were teaching and classroom management.

■ Assessors overturned decisions in 315 cases (0.2 per cent).

■ Teachers were assessed in five areas: knowledge and understanding, teaching and assessment, pupil progress, wider professional effectiveness, and professional characteristics.

4   Comment: performance pay, teacher morale and productivity

A team from Exeter University examined in detail the workings of the performance pay scheme for teachers. The study showed that only 3 per cent of teachers who applied to cross the threshold to a higher scale of pay for an immediate £2,000 rise were turned down. A team of external assessors, appointed by the government and paid £300 per day, had interviewed staff, but spent virtually no time observing them teaching. In only a very small number of cases (1 in 270) did the assessors disagree with the headteacher's judgement on whether the teacher concerned should pass the threshold. Heads spent an average two hours examining each application and, according to the Exeter study, teachers who failed to cross the threshold felt shocked, upset and bitter, while heads who had to give the bad news found the experience stressful and demoralising. Most importantly, the study suggests that three-quarters of heads felt that the threshold had made little or no difference to the way teachers behaved and taught in the classroom. Only one in five believed it had any impact. In summary, the main impact of the performance pay scheme has been to make staff keep more detailed records of childrens' work as evidence to present to assessors.

The risks attached to the development of lower-trust relationships between management and staff as a result of cutbacks will also reflect on attempts to reorganise work. Efforts to introduce elements of employee participation and involvement, such as the Best Value initiative for local authorities, might often be perceived by staff as attempts to intensify work. Data collected by the University of Warwick's 'Trade Unions into the 1990s' project, for example, indicate that there is a lesser incidence of the introduction of quality circles and teamworking into the public sector but a higher incidence of team briefing, suggesting difficulties in establishing more radical change (Waddington and Whitston, 1996). Similarly, the survey reports a higher incidence of grievances over workload and staffing levels in the public sector. A study of work intensification in UK workplaces by Green (2001) also found that there was considerable intensification of work in the public sector throughout the 1990s. In schools, for example, new demands were placed on teachers as a result of the introduction of the National Curriculum and a rise in pupil–teacher ratios, while in universities new external pressure to produce more research output were placed on lecturers. The long-running series of disputes in the Royal Mail since 1988, often initiated by rank-and-file union members against the wishes of the leadership, over the introduction of total quality management (TQM) and team-working is a case in point. Management proposals to introduce these more HRM-based techniques have followed a programme of 'delayering' of management strata and a staff redundancy programme. Industrial relations tensions were therefore heightened in the process such that 'the re-organisation of Royal Mail left the personnel function in a somewhat ambiguous situation within an increasingly complex and politically charged industrial relations environment' (Martinez Lucio and Noon, 1994). While the number of strikes in Royal Mail was especially high in the 1990s, there was a fall in strike rates recorded in 2001. This came after a deal was struck between the employer and the Communication Workers' Union (CWU) whereby Royal Mail agreed not to implement any unagreed changes in working practices at local level in return for a union commitment to suspend industrial action (*People Management*, 25 October 2001).

All of these factors have imposed some limitation on the degree to which new management techniques have been able to be introduced within the public sector. The continued relative resilience of public sector unions, despite their being placed on the defensive, has meant that employers have been forced to negotiate change where they might otherwise have sought to bypass or marginalise unions. Often such change has had to involve re-examining grading structures and realigning pay through job evaluation studies (Waddington and Whitston, 1996). Derecognition of unions in the public sector, or partial derecognition involving managerial grades, has been much rarer than in the private sector, and has been generally confined to those instances where services have been contracted out or privatised (e.g. managerial staff in British Telecom following privatisation). As a result, the climate of adverserial 'industrial' relations, established in particular in the 1970s, has lingered on and processes designed to individualise the employment relationship have proved more difficult to establish.

Chapter summary

This chapter explores the structure and growth of the public sector in the UK. The history from 'model employer' to 'new' Labour is assessed, and the tensions between providing a public service and managing within budgetary constraints are explored. A description of the key industrial relations concerns is given together with a commentary of major disputes.

Questions

1 How can you explain the high density of union membership in the public sector when compared to the private sector?

2 Discuss the problems of introducing 'new public management'. How might the problems be overcome?

Activities

1   Reread Exhibit 14.1 about public sector financing and answer the following questions.

   (a) Why might modern governments be keen to finance public services by private money?

   (b) What problems, if any, might follow from such a strategy?

2   The following questions related to the case study presented in Exhibit 14.2 on performance-related pay for teachers.

   (a) Why did the government face so much opposition from teachers' unions to the introduction of performance-related pay?

   (b) Given the obvious difficulties of the scheme, how might a satisfactory system of performance measurement be established for teachers?

   (c) In introducing the scheme the government has argued that the wider interests of parents and children are at stake. Should public sector trade unions such as the teachers' unions have limitations imposed on them in any action they may take which opposes government policy?

Notes

1   The Private Finance Initiative (PFI) was introduced during the Conservative administration by the Chancellor of the Exchequer in his Autumn Statement in September 1992. The catch-phrase of the initiative was 'private opportunity, public benefit', and the aim was to allow the private sector to assume the management of public services where an improvement in efficiency and a reduction in costs may arise. While the PFI approach may be more expensive than using public finance, ongoing savings may be made by later cost savings in the operation of the service. Despite some opposition to the scheme from Labour prior to its 1997 election victory, the incoming government retained the scheme.

2   The principle that the pay of particular groups of public sector employees is to be determined through comparison with comparable private sector occupations has been superseded since 1979 by the concept of affordability, the idea that pay should be related to the financial circumstances of the employing organisation.

3   Pay review bodies are standing bodies appointed by government and able to take an independent view on medium-term developments in pay for the public service occupations covered. There are pay review bodies for nurses and midwives, doctors and dentists, other health service professionals, school teachers, the armed forces and 'top salaried' senior military officials, civil servants and judges. A total of 1.5 million employees are covered. While this is rather less than one-quarter of the public sector workforce, pay review body awards have influenced pay settlements for other groups within the public sector. Pay review bodies take evidence each year from relevant sources and make recommendations to government. The presumption is that, unless there are compelling reasons to do otherwise, the government will accept the recommendations.

4   The Citizen's Charter initiative was proposed by the government in 1991 through the Citizen's Charter White Paper which emphasised four themes: quality, choice, standards and value in the provision of public services. The objectives were to improve service provision and to instil in providers a more customer-oriented culture. Service providers were required to establish and monitor performance targets along prescribed dimensions, and performance

is subject to independent validation. Charters for particular services were introduced and a central unit established to oversee their development.

5 *Improving Management in Government: The Next Steps* was a report by Sir Robin Ibbs, head of the government's Efficiency Unit, published in 1988 and critical of the impact of the government's management reforms on the civil service. It suggested that the civil service was 'too big and too diverse to be managed as a single unit', and advocated the reorganisation of the executive activities of government (as distinct from policy advice) into separate agencies with specific responsibilities and targets. Headed by chief executives, often recruited from outside the civil service, these agencies were granted greater flexibility in financial and personnel matters. Variations between agencies (in terms of size, activities, financial regimes) in part explain the uneven pace of decentralisation of pay and conditions. Nevertheless, this has been given further impetus by subsequent central government initiatives, and devolution is increasing quite rapidly.

6 The aim of the internal market has been to stimulate greater competition between providers of public services and in this way to improve performance. In the NHS from 1991, for example, the main purchasers of health care (health authorities) were separated from providers of the services (hospitals and community units). The internal market has been supported by devolved budgets and financial management. General practitioners can acquire fundholder status and purchase hospital provision. Similar arrangements now exist across most public sector employers although the major tenets of the internal market in the NHS were substantially downgraded after the election of the Labour government in 1997.

7 In education, the term 'opting out' applies to around 20 per cent of secondary schools that, after a ballot, became grant-maintained schools, no longer subject to local education authority control. All schools are covered by the Local Management of Schools structure of devolved financial management. The policy of opting out of schools has been put on hold by the Labour government.

8 Best Value (BV) was introduced as a new regime for local authorities in England and Wales under the Local Government Act 1999. It was intended as a replacement for the compulsory competitive tendering programme of the outgoing Conservative government. The government's expectations of Best Value is 'continuous improvement' in local authority performance, assessed through changes in service costs and standards, as well as 'better services . . . with significant efficiency improvements'. This involves performance plans, five-yearly reviews of progress with evidence of comparison and competition, and action plans which may involve private finance initiatives. In terms of employee relations, BV authorities are required to adopt a 'partnership' approach to employees and trade unions embodied in a framework agreement signed by the major employers and trade unions.

9 Public sector service organisations were legally obligated under Conservative legislation to allow private contractors to bid for the right to carry out specified services. In the NHS, compulsory competitive tendering (CCT) was introduced initially in 1983 for cleaning, catering and laundry services. In local government, the initiative started in direct labour organisations (e.g. in building work) and was extended into cleaning, refuse collection and maintenance functions by the Local Government Act 1988. The tendering exercise required local authorities to separate the 'client' and 'contractor' roles and hence resulted in a radical restructuring of internal management and organisation in local government. 'Market testing' is closely associated with CCT and was later extended to white-collar central government and local authority services.

Useful websites

www.newdeal.gov.uk **Welfare to Work**   Government website on the Welfare to Work initiatives.
www.pcs.org.uk **Public Commercial and Services**   Website of the trade union for the civil service.
www.ukonline.gov.uk **Statistical information**   Government website which provides statistical and other information.
www.unison.org.uk **Unison**   Website of the trade union Unison (local government employees), with many useful links.

References

Bacon, R. and Eltis, W. (1978) *Britain's Economic Problem: Too Few Producers*, 2nd edn. London: Macmillan.

Blyton, P. and Turnbull, P. (1998) *The Dynamics of Employee Relations*, 2nd edn. London: Macmillan.

Boyne, G. (2000) 'External regulation and Best Value in local government', *Public Money and Management*, July–September.

Carter, B. and Fairbrother, P. (1999) 'The transformation of British public-sector industrial relations: from "model employer" to marketized relations', *Historical Studies in Industrial Relations*, 7: 119–46.

Dickerson, A. and Stewart, M. (1993) 'Is the public sector more strike prone?', *Oxford Bulletin of Economics and Statistics*, 55(3): 253–84.

Edwards, P.K. and Whitston, C. (1991) 'Workers are working harder: effort and shop floor relations in the 1980s', *British Journal of Industrial Relations*, 29(4): 593–600.

Fairbrother, P. (1996) 'Workplace trade unionism in the state sector' in Ackers, P., Smith, C. and Smith, P. (eds) *The New Workplace and Trade Unionism*. London: Routledge.

Farnham, D. and Giles, L. (1995) 'Trade unions in the UK: trends and counter-trends since 1979', *Employee Relations*, 17(2).

Ferner, A. (1994) 'The State as employer' in Hyman, R. and Ferner, A. (eds) *New Frontiers in European Industrial Relations*. London: Blackwell.

Fisher, L. (1999) 'Strong workplace union fights health "Reforms"' in Cohen, S. (ed.), *What's Happening? The Truth about Work and the Myth of Partnership*. London: Trade Union Forum Pamphlet.

Foster, D. and Scott, P. (1998) 'Conceptualising union responses to contracting out municipal services, 1979–97', *Industrial Relations Journal*, 29(2): 137–50.

Fredman, S. and Morris, G. (1989) *The State as Employer: Labour Law in the Public Services*. London: Mansell.

Green, F. (2001) 'It's been a hard day's night: the concentration and intensification of work in late twentieth-century Britain', *British Journal of Industrial Relations*, 39(1): 53–80.

Kelly, J. (1988) *Trade Unions and Socialist Politics*. London: Verso.

Kerr, D. (1997) 'The PFI miracle', *Capital and Class*: 64.

Marsden, D. and French, S. (2000) *What a Performance*. London: London School of Economics.

Martinez Lucio, M. and Noon, M. (1994) 'Organisational change and the tensions of decentralisation: the case of Royal Mail', *Human Resource Management Journal*, 5(2).

Menter, I., Muschamp, Y., Nicholls, P., Ozgal, J. and Pollard, A. (1997) *Work and Identity in the Primary School*. Milton Keynes: Open University Press.

Millward, N., Stevens, M., Smart, D. and Hawes, W.R. (1992) *Workplace Industrial Relations in Transition*. Aldershot: Dartmouth.

Prandy, K., Stewart, A. and Blackburn, R.M. (1982) *White Collar Work*. London: Macmillan.

Seifert, R. (1987) *Teacher Militancy: A History of Teacher Strikes, 1896–1987*. Brighton: Falmer Press.

Seifert, R. (1992) *Industrial Relations in the NHS*. London: Chapman & Hall.

Unison (2001) *Public Services Manifesto*. London: Unison.

Waddington, J. (1992) 'Trade union membership in Britain 1980–87: unemployment and restructuring', *British Journal of Industrial Relations*, 30(2): 287–324.

Waddington, J. and Whitston, C. (1996) 'Empowerment versus intensification – union perspectives of change at the workplace' in Ackers, P., Smith, C. and Smith, P. (eds) *The New Workplace and Trade Unionism*. London: Routledge.

Wigham, E. (1980) *From Humble Petition to Militant Action: A History of the Civil and Public Services Association 1903–1978*. London: CPSA.

Winchester, D. and Bach, S. (1995) 'The public sector' in Edwards, P. (ed.) *Industrial Relations Theory and Practice*, 3rd edn. London: Prentice Hall.

Further reading

Beaumont, P.B. (1992) *Public Sector Industrial Relations*. London: Routledge.

Corby, S. and White, G. (1999) *Employee Relations in the Public Services*. London: Routledge.

Farnham, P. and Horton, S. (1993) *The Political Economy of Public Sector Change*. London: Macmillan.

Millward, N. (1993) *The New Industrial Relations*, London: PSI.

Monbiot, G. (2000) *Captive State: the corporate take-over of Britain*, London: Macmillan.

Rajan, A. and Pearson, R. (1986) *UK Occupation and Employment Trends to 1990*. London: Butterworths.

Salamon, M. (2000) *Industrial Relations*, 4th edn. London: Prentice Hall.

Part Five

Conclusion

Chapter 15

The rediscovery of conflict in the employment relationship

Andy Danford and Paul Stewart

Introduction

In the previous chapters we looked at the importance of employee relations in a number of ways in order to assess the dynamics of the employment relationship from the point of view of the central actors. In trying to encapsulate the extent and depth of the employment relationship it is always tempting to stop at the office door or the factory gate and focus on the immediate set of relations that mark the workplace out as the site of interactions between those buying and selling labour power. An emphasis on the latter is important where we want to demonstrate the peculiar ways in which what goes on at work results from the interactions among various actors in the paid workplace. Yet what goes on in the employment relationship is only partly accounted for by describing what goes on *in work* – whether experienced in a conventional workplace or in the home setting as is the case in home working. Quite apart from the fact that much of what we call work occurs in places where we do not normally receive payment for our efforts (including at home and in the community, for parents, friends and voluntary organisations), there is also the issue of how external social, economic and political relations impact upon workplace behaviour. We return to this later. Nevertheless, we often tend to focus on the employment relationship in paid work since it is the obvious site in which relations between those seeking employment and those offering it are met.

To extend our understanding of the character of employment relations in paid work we need to begin to imagine other themes we might add to what has already been said about the dynamics of the employment relationship. In this concluding chapter, what we want to do is to point out another critical aspect of employment that goes to the heart of the employment relationship across every sector, whatever the occupation or country, whatever the nature of relations between business, state and the wider society. This is the question of conflict, and we take this to be invariably central to all aspects of employment today. If conflict is an ever present feature of workplace relations, it is also everywhere locked into a relationship with consensus-making processes. Here, however, we focus upon the role of conflict in the making of the contemporary workplace. The fact that conflict need not always be evident in the employment relationship does not necessarily presuppose the existence of consensus among the workforce. Looking beyond the factory gate or the office door reminds us of the existence of alternative world-views and of class and cultural communities with quite different views of life from those consensual ones sometimes too readily assumed by managers in the absence of overt conflicts (see Glucksman, 2000; Stephenson and Stewart, 2001).

It would be understandable if students of employee relations were to register surprise at this focus upon conflict at work. After all, the lexicon of work and employment adopted by most of our political leaders, employer representatives, trade union leaders and the media has become dominated by such terms as 'partnership', 'cooperation', 'consensus' and the 'class-free' or 'post-class' society. These shifts in political discourse are reflected in the employment-related agendas of the more influential sociologies of advanced modernity. For example, Bauman (2001) and Beck (1992) have argued that a 'destandardisation of labour' and the emergence of an 'individualised society of employees' have recast the contours and sites of conflict at work and in society. What Bauman refers to as the permanent marriage and stability between capital and labour under Fordism has given way to a new form of 'liquefied modernity' characterised by fragmentation, 'flexibilisation' and a footloose capital that is now concerned more with the production of captive consumers than with conceding workers' rights. As a result, employees cannot resort to collective action, standing shoulder to shoulder to increase the power of individuals, because the new troubles they face are not additive, they simply do not add up to a common cause. Instead, the new risks and uncertainties in the employment relationship, for example, the fear of unemployment, the instability of short-term contracts and the lack of career prospects, though socially produced, must be coped with individually.

This individualisation thesis is both seductive and pessimistic. However, the broad sweep of the argument and the generalisations it produces do not always correspond with concrete reality. For example, in the UK, where there has been much less regulation of the labour market compared with most other European countries, research has shown that the full-time employment contract remains the norm for most employees (Robinson 1999; see also Chapter 13). Similarly, although Bauman, Beck and other 'post-' analysts make explicit the intense risk, uncertainty and insecurity that accompany the 'destandardisation of labour', a more sober assessment is provided by the authors of the current Workplace Employee Relations Survey (WERS). Cully et al.'s (1999) systematic study of employee attitudes presents an overall picture of relative job security experienced by the majority of employees in today's labour market, especially for women and part-time workers.

If we turn to conflict itself, the data on UK labour disputes would appear to support those who advance the individualisation thesis. For example, the Office of National Statistics data for the years 1980 to 2000 show a substantial decline in the incidence of official strikes (Figures 15.1 and 15.2).

Figure 15.1 charts working days lost due to strikes, whereas Figure 15.2 charts the actual number of stoppages. Both show that the number of strikes has been on a downward trend since the early/mid-1980s and that they have reached a fairly constant level since the early 1990s.

However, the reasons for this decline do not lie in the supposed individualisation of the employment relationship. Neither do they necessarily denote a demise in collectivism at work. Instead, the decline in this particular *form* of collectivised conflict resides in other structural and environmental changes in employee relations. For example, during the 1980s and 1990s a recomposition of industrial activity and labour markets resulted in the decline of particular sectors, such as coalmining and engineering, former sites

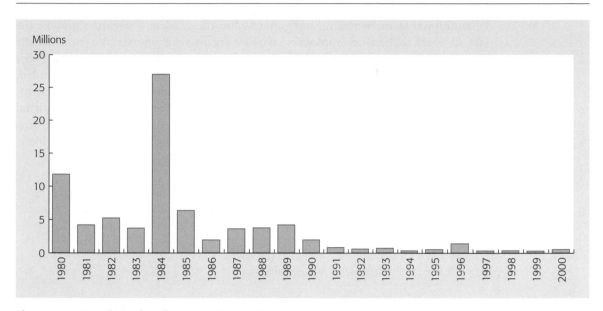

Figure 15.1 **Working days lost, UK, 1980–2000**
Source: Office for National Statistics

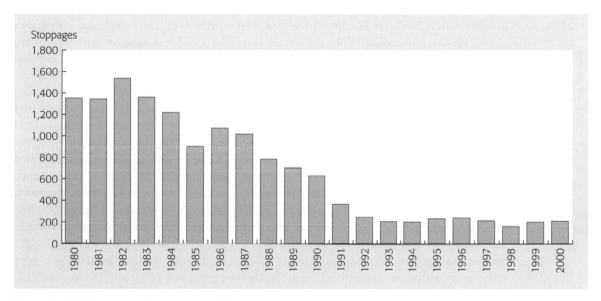

Figure 15.2 **Stoppages in progress, UK, 1980–2000**
Source: Office for National Statistics

of concentrated strike activity and traditional collective militancy. The same period witnessed a significant shift in the balance of power between capital and labour. Two severe economic recessions, bouts of mass unemployment, state attacks on trade union and worker rights, a sharp decline in trade union membership, and the re-emergence of a more confident and aggressive management in industrial relations are all reflected in fewer strikes.

An additional factor which is rarely analysed in the academic literature may be the impact of worker debt on employees' propensity to take industrial action. In the summer of 2001, the total level of consumer debt in the UK stood at record levels: £700 billion. This debt averaged £5,300 per household before mortgages are included. This profound structural change in the financing of consumer spending and the reproduction of labour power has obvious implications for the organisation of any industrial action that runs the risk of cutting off employees' access to this credit resource. It is well summed up in the following comment of an engineering shopfloor worker interviewed in 2002 for an ESRC Future of Work research project:

> As the years went on, you had 11 years of Margaret Thatcher and her Tory policies and people became frightened of putting their heads up above the parapet, because you had a lot more to lose. Finances all changed, the balance of bringing up your family, buying a house and paying a mortgage, the goal posts moved from when I first bought a house back in 1970, to the 1980s and 1990s. When they started to change the formulas for mortgages, for example, people got very, very frightened. (Authors' fieldnotes)

The impact of these different factors on industrial action suggest that both agency and structural change have combined to *suppress* rather than *eradicate* some traditional forms of collective action. However, if this is the case then we might expect the inherent conflict in the employment relationship to re-emerge in different forms. For example, absenteeism constitutes an alternative means of withdrawal from work and employers are increasingly focusing their concern on this. The Confederation of British Industry issued a report in 1997 showing that in 1996, 187 million working days were lost due to sickness (nearly 100 times the amount lost to strike action in that year). This averaged 8.4 working days off per employee and represented 3.7 per cent of total working time. The new salience of absenteeism has been attributed by management consultants and academics alike to a rise in working hours, work intensification and consequent workplace stress.

It is interesting to note how an interest in conflict can be seen to have emerged in two senses. First, it is becoming fashionable once more as an object of study . This is due to the cyclical interest in the character of both employee status and employee interests. The study of employment relations in the 1980s and 1990s focused on employers' interests and circumstances, with the fate of the employee receiving rather less attention. Indeed this was a period in which many assumed that employee interests could be met without the need to resort to conflict. Collectivism, where it existed, was seen to be synonymous with conflict. Secondly, the re-emergence of an interest in conflict is becoming increasingly important because it tells us something about the changing nature of work, company organisation and the wider employment relationship. Specifically, one of the central dimensions of conflict at work today is that it tracks, in an especially close way, the fault lines of new forms and patterns of employment. In so doing, we can say that conflict is also central to the 'new politics of production'.

In using the phrase 'new politics of production' we are referring to the ways in which new patterns of social, organisational and economic relations are emerging in the workplace. These patterns consist in some new forms of working, including teamworking, designed to enhance employee responsibilities for employer and consumer requirements, and interestingly, not only in the obvious external market but inside the company too.

Although now widely recognised as part of the panoply of a firm's necessary response to customer relations, the idea of the employee as internal customer is more than rhetoric. Indeed, we could say that it has two consequences, one intended, the other unintended. First, whereas the idea of the internal customer allows for the devolution of responsibility, the term does not fully account for the impact that the idea of the 'customer' has on employees themselves. Responsibility is fine, but responsibility without authority has very particular consequences.

It is interesting to note that the current WERS data indicate that many UK employees enjoy very little meaningful authority at work. If we consider autonomy and self-management in teams (see Figure 15.3), although the WERS data suggest that in 65 per cent of workplaces employees work in formally designated teams, a much lower proportion of workplaces (35 per cent) operate teams that correspond to a model of semi-autonomous teamworking incorporating a degree of self-management. Moreover, a mere 3 per cent of workplaces operate fully autonomous teams incorporating self-management and the right to appoint team leaders.

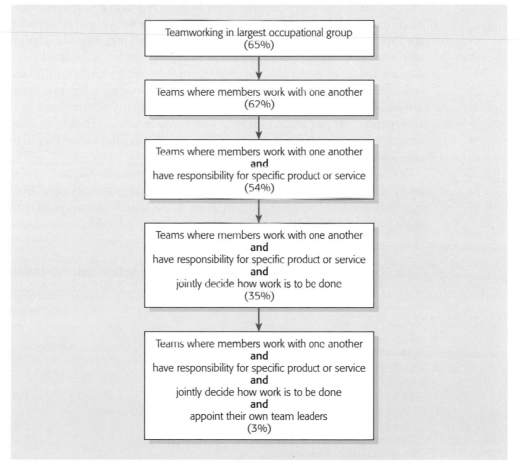

Figure 15.3 From teamworking to fully autonomous teamworking
Source: Cully *et al*. (1999)

Employee consultation rights constitute another mechanism by which employees can exert influence over management decision-making. Again, the WERS data provide a useful source of information on this issue because, as well as collecting data from managers on the range of practices in use, the survey also asked employees to assess these practices. The survey asked employees how often they were asked by managers for their views on five separate workplace issues. These were: future plans for the workforce, staffing issues, working practices, pay, and health and safety. The results are presented in Table 15.1.

The results show that employee participation was low on all five issues. The most widespread participation related to health and safety; nevertheless, on this issue and all others less than one-quarter of employees reported frequent consultation; on staffing and pay issues less than 10 per cent did so. Moreover, over three-quarters of employees felt that they were not frequently consulted on any of the five key employment issues.

One additional effect moreover, is that employees may have limited scope in this context to create formal challenges to management's organisational prerogatives. Secondly, we know from research across the economy as a whole, that contemporary forms and patterns of work and employment increase considerably the intensification of work. Furthermore, this intensification leads to both physical and psychological pressures on employees and the consequent health effects can be seen in the perceived deterioration in the quality of life at work. In addition to teamworking, measures designed to instigate employee responsibility in production include performance-related pay (individualised pay awards), working time accounts, quality circles and continuous improvement schemes. In addition to their stated aim of improving company performance, these are all intended to link employee reward and company performance in such a way that transparency is introduced into the employment nexus. HRM, more broadly, can be seen as a response to the growing requirement for greater rationality in the employment relationship.

If only life and the employment relationship were so simple, but, of course, new forms and patterns of production and innovative management practices (HRM) do not grow out of a social and political vacuum. If we know that antagonisms in the workplace find their origins in the delicate relationships between home-life, community (including the

Table 15.1 Frequent employee participation in workplace decision-making

	Proportion of employees reporting frequent consultation %
Future plans for the workforce	14
Staffing issues, including redundancy	8
Change to working practices	17
Pay issues	5
Health and safety at work	23
Frequent consultation on 3 or more issues	6
Frequent consultation on 2 issues	6
Frequent consultation on 1 issue	11
Frequent consultation on none of these issues	77

Source: adapted from Cully et al. (1999)

wider economy) and work, then in an era of steadily rising productivity and competition, employees will find themselves under increasing duress at work. In the UK, the growing pressures in the world of work have, for many employees, become unsustainable. Francis Green (2001) highlights that work has become more intensive since 1981, with employees indicating that one of the pressures behind intensified effort is peer pressure. The latter is a significant feature of new employment relations.

Many sector studies, notably in the automotive industry, commercial and public services, including health, banking and insurance and postal services, have shown that work is becoming more arduous for all employees. This increasing pressure is creating extraordinary health and safety problems that seriously erode employees' quality of working life. And we can safely assume that many of the health problems caused by the nature of contemporary forms of employment go under-reported. Indeed, according to *Labour Research*:

> Analysis of workers' responses to the Labour Force Survey (LFS) for 1998–1999 put the number of injuries at work at 1.03 million, excluding sickness and injury caused by the effects of certain jobs.
>
> However, these figures are significantly higher than the number of accidents reported by employers.
>
> The HSE [Health and Safety Executive] says that about 70% of accidents are due to management error. (*Labour Research*, February 2001: 5)

Unfortunately, immediate injuries are not the only sign of stress at work. Stress can lead to medium- and long-term health problems. According to the highly regarded voluntary organisation Hazards, which is sponsored by trade union organisations and whose research is sought by government and employers alike, stress can lead to long-term health problems including physical and psychological disability (*Hazards*, 2001). More worryingly for newly employed and younger employees, evidence is now pointing towards 'workplaces of the future' where those in their late thirties may be considered too old because the workplace itself creates long-term and serious injury.

Related to the problem of stress created by new forms and patterns of working is the practice of bullying, an increasingly common form of harassment. We cannot be precise about its extent and variation even if we have become more attuned in recent years to its profoundly debilitating consequences for employees. According to a survey carried by Hoel and Cooper (2000), just under half (47 per cent) of employees in the UK have been witness to some form of bullying at work, and 10 per cent claimed to have been bullied in the six months prior to the survey. (The survey covered a wide range of workplaces and sectors, including, local and central government, postal services and telecommunications, teaching, banking, finance and insurance, the performing arts, and the prison service.) What is worrying, however, is that almost one-quarter said they had been bullied at some point in the previous five years. Disturbingly, while we know the origins of this form of conflict lie in an absence of accountability, confidence and respect, which new forms of work exacerbate, recent data have uncovered a significant degree of management-originated bullying. According to Hoel and Cooper, while 37 per cent of respondents reported bullying originating from colleagues, 68 per cent indicated managers as the source of harassment (15 per cent of people reported being bullied by customers).

According to *Labour Research*, the overall impact of bullying leads to

> an increase in sickness absence, which can have a domino effect which may lead to greater sickness absence; a reduction in staff morale; poor staff performance; staff seeking alternative employment. (*Labour Research*, November 2001, 2001: 9)

These examples drawn from recent evidence suggest that employment is becoming increasingly more stressful, less satisfying and, in many instances, more dangerous. Yet stressful, demanding and difficult jobs are closely bound up with the new patterns of work organisation – teamworking, quality circles, new working time arrangements. The modern workplace demands working patterns which (if not always difficult and boring) are leading increasingly to the rise of a 'new politics of production' in which remuneration becomes less central to employee and trade union demands than issues concerned with quality of life at work.

Alternative possibilities for enhanced quality of working life

If work is becoming increasingly stressful through intensification of effort, how might employees attempt to control the effects of this increased pressure to deliver? One answer is through the strengthening of third-party intermediaries – typically, trade unions – over whom they exert control. This is important in shifting the emphasis away from health and safety and workplace injury as a matter of individual blame. It is not. The problem is the sickness of the organisation, not the individuals who comprise it, and more particularly of the nexus of power relationships that are contained within it, creating increasingly stressful workplaces. As a practical response, one can begin to develop a number of principles that allow for some measure of employee control over working practices, including the effort which goes into their various work activities. These measures will impact directly upon effort associated with time (length of the working day, rest periods and holiday entitlement), effort (how much work in what period of time) and compensation (financial and social, including holiday entitlement on employee terms). These measures should ensure that:

- employee participation in job design is fundamental;
- jobs are designed to avoid mental and physical stress;
- jobs are not designed so that employees are socially and/or psychologically isolated;
- work is adapted to fit the abilities of those responsible for carrying it out.

Moreover, bullying and other forms harassment, including racial, sexual and age-related abuse, should be monitored by employees and their trade union representatives.

While this approach will not in itself resolve the problem of the conflictual workplace, it will allow employees to begin to challenge the powerful assumption of the 1980s and 1990s that the organisation of time and effort was outside their control. While a useful starting point, the focus on the workplace cannot alone account for the stress and injuries suffered by men and women at work since the structure of their daily lives has become increasingly synchronised to the rhythm and tempo of market imperatives. Stress and injury at work increasingly impact on private lives in ways that can affect significantly how men and women are able to cope with their employment. It is in this respect that we can talk about employment in broader environmental terms. In this case, it will be necessary to examine the reciprocal relationships of work, home and community so that people at work may begin to set limits to the way that work is carried out. Questions to be considered will include: who makes decisions over how work is carried out – what are the decision-making processes and who is involved in them? In what way are decisions about staffing levels determined? What role does a union have to play in this? How can employees and their unions become involved in tightening up health and safety at work – how frequently are risk assessments carried out in the workplace? In what ways can the local community be involved in determining shift patterns that can be synchronised to, rather than disrupting, individuals' private, social and community lives?

Given the relationship between economic, social and political power in society, resolving these questions will not abolish health and safety concerns, but addressing them can go some way to identifying the origins of conflict at work. Identifying the basis of the new workplace conflicts can highlight how men and women might begin to challenge the powerful biases against them in employment. It can allow for the beginnings of new alliances between people at work – younger and older workers, men and women, all of different ethnicity – so that they might begin to create workplaces that do not harm and injure them. Addressing the basis of contemporary workplace stress and injury will necessarily form a constitutive part of the new politics of production.

References

Bauman (2001) *The Individualized Society*. Cambridge, Polity Press.

Beck (1992) *Risk Society*, London: Sage.

CBI (1997) *Managing Absence – In Sickness and Health*. CBI Report, April.

Cully, M., Woodland, S., O'Reilly, A. and Dix, G. (1999) *Britain at Work, As Depicted in the 1998 Workplace Employee Relations Survey*. London: Routledge.

Glucksman, M. (2000) *Cottons and Casuals: The Gendered Organisation of Labour in Time and Space*. Durham: Sociology Press.

Green, F. (2001) 'It's been a hard day's night: the concentration and intensification of work in late twentieth-century Britain', *British Journal of Industrial Relations*, 39(1): 53–80.

Hazards (2001) 'When work is a pain', 73 (January/March).

Hoel, H. and Cooper, C. (2000) *Destructive Conflict and Bullying at Work*. Manchester: UMIST.

Robinson, P. (1999) 'Explaining the relationship between flexible employment and labour market regulation' in Felstead, A. and Jewson, N. (eds) *Global Trends in Flexible Labour*. Basingstoke: Macmillan.

Stephenson, C. and Stewart, P. (2001) 'The whispering shadow: collectivism and individualism at Ikeda–Hoover and Nissan', *Sociological Research Online*, www.socresonline.org.uk/6/3/stephenson.html

Index